Program Authors

Peter Afflerbach
Camille Blachowicz
Candy Dawson Boyd
Elena Izquierdo
Connie Juel
Edward Kame'enui
Donald Leu
Jeanne R. Paratore
P. David Pearson
Sam Sebesta
Deborah Simmons
Alfred Tatum
Sharon Vaughn
Susan Watts Taffe
Karen Kring Wixson

Glenview, Illinois • Boston, Massachusetts
Chandler, Arizona • Upper Saddle River, New Jersey

We dedicate Reading Street to
Peter Jovanovich.

His wisdom, courage,
and passion for education
are an inspiration to us all.

ISBN-13: 978-0-328-47051-8
ISBN-10: 0-328-47051-1
2 3 4 5 6 7 8 9 10 V003 14 13 12 11 10
CC1

Any Path, Any Pace

Reading Street

Calle de la Lectura

PEARSON

Who said so?

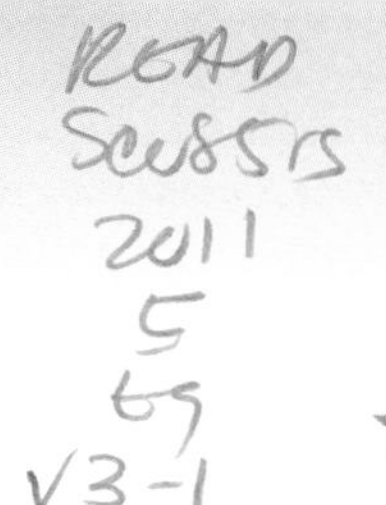

The Leading Researchers,

Program Authors

Peter Afflerbach, Ph.D.
Professor
Department of Curriculum and Instruction
University of Maryland at College Park

Camille L. Z. Blachowicz, Ph.D.
Professor of Education
National-Louis University

Candy Dawson Boyd, Ph.D.
Professor
School of Education
Saint Mary's College of California

Elena Izquierdo, Ph.D.
Associate Professor
University of Texas at El Paso

Connie Juel, Ph.D.
Professor of Education
School of Education
Stanford University

Edward J. Kame'enui, Ph.D.
Dean-Knight Professor of Education and Director
Institute for the Development of Educational Achievement and the Center on Teaching and Learning
College of Education
University of Oregon

Donald J. Leu, Ph.D.
John and Maria Neag Endowed Chair in Literacy and Technology
Director, The New Literacies Research Lab
University of Connecticut

Jeanne R. Paratore, Ed.D.
Associate Professor of Education
Department of Literacy and Language Development
Boston University

P. David Pearson, Ph.D.
Professor and Dean
Graduate School of Education
University of California, Berkeley

Sam L. Sebesta, Ed.D.
Professor Emeritus
College of Education
University of Washington, Seattle

Deborah Simmons, Ph.D.
Professor
College of Education and Human Development
Texas A&M University

Alfred W. Tatum, Ph.D.
Associate Professor and Director of the UIC Reading Clinic
University of Illinois at Chicago

Sharon Vaughn, Ph.D.
H. E. Hartfelder/Southland Corporation Regents Professor
Director, Meadows Center for Preventing Educational Risk
University of Texas

Susan Watts Taffe, Ph.D.
Associate Professor in Literacy
Division of Teacher Education
University of Cincinnati

Karen Kring Wixson, Ph.D.
Professor of Education
University of Michigan

Consulting Authors

Jeff Anderson, M.Ed.
Author and Consultant
San Antonio, Texas

Jim Cummins, Ph.D.
Professor
Department of Curriculum, Teaching and Learning
University of Toronto

Lily Wong Fillmore, Ph.D.
Professor Emerita
Graduate School of Education
University of California, Berkeley

Georgia Earnest García, Ph.D.
Professor
Language and Literacy Division
Department of Curriculum and Instruction
University of Illinois at Urbana-Champaign

George A. González, Ph.D.
Professor (Retired)
School of Education
University of Texas-Pan American, Edinburg

Valerie Ooka Pang, Ph.D.
Professor
School of Teacher Education
San Diego State University

Sally M. Reis, Ph.D.
Board of Trustees Distinguished Professor
Department of Educational Psychology
University of Connecticut

Jon Scieszka, M.F.A.
Children's Book Author
Founder of GUYS READ
Named First National Ambassador for Young People's Literature 2008

Grant Wiggins, Ed.D.
Educational Consultant
Authentic Education
Concept Development

Lee Wright, M.Ed.
Pearland, Texas

Practitioners, and Authors.

Consultant

Sharroky Hollie, Ph.D.
Assistant Professor
California State University
Dominguez Hills, CA

Teacher Reviewers

Dr. Bettyann Brugger
Educational Support Coordinator—Reading Office
Milwaukee Public Schools
Milwaukee, WI

Kathleen Burke
K–12 Reading Coordinator
Peoria Public Schools, Peoria, IL

Darci Burns, M.S.Ed.
University of Oregon

Bridget Cantrell
District Intervention Specialist
Blackburn Elementary School
Independence, MO

Tahira DuPree Chase, M.A., M.S.Ed.
Administrator of Elementary English Language Arts
Mount Vernon City School District
Mount Vernon, NY

Michele Conner
Director, Elementary Education
Aiken County School District
Aiken, SC

Georgia Coulombe
K–6 Regional Trainer/ Literacy Specialist
Regional Center for Training and Learning (RCTL), Reno, NV

Kelly Dalmas
Third Grade Teacher
Avery's Creek Elementary, Arden, NC

Seely Dillard
First Grade Teacher
Laurel Hill Primary School
Mt. Pleasant, SC

Jodi Dodds-Kinner
Director of Elementary Reading
Chicago Public Schools, Chicago, IL

Dr. Ann Wild Evenson
District Instructional Coach
Osseo Area Schools, Maple Grove, MN

Stephanie Fascitelli
Principal
Apache Elementary, Albuquerque Public Schools, Albuquerque, NM

Alice Franklin
Elementary Coordinator, Language Arts & Reading
Spokane Public Schools, Spokane, WA

Laureen Fromberg
Assistant Principal
PS 100 Queens, NY

Kimberly Gibson
First Grade Teacher
Edgar B. Davis Community School
Brockton, MA

Kristen Gray
Lead Teacher
A.T. Allen Elementary School
Concord, NC

Mary Ellen Hazen
State Pre-K Teacher
Rockford Public Schools #205
Rockford, IL

Patrick M. Johnson
Elementary Instructional Director
Seattle Public Schools, Seattle, WA

Theresa Jaramillo Jones
Principal
Highland Elementary School
Las Cruces, NM

Sophie Kowzun
Program Supervisor, Reading/ Language Arts, PreK-5
Montgomery County Public Schools
Rockville, MD

David W. Matthews
Sixth Grade Teacher
Easton Area Middle School
Easton, PA

Ana Nuncio
Editor and Independent Publisher
Salem, MA

Joseph Peila
Principal
Chappell Elementary School
Chicago, IL

Ivana Reimer
Literacy Coordinator
PS 100 Queens, NY

Sally Riley
Curriculum Coordinator
Rochester Public Schools
Rochester, NH

Dyan M. Smiley
Independent Educational Consultant

Michael J. Swiatowiec
Lead Literacy Teacher
Graham Elementary School
Chicago, IL

Dr. Helen Taylor
Director of English Education
Portsmouth City Public Schools
Portsmouth, VA

Carol Thompson
Teaching and Learning Coach
Independence School District
Independence, MO

Erinn Zeitlin
Kindergarten Teacher
Carderock Springs Elementary School
Bethesda, MD

Adapting

In this Teacher's Edition Unit 4, Volume 1

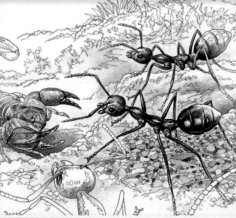

Key
SI Strategic Intervention
OL On-Level
A Advanced
ELL ELL

In the First Stop on Reading Street

GO Digital!

See It!

- Big Question Video
- Concept Talk Video
- Envision It! Animations

Hear It!

- eSelections
- eReaders
- Grammar Jammer
- Leveled Reader Database

Do It!

- Vocabulary Activities
- Story Sort
- 21st Century Skills
- Online Assessment
- Letter Tile Drag and Drop

Meeting Challenges

Key
SI Strategic Intervention
OL On-Level
A Advanced
ELL ELL

Doing the Right Thing

Key
SI Strategic Intervention
OL On-Level
A Advanced
ELL ELL

Inventors and Artists

Key
SI Strategic Intervention
OL On-Level
A Advanced
ELL ELL

Adapting

Key
SI Strategic Intervention
OL On-Level
A Advanced
ELL ELL

Adventurers

Key
- SI Strategic Intervention
- OL On-Level
- A Advanced
- ELL ELL

The Unexpected

Key
SI Strategic Intervention
OL On-Level
A Advanced
ELL ELL

Skills Overview

Key
T Tested Skill
Target Skill

	WEEK 1	WEEK 2
	 **Weslandia** Fiction pp. 26–37 **Under the Back Porch/Keziah** Poetry pp. 42–43	 **Tripping Over the Lunch Lady** Realistic Fiction pp. 52–67 **Square Dancing** Persuasive Text pp. 72–73
Get Ready to Read		
Question of the Week	How do people adapt to difficult situations?	How do people overcome obstacles?
Amazing Words	*discovered, courage, determination, practice, exploration, customize, flexibility, transformation, advancement, dynamic*	*confront, predicament, ingenious, triumphant, application, resilient, modify, conquer, acclimate, persistence*
Word Analysis	Word Endings *-ing, -ed, -s*	Suffixes *-ly, -ian*
Literary Terms	Idiom	Hyperbole
Structure/Features	Resolution	Climax
Read and Comprehend		
Comprehension	T **Skill** Draw Conclusions **Strategy** Questioning Review **Skill** Theme and Setting	T **Skill** Generalize **Strategy** Predict/Set Purpose Review **Skill** Draw Conclusions
Vocabulary	T **Skill** Endings *-s, -ed, -ing* blunders, civilization, complex, envy, fleeing, inspired, rustling, strategy	T **Skill** Unfamiliar Words sprained, frilly, promenading, substitute, Dalmatian
Fluency	Appropriate Phrasing	Accuracy
Language Arts		
Writing	Picture Book Trait: Focus/Ideas	Friendly Letter Trait: Sentences
Conventions	Subject and Object Pronouns	Pronouns and Antecedents
Spelling	Words from Many Cultures	Prefixes *over-, under-, sub-, super-, out-*
Speaking/Listening	How-To Demonstration	Persuasive Speech
Research Skills	Instruction Manual	Telephone Directory

The Big Question

How do people and animals adapt to different situations?

WEEK 3	WEEK 4	WEEK 5	WEEK 6
Exploding Ants Expository Text pp. 83–93 **The Art of Mimicry** Expository Text pp. 98–101	**The Stormi Giovanni Club** Drama pp. 110–125 **The Extra Credit Club** Persuasive Text pp. 130–133	**The Gymnast** Autobiography pp. 142–151 **All About Gymnastics** Online Reference Sources pp. 156–159	**Interactive Review**
How do animals adapt to survive?	How do people adapt to new places?	Why do people try to change themselves?	Connect the Question of the Week to the Big Question
adaptations, predators, defenses, fearsome, mimicry, camouflage, spiny, survival, protrude, formidable	*opportunities, courageous, obstacles, perseverance, familiarize, relocate, engrossed, adjust, surroundings, wanderlust*	*competitive, champion, develop, perfected, routine, rehearse, condition, enhance, fitness, aspire*	Review Amazing Words for Unit 4
Suffix *-ize*	Prefixes *com-, pro-, epi-*	Idioms	
Figurative Language: Metaphor	Dialogue	Figurative Language: Simile	
Headings	Conflict/Resolution	Sequence	
T **Skill** Graphic Sources **Strategy** Important Ideas Review **Skill** Author's Purpose	T **Skill** Generalize **Strategy** Story Structure Review **Skill** Draw Conclusions	T **Skill** Draw Conclusions **Strategy** Visualize Review **Skill** Generalize	Review Draw Conclusions, Generalize, Graphic Sources
T **Skill** Synonyms critical, enables, mucus, scarce, specialize, sterile	T **Skill** Unfamiliar Words cavities, combination, demonstrates, episode, profile, strict	T **Skill** Suffixes *-ion, -ish* bluish, cartwheels, gymnastics, hesitation, limelight, skidded, somersault, throbbing, wincing	Review Endings *-ed, -ing, -s,* Unfamiliar Words, Synonyms, Suffixes *-ion, -ish*
Rate	Expression	Appropriate Phrasing	Review Fluency for Unit 4
Formal Letter Trait: Conventions	Narrative Poetry Trait: Word Choice	Autobiographical Sketch Trait: Voice	
Possessive Pronouns	Indefinite and Reflexive Pronouns	Using *who* and *whom*	Review Unit 4 Conventions
Homophones	Suffixes *-ible, -able*	Negative Prefixes	Review Unit 4 Spelling Patterns
Description	Give Advice	Media Literacy: Interview	
Magazine/Periodical	Thesaurus	Graphs	

Monitor Progress

Don't Wait Until Friday

SUCCESS PREDICTOR	WEEK 1	WEEK 2	WEEK 3	WEEK 4
WCPM **Fluency**	Appropriate Phrasing 120–128 WCPM	Accuracy 120–128 WCPM	Rate 120–128 WCPM	Expression 120–128 WCPM
Vocabulary **Oral Vocabulary/ Concept Development** (assessed informally)	discovered courage determination practice exploration customize flexibility transformation advancement dynamic	confront predicament ingenious triumphant application resilient modify conquer acclimate persistence	adaptations predators defenses fearsome mimicry camouflage spiny survival protrude formidable	opportunities courageous obstacles perseverance familiarize relocate engrossed adjust surroundings wanderlust
Lesson Vocabulary	**T** blunders **T** civilization **T** complex **T** envy **T** fleeing **T** inspired **T** rustling **T** strategy	**T** sprained **T** frilly **T** promenading **T** substitute **T** Dalmatian	**T** critical **T** enables **T** mucus **T** scarce **T** specialize **T** sterile	**T** cavities **T** combination **T** demonstrates **T** episode **T** profile **T** strict
Retelling **Text Comprehension**	**T** **Skill** Draw Conclusions **Strategy** Questioning	**T** **Skill** Generalize **Strategy** Predict/Set Purpose	**T** **Skill** Graphic Sources **Strategy** Important Ideas	**T** **Skill** Generalize **Strategy** Story Structure

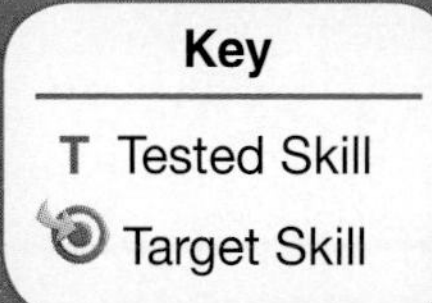

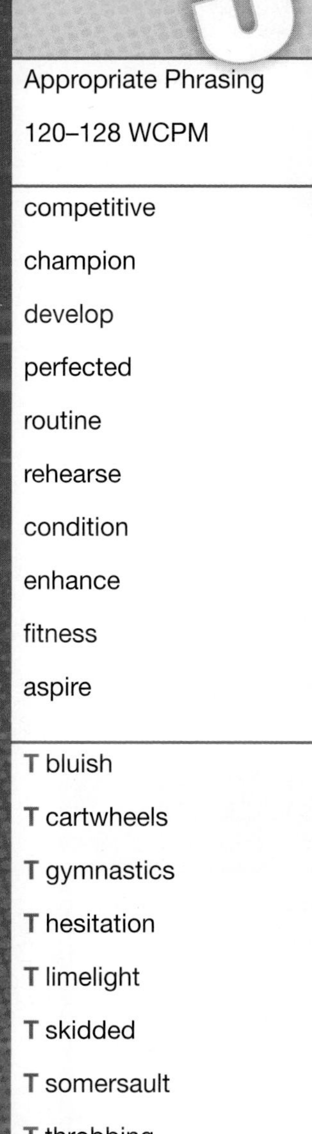

WEEK 5	WEEK 6
Appropriate Phrasing 120–128 WCPM	REVIEW
competitive champion develop perfected routine rehearse condition enhance fitness aspire	
T bluish T cartwheels T gymnastics T hesitation T limelight T skidded T somersault T throbbing T wincing	
T **Skill** Draw Conclusions **Strategy** Visualize	

Online Classroom

Manage Data

- Assign the Unit 4 Benchmark Test for students to take online.
- Online Assessment records results and generates reports by school, grade, classroom, or student.
- Use reports to disaggregate and aggregate Unit 4 skills and standards data to monitor progress.
- Based on class lists created to support the categories important for AYP (gender, ethnicity, migrant education, English proficiency, disabilities, economic status), reports let you track adequate yearly progress every six weeks.

Select a Class: Reading 101

Make Assignments	View Reports and Logs
Assign Tests Search by: Unit GO!	Class Reports View by: Standard GO! Assignment Log View by: Entire Class GO!

Other Resources and Information

Certificates Motivate your students with printable certificates.	The User's Guide and Quick Start Guide get you the help you need fast. Learn how to make the most of the Reading Success Tracker System with our simple to use guides.

Group

- Use results from Unit 4 Benchmark Tests taken online through Online Assessment to measure whether students have mastered the English-Language Arts Content Standards taught in this unit.
- Reports in Online Assessment suggest whether students need Extra Support or Intervention.

Individualized Instruction

- Assessments are correlated to Unit 4 tested skills and standards so that prescriptions for individual teaching and learning plans can be created.
- Individualized prescriptions target instruction and accelerate student progress toward learning outcome goals.
- Prescriptions include remediation activities and resources to reteach Unit 4 skills and standards.

Assessment and Grouping

for Data-Driven Instruction

4-Step Plan for Assessment

1 Diagnose and Differentiate
2 Monitor Progress
3 Assess and Regroup
4 Summative Assessment

STEP 1 Diagnose and Differentiate

Diagnose

To make initial grouping decisions, use the Baseline Group Test, the *Texas Primary Reading Inventory (TPRI),* or another initial placement test. Depending on student's ability levels, you may have more than one of each group.

Baseline Group Tests

Differentiate

If... student performance is  **then...** use the regular instruction and the daily **Strategic Intervention** small group lessons.

If... student performance is  **then...** use the regular instruction and the daily **On-Level** small group lessons.

If... student performance is  **then...** use the regular instruction and the daily **Advanced** small group lessons.

Small Group Time

SI Strategic Intervention

- Daily small group lessons provide more intensive instruction, more scaffolding, more practice, and more opportunities to respond.
- Reteach lessons in the *First Stop on Reading Street* provide more instruction with target skills.
- Leveled readers build background and provide practice for target skills and vocabulary.

OL On-Level

- Explicit instructional routines teach core skills and strategies.
- Daily On-Level lessons provide more practice and more opportunities to respond.
- Independent activities provide practice for core skills and extension and enrichment options.
- Leveled readers provide additional reading and practice for core skills and vocabulary.

A Advanced

- Daily Advanced lessons provide instruction for accelerated learning.
- Leveled readers provide additional reading tied to lesson concepts and skills.

Additional Differentiated Learning Options

Reading Street Response to Intervention Kit

- Focused intervention lessons on the five critical areas of reading: phonemic awareness, phonics, vocabulary, comprehension, and fluency

My Sidewalks on Reading Street

- Intensive intervention for struggling readers

STEP 2 Monitor Progress

Use these tools during lesson teaching to **monitor student progress.**

- **Skill and Strategy** instruction during reading
- **Don't Wait Until Friday** boxes to check retelling, fluency, and oral vocabulary
- **Weekly Assessment** on Day 5 checks comprehension and fluency
- **Reader's and Writer's Notebook** pages at point of use
- **Weekly Tests** assess target skills for the week
- **Fresh Reads** for Fluency and Comprehension

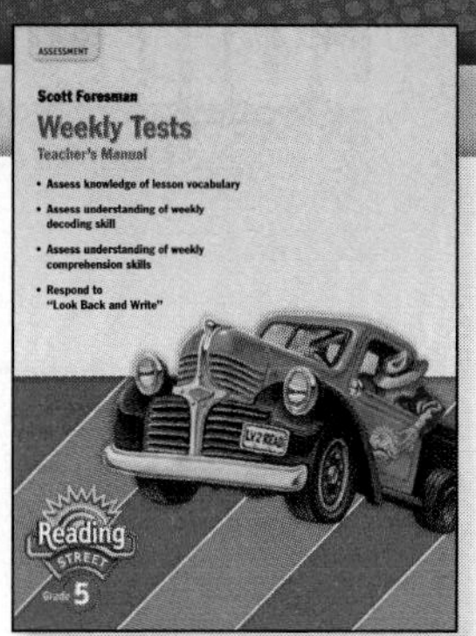

Weekly Tests

Fresh Reads for Fluency and Comprehension

STEP 3 Assess and Regroup

Use these tools during lesson teaching to **assess and regroup.**

- **Weekly Assessments** Record results of weekly assessments in retelling, comprehension, and fluency to track student progress.
- **Unit Benchmark Tests** Administer this assessment to check mastery of unit skills.
- **Regroup** We recommend the first regrouping to be at the end of Unit 2. Use weekly assessment information and Unit Benchmark Test performance to inform regrouping decisions. Then regroup at the end of each subsequent unit.

Unit Assessment Charts in First Stop

Group Baseline Group Test	Regroup Units 1 and 2	Regroup Unit 3	Regroup Unit 4	Regroup Unit 5	End of Year
Weeks 1-6	Weeks 7-12	Weeks 13-18	Weeks 19-24	Weeks 25-30	Weeks 31-36

Outside assessments, such as *DRA, TPRI,* and *DIBELS,* may recommend regrouping at other times during the year.

STEP 4 Summative Assessment

Use these tools after lesson teaching to **assess students.**

- **Unit Benchmark Tests** Use to measure a student's mastery of each unit's skills.
- **End-of-Year Benchmark Test** Use to measure a student's mastery of program skills covered in all six units.

Unit and End-of-Year Benchmark Tests

Concept Launch

Understanding By Design

Grant Wiggins, Ed. D.
Reading Street Author

"A big idea is a concept, theme, or issue that gives meaning and connection to discrete facts and skills…In an education for understanding, a vital challenge is to highlight the big ideas, show how they prioritize the learning, and help students understand their value for making sense of all the 'stuff' of content."

Adapting

Reading Street Online

www.ReadingStreet.com

- Big Question Video
- eSelections
- Envision It! Animations
- Story Sort

How do people and animals adapt to different situations?

Let's Think About Reading!

Weslandia FICTION

How do people adapt to difficult situations?

Paired Selection

Under the Back Porch/Keziah POETRY

Tripping Over the Lunch Lady

REALISTIC FICTION

How do people overcome obstacles?

Paired Selection

Square Dancing: Good for the Heart and Mind

PERSUASIVE TEXT

Exploding Ants EXPOSITORY TEXT

How do animals adapt to survive?

Paired Selection

The Art of Mimicry EXPOSITORY TEXT

The Stormi Giovanni Club DRAMA

How do people adapt to new places?

Paired Selection

The Extra Credit Club PERSUASIVE TEXT

The Gymnast AUTOBIOGRAPHY

Why do people try to change themselves?

Paired Selection

All About Gymnastics ONLINE REFERENCE SOURCES

Small Group Time

Flexible Pacing Plans

Key

SI Strategic Intervention
OL On-Level
A Advanced
ELL ELL

5 Day Plan

DAY 1	• Reinforce the Concept • Read Leveled Readers Concept Literacy Below-Level
DAY 2	• Comprehension Skill • Comprehension Strategy • Revisit Main Selection
DAY 3	• Vocabulary Skill • Revisit Main Selection
DAY 4	• Practice Retelling • Read/Revisit Paired Selection
DAY 5	• Reread for Fluency • Reread Leveled Readers

4 Day Plan

DAY 1	• Reinforce the Concept • Read Leveled Readers Concept Literacy Below-Level
DAY 2	• Comprehension Skill • Comprehension Strategy • Revisit Main Selection
DAY 3	• Vocabulary Skill • Revisit Main Selection
DAY 4	• Practice Retelling • Read/Revisit Paired Selection • Reread for Fluency • Reread Leveled Readers

3 Day Plan

DAY 1	• Reinforce the Concept • Read Leveled Readers Concept Literacy Below-Level
DAY 2	• Comprehension Skill • Comprehension Strategy • Revisit Main Selection
DAY 3	• Practice Retelling • Read/Revisit Paired Selection • Reread for Fluency • Reread Leveled Readers

ELL

5 Day Plan

DAY 1	• Frontload Concept • Preteach Skills • Conventions/Writing
DAY 2	• Review Concept/Skills • Frontload and Read Main Selection • Conventions/Writing
DAY 3	• Review Concept/Skills • Reread Main Selection • Conventions/Writing
DAY 4	• Review Concept/Skills • Read ELL or ELD Reader • Conventions/Writing
DAY 5	• Review Concept/Skills • Reread ELL or ELD Reader • Conventions/Writing

4 Day Plan

DAY 1	• Frontload Concept • Preteach Skills • Conventions/Writing
DAY 2	• Review Concept/Skills • Frontload and Read Main Selection • Conventions/Writing
DAY 3	• Review Concept/Skills • Reread Main Selection • Conventions/Writing
DAY 4	• Review Concept/Skills • Read ELL or ELD Reader • Conventions/Writing

3 Day Plan

DAY 1	• Frontload Concept • Preteach Skills • Conventions/Writing
DAY 2	• Review Concept/Skills • Frontload and Read Main Selection • Conventions/Writing
DAY 3	• Review Concept/Skills • Read ELL or ELD Reader • Conventions/Writing

This Week's ELL Overview

Grade 5 • Unit 4 • Week 1
Weslandia
20a–45s
and DI•16–DI•25

ELL Handbook

- Maximize Literacy and Cognitive Engagement
- Research Into Practice
- Full Weekly Support for Every Selection

Weslandia
- Multi-Lingual Summaries in Five Languages
- Selection-Specific Vocabulary Word Cards
- Frontloading/Reteaching for Comprehension Skill Lessons
- ELD and ELL Reader Study Guides

- Transfer Activities
- Professional Development

Daily Leveled ELL Notes

ELL notes appear throughout this week's instruction and ELL Support is on the DI pages of your Teacher's Edition. The following is a sample of an ELL note from this week.

English Language Learners

Beginning Have students draw a picture to express the meaning of the word. After matching the word and a clue, have them write the word and a word or phrase that reminds them of the meaning.

Intermediate After students match words with clues, they will write a sentence for each word. Have them share sentences with partners.

Advanced Have students write a paragraph or two using the vocabulary words.

Advanced High In addition, have student pairs write synonyms for as many words as they can. (Examples: *blunders-mistakes, envy-jealousy*)

ELL by Strand

The ELL lessons on this week's Support for English Language Learners pages are organized by strand. They offer additional scaffolding for the core curriculum. Leveled support notes on these pages address the different proficiency levels in your class. See pages DI•16–DI•25.

The Three Pillars of ELL Instruction

ELL Strands	Activate Prior Knowledge	Access Content	Extend Language
Vocabulary pp. DI•17–DI•18	Preteach	Reteach	Leveled Writing Activities
Reading Comprehension p. DI•22	Frontloading	Sheltered Reading	After Reading
Phonics, Spelling, and Word Analysis p. DI•20	Preteach	Model	Leveled Practice Activities
Listening Comprehension p. DI•19	Prepare for the Read Aloud	First Listening	Second Listening
Conventions and Writing pp. DI•24–DI•25	Preteach	Leveled Practice Activities	Leveled Writing Activities
Concept Development p. DI•16	Activate Prior Knowledge	Discuss Concept	Daily Concept and Vocabulary Development

This Week's Practice Stations Overview

Six Weekly Practice Stations with Leveled Activities can be found at the beginning of each week of instruction. For this week's Practice Stations, see pp. 20h–20i.

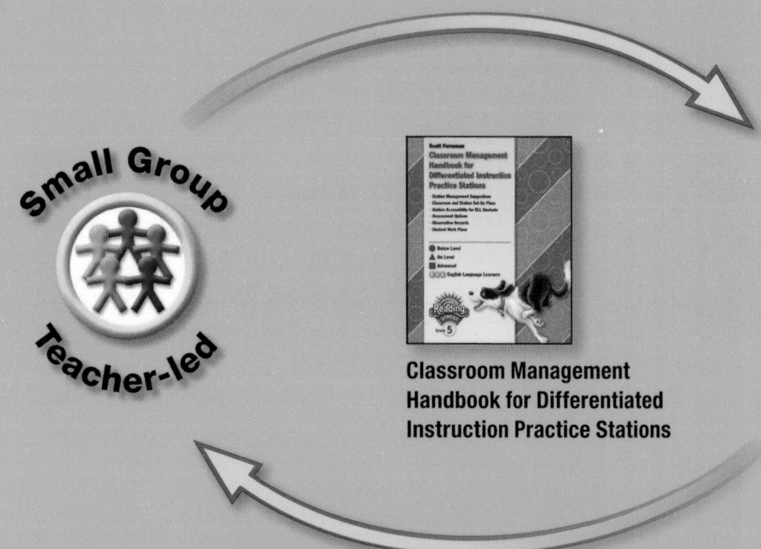

Classroom Management Handbook for Differentiated Instruction Practice Stations

Practice Stations

Daily Leveled Center Activities

 Below
 Advanced
 On-Level

Practice Stations Flip Charts

	 Word Wise	 Word Work	 Words to Know	 Let's Write	 Read for Meaning	 Get Fluent
Objectives	• Spell words with prefixes *un-*, *re-*, and *dis-*.	• Identify words with prefixes *un-*, *re-*, and *dis-*.	• Determine the meaning of words with prefixes *pre-* and *re-*.	• Write a well-organized expository exposition.	• Understand graphic sources.	• Read aloud with accuracy.
Materials	• *Word Wise* Flip Chart Activity 16 • Teacher-made word cards • paper • pencil	• *Word Work* Flip Chart Activity 16 • Word Cards • paper • pencil	• *Words to Know* Flip Chart Activity 16 • Teacher-made word cards • dictionary • paper • pencil	• *Let's Write* Flip Chart Activity 16 • paper • pencil	• *Read for Meaning* Flip Chart Activity 16 • Leveled Readers • paper • pencil	• *Get Fluent* Flip Chart Activity 16 • Leveled Readers

This Week on Reading Street!

Question of the Week

How do people adapt to difficult situations?

Daily Plan

Whole Group

- Draw Conclusions
- Endings *-s, -ed, -ing*
- Fluency/Phrasing
- Research and Inquiry

MONITOR PROGRESS — Success Predictor

Day 1	Days 2–3	Day 4	Day 5
Check Oral Vocabulary	Check Retelling	Check Fluency	Check Oral Vocabulary

Small Group

Teacher-Led

- Reading Support
- Skill Support
- Fluency Practice

Practice Stations

Independent Activities

Customize Literacy More support for a balanced literacy approach, see pp. CL•1–CL•47

Customize Writing More support for a customized writing approach, see pp. CW•1–CW•10

Whole Group

- Writing: Picture Book
- Conventions: Subject and Object Pronouns
- Spelling: Words from Many Cultures

Assessment

- Weekly Tests
- Day 5 Assessment
- Fresh Reads

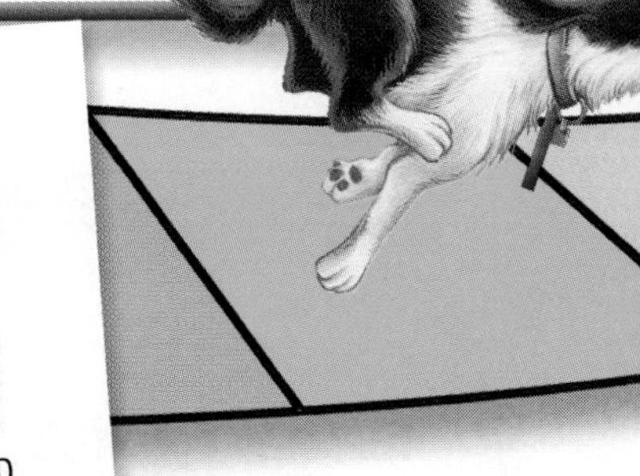

This Week's Reading Selections

Main Selection
Genre: **Fiction**

Paired Selection
Genre: **Poetry**

Leveled Readers

ELL and ELD Readers

Resources on Reading Street!

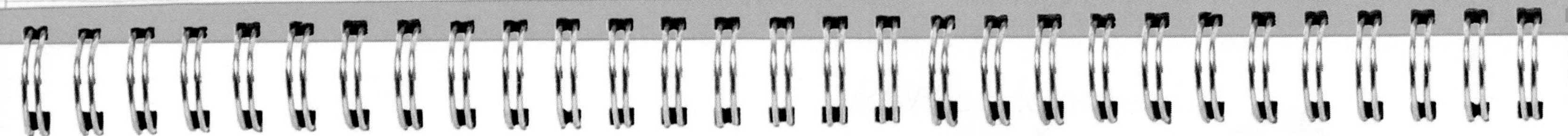

	Build Concepts	Comprehension
Whole Group	 Let's Talk About pp. 20–21	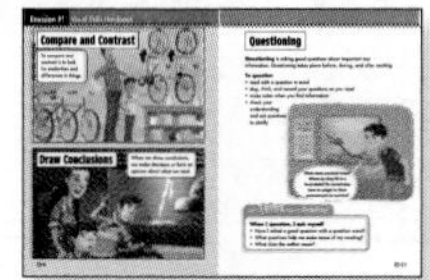 Envision It! Skills/ Strategies 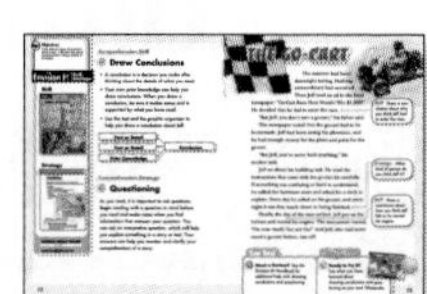 Comprehension Skills Lesson pp. 22–23
 Go Digital	• Concept Talk Video	• Envision It! Animations • eSelections
Small Group and Independent Practice	 Weslandia pp. 26–27  ELL and ELD Readers  Leveled Readers	 Weslandia pp. 26–27  ELL and ELD Readers  Leveled Readers 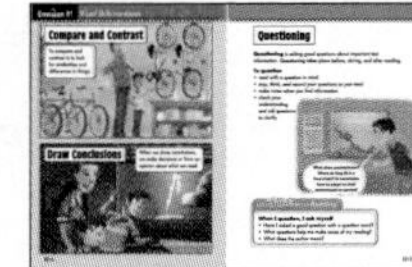 Envision It! Skills/ Strategies  Reader's and Writer's Notebook 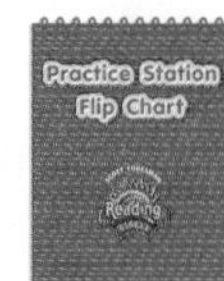 Practice Station Flip Chart
 Go Digital	• eReaders • eSelections	• Envision It! Animations • eSelections • eReaders
Customize Literacy  	• Leveled Readers	• Envision It! Skills and Strategies Handbook • Leveled Readers
Go Digital 	• Concept Talk Video • Big Question Video • eReaders	• Envision It! Animations • eReaders

Question of the Week

How do people adapt to difficult situations?

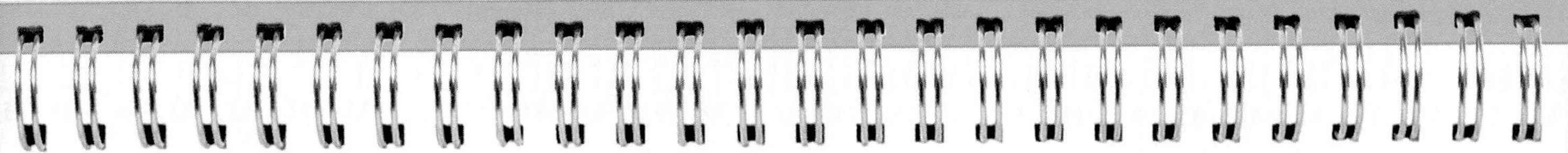

Vocabulary

Envision It! Vocabulary Cards

Vocabulary Skill Lesson pp. 24–25

- Envision It! Vocabulary Cards
- Vocabulary Activities

Envision It! Vocabulary Cards

Weslandia pp. 26–27

Practice Station Flip Chart

Words!

Reader's and Writer's Notebook

- Envision It! Vocabulary Cards
- Vocabulary Activities
- eSelections

- Envision It! Vocabulary Cards

- Vocabulary Activities

Fluency

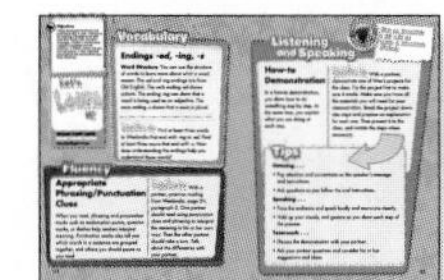

Let's Learn It! pp. 44–45

- eSelections
- eReaders

Weslandia pp. 26–27

Practice Station Flip Chart

Leveled Readers

ELL and ELD Readers

- eSelections
- eReaders

- Leveled Readers

- eReaders

Conventions and Writing

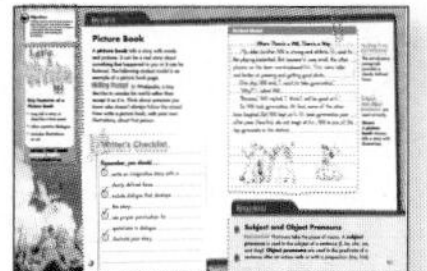

Let's Write It! pp. 40–41

- Grammar Jammer

Reader's and Writer's Notebook

Weslandia pp. 26–27

Practice Station Flip Chart

- Grammar Jammer

- Reader's and Writer's Notebook

- Grammar Jammer

Week 1

My 5-Day Planner for Reading Street!

Don't Wait Until Friday MONITOR PROGRESS

	Check Oral Vocabulary **Day 1** pages 20j–23f	Check Retelling **Day 2** pages 24a–33e
Get Ready to Read	**Concept Talk,** 20j **Oral Vocabulary,** 21a discovered, courage, determination, practice **Listening Comprehension,** Read Aloud, 21b	**Concept Talk,** 24a **Oral Vocabulary,** 24b exploration, customize **Word Analysis,** 24c Word Endings *-ing, -ed, -s* **Literary Terms,** 24d Idiom **Story Structure,** 24d Resolution
Read and Comprehend	**Comprehension Skill,** Draw Conclusions, 21c **Comprehension Strategy,** Questioning, 21c READ **Comprehension,** 22–23 **Model Fluency,** Phrasing, 22–23 **Introduce Lesson Vocabulary,** 23a blunders, civilization, complex, envy, fleeing, inspired, rustling, strategy	**Vocabulary Skill,** Endings, *-s, -ed, -ing,* 24e **Vocabulary Strategy,** Word Structure, 24e **Lesson Vocabulary,** 24–25 blunders, civilization, complex, envy, fleeing, inspired, rustling, strategy READ **Vocabulary,** 24–25 **Model Fluency,** Phrasing, 24–25 READ **Main Selection,** *Weslandia,* 26–33a
Language Arts	**Research and Inquiry,** Identify Questions, 23b **Spelling,** Words from Many Cultures, 23c **Conventions,** Subject and Object Pronouns, 23d **Handwriting,** Cursive Letter *c* and *C,* 23d **Writing,** Picture Book, Introduce, 23e–23f	**Research and Inquiry,** Navigate/Search, 33b **Conventions,** Subject and Object Pronouns, 33c **Spelling,** Words from Many Cultures, 33c **Writing,** Picture Book, Organization, 33d–33e

You Are Here! Unit 4 Week 1

Question of the Week
How do people adapt to difficult situations?

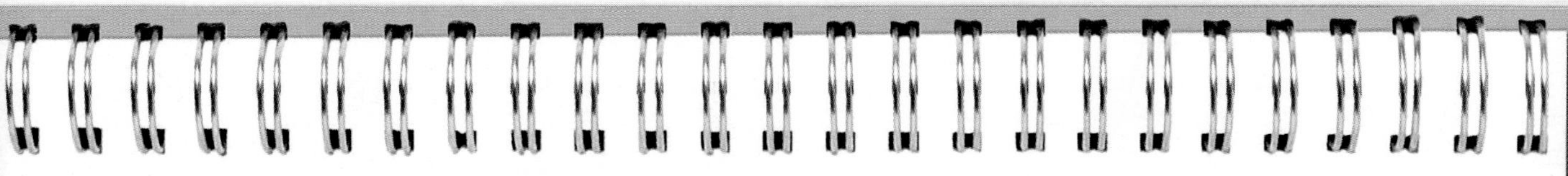

Check Retelling **Day 3** pages 34a–41c	Check Fluency **Day 4** pages 42a–45e	Check Oral Vocabulary **Day 5** pages 45f–45q
Concept Talk, 34a **Oral Vocabulary,** 34b flexibility, transformation **Comprehension Check,** 34c **Check Retelling,** 34d	**Concept Talk,** 42a **Oral Vocabulary,** 42b advancement, dynamic **Genre,** Poetry, 42c	**Concept Wrap Up,** 45f **Check Oral Vocabulary,** 45g discovered, courage, determination, practice, exploration, customize, flexibility, transformation, advancement, dynamic **Amazing Ideas,** 45g Review ◎ Draw Conclusions, 45h Review ◎ Endings *-s, -ed, -ing*, 45h Review Word Analysis, 45i Review Literary Terms, 45i
READ **Main Selection,** *Weslandia,* 34–37a **Retelling,** 38–39 **Think Critically,** 39a **Model Fluency,** Phrasing, 39b **Research and Study Skills,** Instruction Manual, 39c	READ **Paired Selection,** "Under the Back Porch"/ "Keziah," 42–43a **Let's Learn It!** 44–45a Fluency: Phrasing Vocabulary: Endings *-ed, -ing, -s* Listening and Speaking: How-To Demonstration	**Fluency Assessment,** WCPM, 45j–45k **Comprehension Assessment,** ◎ Draw Conclusions, 45l–45m
Research and Inquiry, Analyze, 39d **Conventions,** Subject and Object Pronouns, 39e **Spelling,** Words from Many Cultures, 39e **Let's Write It!** Picture Book, 40–41a **Writing,** Picture Book, Focus/Ideas, 41b–41c	**Research and Inquiry,** Synthesize, 45b **Conventions,** Subject and Object Pronouns, 45c **Spelling,** Words from Many Cultures, 45c **Writing,** Picture Book, Revising, 45d–45e	**Research and Inquiry,** Communicate, 45n **Conventions,** Subject and Object Pronouns, 45o **Spelling Test,** Words from Many Cultures, 45o **Writing,** Picture Book, Subject and Object Pronouns, 45p **Quick Write for Fluency,** 45q

Week 1

Grouping Options for Differentiated Instruction
Turn the page for the small group time lesson plan.

Planning Small Group Time on Reading Street!

Look for this Small Group Time box each day to help meet the individual needs of all your students. Differentiated Instruction lessons appear on the DI pages at the end of each week.

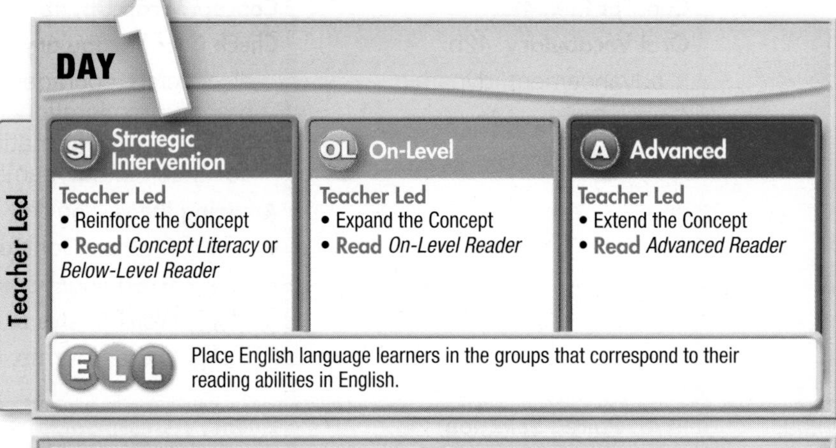

DAY 1

Teacher Led

SI Strategic Intervention	OL On-Level	A Advanced
Teacher Led • Reinforce the Concept • Read *Concept Literacy* or *Below-Level Reader*	Teacher Led • Expand the Concept • Read *On-Level Reader*	Teacher Led • Extend the Concept • Read *Advanced Reader*

ELL Place English language learners in the groups that correspond to their reading abilities in English.

Practice Stations
- Read for Meaning
- Get Fluent
- Word Work

Independent Activities
- Concept Talk Video
- *Reader's and Writer's Notebook*
- Research and Inquiry

ELL

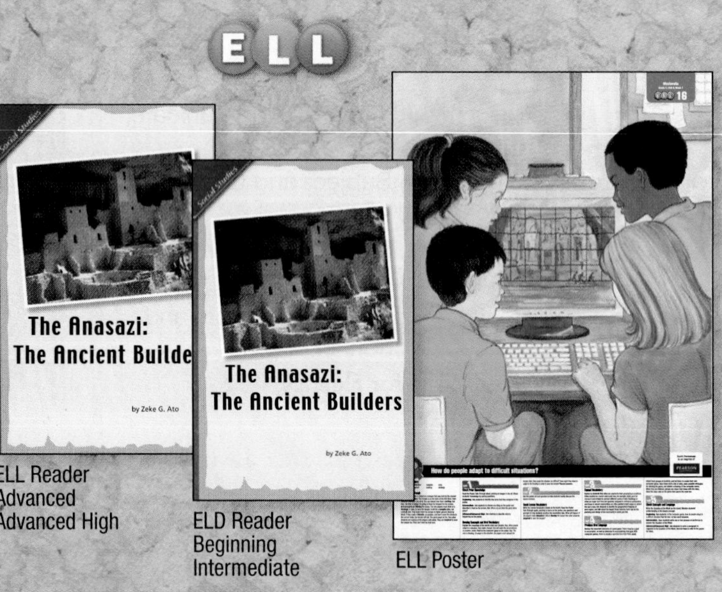

The Anasazi: The Ancient Builders
by Zeke G. Ato
How do people adapt to difficult situations?

ELL Reader Advanced Advanced High

ELD Reader Beginning Intermediate

ELL Poster

	Day 1
SI Strategic Intervention	**Reinforce the Concept,** DI•1–DI•2 Read **Concept Literacy Reader** or **Below-Level Reader**
OL On-Level	**Expand the Concept,** DI•7 Read **On-Level Reader**
A Advanced	**Extend the Concept,** DI•12 Read **Advanced Reader**
ELL English Language Learners	DI•16–DI•25 **Frontload Concept** **Preteach Skills** **Writing**

You Are Here! Unit 4 Week 1

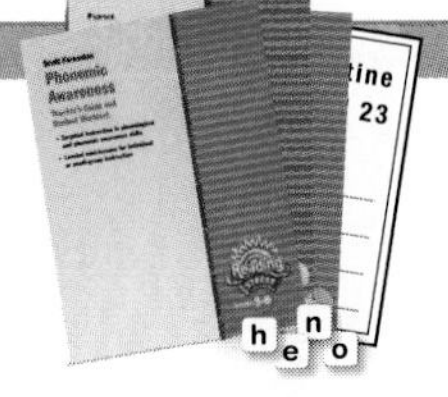

Reading Street Response to Intervention Kit

Reading Street Practice Stations Kit

Question of the Week

How do people adapt to difficult situations?

SI Strategic Intervention

Below-Level Reader

Concept Literacy Reader

Weslandia pp. 26–27

OL On-Level

On-Level Reader

A Advanced

Advanced Reader

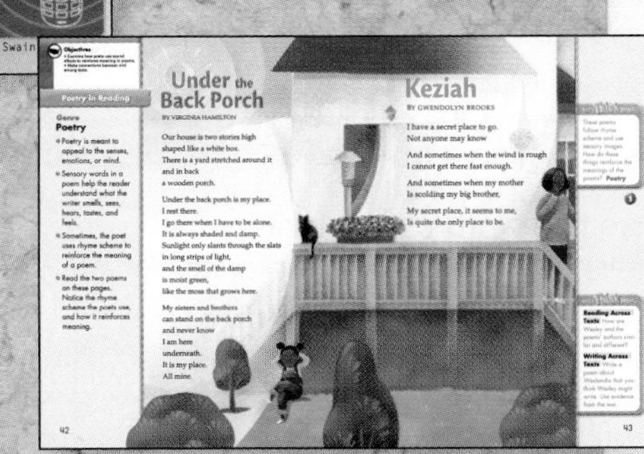

Under the Back Porch/Keziah pp. 42–43

Small Group Weekly Plan

Day 2	Day 3	Day 4	Day 5
Reinforce Comprehension, DI•3 Revisit **Main Selection**	**Reinforce Vocabulary,** DI•4 Read/Revisit **Main Selection**	**Reinforce Comprehension,** Practice Retelling DI•5 Genre Focus Read/Revisit **Paired Selection**	**Practice Fluency,** DI•6 Reread **Concept Literacy Reader** or **Below-Level Reader**
Expand Comprehension, DI•8 Revisit **Main Selection**	**Expand Vocabulary,** DI•9 Read/Revisit **Main Selection**	**Expand Comprehension,** Practice Retelling DI•10 Genre Focus Read/Revisit **Paired Selection**	**Practice Fluency,** DI•11 Reread **On-Level Reader**
Extend Comprehension, DI•13 Revisit **Main Selection**	**Extend Vocabulary,** DI•14 Read/Revisit **Main Selection**	**Extend Comprehension,** Genre Focus DI•15 Read/Revisit **Paired Selection**	**Practice Fluency,** DI•15 Reread **Advanced Reader**
DI•16–DI•25 **Review Concept/Skills** **Frontload Main Selection** **Practice**	DI•16–DI•25 **Review Concept/Skills** Reread **Main Selection** **Practice**	DI•16–DI•25 **Review Concept** Read **ELL/ELD Readers** **Practice**	DI•16–DI•25 **Review Concept/Skills** Reread **ELL/ELD Reader** **Writing**

Week 1

Practice Stations for Everyone on Reading Street!

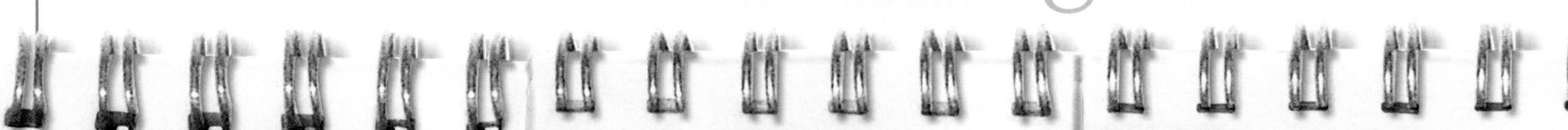

Word Wise
Prefixes *un-*, *re-*, and *dis-*

Objectives
- Spell words with prefixes *un-*, *re-*, and *dis-*.

Materials
- *Word Wise* Flip Chart Activity 16
- Teacher-made word cards
- paper • pencil

Differentiated Activities

● Choose five word cards. Write your words in a list. Circle the prefix in each word. Underline the base word. Write sentences using each of your words. Add other words with these prefixes to your list.

▲ Choose seven word cards, and write your words in a list. Circle the prefix in each word, and write sentences using the words. Add other words with these prefixes to your list.

■ Choose ten word cards, and write your words in a list. Circle the prefix in each word, and write sentences using the words. Add other words with these prefixes to your list.

Technology
- Online Dictionary

Word Work
Prefixes *un-*, *re-*, and *dis-*

Objectives
- Identify words with prefixes *un-*, *re-*, and *dis-*.

Materials
- *Word Work* Flip Chart Activity 16
- Word Cards
- paper • pen

Differentiated Activities

● Find three word cards with each prefix: *un-*, *re-*, and *dis-*. Make a three-column chart with the prefixes as headings. Write your words in the correct column. Say each word.

▲ Find four word cards with each prefix: *un-*, *re-*, and *dis-*. Make a three-column chart with the prefixes as headings, and write your words in the correct column. Say each word.

■ Find five word cards with each prefix: *un-*, *re-*, and *dis-*. Make a three-column chart with the prefixes as headings, and write your words in the correct column. Say each word.

Technology
- Modeled Pronunciation Audio CD

Words to Know
Prefixes *pre-* and *re-*

Objectives
- Determine the meaning of words with prefixes *pre-* and *re-*.

Materials
- *Words to Know* Flip Chart Activity 16
- Teacher-made word cards
- dictionary • paper • pencil

Differentiated Activities

● Choose four word cards. Write the words in a list. Use the prefix to help determine each word's meaning. Check definitions in the dictionary. Write a sentence using each of the words.

▲ Choose six word cards, and write the words in a list. Use the prefix to help determine each word's meaning, and then check each definition in the dictionary. Write sentences using the words.

■ Choose six word cards, and write the words in a list. Use the prefix to help determine each word's meaning, and then check each definition in the dictionary. Write sentences using the words.

Technology
- Online Dictionary

You Are Here! Unit 4 Week 1

Use this week's materials from the Reading Street Leveled Practice Stations Kit to organize your stations.

Key

Below-Level Activities
On-Level Activities
Advanced Activities

Practice Station Flip Chart

Let's Write!

Expository composition

Objectives

- Write a well-organized expository composition.

Materials

- *Let's Write!* Flip Chart Activity 16
- paper • pencil

Differentiated Activities

● Compare two movies that you've enjoyed. Which was better? Write a short paragraph telling why you liked one more than the other. Include specific details to explain how you reached your decision.

▲ Compare two books that you've read. Which was better? Write a short paragraph telling why you preferred one over the other. Include details to explain how you reached your conclusion.

■ Compare and contrast two places you've visited. Which did you prefer? Explain your reasons in a short paragraph that has a strong introduction and conclusion. Include details to support your conclusion.

Technology

- Online Graphic Organizers

Read for Meaning

Graphic sources

Objectives

- Understand graphic sources.

Materials

- *Read for Meaning* Flip Chart Activity 16
- Leveled Readers • paper • pencil

Differentiated Activities

● Choose a book from those provided by your teacher. Think about the graphic sources in the book. Choose one graphic source. Write one sentence telling about the information it provides. Include the type of graphic source it is.

▲ Choose a book from those provided by your teacher. Think about the information provided in the graphic sources. Choose two graphic sources. Write sentences naming the sources and explaining the information they provide.

■ Choose a book from those provided by your teacher. Notice the information provided by the graphic sources. Write a paragraph listing the difference graphic sources in the book. Include details about the information they provide.

Technology

- Leveled Reader Database

Get Fluent

Practice fluent reading.

Objectives

- Read aloud with accuracy.

Materials

- *Get Fluent* Flip Chart Activity 16
- Leveled Readers

Differentiated Activities

● Work with a partner. Choose a Concept Literacy Reader or Below-Level Reader. Take turns reading a page from the book. Use the reader to practice accuracy. Provide feedback as needed.

▲ Work with a partner. Choose an On-Level Reader. Take turns reading a page from the book. Use the reader to practice accuracy. Provide feedback as needed.

■ Work with a partner. Choose an Advanced Reader. Take turns reading a page from the book. Use the reader to practice accuracy. Provide feedback as needed.

Technology

- Leveled Reader Database
- Leveled Reading Street Readers CD-ROM

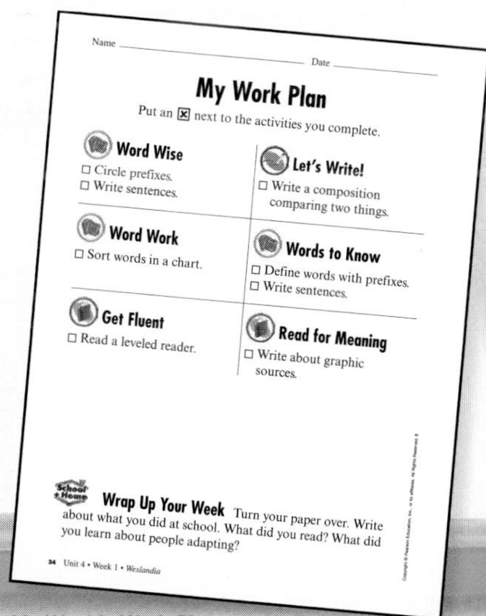
Name Date

My Work Plan

Put an ☒ next to the activities you complete.

Word Wise
☐ Circle prefixes.
☐ Write sentences.

Let's Write!
☐ Write a composition comparing two things.

Word Work
☐ Sort words in a chart.

Words to Know
☐ Define words with prefixes.
☐ Write sentences.

Get Fluent
☐ Read a leveled reader.

Read for Meaning
☐ Write about graphic sources.

Wrap Up Your Week Turn your paper over. Write about what you did at school. What did you read? What did you learn about people adapting?

34 Unit 4 • Week 1 • Weslandia

My Weekly Work Plan

Week 1

Objectives

- Introduce the weekly concept.
- Develop oral vocabulary.

Today at a Glance

Oral Vocabulary
discovered, courage, determination, practice

Comprehension
◉ Draw conclusions
◉ Questioning

Reading
"The Go-Cart"

Fluency
Appropriate phrasing/punctuation cues

Lesson Vocabulary
Tested vocabulary

Research and Inquiry
Identify questions

Spelling
Words from many cultures

Conventions
Subject and object pronouns

Handwriting
Cursive letters *c* and *C*

Writing
Picture book

Concept Talk

Question of the Week

How do people adapt to difficult situations?

Introduce the concept To explore the unit concept of Adapting, this week students will read, write, and talk about how people adapt to difficult situations. Write the Question of the Week on the board.

ROUTINE **Activate Prior Knowledge** **Team Talk**

1. **Think** Have students think about examples of how people can adapt to difficult situations.
2. **Pair** Have pairs of students discuss the Question of the Week. Remind students to consider suggestions from each other.
3. **Share** Call on a few students to share their ideas with the group. Guide the discussion and encourage elaboration with prompts such as:
   - What kinds of difficulties might people have to adapt to?
   - How are these different from everyday difficulties?

Routines Flip Chart

Anchored Talk

Develop oral vocabulary Have students turn to pp. 20–21 in their Student Editions. Look at each of the photos. Then, use the prompts to guide discussion and create the *How people adapt to difficult situations* concept map.

- How does this stone bridge help people adapt to their environment? (allows people to cross) People can meet physical challenges in their environment. Let's add *Physical challenges* to our concept map.
- What challenge does the diver face in his deep-sea exploration? (He must have enough oxygen and a wet suit to remain underwater.) New inventions help people adapt to new and difficult situations. Let's add *Inventing new things* and *New situations* to the concept map.

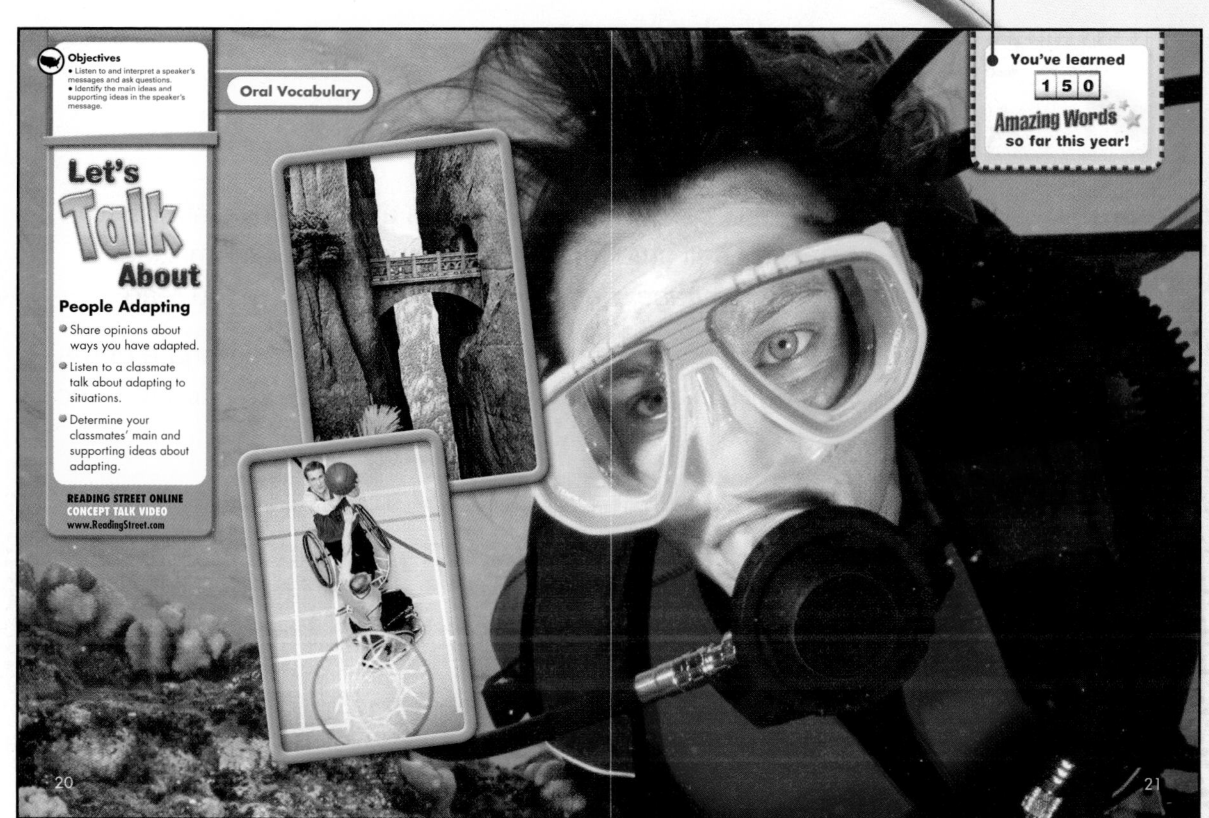

Objectives
Oral Vocabulary
Let's Talk About
People Adapting
Share opinions about ways you have adapted.
Listen to a classmate talk about adapting to situations.
Determine your classmates' main and supporting ideas about adapting.
READING STREET ONLINE
CONCEPT TALK VIDEO
www.ReadingStreet.com
You've learned
1 5 0
Amazing Words
so far this year!
20
21

Student Edition pp. 20–21

Amazing Words

You've learned 1 5 0 words so far

You'll learn 0 1 0 words this week!

discovered	customize
courage	flexibility
determination	transformation
practice	advancement
exploration	dynamic

Writing on Demand

Writing Fluency
Ask students to respond to the photos on pp. 20–21 by writing as well as they can and as much as they can about how people adapt to difficult situations.

- How have the young men in the gymnasium photo adapted to having a disability? (They play basketball using wheelchairs.)
- After discussing the photos, ask: How do people adapt to difficult situations?

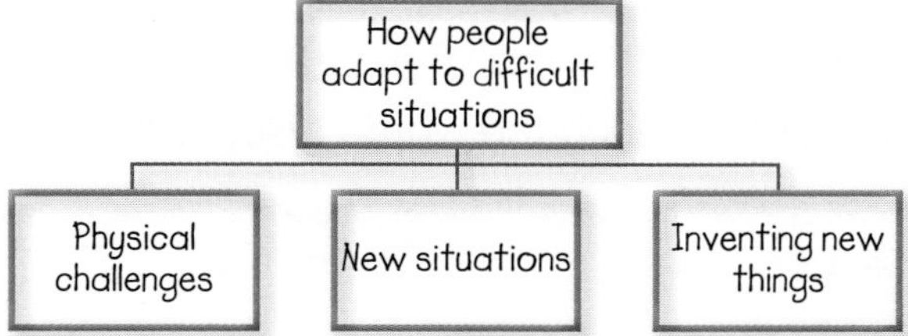

Connect to reading Tell students that this week they will be reading about ways people handle various difficulties. Encourage students to add concept-related words to this week's concept map.

ELL Preteach Concepts Use the Day 1 instruction on ELL Poster 16 to assess and build background knowledge, develop concepts, and build oral vocabulary.

ELL Poster 16

ELL

English Language Learners

ELL Support Additional ELL support and modified instruction is provided in the *ELL Handbook* and in the ELL Support lessons on pp. DI•16–DI•25.

Listening comprehension English learners will benefit from additional visual support to understand the key terms in the concept map. Use the pictures on pp. 20–21 to scaffold understanding.

Frontload for Read Aloud Use the modified Read Aloud on p. DI•19 the ELL Support lessons to prepare students to listen to "Birdsong on a Summer Evening" (p. 21b).

Objectives

- Develop listening comprehension.
- Develop oral vocabulary.

Check Oral Vocabulary
SUCCESS PREDICTOR

Oral Vocabulary
Amazing Words

Introduce Amazing Words "Birdsong on a Summer Evening" on p. 21b is about a boy's efforts to overcome a disability. Tell students to listen for this week's Amazing Words—*discovered, courage, determination, practice*—as you read.

Model fluency As you read "Birdsong on a Summer Evening," model appropriate phrasing by grouping words in a meaningful way and paying attention to punctuation cues.

Teach Amazing Words

Amazing Words Oral Vocabulary Routine

discovered
courage
determination
practice

1. **Introduce** Write the word *determination* on the board. Have students say the word aloud with you. In "Birdsong on a Summer Evening," the narrator needed *determination* to play baseball again. How can you use context clues to determine or clarify the meaning of the word *detemination*? Supply a student-friendly definition.
2. **Demonstrate** Break into groups. Have students consider suggestions from group members to demonstrate understanding. What goals do you think take the most *determination* to achieve? Which famous person do you think showed great *determination* in achieving a goal?
3. **Apply** Ask students to give a personal example of *determination.*

See p. OV•1 to teach the words *discovered, courage,* and *practice.*

Routines Flip Chart

Apply Amazing Words To build oral language, have students discuss the Amazing Words.

MONITOR PROGRESS Check Oral Vocabulary

During discussion, listen for students' use of the Amazing Words.

If... students are unable to use the Amazing Words to discuss the concept,
then... use Oral Vocabulary Routine in the Routines Flip Chart to demonstrate words in different contexts.

Day 1	Days 2–3	Day 4	Day 5
Check Oral Vocabulary	Check Retelling	Check Fluency	Check Oral Vocabulary

Birdsong on a Summer Evening

by Marilyn Helmer

People remember the summer of 1955 because it was one of the hottest on record. Day after day, the sun hung overhead, baking the earth with a heat that lasted right through the night.

For me, it was the summer I had to learn to live with only one arm. The spring before, I'd fallen off my uncle's tractor. After that monster wheel was through with it, the arm was too badly crushed to save. The hardest thing about losing my arm was that I was a baseball man. It was the most important thing in my life back then.

After the accident, [my coach] ignored me. It was as though I'd suddenly become as invisible as my lost arm, but I still went to the park sometimes to watch the games.

And then came Ben. I heard our neighbor Mrs. Shoemaker telling Mom that her nephew was coming to stay for the summer. I hadn't planned to be sitting on the front steps when Ben arrived, but that's exactly where I was. Ben got out of his car and stood there, watching me tossing my baseball up and down in one hand. "Yo there, are you a baseball man?" he called out.

There are some words, like people, that you take to right away. I'd never heard "yo" before and I liked it. I'd never been called a man before, never mind a baseball man, and I liked that, too. I took to Ben right away.

One hot afternoon, I badgered Ben to go swimming. I'd discovered that I could still swim with one arm, and I dragged Ben off to the lake every chance we had. But that day Ben had a different idea. He asked me where the library was.

Our town library was small, but Miss Prinel kept two huge fans going so it was cool inside. A few minutes later [Ben] came over with a book under his arm. He flipped it open and pointed to a picture of a baseball player.

The writing beneath the photograph identified the man as Pete Gray. It went on to say that he was an American League player, an outfielder for the St. Louis Browns in the forties – a man who symbolized sportsmanship, courage, and determination. Like me, he had only one arm.

"Starting this evening, we're gonna practice every day," Ben said.

I stared at him. "Wait a minute," I said.

(continued on p. 45s)

DAY 1 # Read and Comprehend

30–35 mins.

Objectives

- ◎ Draw conclusions and make inferences about text.
- ◎ Ask literal questions of text.
- Read grade-level text with appropriate phrasing.

Skills Trace

◎ **Draw Conclusions**

Introduce U4W1D1; U4W5D1; U6W1D1

Practice U4W1D2; U4W1D3; U4W5D2; U4W5D3; U6W1D2; U6W1D3

Reteach/Review U4W1D5; U4W2D2; U4W2D3; U4W4D2; U4W4D3; U4W5D5; U6W1D5; U6W3D2; U6W3D3; U6W5D2; U6W5D3

Assess/Test Weekly Tests U4W1; U4W5; U6W1

Benchmark Tests U4; U6

KEY:
U = Unit, W = Week, D = Day

Skill ↔ Strategy
◎ Draw Conclusions
◎ Questioning

Student Edition p. EI•6

Introduce drawing conclusions

When you draw a conclusion or make an inference, you make a reasonable judgment or decision based on evidence in the text. How can I draw a sensible conclusion? (by considering all the details I've learned about a subject or situation) The second bullet says that prior knowledge can help me draw a conclusion. What is prior knowledge? (information I already have, based on my reading or experiences) Have students turn to p. EI•6 in the Student Edition to review drawing conclusions. Then read "The Go-Cart" with students.

Model the skill

Think Aloud

Today we're going to read about a boy who successfully builds and races a go-cart. Have students follow along as you read the first paragraph of "The Go-Cart." The first paragraph of "The Go-Cart" includes details about the race. Jeff is having a dull summer and is excited to read about an upcoming event. I can conclude that the prize money is also important to Jeff. He will definitely get involved in this project.

Guide practice

Have students finish reading "The Go-Cart" on their own. After they read, have them use a graphic organizer like the one on p. 22 to identify facts, details, and any prior knowledge they have relating to the story.

Strategy check

Questioning Remind students that if they have difficulty understanding "The Go-Cart," they can use the strategy of asking questions. Model the strategy of generating literal questions to help monitor and adjust comprehension.

Model the strategy

When I started reading the story, I wondered how Jeff managed to build a real go-cart. I didn't understand how he could do this. I asked myself the literal question, "What did Jeff need to do this project?" Then I reread the story aloud and realized that the author mentions Jeff bought a kit of parts that included instructions, and that he asked for help when he needed it. That told me how Jeff was able to build his own go-cart for the race.

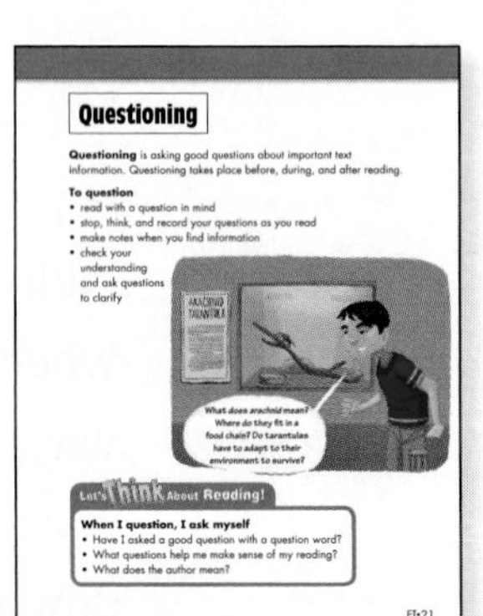

Student Edition p. EI•21

On their own

Use p. 247 in the *Reader's and Writer's Notebook* for additional practice with drawing conclusions.

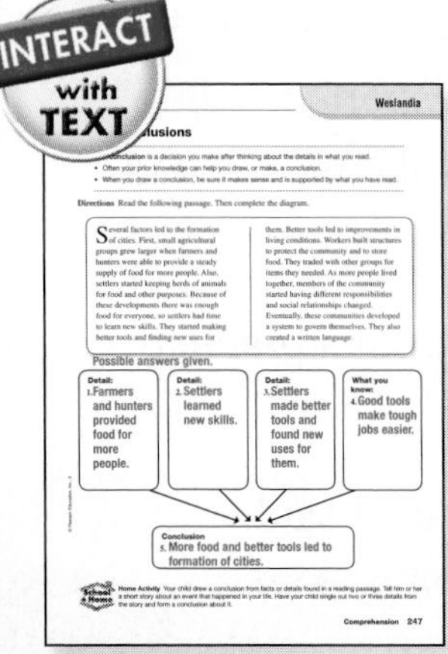

Reader's and Writer's Notebook p. 247

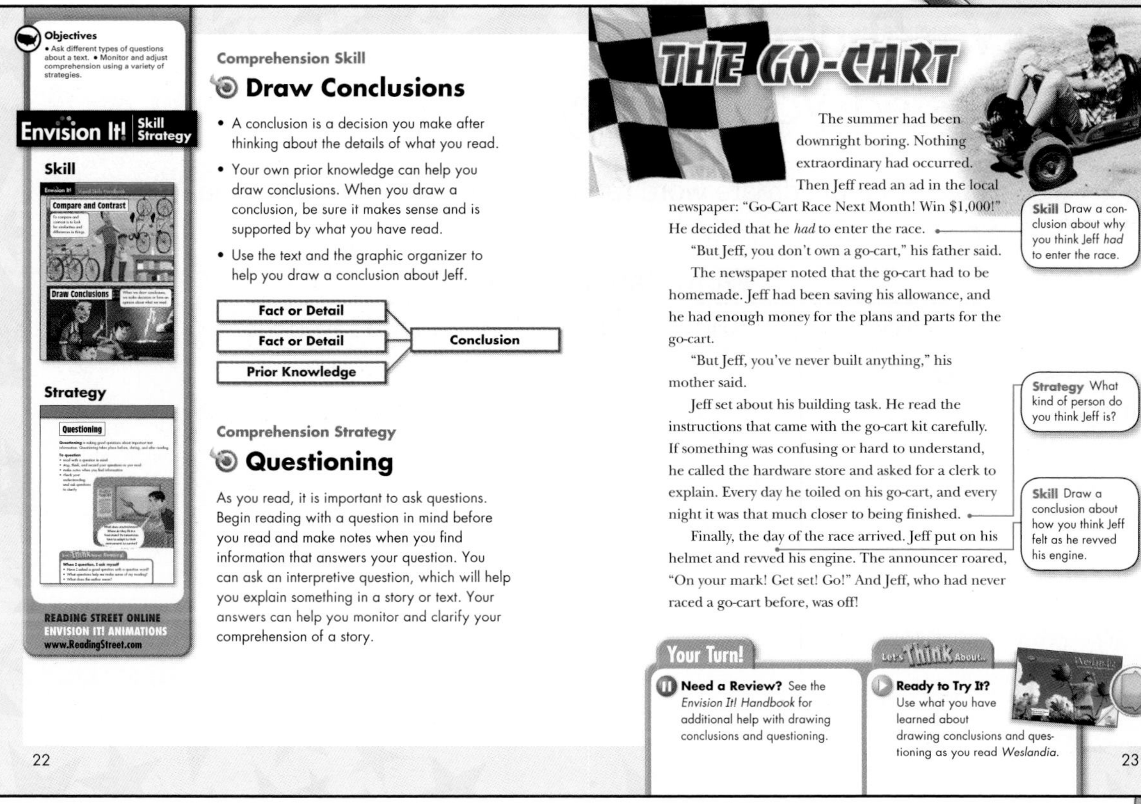

Objectives
• Ask different types of questions about a text. • Monitor and adjust comprehension using a variety of strategies.

Envision It! Skill Strategy

Skill

Strategy

READING STREET ONLINE
ENVISION IT! ANIMATIONS
www.ReadingStreet.com

Comprehension Skill

Draw Conclusions

- A conclusion is a decision you make after thinking about the details of what you read.
- Your own prior knowledge can help you draw conclusions. When you draw a conclusion, be sure it makes sense and is supported by what you have read.
- Use the text and the graphic organizer to help you draw a conclusion about Jeff.

Fact or Detail
Fact or Detail
Prior Knowledge
Conclusion

Comprehension Strategy

Questioning

As you read, it is important to ask questions. Begin reading with a question in mind before you read and make notes when you find information that answers your question. You can ask an interpretive question, which will help you explain something in a story or text. Your answers can help you monitor and clarify your comprehension of a story.

22

THE GO-CART

The summer had been downright boring. Nothing extraordinary had occurred. Then Jeff read an ad in the local newspaper: "Go-Cart Race Next Month! Win $1,000!" He decided that he *had* to enter the race.

"But Jeff, you don't own a go-cart," his father said.

The newspaper noted that the go-cart had to be homemade. Jeff had been saving his allowance, and he had enough money for the plans and parts for the go-cart.

"But Jeff, you've never built anything," his mother said.

Jeff set about his building task. He read the instructions that came with the go-cart kit carefully. If something was confusing or hard to understand, he called the hardware store and asked for a clerk to explain. Every day he toiled on his go-cart, and every night it was that much closer to being finished.

Finally, the day of the race arrived. Jeff put on his helmet and revved his engine. The announcer roared, "On your mark! Get set! Go!" And Jeff, who had never raced a go-cart before, was off!

Skill Draw a conclusion about why you think Jeff *had* to enter the race.

Strategy What kind of person do you think Jeff is?

Skill Draw a conclusion about how you think Jeff felt as he revved his engine.

Your Turn!

Need a Review? See the *Envision It! Handbook* for additional help with drawing conclusions and questioning.

Let's Think About...

Ready to Try It? Use what you have learned about drawing conclusions and questioning as you read *Weslandia*.

23

Student Edition pp. 22–23

Skill Possible response: He knew that he could not pass up such an opportunity to win the money.

Strategy Possible response: determined and creative

Skill Possible response: excited and proud

Academic Vocabulary

draw conclusions to make a decision or opinion that makes sense based on facts and details in a passage, also called an inference

punctuation cues periods, commas, and other marks that give clues to how to group words and phrases to help make the meaning clear

Model Fluency
Appropriate Phrasing

Model fluent reading Have students listen as you read paragraph 2 of "The Go-Cart" with appropriate phrasing. Explain that you will follow punctuation cues to emphasize meaning and read text smoothly.

ROUTINE Oral Rereading

1. **Read** Have students read paragraph 2 of "The Go-Cart" orally.
2. **Reread** To achieve optimal fluency and comprehension, students should reread the text three to four times with appropriate phrasing.
3. **Corrective Feedback** Have students read aloud without you. Provide feedback about their phrasing and encourage them to note punctuation that shows when to pause or come to a stop. Listen for use of appropriate phrasing.

Routines Flip Chart

English Language Learners

Draw conclusions Before students read "The Go-Cart," ask them to share what they know about a go-cart. Have them study the picture carefully and name the characteristics they see. If necessary, provide them with additional information. Ask students how a ride in a go-cart would feel.

DAY 1 Read and Comprehend

Objectives

- Activate prior knowledge of words.
- Identify questions for research.

Vocabulary
Tested Vocabulary

Lesson vocabulary

Have students create word rating charts using the categories *Know, Have Seen,* and *Don't Know.*

Activate prior knowledge

Word Rating Chart

Word	Know	Have Seen	Don't Know
blunders			✔
civilization	✔		
complex		✔	
envy	✔		
fleeing			
inspired			
rustling			
strategy			

Read each word to students and have them rate their knowledge of the word by placing a checkmark in one of the three columns: *Know* (know and can use); *Have Seen* (have seen or heard the word; don't know meaning)*; Don't Know* (don't know the word).

Have students provide sentences for the words they checked in the *Know* column. By the end of the week, have them revise their charts and demonstrate their understanding by using each word in a sentence.

Preteach Academic Vocabulary

ELL **Academic Vocabulary** Write the following words on the board:

draw conclusions	**fiction**
subject pronoun	**punctuation cues**
object pronoun	**instruction manual**

Have students share what they know about this week's Academic Vocabulary. Use the students' responses to assess their prior knowledge. Preteach the Academic Vocabulary by providing a student-friendly description, explanation, or example that clarifies the meaning of each term. Then ask students to restate the meaning of the Academic Vocabulary term in their own words.

Research and Inquiry
Identify Questions

Teach Discuss the Question of the Week: *How do people adapt to difficult situations?* Tell students they will investigate how people in ancient civilizations adapted to the challenges of their world. They will summarize and illustrate their findings and then present them to the class on Day 5.

Model Think Aloud: First I need to decide on the topic I'll research. I'll start by forming questions about ancient civilizations. I'm interested in finding out about the Mayan civilization. I know that this was a highly developed culture, so some inquiry questions could be, *How did the Maya farm their land? What did they do when they were not working?*

Guide practice After students have chosen topics, explain that tomorrow they will research their questions in print resources and online. Help students create a research plan for collecting information from print and electronic reference texts.

On their own Have students work in pairs to formulate open-ended questions.

21st Century Skills

Weekly Inquiry Project

Day 1	Identify Questions
Day 2	Navigate/Search
Day 3	Analyze
Day 4	Synthesize
Day 5	Communicate

Small Group Time

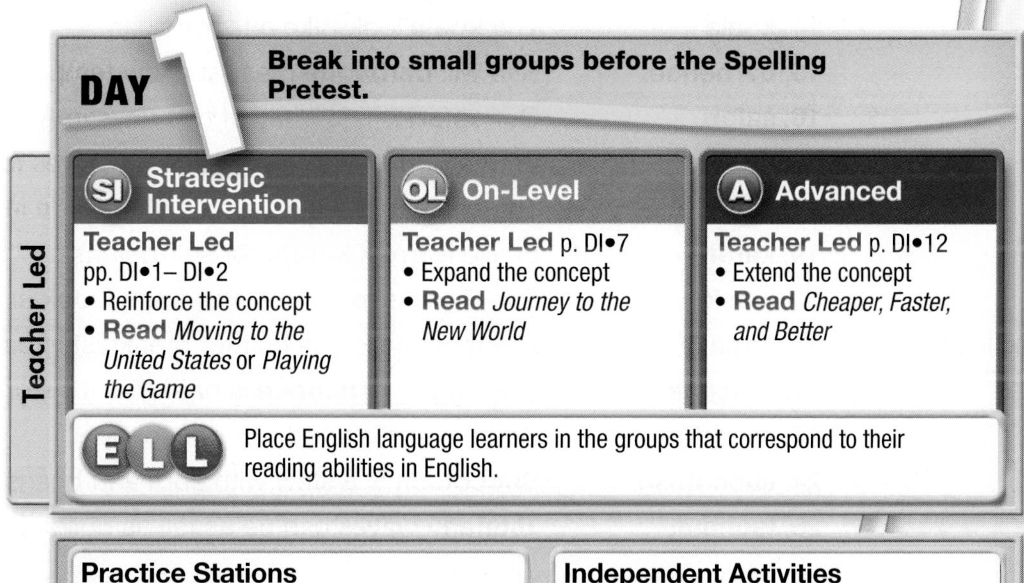

DAY 1 Break into small groups before the Spelling Pretest.

Teacher Led

SI Strategic Intervention	OL On-Level	A Advanced
Teacher Led pp. DI•1– DI•2 • Reinforce the concept • **Read** *Moving to the United States* or *Playing the Game*	**Teacher Led** p. DI•7 • Expand the concept • **Read** *Journey to the New World*	**Teacher Led** p. DI•12 • Extend the concept • **Read** *Cheaper, Faster, and Better*

ELL: Place English language learners in the groups that correspond to their reading abilities in English.

Practice Stations
- Read for Meaning
- Get Fluent
- Word Work

Independent Activities
- Concept Talk Video
- *Reader's and Writer's Notebook*
- Vocabulary Activities

ELL

English Language Learners

Multilingual vocabulary Students can apply knowledge of their home languages to acquire new English vocabulary by using the Multilingual Vocabulary Lists (*ELL Handbook*, pp. 431).

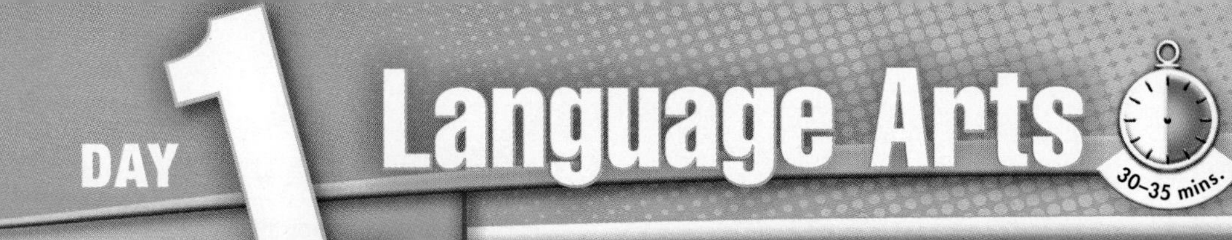

Objectives

- Pretest words from many cultures.
- Identify subject and object pronouns.
- Write cursive capital letter *C* and lowercase *c* in words.

Spelling Pretest
Words from Many Cultures

Introduce Many words in English come from other languages and may have unexpected spellings. Write *banquet*. In French, this word is pronounced *bankay* with a long *a*, but in English, it is pronounced *bankwet*. This week we will work on spelling words from other cultures.

Pretest Use these sentences to administer the spelling pretest. Say each word, read the sentence, and repeat the word.

1. khaki	Explorers often wear **khaki** clothing in the jungle.
2. hula	The **hula** is a native folk dance of Hawaii.
3. banana	A big, yellow **banana** is my favorite dessert.
4. ballet	The Nutcracker **ballet** is a fun story in dance.
5. waltz	Tony is the best dancer of the Mexican **waltz.**
6. tomato	The **tomato** was cultivated first in Mexico.
7. vanilla	The Aztecs used **vanilla** to add flavor.
8. canyon	A river can create a street of water called a **canyon.**
9. yogurt	Bill enjoys **yogurt** for a daily snack.
10. banquet	My uncle loves the food at the holiday **banquet.**
11. macaroni	**Macaroni** with cheese is Maria's favorite pasta.
12. polka	The **polka** is a lively dance folk dance.
13. cobra	A **cobra** snake is dangerous.
14. koala	The **koala** looks like a teddy bear.
15. barbeque	Rita will **barbeque** meat at a low temperature.
16. safari	Our **safari** is a journey of two days in Africa.
17. buffet	With a **buffet**, we could serve ourselves food.
18. stampede	The crash made the animals **stampede** in fright.
19. karate	Emilio learned **karate** for self-defense.
20. kiosk	She like to shop at a small, open **kiosk** at the mall.

Challenge words

21. papaya	The most delicious fruit for breakfast is **papaya.**
22. artichoke	Cooking an **artichoke** is hard, but it's worth it!
23. sauerkraut	**Sauerkraut** is good use of cabbage.
24. succotash	**Succotash** is a stew with corn and beans.
25. tsunami	**Tsunami** waves can be as tall as buildings.

Self-correct After the pretest, you can either display the correctly spelled words or spell them orally. Have students self-correct their pretests by writing misspelled words.

On their own For additional practice, use *Let's Practice It!* p. 184 on the *Teacher Resources DVD-ROM.*

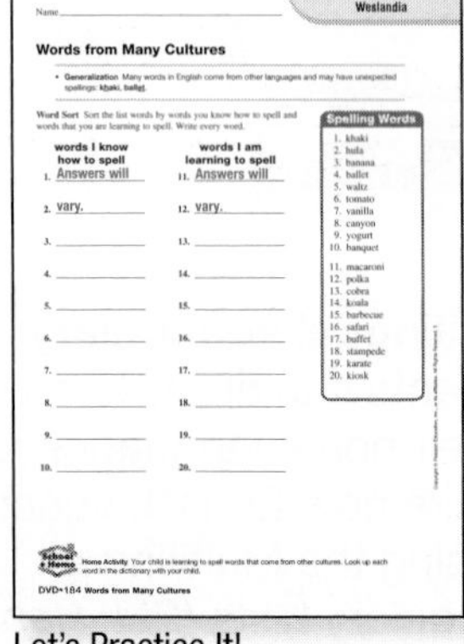
Words from Many Cultures

Let's Practice It!
TR DVD•184

Conventions
Subject and Object Pronouns

Teach Display Grammar Transparency 16, and read aloud the explanation and examples in the box. Then display this sentence: *He was an outcast from the civilization around him*.

In this sentence, *he* is a subject pronoun, and *him* is an object pronoun. *He* is the subject of the sentence, and *him* is the object of the preposition *around*.

Grammar Transparency 16, TR DVD

Model Read aloud the information in the box. Complete numbers 1 and 2.

Guide practice Guide students to complete items 3–10. Apply the definition for subject and object pronouns to show how you determined the appropriate pronouns. Record the correct responses on the transparency.

Daily Fix-It Use Daily Fix-It numbers 1 and 2 in the right margin.

Connect to oral language Have students read sentences 11–16 on the transparency and underline the pronoun to correctly complete each sentence.

Handwriting
Cursive Letter *c* and *C*

Model letter formation Display the capital cursive letter *C* and the lowercase letter *c*. Follow the stroke instruction pictured to model letter formation.

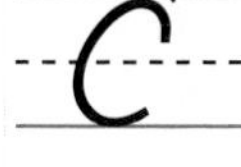

Model legibility Explain that writing legibly means letters are the correct size, form, and slant. The writing has smoothness: the lines are not shaky or jagged. Model writing this sentence smoothly: *Charles played cymbals in the Chicago City band*. Make sure the letters aren't too light, dark, or jagged.

Guide practice Have students write these sentences. *Carol cited Cicero as her source. Charles chose Sid Caesar as his source*. Circulate around the room, guiding students.

Academic Vocabulary

object pronoun a pronoun that is used after action verbs or as objects of prepositions: *me, you, him, her, it, us, them*

subject pronoun a pronoun that is used as the subject of a sentence: *I, you, he, she, it, we, they*

Daily Fix-It

1. Caleb told we about a book he red. *(us; read.)*
2. It were about islands with natives and bannana trees. *(was; banana)*

English Language Learners

Cognates Point out the Spanish cognates for this week's lesson in spelling. Note that more than half of this week's spelling words have cognates because the words come from different cultures.

ballet/ballet
hula/hula
tomato/tomate
vanilla/vainilla
yogurt/yogur
macaroni/macarrones
polka/polca
banquet/banquete
cobra/cobra
koala/koala
karate/karate
papaya/papaya
sauerkraut/sauerkraut
succotash/succotash
tsunami/tsunami

DAY 1 Language Arts

Objective

- Understand and identify the features of a picture book.

MINI-LESSON

5 Day Planner

Guide to Mini-Lessons

DAY 1	Read Like a Writer
DAY 2	Creating a Story Chart
DAY 3	Defining Focus Clearly
DAY 4	Revising Strategy: Adding
DAY 5	Proofread for Pronouns

Writing—Picture Book

Introduce

MINI-LESSON

Read Like a Writer

INTERACT with TEXT

Reader's and Writer's Notebook p. 248

- **Introduce** This week you will write a picture book about a character who doesn't always follow a crowd. A picture book is an illustrated story. It includes a clear focus, characters, setting, and a plot, or series of events. After writing the story, we add pictures to illustrate and provide visual portrayals of significant events.

  Prompt In *Weslandia,* a boy decides to remake his world rather than accept it as it is. Think about someone you know who doesn't always follow the crowd. Now write a picture book, with your own illustration, about that person.

  Trait Focus/Ideas: Clearly Defined Focus

  Mode Narrative

- **Examine Model Text** Picture books combine visual and written elements to tell a story. Let's look at a narrative about a boy with an imaginary twin. Pay particular attention to the key features of the story that an author and artists might choose to illustrate. Have students read *The Boy in the Mirror* on p. 248 of the *Reader's and Writer's Notebook*.

- **Key Features** Explain that a picture book is an illustrated story. It can describe a true or fictional event. Tell students that picture books oftentimes will use dialogue to bring the story to life. Point out the dialogue as you read together. Comment on how it makes the characters more realistic.

  As we read the story, we can select the events that an artist would want to illustrate in order to better convey the story's main ideas. Have students select key events in the story that a picture might make clearer to a reader.

Review key features

Review the key features of a picture book with students. You may want to post the key features in the classroom for students to reference as they work on their picture books.

Key Features of a Picture Book

- may tell a story or describe a true event
- often contains dialogue
- includes illustrations or art

ROUTINE Quick Write for Fluency

Team Talk

1. **Talk** Have pairs take two or three minutes to discuss the features of an illustrated narrative, or picture book.
2. **Write** Each person writes a short paragraph explaining the relationship of narrative elements to the illustrations.
3. **Share** Partners read their paragraphs to each other.

Routines Flip Chart

Wrap Up Your Day

- ✔ **Build Concepts** What did you learn about the relationship between illustrations and narrative in a picture book?
- ✔ **Oral Vocabulary** Have students use the Amazing Words they learned in context sentences.
- ✔ **Homework** Send home this week's Family Times newsletter in *Let's Practice It!* pp. 185–186 on the *Teacher Resources DVD-ROM*.

Let's Practice It!
TR DVD•185–186

Let Me Check MY List

Encourage students to keep lists of words they come across that are exciting or interesting to them. They can use their lists to increase their vocabulary and incorporate them in their own writing. This is a great way to improve vocabulary and word choice.

ELL

English Language Learners

Picture Book Make sure that students understand the meaning of picture book. Emphasize that the illustrations are important in telling the story in a picture book. List examples of picture books with which students may be familiar. Explain how these examples reflect the features of a picture book. *(A story is narrated with many pictures to illustrate characters, setting, and events.)*

Preview DAY 2

Tell students that tomorrow they will read about a boy who creates his own world.

Objectives
- Expand the weekly concept.
- Develop oral vocabulary.

Today at a Glance

Oral Vocabulary
exploration, customize

Word Analysis
Endings *-s, -ed, -ing*

Literary Terms
Idioms

Story Structure
Resolution

Lesson Vocabulary
Endings *-s, -ed, -ing*

Reading
"Long-Ago Lives"
Weslandia

Fluency
Appropriate phrasing-punctuation cues

Research and Inquiry
Navigate/Search

Spelling
Words from many cultures

Conventions
Subject and object pronouns

Writing
Picture book

Concept Talk

Question of the Week
How do people adapt to difficult situations?

Expand the concept Remind students of the Question of the week. Tell students that today they will begin reading *Weslandia.* As they read, encourage students to think about how the characters adapt to their situations.

Anchored Talk

Develop oral vocabulary Use the photos on pp. 20–21 and the Read Aloud, "Birdsong on a Summer Evening," to talk about the Amazing Words—*discovered, courage, determination,* and *practice.* Add these and other concept-related words to the concept map to develop students' knowledge of the topic. Have students get into groups. Then have them use the following questions to elicit and consider suggestions from each group member and develop their understanding of the concept.

- What had Ben *discovered* about playing ball despite having a disability?
- What can people learn when they *practice* a new activity?
- How does a display of *determination* and *courage* help us adapt?

Oral Vocabulary
Amazing Words

Amazing Words

discovered	customize
courage	flexibility
determination	transformation
practice	advancement
exploration	dynamic

Amazing Words Oral Vocabulary Routine

Teach Amazing Words

1. **Introduce** Write the Amazing Word *exploration* on the board. Have students say it aloud with you. Relate *exploration* to the photographs on pp. 20–21 and "Birdsong on a Summer Evening." What might lead someone to an *exploration* of a new skill or idea? How does the *exploration* of our own abilities help us grow? Have students use the context clues to determine the definition of the word. (*Exploration* means a journey to discover something new.)
2. **Demonstrate** Have students answer questions to demonstrate understanding. What did Columbus's *exploration* of the New World lead to? How might the *exploration* of another culture broaden your ideas about the world?
3. **Apply** Have students apply their understanding. What *exploration* would you like to take part in?

See p. OV•1 to teach *customize.*

Routines Flip Chart

Apply Amazing Words

Help students establish a purpose for reading as they read "Long-Ago Lives" on p. 25. Have them think about the *exploration* of new possibilities and about how we can *customize* objects to help us attain goals.

Connect to reading

Explain that today students will read about how people of long ago played an interesting sport. As they read, they should think about how this week's Question of the Week and the Amazing Words *exploration* and *customize* apply to the challenge of adapting to fit particular needs.

ELL Reinforce Vocabulary Use the Day 2 instruction on ELL Poster 16 to teach lesson vocabulary and the lesson concept.

ELL Poster 16

Objectives

- Add endings to base words to alter their use.
- Understand common idioms.
- Understand that stories are structured to reach a resolution.

Word Analysis
Endings *-s, -ed, -ing*

Teach endings Tell students that the endings *-s, -ed,* and *-ing* can be added to base words to change how the words are used in sentences. Have students practice working with base words and endings using the chart below.

Model Think Aloud Write the word *inspired* on the board. This word will appear in *Weslandia*. I don't recognize a base word in *inspired*, but I do see an *-ed* ending. I remember that sometimes the base word drops the final *e* when an ending is added. If I drop the *-ed* and add the final *e* back on, the base word is *inspire*, which means "to fill with a thought or feeling." So, *inspired* means "filled with a thought or feeling."

Base word + *-s, -ed, -ing*

blunder	blunders	blundered	blundering
civilization (civilize)			
envy			
flee			
inspire			
rustle			

Guide practice Have students add *-s, -ed,* and *-ing,* to the base words listed in the chart. Discuss how the endings change the function of the words in the sentences.

On their own Have students use a dictionary to check the spellings and meanings of the newly-formed words. Then have students make sentences with the words. Follow the Strategy for Meaningful Word Parts to teach the word *fleeing*.

ROUTINE **Strategy for Meaningful Word Parts**

1. **Look for meaningful word parts** Display the word *fleeing*. Underline *flee* and circle *-ing*.
2. **Connect to meaning** I see the word *flee* and I see the *-ing*. I know that *flee* means "to run away," and I know that the ending *-ing* is used for actions that are happening now.
3. **Read the word** Blend the meaningful word parts together to read the word *fleeing* and determine that its meaning is "running away from."

Continue the Routine with the words *envy* and *rustle*.

Routines Flip Chart

Literary Terms
Idioms

Teach idioms

Tell students that an idiom is a phrase or expression whose meaning cannot be understood from the ordinary meaning of the words that form it. Explain that context clues will sometimes help you to figure out the meaning of an idiom.

Model idioms

Think Aloud Let's look back at "The Go-Cart" on page 23. I see the phrase *set about* in paragraph 5. What could *set about* mean? It looks like Jeff is starting to work on the go-cart. So *set about* seems to mean "began doing something."

Guide practice

Find an example of an idiom in *Weslandia*. Be sure to point out that the dictionary offers explanations of some idioms.

On their own

Have students identify and explain the meaning of idioms in other selections of their Student Edition or share idioms they have said or heard in their own lives.

Story Structure
Resolution

Teach resolution

The plot of a fiction story contains a conflict that must find a **resolution** or solution in order to satisfy a reader's expectations. Recognizing conflict and resolution helps readers to better understand a story and foreshadow what might happen next.

Model the strategy

Think Aloud I know that a problem or conflict in *A Summer's Trade* was that Tony used the money he was saving for a saddle to buy back his sick grandmother's bracelet. I know that this problem was resolved when his grandmother got well and traded her next rug for the saddle.

Guide practice

Discuss with students the story structure of another fiction story, such as *The Ch'i-lin Purse*. Have students describe the main problem in the story and the resolution. Ask students to describe how the problem advances the plot and gives rise to future events.

On their own

Have students preview the illustrations of *Weslandia* and tell how the pictures provide clues about the actions that give rise to the conflict and resolution of the story.

Academic Vocabulary

fiction stories that tell of imaginary people and happenings

Objectives

- Determine the meaning of grade-level words by using endings and word structure.
- Read grade-level text with appropriate phrasing.

Vocabulary Strategy for Endings *-s, -ed,* and *-ing*

Student Edition p. W•4

Teach word structure

Envision It!

Tell students to use the strategy of word structure when they encounter a word with the ending *-s, -ed,* or *-ing*. They should first determine what the base word is. Explain that both nouns and verbs can end in *-s*, but that *-ed* and *-ing* can also be added to verbs to show time or tense, and to nouns to create adjectives. Refer students to *Words*! on p. W•4 in the Student Edition for additional practice with base words.

Model the strategy

Think Aloud Write on the board: *We are likely to imagine them fleeing for their lives from enemies or wild beasts*. I haven't seen the word *fleeing* before, but I can guess from the word structure that it is a verb. The context suggests running in fear from something, so I'm thinking that the base word *flee* means "run away." With the ending, or affix, *-ing*, it means "escaping."

Guide practice

Write this sentence on the board: *Stand on one of those ancient ball courts and you can almost feel the excitement of the crowd or hear the rustling of a feather headdress.* Have students determine the meaning of *rustling* by examining its structure and using context clues. If they are unable to identify the *-ing* ending and its relationship to the base word, then have them look up the word in a dictionary or glossary. For additional support, use *Envision It! Pictured Vocabulary Cards* or *Tested Vocabulary Cards.*

On their own

Read "Long-Ago Lives" on p. 25. Have students use word structure clues to determine the meaning of other words in the passage. For additional practice use *Reader's and Writer's Notebook* p. 249.

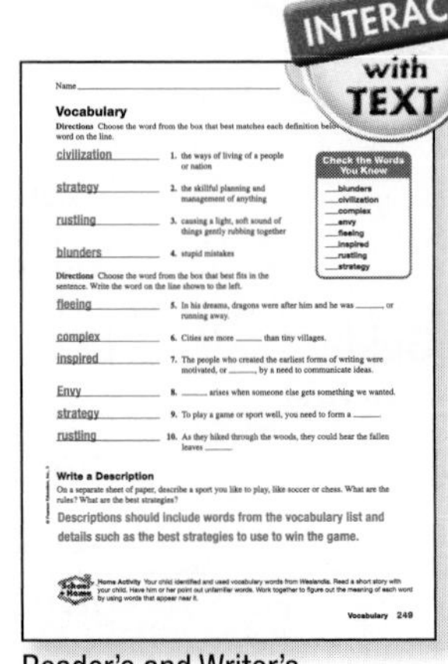

Reader's and Writer's Notebook p. 249

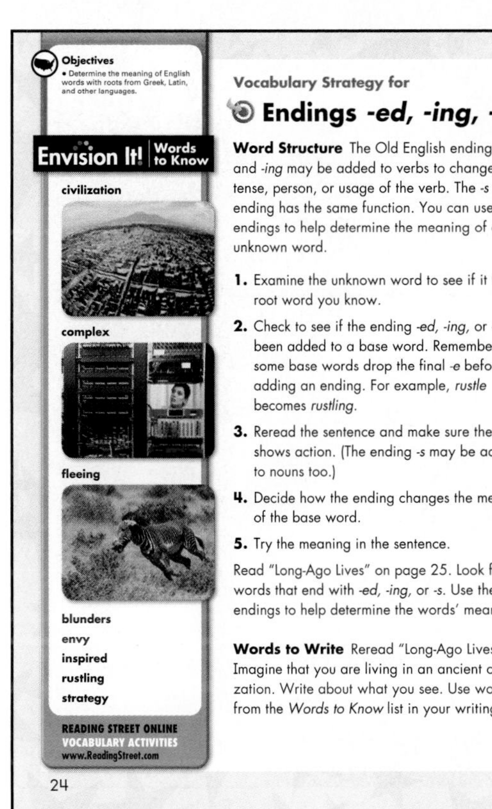

Objectives
• Determine the meaning of English words with roots from Greek, Latin, and other languages.

Envision It! Words to Know

civilization

complex

fleeing

blunders
envy
inspired
rustling
strategy

READING STREET ONLINE
VOCABULARY ACTIVITIES
www.ReadingStreet.com

Vocabulary Strategy for

Endings *-ed, -ing, -s*

Word Structure The Old English endings *-ed* and *-ing* may be added to verbs to change the tense, person, or usage of the verb. The *-s* ending has the same function. You can use endings to help determine the meaning of an unknown word.

1. Examine the unknown word to see if it has a root word you know.
2. Check to see if the ending *-ed, -ing,* or *-s* has been added to a base word. Remember that some base words drop the final *-e* before adding an ending. For example, *rustle* becomes *rustling.*
3. Reread the sentence and make sure the word shows action. (The ending *-s* may be added to nouns too.)
4. Decide how the ending changes the meaning of the base word.
5. Try the meaning in the sentence.

Read "Long-Ago Lives" on page 25. Look for words that end with *-ed, -ing,* or *-s.* Use the endings to help determine the words' meanings.

Words to Write Reread "Long-Ago Lives." Imagine that you are living in an ancient civilization. Write about what you see. Use words from the *Words to Know* list in your writing.

24

LONG-AGO LIVES

We do not usually envy the lives of people who lived thousands of years ago. We are likely to imagine them fleeing for their lives from enemies or wild beasts. Any civilization without excellent shopping, television, and computers seems far too primitive for us.

However, we have learned much about early cultures. What we have learned shows us that their world was often complex, not simple. They were not all that different from us. For example, two thousand years ago the Mayan people played a ball game. The game was played by teams on stone courts with special goals. Players needed great strength and skill. The strategy was to send a heavy ball through a high stone ring using only hips, knees, and elbows. Kings might play this game, for which the stakes were very high. No one wanted to make any blunders because the loser might lose his head!

This game may have inspired our modern game of soccer. Stand on one of those ancient ball courts and you can almost feel the excitement of the crowd or hear the rustling of a feather headdress.

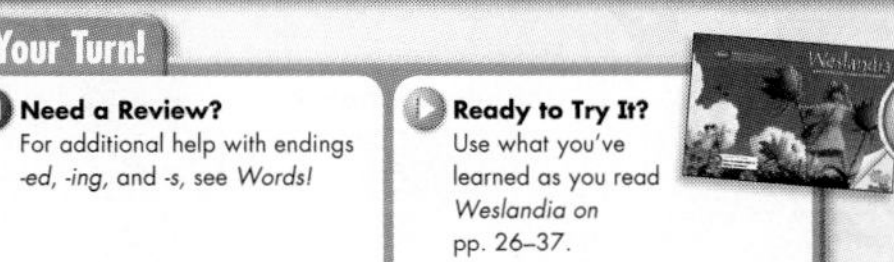

Your Turn!

Need a Review? For additional help with endings *-ed, -ing,* and *-s,* see *Words!*

Ready to Try It? Use what you've learned as you read *Weslandia* on pp. 26–37.

25

Student Edition pp. 24–25

Reread for Fluency
Appropriate Phrasing

Model fluent reading Read paragraph 2 of "Long-Ago Lives" aloud, pausing at commas and coming to a full stop at periods. Tell students that you are reading the passage with appropriate phrasing to enhance comprehension and to convey meaning, using punctuation cues to guide you as you read.

ROUTINE Oral Reading

1. **Read** Have students read paragraph 2 of "Long-Ago Lives" orally.
2. **Reread** To achieve optimal fluency and comprehension, students should reread the text three or four times.
3. **Corrective Feedback** Have students read aloud without you. Provide feedback about their phrasing and encourage them to note punctuation that shows when to pause or come to a stop. Listen for use of appropriate phrasing.

Routines Flip Chart

Lesson Vocabulary

blunders stupid mistakes

civilization the ways of living of a people or nation

complex made up of a number of parts; hard to understand

envy feeling of discontent because another person has what you want

fleeing to be running away

inspired to be filled with a thought or feeling; influenced

rustling causing a light, soft sound of things gently rubbing together

strategy the skillful planning and management of anything

Differentiated Instruction

SI Strategic Intervention
Have students identify the word endings from this week's lesson vocabulary. Help students identify how these endings change the root words.

English Language Learners
Vocabulary Point out how a word's meaning can be expressed with other words. Repeat the sentence: *The strategy was to send a ball through a high stone ring.* Then have students suggest other words for *strategy*.

Build Academic Vocabulary
Use the lesson vocabulary pictured on p. 24 to teach the meanings of *civilization, complex,* and *envy*. Call on pairs to write the words on sticky notes and use them to label images of the words on the ELL poster.

DAY 2 Read and Comprehend

Objectives

- Understand the elements of fiction.
- Use illustrations to preview and predict.
- Set a purpose for reading.

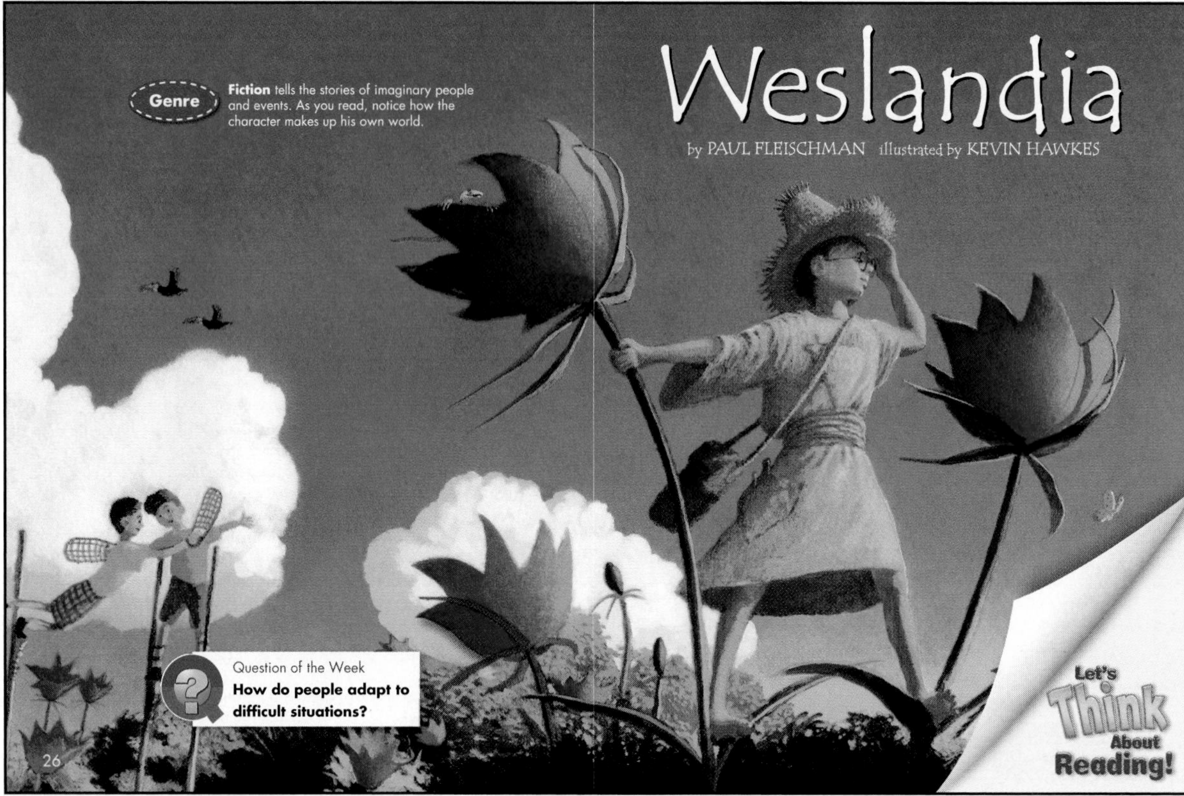

Student Edition pp. 26–27

Build Background

Discuss gardening

Team Talk Have students turn to a partner and discuss the Question of the Week and these questions about gardening. Have them elicit and consider each other's suggestions.

- How did people grow crops in the past?
- How might farmers of long ago have adapted to working conditions?
- What could be rewarding about having your own garden?

Connect to selection

Have students discuss their answers with the class. Encourage them to ask questions to clarify the speaking student's perspective. Possible responses: They planted seeds of plants found locally. They might have had difficulty with irrigation and crop failure from pests or weather. It would be satisfying to grow just what you like and to be able to see tangible results of your hard work. For additional opportunities to build background, use the Background Building Audio.

Prereading Strategies

Genre Explain that **fiction** tells stories of imaginary people and events. Fiction may contain characters and events that are realistic or ones that seem odd or dreamlike.

Preview and predict Have students preview *Weslandia* by looking at the title and illustrations. Have them predict what they will find out as they read.

Set purpose Prior to reading, have students set their own purposes for reading this selection. To help students set a purpose, ask them to think about what people do to adapt to difficult situations.

INTERACT with TEXT

Have students use p. 22 in the *Reader's and Writer's Notebook* to review and use the strategy of questioning.

Small Group Time

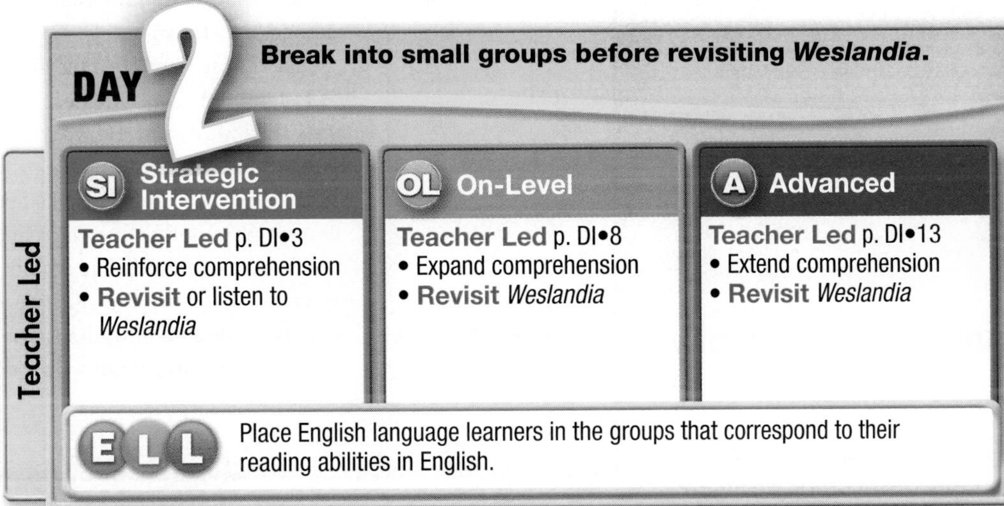

DAY 2 Break into small groups before revisiting *Weslandia*.

Teacher Led

SI Strategic Intervention	OL On-Level	A Advanced
Teacher Led p. DI•3 • Reinforce comprehension • **Revisit** or listen to *Weslandia*	**Teacher Led** p. DI•8 • Expand comprehension • **Revisit** *Weslandia*	**Teacher Led** p. DI•13 • Extend comprehension • **Revisit** *Weslandia*

ELL Place English language learners in the groups that correspond to their reading abilities in English.

Practice Stations	Independent Activities
• Words to Know • Get Fluent • Word Wise	• Background Building Audio • *Reader's and Writer's Notebook* • Research and Inquiry

Differentiated Instruction

 Strategic Intervention

Set purpose Work with students to set a purpose for reading, or if time permits, have students work with partners to set purposes.

 Advanced

Have students write two or three sentences about how crop farming has changed over time.

Multidraft Reading

For **Whole Group** instruction, choose one of the reading options below. For each reading, have students set the purpose indicated.

Option 1
Day 2 Read the selection. Use Guide Comprehension to monitor and clarify understanding.
Day 3 Reread the selection. Use Extend Thinking to develop higher-order thinking skills.

Option 2
Day 2 Read the first half of the selection, using both Guide Comprehension and Extend Thinking instruction.
Day 3 Read the second half of the selection, using both Guide Comprehension and Extend Thinking instruction.

ELL

English Language Learners

Build background To build background, review the selection summary in English (*ELL Handbook*, p. 121). Use the Retelling Cards to provide visual support for the summary.

DAY 2 Read and Comprehend

Objectives

- Ask questions to monitor, adjust, and improve comprehension of text.

OPTION 1 Guide Comprehension Skills and Strategies

Teach Questioning

Questioning Write on the board: *How does Wesley feel about being different*? Explain that this is an interpretive, or inferential question because the answer is not written in the text. There is no sentence that says how he feels about standing out. The reader infers it after reading these pages. Have students answer this interpretive question using pp. 28–29.

Corrective Feedback

If... students are unable to answer an interpretive question,
then... model answering interpretive questions based on inferences from the text.

Model the Strategy

Think Aloud: A question I could ask here is *How does Wesley feel about being different?* Is there a sentence that actually says this? (no) I can infer that he is unhappy based on details in the story.

"Of course he's miserable," moaned Wesley's mother. "He sticks out."

"Like a nose," snapped his father.

Listening through the heating vent, Wesley knew they were right. He was an outcast from the civilization around him.

He alone in his town disliked pizza and soda, alarming his mother and the school nurse. He found professional football stupid. He'd refused to shave half his head, the hairstyle worn by all the other boys, despite his father's bribe of five dollars.

Passing his neighborhood's two styles of

Let's Think About...

Why does Wesley feel like an outcast?
Questioning

1

28

Student Edition pp. 28–29

Let's Think About...

1. Wesley feels like an outcast because he's different from other people in his town.
2. I think his project will be finding a way to get along with the other children.

OPTION 2 Extend Thinking Think Critically

Higher-Order Thinking Skills

Questioning • Analysis Ask yourself a literal question about page 29. How could this question be answered based on the text? Possible question: What does Wesley find interesting about his school day? Possible response: He finds the lesson about agriculture in other civilizations interesting.

The text states that he is an outcast and has no friends. His parents think he is miserable because he stands out. If I were Wesley, I would feel lonely and sad. But Wesley refuses to be like all the others, so I also think he likes being different.

On Their Own

Have students reread pp. 28–29 and ask additional interpretive questions.

housing—garage on the left and garage on the right—Wesley alone dreamed of more exciting forms of shelter. He had no friends, but plenty of tormentors.

Fleeing them was the only sport he was good at.

Each afternoon his mother asked him what he'd learned in school that day.

"That seeds are carried great distances by the wind," he answered on Wednesday.

"That each civilization has its staple food crop," he answered on Thursday.

"That school's over and I should find a good summer project," he answered on Friday.

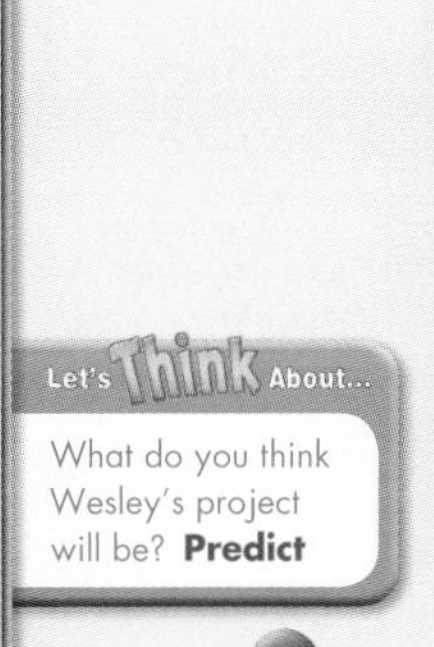

Let's Think About...
What do you think Wesley's project will be? **Predict**

2

29

Idioms • Analysis What does the idiom *sticks out* on page 28 mean? In what ways does Wesley "stick out"? Possible response: It means that a person is different in a way that other people notice. Wesley sticks out because he does not like pizza, soda, or professional football, and he refuses to cut his hair the way everyone else does.

Character and Plot • Analysis Infer what the author means when he says, *Wesley alone dreamed of more exciting forms of shelter.* What does this tell you about Wesley? How does this inference about Wesley's life foreshadow what might happen in the story? Possible response: Wesley thinks the neighborhood homes look boring and too similar. He thinks more imaginatively than other people in his neighborhood. Wesley might build a new, more creative form of shelter later in the story.

Differentiated Instruction

Advanced

Critical thinking Have students discuss the ways that seeds become plants. Have them answer the question: What are some things that help seeds take root in the soil?

ELL

English Language Learners

Activate prior knowledge Ask volunteers to name plants that give us food or clothing. Make a list on the board of students' responses.

Objectives

- Describe incidents that advance the story to draw conclusions.

OPTION 1 Skills and Strategies, continued

Teach Draw Conclusions

Draw Conclusions Have students read about Wesley's grand plan on p. 30. Then ask students why they think Wesley doesn't plant seeds himself. (He will let nature take its course; the wind blows local seeds into his garden.)

Corrective Feedback

If... students are unable to draw a conclusion based on the story up to this point,
then... model how to draw a logical conclusion.

Name________________ Westandia

Draw Conclusions

- A **conclusion** is a decision you make after thinking about the details in what you read.
- Often your prior knowledge can help you draw, or make, a conclusion.
- When you draw a conclusion, be sure it makes sense and is supported by what you have read.

Directions Read the following passage. Then answer the questions below.

When Kyoung first arrived in the United States, he saw tall buildings, cars, and people. It looked just like he'd seen in the movies. Everyone and everything moved very quickly. There also was so much more of everything than in his village in his old country. It wasn't until he got to his new home in Maryville that time seemed to slow down.

At school, students didn't talk to him much because he didn't speak English. His teacher suggested that he have a different student buddy each week. The students talked to him more. They asked about his life before he came to the United States. He tried to explain, but it was difficult. The cultures were very different and he was still learning English. Nevertheless, he told them a little each time they asked.

Possible answers given.

1. How do you think Kyoung felt when he first reached the U.S.?
   He may have felt excited, and a little frightened and homesick.
2. What parts of the text helped you reach the conclusion you described above?
   The passage describes how the U.S. seems like a movie, and how everything is big and fast-moving.
3. What things that you already knew helped you reach the conclusion you described above?
   Big cities are often amazing to people from the countryside.
4. Do you think pairing Kyoung with other students was a good idea?
   Yes; students began to feel more comfortable with him.
5. How do you think Kyoung felt when other students asked him about his past? Is your conclusion based on the passage, on your own experience, or both?
   Happy to be asked; I based my answer on the text and on how I would feel if I were Kyoung.

Home Activity Your child drew conclusions from the details of a brief story. Read an article or story with your child about a faraway place. Ask him or her questions about how someone from there of your child's age might adapt to life in the United States.

Comprehension DVD•187

Let's Practice It!
TR DVD•187

Model the Skill

Think Aloud How could I draw a conclusion based on this part of the story? I know Wesley has been learning about other civilizations and how they grow crops. He's learned that the wind carries seeds.

As always, his father mumbled, "I'm sure you'll use that knowledge often."

Suddenly, Wesley's thoughts shot sparks. His eyes blazed. His father was right! He could actually *use* what he'd learned that week for a summer project that would top all others. He would grow his own staple food crop—and found his own civilization!

The next morning he turned over a plot of ground in his yard. That night a wind blew in from the west. It raced through the trees and set his curtains snapping. Wesley lay awake, listening. His land was being planted.

Five days later the first seedlings appeared.

Let's Think About...

What clues here tell you how Wesley's land was being planted? Reread to find out.
Important Ideas

30

Student Edition pp. 30–31

OPTION 2 Think Critically, continued

Higher-Order Thinking Skills

Draw Conclusions • Synthesis How does the information on the bottom of page 31 support Wesley's views about growing plants? What conclusion can you draw about his plan? Possible response: His plants are growing quickly without his help. I can conclude that Wesley's gardening plan is firmly based on the knowledge he learned in school and that it will be very successful.

Let's Think About...

3. The text says that while Wesley lay awake listening to the wind, his land was being planted.
4. Probably because they were just small seedlings, or they weren't planted in rows.

So, I can conclude that he doesn't plant any seeds because he respects what nature can do on its own. What does Wesley want to do? (He wants to grow plants and crops the way people did long ago and still do in some cultures.)

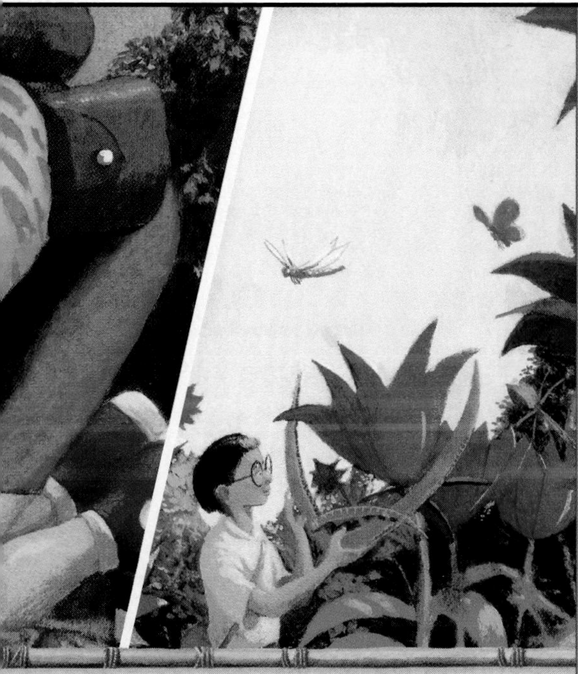

"You'll have almighty bedlam on your hands if you don't get those weeds out," warned his neighbor.

"Actually, that's my crop," replied Wesley. "In this type of garden there are no weeds."

Following ancient tradition, Wesley's fellow gardeners grew tomatoes, beans, Brussels sprouts, and nothing else. Wesley found it thrilling to open his land to chance, to invite the new and unknown.

The plants shot up past his knees, then his waist. They seemed to be all of the same sort. Wesley couldn't find them in any plant book.

"Are those tomatoes, beans, or Brussels sprouts?" asked Wesley's neighbor.

Let's Think About...
Why does the neighbor think that Wesley's garden is full of weeds?
Questioning

4

31

Cause and Effect • Analysis What caused the seeds to take root so easily? Possible response: Wesley turned over the soil, preparing it for planting.

Monitor and Clarify • Analysis Reread page 31 aloud. Then use the information you reread to infer why the other neighborhood gardeners only plant tomatoes, beans, and brussels sprouts. Possible response: They are planting the same vegetables as everyone else without questioning this custom.

On Their Own

Have students reread pp. 30–31 to draw further conclusions about Wesley's project. For additional practice with drawing conclusions, see *Let's Practice It!* p. 187 on the *Teacher Resources DVD-ROM.*

Differentiated Instruction

 Strategic Intervention

Draw conclusions Remind students that conclusions must be based on the information in the text and/or on their prior knowledge. Have students write a sentence in which they draw a conclusion about Wesley's neighbors. Then have them share their sentences with a partner.

English Language Learners

Unknown words Focus students' attention on the word *tradition* on p. 31. Explain that this word means "a long-held custom, habit or belief." Ask students what most gardeners seem to believe about planting vegetables. Then ask students to name a tradition followed in their own family or neighborhood.

Questioning Ask pairs of students to answer the question: What does Wesley's neighbor warn him about on p. 31? (Weeds taking over the garden.) Then have them formulate and answer another question about what makes Wesley's garden different from many others.

Objectives

◎ Determine the meanings of words with endings.

OPTION 1 Skills and Strategies, continued

Teach Endings *-s, -ed, -ing*

◎ **Endings *-s, -ed, -ing*** Have students read the last two paragraphs on p. 32, noting the *-ing* ending on the words *blushing* and *breakfasting.* Ask them the meaning of each word.

Corrective Feedback

If... students are unable to offer a definition of each word with an *-ing* ending,
then... model how to analyze the word structure.

Reader's and Writer's Notebook p. 253

Model the Skill

I know that I can find the base word by separating it from the *-ing* ending. I'll look at the word *blushing.*

"None of the above," replied Wesley.

Fruit appeared, yellow at first, then blushing to magenta. Wesley picked one and sliced through the rind to the juicy purple center. He took a bite and found the taste an entrancing blend of peach, strawberry, pumpkin pie, and flavors he had no name for.

Ignoring the shelf of cereals in the kitchen, Wesley took to breakfasting on the fruit. He dried half a rind to serve as a cup, built his own squeezing device, and drank the fruit's juice throughout the day.

Let's Think About... How does the description help you visualize the fruit Wesley is eating? **Visualize** 5

32

Student Edition pp. 32–33

Let's Think About...

5 The fruit is described as magenta with a purple, juicy center. I can visualize that it looks a little bit like a peach.

6 Wesley learned how to do all these things in school.

◎ **Draw Conclusions • Synthesis** Based on the story, what can you infer about Wesley? What evidence from the text supports your inference?

OPTION 2 Think Critically, continued

Higher-Order Thinking Skills

◎ **Word Endings *-ed, -s, -ing* • Analysis** Use word structure to determine the meaning of the word *appeared* on page 32. Possible response: *Appeared* has the *-ed* ending. The base word is *appear*. The meaning of *appear* is "to come into sight," so *appeared* means "came into sight."

Without the *-ing* ending, the word is *blush.* Is that a noun or a verb in this sentence? (a verb) What does it mean? (to turn red or rosy) If I add back the *-ing* ending, the word means "turning a red or rosy color."

On Their Own

Have students analyze the structure of *breakfasting.* Ask them to define the word and identify the part of speech. For additional practice, use *Reader's and Writer's Notebook* p. 253.

Pulling up a plant, he found large tubers on the roots. These he boiled, fried, or roasted on the family barbecue, seasoning them with the plant's highly aromatic leaves.

It was hot work tending his crop. To keep off the sun, Wesley wove himself a hat from strips of the plant's woody bark. His success with the hat inspired him to devise a spinning wheel and loom on which he wove a loose-fitting robe from the stalks' soft inner fibers.

Unlike jeans, which he found scratchy and heavy, the robe was comfortable, reflected the sun, and offered myriad opportunities for pockets.

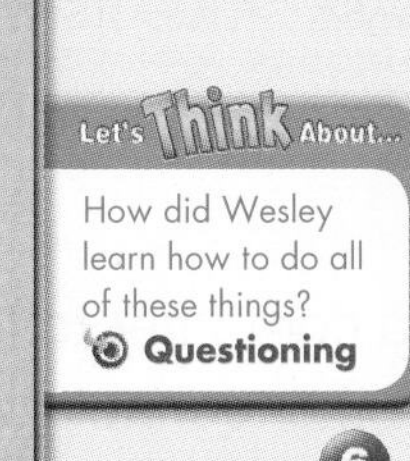

Let's Think About...

How did Wesley learn how to do all of these things?
Questioning

6

33

Possible response: He is intelligent, innovative, and determined. Also, he is not afraid to try new things. Welsey makes his own food, clothes, shelter, and games.

Background Knowledge • Evaluation • Text to Self We see that Wesley becomes completely involved in his gardening project. Does this project remind you of a hobby or activity that you greatly enjoy? Explain how. Answers will vary, but students should explain how Wesley's gardening reminds them of something they enjoy.

Check Predictions Have students look back at the predictions they made earlier and discuss whether they were accurate. Then have students preview the rest of the selection and either adjust their predictions accordingly or make new predictions.

Differentiated Instruction

Strategic Intervention

Word endings If students have trouble determining word meaning through word structure, have them work with a partner to look up each base word in a printed or electronic dictionary. Then have them modify the meaning of the base word as they add each word ending. Students can make a T-chart with the meanings of base words and words with word endings.

Advanced

Extend critical thinking Have students discuss what new "civilization" they would create.

Connect to Social Studies

Staple crops vary from region to region. Wheat is a staple crop for the United States. Rice is a staple in Asia and many other countries, while sweet potatoes and cassava are staples in many parts of Africa.

ELL

English Language Learners

Active prior knowledge Have students work in small groups to list words that relate to particular hobbies. Ask students which words they would have to use to explain how to do a favorite activity.

If you want to teach this selection in two sessions, stop here.

Objectives

- Find pertinent information from online sources.
- Identify subject and object pronouns.
- Spell words from many cultures.

Research and Inquiry
Navigate/Search

Teach Have students collect information about the ancient civilization they chose. Encourage them to use electronic and print encyclopedias as they begin their research. They may also find other reference texts in the library.

Model Think Aloud When looking for information about how the Maya spent time when they were not working, I found a college student's blog about a trip to the Yucatán peninsula in Mexico. Although I'm not going to use that Web site, it had a link to an article by the student's professor. The professor recently published an article about the lives of children in the Mayan civilization. I'm going to bookmark that site. I'll record my notes in a word-processing program to make it easier for me to see how the ideas are connected and flow from one general idea to another.

Guide practice Have students continue their review of resources they identified. Have them evaluate the relevance, validity, and reliability of the sources they use for their research. For example, personal blogs may not contain much useful or reliable information. Direct them instead to authoritative sites, such as those associated with government agencies and educational institutions. Similarly, a well-regarded magazine that often features articles about ancient civilizations will probably contain more valid information than a personal newsletter. Ask students why it is important to use valid, reliable sources.

On their own Ask students to use a computer to take notes as they gather information. They should use the technology to help them see how ideas relate to each other. They should also record the source of each of their notes. Remind them to write down the title, author and page number of each print resource for their Works Cited page. They should record the title, author, Web address, and date each Web site was last modified.

Conventions
Subject and Object Pronouns

Teach Remind students of subject and object pronoun rules. When the pronoun is the subject of a sentence, it is a subject pronoun. When the pronoun is used after an action verb or as the object of a preposition, it is an object pronoun.

Guide practice Explain that subject and object pronouns allow writers to avoid repeating nouns.

Repetitive: The twins said that the twins would help in the garden.

Better: The twins said that they would help in the garden.

Daily Fix-It Use Daily Fix-It numbers 3 and 4 in the right margin.

Connect to oral language Have students look for subject and object pronouns in *Weslandia.* (subject pronouns: *He, they*, p. 28; *you*, p. 31; object pronouns: *them,* p. 31; *him* p. 33*)*

On their own For additional practice, use the *Reader's and Writer's Notebook* p. 250.

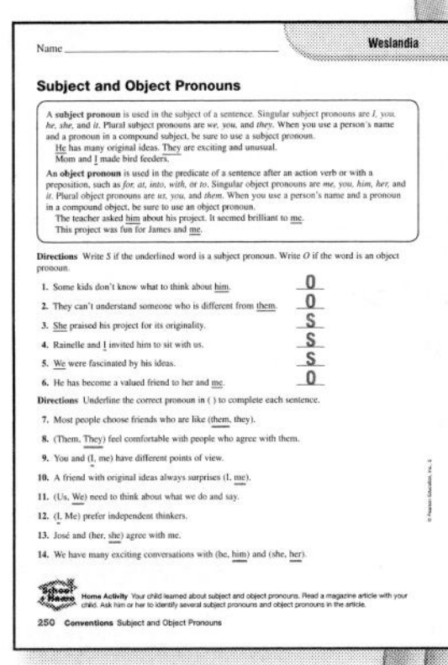

Name ______ Weslandia

Subject and Object Pronouns

A **subject pronoun** is used in the subject of a sentence. Singular subject pronouns are *I, you, he, she,* and *it.* Plural subject pronouns are *we, you,* and *they.* When you use a person's name and a pronoun in a compound subject, be sure to use a subject pronoun.
He has many original ideas. They are exciting and unusual.
Mom and I made bird feeders.

An **object pronoun** is used in the predicate of a sentence after an action verb or with a preposition, such as *for, at, into, with,* or *to.* Singular object pronouns are *me, you, him, her,* and *it.* Plural object pronouns are *us, you,* and *them.* When you use a person's name and a pronoun in a compound object, be sure to use an object pronoun.
The teacher asked him about his project. It seemed brilliant to me.
This project was fun for James and me.

Directions Write *S* if the underlined word is a subject pronoun. Write *O* if the word is an object pronoun.

1. Some kids don't know what to think about him. O
2. They can't understand someone who is different from them. O
3. She praised his project for its originality. S
4. Rainelle and I invited him to sit with us. S
5. We were fascinated by his ideas. S
6. He has become a valued friend to her and me. O

Directions Underline the correct pronoun in ( ) to complete each sentence.

7. Most people choose friends who are like (them, they).
8. (Them, They) feel comfortable with people who agree with them.
9. You and (I, me) have different points of view.
10. A friend with original ideas always surprises (I, me).
11. (Us, We) need to think about what we do and say.
12. (I, Me) prefer independent thinkers.
13. José and (her, she) agree with me.
14. We have many exciting conversations with (he, him) and (she, her).

Home Activity Your child learned about subject and object pronouns. Read a magazine article with your child. Ask him or her to identify several subject pronouns and object pronouns in the article.

250 **Conventions** Subject and Object Pronouns

Reader's and Writer's Notebook p. 250

Spelling
Words from Many Cultures

Teach Remind students that words from different cultures may have unusual spellings for some sounds. Yet, they can still use spelling rules and common patterns to help them to spell these words.

Guide practice Write *hula* and underline the final *-a*. Today we are going to look for words that end in the short *a* sound. In the word *hula*, the *a* at the end of the word has the short *a* sound. Have students work in pairs. They should read each spelling word and listen for the short *a* sound at the end. Have students identify and group the list words that end in the short *a* sound.

On their own For additional practice, use the *Reader's and Writer's Notebook* p. 251.

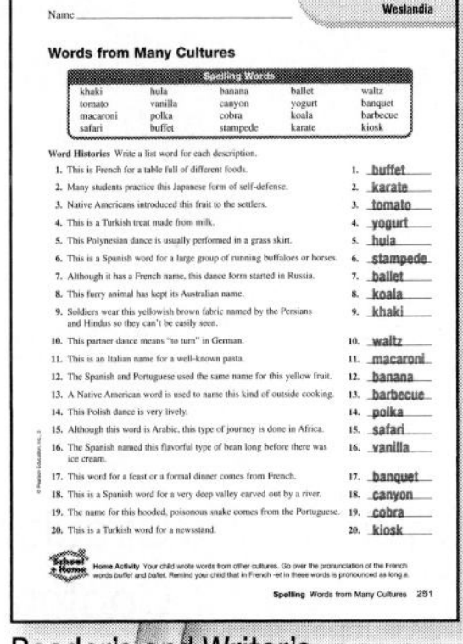

Name ______ Weslandia

Words from Many Cultures

Spelling Words				
khaki	hula	banana	ballet	waltz
tomato	vanilla	canyon	yogurt	banquet
macaroni	polka	cobra	koala	barbecue
safari	buffet	stampede	karate	kiosk

Word Histories Write a list word for each description.

1. This is French for a table full of different foods. 1. buffet
2. Many students practice this Japanese form of self-defense. 2. karate
3. Native Americans introduced this fruit to the settlers. 3. tomato
4. This is a Turkish treat made from milk. 4. yogurt
5. This Polynesian dance is usually performed in a grass skirt. 5. hula
6. This is a Spanish word for a large group of running buffaloes or horses. 6. stampede
7. Although it has a French name, this dance form started in Russia. 7. ballet
8. This furry animal has kept its Australian name. 8. koala
9. Soldiers wear this yellowish brown fabric named by the Persians and Hindus so they can't be easily seen. 9. khaki
10. This partner dance means "to turn" in German. 10. waltz
11. This is an Italian name for a well-known pasta. 11. macaroni
12. The Spanish and Portuguese used the same name for this yellow fruit. 12. banana
13. A Native American word is used to name this kind of outside cooking. 13. barbecue
14. This Polish dance is very lively. 14. polka
15. Although this word is Arabic, this type of journey is done in Africa. 15. safari
16. The Spanish named this flavorful type of bean long before there was ice cream. 16. vanilla
17. This word for a feast or a formal dinner comes from French. 17. banquet
18. This is a Spanish word for a very deep valley carved out by a river. 18. canyon
19. The name for this hooded, poisonous snake comes from the Portuguese. 19. cobra
20. This is a Turkish word for a newsstand. 20. kiosk

Home Activity Your child wrote words from other cultures. Go over the pronunciation of the French words buffet and ballet. Remind your child that in French -et in these words is pronounced as long a.

Spelling Words from Many Cultures 251

Reader's and Writer's Notebook p. 251

Daily Fix-It

3. The natives had lived on the iland for centurys. (*island; centuries*)
4. Them ate the roots, leaves, and fruits of a plant that growed there. (*They; grew*)

ELL

English Language Learners

Conventions To provide students with practice on subject and object pronouns, use the modified grammar lessons in the *ELL Handbook* and the Grammar Jammer online at: www.ReadingStreet.com

Objectives

- Begin to plan a story for a picture book.

Writing—Picture Book

Writer's Craft: Organization

Introduce the prompt Remind students that the selection they'll be reading this week, *Weslandia,* is a picture book. Review the key features of a picture book. Remind students to keep these features in mind as they plan their writing. Display and read aloud the writing prompt.

> **Writing Prompt**
>
> In *Weslandia,* a boy decides to remake his world rather than accept it as it is. Think about someone you know who doesn't always follow the crowd. Now write a picture book, with your own illustrations, about that person.

Select a focus Think Aloud Our topic for our picture book is someone we know who doesn't always follow a crowd. Now, we need to select a character who will be the focus of our narrative. Let's make a chart of possible characters who have their own way of doing things. I know a man who works in a movie theater who imagines that his own life is a movie. I will write *a man who works in a movie theater* in the *Character* column and I will write *imagines that his life is a movie* in the *How They Are Different* column.

Gather information Remind students that they can do research to help them find more information. They can interview people who know about their main character. Remember to keep this chart as the students will refer back to it tomorrow as they draft.

Characters	How They Are Different
The man who works in the movie theatre	Imagines that his own life is a movie
Grandpa Bob	Started his own company
My friend Kami	Made a huge replica of a castle in her basement

Corrective feedback Circulate around the room as students use the chart to choose characters. Conference with students who are having trouble coming up with ideas. Ask each struggling student to consider people they may not know well for the main character.

MINI-LESSON

Creating a Story Chart

Tell students that they will now focus on a particular character for their stories. Display a story chart. Tell students that this story chart will help them organize their ideas.

Now that I have selected a topic, I will think of ways to tell the story of the man who works in a movie theater. Since I know that a story has characters and a setting and follows a sequence of events, I will use this chart to organize my ideas.

I begin my story chart by writing down my characters. The man who works in the theater is named Herb Trew. I'll also include characters that Herb works with and a regular customer who watches many movies. I will describe the setting as a small movie theater in a quiet town where nothing happens.

Continue modeling how to complete story chart. Have students begin their own story charts by using the form on p. 252 of their *Reader's and Writer's Notebook.* Explain that they will complete their own story charts with elements they would like to include in their picture books.

Differentiated Instruction

Advanced

Challenge students to write a story that involves two people who fit the description in the writing prompt. Have them compare and contrast these characters within the story.

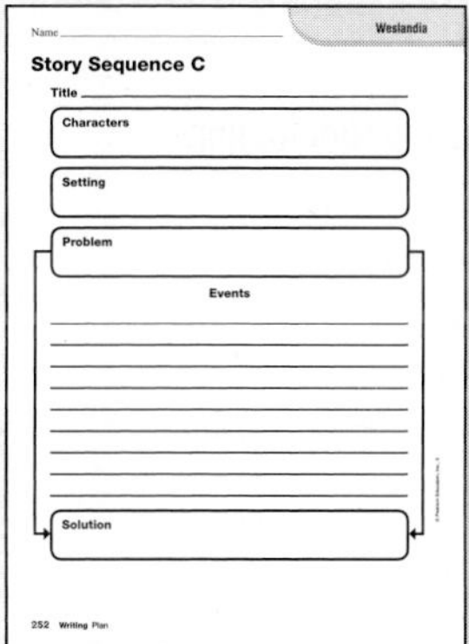

Reader's and Writer's Notebook p. 252

ROUTINE

Quick Write for Fluency

Team Talk

1. **Talk** Have pairs discuss their character ideas.
2. **Write** Each person writes a short description of their character.
3. **Share** Partners read each other's descriptions.

Routines Flip Chart

Teacher Tip

Do a periodic check of students' quick writes to make sure they are on task and communicating effectively with their partners.

Wrap Up Your Day

- ✔ **Build Concepts** Have students discuss why Wesley might want to create his own world.
- ✔ **Draw Conclusions** What conclusions can you draw about Wesley's parents?
- ✔ **Questioning** What questions do you have about what is involved in starting your own civilization?

Preview DAY 3

Tell students that tomorrow they will read more about Welsey's new society.

Objectives
- Expand the weekly concept.
- Develop oral vocabulary.

Today at a Glance

Oral Vocabulary
flexibility, transformation

Comprehension Check/Retelling
Discuss questions

Reading
Weslandia

Think Critically
Retelling

Fluency
Appropriate phrasing/punctuation cues

Research and Study Skills
Instruction manual

Research and Inquiry
Analyze

Spelling
Words from many cultures

Conventions
Subject and object pronouns

Writing
Picture book

Concept Talk

Question of the Week

How do people adapt to difficult situations?

Expand the concept Remind students of the Question of the Week. Discuss how the question relates to someone who wants to create his own world. Tell students that today they will read about how Wesley adapts to the world around him. Encourage students to think about how Wesley customizes his new world to suit his needs.

Anchored Talk

Develop oral vocabulary Use the illustrations to review pp. 26–33 of *Weslandia*. Discuss the Amazing Words *exploration* and *customize,* which both have affixes. Add these and other concept-related words to the concept map. Have students get into groups. Then have them use the following questions to identify points of agreement among group members and develop their understanding of the concept.

- Wesley's *exploration* of the garden helped him to appreciate nature's gifts. What are other ways that *exploration* can lead to adaptation?
- Think about how Wesley managed to *customize* his wardrobe with a lightweight robe woven from plant fibers. How else could people *customize* their clothing in order to adapt to their location?

Oral Vocabulary
Amazing Words

Amazing Words

discovered	customize
courage	flexibility
determination	transformation
practice	advancement
exploration	dynamic

Teach Amazing Words

Amazing Words Oral Vocabulary Routine

1. **Introduce** Write the word *transformation* on the board. Have students say it with you. Yesterday, we learned that a person can undergo a personal *transformation* that leads to success. Have students use context clues to determine a definition of *transformation*. Remind them to look for affixes that can help them understand the word's meaning. (A *transformation* is a great change in appearance or form.)
2. **Demonstrate** Have students answer questions to demonstrate understanding. How did Wesley undergo a *transformation*? (He changed his whole world through imagination.)
3. **Apply** Have students apply their understanding. Has someone you know recently undergone a striking *transformation*?

See p. OV•1 to teach *flexibility*.

Routines Flip Chart

Apply Amazing Words

Help students establish purposes for reading as they read pp. 34–37 of *Weslandia*. Have them consider how the Amazing Words *transformation* and *flexibility* apply to the changes Wesley made to his garden and to his life in general.

Connect to reading

Explain that today students will read about a boy who uses his imagination and creativity to change his own world. As they read, students should think about how this week's Question of the Week and the Amazing Words *transformation* and *flexibility* apply to Wesley's project.

ELL Expand Vocabulary Use the Day 3 instruction on ELL Poster 16 to help students expand vocabulary.

ELL Poster 16

Get Ready to Read

Objectives

- Draw conclusions to aid comprehension.
- Use the questioning strategy to aid comprehension.
- Use endings and word structure to determine the meanings of words.

Comprehension Check

Have students discuss each question with a partner. Ask several pairs to share their responses.

Genre • Analysis

Why do you think the author included realistic details about growing and using food crops in this story? Possible response: It makes Wesley's project seem more realistic, even though there are elements of fantasy in the story.

Draw conclusions • Evaluation

In the story, Wesley is able to use his staple crop as the basis of his summer diet. Evaluate Wesley's diet. Is it possible to be healthy while eating only one variety of plant? How could you find out? Possible response: Not usually, but Wesley eats different parts of his plants, which seem to have the nutritional value of several different plants; I could use the Internet and look up *staple crops* and *nutrition*.

Questioning • Evaluation

Ask yourself a few questions to evaluate Wesley's crop. Possible response: What staple crops yield food, fiber for making clothing, and building materials? How is Wesley's crop similar? How is it different? What conclusions can I make about his crop?

Endings • Analysis

Turn to page 28 and find words with *-ing, -ed,* and *-s* endings. Then use word structure to determine the meaning of each word. Possible response: The words *moaned* and *disliked* took place in the past. The *-ing* in *listening* and *heating* indicates a part of speech. The *-s* in *dollars* and *boys* indicates that there is more than one.

Connect text to self

Wesley allowed nature to take charge in planting his garden. What would you have done if you were starting a garden that would grow only plants found in your region of the country? Possible responses: I would do what Wesley did; I would research local crops and plant several varieties of these.

Strategy Response Log

INTERACT with TEXT

Have students write questions about Wesley, his civilization, and his crop in *Weslandia* on p. 22 in the *Reader's and Writer's Notebook*.

Check Retelling

Have students retell the first part of *Weslandia*. Encourage students to summarize the main ideas and order of events in their retellings. Make sure they maintain meaning and logical order.

Corrective feedback

If... the students leave out important details,
then... have students look back through the illustrations in the selection.

Small Group Time

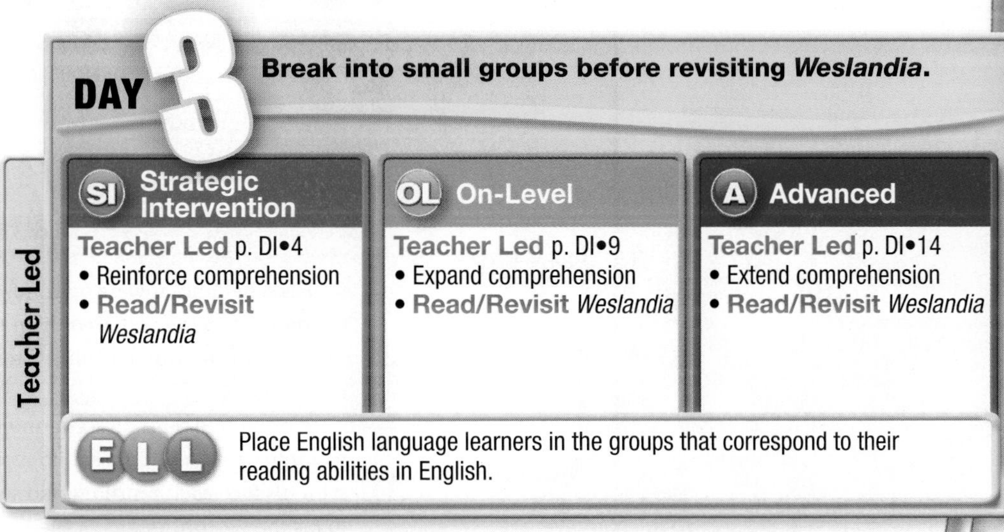

DAY 3
Break into small groups before revisiting *Weslandia*.
Teacher Led
SI Strategic Intervention
Teacher Led p. DI•4
• Reinforce comprehension
• Read/Revisit *Weslandia*
OL On-Level
Teacher Led p. DI•9
• Expand comprehension
• Read/Revisit *Weslandia*
A Advanced
Teacher Led p. DI•14
• Extend comprehension
• Read/Revisit *Weslandia*
ELL
Place English language learners in the groups that correspond to their reading abilities in English.

Practice Stations
- Let's Write
- Get Fluent
- Word Work

Independent Activities
- AudioText of *Weslandia*
- *Reader's and Writer's Notebook*
- Research and Inquiry

English Language Learners

Check retelling To support retelling, review the multilingual summary for *Weslandia* with the appropriate Retelling Cards to scaffold understanding.

Objectives

- Identify and explain how theme and setting play an important role in a fictional story.

OPTION 1 Skills and Strategies, continued

Teach Theme and Setting

Review Literary Elements: Theme and Setting The setting of a story is the time and place in which events take place. Sensory details can help make the setting come alive for the reader. The theme is the main message of the story. Identify the setting and theme of *Weslandia*. (a town in the present time; the importance of thinking for yourself)

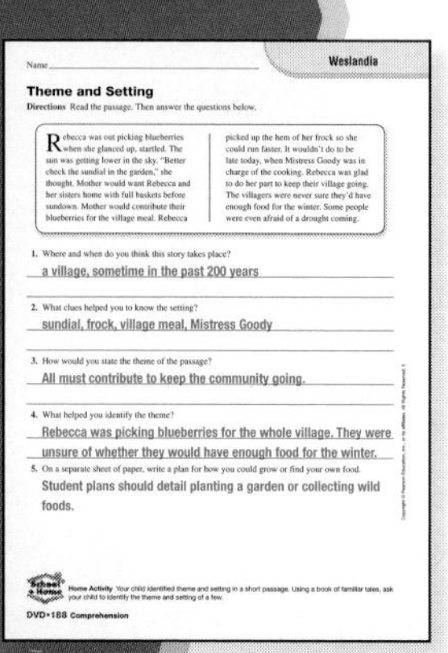

Name

Weslandia

Theme and Setting

Directions Read the passage. Then answer the questions below.

Rebecca was out picking blueberries when she glanced up, startled. The sun was getting lower in the sky. "Better check the sundial in the garden," she thought. Mother would want Rebecca and her sisters home with full baskets before sundown. Mother would contribute their blueberries for the village meal. Rebecca picked up the hem of her frock so she could run faster. It wouldn't do to be late today, when Mistress Goody was in charge of the cooking. Rebecca was glad to do her part to keep their village going. The villagers were never sure they'd have enough food for the winter. Some people were even afraid of a drought coming.

1. Where and when do you think this story takes place?
 a village, sometime in the past 200 years
2. What clues helped you to know the setting?
 sundial, frock, village meal, Mistress Goody
3. How would you state the theme of the passage?
 All must contribute to keep the community going.
4. What helped you identify the theme?
 Rebecca was picking blueberries for the whole village. They were unsure of whether they would have enough food for the winter.
5. On a separate sheet of paper, write a plan for how you could grow or find your own food.
 Student plans should detail planting a garden or collecting wild foods.

Home Activity Your child identified theme and setting in a short passage. Using a book of familiar tales, ask your child to identify the theme and setting of a few.

DVD•188 Comprehension

Let's Practice It!
TR DVD•188

Corrective Feedback

If... students have difficulty identifying the setting and theme,
then... model how to identify the story's setting and message.

Model the Skill

Think Aloud The text and illustrations tell me that the story takes place in a small town with homes and yards. What does the author seem to be saying about finding satisfaction and happiness?

Let's Think About...

Do you think Wesley's relationship with his schoolmates will change? Why do you think that? **Predict**

His schoolmates were scornful, then curious. Grudgingly, Wesley allowed them ten minutes apiece at his mortar, crushing the plant's seeds to collect the oil.

This oil had a tangy scent and served him both as suntan lotion and mosquito repellent. He rubbed it on his face each morning and sold small amounts to his former tormentors at the price of ten dollars per bottle.

"What's happened to your watch?" asked his mother one day.

Wesley admitted that he no longer wore it. He told time by the stalk that he used as a sundial and

34

Student Edition pp. 34–35

Multidraft Reading

Double Day Read!

If you chose...

Option 1 Return to Extend Thinking instruction starting on p. 28–29.
Option 2 Read pp. 34–37.
Use the Guide Comprehension and Extend Thinking instruction.

OPTION 2 Think Critically, continued

Higher-Order Thinking Skills

Review Theme and Setting • Analysis On page 35, we find out that Wesley invents his own sports. How does this detail support the story's theme? Possible response: By thinking for himself, Welsey created sports that he actually enjoys playing.

Let's Think About...

7 Yes, I think his schoolmates will want to be included in what he is doing.

8 because there are eight petals on the plant's flowers

(You have to pursue your own interests and goals and not worry about what other people think.) How does the setting help you adjust your understanding of the theme? (I know that having a yard gives Wesley a place for his garden and the opportunity to be creative there. This makes the whole story, and the theme, possible.)

On Their Own

Have students use a graphic organizer to make notes about setting and theme. For additional practice, use *Let's Practice It!* p. 188 on the *Teacher Resources DVD-ROM.*

had divided the day into eight segments—the number of petals on the plant's flowers.

He'd adopted a new counting system as well, based likewise upon the number eight. His domain, home to many such innovations, he named "Weslandia."

Uninterested in traditional sports, Wesley made up his own. These were designed for a single player and used many different parts of the plant. His spectators looked on with envy.

Realizing that more players would offer him more scope, Wesley invented other games that would include his schoolmates, games rich with

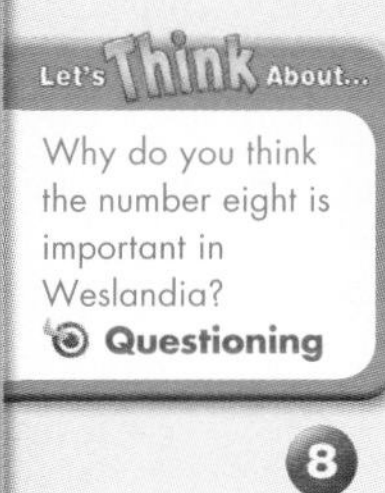

Let's Think About...
Why do you think the number eight is important in Weslandia?
Questioning

8

35

Main Idea and Details • Synthesis On pages 34–35, we learn that Wesley has invented his own way of telling time. This detail supports what main idea? Possible response: This detail supports the main idea that Wesley is creating a new civilization.

Summarize • Analysis Summarize how the opinions of Wesley's schoolmates have changed since the beginning of the story. Possible response: At first, his classmates teased and tormented Wesley because they thought he was weird. But slowly, they have become interested in Wesley's unique summer project, and now they want to share in the fun.

Differentiated Instruction

 Strategic Intervention

Identify theme Tell students that by keeping track of details and events, they can discover the story's theme, or the main message the author is trying to tell you. Model identifying the significant details and events of this story and how they relate to the theme.

A Advanced

Creative thinking Have students brainstorm a way to make a sundial using classroom materials.

ELL

English Language Learners

Vocabulary: Content words Have students note words that relate to Wesley's return to earlier customs, such as *mortar, sundial,* and *counting system*. In pairs, have students look at these words in context and then explain what they mean. Ask: Why do these things have a special meaning for Wesley? When and where might these things be used?

Read and Comprehend

OPTION 1 Skills and Strategies, continued

Objectives

- Use details from the story to draw conclusions.

Teach Draw Conclusions

Draw Conclusions Have students read the last two lines on p. 37. Then ask students to draw conclusions about Wesley's mood when school restarts at the end of the summer.

Corrective Feedback

If... students are unable to draw conclusions about Wesley's mood, **then...** model using details to draw conclusions.

Model the Skill

Think Aloud What makes me conclude that Wesley is going to be happier this school year? (His classmates changed their opinion of him over the summer.)

strategy and complex scoring systems. He tried to be patient with the other players' blunders.

August was unusually hot. Wesley built himself a platform and took to sleeping in the middle of Weslandia. He passed the evenings playing a flute he'd fashioned from a stalk or gazing up at the sky, renaming the constellations.

His parents noted Wesley's improved morale. "It's the first time in years he's looked happy," said his mother.

Wesley gave them a tour of Weslandia.

"What do you call this plant?" asked his father.

36

Student Edition pp. 36–37

Let's Think About...

9 I think Wesley will learn ideas in school that he can use to make Weslandia bigger and better. I predict Wesley will have a lot of friends who will want to help out.

OPTION 2 Think Critically, continued

Higher-Order Thinking Skills

Draw Conclusions • Analysis Do you think that Wesley will maintain or abandon his garden when school starts? What details from the story serve as evidence for this inference? Possible response: I think that Wesley will maintain his garden because he loves it, and it is so important to him. The story shows that Wesley is someone who stands his ground and doesn't let the opinions of others influence his thinking. He's not one to abandon something just because it's hard or unpopular.

What details from the story support this conclusion? (His classmates worked with Wesley's mortar, they bought his suntan lotion and mosquito repellent, and they played his new games.)

On Their Own

Have students look at the illustrations on pp. 28–29 and 35. Ask them to explain how these illustrations help us draw conclusions about how Wesley's relationship with his classmates has changed.

Not knowing its name, Wesley had begun calling it "swist," from the sound of its leaves rustling in the breeze.

In like manner, he'd named his new fabrics, games, and foods, until he'd created an entire language.

Mixing the plant's oil with soot, Wesley made a passable ink. As the finale to his summer project, he used the ink and his own eighty-letter alphabet to record the history of his civilization's founding.

In September, Wesley returned to school...
He had no shortage of friends.

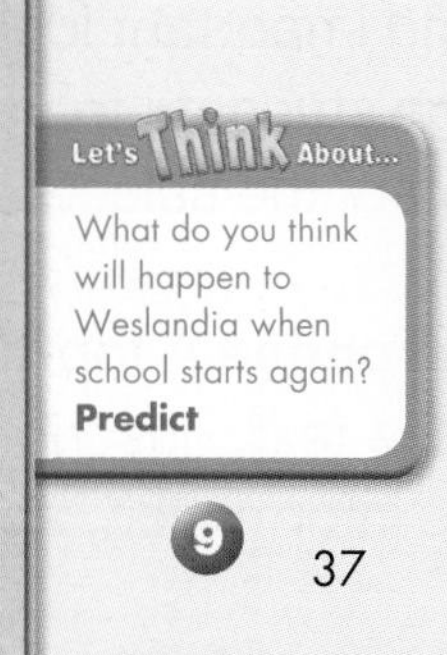

Let's Think About...
What do you think will happen to Weslandia when school starts again?
Predict

9 37

Questioning • Analysis What is an evaluative question I could ask about Wesley's summer project to help monitor and clarify my understanding of the story? Possible response: Would I ever want to live for a summer like Wesley did?

Comprehension Check

Spiral Review

Main Idea and Details • Evaluation On page 37, we are told how Wesley passed a hot August. How could I support the conclusion that Wesley had adapted to the natural world, like people of older civilizations? Possible response: Wesley dealt with the heat by sleeping outdoors where it was cooler and by making cooler clothes and suntan lotion.

Check Predictions Have students return to the predictions they made earlier and confirm whether they were accurate.

Differentiated Instruction

SI Strategic Intervention

Draw conclusions Have students work in pairs to draw conclusions and to clarify any misunderstandings about the text.

A Advanced

Extend critical thinking Have students use details from the story to describe how Wesley's parents feel about his summer project.

Connect to Social Studies

Traditionally, Amish people live a simple, self-sufficient life that is different from much of American society. They make their own clothes and live off their own land. They travel by horse and buggy instead of by car and use candles instead of electricity.

Six Pillars of Character

Fairness We show fairness when we play by the rules, share, and listen to others. Have students discuss how Wesley displays fairness when he interacts with his classmates.

ELL

English Language Learners

Using illustrations Have students use the illustration on pp. 36–37 to point to and identify some of the objects found in Weslandia.

DAY 3 Read and Comprehend

Objectives

- ◎ Use illustrations to draw conclusions.
- ◎ Ask questions of text.

Check Retelling
SUCCESS PREDICTOR

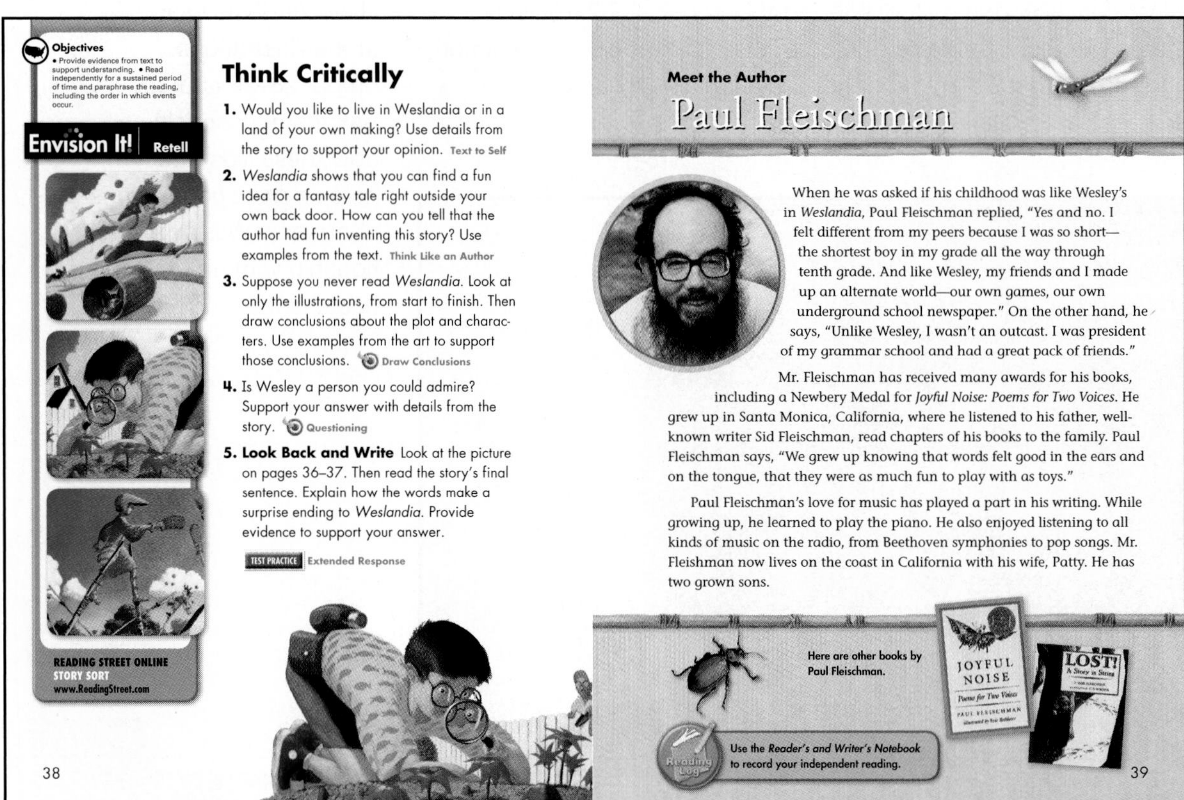

Objectives
• Provide evidence from text to support understanding. • Read independently for a sustained period of time and paraphrase the reading, including the order in which events occur.

Envision It! | Retell

READING STREET ONLINE
STORY SORT
www.ReadingStreet.com

Think Critically

1. Would you like to live in Weslandia or in a land of your own making? Use details from the story to support your opinion. *Text to Self*
2. *Weslandia* shows that you can find a fun idea for a fantasy tale right outside your own back door. How can you tell that the author had fun inventing this story? Use examples from the text. *Think Like an Author*
3. Suppose you never read *Weslandia.* Look at only the illustrations, from start to finish. Then draw conclusions about the plot and characters. Use examples from the art to support those conclusions. *Draw Conclusions*
4. Is Wesley a person you could admire? Support your answer with details from the story. *Questioning*
5. **Look Back and Write** Look at the picture on pages 36–37. Then read the story's final sentence. Explain how the words make a surprise ending to *Weslandia.* Provide evidence to support your answer.

TEST PRACTICE Extended Response

38

Meet the Author
Paul Fleischman

When he was asked if his childhood was like Wesley's in *Weslandia*, Paul Fleischman replied, "Yes and no. I felt different from my peers because I was so short—the shortest boy in my grade all the way through tenth grade. And like Wesley, my friends and I made up an alternate world—our own games, our own underground school newspaper." On the other hand, he says, "Unlike Wesley, I wasn't an outcast. I was president of my grammar school and had a great pack of friends."

Mr. Fleischman has received many awards for his books, including a Newbery Medal for *Joyful Noise: Poems for Two Voices.* He grew up in Santa Monica, California, where he listened to his father, well-known writer Sid Fleischman, read chapters of his books to the family. Paul Fleischman says, "We grew up knowing that words felt good in the ears and on the tongue, that they were as much fun to play with as toys."

Paul Fleischman's love for music has played a part in his writing. While growing up, he learned to play the piano. He also enjoyed listening to all kinds of music on the radio, from Beethoven symphonies to pop songs. Mr. Fleischman now lives on the coast in California with his wife, Patty. He has two grown sons.

Here are other books by Paul Fleischman.

Use the *Reader's and Writer's Notebook* to record your independent reading.

39

Student Edition pp. 38–39

Plan to Assess Retelling

- ☑ **This week assess Strategic Intervention students.**
- ☐ **Week 2** Assess Advanced students.
- ☐ **Week 3** Assess Strategic Intervention students.
- ☐ **Week 4** Assess On-Level students.
- ☐ **Week 5** Assess any students you have not yet checked during this unit.

Retelling

Envision It!

Have students work in pairs to retell the selection, using the Envision It! Retelling Cards as prompts. Remind students that they should accurately describe the plot and important ideas and use key vocabulary in their retellings. Encourage students to use their retellings to monitor and adjust their comprehension of the selection.

Scoring rubric

Top-Score Response A top-score response makes connections beyond the text, describes the plot and important ideas using accurate information, and draws conclusions from the text.

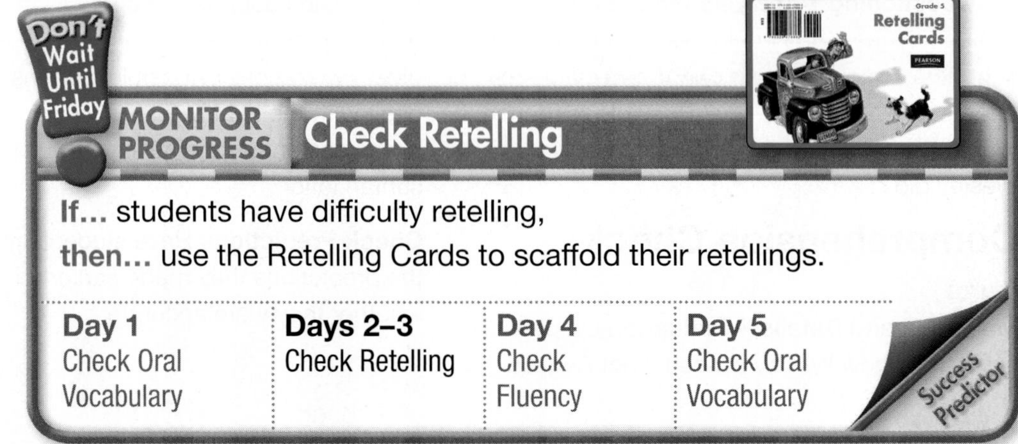

Don't Wait Until Friday **MONITOR PROGRESS** **Check Retelling**

If… students have difficulty retelling,
then… use the Retelling Cards to scaffold their retellings.

Day 1	Days 2–3	Day 4	Day 5
Check Oral Vocabulary	Check Retelling	Check Fluency	Check Oral Vocabulary

Success Predictor

Think Critically

Text to self

1. Responses will vary, but students may say that while Weslandia would be fun to visit, it could also be lonely without friends and family.

Think like an author

2. He must have had fun describing a new fruit and thinking about how to make a flute from a stalk.

Draw conclusions

3. Wesley is an unusual boy who plants a garden in his own way. The garden becomes his world, and from its plants, Wesley gets materials to create things.

Questioning

4. Yes, I admire him. His personality and imagination make him interesting and likable.

5. **Look Back and Write** To build writing fluency, assign a 10–15 minute time limit.

Suggest that students use a prewriting strategy, such as brainstorming or using a graphic organizer, to organize their ideas. Remind them to establish a topic sentence and support it with facts, details, or explanations. As students finish, encourage them to reread their responses, revise for organization and support, and proofread for errors in grammar and conventions.

Scoring rubric

Top-Score Response A top-score response uses details to tell about Wesley and the results of his project.

A top-score response should include:

- Wesley was lonely and turned to his own imagination.
- He was inventive and used his knowledge for practical ends.
- He realized that creating his civilization was a great summer project.
- Being himself at first brought him trouble, but by the end brought him friends.

Differentiated Instruction

Strategic Intervention

Draw conclusions Have students work in pairs to brainstorm a list of reasons why Wesley created his own civilization.

Meet the Author

Have students read about author Paul Fleischman on p. 39. Ask them how he expresses his admiration of independence in *Weslandia.*

Independent Reading

After students enter their independent reading information into their Reading Logs, have them paraphrase a portion of the text they have just read. Remind students that when we paraphrase, we express the meaning of a passage, using other words and maintaining logical order.

ELL

English Language Learners

Retelling Use the Retelling Cards to discuss the selection with students. Place the cards in an incorrect order and have volunteers correct the mistake. Then have students explain where each card should go as they describe the sequence of the selection.

Retelling Success Predictor

Read and Comprehend

Objectives

- Read grade-level text with appropriate phrasing.
- Reread for fluency.
- Understand how to read and use instruction manuals.

Model Fluency
Appropriate Phrasing

Model fluent reading

Have students turn to p. 30 of *Weslandia*. Have students follow along as you read this page. Tell them to listen to the excited tone of your voice when reading sentences that end with an exclamation point. Also, tell students to note how you pause at the dash. Adjust your phrasing using all punctuation cues.

Guide practice

Have the students follow along as you read the page again. Then have them reread the page as a group without you until they read with the right phrasing and with no mistakes. Ask questions to be sure students comprehend the text. Continue the same way on p. 31.

Reread for Fluency

Corrective feedback

If... students are having difficulty reading with correct phrasing,
then... prompt:

- Where can we break up this sentence? Which words are related?
- Read the sentence again. Pause after each group of words.
- Tell me the sentence. Now read it with pauses after each group of words.

ROUTINE **Oral Rereading**

1. **Read** Have students read pp. 32–33 of *Weslandia* orally.
2. **Reread** To achieve optimal fluency, students should reread the text three to four times with appropriate phrasing.
3. **Corrective Feedback** Have students read aloud without you. Provide feedback about their phrasing and encourage them to note punctuation that shows when to pause or come to a stop. Listen for use of appropriate phrasing.

Routines Flip Chart

Research and Study Skills
Instruction Manual

Teach

Ask students how they might find information on how to play a game or program a new phone. Students may mention reading an instruction manual. Review these terms:

- A **manual** is meant to be conveniently carried around and contains instructions on how to do something. It can also be called a handbook.
- **Instructions** can help you complete a task, solve a problem, or perform a specific procedure. The instructions may be for immediate use or for reference at a later time.
- Manuals often have different text features, such as a table of contents, a glossary, and illustrations, to give an overview of the contents, to locate information, and to make the instructions easier to understand.
- The instructions should be read completely before you begin. To follow the instructions, read the first step, do what it says, then go on to the next step. Try to visualize each step as you go.
- Manuals often contain warnings about a procedure, explaining any danger involved. These are marked with an exclamation mark or the word WARNING or CAUTION.

Provide groups with examples of different kinds of instruction manuals. Have each group show its manual to the class and explain what kind of instructions it gives. If possible, have students do the procedure described in the manual.

Guide practice

Discuss these questions:

How are all these instruction manuals similar? (They each explain the steps of a process.)

How do you know what to do first? (The manual lists the steps in order.)

Why is it important to read the whole manual carefully? (You will find warnings and additional information.)

On their own

Have students complete pp. 254–255 of the *Reader's and Writer's Notebook,* using text features to locate specific information.

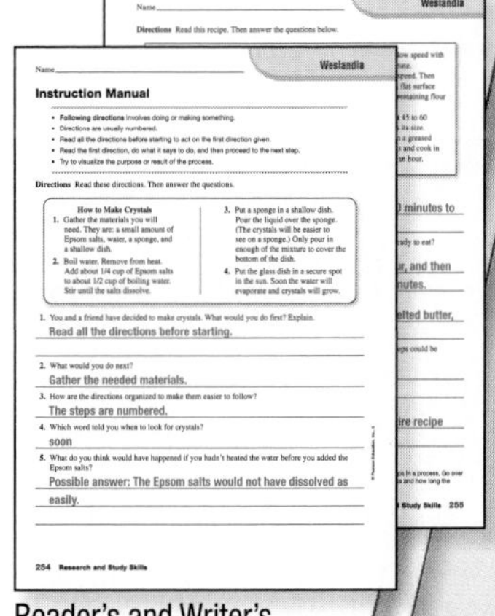
Name

Weslandia

Instruction Manual

- **Following directions** involves doing or making something.
- Directions are usually numbered.
- Read all the directions before starting to act on the first direction given.
- Read the first direction, do what it says to do, and then proceed to the next step.
- Try to visualize the purpose or result of the process.

Directions Read these directions. Then answer the questions.

How to Make Crystals

1. Gather the materials you will need. They are: a small amount of Epsom salts, water, a sponge, and a shallow dish.
2. Boil water. Remove from heat. Add about 1/4 cup of Epsom salts to about 1/2 cup of boiling water. Stir until the salts dissolve.
3. Put a sponge in a shallow dish. Pour the liquid over the sponge. (The crystals will be easier to see on a sponge.) Only pour in enough of the mixture to cover the bottom of the dish.
4. Put the glass dish in a secure spot in the sun. Soon the water will evaporate and crystals will grow.

1. You and a friend have decided to make crystals. What would you do first? Explain.
Read all the directions before starting.
2. What would you do next?
Gather the needed materials.
3. How are the directions organized to make them easier to follow?
The steps are numbered.
4. Which word told you when to look for crystals?
soon
5. What do you think would have happened if you hadn't heated the water before you added the Epsom salts?
Possible answer: The Epsom salts would not have dissolved as easily.

254 Research and Study Skills

Name

Weslandia

Directions Read this recipe. Then answer the questions below.

Reader's and Writer's Notebook pp. 254–255

Academic Vocabulary

Instruction manual An instruction manual gives detailed steps about how to make or do something. Instruction manuals make every step of a process clear.

English Language Learners

Professional Development: What ELL experts say about interaction: "Teachers can provide their students, irrespective of background, experiences with academic language by reading to them, and discussing readings, instructional activities, and experiences. By drawing children into instructional conversations focused on the language they encounter in their school texts and other materials, teachers get children to notice language itself and to figure out how it works." — Dr. Jim Cummins

Instruction manuals Have students create a simple instruction manual by working in small groups. Some options: a recipe; a guide to using a pencil sharpener safely; a manual about operating an electronic game.

Objectives

- Analyze data for usefulness.
- Identify subject and object pronouns.
- Spell frequently misspelled words.

Research and Inquiry
Analyze

Teach Tell students that today they will analyze their findings. Have them ask themselves questions to refine the focus of their inquiry topic.

Model Think Aloud Originally, I thought that I'd find out about how the Maya amused themselves. Then I read an article explaining that some Mayan games were taken very seriously and were not played by children. So I asked myself, *How can I change my topic fit what I found?* I will refocus my inquiry question, based on what I learned from the historian and from my online research. Now my inquiry question is *What games did Mayan children play?*

Guide practice Have students analyze their findings. Remind students to ask you or ask other students if they need help refining their research question.

Because students will be relying on many sources of information, discuss the difference between plagiarism and paraphrasing. Have students describe the difference and discuss why it is important to have a Works Cited page.

On their own Remind students that they will need to use drawing tools or clip art from the computer to illustrate their summaries. Ask them to make sure they have a model or an idea for their illustration.

Have students work in small groups to record ideas about the ancient civilization they have researched. They can help one another select clip art or experiment with drawing programs to illustrate their summaries. Illustrations should echo the main points in their summaries.

Conventions
Subject and Object Pronouns

Review Remind students that this week they learned about subject and object pronouns. Review definitions and examples of subject and object pronouns.

- A pronoun used as the subject of a sentence is a subject pronoun. *I, you, he, she, it, we,* and *they* are subject pronouns.
- A pronoun used after action verbs or as objects of prepositions are object pronouns. *Me, you, him, her, it, us,* and *them* are object pronouns.

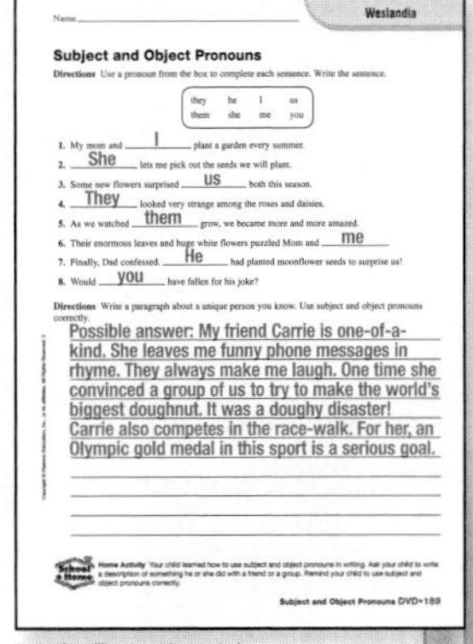
Let's Practice It!
TR DVD•189

Daily Fix-It Use Daily Fix-It numbers 5 and 6 in the right margin.

Connect to oral language Display the following sentences and have students read from the board, guiding them to select the appropriate pronoun:

Dan and he/him found a dollar on the floor. (he)
Jane and I/me like walnuts. (I)
Dad asked Phil and I/me to shell the nuts. (me)

On their own For additional practice, use *Let's Practice It!* p. 189 on the *Teacher Resources DVD-ROM.*

Spelling
Words from Many Cultures

Frequently misspelled words The words *again, our,* and *are* are words that students often misspell. I'm going to read a sentence. Choose the right word to complete the sentence and then write it correctly. Have students check their own work with a dictionary or electronic spelling source.

1. Do you think _____ team will win? (our)
2. We _____ going to visit a museum. (are)
3. I will enter the talent contest _____. (again)

On their own For additional practice, use the *Reader's and Writer's Notebook* p. 256.

Differentiated Instruction

SI Strategic Intervention
Provide students with this strategy to identify the correct pronoun in a phrase such as *Jane and I* or *Terry and her.* Say the sentence with just the pronoun and not the rest of the phrase. *Examples: I climbed the mountain. Jane and I climbed the mountain. Jane showed her our pictures. Jane showed Terry and her our pictures.*

Daily Fix-It

5. If I went to a jungel I would take a safarie. *(jungle; safari)*
6. Help! There's a crockodile in the pool. *(crocodile; pool!)*

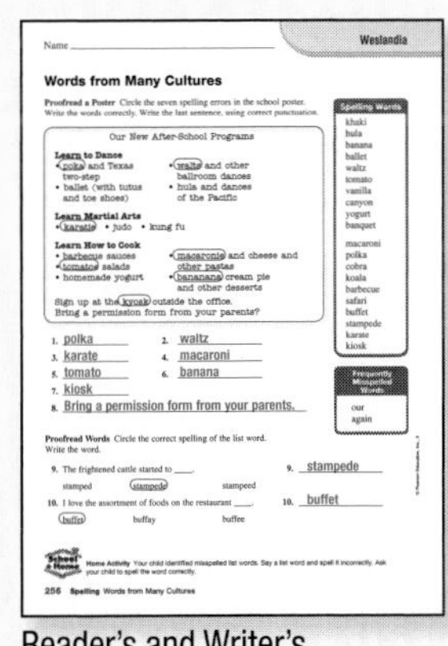
Reader's and Writer's Notebook p. 256

Objectives

- Understand the criteria for writing a picture book.

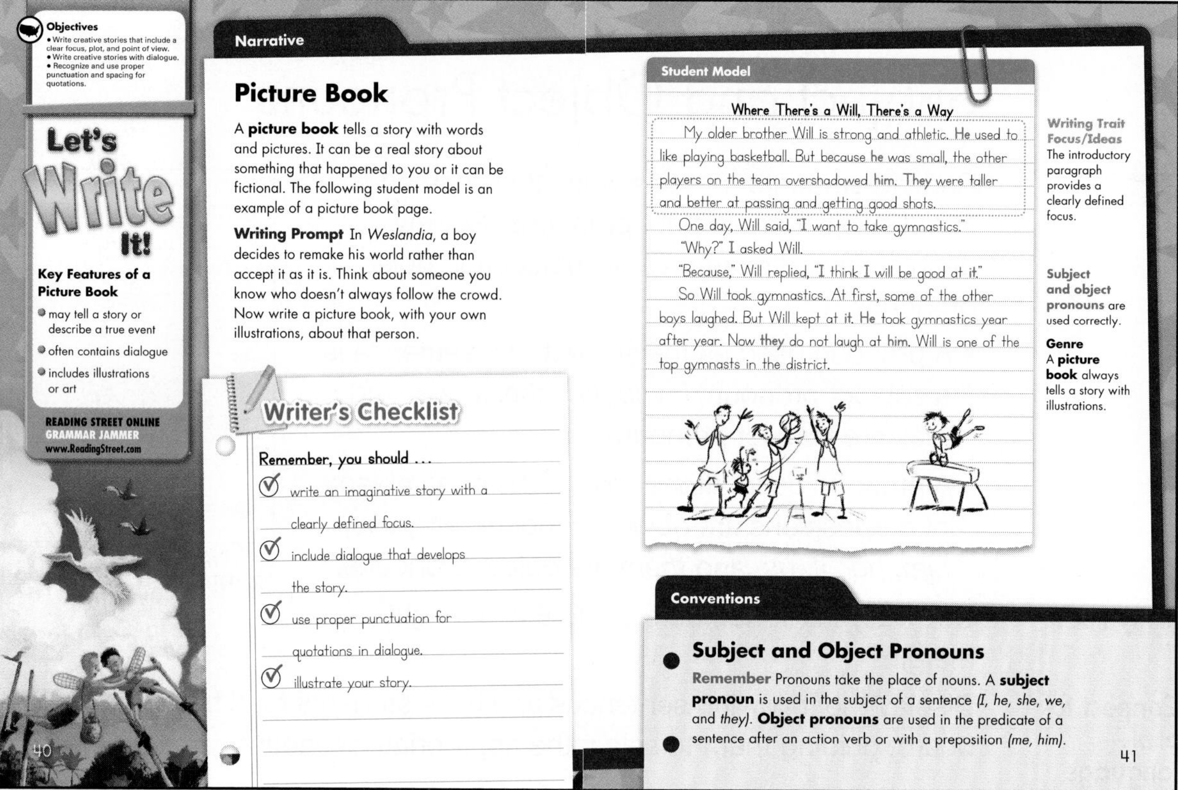

Objectives
- Write creative stories that include a clear focus, plot, and point of view.
- Write creative stories with dialogue.
- Recognize and use proper punctuation and spacing for quotations.

Let's Write It!

Key Features of a Picture Book
- may tell a story or describe a true event
- often contains dialogue
- includes illustrations or art

READING STREET ONLINE
GRAMMAR JAMMER
www.ReadingStreet.com

Narrative

Picture Book

A **picture book** tells a story with words and pictures. It can be a real story about something that happened to you or it can be fictional. The following student model is an example of a picture book page.

Writing Prompt In *Weslandia*, a boy decides to remake his world rather than accept it as it is. Think about someone you know who doesn't always follow the crowd. Now write a picture book, with your own illustrations, about that person.

Writer's Checklist

Remember, you should ...
- write an imaginative story with a clearly defined focus.
- include dialogue that develops the story.
- use proper punctuation for quotations in dialogue.
- illustrate your story.

40

Student Model

Where There's a Will, There's a Way

My older brother Will is strong and athletic. He used to like playing basketball. But because he was small, the other players on the team overshadowed him. They were taller and better at passing and getting good shots.

One day, Will said, "I want to take gymnastics."

"Why?" I asked Will.

"Because," Will replied, "I think I will be good at it."

So Will took gymnastics. At first, some of the other boys laughed. But Will kept at it. He took gymnastics year after year. Now they do not laugh at him. Will is one of the top gymnasts in the district.

Writing Trait Focus/Ideas The introductory paragraph provides a clearly defined focus.

Subject and object pronouns are used correctly.

Genre A **picture book** always tells a story with illustrations.

Conventions

Subject and Object Pronouns

Remember Pronouns take the place of nouns. A **subject pronoun** is used in the subject of a sentence (*I, he, she, we,* and *they*). **Object pronouns** are used in the predicate of a sentence after an action verb or with a preposition (*me, him*).

41

Student Edition pp. 40–41

Let's Write It!
Picture Book

Teach

Use pp. 40–41 in the Student Edition. Direct students to read the key features of a picture book which appear on p. 40. Remind students that they can refer to the information in the Writer's Checklist as they write their own picture book.

Read the student model on p. 41. Point out the use of dialogue in the story.

Connect to conventions

Remind students that writers often use pronouns to avoid repetition of nouns and names in compositions. Point out the correct use of subject and object pronouns in the model.

Writing—Picture Book
Writing Trait: Focus/Ideas

Display rubric

Display Scoring Rubric 16 from the *Teacher Resources DVD* and go over the criteria for each trait under each score. Then, using the model in the Student Edition, choose students to explain why the model should score a 4 for one of the traits. If a student offers that the model should score below 4 for a particular trait, the student should offer support for that response. Remind students that this is the rubric that will be used to evaluate narrative in the picture book they write.

Scoring Rubric: Picture Book

	4	3	2	1
Focus/Ideas	Focused narrative	Somewhat focused narrative	Narrative with unclear focus	Writing lacks clarity or development
Organization	Carefully ordered plot with clearly illustrated events; strong dialogue	Plot is understand-able and some events illustrated; good dialogue	Plot is not clear and events not illustrated; dialogue hard to follow	No plot; no illustrations; no dialogue
Voice	Involved throughout	Involved most of the time	Tries to be involved	No involvement
Word Choice	Very descriptive; includes many sensory details	Clear language; includes some sensory details	Some vague or repetitive words; contains few sensory details	Incorrect or limited word choice; no sensory details
Sentences	Good variety of sentences	Some variety in sentences	Too many short, choppy sentences	No variety in sentences
Conventions	Excellent control; correct use of subject and object pronouns	Good control; few errors; correct subject and object pronouns used	Several errors; subject and object pronouns often used incorrectly	Many major errors; no understanding of subject and object pronouns

Story chart

Have students get out the story charts they worked on yesterday. If their charts are incomplete, have them brainstorm with a partner to complete them.

Write

You will be using your story chart as you write the draft of your picture book. When you are drafting, don't worry if your story does not sound exactly as you want it. You will have a chance to revise tomorrow.

Differentiated Instruction

Advanced

Humor Challenge students to use elements of humor, such as satire, in their stories. Provide them with examples from current picture books.

English Language Learners

Support drafting Encourage students to focus on the characters and events in their narratives rather than worry whether every word is correct. Ask students questions about a time when they saw someone who did not follow the crowd. Base your questions on some of the key features of a picture book. *(Who were the people involved? Where were they? What happened?)* Keep in mind that in other cultures, a story may focus on characters and setting rather than plot. Suggest that they make notes as they answer these questions.

Objectives

- Write a clearly focused draft of a picture book.

Writing, continued
Writer's Craft: Focus/Ideas

MINI-LESSON

Defining Focus Clearly

- **Introduce** Explain to students that a picture book should have a clear focus that is supported by character descriptions and plot events. Display the Drafting Tips for students. Remind them that the purpose of drafting is to get their ideas down in a focused and organized way. Then display Writing Transparency 16A.

Herb Trew worked at the Rose Theater. Each day he waited for the movie to end and the people to leave. "Good riddance," Herb Trew grumbled. Then he went up and down every aisle cleaning, muttering to himself. He used to like his job. The smell of the popcorn no longer made him feel happy and comfortable the way it used to. He often stood in the empty theater and thought he had the most boring job in the whole world.

Writing Transparency 16A, TR DVD

Drafting Tips

✔ Create a clear focus for your story. Ask yourself what you want the readers to discover by reading your story.

✔ Create the characters, setting, and plot events that support your focus.

✔ Don't worry about grammar and mechanics when drafting. You'll concentrate on them during the proofreading stage.

Think Aloud I'm going to write a story about a man who works in a movie theater and dreams that his life is a movie. That will be my main focus. I will refer to my story chart to make sure I include details about my characters and the setting, as well as the plot. I'll begin by introducing the setting and my main character. Next I want to show readers that Herb is unhappy. I'll make him sound impatient and lonely. Herb is bored with his job, so I'll make it sound unappealing. Finally, I'll summarize Herb's unhappiness. All of these details support the fact that Herb wants to live in a movie-like life.

Tell students they will now draft their narratives. Remind students not to worry if their narrative is not as descriptive as they would like; they can work on making it more descriptive in the next step in the writing process, revising. Circulate around the room, reviewing students' drafts before they revise their work tomorrow.

ROUTINE **Quick Write for Fluency** Team Talk

1. **Talk** Have students work in pairs and ask each other questions about their story's focus.
2. **Write** Each person writes a short paragraph describing the story's focus.
3. **Share** Partners check each other's paragraph for the correct use of subject and object pronouns.

Routines Flip Chart

Wrap Up Your Day

- **Build Concepts** Have students discuss how Wesley's life has changed since he created his own civilization.
- **Draw Conclusions** What conclusions can you draw about how Wesley feels at the end of the summer?
- **Questioning** What questions do you have about the author's purpose for writing this story?

Differentiated Instruction

SI Strategic Intervention

Character and Conflict During drafting, have students clearly describe their main character and the story's conflict. Explain that understanding what drives their character to create his or her imaginary life will help them develop their story. Ask students specific questions about the conflict in their story. *(Why is he unhappy? What about his situation makes him wish he were somewhere else? What does the character's job feel like?)*

Tell students that tomorrow they will read two poems about special hiding places.

Objectives
- Expand the weekly concept.
- Develop oral vocabulary.

Today at a Glance

Oral Vocabulary
advancement, dynamic

Genre
Poetry

Reading
"Under the Back Porch"
"Keziah"

Let's Learn It!
Fluency: Appropriate phrasing/punctuation cues
Vocabulary: Endings
Listening and Speaking: How-to demonstration

Research and Inquiry
Synthesize

Spelling
Words from many cultures

Conventions
Subject and object pronouns

Writing
Picture book

Concept Talk

Question of the Week

How do people adapt to difficult situations?

Expand the concept Remind students that this week they have read about people who have adapted to difficult situations. Tell students that today they will explore the genre of poetry and compare two poems about personal transformation.

Anchored Talk

Develop oral vocabulary Use the illustrations to review pp. 34–37 of *Weslandia*. Discuss the Amazing Words *flexibility* and *transformation*. Add these and other concept-related words to the concept map. Have students break into groups. Then have them use the following questions to identify points of disagreement among group members, use context to determine or clarify the meaning of the unfamiliar Amazing Words, and develop their understanding of the concept.

- Think about some ways in which Wesley showed *flexibility*. When might you need to show *flexibility* in order to achieve a goal and adapt to a difficult situation?
- The *transformation* of Wesley's garden led to other changes in Wesley's world. How can positive experiences lead to a wonderful *transformation* in a person's life?

Strategy Response Log

INTERACT with TEXT

Have students write questions about Wesley and Weslandia on p. 22 in *Reader's and Writer's Notebook.* Then have students work with a partner to answer their own questions.

Oral Vocabulary
Amazing Words

Amazing Words

discovered	customize
courage	flexibility
determination	transformation
practice	advancement
exploration	dynamic

Amazing Words Oral Vocabulary Routine

Teach Amazing Words

1 **Introduce** Write the Amazing Word *advancement* on the board. Have students say it aloud with you. We read about how a civilization shows *advancement* when it grows staple crops. What word ending, or affix, helps me understand this word? (There is a suffix, *-ment*, added to the word *advance*, making the word a noun meaning "a development or improvement.")

2 **Demonstrate** Have students answer questions to demonstrate understanding. How does the planting of crops for food lead to a culture's *advancement*? (It allows the people to concentrate on other goals, with a food supply assured.)

3 **Apply** Have students apply their understanding. What other *advancement* might a civilization make?

See p. OV•1 to teach *dynamic*.

Routines Flip Chart

Apply Amazing Words

To help students establish a purpose for reading as they read "Under the Back Porch" and "Keziah" on pp. 42–43, have them think about why finding a special place can lead to the advancement of a person's individual goals.

Connect to reading

As students read today's selection about a child who has a special hiding place, have them think about how the Question of the Week and the Amazing Words *advancement* and *dynamic* apply to having a special place.

ELL **Produce Oral Language** Use the Day 4 instruction on ELL Poster 16 to extend and enrich language.

ELL Poster 16

Objectives

- Understand how sensory details impact poetry.

Let's Think About Genre

Poetry: Sensory Details

Introduce the genre

Explain to students that poetry is a special genre of literature. A poem is designed to express deep meaning or thought. Ask students to share what they already know about poetry, and whether they have any favorite poems.

Discuss the genre

Poems include images made up of sensory details. These are details that appeal to one or more of our fives senses: sight, hearing, touch, taste, and smell. Sensory details help us visualize or in other ways experience what the poem is about. A poem may include a rhyme scheme, but it always has rhythm.

Ask the following questions:

- How is a poem different from a work of fiction? Possible response: A poem is written in lines, not sentences; it may rhyme; it expresses meaning.
- What sense does rhyme scheme appeal to, and how does it reinforce the meaning of the poem? Possible response: hearing; it draws attention to important words and ideas.
- What is one difference between rhythm and alliteration? Possible response: Rhythm has to do with the syllables of words and alliteration has to do with the beginnings of words.
- What kinds of sensory details would you expect to find in a poem about the joys of spending time alone? Possible response: details about how the place looks, feels, sounds, and smells

Guide practice

Have students fill in the chart with sensory details they experience when they are in the classroom.

Sight	Hearing	Touch	Smell

Connect to reading

Tell students that they will now read two poems with narrators, or speakers, who use the pronoun "I." Have students evaluate the impact of the sensory details and imagery in the poems.

Small Group Time

DAY 4 **Break into small groups before reading or revisiting "Under the Back Porch" and "Keziah."**

Teacher Led

SI Strategic Intervention	OL On-Level	A Advanced
Teacher Led p. DI•5 • Practice retelling • Genre focus • **Read/Revisit** "Under the Back Porch" and "Keziah"	Teacher Led p. DI•10 • Practice retelling • Genre focus • **Read/Revisit** "Under the Back Porch" and "Keziah"	Teacher Led p. DI•15 • Genre focus • **Read/Revisit** "Under the Back Porch" and "Keziah"

Place English language learners in the groups that correspond to their reading abilities in English.

Practice Stations
- Read for Meaning
- Get Fluent
- Words to Know

Independent Activities
- AudioText: "Under the Back Porch" and "Keziah"
- *Reader's and Writer's Notebook*
- Research and Inquiry

Objectives

- Understand sensory details in poetry.

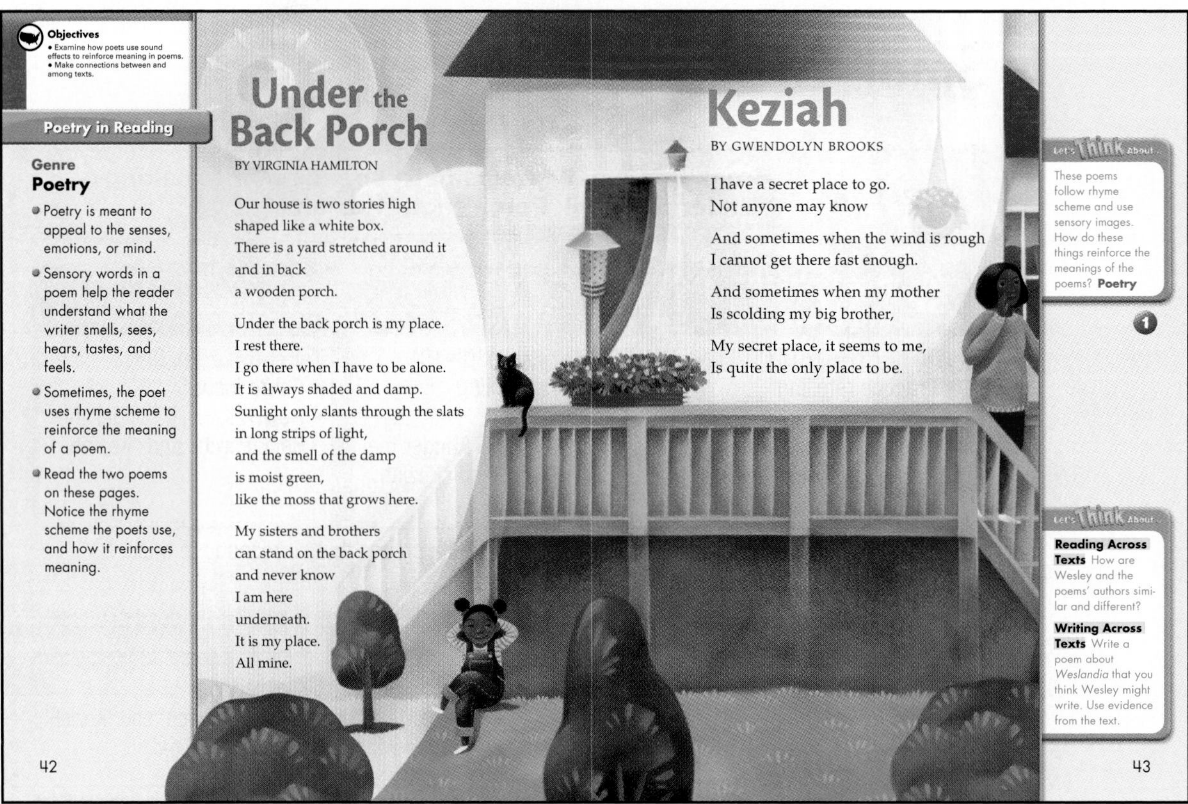
Objectives
• Examine how poets use sound effects to reinforce meaning in poems.
• Make connections between and among texts.

Poetry in Reading

Genre
Poetry

- Poetry is meant to appeal to the senses, emotions, or mind.
- Sensory words in a poem help the reader understand what the writer smells, sees, hears, tastes, and feels.
- Sometimes, the poet uses rhyme scheme to reinforce the meaning of a poem.
- Read the two poems on these pages. Notice the rhyme scheme the poets use, and how it reinforces meaning.

Under the Back Porch

BY VIRGINIA HAMILTON

Our house is two stories high
shaped like a white box.
There is a yard stretched around it
and in back
a wooden porch.

Under the back porch is my place.
I rest there.
I go there when I have to be alone.
It is always shaded and damp.
Sunlight only slants through the slats
in long strips of light,
and the smell of the damp
is moist green,
like the moss that grows here.

My sisters and brothers
can stand on the back porch
and never know
I am here
underneath.
It is my place.
All mine.

42

Keziah

BY GWENDOLYN BROOKS

I have a secret place to go.
Not anyone may know

And sometimes when the wind is rough
I cannot get there fast enough.

And sometimes when my mother
Is scolding my big brother,

My secret place, it seems to me,
Is quite the only place to be.

Let's Think About...
These poems follow rhyme scheme and use sensory images. How do these things reinforce the meanings of the poems? **Poetry**

1

Let's Think About...
Reading Across Texts How are Wesley and the poems' authors similar and different?
Writing Across Texts Write a poem about *Weslandia* that you think Wesley might write. Use evidence from the text.

43

Student Edition pp. 42–43

Guide Comprehension

Teach the genre

Poetry: Sensory Details Have students read "Under the Back Porch" and "Keziah" on pp. 42–43. As they read, have them look for sensory details in the poems. Then say: Find an example of a sensory detail in one of these poems.

Corrective feedback

If... students are unable to find an example of a sensory detail,
then... use the model to guide students to identify sensory details.

Model the Skill

Think Aloud I know that sensory details appeal to one or more of our five senses. In "Under the Back Porch," the speaker says, *the smell of the damp is moist green.* This imagery appeals to my senses of smell, touch, and sight.

On their own

Have students identify additional examples of sensory details and imagery and then evaluate their impact in the poems.

Extend Thinking
Think Critically

Higher-order thinking skills

Genre • Analysis What overall feeling or idea do you get from the sensory details in "Under the Back Porch"? Possible response: I get the feeling that it would be nice to be under the porch because it is cool, shady, and smells pleasantly of moss.

Theme and Setting • Evaluation Evaluate how the setting of each poem contributes to the author's theme or message about the pleasure of being in a quiet, secret place? Possible response: The setting of the first poem is a house or yard in the suburbs or countryside. The secret place in the second poem seems to be outside, and both settings give a feeling of peacefulness, quiet, and solitude. The descriptions of the settings make a big impact on messages of the poems.

Let's Think About...

1 Rhyme scheme appeals to the reader's hearing and draws attention to important words and ideas. Sensory details bring the poems to life by helping readers visualize what is happening. These images allow readers to experience the same sights, sounds, smells, and feelings that the poems' narrators experience.

Reading Across Texts

Have students use a Venn diagram to compare and contrast Wesley and the poems' narrators.

Writing Across Texts

Students' poems should reflect Wesley's personality and actions from *Weslandia*.

Differentiated Instruction

Strategic Intervention

Poetry In a small group setting, review the poems on pp. 42–43. Use the chart of the senses. Have students fill out the chart with words and phrases from both poems. Ask: Which poem uses more sensory details? ("Under the Back Porch")

Advanced

Have students add another stanza to "Keziah," using at least one example of phrases that include sensory details that create imagery.

English Language Learners

Genre Remind students that a poem can tell a story. Ask: Who is telling the story in each poem? What does the speaker want us to know about her special place and why she goes there? (privacy, healing, enjoyment) Write the reasons on the board. Then ask: What words does the speaker use to tell why this place appeals to or is important to her? List all suggestions.

- Discuss the meaning of the word *secret.* Point out that the definition is "known only to oneself or a few." Ask: Why does Keziah want to keep others from knowing about her secret place?

DAY 4 Read and Comprehend

Objectives

- Read with fluency.
- Use endings and word structure to identify meanings of words.
- Give oral presentations.

Check Fluency
SUCCESS PREDICTOR

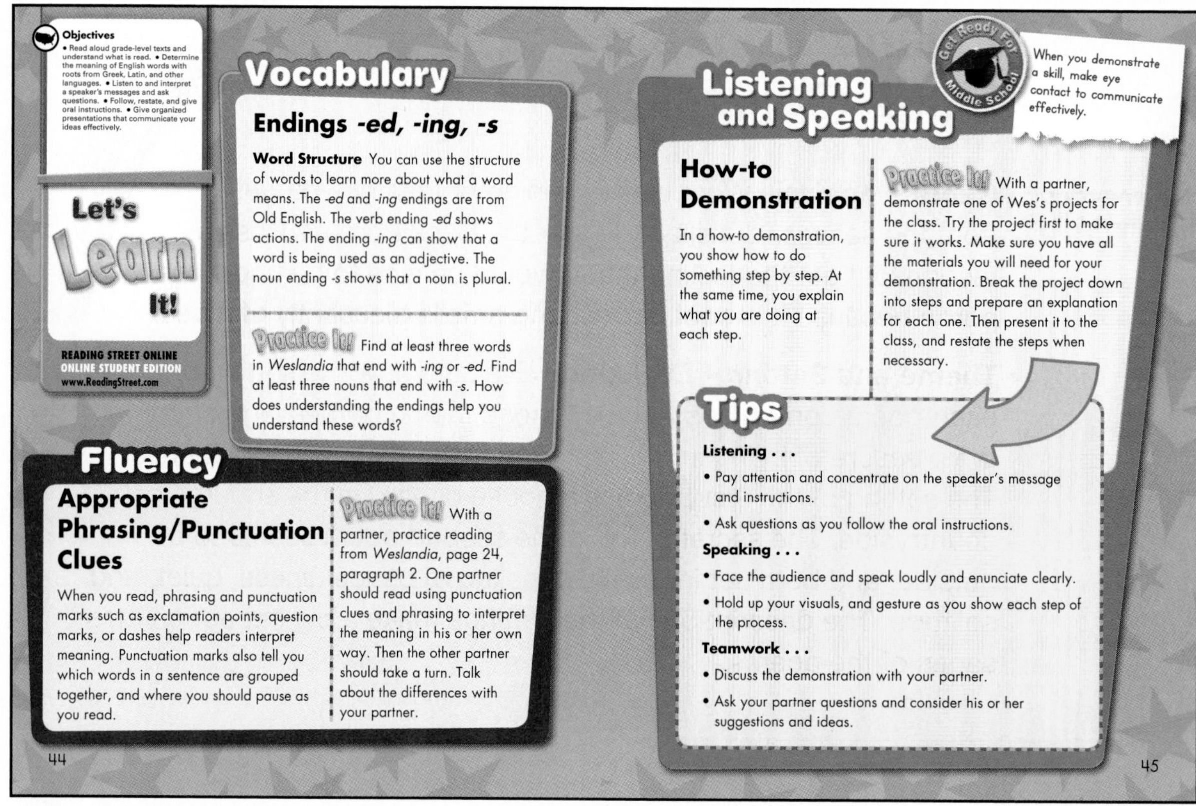

Objectives
• Read aloud grade-level texts and understand what is read. • Determine the meaning of English words with roots from Greek, Latin, and other languages. • Listen to and interpret a speaker's messages and ask questions. • Follow, restate, and give oral instructions. • Give organized presentations that communicate your ideas effectively.

Let's Learn It!

READING STREET ONLINE
ONLINE STUDENT EDITION
www.ReadingStreet.com

Vocabulary

Endings *-ed, -ing, -s*

Word Structure You can use the structure of words to learn more about what a word means. The *-ed* and *-ing* endings are from Old English. The verb ending *-ed* shows actions. The ending *-ing* can show that a word is being used as an adjective. The noun ending *-s* shows that a noun is plural.

Practice It! Find at least three words in *Weslandia* that end with *-ing* or *-ed*. Find at least three nouns that end with *-s*. How does understanding the endings help you understand these words?

Fluency

Appropriate Phrasing/Punctuation Clues

When you read, phrasing and punctuation marks such as exclamation points, question marks, or dashes help readers interpret meaning. Punctuation marks also tell you which words in a sentence are grouped together, and where you should pause as you read.

Practice It! With a partner, practice reading from *Weslandia*, page 24, paragraph 2. One partner should read using punctuation clues and phrasing to interpret the meaning in his or her own way. Then the other partner should take a turn. Talk about the differences with your partner.

Listening and Speaking

Get Ready For Middle School

When you demonstrate a skill, make eye contact to communicate effectively.

How-to Demonstration

In a how-to demonstration, you show how to do something step by step. At the same time, you explain what you are doing at each step.

Practice It! With a partner, demonstrate one of Wes's projects for the class. Try the project first to make sure it works. Make sure you have all the materials you will need for your demonstration. Break the project down into steps and prepare an explanation for each one. Then present it to the class, and restate the steps when necessary.

Tips

Listening . . .
- Pay attention and concentrate on the speaker's message and instructions.
- Ask questions as you follow the oral instructions.

Speaking . . .
- Face the audience and speak loudly and enunciate clearly.
- Hold up your visuals, and gesture as you show each step of the process.

Teamwork . . .
- Discuss the demonstration with your partner.
- Ask your partner questions and consider his or her suggestions and ideas.

44 45

Student Edition pp. 44–45

Fluency
Appropriate Phrasing

Guide Practice Use the Student Edition activity as an assessment tool. Make sure the reading passage is at least 200 words in length. As students read aloud with partners, walk around to make sure their phrasing makes word groupings meaningful and that they follow punctuation cues.

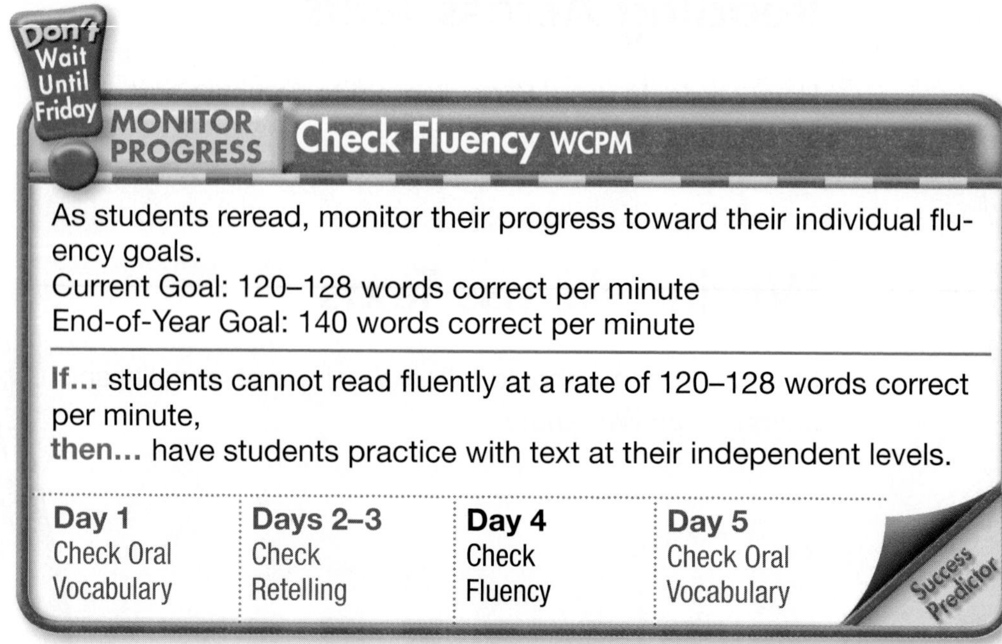

Don't Wait Until Friday

MONITOR PROGRESS **Check Fluency** WCPM

As students reread, monitor their progress toward their individual fluency goals.
Current Goal: 120–128 words correct per minute
End-of-Year Goal: 140 words correct per minute

If... students cannot read fluently at a rate of 120–128 words correct per minute,
then... have students practice with text at their independent levels.

Day 1	Days 2–3	Day 4	Day 5
Check Oral Vocabulary	Check Retelling	Check Fluency	Check Oral Vocabulary

Success Predictor

Vocabulary

Endings

Teach endings *-ing, -ed, -s*

Word Structure Write these words from pp. 28 and 29 of *Weslandia* on the board:

moaned sticks snapped heating housing

Explain that word affixes can help determine the meaning of words. Point out that the *-ing* affix in *heating* and *housing* can mean either that the word is a verb or an adjective. The *-s* affix in *sticks* means that the word is a plural noun or a verb. The *-ed* affix in *moaned* and *snapped* means that the actions happened in the past.

Guide practice

Have students determine the part of speech of each word listed above as it is used in *Weslandia*.

On their own

Walk around the room to make sure that student pairs can correctly identify the meaning and part of speech of the words.

Listening and Speaking

How-to Demonstration

Teach

Tell students that in order for a how-to demonstration to be effective, they must be organized and know each step of the process in the correct sequence. Remind students performing the demonstration that they should have all materials needed for the activity on hand and be sure to break the steps down so that instruction is clear and logical. The students should follow their own oral instructions in sequence during their demonstration. They should also restate the steps so the audience can more easily follow the demonstration.

Guide practice

Remind presenting students that good speakers maintain eye contact with listeners, speak at an appropriate rate and volume with clear enunciation, make natural gestures with their hands and body, and use proper conventions of language while speaking. Remind the students in the audience to listen attentively to the presentation and to take notes to help them accurately interpret the speaker's message.

On their own

Have students give their how-to demonstrations with their partners.

Demonstrating

Remind students that they should concentrate on the steps of the instructions as both presenters and audience. Tell students that any visuals used in a demonstration can clarify spoken information and steps in a process.

ELL

English Language Learners

Practice with word endings
Assist pairs of students in identifying how word endings can signal grammatical function in a sentence. Review parts of speech, including nouns, adjectives, and verbs. Review how these parts of speech incorporate the endings *-ed*, *-ing,* and *-s*. Have students circle these endings and identify the function of each word on the board.

Objectives

- Use illustrations and captions to support text in writing.
- Review subject and object pronouns.
- Spell words from many cultures.

Research and Inquiry
Synthesize

Teach Have students synthesize their findings into a written summary. They should use a word processor as they summarize. Remind them that they will need to include a Works Cited page to acknowledge their sources.

Guide practice Students should use illustrations and clip art to expand upon important information about their ancient civilizations. Suggest that students use drawing tools or clip art to create their illustrations. Students should create informative captions for the illustrations or clip art they have chosen.

On their own Have students put the finishing touches on their summaries and use the spell-check function in their word-processing programs to check for misspelled words.

Remind them that they still need to reread their summaries to check that the spelling and grammar is correct. Since the spell-check program only looks from misspellings, some words may be spelled correctly but not used properly. Ask students to describe the limitations of the spell-check program.

Conventions
Subject and Object Pronouns

Test practice Remind students that grammar skills, such as recognizing and using subject and object pronouns correctly, are often assessed on important tests.

Have students compare subject and object pronouns side by side. Read a sentence with a subject pronoun. *(We went to the store yesterday.)* Then ask students to make up a sentence using the same form of object pronoun. (first person plural—*Johnny took us to the store yesterday.*)

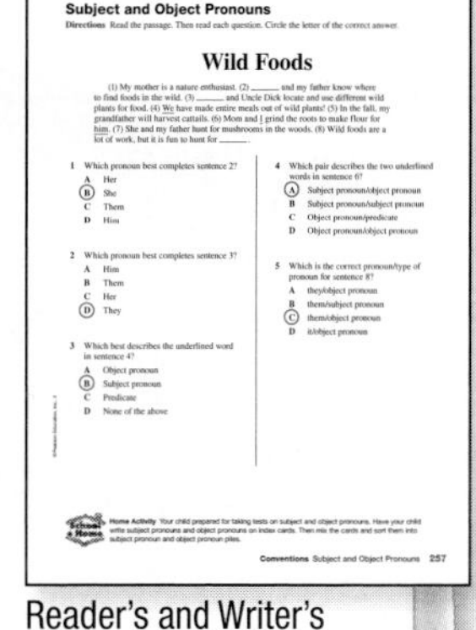
Reader's and Writer's Notebook p. 257

Repeat the activity beginning with a sentence with an object pronoun *(I know him very well)* and asking students to compose a sentence with the same form of subject pronoun. (third person masculine: *He is a great basketball player.*)

Daily Fix-It Use Daily Fix-It numbers 7 and 8 in the right margin.

On their own For additional practice, use the *Reader's and Writer's Notebook* p. 257.

Spelling
Words from Many Cultures

Practice spelling strategy Remind students that spelling patterns and rules can help them even on cultural words. Have partners take turns quizzing each other on spelling the list words. Have one student dictate as the other writes each word. Have them review each other's work, using print or electronic resources to help, and continue quizzing and checking until each partner spells all the words correctly.

On their own For additional practice, use *Let's Practice It!* p. 190 on the *Teacher Resources DVD-ROM.*

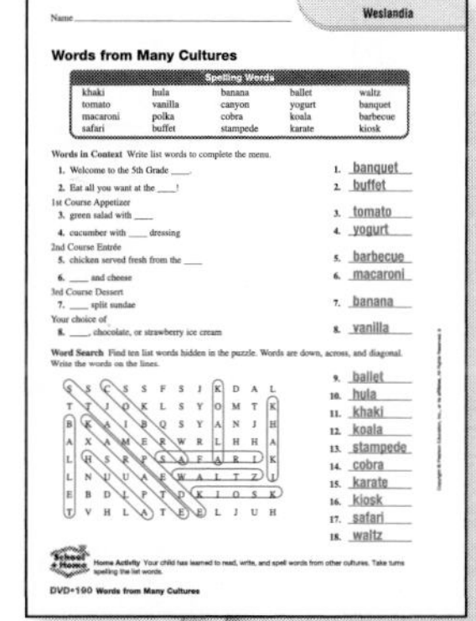
Let's Practice It! TR DVD•190

Daily Fix-It

7. Paul and him wrote a book on finding food in the wild! *(he; wild.)*
8. The section on edible Flowers are interesting. *(flowers is)*

Objectives

- Revise the draft of the picture book narrative.
- Apply the revising technique of adding.
- Add elements such as sensory details, vivid descriptions, and dialogue suitable for illustrations.

Writing—Picture Book
Revising Strategy

MINI-LESSON

Revising Strategy: Adding

- Yesterday we drafted a narrative for a picture book. Today we will revise our drafts to make the writing more interesting and suitable for illustration.
- Display Writing Transparency 16B. Remind students that revising does not include corrections of grammar and mechanics. Tell them that this will be done during proofreading. Then introduce the revising strategy of adding. When we revise, we ask, *Have I described the scene and actions vividly? Have I included enough sensory details? Is there dialogue?* The revising strategy of adding is one way to include elements that focus on the illustration of the narrative. Let's look at the paragraph I drafted yesterday. Instead of telling readers Herb doesn't like his job at the movie theater, I can add sensory details to show how bored and lonely Herb is. This emphasizes Herb's loneliness and makes the reader feel alone. Tell students that they can also add dialogue to make the writing come to life. Write in an example of dialogue and repeat it aloud. Now have students revise their drafts from yesterday using the revising strategy of adding.

Writing Transparency 16B, TR DVD

Revising Tips

- ✔ Add information to make sure that the focus of the story is well-supported.
- ✔ Make sure writing is well-organized and engaging.
- ✔ Add more sensory details, vivid descriptions, and dialogue that will add interest and excitement to the picture book.

Peer conferencing

Peer Revision Have pairs of students exchange papers for peer review. Each student reads his partner's paper and writes a short paragraph summarizing the feelings that the author is describing.

Review the Revising Tips with the class. Then have students revise their drafts from yesterday, focusing on the revising strategy of adding.

Corrective feedback

Circulate around the room to monitor students and have conferences with students as they revise. Remind students who are correcting errors that they will have time to edit tomorrow. They should be working on content and organization today.

ROUTINE **Quick Write for Fluency** Team Talk

1. **Talk** Pairs discuss the illustrations in *Weslandia* and how they help to make the narrative more understandable.
2. **Write** Students write a paragraph describing the type of pictures they would like to see illustrate their narratives.
3. **Share** Partners read each other's paragraphs and comment on whether they agree or disagree with the choice of illustrations.

Routines Flip Chart

English Language Learners

Modify the Prompt Allow beginning English speakers to work with a partner, dictating their compositions as their partner records them as a list. In the revising step, have students add words to make their narratives more descriptive.

Differentiated Instruction If students have trouble writing their compositions, then suggest that they respond orally to the prompt.

Wrap Up Your Day

- ✔ **Build Concepts** Have students discuss any special places that they have.
- ✔ **Oral Vocabulary** Monitor students' use of oral vocabulary as they respond to the question, *How might you create a special place of your own?*
- ✔ **Text Features** Discuss how stanzas help students understand text.

Remind students to think about how people adapt to difficult situations.

Objectives
- Review the weekly concept.
- Review oral vocabulary.

Today at a Glance

Oral Vocabulary

Comprehension
◎ Draw conclusions

Lesson Vocabulary
◎ Endings *-s,-ed,-ing*

Word Analysis
Endings *-ing,-ed,-s*

Literary Terms
Idioms

Assessment
Fluency
Comprehension

Research and Inquiry
Communicate

Spelling
Words from many cultures

Conventions
Subject and object pronouns

Writing
Picture book

Check Oral Vocabulary
SUCCESS PREDICTOR

Concept Wrap Up

Question of the Week

How do people adapt to difficult situations?

Review the concept Have students look back at the reading selections to find examples that demonstrate how people adapt to challenges.

Review Amazing Words Display and review this week's concept map. Remind students that this week they have learned ten Amazing Words related to people adapting. Have students use the Amazing Words and the concept map to answer the question *How do people adapt to difficult situations*?

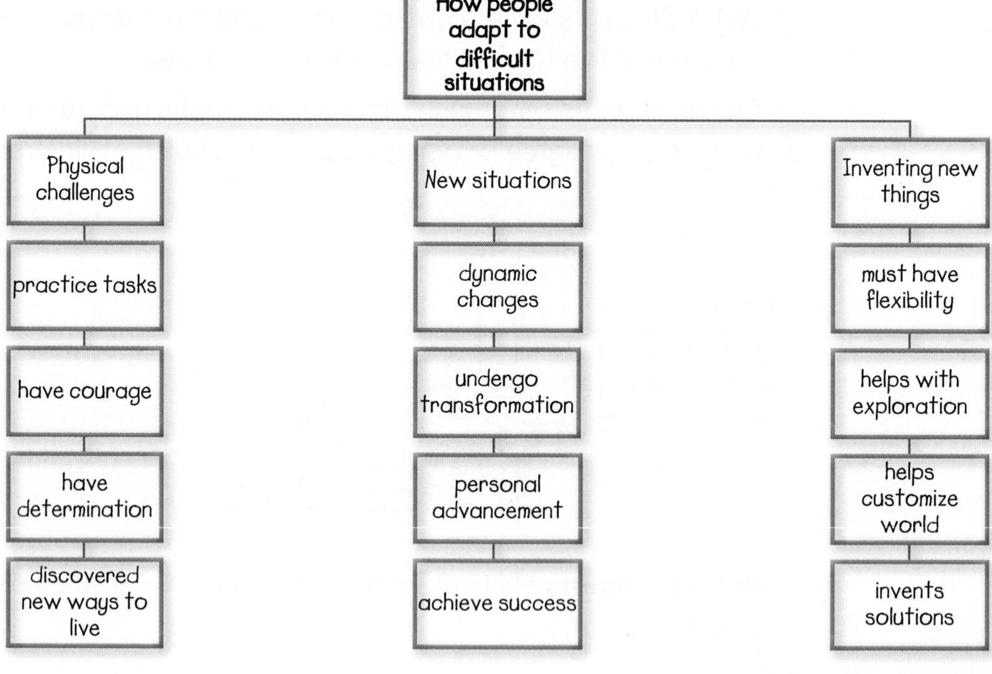

ELL Check Concepts and Language Use the Day 5 instruction on ELL Poster 16 to monitor students' understanding of the lesson concept.

ELL Poster 16

Amazing Ideas

Connect to the Big Question Have pairs of students elicit and consider suggestions from each other about how the Question of the Week connects to the Big Question: *How do people and animals adapt to different situations?* Tell students to use the concept map and what they have learned from this week's Anchored Talks and reading selections to form an Amazing Idea—a realization or "big idea" about Adapting. Remind partners to pose and answer questions with appropriate details and to give suggestions that build on each other's ideas. Then ask each pair to share their Amazing Idea with the class.

Amazing Ideas might include these key concepts:

- Determination is a key ingredient to success in adapting, especially when the challenge is a difficult one.
- People throughout the ages have faced difficult situations and have managed to adapt to them.
- We can all learn about our hidden strengths when we are forced to adapt to a difficult situation.

Write about it Have students write a few sentences about their Amazing Idea, beginning with "This week I learned…"

It's Friday

MONITOR PROGRESS Check Oral Vocabulary

Have individuals use this week's Amazing Words to describe a time when they had to adapt to a difficult situation. Monitor students' ability to use the Amazing Words and note which words you need to reteach.

If... students have difficulty using the Amazing Words,

then... reteach using the Oral Vocabulary Routine, pp. 21a, 24b, 34b, 42b, OV•1.

Day 1	Days 2–3	Day 4	Day 5
Check Oral Vocabulary	Check Retelling	Check Fluency	Check Oral Vocabulary

Success Predictor

Amazing Words

discovered	customize
courage	flexibility
determination	transformation
practice	advancement
exploration	dynamic

English Language Learners

Concept Map Work with students to add new words to the concept map.

DAY 5 Wrap Up your Week

20–25 mins.

Objectives

- ◎ Review drawing conclusions.
- Review using word structure to determine the meaning of unknown words.
- ◎ Review word endings -ing, -ed, -s.
- Review common idioms.

Comprehension Review

Draw Conclusions

Student Edition p. EI•6

Teach draw conclusions Review the definition of drawing conclusions on p. 22. Remind students that reasonable conclusions are supported by evidence in a text and sometimes inferred by their own prior knowledge. For additional support have students review p. EI•6 on drawing conclusions.

Envision It!

Guide practice Have partners identify the conclusions and evaluate whether they are well supported. Have student pairs draw conclusions based on events and information in *Weslandia*. Then have pairs identify textual evidence that supports their conclusions.

On their own For additional practice with drawing conclusions, use *Let's Practice It!* p. 191 on the *Teacher Resources DVD-ROM*.

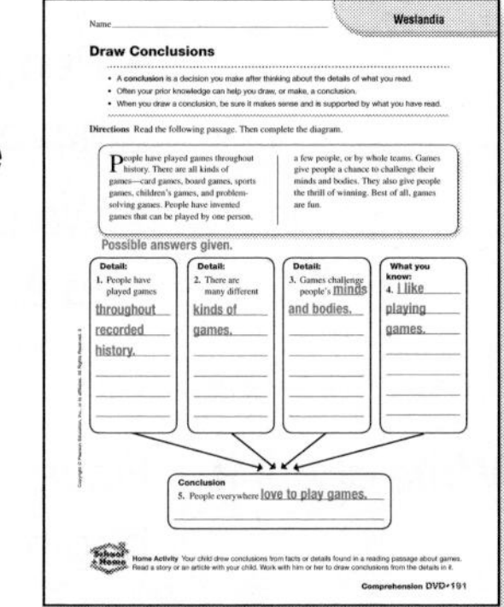
Name

Weslandia

Draw Conclusions

- A **conclusion** is a decision you make after thinking about the details of what you read.
- Often your prior knowledge can help you draw, or make, a conclusion.
- When you draw a conclusion, be sure it makes sense and is supported by what you have read.

Directions Read the following passage. Then complete the diagram.

People have played games throughout history. There are all kinds of games—card games, board games, sports games, children's games, and problem-solving games. People have invented games that can be played by one person, a few people, or by whole teams. Games give people a chance to challenge their minds and bodies. They also give people the thrill of winning. Best of all, games are fun.

Possible answers given.

Detail:	Detail:	Detail:	What you know:
1. People have played games throughout recorded history.	2. There are many different kinds of games.	3. Games challenge people's minds and bodies.	4. I like playing games.

Conclusion
5. People everywhere love to play games.

Home Activity Your child drew conclusions from facts or details found in a reading passage about games. Read a story or an article with your child. Work with him or her to draw conclusions from the details in it.

Comprehension DVD•191

Let's Practice It!
TR DVD•191

Vocabulary Review

Endings *-s, -ed, -ing*

Teach endings *-s, -ed, -ing* Remind students to look at word structure, word affixes in particular, to determine or clarify the meanings of unknown or unfamiliar words.

Guide practice Review with students how to find the meaning of a word by looking for meaningful word parts. Explain that endings give clues to meaning.

On their own Have students work with partners to write sentences containing words with the endings *-ing, -ed,* and *-s*. Partners can trade sentences and identify the word endings that help them determine each word's meaning.

Word Analysis Review

Endings *-ing, -ed, -s*

Teach endings *-ing, -ed, -s* Review how the affixes *-ing, -ed,* and *-s* can be added to base words. Discuss how adding these affixes can change the part of speech of the base word.

Guide practice Display the following words: *trampled, disturbing, investigators*. Use the Strategy for Meaningful Word Parts to teach the word *trampled*.

ROUTINE Strategy for Meaningful Word Parts

1. **Introduce the Word Parts** Display the word *trampled*. Underline the base word *trample* and circle the affix *-ed*.
2. **Connect to Meaning** I see the base word *trample* and I see the affix *-ed*. I know *trample* means "to crush underfoot." Adding the *-ed* makes the verb past tense. The new word means "crushed underfoot."
3. **Read the Word** Blend the meaningful word parts together to read the word *trampled*.

Routines Flip Chart

On their own Have students work in pairs to circle the affixes in *disturbing* and *investigators*. Then have them determine the meaning of each word.

Literary Terms Review

Idioms

Teach Idioms Have students review *Weslandia* on p. 31. Remind students that an idiom is a group of words that cannot be understood by their literal meaning. For example, *pulling your leg* is an idiom that means "to make a joke."

Guide practice Find an example of idiom from *Weslandia*. Discuss why the author uses that idiom (*shot up*) in place of literal language ("grew quickly").

On their own Have students make a T-chart with the headings *Idiom* and *Meaning*. Ask them to identify common idioms from the reading selections and then record their meaning in the T-chart.

Lesson Vocabulary

blunders stupid mistakes
civilization the ways of living of a people or nation
complex made up of a number of parts; hard to understand
envy feeling of discontent because another person has what you want
fleeing to be running away
inspired to be filled with a thought or feeling; influenced
rustling causing a light, soft sound of things gently rubbing together
strategy the skillful planning and management of anything

ELL

English Language Learners

Draw conclusions If students have trouble drawing conclusions, look at their inferential statements and ask, What makes you think this? Which part of the story supports your conclusion? Which words in particular lead to this conclusion?

Words with endings Supply students with a list of words with endings *-ing, -ed,* and *-s*. Have students circle the ending of each word. Ask them to use the word in a sentence.

Objectives

- Read grade-level text with fluency.

Assessment

Check words correct per minute

Fluency Make two copies of the fluency passage on p. 45k. As the student reads the text aloud, mark mistakes on your copy. Also mark where the student is at the end of one minute. To check the student's comprehension of the passage, have him or her retell what was read. To figure words correct per minute (WCPM), subtract the number of mistakes from the total number tof words read in one minute.

Corrective feedback

If... students cannot read fluently at a rate of 120–128 WCPM or with comprehension,
then... make sure they practice with text at their independent reading level. Provide additional fluency practice by pairing nonfluent readers with fluent readers.

If... students already read at 140 WCPM,
then... have them read a book of their choice independently.

Plan to Assess Fluency

- ☑ **This week assess Advanced students.**
- ☐ **Week 2** Assess Strategic Intervention students.
- ☐ **Week 3** Assess On-Level students.
- ☐ **Week 4** Assess Strategic Intervention students.
- ☐ **Week 5** Assess any students you have not yet checked during this unit.

Set individual goals for students to enable them to reach the year-end goal.

- Current Goal: 120–128 WCPM
- Year-End Goal: 140 WCPM

Small Group Time

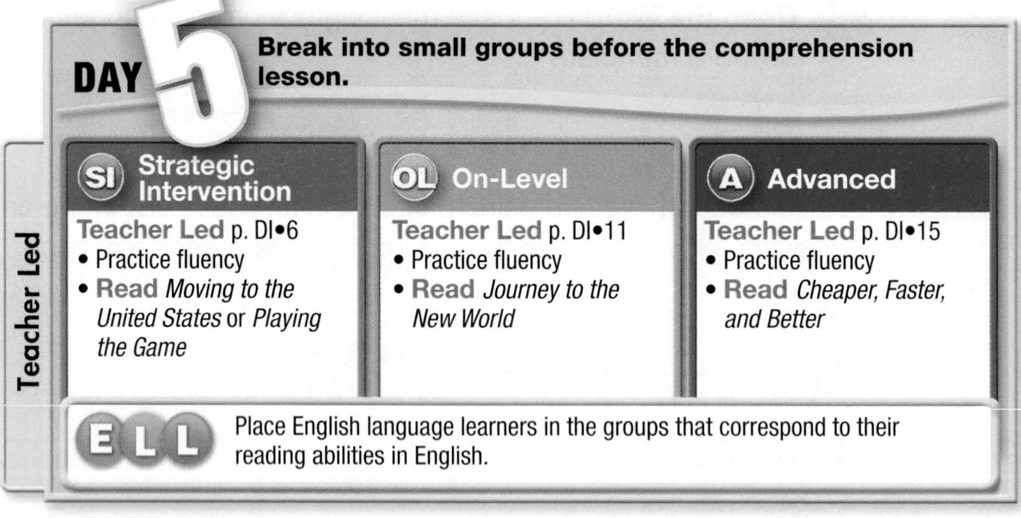

DAY 5
Break into small groups before the comprehension lesson.
Teacher Led
SI Strategic Intervention
Teacher Led p. DI•6
• Practice fluency
• Read Moving to the United States or Playing the Game
OL On-Level
Teacher Led p. DI•11
• Practice fluency
• Read Journey to the New World
A Advanced
Teacher Led p. DI•15
• Practice fluency
• Read Cheaper, Faster, and Better
ELL
Place English language learners in the groups that correspond to their reading abilities in English.

Practice Stations
- Words to Know
- Get Fluent
- Read for meaning

Independent Activities
- Grammar Jammer
- Concept Talk Video
- Vocabulary Activities

Name ______________________________

Four Seasons

When Leo moved from the mountains of Georgia to sunny California, he 12
knew that he would miss the four seasons. But, he loved their home that was 27
the color of a mango. 32

The kitchen was painted seafoam green. The living room was painted 43
pumpkin orange. His mother's room was ripe-banana yellow. Leo's room was 54
white. And he didn't love his room with its four, boring, white walls. 67

"So, paint it," his mother said. 73

Leo did. On one wall, he painted a forest with pastel flowers just opening 87
up. He painted a pond with a mother duck and five babies. 99

On another wall, Leo painted a forest, but the trees were full of rich, 113
green leaves. On the pond bank, he painted himself holding a fishing pole. 126

On the third wall, Leo painted the same forest but this time the leaves 140
were orange, red, and yellow. Large, brown cattails grew around the pond. 152
Leo painted a flock of birds flying south. 160

On the fourth wall, Leo painted the same forest, but the trees were bare. 174
The pond was frozen, and Leo painted himself skating across the surface. 186

The boring, white walls were gone. And Leo could see the four seasons 199
anytime he wanted. 202

MONITOR PROGRESS

- **Check Fluency**

Objectives

- Read grade-level text with comprehension.

Assessment

Check draw conclusions

Drawing Conclusions Use "The Sea Queen" on p. 45m to check students' understanding of drawing conclusions about a text. Make sure students always support their conclusions with textual evidence.

1. What does the following sentence tell you about Maria? "Each week she waited and watched with envy as exciting people got to do exciting things on her favorite reality television show." (Maria feels that her life is boring compared to the lives of other people.)
2. Use what you've read and your prior knowledge to draw a conclusion about how Maria now feels about her life. (After Maria's adventure in the sea cave, she feels important and exciting. The phrase "So much for being bored" supports my conclusion that her life had changed.)
3. What conclusion can you infer about why Maria felt she had to sit in the sea grass chair? What evidence from the text supports your conclusion? (She felt it was meant for her and that her adventure would begin once she sat in the chair. The sentence "As she sat down an amazing thing happened" supports my conclusion that her adventure would begin once she sat in the chair.)

Corrective feedback

If... students are unable to answer the comprehension questions, **then...** use the Reteach lesson in the *First Stop* book.

Name ______________________________

The Sea Queen

Maria had only one week left before school started again and, so far, not one exciting thing had happened. Maria had been sure that something great, maybe something even magnificent, would happen to her. Each week she waited and watched with envy as exciting people got to do exciting things on her favorite reality television show.

"I bet if they made a reality show about me it would be called 'The Boring Life of Maria,'" she told her mom one evening.

"I think that might change," her mother said. "You get to spend this last week with Grandma Sandy in her beach house."

On Monday, Grandma Sandy told Maria to go exploring. Maria was walking across the warm sand thinking about her boring life when she spotted a large patch of sea grass. The sea grass seemed to be calling to her and beckoning her to come closer.

To Maria's surprise, the sea grass covered a hidden door. The handle was a seashell. She opened the door and found herself inside a cave painted blue and green. In the middle of the cave was a large chair made of woven sea grasses and decorated with shells.

Maria knew that she had to sit in the chair. As she sat down an amazing thing happened. Hundreds of sea creatures came forth. "Queen!" they called out to her.

Maria visited the sea cave every day. She learned the names of all the creatures who called her queen. So much for being bored, she thought. On her last day, the creatures presented her with the official notice that Maria would be their queen forever.

MONITOR PROGRESS

• Draw Conclusions

Objectives

- Communicate inquiry results.
- Administer spelling test.
- Review subject and object pronouns.

Research and Inquiry
Communicate

Present ideas Have students present their summaries and illustrations. Make sure they explain how the illustration relates to their summary and what factual information is evident in the illustration. They should either read the summary aloud or highlight a few key points about their ancient civilization.

Listening and speaking Remind students how to be good speakers and how to communicate effectively with their audience.

- Speak clearly and loudly, using a normal speaking rate.
- Keep eye contact with audience members and gesture naturally.
- Point to your illustration as you talk about it.
- Use good grammar and language appropriate for your audience to be sure ideas are clear to everyone.
- Respond to questions with appropriate details.

Remind students of these tips for being a good listener.

- Pay close attention to be sure you can understand and interpret the speaker's verbal and nonverbal messages.
- Make sure you understand any factual information presented in the illustration. Some illustrations may include historical places or people. There also may be some clues about of the culture evident in the illustration.
- Wait until the speaker has finished before raising your hand to ask a relevant question.
- Be polite, even if you disagree.

Spelling Test
Words from Many Cultures

Spelling test To administer the spelling test, refer to the directions, words, and sentences on p. 23c.

Conventions
Extra Practice

Teach Remind students that subject and object pronouns allow writers to avoid repeating nouns.

- A pronoun used as the subject of a sentence is a subject pronoun. *I, you, he, she, it, we,* and *they* are subject pronouns.
- A pronoun used after action verbs or as objects of prepositions are object pronouns. *Me, you, him, her, it, us,* and *them* are object pronouns.

Guide practice Have students work with a partner to substitute pronouns for the nouns in the following sentences. Guide students in selecting the correct pronouns.

Cara is watching Jim.	(She is watching him.)
Jim is laughing with Cara.	(He is laughing with her.)
You and I will meet Jim and Cara.	(We will meet them.)

Daily Fix-It Use Daily Fix-It numbers 9 and 10 in the right margin.

On their own Have students rearrange the words in these sentences so that the appropriate subject and object pronouns are used correctly.

1. **them couldn't any in find Wesley book plant**
   (Wesley couldn't find them in any plant book.)
2. **gave a of tour Wesley Weslandia them**
   (Wesley gave them a tour of Westlandia.)

For additional practice, use *Let's Practice It!* p. 192 on the *Teacher Resources DVD-ROM.*

Daily Fix-It

9. The tamato was an early food of South american natives. *(tomato; American)*
10. Chocolate also comed to us, from Native Americans. *(came; us from)*

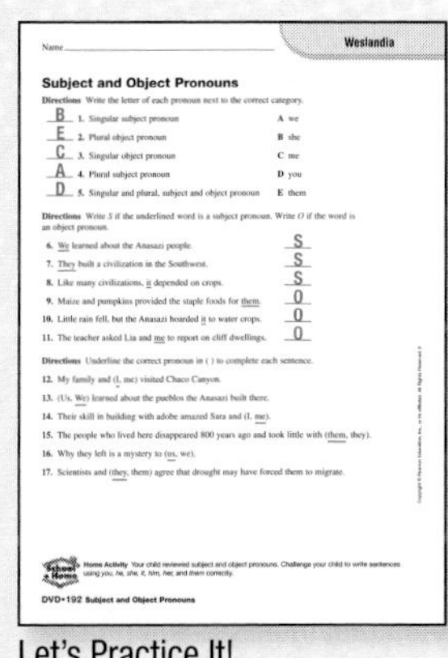

Name ____________ Weslandia

Subject and Object Pronouns

Directions Write the letter of each pronoun next to the correct category.

B 1. Singular subject pronoun — A we
E 2. Plural object pronoun — B she
C 3. Singular object pronoun — C me
A 4. Plural subject pronoun — D you
D 5. Singular and plural, subject and object pronoun — E them

Directions Write *S* if the underlined word is a subject pronoun. Write *O* if the word is an object pronoun.

6. We learned about the Anasazi people. S
7. They built a civilization in the Southwest. S
8. Like many civilizations, it depended on crops. S
9. Maize and pumpkins provided the staple foods for them. O
10. Little rain fell, but the Anasazi hoarded it to water crops. O
11. The teacher asked Lia and me to report on cliff dwellings. O

Directions Underline the correct pronoun in ( ) to complete each sentence.

12. My family and (I, me) visited Chaco Canyon.
13. (Us, We) learned about the pueblos the Anasazi built there.
14. Their skill in building with adobe amazed Sara and (I, me).
15. The people who lived here disappeared 800 years ago and took little with (them, they).
16. Why they left is a mystery to (us, we).
17. Scientists and (they, them) agree that drought may have forced them to migrate.

Home Activity Your child reviewed subject and object pronouns. Challenge your child to write sentences using *you, he, she, it, him, her,* and *them* correctly.

DVD•192 Subject and Object Pronouns

Let's Practice It!
TR DVD•192

Objectives

- Proofread for correct usage of subject and object pronouns.
- Create final draft.
- Select scenes and events for illustrations.

Writing—Picture Book
Subject and Object Pronouns

Review Revising Remind students that yesterday they revised their drafts, paying particular attention to adding sensory details, vivid descriptions, and dialogue. Today, students will proofread their narratives and select the scenes and events that they will illustrate for their picture books.

MINI-LESSON

Proofread for Pronouns

- **Teach** When we proofread, we look for errors in mechanics such as spelling, capitalization, punctuation, and grammar. Today we will focus on using subject and object pronouns correctly. Let's look at a couple of paragraphs from our narrative about a character who dreams about an imaginary life. Display Writing Transparency 16C.

Writing Transparency 16C, TR DVD

- **Model** First I will look for subject and object pronouns. In the third sentence, I see that I have repeated the character's name, Herb Trew. I can use the subject pronoun *he* to replace *Herb Trew.* In the second sentence of the second paragraph, I used the subject pronoun *he*, but the pronoun follows an action verb so I should use the object pronoun *him* instead. Now, I will look for errors in spelling, punctuation, capitalization, and grammar. Explain to students that they should reread their narratives several times, each time looking for different types of errors.

Proofread Display the Proofreading Tips. Ask students to proofread their compositions, using the Proofreading Tips and paying particular attention to proper use of subject and object pronouns. When students have finished editing their own work, have pairs proofread one another's narratives and evaluate picture choices.

Proofreading Tips

- ✔ Be sure your subject and object pronouns are correct.
- ✔ Check spelling, grammar, and punctuation.
- ✔ Make sure dialogue is punctuated correctly.

Present

Have students incorporate revisions and proofreading edits into their narrative to create a final draft. Student should then go through their narrative to select particular scenes and events they wish to illustrate.

A good rule of thumb is one illustration per paragraph. Have students fold letter-size unlined paper in half to form blank half-pages and write one paragraph of their narrative on each page. Students may then draw or sketch a picture that illustrates that particular paragraph. Some students may wish to use stick figures to represent their characters. Students can choose dialogue from their narratives and put them in balloons. After they complete the individual drawings and accompanying narrative, they may wish to assemble their work into a complete picture book.

ROUTINE **Quick Write for Fluency** Team Talk

1. **Talk** Pairs discuss what they have learned about what it is like to not follow the crowd.
2. **Write** Each student writes a paragraph about how their main character did not follow the crowd.
3. **Share** Partners read each other's paragraphs.

Routines Flip Chart

Focus Your Editing

In the editing process, students can easily get bogged down by everything that needs to be fixed. Editing one aspect at a time helps students focus their efforts.

Teacher Note

Writing Self-Evaluation Guide Make copies of the Writing Self-Evaluation Guide on p. 39 of the *Reader's and Writer's Notebook* and hand out to students.

English Language Learners

Poster Preview Prepare students for next week by using Week 2 ELL Poster 17. Read the Poster Talk-Through to introduce the concept and vocabulary. Ask students to identify and describe objects and actions in the art.

Selection Summary Send home the summary of *Tripping Over the Lunch Lady* in English and the students' home languages, if available. Students can read the summary with family.

Preview NEXT WEEK

How do people overcome obstacles? You will be reading about a clumsy girl who sets her sights on square dancing.

Assessment Checkpoints for the Week

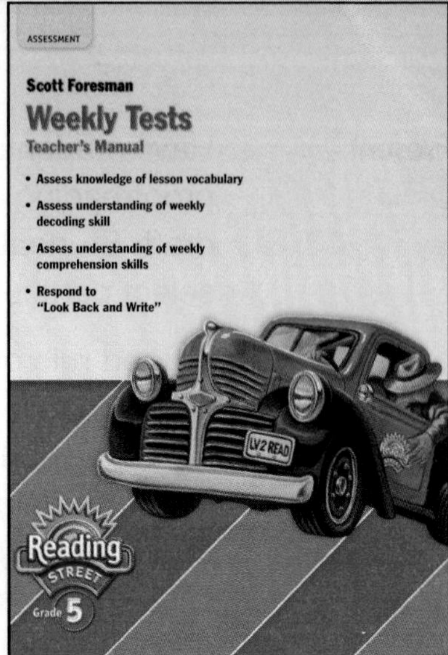

Weekly Tests

Weekly Assessment

Use pp. 111–118 of *Weekly Tests* to check:

✔ **Word Analysis** Endings *-ing, -ed, -s*

✔ **Comprehension Skill** Draw Conclusions

✔ Review **Comprehension Skill** Literary Elements: Theme and Setting

✔ **Lesson Vocabulary**

blunders	fleeing
civilization	inspired
complex	rustling
envy	strategy

Advanced

On-Level

Strategic Intervention

Differentiated Assessment

Use pp. 91–96 of *Fresh Reads for Fluency and Comprehension* to check:

✔ **Comprehension Skill** Draw Conclusions

✔ Review **Comprehension Skill** Literary Elements: Theme and Setting

✔ **Fluency** Words Correct Per Minute

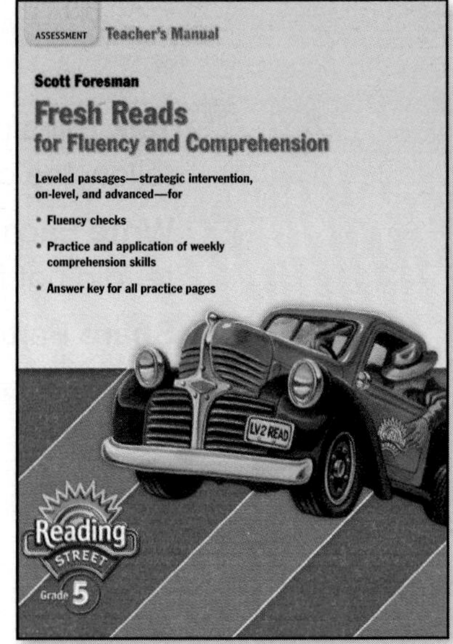

Fresh Reads for Fluency and Comprehension

Managing Assessment

Use *Assessment Handbook* for:

✔ **Weekly Assessment Blackline Masters for Monitoring Progress**

✔ **Observation Checklists**

✔ **Record-Keeping Forms**

✔ **Portfolio Assessment**

Assessment Handbook

Read Aloud (continued)

Birdsong on a Summer Evening

Continued from p. 21b

“Maybe this Pete Gray could do it, but he probably practiced his brains out. How am I supposed to do that when I don’t even have a team to play with?”

Ben looked me straight in the eye. “You’re either a baseball man, or you’re not,” he said. He closed the book with a bang. “You don’t get nothin’ for nothin’ in this world. We’re gonna practice together, just you and me. We’re gonna get you ready for the team.”

That was what Ben did for me that summer. We went to the park every evening. I can’t say it was easy. People would stop and watch us. I hated that.

Ben would pull my attention back to what we were doing. “Pay them no mind,” he’d say. “You want something bad enough, you gotta work for it. You want to be a baseball man, you gotta practice.”

At first I couldn’t throw and I couldn’t hit anything at all. Ben kept me at it, and I learned. Soon I was hitting as many as I was missing. It was slow going, but I got better.

When I came home one night, Mom told me that [my coach] had called. He’d left a message that I should come to the ballpark the next afternoon. He was putting a team together and he wanted me.

So I went to the meeting—and joined the team and played baseball again.

Pacing Small Group Instruction

5-Day Plan

DAY 1	• Reinforce the concept • Read Leveled Readers Concept Literacy Below Level
DAY 2	• Draw Conclusions • Questioning • Revisit Student Edition pp. 26–33
DAY 3	• Endings • Revisit Student Edition pp. 34–37
DAY 4	• Practice Retelling • Read/Revisit Student Edition pp. 42–43
DAY 5	• Reread for fluency • Reread Leveled Readers

3- or 4-Day Plan

DAY 1	• Reinforce the concept • Read Leveled Readers
DAY 2	• Draw Conclusions • Questioning • Revisit Student Edition pp. 26–33
DAY 3	• Endings • Revisit Student Edition pp. 34–37
DAY 4	• Practice Retelling • Read/Revisit Student Edition pp. 42–43 • Reread for fluency • Reread Leveled Readers

3-Day Plan: Eliminate the shaded box.

DAY 1

Build Background

- **Reinforce the Concept** Connect to the weekly question *How do people adapt to difficult situations?* Talk with students about changes they have had to face, such as moving to a new town, starting at a new school, or getting a new brother or sister. Point out that most people have to face some big changes at some time in their lives. This week's concept is *people adapting.* When you face big changes, you have to adapt by changing to fit different conditions and situations. For example, if you are starting at a new school, you need to learn new rules, where to go for lunch, and how to make new friends. You can't keep doing the same old things you used to do. Discuss the words on the concept map on p. 20–21 in the Teacher Edition.
- **Connect to Reading** Ask students how they used what they already know to help them adapt to a new situation. For instance, what did they know about making friends that helped them make new ones? This week you will read about ways that people adapt to difficult situations. Using what you already know can help you adapt.

Objectives

- Interpret a speaker's messages (both verbal and nonverbal).

DAY 1

For a complete literacy instructional plan and additional practice with this week's target skills and strategies, see the **Leveled Reader Teaching Guide.**

Concept Literacy Reader

- **Read** *Moving to the United States*
- **Before Reading** Preview the selection with students, focusing on key concepts and vocabulary. Then have them set a purpose for reading.
- **During Reading** Read the first two pages of the selection aloud while students track the print. Then have students finish reading the selection with a partner.
- **After Reading** After students finish reading the selection, connect it to the weekly question *How do people adapt to difficult situations?*

Below-Level Reader

- **Read** *Playing the Game*
- **Before Reading** Use a picture walk to guide students through the text, focusing on key concepts and vocabulary. Then have students set a purpose for reading.
- **During Reading** Do a choral reading of pp. 6–9. If students are able, have them read and discuss the remainder of the book with a partner. Have partners discuss the following questions:
  - How did Ella and Pete adapt to their new neighborhood? *(They joined in the game the kids played.)*
  - What did Ella and Pete do when they played with the other kids in the park? *(They made up a new plan to win the game.)*
- **After Reading** Have students look at and discuss the concept map. Connect the Below-Level Reader to the weekly question *How do people adapt to difficult situations?*

Playing the Game
by Adam McClellan
illustrated by Dan Grant

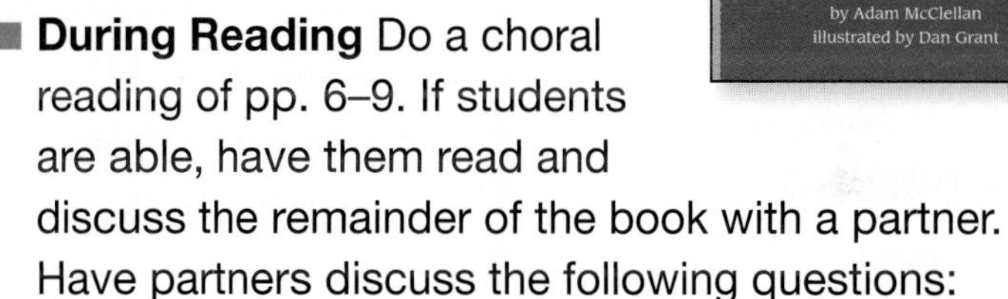
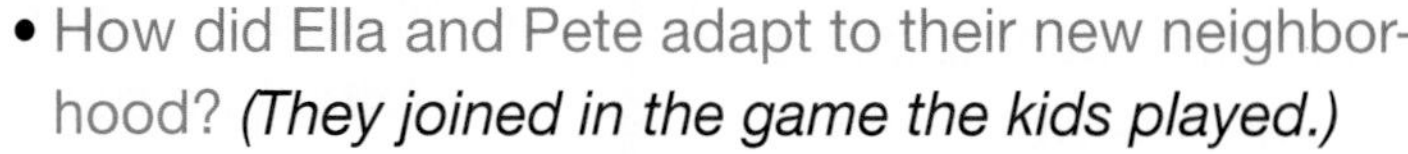

MONITOR PROGRESS

If... students have difficulty reading the selection with a partner,
then... have them follow along as they listen to the Leveled Readers DVD-ROM.

If... students have trouble understanding ways that Ella and Pete adapted to the new game,
then... reread pp. 20–22 and discuss their choices together.

Objectives

- Interpret a speaker's messages (both verbal and nonverbal).

Reinforce Comprehension

Skill Draw Conclusions Review with students *Envision It!* p. EI•6 on Draw Conclusions. Then use p. 22 to review the definition of draw conclusions.

Strategy Questioning Review the definition of questioning. Remind students to ask themselves questions as they read about what the characters are doing and why they are doing it. These questions can help students draw conclusions about events in the story. For additional support, refer students to *Envision It!* p. EI•21.

Revisit *Weslandia* on pp. 26–33. Have students begin reading the story aloud with a partner. As they read, have them apply the comprehension skill and strategy to the story.

- What do you know about Wesley so far? *(He doesn't like pizza, soda, and football; he doesn't shave his head; and he is good at running away.)*
- Based on these details, what conclusion about Wesley can you draw? *(He is different from most other boys.)*
- How did the other kids react to Wesley's summer project? *(They first spied on him, and then they wanted to join in on what he was doing.)*
- What conclusion can you draw about how Wesley is adapting to his difficult situation? *(When he didn't fit into the civilization around him, he cleverly started his own.)*

Use the During Reading Differentiated Instruction for additional support for struggling readers.

MONITOR PROGRESS

If… students have difficulty reading along with the group,
then… have them follow along as they listen to the AudioText.

Objectives

- Ask literal questions of text.

Student Edition p. EI•6

More Reading

Use additional Leveled Readers or other texts at students' instructional levels to reinforce this week's skills and strategies. For text suggestions, see the Leveled Reader Database or the Leveled Readers Skills Chart on pp. CL 24–CL 29.

DAY 3

Reinforce Vocabulary

Endings/Word Structure Point out to students that the ending *-ed* can be added to verbs to change the tense from present to past. Write the following sentence from *Weslandia* on the board: "What happened to your watch?" Underline the word *happened*.

I see the base word is *happen,* which means "an action that takes place." Then I see that the ending *-ed* has been added to the base word. The ending changes the meaning to the past tense. So, *happened* means "an action that took place in the past."

Revisit *Weslandia* on pp. 34–37. Review *Words!* on p. W•4. As students finish reading *Weslandia*, encourage them to use word endings to determine when an action took place. Point out the word *reflected* on page 33.

- What is the base word? *(reflect)* How does the *-ed* ending change the meaning of the base word? *(It shows the action happened in the past.)*
- Look at the word *offered* on this page. What does the base word *offer* mean? *("give something to someone")* When did this action take place? *(in the past)*

Use the During Reading Differentiated Instruction for additional support for struggling readers.

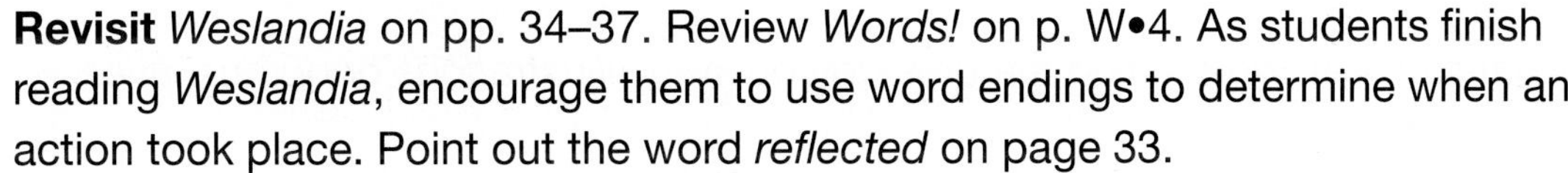

MONITOR PROGRESS

If... students need more practice with the lesson vocabulary,
then... use *Envision It! Pictured Vocabulary Cards.*

Objectives

- Recognize an ending on a word.

Student Edition p. W•4

More Reading

Use additional Leveled Readers or other texts at students' instructional levels to reinforce this week's skills and strategies. For text suggestions, see the Leveled Reader Database or the Leveled Readers Skills Chart on pp. CL 24–CL 29.

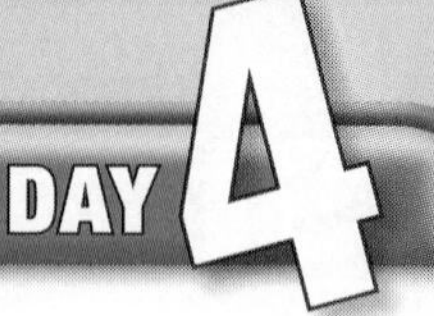

Practice Retelling

- **Retell** Have students work in pairs and use the Retelling Cards to retell *Weslandia*. Monitor their retellings and prompt students as needed. If students struggle, model a fluent retelling.

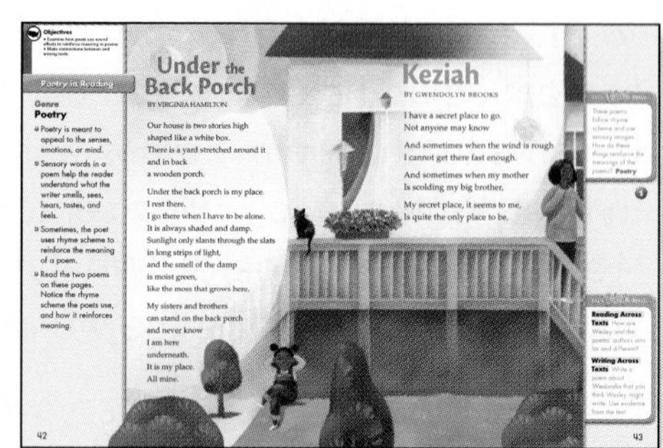

Genre Focus

- **Before Reading or Revisiting** "Under the Back Porch" and "Keziah" on pp. 42–43, read aloud the genre information about poetry on p. 42. Then have students preview "Under the Back Porch" and "Keziah." Ask:

• What pictures, words, and features do you see? *(illustrations of poems, titles, lines of poetry)*

• Look at the illustration. What do the two people seem to be doing? *(standing on or sitting under a porch)*

Then have students set a purpose for reading based on their preview.

- **During Reading or Revisiting** Have students do a choral reading of the poems. Stop to point out that images in the lines are used to express thoughts and feelings.

- **After Reading or Revisiting** Have students share their reactions to the poems. Then guide them through the Reading Across Texts and Writing Across Texts activities.

• How are Wesley and the girls in the poems alike? *(None of them seem to fit in with the people around them. They each find their own way of being themselves.)*

• How are they different? *(Wesley creates his own civilization; the girls just want to be alone.)*

MONITOR PROGRESS

If... students have difficulty retelling the selection,
then... have them review the story using the illustrations.

Objectives

• Analyze how poets use sound effects to reinforce meaning in poems.

For a complete literacy instructional plan and additional practice with this week's target skills and strategies, see the **Leveled Reader Teaching Guide.**

Concept Literacy Reader

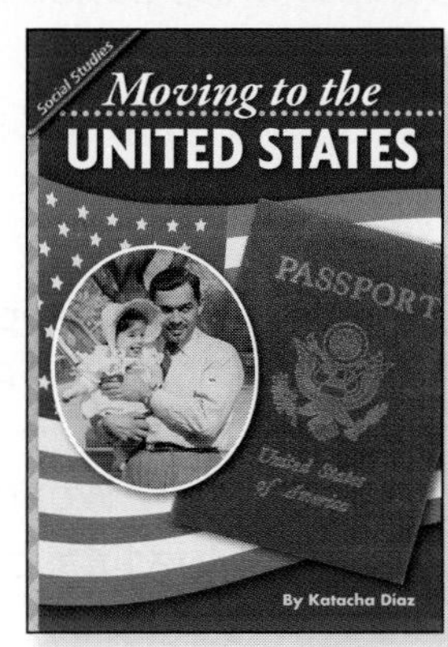

Moving to the United States

- **Model** Model the fluency skill of appropriate phrasing and punctuation cues for students. Ask students to listen carefully as you read aloud the first two pages of the selection. Have students note the grouping of your words and the rise and fall of your voice.
- **Fluency Routine**

1. Have students reread passages from *Moving to the United States* with a partner.
2. For optimal fluency, students should reread three to four times.
3. As students read, monitor fluency and provide corrective feedback. Encourage students to use punctuation cues, such as commas and periods, to determine where to pause.

See *Routines Flip Chart* for more help with fluency.

- **Retell** Have students retell *Moving to the United States.* Prompt as necessary.

Below-Level Reader

Playing the Game

- **Model** Ask students to listen carefully as you read aloud one or two pages of *Playing the Game* that have different types of punctuation. Emphasize appropriate phrasing by observing punctuation cues.
- **Fluency Routine**

1. Have students reread passages from *Playing the Game* with a partner or individually.
2. For optimal fluency, students should reread three to four times.
3. As students read, monitor fluency and provide corrective feedback. Remind students to pause at commas and raise their voices slightly to indicate a question. Discuss how this creates a more natural rhythm, especially in dialogue.

See *Routines Flip Chart* for more help with fluency.

- **Retell** For additional practice, have students retell *Playing the Game* page-by-page, using the illustrations. Prompt as necessary.

- What happens in this part?
- What is the problem in the story?

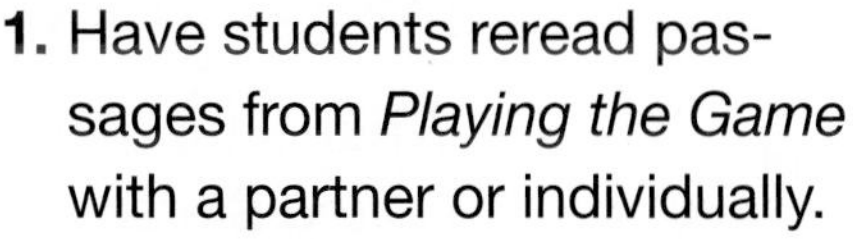

MONITOR PROGRESS

If... students have difficulty reading fluently,
then... provide additional fluency practice by pairing nonfluent readers with fluent ones.

Objectives
- Read aloud grade-level stories with fluency.

Small Group Time

Pacing Small Group Instruction

5-Day Plan

DAY 1	• Expand the concept • Read On-Level Reader
DAY 2	• Draw Conclusions • Questioning • Revisit Student Edition pp. 26–33
DAY 3	• Endings • Revisit Student Edition pp. 34–37
DAY 4	• Practice Retelling • Read/Revisit Student Edition pp. 42–43
DAY 5	• Reread for fluency • Reread On-Level Reader

3- or 4-Day Plan

DAY 1	• Expand the concept • On-Level Reader
DAY 2	• Draw Conclusions • Questioning • Revisit Student Edition pp. 26–33
DAY 3	• Endings • Revisit Student Edition pp. 34–37
DAY 4	• Practice Retelling • Read/Revisit Student Edition pp. 42–43 • Reread for fluency • Reread On-Level Reader

3-Day Plan: Eliminate the shaded box.

OL On-Level

DAY 1

Build Background

■ **Expand the Concept** Discuss the weekly question *How do people adapt to difficult situations?* and expand the concept. How can people adapt to new situations that are so different from what they have known before? Discuss the meanings of the words on the concept map on p. 20–21 in the Teacher Edition.

On-Level Reader

For a complete literacy instructional plan and additional practice with this week's target skills and strategies, see the **Leveled Reader Teaching Guide.**

■ **Before Reading** *Journey to the New World*, have students preview the reader by looking at the title, cover, and pictures in the book. Ask:

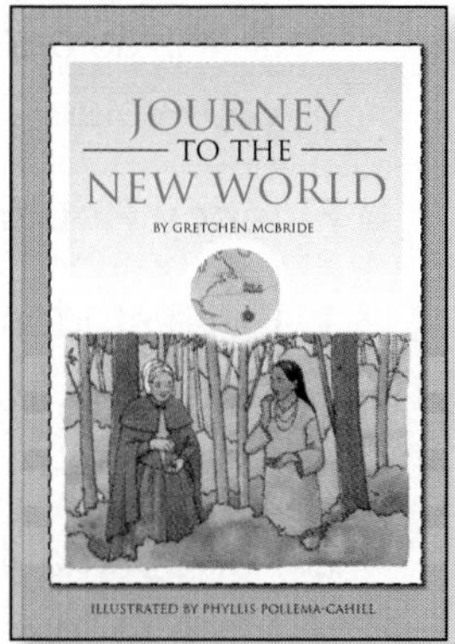

Journey to the New World

- What is the topic of this book? *(immigrants arriving in the United States)*
- Do you think it was easy or difficult for people to establish settlements in the New World? Why? *(difficult, because they left everything they knew and came to a completely new place where everything was different)*

Have students create a web with the label *Starting a New Settlement.* This book tells about the adventure that Jane and her family had as they moved to Virginia. As you read, look for key words that describe Jane's new home. Record them in your web.

■ **During Reading** Read aloud the first six pages of the book as students follow along. Then have them finish reading the book on their own. Remind students to add words to their web as they read.

■ **After Reading** Have partners compare the words on their web.

- How did settlers build their homes in the New World? *(They used tree logs, sap, and grasses.)*
- What were some of the problems and difficulties they had to overcome to adapt to the New World? *(They needed to plant crops, protect themselves against storms, and make friends with the Indians.)*

Objectives

- Interpret a speaker's messages (both verbal and nonverbal).

On-Level

DAY 2

Expand Comprehension

Skill Draw Conclusions Use p. 22 to review the definition of draw conclusions. For additional review, see p. EI•6 in *Envision It!* A conclusion is a decision or opinion you make after thinking about the details in what you read or hear. You can ask questions as you read to help you draw conclusions.

Strategy Questioning Review the definition of questioning. Encourage students to ask questions and draw conclusions as they read. During reading, use the Extend Thinking questions for additional support. For further support, refer students to *Envision It!* p. EI•21.

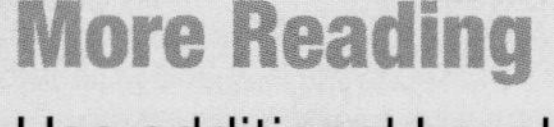

Student Edition p. EI•6

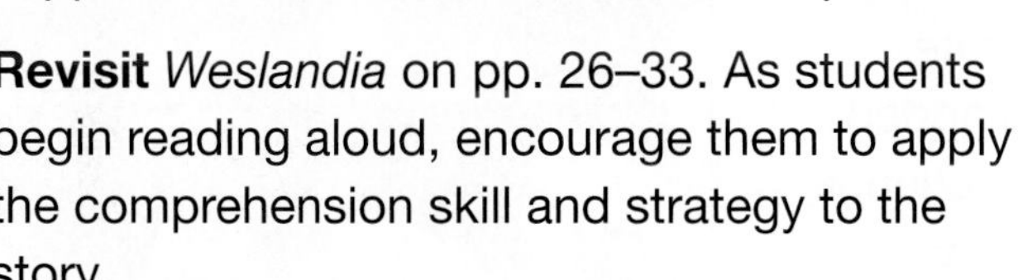

Revisit *Weslandia* on pp. 26–33. As students begin reading aloud, encourage them to apply the comprehension skill and strategy to the story.

- Wesley's parents say he "sticks out." What details does the story give that support their conclusion? *(He doesn't like pizza or soda, he doesn't shave his head, and he hates football.)*
- As Wesley works on his summer project, why do you think the other kids stopped tormenting him? *(They got involved in his civilization.)*

More Reading

Use additional Leveled Readers or other texts at students' instructional levels to reinforce this week's skills and strategies. For text suggestions, see the Leveled Reader Database or the Leveled Readers Skills Chart on pp. CL 24–CL 29.

Objectives

- Ask literal questions of text.

Expand Vocabulary

Word Endings/Word Structure Write the word *roasted* on the board as you say it aloud.

- What is the base word? *(roast)*
- How does the word ending *-ed* change the base word? *(It changes the meaning from present to past tense.)*

Revisit *Weslandia* on pp. 34–37. Ask students to turn to p. 35 and tell you all the words with the *-ed* word ending. Write the words on the board: *divided, adopted, based, named, uninterested, designed, used, looked, invented.* Point out that for the base words that end in *e*—*divide, base, name,* and *use*—only the word ending *-d* is added. Explain that both endings *-ed* and *-d* change the meaning of a verb to the past tense.

Then review the meaning of the words in their context. Point out that not every word with the *-ed* ending is used as the past tense of a verb. For example, in the sentence "Uninterested in traditional sports, Wesley made up his own" the word *uninterested* is used as an adjective to describe Wesley.

As students finish reading *Weslandia*, have them use word endings to help understand when actions took place as they read. Then ask students to recall what happened in the selection. Encourage them to think critically.

- What conclusion can you draw about how Wesley handled his situation? *(He showed cleverness and creativity by making his own world instead of being angry about not fitting in.)*
- Why do you think it was important for Wesley to accomplish what he did without help from his parents? *(He is original and creative and likes to do things his own way.)*

Objectives

- Recognize an ending on a word.

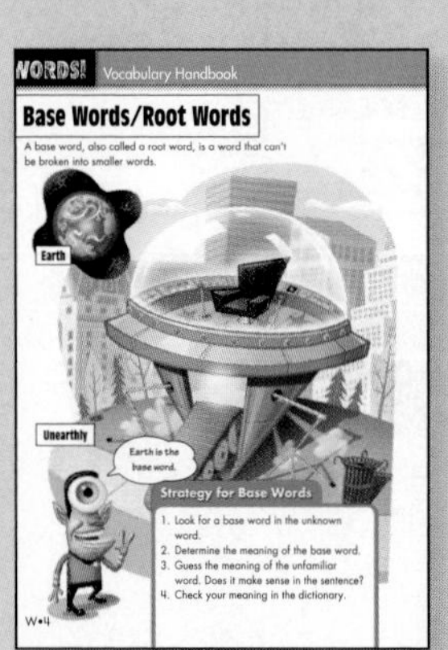

Student Edition p. W•4

More Reading

Use additional Leveled Readers or other texts at students' instructional levels to reinforce this week's skills and strategies. For text suggestions, see the Leveled Reader Database or the Leveled Readers Skills Chart on pp. CL 24–CL 29.

DAY 4

Practice Retelling

- **Retell** To assess students' comprehension, use the Retelling Cards. Monitor retelling and prompt students as needed.

Genre Focus

- **Before Reading or Revisiting** "Under the Back Porch" and "Keziah" on pp. 42–43, read aloud the genre information about poetry on p. 42. Have students preview the poems and set a purpose for reading. Ask:

• What features do you see in the poems that are different from stories you read? *(no paragraphs, only lines arranged on the page, illustrations taking up most of the space)*

• What differences do you see between the two poems? *(One has stanzas, and the other is free verse.)*

- **During Reading or Revisiting** Have students read along with you while tracking the print.

• What senses do the writers appeal to? *(sight, smell, touch)*

• What feelings do the poems create? *(a sense of safety and of delight in a secret place)*

• When does the speaker in both poems want to be alone? *(possible answers: when there is too much noise in the family, when things get difficult, or when she needs a place to call her very own)*

• Read the lines "And sometimes when the wind is rough / I cannot get there fast enough." Do you think the speaker is talking about the weather? Explain. *(No. The speaker is using the weather to talk about when she is feeling bad or when things are really difficult for her.)*

• What sound device is in "Keziah"? *(rhyme)* What is the effect? *(The rhyming lines gives the poem a musical, memorable quality.)*

- **After Reading or Revisiting** Have students share their reaction to the poems. Then have them write a short poem about their own secret place.

Objectives

• Analyze how poets use sound effects to reinforce meaning in poems.

On-Level Reader

- **Model** Read aloud one or two pages of the On-Level Reader *Journey to the New World* that have different types of punctuation. Emphasize appropriate phrasing and punctuation cues. Have students notice that you pause at commas and raise your voice slightly to indicate a question. Discuss how observing punctuation by adjusting tone of voice creates expression.

- **Fluency Routine**

  1. Have students reread passages from *Journey to the New World* with a partner.
  2. For optimal fluency, students should reread passages three to four times.
  3. As students read, monitor fluency and provide corrective feedback. Have students note the grouping of your words into phrases and the rise and fall of your voice. Discuss how reading with a natural rhythm is much more pleasing than reading word-by-word.

See *Routines Flip Chart* for more help with fluency.

- **Retell** For additional practice, have students use headings and photographs as a guide to retell *Journey to the New World*. Prompt as necessary.

- What is this selection mostly about?
- What did you learn from reading this selection?

Objectives

- Read aloud grade-level stories with fluency.

DAY 1

Build Background

- **Extend the Concept** Expand on the weekly question *How do people adapt to difficult situations?* In history, how have people learned to adapt to strange, new, or difficult situations? For example, think about arriving in a strange new land without any modern conveniences. What knowledge might people use to help them survive? *(They might have knowledge of how to build shelter, find water, make fire, find food, and cook it.)*

Advanced Reader

For a complete literacy instructional plan and additional practice with this week's target skills and strategies, see the **Leveled Reader Teaching Guide.**

- **Before Reading** *Cheaper, Faster, and Better,* introduce the book. Today you will read about how people adapted to changes in technology. Have students look at the illustrations in the book and use them to predict what will happen in the text. Then have students set a purpose for reading.
- **During Reading** Have students read the Advanced Reader independently.

Encourage them to think critically. For example, ask:

- What does the word *adapt* mean, and how can you apply that to technology?
- How did your parents adapt to changes in technology?
- How have their lives changed because of it?

- **After Reading** Have students review the concept map and explain how *Cheaper, Faster, and Better* helps students answer the weekly question *How do people adapt to difficult situations?* Prompt as necessary.
- **Now Try This** Assign "Now Try This" at the end of the Advanced Reader.

Objectives

- Interpret a speaker's messages (both verbal and nonverbal).

Pacing Small Group Instruction

15–20 mins.

5-Day Plan

DAY 1	• Extend the concept • Read Advanced Reader
DAY 2	• Draw Conclusions • Questioning • Revisit Student Edition pp. 26–33
DAY 3	• Endings • Revisit Student Edition pp. 34–37
DAY 4	• Poetry • Read/Revisit Student Edition pp. 42–43
DAY 5	• Reread for fluency • Reread Advanced Reader

3- or 4-Day Plan

DAY 1	• Extend the concept • Advanced Reader
DAY 2	• Draw Conclusions • Questioning • Revisit Student Edition pp. 26–33
DAY 3	• Endings • Revisit Student Edition pp. 34–37
DAY 4	• Poetry • Read/Revisit Student Edition pp. 42–43 • Reread for fluency • Reread Advanced Reader

3-Day Plan: Eliminate the shaded box.

More Reading

Use additional Leveled Readers or other texts at students' instructional levels to reinforce this week's skills and strategies. For text suggestions, see the Leveled Reader Database or the Leveled Readers Skills Chart on pp. CL 24–CL 29.

Extend Comprehension

Skill Draw Conclusions Tell students that drawing conclusions is similar to making inferences. Have students describe someone they know who is similar to Wesley. What can they infer about how that person might handle difficult situations?

Strategy Questioning Review the definition of questioning, and remind students to ask questions as they read the rest of *Weslandia*. Have students write down questions, exchange questions with a partner, and answer each other's questions. For example:

- Are there better ways that Wesley could be handling his situation?
- What would you tell him to do if you were his friend?

During reading, use the Extend Thinking questions and the During Reading Differentiated Instruction for additional support.

Revisit *Weslandia* on pp. 26–33. As students begin reading *Weslandia*, have them apply the comprehension skill and strategy.

- How does Wesley start to change his life? *(He starts making his own clothes and growing his own food.)*
- What conclusions can you draw about how Wesley adapts to his situation? *(Instead of becoming angry or sulking, Wesley starts using what he knows to do something he's interested in.)*

Critical Thinking Encourage students to think critically as they read *Weslandia*.

- What kind of student do you think Wesley was?
- What would Wesley be like as an adult?

Objectives

- Ask literal questions of text.

DAY 3

Extend Vocabulary

Endings/Word Structure Write the following sentence on the board, underlining the words *allowed* and *crushing*. "Wesley allowed them ten minutes apiece at his mortar, crushing the plant's seeds to collect the oil."

- How does knowing the meaning of the ending *-ed* help you understand the meaning of the word? *(It tells me the action happened in the past.)*
- What does the ending *-ing* in the word *crushing* tell you? *(It tells me the action that is happening right now or continuously.)*

Then ask students to turn to p. 36 and call out words with *-ing* endings. Write them on the board: *scoring, sleeping, playing, gazing, renaming*. Point out that when the base word ends in *e*—as in *score* and *gaze*—the *e* is dropped before the ending *-ing* is added.

Review the meaning of the words in context. Explain that *-ing* words are often used as adjectives *(scoring system)* as well as verbs that show action *(playing, gazing, renaming).*

Revisit *Weslandia* on pp. 34–37. As students finish reading the selection, remind them to use their knowledge of word endings to help them understand when an action took place.

Critical Thinking Have students recall what happened in the selection. Encourage them to think critically. For example, ask:

- In what ways does Wesley change or remain the same throughout the story?
- What generalization can you make about Wesley's character?

Objectives

- Recognize an ending on a word.

More Reading

Use additional Leveled Readers or other texts at students' instructional levels to reinforce this week's skills and strategies. For text suggestions, see the Leveled Reader Database or the Leveled Readers Skills Chart on pp. CL 24–CL 29.

Genre Focus

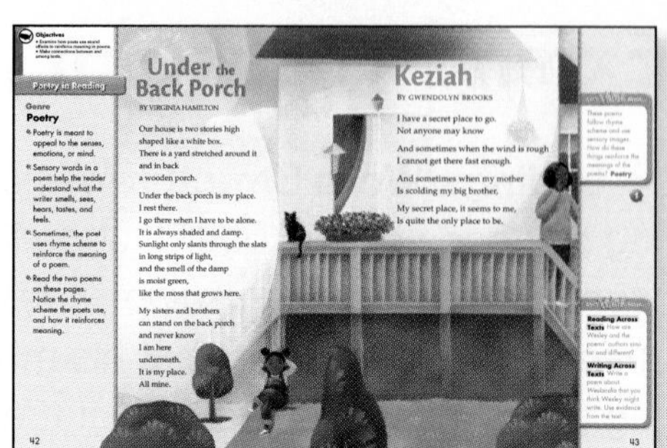

- **Before Reading or Revisiting** "Under the Back Porch" and "Keziah" on pp. 42–43, read the genre information on p. 42. Ask students to use the layout and illustrations to preview the poems and set a purpose before reading.
- **During Reading or Revisiting** Ask students to notice which sensory words, rhythms, or rhymes the authors of these two poems use.

How do sensory words and the rhythm and rhymes affect your feelings about the subject of the poem? *(Students may say that the images in both poems help them feel how safe and secure the secret places are. The rhyme adds emphasis to the speaker's words about escaping from a difficult or tense situation.)*

- **After Reading or Revisiting** Have students discuss Reading Across Texts. Then have them do Writing Across Texts independently.

Objectives

- Analyze how poets use sound effects to reinforce meaning in poems.

- **Reread for Fluency** Have students silently reread passages from the Advanced Reader *Cheaper, Faster, and Better*. Then have them reread aloud with a partner or individually. As students read, monitor fluency and provide corrective feedback. If students read fluently on the first reading, they do not need to reread three to four times. Assess the fluency of students in this group using p. 45j.
- **Retell** Have students summarize the main idea and key details from the Advanced Reader *Cheaper, Faster, and Better.*
- **Now Try This** Have students complete their projects. You may wish to review their work to see if they need additional ideas. Have them share their finished work with classmates.

Objectives

- Read aloud grade-level stories with fluency.

Support for English Language Learners

The ELL lessons are organized by strands. Use them to scaffold the weekly curriculum of lessons or during small group time instruction.

Academic Language

Students will hear or read the following academic language in this week's core instruction. As students encounter the vocabulary, provide a simple definition or concrete example. Then ask students to suggest an example or synonym of the word and identify available cognates.

Skill Words	draw conclusions fiction subject pronoun object pronoun	singular plural punctuation clues dialogue
Concept Words	adapt imagine	courage

**Spanish cognates in parentheses*

Concept Development

How do people adapt to difficult situations?

■ **Preteach Concept**

- **Prior Knowledge** Have students turn to pages 20–21 in the Student Edition. Call attention to the picture of the scuba diver and tap into students' knowledge of scuba diving. What is that man doing? How someone stay underwater for a long time? How does the breathing mask he's wearing help him stay underwater?
- **Discuss Concept** Elicit students' knowledge and experience of adapting to difficult situations. Look at the bridge. Why do you think people built that bridge? What problem did it solve? Can you think of other ways that people have helped themselves in difficult situations? Supply background information as needed.
- **Poster Talk-Through** Read aloud the Poster Talk-Through on ELL Poster 16 and work through the Day 1 activities.

■ **Daily Concept and Vocabulary Development** Use the daily activities on ELL Poster 16 to build concept and vocabulary knowledge.

Objectives

- Internalize new basic and academic language by using and reusing it in meaningful ways in speaking and writing activities that build concept and language attainment.

Content Objectives

- Use concept vocabulary related to how people adapt to difficult situations.

Language Objectives

- Express ideas in response to art and discussion.

Daily Planner

DAY 1	• **Frontload Concept** • **Preteach** Comprehension Skill, Vocabulary, Phonics/Spelling, Conventions • **Writing**
DAY 2	• **Review Concept,** Vocabulary, Comprehension Skill • **Frontload Main Selection** • **Practice** Phonics/Spelling, Conventions/Writing
DAY 3	• **Review Concept,** Comprehension Skill, Vocabulary, Conventions/Writing • **Reread Main Selection** • **Practice** Phonics/Spelling
DAY 4	• **Review Concept** • **Read ELL/ELD Readers** • **Practice** Phonics/Spelling, Conventions/Writing
DAY 5	• **Review Concept,** Vocabulary, Comprehension Skill, Phonics/Spelling, Conventions • **Reread ELL/ELD Readers** • **Writing**

**See the ELL Handbook for ELL Workshops with targeted instruction.*

Concept Talk Video

Use the Concept Talk Video Routine (*ELL Handbook,* page 477) to build background knowledge about adapting to difficult situations. For more listening practice, see *Use Classroom Resources* (*ELL Handbook,* pages 406–407).

Language Objectives

- Understand and use basic vocabulary.
- Learn meanings of grade-level vocabulary.

ELL Workshop

Provide opportunities for students to give information using high frequency, high-need, and concrete vocabulary. *Give a Speech* (*ELL Handbook,* pages 412–413) supports students with speaking.

ELL Workshop

Provide opportunities for students to give information using new abstract and content-based vocabulary. *Give a Speech* (*ELL Handbook,* pages 412–413) supports students with their speaking.

ELL English Language Learners

Basic Vocabulary

- **High-Frequency Words** Use the vocabulary routines and the high-frequency word list on page 452 of the *ELL Handbook* to systematically teach newcomers the first 300 sight words in English. Students who began learning ten words per week at the beginning of the year are now learning words 151–160.

Lesson Vocabulary

- **Preteach** Introduce the Lesson Vocabulary using this routine:

1. Distribute copies of this week's Word Cards (*ELL Handbook*, page 119).
2. Display ELL Poster 16 and reread the Poster Talk-Through.
3. Using the poster illustrations, model how a word's meaning can be expressed with other similar words: People are *fleeing,* or running away, in the game.
4. Use these sentences to reveal the meaning of the other words.
   - The difficult directions on the computer were too *complex* to understand. (hard)
   - The coach had a *strategy* to win the soccer game. (plan)
   - The team lost the game because we made many *blunders*. (silly mistakes)
   - The leaves of the tree made a *rustling* sound in the breeze. (sound caused by things moving against each other)
   - After I heard the beautiful music, I was *inspired* to learn to play. (influenced)
   - The Aztec people built a great *civilization* in Mexico. (society)
   - Mario looked at Jo's toy with *envy*. (longing)

Objectives

- Use visual, contextual, and linguistic support to enhance and confirm understanding of increasingly complex and elaborated spoken language.

ELL English Language Learners

- **Reteach** Display the Word Cards on the board and review the meaning of each word. Use the questions below to confirm students' understanding of each word.
  - If you are *fleeing*, are you running away from something? (yes)
  - If something is *complex*, is it easy to understand? (no)
  - Are *blunders* mistakes? (yes)
  - Is *envy* a happy feeling? (no)
  - True or False: A *civilization* is a group of people living in a similar way. (true)
  - True or False: When you have a *strategy*, you have no plan. (false)
  - If you are *inspired* to do something, do you really want to do it? (yes)
  - Is a *rustling* sound usually loud? (no)
- **Writing** Distribute copies of the Word Cards and eight blank cards to pairs of students. Have partners write a clue or draw a simple picture on a blank card for each word.
  - Have students mix the Word Cards and clue cards together and lay them facedown, spread out. Students can take turns choosing two cards, trying to match a word with its clue. Have students explain their choices to each other. Once the match is made, students should use the word in an oral sentence. Circulate to help student pairs.

Beginning Have students draw a picture to express the meaning of the word. After matching the word and a clue, have them write the word and a word or phrase that reminds them of the meaning.

Intermediate After students match words with clues, they will write a sentence for each word. Have them share sentences with partners.

Advanced Have students write a paragraph or two using the vocabulary words.

Advanced High In addition, have student pairs write synonyms for as many words as they can. (Examples: *blunders-mistakes, envy-jealousy*)

Objectives

- Use strategic learning techniques such as concept mapping, drawing, memorizing, comparing, contrasting, and reviewing to acquire basic and grade-level vocabulary.

Language Objectives

- Produce drawings, phrases, or short sentences to show an understanding of Lesson Vocabulary.

ELL Teacher Tip

Distribute the multilingual vocabulary list for *Weslandia*. Have students who speak Spanish, Cantonese or Mandarin (Chinese) Vietnamese, Korean, or Hmong find the English words and their translations in their home language. What other words in your home language match these English words? Have students find the English words in context in *Weslandia* and check their understanding against their list of home language words.

ELL Workshop

Support students' ability to take notes to demonstrate listening comprehension of the Read Aloud. Practice with *Take Notes/Create an Outline* (*ELL Handbook*, pages 410–411).

Content Objectives

- Monitor and adjust oral comprehension.

Language Objectives

- Discuss oral passages.
- Use a graphic organizer to take notes.

ELL Teacher Tip

Provide Wait Time English language learners often need extra time to process questions in English and to formulate responses. Allowing students time to think in English demands both concentration and patience. Tell students to take time to think about their answers. Encourage them to ask questions about words or ideas they do not understand.

Listening Comprehension

Read Aloud

A Baseball Man

When I was eleven years old, I loved to play baseball. It was the most important thing in my life. But I had an accident and I lost my arm. I thought I could not play baseball anymore. My coach seemed to forget about me. Sometimes I went to the park to watch my team play games. But, I was never asked to play.

Then, Ben came to stay for the summer. Ben was the nephew of our neighbor. Ben saw me tossing a baseball up and down in one hand. He could see that I had only one arm. "Are you a baseball man?" he asked. I loved the sound of the words *baseball man*. And no one had ever called me a "man" before. I liked Ben right away. We became friends.

One day, Ben showed me a picture of a famous baseball player. His name was Pete Gray and he had only one arm. Ben told me that Pete Gray had courage and determination. Ben said that I too could play with one arm.

At first, I did not think I could do it. But, every evening Ben and I practiced baseball together in the park. At first, I could not catch or throw the ball. But, I kept trying. It took a long time, but I got better.

One day the coach told me to come to the ballpark. He wanted me to play on the baseball team. I was thrilled.

Prepare for the Read Aloud The modified Read Aloud above prepares students for listening to the oral reading "Birdsong on a Summer Evening" on page 21b.

- **First Listening: Listen to Understand** Write the title of the Read Aloud on the board. This story is about a boy who has to adapt to a difficult situation in his life. Listen to find out how he does it. Who helps him to adapt?
- **Second Listening: Listen to Check Understanding** Using Story Map B (*ELL Handbook,* page 484), work with students to list the characters, the setting, and the main events of the story. Fill in the chart with student answers.

Objectives

- Demonstrate listening comprehension of increasingly complex spoken English by following directions, retelling or summarizing spoken messages, responding to questions and requests, collaborating with peers, and taking notes commensurate with content and grade-level needs.

Phonics and Spelling

■ **Words Ending in *-ed, -ing*** Use Sound-Spelling Cards 118, 119, 120, and 126 to teach the sounds, pronunciations, and spellings of *-ed* and *-ing*.

- Display card 118 to teach *-ed*. This is *filled*. Say it with me: *filled*. Point to the letters *ed*. The sound /d/ is spelled *ed*. Have students say /d/ several times as you point to *ed*. Repeat the routine above with card 119 (*twisted*) and card 120 (*jumped*).
- Display card 126 to teach *-ing*. This is *drinking*. Say it with me: *drinking*. Point to the letters *ing*. The sounds /i/ /ng/ are spelled *ing*. Have students say /i/ /ng/ several times as you point to *ing*. What is the sound for these letters?

For more practice pronouncing these sounds, use the Modeled Pronunciation Audio CD Routine (*ELL Handbook,* page 478).

Word Analysis: Inflected Endings *-s, -ed, -ing*

■ **Preteach and Model** Remind students that the inflected endings *-s, -ed,* and *-ing* are added to verbs to change the tense or time. Write the vocabulary words *fleeing* and *rustling* on the board. Say each word aloud and have students repeat it several times. Write *flee* and *rustle* on the board. Then write these sentences: *The boy is fleeing from his enemies. The leaves on the tree are rustling in the wind.* Demonstrate how the final *-e* in *rustle* is dropped before adding *-ing*.

■ **Practice** Display these rules: To make the *-ing* form of a verb, add *-ing* to most verbs. Drop the silent *e* at the end of the verb before adding *-ing*. Write these verbs on the board: *work, drive, exercise, blunder*. Have students add *-ing* to each of these words.

Beginning/Intermediate Have students work in mixed pairs to add the ending *-ing* to each of the verbs. Then have intermediate students use the verb in a sentence and practice repeating it with the beginning student.

Advanced/Advanced High Have students add all three inflected endings to the verbs on the board. Challenge them to write a sentence about making a blunder while working, driving, or exercising.

Objectives

- Distinguish sounds and intonation patterns of English with increasing ease.
- Use visual, contextual, and linguistic support to enhance and confirm understanding of increasingly complex and elaborated spoken language.

Content Objectives

- Identify inflected endings *-s, -ed, -ing.*
- Identify final syllables *-ed* and *-ing.*

Language Objectives

- Apply phonics and decoding skills to spelling.
- Understand use of verb endings.

Transfer Skills

Verb Endings English verb endings differ from verb endings in languages such as Spanish and Polish, which use different endings for person and number. Students may need practice adding *-s* and *-es* to present tense verbs with third-person singular subjects. In Chinese, Hmong, and Vietnamese, verbs do not change to show the tense. Adverbs or expressions of time indicate when an action is taking place.

ELL Teaching Routine

For more practice with word endings, use the Word Parts Strategy (*ELL Handbook,* page 473).

English Language Learners

Content Objectives

- Understand how to draw conclusions.
- Use questions to draw conclusions.

Language Objectives

- Discuss how to draw a conclusion.

ELL Workshop

Encourage students to ask questions to monitor their understanding of instruction of comprehension skills. Use *Ask Clarifying Questions* (*ELL Handbook,* pages 404–405) for practice.

Comprehension
Draw Conclusions

- **Preteach** Good readers draw conclusions as they read. When you draw conclusions, you combine what you know with information and details from the text. A conclusion is a decision you make after combining your knowledge with details from the text. Have students turn to Envision It! on page EI•18 in the Student Edition. Read aloud the definition of *inferring*. Tell students that drawing conclusions is one kind of inferring. Look at the picture on this page. The girl is drawing a conclusion about the volcano. What conclusion did she draw? Have students read the information on the page. What questions should you ask yourself so that you can draw conclusions as you read?

- **Reteach** Give each student a copy of Picture It! (*ELL Handbook,* p. 120). The pictures and the text on this page will help you draw a conclusion about what is happening in the story. Have students read the text aloud. After each reading have students draw conclusions. (*Detail:* Veronique is at a starting line. *Detail:* She took off like a rocket. *What I Know:* Runners usually take off fast when they say go. *Conclusion:* Veronique must be in a race.)

Beginning Reread the passage aloud with students. Guide them to underline important details to support any conclusions. Then have them read the details aloud.

Intermediate/Advanced/Advanced High Have students reread the passage. Have them underline details that support their conclusion. Then have them fill in the graphic organizer on the page.

MINI-LESSON

Social Language

Tell students that the word *draw* has many meanings. When we draw a conclusion, we "pull out" details from the text and illustrations. We put these details together with what we know. Then we draw or make a conclusion. What other meanings can the word *draw* have? (to draw a picture, to draw water from a well, to draw a card from a deck of cards)

Objectives

- Understand the general meaning, main points, and important details of spoken language ranging from situations in which topics, language, and contexts are familiar to unfamiliar.

Reading Comprehension
Weslandia

Student Edition pp. 26–27

■ **Frontloading** Read aloud the title and ask students what the word *Weslandia* might mean. *Weslandia* has the word *land* in it. I wonder if it could be a place. Let's look through the selection to find clues. Guide students on a picture walk through *Weslandia*. Ask students to predict whether Weslandia is a place or a person. During reading, pause and invite students to adjust their predictions. Provide students with a two-column chart to fill out as they read the selection. Supply these headings: *What is Weslandia? What is it like?*

Sheltered Reading Ask questions such as the following to guide students' comprehension:

- p. 28: Why does Wesley feel like someone who does not belong with other kids? (He acts and looks different from the other kids.)
- p. 29: How do the other kids treat him? (They chase him and throw things at him.)
- p. 30–33: What kind of plant does Wesley grow? (a plant with red flowers) What is unusual about this plant? (It grows taller than the boy.)
- p. 34–37: How can you tell that the other kids like Wesley's garden? (They play games with him among the plants.) Do you think Wesley has friends now? (yes)

■ **Fluency: Appropriate Phrasing: Punctuation Clues** Remind students that commas in a sentence tell you when to pause, or stop for a second. Read aloud page 28 of the story, except for the last line. Model pausing at commas. Ask students for unfamiliar words and model how to pronounce them. Reread the page aloud. Then, assign an appropriate number of lines for students to practice according to their proficiency level. Have each student read their lines to the class, beginning with the most proficient speakers. For more practice, use the Fluency: Choral Reading Routine (*ELL Handbook,* page 474).

After Reading Guide students in summarizing the text using the Retelling Cards. Assign each student a task based on proficiency level. Beginning students can rearrange cards in the correct order. Intermediate and advanced students can be assigned a card and retell that part of the selection.

Objectives

- Ask and give information ranging from using a very limited bank of high-frequency, high-need, concrete vocabulary, including key words and expressions needed for basic communication in academic and social contexts, to using abstract and content-based vocabulary during extended speaking assignments.
- Read linguistically accommodated content area material with a decreasing need for linguistic accommodations as more English is learned.

Content Objectives

- Monitor and adjust comprehension.
- Make and adjust predictions.

Language Objectives

- Use commas as clues to pause in oral reading.
- Summarize text using visual support.

Graphic Organizer

Two-Column Chart

What is Weslandia?	What is it like?

Audio Support

Students can prepare for reading *Weslandia* by using the eSelection or the AudioText CD. See the AudioText CD Routine (*ELL Handbook,* page 477) for suggestions on using these learning tools.

ELL Teaching Routine

For more practice summarizing, use the Retelling/Summarizing Narrative Routine (*ELL Handbook,* page 475).

ELL Workshop

For assistance with English language structures, see *Take Notes/Create an Outline* (*ELL Handbook,* pages 410–411).

Support for English Language Learners

For additional leveled instruction, see the **ELL/ELD Reader Teaching Guide.**

Comprehension

The Anasazi: The Ancient Builders

■ **Before Reading** Distribute copies of the ELL and ELD Readers, *The Anasazi: The Ancient Builders,* to students at their reading level.

- **Preview** Read the title aloud with students: This is a nonfiction text about a Native American civilization of long ago. Invite students to look through pictures and name what they see. Have them predict what the land and climate the Anasazi lived in was like based on the picture clues and their prior knowledge.
- **Set a Purpose for Reading** Let's read to find out what the environment of the Anasazi people was like and how they adapted to it.

■ **During Reading** Follow this Reading Routine for both reading groups.

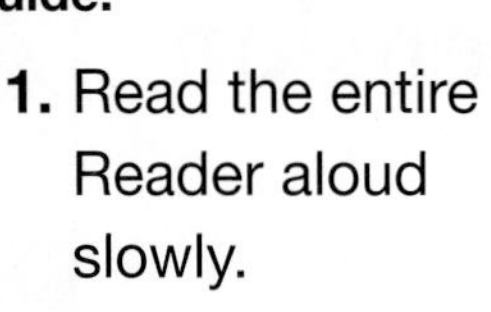

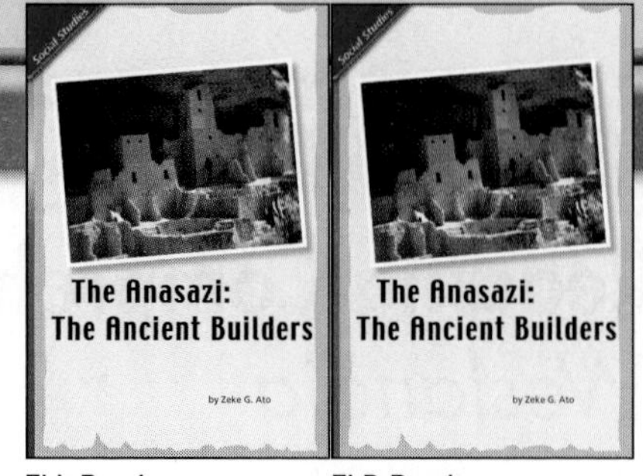

ELL Reader ELD Reader

1. Read the entire Reader aloud slowly.
2. Reread pp. 1–4, pausing to build background or model comprehension. Have beginning students finger-point as you read. Use the questions in the chart below to check students' comprehension.
3. Have students take turns rereading pp. 1–4 orally in pairs, taking turns to read pages.
4. Repeat steps 2–3 for pages 5–8 and then 9–12 of the Reader.

■ **After Reading** Use the exercises on the inside back cover of each Reader and invite students to share their writing. In a whole-group discussion, ask students How did the Anasazi adapt to their difficult environment? Record their answers on the board and invite them to point to pictures in the book to support their answers.

ELD Reader Beginning/Intermediate

■ **pp. 2–4** What is the high desert like? Read one or two sentences that tell you the answer. (a place with a lot of mountains and flat hills)

■ **pp. 9–12** What was one of the crops the Anasazi grew? (corn)

Writing Why do you think the Anasazi people disappeared? Find the sentence in the book that tells you why. Copy the sentence. Then read it aloud to your partner.

ELL Reader Advanced/Advanced High

■ **pp. 2–4** What is the high desert? (a land of mountains and flat hills called *mesas*)

■ **pp. 9–12** What were the major crops of the Anasazi? (corn, beans, squash)

Study Guide Distribute copies of the ELL Reader Study Guide (*ELL Handbook,* page 124). Scaffold comprehension by helping students look back through the Reader in order to fill in the graphic organizer. Review their responses together. (See *ELL Handbook,* pp. 209–212.)

Objectives

- Read linguistically accommodated content area material with a decreasing need for linguistic accommodations as more English is learned.

Conventions
Subject and Object Pronouns

- **Preteach** Display the following sentences on the board: *Jeff talked to him. She ran home. They ate dinner. Maria cooked it.* Remind students that a subject pronoun represents the subject in a sentence. Explain that an object pronoun stands for what or who receives the action. Guide students to identify each pronoun and tell whether it is a subject pronoun or an object pronoun. (*him,* object; *she,* subject; *They,* subject; *it,* object)

- **Practice** Have students create new sentences using pronouns from the board. Remind them to refer to the chart to find out if the pronoun is a subject or object.

Beginning Have students point to the subject and object pronouns and say them aloud. Ask students to explain the difference between them.

Intermediate Have students fill in sentence frames in which there are blanks where a subject or object pronoun should appear. Ask them to identify which kind of pronoun is called for in each blank.

Advanced/Advanced High Have students write sentences using the pronouns from the board as subject and object pronouns. Then have them blank out one pronoun in each sentence to create a sentence frame for intermediate students to fill in with the correct pronoun.

- **Reteach** Display the following paragraph on the board: *I talked to Maria and Jim. They were nice. I showed them my camera. It was new. I took a picture of them.* Ask students to identify subject and object pronouns.

- **Practice** Use the sentences above for different levels of proficiency.

Beginning Have students point to the subject and object pronouns in each sentence in the paragraph. Then have them copy the sentences.

Intermediate Have students work in pairs to create additional sentences for the paragraph and share them with the class.

Advanced/Advanced High Have students choose one or two nouns from the Lesson Vocabulary words and write a paragraph using them as both subject and object pronouns.

Objectives

- Employ increasingly complex grammatical structures in content area writing commensurate with grade level expectations such as (i) using correct verbs, tenses, and pronouns/antecedents; (ii) using possessive case (apostrophe -s) correctly; and, (iii) using negatives and contractions correctly.

Content Objectives

- Identify subject and object pronouns.
- Understand that a pronoun can be used as a subject or object of the verb.

Language Objectives

- Practice using subject and object pronouns in speaking.
- Write sentences using subject and object pronouns.

Transfer Skills

Subject Pronouns

In Spanish, unlike English, speakers may omit the subject pronoun because Spanish verbs can indicate the subject. Have them work with a partner to correct this error.

Object Pronouns

Spanish, Chinese, and Vietnamese speakers may use subject pronouns as objects (*Give the book to she.*) until practice in English clarifies the different pronoun forms.

Grammar Jammer

For more practice with pronouns, use the Grammar Jammer for this target skill. See the Grammar Jammer Routine (*ELL Handbook,* page 478) for suggestions on using this learning tool.

Support for English Language Learners

Content Objectives

- Identify dialogue in fiction.
- Understand idioms.

Language Objectives

- Write a short dialogue.
- Share feedback for editing and revising.

ELL Teaching Routine

For practice spelling words related to difficult situations, use the Spelling Routine (*ELL Handbook,* page 476).

ELL Workshop

Students can collaborate with peers to discuss their writing. *Discuss with Classmates* (*ELL Handbook,* pages 418–419) provides assistance with discussion.

ELL English Language Learners

Dialogue

- **Introduce** Stories contain dialogue or conversations between characters. Display the model and read it aloud. Have students turn to page 28 of the selection and the lines of dialogue between Wesley's mother and father. Who are they talking about? (Wesley) What does "He sticks out" mean? (He is different from the other kids.) How does a nose "stick out"? (It sticks out from your face.) Point out that the father is making a joke.

Writing Model

"Of course he's miserable," moaned his mother. "He sticks out."

"Like a nose," snapped his father.

Practice Have students find other examples of dialogue in *Weslandia*. Discuss how dialogue is written. When each person in the story speaks, the writer begins on a new line. The writer puts quotation marks around the exact words that the person speaks. What punctuation mark separates the exact words or quotation and the words that identify the speaker? (comma)

- **Write** Have students write a dialogue between themselves and Wesley. First they will write a question they want to ask Wesley. Then they will write Wesley's answer.

Beginning Have student pairs make up a question to ask Wesley. Then have them dictate the question to a more proficient student who will write it down. Beginners may then copy the written question.

Intermediate Supply students with a sentence frame: Why did you _____? Have partners work together to write a question and an answer from Wesley. Have pairs exchange papers and provide feedback for revising and editing.

Advanced/Advanced High Have students work in pairs to write an interview or several short questions and answers between themselves and Wesley. Then have pairs exchange papers and provide feedback for revising and editing. Ask students to explain how their dialogues could help a reader draw a conclusion about Wesley.

Objectives

- Narrate, describe, and explain with increasing specificity and detail as more English is acquired.
- Narrate, describe, and explain with increasing specificity and detail to fulfill content area writing needs as more English is acquired.

This Week's ELL Overview

Grade 5 • Unit 4 • Week 2
Tripping Over the Lunch Lady
46a–75r and DI•41–DI•50

ELL Handbook

- Maximize Literacy and Cognitive Engagement
- Research Into Practice
- Full Weekly Support for Every Selection

Tripping Over the Lunch Lady
- Multi-Lingual Summaries in Five Languages
- Selection-Specific Vocabulary Word Cards
- Frontloading/Reteaching for Comprehension Skill Lessons
- ELD and ELL Reader Study Guides

- Transfer Activities
- Professional Development

Daily Leveled ELL Notes

ELL notes appear throughout this week's instruction and ELL Support is on the DI pages of your Teacher's Edition. The following is a sample of an ELL note from this week.

English Language Learners

Beginning Read the words aloud with students. Then have students underline the smaller words contained in these words.

Intermediate Have students underline the smaller words and then use the smaller word in an oral sentence.

Advanced Have students work in pairs to identify the smaller words. Have them define the words and write sentences with them.

Advanced High Have students tell how knowing that some smaller words are contained in longer ones in English can help them as they read. Encourage them to begin their statement this way: *When I read and find a word I'm not sure of, I can _____.*

ELL by Strand

The ELL lessons on this week's Support for English Language Learners pages are organized by strand. They offer additional scaffolding for the core curriculum. Leveled support notes on these pages address the different proficiency levels in your class. See pages DI•41–DI•50.

The Three Pillars of ELL Instruction

ELL Strands	Activate Prior Knowledge	Access Content	Extend Language
Vocabulary pp. DI•42–DI•43	Preteach	Reteach	Leveled Writing Activities
Reading Comprehension p. DI•47	Frontloading	Sheltered Reading	After Reading
Phonics, Spelling, and Word Analysis p. DI•45	Preteach	Teach/Model	Leveled Practice Activities
Listening Comprehension p. DI•44	Prepare for the Read Aloud	First Listening	Second Listening
Conventions and Writing pp. DI•49–DI•50	Preteach	Practice	Leveled Writing Activities
Concept Development p. DI•41	Activate Prior Knowledge	Discuss Concept	Daily Concept and Vocabulary Development

This Week's Practice Stations Overview

Grade 5 • Unit 4 • Week 2
Tripping Over the Lunch Lady
46a–75r

Six Weekly Practice Stations with Leveled Activities can be found at the beginning of each week of instruction. For this week's Practice Stations, see pp. 46h–46i.

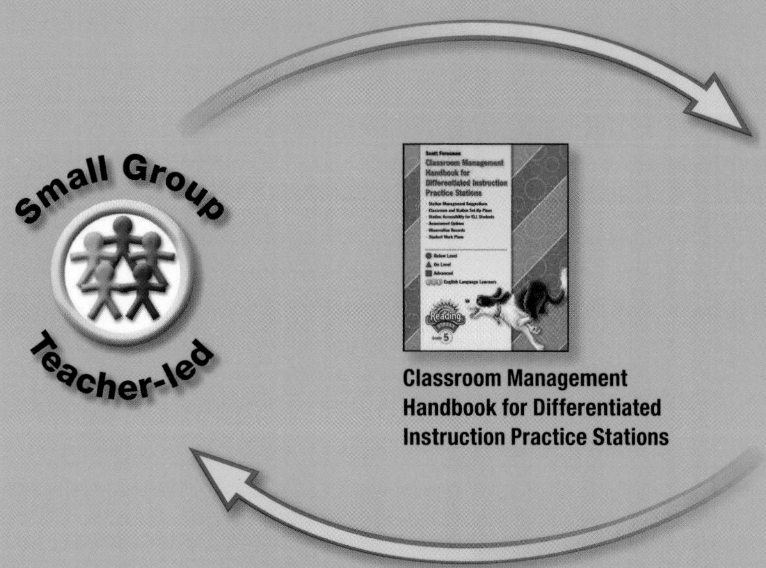

Classroom Management Handbook for Differentiated Instruction Practice Stations

Practice Stations

Daily Leveled Center Activities

Below
Advanced
On-Level

Practice Stations Flip Charts

	 **Word Wise**	 **Word Work**	 **Words to Know**	 **Let's Write**	 **Read for Meaning**	 **Get Fluent**
Objectives	• Spell words from different cultures.	• Identify words from different cultures.	• Determine the meaning of words with endings *-s, -ed, -ing.*	• Write a picture book.	• Draw conclusions based on information you read.	• Read aloud using appropriate phrasing.
Materials	• *Word Wise* Flip Chart Activity 17 • Teacher-made word cards • dictionary • paper • pencil	• *Word Work* Flip Chart Activity 17 • Teacher-made word cards • paper • pencil	• *Words to Know* Flip Chart Activity 17 • magazines • dictionary • paper • pencil	• *Let's Write* Flip Chart Activity 17 • paper • pencil • crayons or markers	• *Read for Meaning* Flip Chart Activity 17 • Leveled Readers • paper • pencil	• *Get Fluent* Flip Chart Activity 17 • Leveled Reader

This Week on Reading Street!

Question of the Week

How do people overcome obstacles?

Daily Plan

Whole Group

- Generalize
- Unfamiliar Words
- Fluency/Accuracy
- Research and Inquiry

MONITOR PROGRESS Success Predictor

Day 1	Days 2–3	Day 4	Day 5
Check Oral Vocabulary	Check Retelling	Check Fluency	Check Oral Vocabulary

Small Group

Teacher-Led

- Reading Support
- Skill Support
- Fluency Practice

Practice Stations

Independent Activities

Customize Literacy More support for a balanced literacy approach, see pp. CL•1–CL•47

Customize Writing More support for a customized writing approach, see pp. CW•1–CW•10

Whole Group

- Writing: Friendly Letter
- Conventions: Pronouns and Antecedents
- Spelling: Prefixes

Assessment

- Weekly Tests
- Day 5 Assessment
- Fresh Reads

You Are Here! Unit 4 Week 2

This Week's Reading Selections

Main Selection
Genre: **Realistic Fiction**

Paired Selection
Genre: **Persuasive Text**

Leveled Readers

ELL and ELD Readers

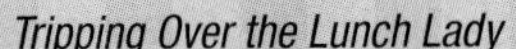

Resources on Reading Street!

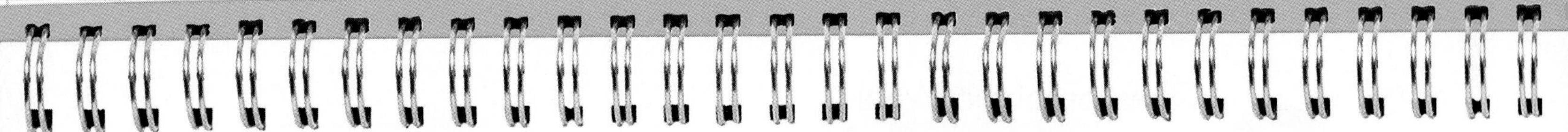

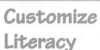

	Build Concepts	Comprehension
Whole Group	 Let's Talk About pp. 46–47	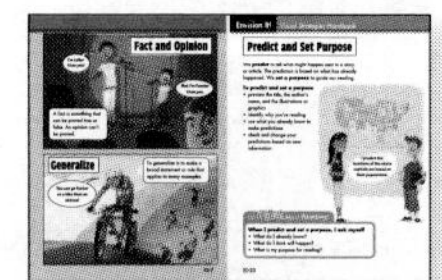 Envision It! Skills/ Strategies 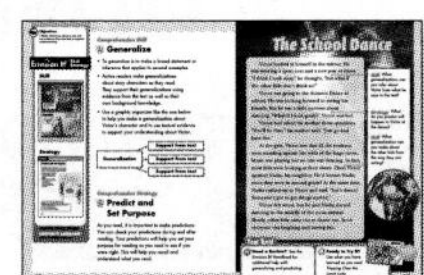 Comprehension Skills Lesson pp. 48–49
 Go Digital	• Concept Talk Video	• Envision It! Animations • eSelections
Small Group and Independent Practice	 Tripping Over the Lunch Lady pp. 52–53  ELL and ELD Readers  Leveled Readers	 Tripping Over the Lunch Lady pp. 52–53  ELL and ELD Readers  Leveled Readers 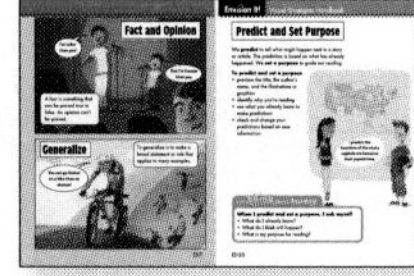 Envision It! Skills/ Strategies  Reader's and Writer's Notebook 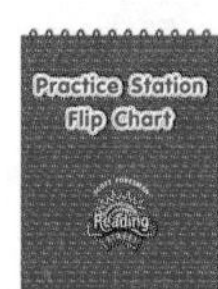 Practice Station Flip Chart
 Go Digital	• eReaders • eSelections	• Envision It! Animations • eSelections • eReaders
Customize Literacy	• Leveled Readers	• Envision It! Skills and Strategies Handbook • Leveled Readers
 Go Digital	• Concept Talk Video • Big Question Video • eReaders	• Envision It! Animations • eReaders

Question of the Week

How do people overcome obstacles?

Vocabulary	Fluency	Conventions and Writing
 Envision It! Vocabulary Cards 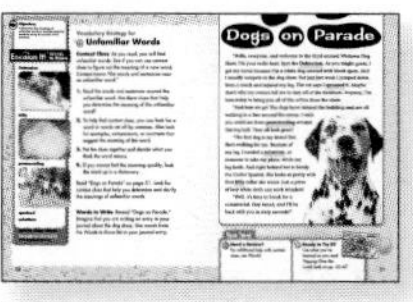 Vocabulary Skill Lesson pp. 50–51	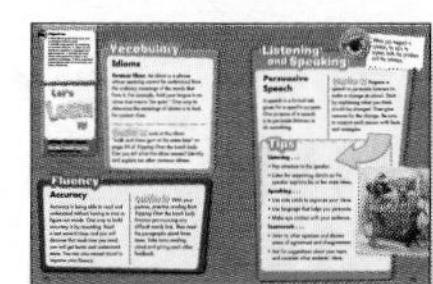 Let's Learn It! pp. 74–75	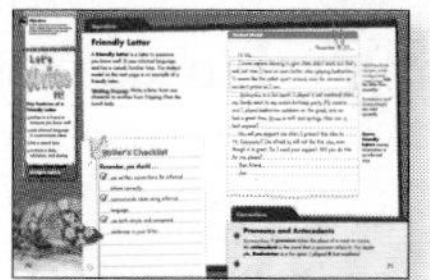 Let's Write It! pp. 70–71
• Envision It! Vocabulary Cards • Vocabulary Activities	• eSelections • eReaders	• Grammar Jammer
 Envision It! Vocabulary Cards  Tripping Over the Lunch Lady pp. 52–53  Practice Station Flip Chart  Words! W•7 Reader's and Writer's Notebook	  Tripping Over the Lunch Lady pp. 52–53  Practice Station Flip Chart  ELL and ELD Readers  Leveled Readers	 Reader's and Writer's Notebook  Tripping Over the Lunch Lady pp. 52–53 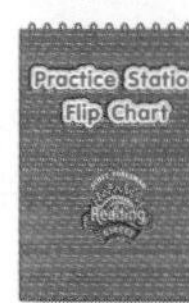 Practice Station Flip Chart
• Envision It! Vocabulary Cards • Vocabulary Activities • eSelections	• eSelections • eReaders	• Grammar Jammer
• Envision It! Vocabulary Cards	• Leveled Readers	• Reader's and Writer's Notebook
• Vocabulary Activities	• eReaders	• Grammar Jammer

My 5-Day Planner for Reading Street!

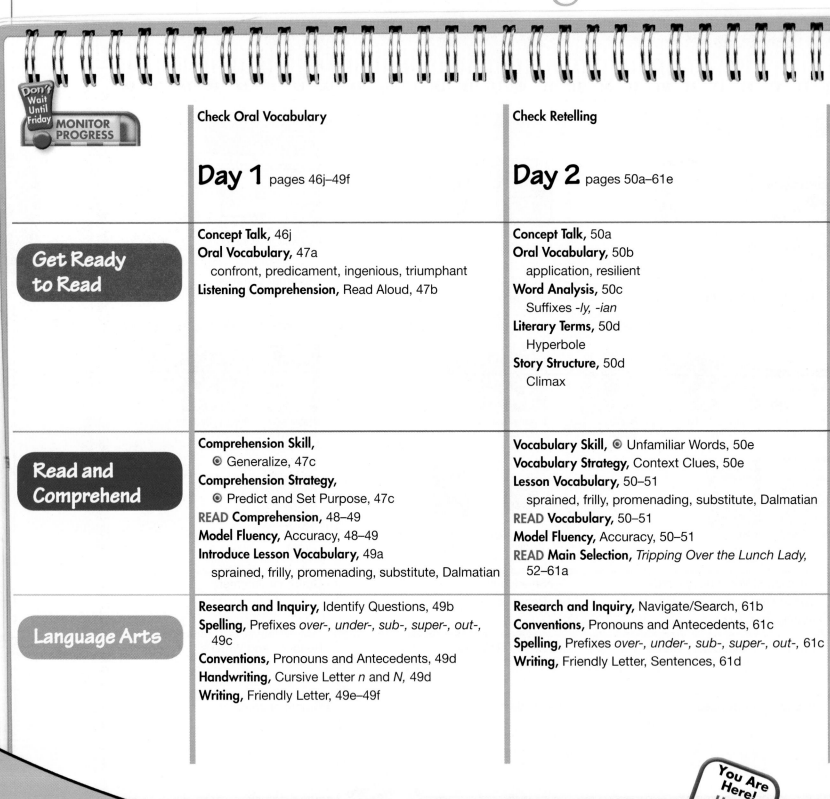

Don't Wait Until Friday MONITOR PROGRESS

	Check Oral Vocabulary **Day 1** pages 46j–49f	Check Retelling **Day 2** pages 50a–61e
Get Ready to Read	**Concept Talk,** 46j **Oral Vocabulary,** 47a confront, predicament, ingenious, triumphant **Listening Comprehension,** Read Aloud, 47b	**Concept Talk,** 50a **Oral Vocabulary,** 50b application, resilient **Word Analysis,** 50c Suffixes *-ly, -ian* **Literary Terms,** 50d Hyperbole **Story Structure,** 50d Climax
Read and Comprehend	**Comprehension Skill,** ◎ Generalize, 47c **Comprehension Strategy,** ◎ Predict and Set Purpose, 47c READ **Comprehension,** 48–49 **Model Fluency,** Accuracy, 48–49 **Introduce Lesson Vocabulary,** 49a sprained, frilly, promenading, substitute, Dalmatian	**Vocabulary Skill,** ◎ Unfamiliar Words, 50e **Vocabulary Strategy,** Context Clues, 50e **Lesson Vocabulary,** 50–51 sprained, frilly, promenading, substitute, Dalmatian READ **Vocabulary,** 50–51 **Model Fluency,** Accuracy, 50–51 READ **Main Selection,** *Tripping Over the Lunch Lady,* 52–61a
Language Arts	**Research and Inquiry,** Identify Questions, 49b **Spelling,** Prefixes *over-, under-, sub-, super-, out-,* 49c **Conventions,** Pronouns and Antecedents, 49d **Handwriting,** Cursive Letter *n* and *N,* 49d **Writing,** Friendly Letter, 49e–49f	**Research and Inquiry,** Navigate/Search, 61b **Conventions,** Pronouns and Antecedents, 61c **Spelling,** Prefixes *over-, under-, sub-, super-, out-,* 61c **Writing,** Friendly Letter, Sentences, 61d

You Are Here! Unit 4 Week 2

Question of the Week

How do people overcome obstacles?

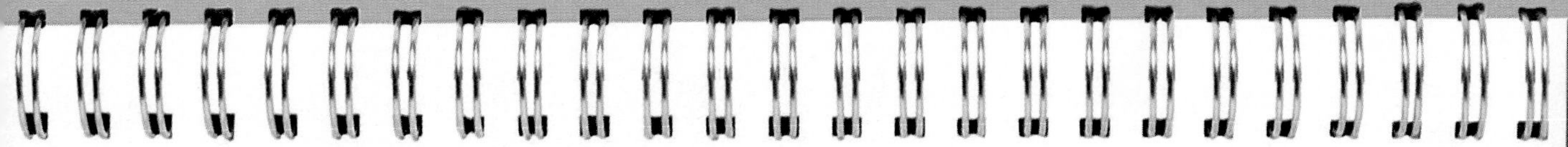

Check Retelling	Check Fluency	Check Oral Vocabulary
Day 3 pages 62a–71c	**Day 4** pages 72a–75e	**Day 5** pages 75f–75q
Concept Talk, 62a **Oral Vocabulary,** 62b modify, conquer **Comprehension Check,** 62c **Check Retelling,** 62d	**Concept Talk,** 72a **Oral Vocabulary,** 72b acclimate, persistence **Genre,** Persuasive Text, 72c	**Concept Wrap Up,** 75f **Check Oral Vocabulary,** 75g confront, predicament, ingenious, triumphant, application, resilient, modify, conquer, acclimate, persistence **Amazing Ideas,** 75g Review ◎ Generalize, 75h Review ◎ Unfamiliar Words, 75h Review Word Analysis, 75i Review Literary Terms, 75i
READ Main Selection, *Tripping Over the Lunch Lady,* 62–67a **Retelling,** 68–69 **Think Critically,** 69a **Model Fluency,** Accuracy, 69b **Research and Study Skills,** Telephone Directory, 69c	**READ Paired Selection,** "Square Dancing: Good for the Heart and Mind," 72–73a **Let's Learn It!** 74–75a Fluency: Accuracy Vocabulary: Idioms Listening and Speaking: Persuasive Speech	**Fluency Assessment,** WCPM, 75j–75k **Comprehension Assessment,** ◎ Generalize, 75l–75m
Research and Inquiry, Analyze, 69d **Conventions,** Pronouns and Antecedents, 69e **Spelling,** Prefixes *over-, under-, sub-, super-, out-,* 69e **Let's Write It!** Friendly Letter, 70–71a **Writing,** Friendly Letter, Sentences, 71b–71c	**Research and Inquiry,** Synthesize, 75b **Conventions,** Pronouns and Antecedents, 75c **Spelling,** Prefixes *over-, under-, sub-, super-, out-,* 75c **Writing,** Friendly Letter, Revising, 75d–75e	**Research and Inquiry,** Communicate, 75n **Conventions,** Pronouns and Antecedents, 75o **Spelling Test,** Prefixes *over-, under-, sub-, super-, out-,* 75o **Writing,** Friendly Letter, Conventions, 75p **Quick Write for Fluency,** 75q

Week 2

Grouping Options for Differentiated Instruction

Turn the page for the small group time lesson plan.

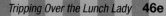

Planning Small Group Time on Reading Street!

Look for this Small Group Time box each day to help meet the individual needs of all your students. Differentiated Instruction lessons appear on the DI pages at the end of each week.

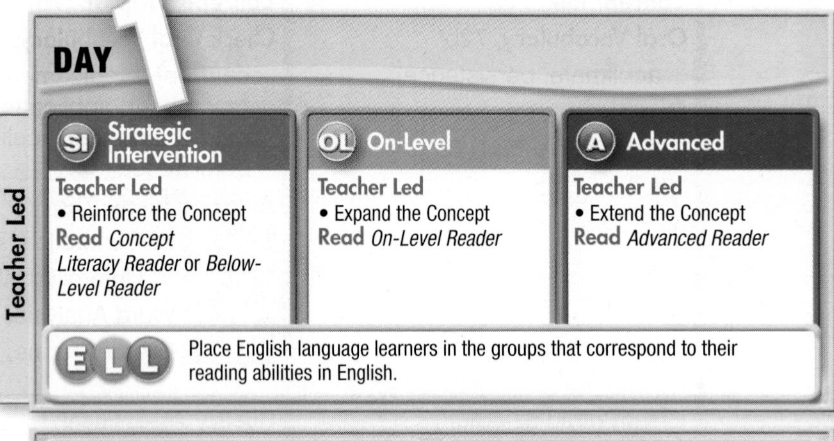

DAY 1

Teacher Led

SI Strategic Intervention	OL On-Level	A Advanced
Teacher Led • Reinforce the Concept Read *Concept Literacy Reader* or *Below-Level Reader*	Teacher Led • Expand the Concept Read *On-Level Reader*	Teacher Led • Extend the Concept Read *Advanced Reader*

ELL Place English language learners in the groups that correspond to their reading abilities in English.

Practice Stations	Independent Activities
• Read for Meaning • Get Fluent • Word Work	• Concept Talk Video • *Reader's and Writer's Notebook* • Research and Inquiry

ELL

ELL Reader
Advanced
Advanced High

ELD Reader
Beginning
Intermediate

ELL Poster

	Day 1
SI Strategic Intervention	**Reinforce the Concept,** DI•26–DI•27 Read **Concept Literacy Reader** or **Below-Level Reader**
OL On-Level	**Expand the Concept,** DI•32 Read **On-Level Reader**
A Advanced	**Extend the Concept,** DI•37 Read **Advanced Reader**
ELL English Language Learners	DI•41–DI•50 **Frontload Concept** **Preteach Skills** **Writing**

You Are Here! Unit 4 Week 2

Reading Street Response to Intervention Kit

Reading Street Practice Stations Kit

Question of the Week
How do people overcome obstacles?

SI Strategic Intervention

Below-Level Reader

Concept Literacy Reader

Tripping Over the Lunch Lady pp. 52–53

OL On-Level

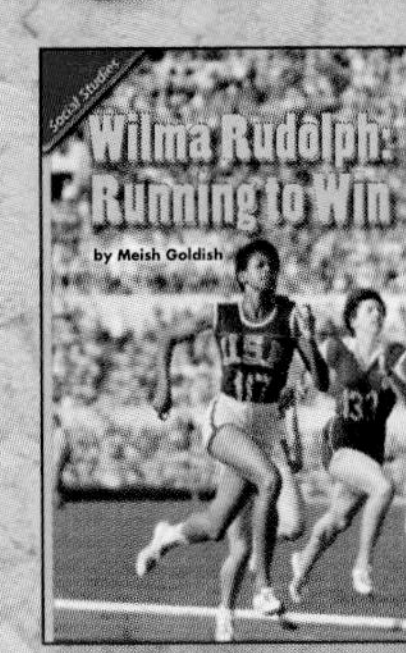

On-Level Reader

A Advanced

Advanced Reader

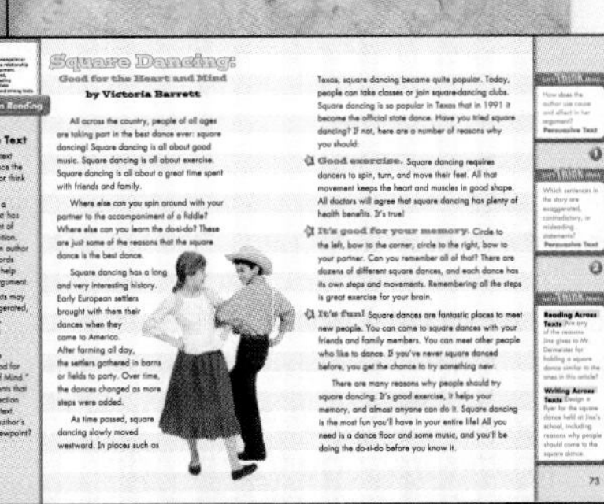

Square Dancing pp. 72–73

Small Group Weekly Plan

Day 2	Day 3	Day 4	Day 5
Reinforce Comprehension, DI•28 Revisit **Main Selection**	**Reinforce Vocabulary,** DI•29 Read/Revisit **Main Selection**	**Reinforce Comprehension,** Practice Retelling DI•30 Genre Focus Read/Revisit **Paired Selection**	**Practice Fluency,** DI•31 Reread **Concept Literacy Reader** or **Below-Level Reader**
Expand Comprehension, DI•33 Revisit **Main Selection**	**Expand Vocabulary,** DI•34 Read/Revisit **Main Selection**	**Expand Comprehension,** Practice Retelling DI•35 Genre Focus Read/Revisit **Paired Selection**	**Practice Fluency,** DI•36 Reread **On-Level Reader**
Extend Comprehension, DI•38 Revisit **Main Selection**	**Extend Vocabulary,** DI•39 Read/Revisit **Main Selection**	**Extend Comprehension,** Genre Focus DI•40 Read/Revisit **Paired Selection**	**Practice Fluency,** DI•40 Reread **Advanced Reader**
DI•41–DI•50 **Review Concept/Skills** **Frontload Main Selection** **Practice**	DI•41–DI•50 **Review Concept/Skills** Reread **Main Selection** **Practice**	DI•41–DI•50 **Review Concept** Read **ELL/ELD Readers** **Practice**	DI•41–DI•50 **Review Concept/Skills** Reread **ELL/ELD Reader** **Writing**

Week 2

Practice Stations for Everyone on Reading Street!

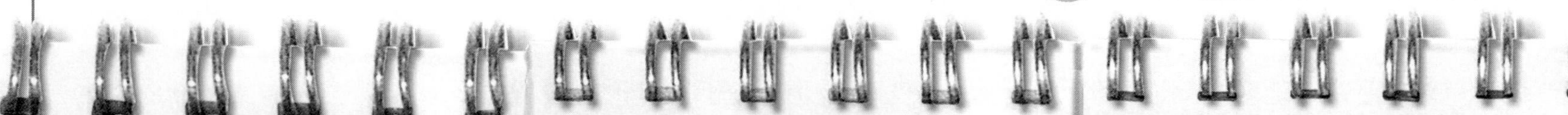

Word Wise
Word Origins

Objectives
- Spell words from different cultures.

Materials
- *Word Wise* Flip Chart Activity 17
- Teacher-made word cards
- dictionary
- paper
- pencil

Differentiated Activities

● Choose five word cards. Write your words in a list. Write sentences using each of the words. Think of other words you know from different cultures. Add them to your list.

▲ Choose seven word cards, and write the words in a list. Use a dictionary to look up the origin of each word. Write sentences using each of your words. List the words on a sheet of paper.

■ Choose ten word cards, and write the words in a list. Check the origin of each word in a dictionary. Write sentences using each of the words. Add other words from different cultures to your list.

Technology
- Online Dictionary

Word Work
Word Origins

Objectives
- Identify words from different cultures.

Materials
- *Word Work* Flip Chart Activity 17
- Teacher-made word cards
- paper
- pencil

Differentiated Activities

● Choose six word cards. Write the words in a list. Quietly say each word aloud. Use your words to write a short, fictional story about an adventure.

▲ Choose eight word cards, and write the words in a list. Quietly say each word aloud. Use your words to write a short, fictional story about an adventure.

■ Choose ten word cards, and write your words in a list. Quietly say each word aloud. Use your words to write a short, fictional story about an adventure.

Technology
- Modeled Pronunciation Audio CD

Words to Know
Endings *-s, -ed, -ing*

Objectives
- Determine the meaning of words with endings *-s, -ed, -ing*.

Materials
- *Words to Know* Flip Chart Activity 17
- magazines
- dictionary
- paper
- pencil

Differentiated Activities

● Use a magazine to find two verbs with each ending: *-s, -ed,* and *-ing*. Write the words in a list. Check each word's meaning in a dictionary. Write sentences using each of the words.

▲ Make a three-column chart with headings *-s, -ed,* and *-ing*. Use a magazine to find three verbs for each column. Check word meanings in a dictionary. Write sentences using the words.

■ Make a three-column chart with headings *-s, -ed,* and *-ing*. Use a magazine to find three verbs for each column. Check word meanings in a dictionary. Write sentences using the words.

Technology
- Online Dictionary

Use this week's materials from the Reading Street Leveled Practice Stations Kit to organize this week's stations.

Key

Below-Level Activities

On-Level Activities

Advanced Activities

Practice Station Flip Chart

Let's Write!

Picture Book

Objectives

- Write a picture book.

Materials

- *Let's Write!* Flip Chart Activity 17
- paper
- pencil
- crayons or markers

Differentiated Activities

● Think about a person who makes people laugh. Write a picture book that tells about this person. Focus on what makes this person special. Include a drawing of the person with your book.

▲ Write a picture book telling about a person you know who has an interesting hobby. Focus on explaining why the person and the hobby are special. Include an illustration of the person.

■ Write a picture book that tells about a person with an interesting skill or ability. Include details focusing on how the person developed this skill or ability, and draw an illustration of the person.

Technology

- Online Graphic Organizers

Read for Meaning

Draw Conclusions

Objectives

- Draw conclusions based on information you read.

Materials

- *Read for Meaning* Flip Chart Activity 17
- Leveled Readers
- paper
- pencil

Differentiated Activities

● Choose and read a book from those your teacher provided. Draw a conclusion based on what you read. Write one sentence stating your conclusion. Write one sentence with information from the story to support your conclusion.

▲ Choose and read a book from those your teacher provided. Draw a conclusion based on the information. Write a short paragraph that states your conclusion. Include information to support your conclusion.

■ Choose and read a book from those your teacher provided. Think about two conclusions you can draw. Write a short paragraph that explains each conclusion. Include at least one detail to support each of the conclusions.

Technology

- Leveled-Reader Database

Get Fluent

Practice fluent reading.

Objectives

- Read aloud using appropriate phrasing.

Materials

- *Get Fluent* Flip Chart Activity 17
- Leveled Readers

Differentiated Activities

● Work with a partner. Choose a Concept Literacy Reader or Below-Level Reader. Take turns reading a page from the book. Use the reader to practice appropriate phrasing. Provide feedback as needed.

▲ Work with a partner. Choose an On-Level Reader. Take turns reading a page from the book. Use the reader to practice appropriate phrasing. Provide feedback as needed.

■ Work with a partner. Choose an Advanced Reader. Take turns reading a page from the book. Use the reader to practice appropriate phrasing. Provide feedback as needed.

Technology

- Leveled Reader Database
- Reading Street Readers CD-ROM

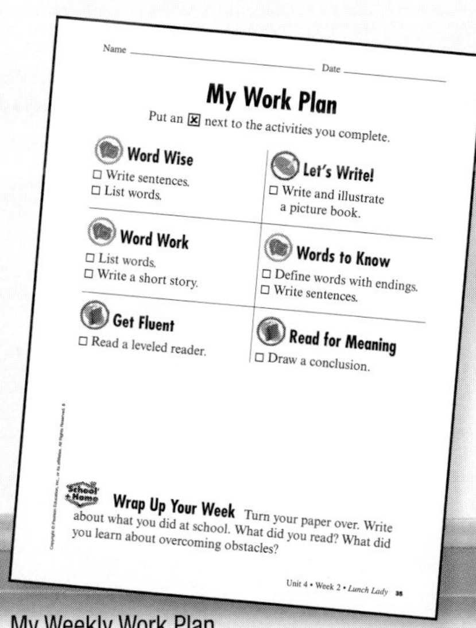
Name ____ Date ____

My Work Plan

Put an ☒ next to the activities you complete.

Word Wise
☐ Write sentences.
☐ List words.

Let's Write!
☐ Write and illustrate a picture book.

Word Work
☐ List words.
☐ Write a short story.

Words to Know
☐ Define words with endings.
☐ Write sentences.

Get Fluent
☐ Read a leveled reader.

Read for Meaning
☐ Draw a conclusion.

Wrap Up Your Week Turn your paper over. Write about what you did at school. What did you read? What did you learn about overcoming obstacles?

Unit 4 • Week 2 • Lunch Lady

My Weekly Work Plan

Week 2

Objectives
- Introduce the weekly concept.
- Develop oral vocabulary.

Today at a Glance

Oral Vocabulary
confront, predicament, ingenious, triumphant

Comprehension
◉ Generalize
◉ Predict and set purpose

Reading
"The School Dance"

Fluency
Accuracy

Lesson Vocabulary
Tested vocabulary

Research and Inquiry
Identify questions

Spelling
Prefixes *over-, under-, sub-, super-, out-*

Conventions
Pronouns and antecedents

Handwriting
Cursive letters *n* and *N*

Writing
Friendly letter

Concept Talk

Question of the Week

How do people overcome obstacles?

Introduce the concept To further explore the concept of Adapting, this week students will read, write, and talk about ways people adapt to overcome obstacles.

ROUTINE — Activate Prior Knowledge — Team Talk

1. **Think** Have students think about obstacles that people have to overcome in their lives.
2. **Pair** Have pairs of students discuss the Question of the Week by considering suggestions from each other.
3. **Share** Call on a few students to share their ideas and comments with the group. Guide the discussion and encourage elaboration with prompts such as:
   - What types of obstacles do people sometimes have to overcome?
   - What obstacles have you or has someone you know been able to overcome?

Routines Flip Chart

Anchored Talk

Develop oral vocabulary Have students turn to pp. 46–47 in their Student Editions. Look at each of the photos. Then, use the prompts to guide discussion and create the *How people overcome obstacles* concept map.

- What obstacles might the Eskimo family face? (They have to face long, hard winters.) Their winters are harsh. Harsh conditions are only one type of obstacle. Let's add *Types of obstacles* to our concept map.
- What obstacles might a blind person face? (The person's physical disability makes it harder for him or her to read.) What qualities might a person with disabilities have to possess to overcome obstacles? (determination, strength) Let's add *Qualities and actions* to our concept map.

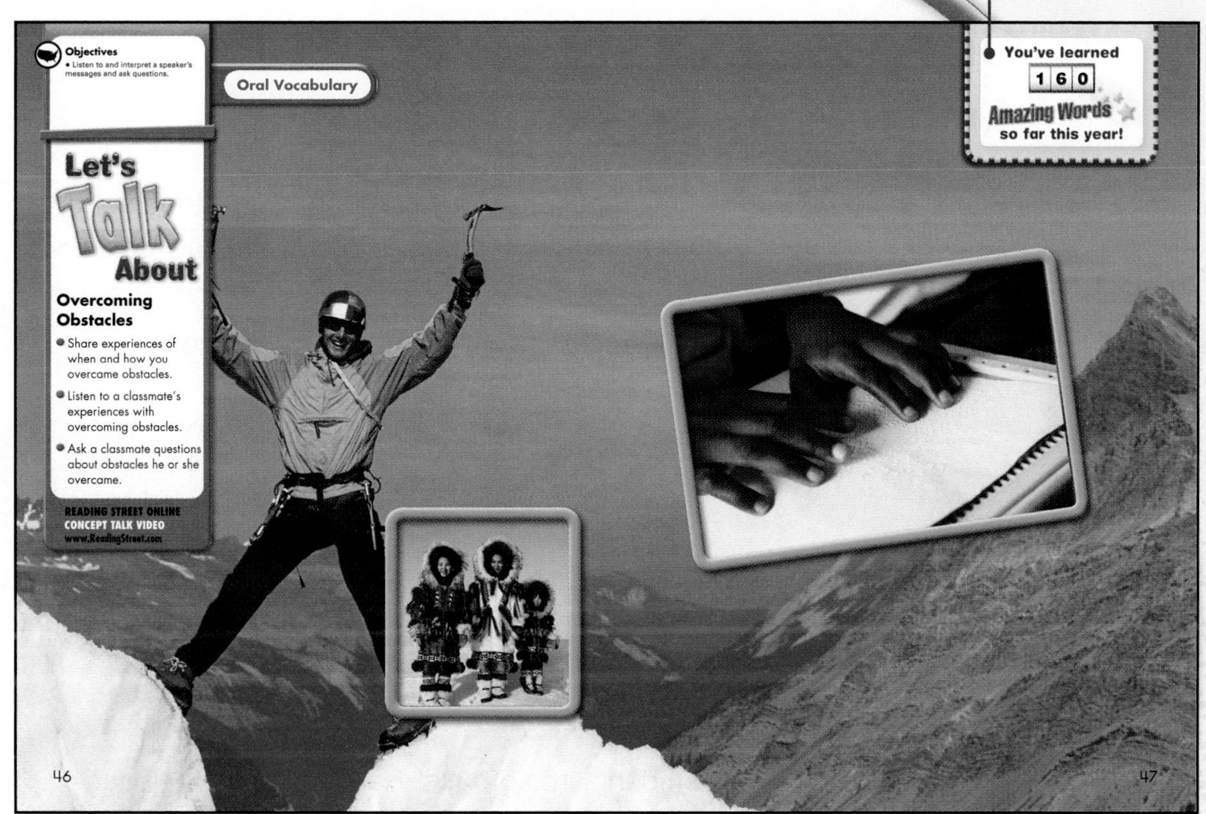

Objectives
• Listen to and interpret a speaker's messages and ask questions.
Oral Vocabulary
Let's Talk About
Overcoming Obstacles
• Share experiences of when and how you overcame obstacles.
• Listen to a classmate's experiences with overcoming obstacles.
• Ask a classmate questions about obstacles he or she overcame.
READING STREET ONLINE
CONCEPT TALK VIDEO
www.ReadingStreet.com
You've learned 160 Amazing Words so far this year!
46
47

Student Edition pp. 46–47

- What obstacles might a mountain climber face? (A mountain climber faces a physical challenge.) How might the climber feel after making it to the top of the mountain? (happy) Let's add *Results of overcoming* to our concept map.
- After discussing the photos, ask: How do people overcome obstacles?

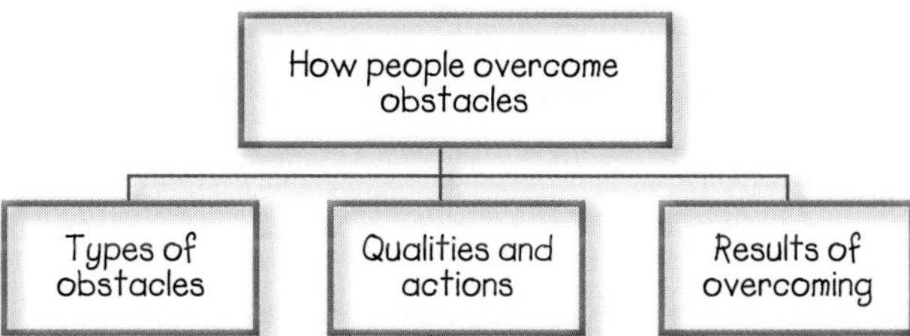

Connect to reading Tell students that this week they will be reading about different people who are able to overcome obstacles.

ELL Preteach Concepts Use the Day 1 instruction on ELL Poster 17 to assess and build background knowledge, develop concepts, and build oral vocabulary.

ELL Poster 17

Amazing Words

You've learned 160 words so far.

You'll learn 010 words this week!

confront	resilient
predicament	modify
ingenious	conquer
triumphant	acclimate
application	persistence

Writing on Demand

Writing Fluency

Ask students respond to the photos on pp. 46–47 by writing as well as they can about how people can overcome obstacles.

ELL

English Language Learners

ELL support Additional ELL support and modified instruction is provided in the *ELL Handbook* and in the ELL Support lessons on pp. DI•41–DI•50.

Listening comprehension English learners will benefit from additional visual support to understand the key terms in the concept map. Use the pictures on pp. 46–47 to scaffold understanding.

Frontload for Read Aloud Use the modified Read Aloud on p. DI•44 of the ELL Support lessons to prepare students to listen to "Sense" (p. 47b).

Objectives
- Develop listening comprehension.
- Develop oral vocabulary.

Check Oral Vocabulary
SUCCESS PREDICTOR

Oral Vocabulary
Amazing Words

Introduce Amazing Words "Sense" on p. 47b is a story about a famous composer. Tell students to listen for this week's Amazing Words — *confront, predicament, ingenious, triumphant* — as you read.

Model fluency As you read "Sense," model accuracy with smooth, fluent reading.

Teach Amazing Words

Amazing Words Oral Vocabulary Routine

confront
predicament
ingenious
triumphant

1. **Introduce** Write the word *predicament* on the board. Have students say the word aloud with you. In "Sense," Beethoven has a terrible *predicament*. What context clues can you find to help you understand the meaning of the word? Supply a student-friendly definition.
2. **Demonstrate** Break students into groups. Have students elicit suggestions from group members to demonstrate understanding in a student-led discussion using these questions. Is it a *predicament* when you have to do your homework? (no) Is it a *predicament* when you forget to bring your homework to school? (yes)
3. **Apply** Ask students to give an example of when they have been in a *predicament.*

See p. OV•2 to teach *confront, ingenious,* and *triumphant*.

Routines Flip Chart

Apply Amazing Words To build oral language, have students discuss the Amazing Words.

MONITOR PROGRESS **Check Oral Vocabulary**

During discussion, listen for students' use of Amazing Words.

If... students are unable to use the Amazing Words to discuss the concept,

then... use the Oral Vocabulary Routine in the Routines Flip Chart to demonstrate words in different contexts.

Day 1	**Days 2–3**	**Day 4**	**Day 5**
Check Oral Vocabulary	Check Retelling	Check Fluency	Check Oral Vocabulary

Sense

It was getting worse, bit by bit. At first he tried to ignore it. To fake his way through conversations with people. To go on with his work as if it didn't really matter. And then he tried doctors. One by one they came with their fancy cures. One by one they failed. Every day he woke up to a silence broken only by his own heart, beating in terror. He hoped against hope that things would someday return to normal. He just could not bring himself to confront the truth. He—he of all people—*could not hear.*

He could not hear the flute playing in the distance, or the voices of those he loved. Worst of all, he could not hear his beloved piano. "What do you do," he wondered, "when the most important thing you have is gone? How do you survive?" He began to isolate himself from other people, worried that they would discover his secret. "Speak louder! Shout!" he longed to tell them. But how could he admit it? Hearing was the one sense that should be strongest in him above all other people. He began to believe that he simply could not go on. But something stopped him from giving up.

He believed in his work. He had a gift, and that gift must not be thrown away. Even when the sense he needed most for it had failed him. So he made a decision. The predicament would not go away. He had to accept it. But he would cope with it in ingenious ways. He used ear trumpets to amplify voices. He cut the legs off his piano so he could lie on the floor and hear its vibrations. Eventually, he asked people to write their questions to him in special books. He read their messages and responded to them aloud, almost as if he were having a conversation. He relied on the power of his memory and the strength of his talent to create masterpieces he could hear only in his own mind.

Finally, he shared with the world one of his most important works: the Ninth Symphony. When it was finished, he had to be turned around to face the audience. He was completely deaf. He could not hear a bit of their thunderous applause. And he could not hear them shout his name, the name of one of the greatest, most triumphant musical composers of all time: Ludwig van Beethoven.

DAY 1 Read and Comprehend

30–35 mins.

Objectives

- Generalize to aid comprehension.
- Use the predict and set purpose strategy to aid comprehension.
- Read grade-level text with accuracy.

Skills Trace

Generalize

Introduce U4W2D1; U4W4D1; U5W5D1

Practice U4W2D2; U4W2D3; U4W4D2; U4W4D3; U5W5D2; U5W5D3

Reteach/Review U4W2D5; U4W4D5; U5W5D3; U5W5D5; U6W1D3

Assess/Test Weekly Tests U4W2; U4W4; U5W5

Benchmark Tests U4

KEY:

U=Unit W=Week D=Day

Skill ↔ Strategy

Generalize

Predict and Set Purpose

Student Edition p. EI•7

Introduce generalize

To generalize is to make a broad statement or inference that applies to many examples. You could say most schools hold dances. Which word is a clue that this is a generalization? *(most)* You can make generalizations about story characters as you read too. What can help me make a generalization about a character? (evidence from the text and background knowledge) Have students turn to p. EI•7 in the Student Edition to review generalizing. Then read "The School Dance" with students.

Envision It!

Model the skill

Today we are going to read about a boy who is going to a school dance. After I read the first two paragraphs, what generalization can I make about Victor? (He is usually nervous about what others think about him.) I can find evidence from the text to support my generalization. What evidence can you find? (It says he was worried, and he asked a lot of questions.)

Guide practice

Have students finish reading "The School Dance" on their own. After they read, ask them to infer their own generalization about the story. Have them use a graphic organizer like the one on p. 48 and support their generalization with information from the text.

Strategy check

Predict and Set Purpose Remind students that if they have difficulty understanding "The School Dance," they can use the strategy of predict and set purpose. Model predicting to aid comprehension.

Model the strategy

After reading the first two paragraphs, I can make a prediction about what will happen to Victor at the dance. I think that because Victor is so worried, he will not have a good time. I can now set a purpose for reading the rest of the story: to find out if Victor will have a good time at the dance. Have students read the rest of the story with this purpose in mind. Then have students review the strategy of predict and set purpose on p. EI•20 of the Student Edition.

Envision It!

Student Edition p. EI•20

On their own

Use p. 258 in the *Reader's and Writer's Notebook* for additional practice with generalization.

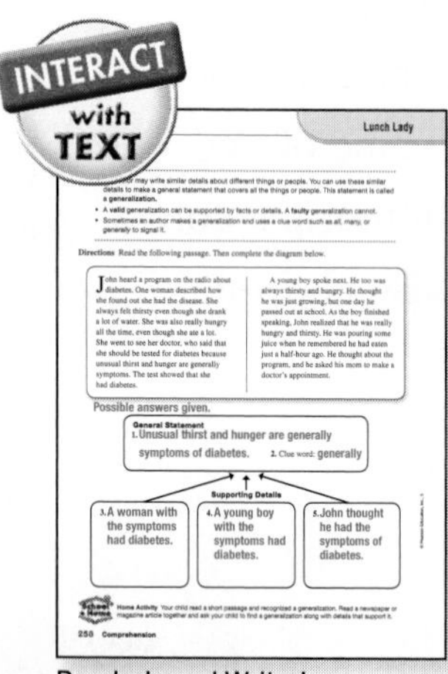

Reader's and Writer's Notebook, p. 258

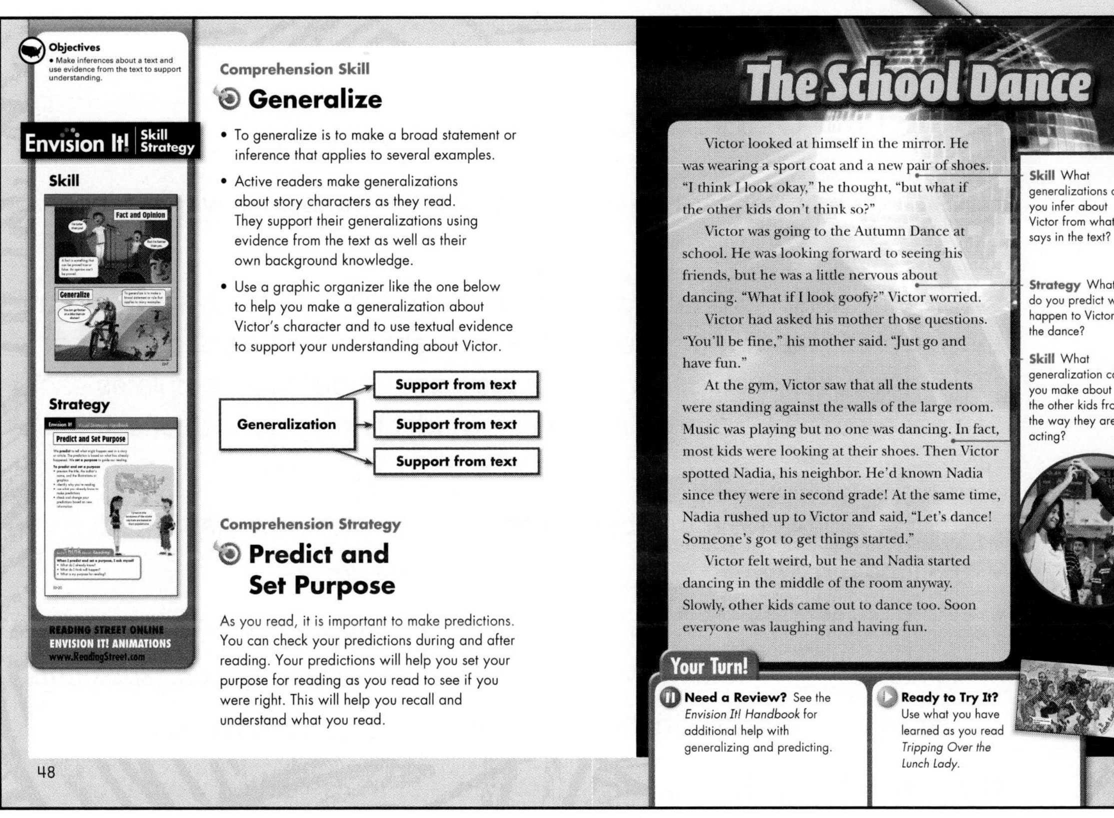

Objectives
• Make inferences about a text and use evidence from the text to support understanding.

Envision It! | Skill Strategy

Skill

Fact and Opinion

Generalize

Strategy

Predict and Set Purpose

READING STREET ONLINE
ENVISION IT! ANIMATIONS
www.ReadingStreet.com

Comprehension Skill

Generalize

- To generalize is to make a broad statement or inference that applies to several examples.
- Active readers make generalizations about story characters as they read. They support their generalizations using evidence from the text as well as their own background knowledge.
- Use a graphic organizer like the one below to help you make a generalization about Victor's character and to use textual evidence to support your understanding about Victor.

Generalization → Support from text; Support from text; Support from text

Comprehension Strategy

Predict and Set Purpose

As you read, it is important to make predictions. You can check your predictions during and after reading. Your predictions will help you set your purpose for reading as you read to see if you were right. This will help you recall and understand what you read.

48

The School Dance

Victor looked at himself in the mirror. He was wearing a sport coat and a new pair of shoes. "I think I look okay," he thought, "but what if the other kids don't think so?"

Victor was going to the Autumn Dance at school. He was looking forward to seeing his friends, but he was a little nervous about dancing. "What if I look goofy?" Victor worried.

Victor had asked his mother those questions. "You'll be fine," his mother said. "Just go and have fun."

At the gym, Victor saw that all the students were standing against the walls of the large room. Music was playing but no one was dancing. In fact, most kids were looking at their shoes. Then Victor spotted Nadia, his neighbor. He'd known Nadia since they were in second grade! At the same time, Nadia rushed up to Victor and said, "Let's dance! Someone's got to get things started."

Victor felt weird, but he and Nadia started dancing in the middle of the room anyway. Slowly, other kids came out to dance too. Soon everyone was laughing and having fun.

Skill What generalizations can you infer about Victor from what he says in the text?

Strategy What do you predict will happen to Victor at the dance?

Skill What generalization can you make about the other kids from the way they are acting?

Your Turn!

Need a Review? See the *Envision It! Handbook* for additional help with generalizing and predicting.

Ready to Try It? Use what you have learned as you read *Tripping Over the Lunch Lady*.

49

Student Edition pp. 48–49

Skill Possible response: He is insecure and always worries about what others think about him.

Strategy Possible response: He will get over his nervousness and have fun.

Skill Possible response: All of the kids are insecure and nervous too.

Academic Vocabulary

generalize to make a broad statement or rule that applies to several examples

Model Fluency

Accuracy

Model fluent reading Have students listen as you read paragraph 1 of "The School Dance" with accuracy. Explain that you will read the words carefully so that you're reading without making any mistakes.

ROUTINE Paired Reading

1. **Select a passage** For "The School Dance," use the whole passage.
2. **Reader 1** Students read the entire passage, switching readers at the end of paragraph 3.
3. **Reader 2** Partners reread the passage. This time the other student begins.
4. **Reread** For optimal fluency, have partners continue to read three or four times.
5. **Corrective Feedback** Listen as students read. Provide feedback about their accuracy and encourage them to read the words with no mistakes.

Routines Flip Chart

ELL

English Language Learners

Generalize Talk about the weather. Have volunteers fill in these sentences: *When it rains, it is always ____ outside. In the summer, it is always ___ outside.*

Explain that these are generalizations. Point out that the word *always* is a clue that the sentence is a generalization.

Objectives

- Activate prior knowledge of words.
- Identify questions for research.

Vocabulary
Tested Vocabulary

Lesson vocabulary Have students complete sentences by filling in the blanks with lesson words.

Activate prior knowledge Display the lesson words and discuss what students already know about these words. Then write incomplete sentences on the board, such as those below. Have students identify the lesson word that completes each sentence and makes sense in context. Students may need to check the glossary.

- She tripped over the tree branch and _______ her ankle. *(sprained)*
- The little girl wore a ______ dress to the party. *(frilly)*
- The models were ______ at the fashion show. *(promenading)*
- We had a ______ teacher when our regular teacher was sick. *(substitute)*
- That big, white dog with the dark spots is a______. *(Dalmatian)*

Synonyms Have students think of synonyms for some of the selection words. List the synonyms on the board.

At the end of the week, students can review these fill-in-the-blank sentences or create their own with a partner.

Preteach Academic Vocabulary

Academic Vocabulary Write the following words on the board:

generalize	**antecedent**
essay	**friendly letter**
climax	**compound sentence**

Have students share what they know about this week's Academic Vocabulary. Use the students' responses to assess their prior knowledge. Preteach the Academic Vocabulary by providing a student-friendly description, explanation, or example that clarifies the meaning of each term. Then ask students to restate the meaning of the Academic Vocabulary term in their own words.

Research and Inquiry
Identify Questions

Teach Discuss the Question of the Week: *How do people overcome obstacles?* Tell students that they will research a famous person who has overcome an obstacle and write a brief description of the person. They will include a drawing or photograph of the person in a presentation on Day 5.

Model 
Think Aloud I'll start by thinking about obstacles people face. Some people have physical disabilities, and others have learning disabilities. I would like to learn more about how people face dyslexia, which is a reading disability. A question could be *What famous person faced dyslexia and how did he or she overcome it?* I know that Nolan Ryan, a baseball player, overcame dyslexia. I will research him.

Guide practice Have students work in groups. They should consult with each other as they brainstorm, decide on a topic, and formulate open-ended inquiry questions. Explain that tomorrow they will conduct research using online sources and periodicals.

On their own Have students generate research plans for tomorrow.

Small Group Time

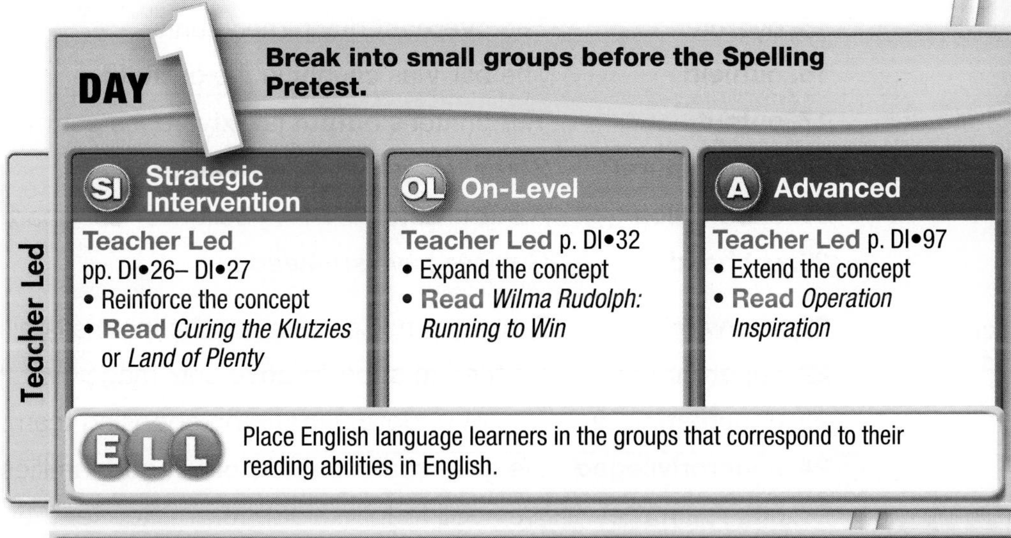

DAY 1 Break into small groups before the Spelling Pretest.

Teacher Led

SI Strategic Intervention	OL On-Level	A Advanced
Teacher Led pp. DI•26– DI•27 • Reinforce the concept • Read *Curing the Klutzies* or *Land of Plenty*	Teacher Led p. DI•32 • Expand the concept • Read *Wilma Rudolph: Running to Win*	Teacher Led p. DI•97 • Extend the concept • Read *Operation Inspiration*

ELL Place English language learners in the groups that correspond to their reading abilities in English.

Practice Stations	Independent Activities
• Read for Meaning • Get Fluent • Word Work	• Concept Talk Video • *Reader's and Writer's Notebook* • Vocabulary Activities

INTERNET GUY
Don Leu

21st Century Skills

Weekly Inquiry Project

Day 1	Identify Questions
Day 2	Navigate/Search
Day 3	Analyze
Day 4	Synthesize
Day 5	Communicate

Differentiated Instruction

Advanced
Have students brainstorm a list of famous people they think may have overcome a learning or physical challenge. Have them determine the keywords they could use to help them with the list.

English Language Learners
Multilingual vocabulary
Students can apply knowledge of their home languages to acquire new English vocabulary by using the Multilingual Vocabulary Lists (*ELL Handbook*, pp. 431–444).

Objectives

- Pretest words with prefixes *over-, under-, sub-, super-,* and *out-*.
- Identify and use pronouns and antecedents.
- Write cursive capital letter *N* and lowercase *n* in words.

Spelling Pretest

Prefixes *over-, under-, sub-, super-, out-*

Introduce Remind students that prefixes are word parts. This week we will work on spelling words with the prefixes *over-, under-, sub-, super-,* and *out-*. These prefixes do not change the spelling of the base word.

Pretest Use these sentences to administer the spelling pretest. Say each word, read the sentence, and repeat the word.

1. overlook	Some details are easy to **overlook.**
2. underline	**Underline** the verb in each sentence.
3. subway	The **subway** train goes fast.
4. subset	A **subset** is part of a larger set.
5. supermarket	Our **supermarket** is huge.
6. outlet	The new store is a shoe **outlet.**
7. underground	**Underground** tunnels are dark.
8. overboard	We threw crumbs **overboard.**
9. undercurrent	The ocean's **undercurrent** is strong.
10. superstar	Fans ran after the **superstar.**
11. overtime	I worked **overtime** last week.
12. supersonic	The **supersonic** jet is loud.
13. submarine	The **submarine** finally surfaced.
14. undercover	The police work **undercover** to solve crimes.
15. overcast	The **overcast** day turned sunny.
16. outfield	The ball was caught in the **outfield.**
17. output	The printer's **output** is sixty pages per minute.
18. supernatural	Some things seem **supernatural.**
19. subdivision	A **subdivision** is being built near our apartment.
20. subheads	Outlines have **subheads.**

Challenge words

21. overwhelm	Too much noise can **overwhelm** small children.
22. superimpose	He tried to **superimpose** one image over the other.
23. underestimate	Do not **underestimate** the opposing team.
24. underprivileged	We gave coats to **underprivileged** families.
25. subcommittee	We need to form a **subcommittee** for that issue.

Self-correct After the pretest, you can either display the correctly spelled words or spell them orally. Have students self-correct their pretests by writing misspelled words.

On their own For additional practice, use *Let's Practice It!* p.193 on the *Teacher Resources DVD-ROM.*

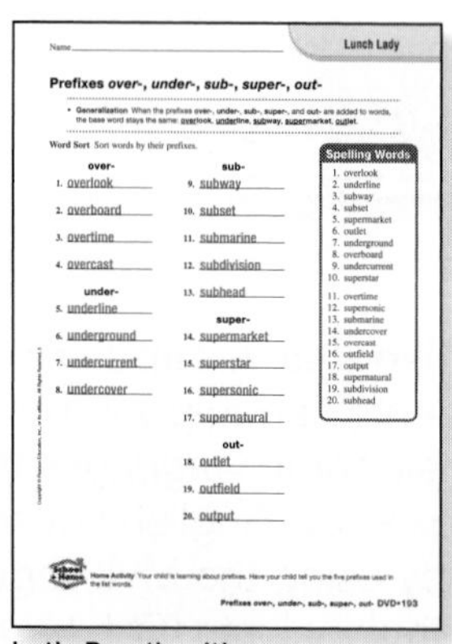
Name ______ Lunch Lady

Prefixes *over-, under-, sub-, super-, out-*

- **Generalization** When the prefixes over-, under-, sub-, super-, and out- are added to words, the base word stays the same: overlook, underline, subway, supermarket, outlet.

Word Sort Sort words by their prefixes.

over-
1. overlook
2. overboard
3. overtime
4. overcast

under-
5. underline
6. underground
7. undercurrent
8. undercover

sub-
9. subway
10. subset
11. submarine
12. subdivision
13. subhead

super-
14. supermarket
15. superstar
16. supersonic
17. supernatural

out-
18. outlet
19. outfield
20. output

Spelling Words: 1. overlook 2. underline 3. subway 4. subset 5. supermarket 6. outlet 7. underground 8. overboard 9. undercurrent 10. superstar 11. overtime 12. supersonic 13. submarine 14. undercover 15. overcast 16. outfield 17. output 18. supernatural 19. subdivision 20. subhead

School + Home **Home Activity** Your child is learning about prefixes. Have your child tell you the five prefixes used in the list words.

Prefixes over-, under-, sub-, super-, out- DVD•193

Let's Practice It!
TR DVD•193

Conventions
Pronouns and Antecedents

Teach Display Grammar Transparency 17. Read aloud the definitions of *pronoun* and *antecedent* at the top. Then display this sentence: *Mr. Deimeister is a good gym teacher, but he gets hurt several times when students or things fall on him.* Explain that in this sentence the underlined pronouns *he* and *him* refer to the noun, or person, *Mr. Deimeister. Mr. Deimeister* is the **antecedent** of *he* and *him.*

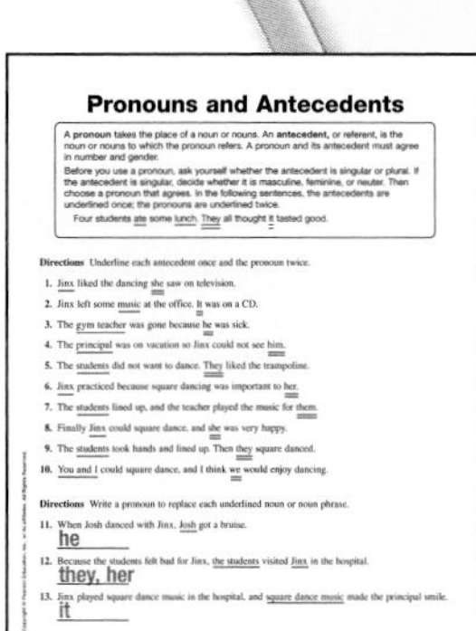

Pronouns and Antecedents

A **pronoun** takes the place of a noun or nouns. An **antecedent,** or referent, is the noun or nouns to which the pronoun refers. A pronoun and its antecedent must agree in number and gender.

Before you use a pronoun, ask yourself whether the antecedent is singular or plural. If the antecedent is singular, decide whether it is masculine, feminine, or neuter. Then choose a pronoun that agrees. In the following sentences, the antecedents are underlined once; the pronouns are underlined twice.

Four students ate some lunch. They all thought it tasted good.

Directions Underline each antecedent once and the pronoun twice.

1. Jinx liked the dancing she saw on television.
2. Jinx left some music at the office. It was on a CD.
3. The gym teacher was gone because he was sick.
4. The principal was on vacation so Jinx could not see him.
5. The students did not want to dance. They liked the trampoline.
6. Jinx practiced because square dancing was important to her.
7. The students lined up, and the teacher played the music for them.
8. Finally Jinx could square dance, and she was very happy.
9. The students took hands and lined up. Then they square danced.
10. You and I could square dance, and I think we would enjoy dancing.

Directions Write a pronoun to replace each underlined noun or noun phrase.

11. When Josh danced with Jinx, Josh got a bruise. he
12. Because the students felt bad for Jinx, the students visited Jinx in the hospital. they, her
13. Jinx played square dance music in the hospital, and square dance music made the principal smile. it

Unit 4 Tripping Over the Lunch Lady — Grammar 17

Grammar Transparency 17, TR DVD

Model Identify the antecedent and pronoun in sentences 1, 2, and 3. Apply the definitions for antecedents and pronouns to show how you determined the correct answer.

Guided practice Work through the remaining sentences.

Daily Fix-It Use Daily Fix-It numbers 1 and 2 in the right margin.

Connect to oral language Have students read sentences 11 to 13 on the transparency and explain which pronoun is correct to use as a replacement in each sentence.

Handwriting
Cursive Letter *n* and *N*

Model letter formation Display the uppercase cursive letter *N* and the lowercase letter *n.* Follow the stroke instruction pictured to model letter formation.

Model letter shape Explain that writing legibly involves forming the letter shapes properly. For example, you do not want to make an extra loop when retracing the first line on the left side of capital letter *N* back up. Write the following sentence: *Neil went to Nantucket.* Be sure to join both the capital *N* and the lowercase *n* to the letters that follow them and to model the correct shape.

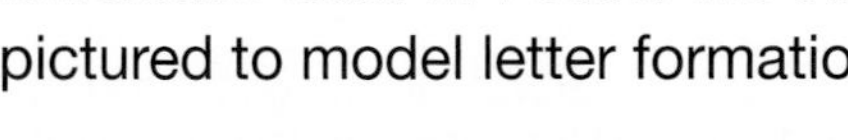

Guide practice Have students write these phrases: *nice Nancy; nervous Nick; Nurse Nina.* Circulate around the room, guiding students.

Academic Vocabulary

antecedent the noun or nouns to which a pronoun refers

Daily Fix-It

1. The gum in Tony's mouth went down his throat and almost chocked her. *(choked; him)*
2. The lady square dancer had a smile on their face as she swinged her partner. *(her; swung)*

English Language Learners

Language production: Subject and object pronouns Review pronouns that are used to name females and males, while also making the pronoun-antecedent connection more clear. Begin by asking students to point to a *she.* Remind students that *she* is a subject pronoun. Ask them the name of the student, explaining that *she* is the pronoun that refers to this antecedent. Then ask students to give you the object pronoun that matches *she.* Explain that *her* is also a pronoun referring to the antecedent. Repeat with *he.*

DAY 1 Language Arts

Objectives

- Understand and identify the features of a friendly letter.

MINI-LESSON

5 Day Planner
Guide to Mini-Lessons

DAY 1	Read Like a Writer
DAY 2	Sentence Variety
DAY 3	Casual Tone
DAY 4	Revising Strategy: Adding
DAY 5	Proofread for Conventions

Writing—Friendly Letter
Introduce

MINI-LESSON

Read Like a Writer

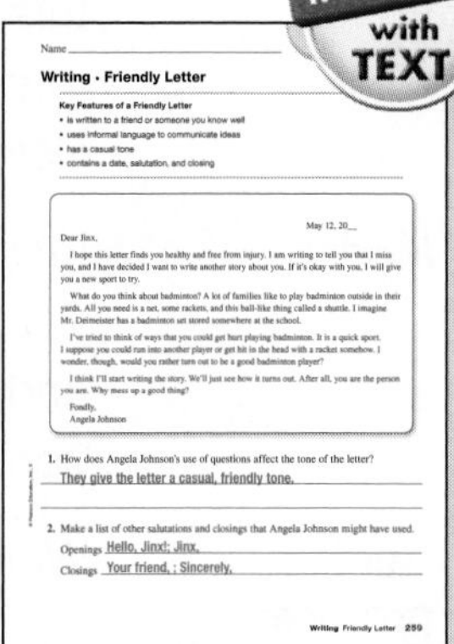

Reader's and Writer's Notebook p. 259

- **Introduce** This week you will write a **friendly letter.** Usually, you send friendly letters to people you know well. The tone of a friendly letter is casual rather than formal. However, a friendly letter still includes the important letter parts.

Prompt	Write a letter from one character to another from *Tripping Over the Lunch Lady.*
Trait	Sentences
Mode	Narrative

- **Examine Model Text** Let's read a friendly letter written from the author of *Tripping Over the Lunch Lady* to her main character, Jinx. Explain that although friendly letters can be light-hearted, they still convey important ideas and information. Have students read the letter on p. 259 of their *Reader's and Writer's Notebook.*

- **Key Features** Friendly letters have the **date** at the top. Point to the date and circle the comma, reminding students to punctuate the date correctly. Then, the letter opens with a **salutation,** or greeting, which is followed by a comma.

The body of a friendly letter is made up of several paragraphs. Each paragraph is about one idea, and using a variety of sentences makes the paragraph more interesting to read. Point out that sentence 1 in the opening paragraph is a simple sentence, sentence 2 is a compound sentence, and sentence 3 begins with an introductory clause. Have students analyze the other paragraphs and label the types of sentences. Discuss the **casual tone** of the letter.

Finally, the letter ends with a **closing.** Circle the comma in the closing, and have students circle the letter writer's name.

Review key features

Review the key features of a friendly letter with students. You may want to post the key features in the classroom for students to refer to as they work on their compositions.

Key Features of a Friendly Letter

- written to a friend or someone you know well
- uses informal language to communicate ideas
- has a casual tone
- contains a date, salutation, and closing

ROUTINE Quick Write for Fluency — Team Talk

1. **Talk** Have pairs take two or three minutes to discuss the features of a friendly letter.
2. **Write** Each person writes a short paragraph naming someone to whom they might send a friendly letter, telling why they chose that person, and suggesting the types of information they might include in the letter.
3. **Share** Partners trade papers and read one another's paragraphs.

Routines Flip Chart

Wrap Up Your Day

- ✔ **Build Concepts** What did you learn about how people adapt to face challenges?
- ✔ **Oral Vocabulary** Have students use the Amazing Words they learned in context sentences.
- ✔ **Homework** Send home this week's Family Times newsletter on *Let's Practice It!* pp. 194–195 on the *Teacher Resources DVD-ROM.*

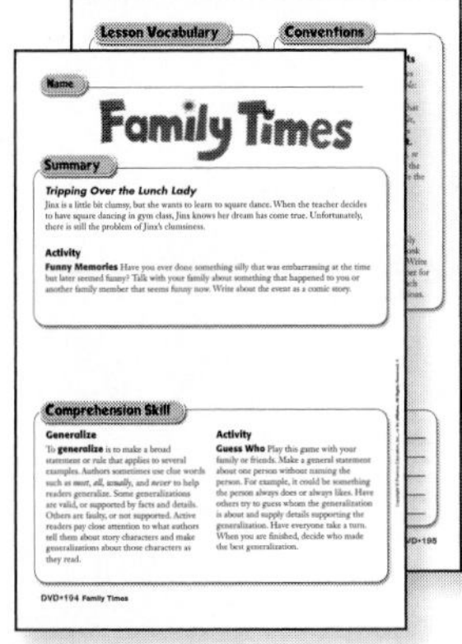
Let's Practice It!
TR DVD•194–195

Write Guy
Jeff Anderson

Register Swap

Even if they don't know what to call them, students often know the difference between formal and informal registers. Discuss with students the types of audiences and situations where they might use informal language and those where they might use formal language. Making this explicit distinction helps students get a deeper understanding of purpose and audience.

Academic Vocabulary

friendly letter a letter written in a friendly tone to a friend or acquaintance

English Language Learners

Informal Language Read the writing model, pausing to point out examples of informal language. Explain what makes the examples feel informal. For example, the third sentence of the opening paragraph uses the contraction *it's* and the informal word *okay.*

Preview DAY 2

Tell students that tomorrow they will read about a clumsy girl who gets hurt in gym class.

Objectives

- Expand the weekly concept.
- Develop oral vocabulary.

Today at a Glance

Oral Vocabulary
application, resilient

Word Analysis
Suffixes *-ly, -ian*

Literary Terms
Hyperbole

Story Structure
Climax

Lesson Vocabulary
Unfamiliar words

Reading
"Dogs on Parade"
Tripping Over the Lunch Lady

Fluency
Accuracy

Research and Inquiry
Navigate/Search

Spelling
Prefixes *over-, under-, sub-, super-, out-*

Conventions
Pronouns and antecedents

Writing
Friendly letter

Concept Talk

Question of the Week

How do people overcome obstacles?

Expand the concept

Remind students of the Question of the Week. Tell students that today they will begin reading *Tripping Over the Lunch Lady*. As they read, encourage students to think about how people they know have overcome obstacles.

Anchored Talk

Develop oral vocabulary

Use the photos on pp. 46–47 and the Read Aloud, "Sense," to talk about the Amazing Words: *confront, predicament, ingenious,* and *triumphant*. Add these and other concept-related words to the concept map to develop students' knowledge of the topic. Discuss the following questions.

- Have you ever had to *confront* a *predicament*? What was it? Possible response: I wanted to play soccer and take piano lessons, but both were on the same day.
- Were you able to come up with an *ingenious* way to solve your problem? What was it? Possible response: I joined the soccer team and was able to schedule my piano lessons for another day.
- How were you able to be *triumphant* over your problem or obstacle? Possible response: I practiced very hard at both skills. My soccer team won the tournament, and I did well at my piano recital too.

Oral Vocabulary
Amazing Words

Amazing Words

confront	resilient
predicament	modify
ingenious	conquer
triumphant	acclimate
application	persistence

Amazing Words Oral Vocabulary Routine

Teach Amazing Words

1. **Introduce** Write the Amazing Word *resilient* on the board. Have students say it aloud with you. Relate *resilient* to the photographs on pp. 46–47 and "Sense." In these pictures, do the people have to be *resilient* to overcome their obstacles? Did Beethoven have to be *resilient* to overcome going deaf? Have students use context clues to determine the definition of the word. (To be resilient means to be able to recover from hard times or adapt to change.)
2. **Demonstrate** Have students answer questions to demonstrate understanding. How does the blind child show that she is *resilient*? (by learning how to read with Braille) How did Beethoven show that he was *resilient*? (He was able to write the Ninth Symphony even though he could not hear it.)
3. **Apply** Have students apply their understanding. How have you had to be resilient in your life?

See p. OV•2 to teach *application*.

Routines Flip Chart

Apply Amazing Words

As students read "Dogs on Parade" on p. 51, have them think about how *resilient* the narrator is in his *application* of his talents in a new direction.

Connect to reading

Explain that today students will read about a clumsy girl who wants to learn to square dance. Help students establish a purpose for reading. As they read, they should think about how the Question of the Week and the Amazing Words, *resilient* and *application* apply to a clumsy, accident-prone girl.

ELL Reinforce Vocabulary Use the Day 2 instruction on ELL Poster 17 to teach lesson vocabulary and discuss the lesson concept.

Poster 17

Objectives

- Use the meanings of the suffixes *-ly* and *-ian* to determine the meanings of unfamiliar words.
- Understand how hyperbole is used in fiction.
- Understand story structure by recognizing the climax of a story.

Word Analysis
Suffixes *-ly, -ian*

Teach suffixes *-ly, -ian*

Tell students that suffixes are letters added to the end of a word that change the word's meaning or part of speech. When added to a word, the suffix *-ly* forms adjectives or adverbs that mean "having the qualities of, happening at intervals of" or denotes manner or degree. The suffix *-ian* forms adjectives or nouns that mean "of or from a certain place or group." Have students choose one word from the Base Word column and add a suffix from the Suffix column to build a new word. Point out how sometimes one or more letters gets dropped when adding a suffix.

Model the skill

I will choose the word *happy* from the Base Word column and look for a suffix in the Suffix column that can form a new word. I can add the suffix *-ly* to *happy* to make the word *happily*. *Happily* is an adjective that means "in a happy manner."

Base Word				Suffix
happy	frill	perfect	safe	*-ly*
library	accidental	music	electric	*-ian*

Guide practice

Have students combine words from both columns to build new words.

On their own

Have students use the suffixes to determine the meaning of the new words they created. Then have them use a printed or electronic dictionary to confirm the meaning of each word and determine the word's part of speech before and after the addition of the suffix. Follow the Strategy for Meaningful Word Parts to teach the word *frilly*.

ROUTINE — **Strategy for Meaningful Word Parts**

1. **Introduce word parts** Circle the base word and suffix. I will circle *frill* and *-ly*. Notice how the word and suffix share the letter *l*.
2. **Connect to meaning** Define each part. *Frill* is a ruffle. The suffix *-ly* means "having the qualities of."
3. **Read the word** Blend the meaningful word parts together to read *frilly*. Then blend the meanings to find the meaning of *frilly*. *Frilly* is "something with the quality of ruffles."

Continue the routine with the words *musician* and *safely*.

Routines Flip Chart

Literary Terms
Hyperbole

Teach hyperbole

Tell students that hyperbole, or exaggeration, is a type of figurative language. An author uses hyperbole when he or she overstates something or makes it greater than it actually is. It is used to emphasize a point and not to deceive, and is found in fiction, especially in tall tales. It is often funny.

Model hyperbole

Let's look at "The School Dance." I don't see any exaggeration in this passage. Can you think of ways to add exaggeration to this story? (Answers will vary but could include that Victor felt so weird dancing that he thought his head was spinning around the room.)

Guide practice

From *Tripping Over the Lunch Lady*, read the sixth paragraph on p. 56. Explain that it is probably an exaggeration that the character's entire life changed by seeing something on television.

On their own

Have students look for examples of hyperbole in their Student Edition.

Story Structure
Climax

Teach climax

One of the main components of a story is the plot, or the events or incidents that happen in the story. One major point in the plot is the **climax,** the point when the conflict is directly confronted.

Model the strategy

I know that a story has a plot that centers around a conflict or problem. The climax is when this conflict is confronted. When I review "The School Dance," I see that the climax comes when his friend Nadia asks him to dance. Victor has to decide if he will dance or not.

Guide practice

Discuss the importance of looking for the conflict in a story. Once they understand the problem, then they can continue to read to see the conflict resolved.

On their own

Have students preview the illustrations in *Tripping Over the Lunch Lady*. Ask students how certain illustrations show events that foreshadow or give rise to future events shown in illustrations at the end of the story.

Academic Vocabulary

climax the point in a plot when the conflict is directly confronted

Objectives

- Use context clues to determine the meanings of unfamiliar words.
- Read grade-level text with accuracy.

Vocabulary Strategy for Unfamiliar Words

Context Clues

Context clues are the words and sentences found around an unknown word that may help you figure out a word's meaning.

Strategy for Context Clues

1. Look for clues in the words and phrases around the unknown word.
2. Take a guess at the word's meaning. Does it make sense in the sentence?
3. Use a dictionary to check your guess.

W•7

Student Edition p. W•7

Teach unfamiliar words

Envision It!

Tell students that when they encounter an unfamiliar word, they can use the strategy of looking for context clues to determine the word's meaning. Explain how the words and sentences around an unfamiliar word can help students understand its meaning. Refer students to *Words!* on p. W•7 in the Student Edition for additional practice.

Model the strategy

Think Aloud

Write on the board: *Her sprained ankle was bandaged, but Marcie said it didn't hurt very much anymore.* I can figure out the meaning of sprained by looking at the other words in the sentence. I can tell from the context her ankle was bandaged and that it hurt. So I can determine that *sprained* must mean that she injured her ankle.

Guide practice

Read these sentences from "Dogs on Parade": *I'm your radio host, Spot the Dalmatian. As you might guess, I got my name because I'm a white dog covered with black spots*. Have students determine the meaning of Dalmatian using context clues. For additional support, use Envision It! Pictured Vocabulary Cards or Tested Vocabulary Cards.

On their own

Read "Dogs on Parade" on p. 51. Have students list the context words that give clues to the meanings of *promenading, substitute* and *frilly* in this selection. For additional practice, use the *Reader's and Writer's Notebook* p. 260.

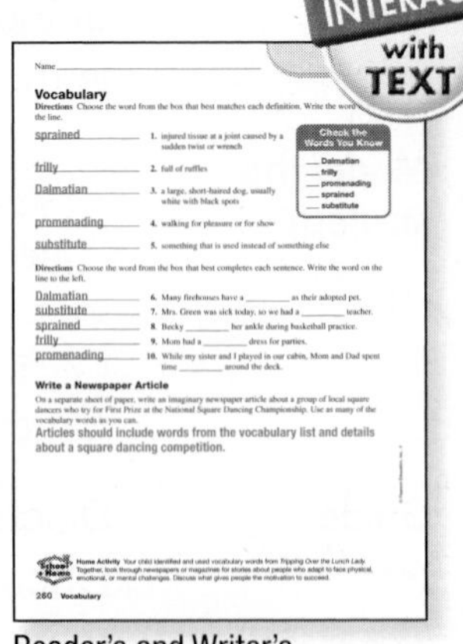

INTERACT with TEXT

Name ______

Vocabulary

Directions Choose the word from the box that best matches each definition. Write the word on the line.

Check the Words You Know: ___ Dalmatian ___ frilly ___ promenading ___ sprained ___ substitute

sprained 1. injured tissue at a joint caused by a sudden twist or wrench
frilly 2. full of ruffles
Dalmatian 3. a large, short-haired dog, usually white with black spots
promenading 4. walking for pleasure or for show
substitute 5. something that is used instead of something else

Directions Choose the word from the box that best completes each sentence. Write the word on the line to the left.

Dalmatian 6. Many firehouses have a ______ as their adopted pet.
substitute 7. Mrs. Green was sick today, so we had a ______ teacher.
sprained 8. Becky ______ her ankle during basketball practice.
frilly 9. Mom had a ______ dress for parties.
promenading 10. While my sister and I played in our cabin, Mom and Dad spent time ______ around the deck.

Write a Newspaper Article

On a separate sheet of paper, write an imaginary newspaper article about a group of local square dancers who try for First Prize at the National Square Dancing Championship. Use as many of the vocabulary words as you can.

Articles should include words from the vocabulary list and details about a square dancing competition.

Home Activity Your child identified and used vocabulary words from *Tripping Over the Lunch Lady*. Together, look through newspapers or magazines for stories about people who adapt to face physical, emotional, or mental challenges. Discuss what gives people the motivation to succeed.

260 Vocabulary

Reader's and Writer's Notebook p. 260

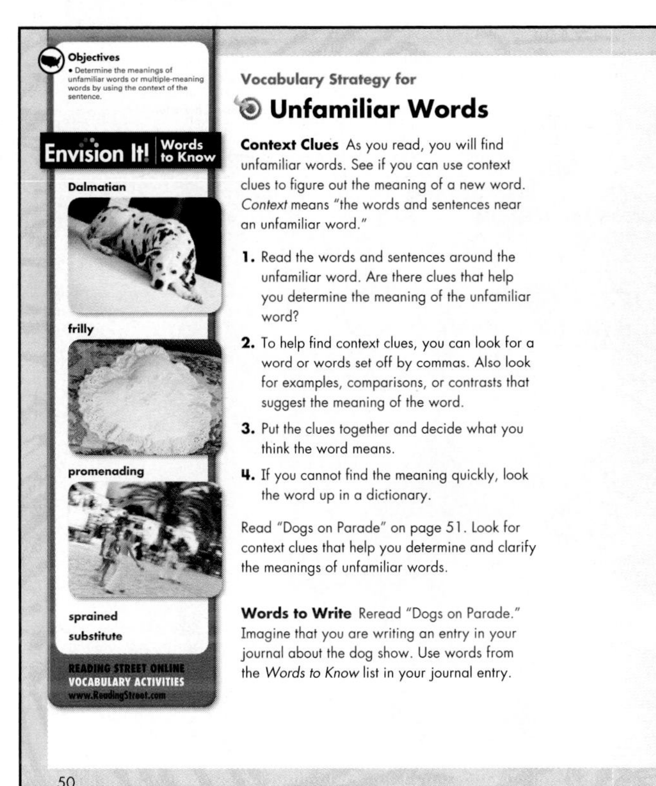

Objectives

• Determine the meanings of unfamiliar words or multiple-meaning words by using the context of the sentence.

Envision It! Words to Know

Dalmatian

frilly

promenading

sprained

substitute

READING STREET ONLINE VOCABULARY ACTIVITIES www.ReadingStreet.com

Vocabulary Strategy for

Unfamiliar Words

Context Clues As you read, you will find unfamiliar words. See if you can use context clues to figure out the meaning of a new word. *Context* means "the words and sentences near an unfamiliar word."

1. Read the words and sentences around the unfamiliar word. Are there clues that help you determine the meaning of the unfamiliar word?
2. To help find context clues, you can look for a word or words set off by commas. Also look for examples, comparisons, or contrasts that suggest the meaning of the word.
3. Put the clues together and decide what you think the word means.
4. If you cannot find the meaning quickly, look the word up in a dictionary.

Read "Dogs on Parade" on page 51. Look for context clues that help you determine and clarify the meanings of unfamiliar words.

Words to Write Reread "Dogs on Parade." Imagine that you are writing an entry in your journal about the dog show. Use words from the *Words to Know* list in your journal entry.

50

Dogs on Parade

"Hello, everyone, and welcome to the third annual Westown Dog Show. I'm your radio host, Spot the Dalmatian. As you might guess, I got my name because I'm a white dog covered with black spots. And I usually compete in the dog show. But just last week I jumped down from a couch and injured my leg. The vet says I sprained it. Maybe that's why my owners tell me to stay off of the furniture. Anyway, I'm here today to bring you all of the action from the show.

"And here we go! The dogs have entered the building and are all walking in a line around the arena. I wish you could see them promenading around this big hall. They all look great!

"The first dog is my friend Dot. She's walking for me. Because of my leg, I needed a substitute, or someone to take my place, while my leg heals. And right behind her is Sandy the Cocker Spaniel. She looks so pretty with that frilly collar she wears. Just a piece of lacy white cloth can work wonders!

"Well, it's time to break for a commercial. Stay tuned, and I'll be back with you in sixty seconds!"

Your Turn!

Need a Review? For additional help with context clues, see *Words!*

Ready to Try It? Use what you've learned as you read *Tripping Over the Lunch Lady* on pp. 52–67.

51

Student Edition pp. 50–51

Lesson Vocabulary

Dalmatian a dog that has a white coat with black or brown spots

frilly clothing that has ruffles

promenading to be walking for show

sprained to be injured by a sudden twist

substitute a person or thing taking the place of another

Differentiated Instruction

Strategic Intervention

Unknown Words Have students work in pairs to look for context clues for the meaning of *substitute* in "Dogs on Parade." Have students look for words set off by commas as a clue to the definition. Ask students to share their definitions. Then have them write a sentence using the word *substitute*.

Reread for Fluency

Accuracy

Model fluency Read paragraph 2 of "Dogs on Parade" aloud making sure that your reading is accurate. Tell students that you are reading the passage carefully so that you don't make any mistakes.

ROUTINE Paired Reading

1. **Select a passage** For "Dogs on Parade," use the whole passage.
2. **Reader 1** Students read the entire passage, switching readers at the end of the second paragraph.
3. **Reader 2** Partners reread the passage. This time the other student begins.
4. **Reread** For optimal fluency and comprehension, have partners continue to reread aloud three or four times.
5. **Corrective Feedback** Listen as students read. Provide feedback about their accuracy and encourage them to read the words with no mistakes.

Routines Flip Chart

English Language Learners

Build Academic Vocabulary Use the pictures of the lesson vocabulary on p. 50 to teach the meanings of *Dalmatian, frilly,* and *promenading*. Call on pairs to write the words on sticky notes and use them to label images of the words on the ELL Poster.

Objectives

- Understand the elements of realistic fiction.
- Use illustrations to preview and predict.
- Set a purpose for reading.

Student Edition pp. 52–53

Build Background

Discuss overcoming obstacles

Team Talk Have students turn to a partner and discuss the Question of the Week and these questions about overcoming obstacles. Have them elicit and consider each other's suggestions.

- What are some obstacles you have overcome in your life?
- What would you tell a friend who was trying to overcome the obstacle of not doing well in math class?
- How might someone overcome the obstacle of not being good at a certain sport?

Connect to selection

Have students discuss their answers with the class. Possible responses: I have overcome the obstacle of not being good at baseball. I would tell my friend to study hard in math and ask the teacher for help. I would also help them understand their homework. To get better at a certain sport, you could practice more. You could also try to find a sport that you are better at. For additional opportunities to build background, use the Background Building Audio.

Prereading Strategies

Genre Explain that **realistic fiction** has characters, settings, and actions that seem real, but the author has made them up.

Have students preview the selection by looking at its illustrations. Have them predict what they think the story will be about.

Set purpose Prior to reading, have students set their own purposes for reading this selection. To help students set a purpose, ask them to think about what they have done to overcome obstacles in their own lives.

Strategy Response Log

INTERACT with TEXT

Have students use the Strategy Response Log on p. 23 in the *Reader's and Writer's Notebook* to identify the characteristics of realistic fiction. As they read, have them look for characteristics of the genre.

Small Group Time

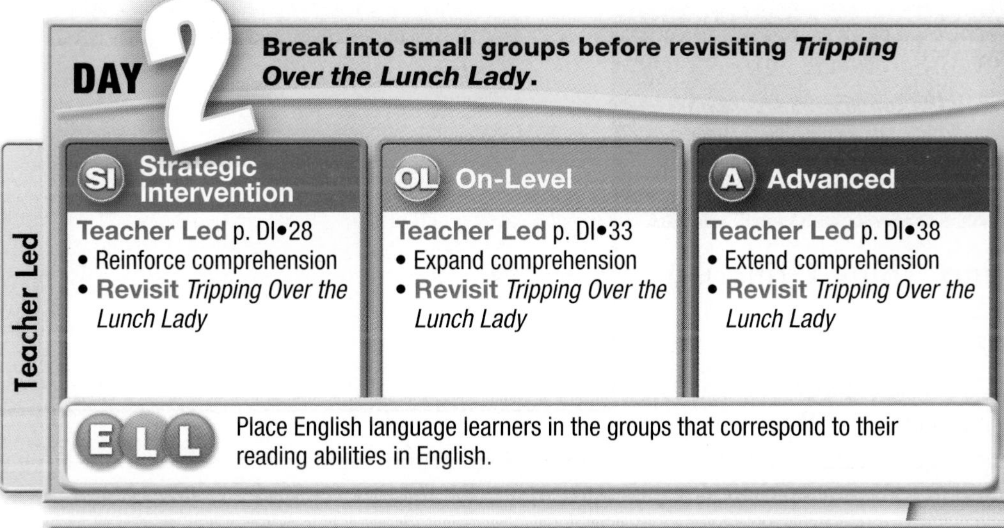

DAY 2 **Break into small groups before revisiting *Tripping Over the Lunch Lady*.**

Teacher Led

SI Strategic Intervention	OL On-Level	A Advanced
Teacher Led p. DI•28 • Reinforce comprehension • **Revisit** *Tripping Over the Lunch Lady*	**Teacher Led** p. DI•33 • Expand comprehension • **Revisit** *Tripping Over the Lunch Lady*	**Teacher Led** p. DI•38 • Extend comprehension • **Revisit** *Tripping Over the Lunch Lady*

ELL Place English language learners in the groups that correspond to their reading abilities in English.

Practice Stations	Independent Activities
• Words to Know • Get Fluent • Word Wise	• Background Building Audio • *Reader's and Writer's Notebook* • Research and Inquiry

Differentiated Instruction

 **Strategic Intervention**

Work with students to set a purpose for reading, or if time permits, have students work with partners to set purposes.

 **Advanced**

Have students learn about athletes who had to overcome an obstacle to be successful.

Multidraft Reading

For **Whole Group** instruction, choose one of the reading options below. For each reading, have students set the purpose indicated.

Option 1

Day 2 Read the selection. Use Guide Comprehension to monitor and clarify understanding.

Day 3 Reread the selection. Use Extend Thinking to develop higher-order thinking skills.

Option 2

Day 2 Read the first half of the selection, using both Guide Comprehension and Extend Thinking instruction.

Day 3 Read the second half of the selection, using both Guide Comprehension and Extend Thinking instruction.

English Language Learners

Build Background To build background, review the selection summary in English (*ELL Handbook,* p. 127). Use the Retelling Cards to provide visual support for the summary.

DAY 2 Read and Comprehend

Objectives

◎ Generalize to aid comprehension.

OPTION 1 Guide Comprehension Skills and Strategies

Teach Generalize

◎ **Generalize** Have students read p. 54. Sometimes when you read, you are given ideas about several things or people and you can make a statement about all of them together. This statement is called a *generalization.* You can use clue words, such as *most, all, always,* and *never,* to help you make your own generalizations and identify generalizations in what you read. Ask students what generalization they can infer about Jinx. (Jinx is always having accidents.)

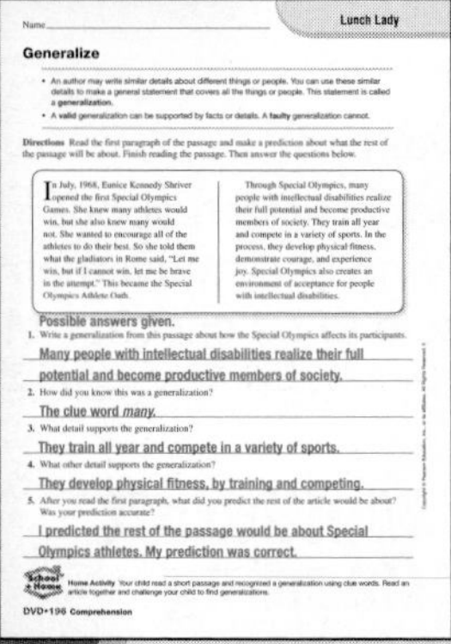

Name________ Lunch Lady

Generalize

- An author may write similar details about different things or people. You can use these similar details to make a general statement that covers all the things or people. This statement is called a **generalization**.
- A **valid** generalization can be supported by facts or details. A **faulty** generalization cannot.

Directions Read the first paragraph of the passage and make a prediction about what the rest of the passage will be about. Finish reading the passage. Then answer the questions below.

In July, 1968, Eunice Kennedy Shriver opened the first Special Olympics Games. She knew many athletes would win, but she also knew many would not. She wanted to encourage all of the athletes to do their best. So she told them what the gladiators in Rome said, "Let me win, but if I cannot win, let me be brave in the attempt." This became the Special Olympics Athlete Oath.

Through Special Olympics, many people with intellectual disabilities realize their full potential and become productive members of society. They train all year and compete in a variety of sports. In the process, they develop physical fitness, demonstrate courage, and experience joy. Special Olympics also creates an environment of acceptance for people with intellectual disabilities.

Possible answers given.

1. Write a generalization from this passage about how the Special Olympics affects its participants.
   Many people with intellectual disabilities realize their full potential and become productive members of society.
2. How did you know this was a generalization?
   The clue word *many.*
3. What detail supports the generalization?
   They train all year and compete in a variety of sports.
4. What other detail supports the generalization?
   They develop physical fitness, by training and competing.
5. After you read the first paragraph, what did you predict the rest of the article would be about? Was your prediction accurate?
   I predicted the rest of the passage would be about Special Olympics athletes. My prediction was correct.

School + Home **Home Activity** Your child read a short passage and recognized a generalization using clue words. Read an article together and challenge your child to find generalizations.

DVD•196 Comprehension

Let's Practice It!
TR DVD•196

Corrective Feedback

If... students are not able to infer a generalization,
then... model generalizing.

Model the Skill

Think Aloud When we read p. 54, we learn a lot about Jinx. What are some things we find out? (Possible response: She falls down stairs, breaks her arm, and falls off the trampoline.)

I'm never going to be a gymnast.

You know how people say that some folks can't walk and chew gum at the same time? Oh yeah, they were talking about me.

I fall down stairs and roll out of bed onto the floor. I drop things on my toes and get trapped in closets. I've broken my arm making cookies. Don't ask. I even got locked in my own locker once. I wanted to see what it was like inside, and had to stay there till the end of school for the janitor to let me out.

Do you know how embarrassing it is to be caught in a locker? Just ask me.

I'm especially not good with my feet *off* the ground. I was telling Mr. Deimeister just that, about the time I went flying off the trampoline over Tony Friedman's head yesterday and scared him so bad (he wasn't spotting for me but was talking to Gus Jackson about what they were going to do after school) that he choked on some gum he wasn't supposed to have in his mouth.

Right around the time he was having the Heimlich done on him and Gus was screaming to apply direct pressure (luckily we'd just had a first-aid class the period before gym), I realized that what everybody calls me is probably true.

Jinx.

That's how everyone refers to me. My own parents, even.

Mom thinks it's cute. My uncle Jeff began calling me Jinx when I started crawling backward as a baby and getting stuck in boxes, under tables, and even, the story goes, a pair of my dad's boots.

54

Student Edition pp. 54–55

Genre • Evaluation Evaluate the events in the story so far. Do you think that the things that happen to Jinx could really happen? How does this tie into the genre of the story? Yes, the events might be a little exaggerated, but these things could really happen. The genre of the story is realistic fiction, which means that the story is made up, but that the things that happen in the story could possibly happen in real life.

OPTION 2 Extend Thinking Think Critically

Higher-Order Thinking Skills

◎ **Generalize • Synthesis** What is one generalization you can infer about the people around Jinx? What evidence from the text supports this generalization? The people around Jinx usually get hurt, but they still like Jinx and want to be her friend. She made Tony Friedman choke on his gum, and everyone calls her Jinx. Jinx's mom thinks her clumsiness is cute.

From all this information, I can make a generalization about Jinx. She is always having accidents.

55

Review **Draw Conclusions • Evaluation** Is *Jinx* a good nickname for the main character? Why or why not? Jinx gets into a lot of accidents that hurt other people. The word *jinx* means "to bring bad luck."

On Their Own

Have students reread p. 54 and make a list of all the things that happened to Jinx that lead to the generalization above. For additional practice, use *Let's Practice It!* p. 196 on the *Teacher Resources DVD-ROM.*

Differentiated Instruction

SI Strategic Intervention

Vocabulary Review the definition of *jinx* (something that brings bad luck). Ask students to reread p. 54 to find an example of how Jinx was bad luck for someone else. (She scared Tony Friedman and he choked on his gum.)

ELL

English Language Learners

Activate prior knowledge Ask students if they know anyone like Jinx who is not coordinated and does not do well in gym. Do they know anyone who has a lot of accidents? Encourage discussion about the people they may know with these characteristics and compare them to Jinx.

Read and Comprehend

Objectives

- Use the strategy of predict and set purpose to aid comprehension.

OPTION 1 Skills and Strategies, continued

Teach Predict and Set Purpose

Predict and Set Purpose Have students read pp. 56–57 and predict what will happen with Jinx's square dancing idea. (She might get hurt or hurt someone else while square dancing.) Based on their predictions, ask students what purpose they can set for reading the rest of the story.

Corrective Feedback

If... students are unable to make a prediction and set a purpose,
then... model predicting and setting purposes.

Model the Strategy

Think Aloud: Think about what you already know about Jinx. Do you think that square dancing will go well for her? (No, I don't think it will.) What can you predict about Jinx and square dancing?

Dad pats me on the head like an old skunky stray and says Uncle Jeff was just like me.

Yeah, right.

Uncle Jeff drives a Porsche and lives in a cabin in the woods with a hot tub.

I'm too uncoordinated to ever drive a car, and I'm pretty sure a hot tub is just a bad accident waiting to happen. I love Uncle Jeff anyway, though. I guess he might have been a jinx back in the day. But hey, he must have grown out of it, which doesn't necessarily mean I will.

I'm never going to be able to keep my feet together and fly perfectly on the trampoline. I'm never going to be able to make a basket without breaking somebody's bones (the doctors did do a good job on Mr. Deimeister's nose, though). I'm never going to run like my sister or kick a soccer ball like my brother without falling, throwing up, or pulling a muscle on me or somebody else. My dad won't even let me use a steak knife. I still have to cut meat with one of those plastic picnic things that sort of look like a knife.

But a while ago everything changed—my whole life, even, because of something I saw on the Folk Arts Channel. A couple days after that, a picture in an album made it feel exactly right.

56

Student Edition pp. 56–57

Review **Draw Conclusions • Evaluation** Jinx draws the conclusion that she will become a square dance star because she thinks the woman on television was sending her a message and she found a picture of her mother square dancing. Do you think that her conclusion is accurate? Why or why not?

OPTION 2 Think Critically, continued

Higher-Order Thinking Skills

Predict and Set Purpose • Synthesis How can making predictions and setting a purpose for reading help you better understand the text? Possible response: You know what to look for when you are reading so that you do not miss any details that might be important to the story.

(She will probably get hurt or hurt someone else doing it.) What do you want to find out as you continue to read? (if Jinx gets hurt or hurts someone else during square dancing) Setting a purpose to read will help you understand the story better and make it more interesting.

On Their Own

Have students reread p. 57. Ask them to make another prediction about Jinx.

Connect to Social Studies

Square dancing began in New England. The first settlers brought their national dances with them. After a week of hard work, they would gather on Saturday nights and dance as they did back home. As the communities grew, people from different backgrounds added their dances to the mix. This is how square dancing became the rich and varied dance that it is today.

Yes, ladies and gentlemen, boys and girls, people I've run over, stepped on, and tripped up . . . I am going to be a square dance star.

The dancers on television floated over the floor, arm in arm. They smiled, laughed, and nobody fell into anybody else or sprained anything. They were all so happy and even seemed to really like each other. And then I saw this woman who looked just like my mom. She could have been my mom, she looked so much like her. Then in the middle of a swing around she looked the camera in the eye and smiled at me. Honest, it was as if she looked right at me to say: "You could be me, and look—I can do this."

Wow.

It was a couple of days later when a picture fell out of a photo album I'd just dropped in the fish tank (I rescued everything pretty quick, except now our goldfish hide when I come close to the tank), but there in living color was a picture of my mom arm in arm with this kid with hair way down his back—square dancing.

It was in my genes.

I knew then it was meant to be.

57

Possible response: No, I do not think her conclusion is accurate because seeing someone on TV or finding a picture is not good evidence on which to base a conclusion. Her history of being clumsy is much more important to consider when drawing a conclusion.

Author's Purpose • Analysis Find an example of exaggeration on page 57. Explain why the author would use exaggeration in this type of story. Possible response: Jinx says that the goldfish hide when she comes by. That is an exaggeration because goldfish are probably not smart enough to do that. The author probably used exaggeration to be funny and to show just how clumsy Jinx is.

ELL

English Language Learners

Vocabulary Discuss the meaning of *sprained* on p. 57. Demonstrate by walking around the room limping. Then ask students if they have ever injured themselves as a result of clumsiness and to describe their experiences.

Objectives

- Draw conclusions to aid comprehension.

OPTION 1 Skills and Strategies, continued

Teach Draw Conclusions

Review **Draw Conclusions** Have students read p. 59. Based on the fact that Mr. Deimeister backed away from Jinx, what conclusion can you draw about his feelings toward her? (He was afraid he was going to get hurt again.)

Corrective Feedback

If... students are having difficulty drawing conclusions,
then... model using events in the story to infer and draw conclusions.

Let's Practice It!
TR DVD•197

Model the Skill

Think Aloud Why would someone back away from another person? (Possible response: if he or she is afraid) Why would Mr. Deimeister be afraid of Jinx?

Student Edition pp. 58–59

OPTION 2 Think Critically, continued

Higher-Order Thinking Skills

Review **Draw Conclusions • Analysis** Why might Jinx be so excited about having a square dancing class? Possible response: Jinx thinks she will be good at square dancing. She thinks that it will give her a chance to finally be good at something in gym.

Generalize • Synthesis What generalization can you make about Mr. Deimeister? Possible response: He does not often listen to Jinx, and he is afraid of her.

(Earlier in the story, it said that Jinx had broken Mr. Deimeister's nose.) So, what conclusion can you draw about how Mr. Deimeister feels about Jinx? (Possible response: He is afraid of her.)

And not only am I going to be a star, I'm going to be the fifth-grade school gym square dance champ of the whole world. And nobody's going to stop me—ouch . . .

It's a hard thing to change people's minds about how things are done and to get them to do something new.

This is how it went with Mr. Deimeister when I went to his office and told him what might be the most wonderful thing since kneepads and bandages.

"What?" he said, sort of backing away from me like he always does.

"Square dancing, Mr. Deimeister. Square dancing. It's fun and it's good exercise for everybody. I saw it on the Folk Arts Channel and practiced with a huge stuffed teddy bear."

"What?"

"It was real cool the way the guys swung the girls and everybody skipped and twirled around the room. I think it would be good for us all to learn a new skill, learn to dance with partners ('cause usually the boys don't want to), and get a good workout."

"What?"

"We wouldn't have to wear the frilly dresses or bow ties like they did on TV. I think our regular gym clothes would be okay. Do you think they have square dance music in the band room?"

"What?"

I think a few more meetings with Mr. Deimeister will get him to come around to the square dance way. So later that day I dropped off some square dance music at his office. He wasn't there and I accidentally dropped a ten-pound weight I was moving off his desk onto a fishing pole that fell on the floor. There was a stuffed fish over his desk.

Scary.

59

Predict and Set Purpose • Analysis
What prediction can you make about what will happen next in the story? Possible responses: Mr. Deimeister won't let the class do square dancing. Jinx will keep asking Mr. Deimeister to have square dancing. If the class does square dance, Jinx might get hurt or hurt someone else.

On Their Own

Have students reread p. 59. Ask them to use the text to infer or draw a conclusion about how Jinx feels about Mr. Deimeister. For additional practice, use *Let's Practice It!* p. 197 on the *Teacher Resources DVD-ROM.*

Differentiated Instruction

SI Strategic Intervention

Draw conclusions Work with students in small groups to help them draw a conclusion about how Mr. Deimeister feels about Jinx. Write three headings on the board: *What I Already Know*, *Clues From Text*, and *Conclusions*. Ask volunteers for answers to fill in the chart. (Students know that Jinx has broken Mr. Deimeister's nose; they learn that he backs away from Jinx; they can conclude that he is afraid of Jinx.)

ELL English Language Learners

Generalize Read aloud paragraphs 3–10 on p. 59. Emphasize Mr. Deimeister's responses *(What?)* After the first three paragraphs have students read his response with you. Ask if Mr. Deimeister was listening to Jinx. (No, he was not.) Review the definition of *generalize* and then have students work as a group to make a generalization about Mr. Deimeister and Jinx.

DAY 2 Read and Comprehend

Objectives

◎ Use context clues to understand unfamiliar words.

OPTION 1 Skills and Strategies, continued

Teach Unfamiliar Words

Unfamiliar Words Have a volunteer read aloud the third paragraph on p. 60. Ask students if they know the meaning of *promenading*. Have them find the context clues that will help them understand the meaning of the word.

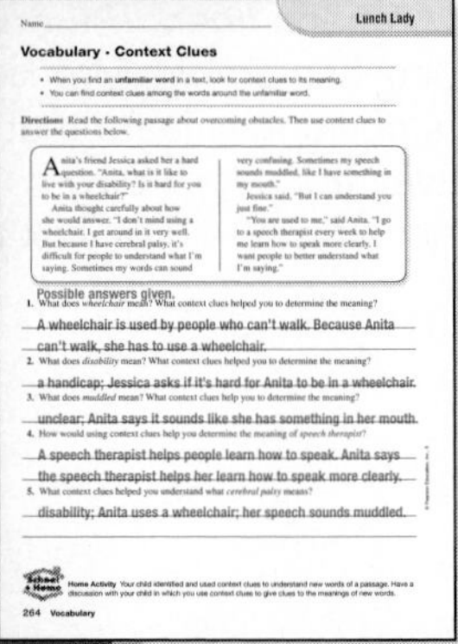

Name ______ Lunch Lady

Vocabulary • Context Clues

- When you find an **unfamiliar word** in a text, look for context clues to its meaning.
- You can find context clues among the words around the unfamiliar word.

Directions Read the following passage about overcoming obstacles. Then use context clues to answer the questions below.

Anita's friend Jessica asked her a hard question. "Anita, what is it like to live with your disability? Is it hard for you to be in a wheelchair?"

Anita thought carefully about how she would answer. "I don't mind using a wheelchair. I get around in it very well. But because I have cerebral palsy, it's difficult for people to understand what I'm saying. Sometimes my words can sound very confusing. Sometimes my speech sounds muddled, like I have something in my mouth."

Jessica said, "But I can understand you just fine."

"You are used to me," said Anita. "I go to a speech therapist every week to help me learn how to speak more clearly. I want people to better understand what I'm saying."

Possible answers given.

1. What does *wheelchair* mean? What context clues helped you to determine the meaning?
   A wheelchair is used by people who can't walk. Because Anita can't walk, she has to use a wheelchair.
2. What does *disability* mean? What context clues helped you to determine the meaning?
   a handicap; Jessica asks if it's hard for Anita to be in a wheelchair.
3. What does *muddled* mean? What context clues help you to determine the meaning?
   unclear; Anita says it sounds like she has something in her mouth.
4. How would using context clues help you determine the meaning of *speech therapist*?
   A speech therapist helps people learn how to speak. Anita says the speech therapist helps her learn how to speak more clearly.
5. What context clues helped you understand what *cerebral palsy* means?
   disability; Anita uses a wheelchair; her speech sounds muddled.

Home Activity Your child identified and used context clues to understand new words of a passage. Have a discussion with your child in which you use context clues to give clues to the meanings of new words.

264 Vocabulary

Reader's and Writer's Notebook p. 264

Corrective Feedback

If... students are unable to figure out the meaning of *promenading*, **then...** model using context clues to define unfamiliar words.

Model the Skill

Think Aloud What clue words or phrases on page 60 can help you figure out the meaning of *promenading*? (dancing, two feet safely planted on the wooden floor)

I thought we'd be dancing by now, but days after my meeting with Mr. Deimeister we're still on the trampoline that decided a long time ago it didn't like me. Evil is what it is. Evil. And it won't even take pity on my poor classmates, who have to keep catching me and throwing me back on it.

Mr. Deimeister keeps yelling, "Spot Jinx, spot Jinx!"

I'm feeling like a clumsy Dalmatian with all the spot Jinx going on. And I'm thinking how happy I'd be if my two feet were safely planted on the wooden floor, promenading down the court. Square dancing would save me.

I'd be the world's best square dancer. Maybe I could even stop wars and hunger with square dancing. I'd go to other countries and dance with my square dance group that would not include any of the people who back away when I use a fork in the lunchroom or have their arms stretched out to catch me when I'm going down the stairs to art class.

Maybe I'd get some award for ending unhappiness in the world by spreading square dance love all over the planet.

Maybe I'd change the whole wide wor—

"Spot Jinx!"

And maybe I'll do that after I come back from the nurse's office.

"I don't really want to square dance, Jinx."

Victoria is my best friend and I was counting on her to help me in the gym square dance campaign. Anyway, she's a good dancer and hasn't broken Mr. Deimeister's nose.

60

Student Edition pp. 60–61

OPTION 2 Think Critically, continued

Higher-Order Thinking Skills

Unfamiliar Words • Synthesis Use context clues to determine the meaning of the word *campaign* on page 60, paragraph 10. Jinx has been doing many things to try to convince Mr. Deimeister to have a square dancing class in gym. A *campaign* is a set of activities a person does to achieve a goal or get something done.

Generalize • Synthesis Based on what you have read of the story so far, what new generalization you can infer about Jinx? Possible responses: She is a very determined person. She never stops talking about square dancing.

What does Jinx want to do? (square dance on the gym floor) We know that Jinx wants to dance. Dances have specific movements. I think *promenading* is a special square-dancing move.

“C’mon, Vic. You have to be with me on this. I’m sick of dodge ball and volleyball. I broke half the gym windows and knocked out two people before Mr. Deimeister sat me on the bench to watch the clock.”

“I still don’t want to square dance, Jinx. We’ll look stupid. The boys won’t do it and all the girls will end up dancing together with the boys laughing at us.”

Victoria pulls her braids back and blows a big bubble. Señora Smith comes over and taps her on the shoulder.

“No gum in Spanish class. How can you learn a new language with Super Bubble in your mouth?”

When Vic swallows the gum, Señora Smith makes a face and goes back to teaching us how to ask for a bathroom in Spanish.

“So what if they laugh. It’ll be fun. Our feet will be on the ground and there won’t be any round hard balls to knock anybody down or break anything. Help me out. This could be great.”

My best friend forever, Vic will be.

She’s going to the gym during our free period to practice with me.

We’ll be square dance champions of the world when we finish.

Square dancing forever.

61

On Their Own

Ask students to find the context clues that help them figure out the meaning of *Dalmatian* on p. 60, paragraph 3. For more practice, use *Reader’s and Writer’s Notebook* p. 264.

Background Knowledge • Synthesis • Text to Self Describe someone you know who is clumsy like Jinx. Possible response: My little sister is just learning to walk, and she is always falling down and knocking things over.

Check Predictions Have students look back at the predictions they made earlier and discuss whether they were accurate. Then have students preview the rest of the selection and either adjust their predictions accordingly or make new predictions.

Differentiated Instruction

Strategic Intervention

Generalize Work with students in small groups to help them make a new generalization about Jinx. Write on the board: *Generalization.* Draw three lines from the word. Ask volunteers for three details about Jinx and square dancing. Write the answers on the board. Help students make a generalization based on the three details.

Advanced

Vocabulary Have students compare and contrast the meanings of *spot* as used on p. 60, paragraphs 2 and 3. Ask students to decide why the author wrote these two paragraphs this way.

ELL

English Language Learners

Vocabulary Use the picture of the volleyball net on p. 61 to teach the meaning of the word. Ask students to find the context clues on pp. 60–61 that help them understand how to play volleyball.

Predict Have students look back at the pictures on pp. 52–61. Then have them make predictions about how the story will end based solely on the pictures they have seen so far.

If you want to teach this selection in two sessions, stop here.

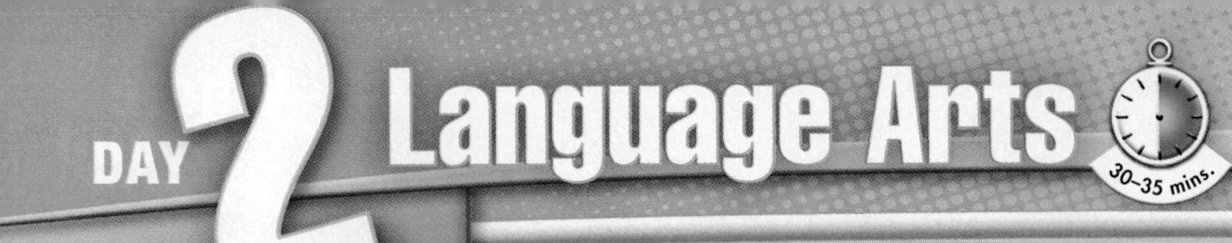

Objectives

- Find pertinent information from print, online, and personal sources.
- Recognize and correctly use pronouns and antecedents.
- Practice correctly spelling words with the prefixes *over-*, *under-*, *sub-*, *super-*, and *out-*.

Research and Inquiry
Navigate/Search

Teach Have students follow their research plan to collect information about a famous person who has overcome an obstacle. In addition to periodicals, they can search the Internet using keywords that relate to their inquiry questions.

Model Think Aloud When looking for information about dyslexia, I found that it is the most common learning disability people face. I used the keywords *Nolan Ryan dyslexia* to lead me to more specific information. I found several links, including newspaper articles about Nolan Ryan. I'm also going to ask other people, such as my doctor, to tell me what they know about dyslexia. The resource room teacher works with a lot of students with dyslexia, so I am going to talk to him too.

Guide practice Have students evaluate the relevance, validity, and reliability of sources for their research. Explain that a doctor may be a reliable source when talking about an illness or a learning disability but not when talking about sports statistics. Discuss and suggest reliable sources for this inquiry project.

On their own Have students search for pictures and other visual aids appropriate for their description. They may use a picture of the person they are studying, or they may use a diagram or other visual aid that tells about the physical or mental obstacle.

Conventions
Pronouns and Antecedents

Teach Write these sentences on the board. *Jinx said that Jinx would like to be a square dancer. Mr. Deimeister broke some of Mr. Deimeister's ribs in a fishing accident.* Explain how much less awkward the sentences would be if they used pronouns. Cross out the second *Jinx* in the first sentence, and ask students what pronoun you should use to refer back to the antecedent. Fix the second sentence in the same way.

Guide practice Explain that sometimes using a pronoun can make sentence meaning unclear. If a pronoun's antecedent is unclear, the sentence should be rewritten.

Unclear: Dad and Amir exercise daily in his room.

Clear: Dad and Amir exercise daily in Amir's room.

Daily Fix-It Use Daily Fix-It numbers 3 and 4 in the right margin.

Connect to oral language Have students look for and read aloud sentences that have pronouns and their antecedents on p. 59 of *Tripping Over the Lunch Lady.* (third paragraph; eleventh paragraph, first sentence)

On their own For additional practice, use *Reader's and Writer's Notebook* p. 261.

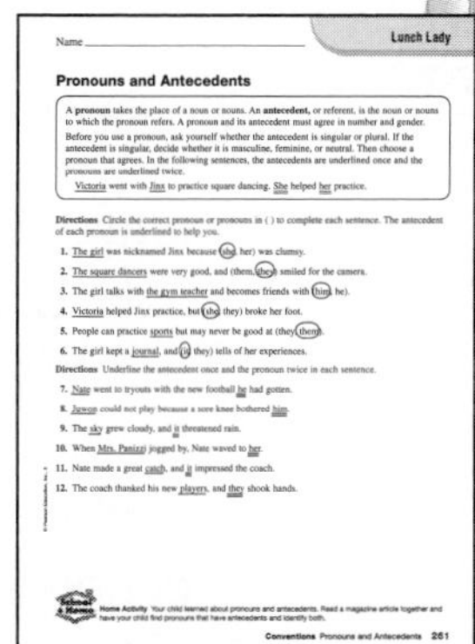

Name ______ Lunch Lady

Pronouns and Antecedents

A **pronoun** takes the place of a noun or nouns. An **antecedent,** or referent, is the noun or nouns to which the pronoun refers. A pronoun and its antecedent must agree in number and gender. Before you use a pronoun, ask yourself whether the antecedent is singular or plural. If the antecedent is singular, decide whether it is masculine, feminine, or neutral. Then choose a pronoun that agrees. In the following sentences, the antecedents are underlined once and the pronouns are underlined twice.

Victoria went with Jinx to practice square dancing. She helped her practice.

Directions Circle the correct pronoun or pronouns in ( ) to complete each sentence. The antecedent of each pronoun is underlined to help you.

1. The girl was nicknamed Jinx because (she, her) was clumsy.
2. The square dancers were very good, and (them, they) smiled for the camera.
3. The girl talks with the gym teacher and becomes friends with (him, he).
4. Victoria helped Jinx practice, but (she, they) broke her foot.
5. People can practice sports but may never be good at (they, them).
6. The girl kept a journal, and (it, they) tells of her experiences.

Directions Underline the antecedent once and the pronoun twice in each sentence.

7. Nate went to tryouts with the new football he had gotten.
8. Jewon could not play because a sore knee bothered him.
9. The sky grew cloudy, and it threatened rain.
10. When Mrs. Panizzi jogged by, Nate waved to her.
11. Nate made a great catch, and it impressed the coach.
12. The coach thanked his new players, and they shook hands.

Home Activity Your child learned about pronouns and antecedents. Read a magazine article together and have your child find pronouns that have antecedents and identify both.

Conventions Pronouns and Antecedents 261

Reader's and Writer's Notebook p. 261

Spelling
Prefixes *over-, under-, sub-, super-, out-*

Teach Remind students of the rule that when the prefixes *over-, under-, sub-, super-,* and *out-* are added to words, the spelling and pronunciation of the base word stay the same.

Guide practice Write *sub-* and *super-* on the board. Point out that *sub-* has one syllable, whereas *super-* has two. Have students work in pairs to read each spelling word, identify the prefix, and then write the word in the proper list: words with one-syllable prefix, words with two-syllable prefix.

On their own For additional practice, use *Reader's and Writer's Notebook* p. 262.

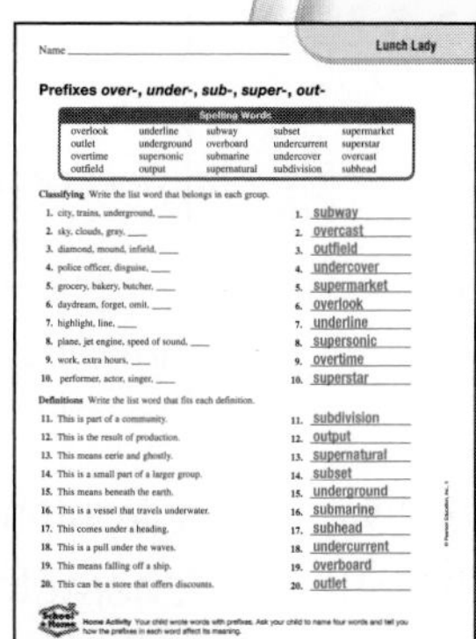

Name ______ Lunch Lady

Prefixes *over-, under-, sub-, super-, out-*

Spelling Words				
overlook	underline	subway	subset	supermarket
outlet	underground	overboard	undercurrent	superstar
overtime	supersonic	submarine	undercover	overcast
outfield	output	supernatural	subdivision	subhead

Classifying Write the list word that belongs in each group.

1. city, trains, underground, ___ 1. subway
2. sky, clouds, gray, ___ 2. overcast
3. diamond, mound, infield, ___ 3. outfield
4. police officer, disguise, ___ 4. undercover
5. grocery, bakery, butcher, ___ 5. supermarket
6. daydream, forget, omit, ___ 6. overlook
7. highlight, line, ___ 7. underline
8. plane, jet engine, speed of sound, ___ 8. supersonic
9. work, extra hours, ___ 9. overtime
10. performer, actor, singer, ___ 10. superstar

Definitions Write the list word that fits each definition.

11. This is part of a community. 11. subdivision
12. This is the result of production. 12. output
13. This means eerie and ghostly. 13. supernatural
14. This is a small part of a larger group. 14. subset
15. This means beneath the earth. 15. underground
16. This is a vessel that travels underwater. 16. submarine
17. This comes under a heading. 17. subhead
18. This is a pull under the waves. 18. undercurrent
19. This means falling off a ship. 19. overboard
20. This can be a store that offers discounts. 20. outlet

Home Activity Your child wrote words with prefixes. Ask your child to name four words and tell you how the prefixes in each word affect its meaning.

262 **Spelling** Prefixes over-, under-, sub-, super-, out-

Reader's and Writer's Notebook p. 262

Daily Fix-It

3. When the kids was on the trampoline, Jinx just liked to watch they. *(were; them)*
4. The folk arts Channel was on, and they showed different kinds of dancers. *(Folk Arts; it)*

ELL

English Language Learners

Conventions To provide students with practice on pronouns and antecedents, use the modified grammar lessons in the *ELL Handbook* and the Grammar Jammer! online at: www.ReadingStreet.com

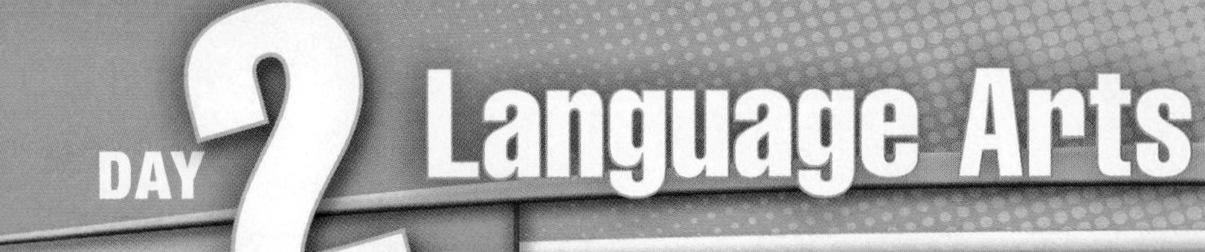

Objectives

- Decide on the writer and recipient of an informal letter.
- Reveal writer's informal speaking voice in a variety of written sentences.

Writing—Friendly Letter
Writing Trait: Sentences

Introduce the prompt

Explain to students that the selection they are reading this week, *Tripping Over the Lunch Lady,* is a funny story told by the main character, Jinx. The language of the story sounds like Jinx talking—informal and casual. Remind students that this is the same tone you use to write a friendly letter. Review the key features of a friendly letter: it is written to someone you know; it has a casual tone; it uses informal language; and it contains a date, salutation, and closing. Remind students to think about these features as they plan their writing. Then explain that they will begin the writing process for a friendly letter today. Read aloud the writing prompt.

Writing Prompt

Write a letter from one character to another from *Tripping Over the Lunch Lady.*

Select the characters

To help us decide who the letter writer and letter receiver will be, we can list some facts about each story character. We can list the information in a chart, with the characters' names across the top and some categories of things we know about the characters down the side. Display a four-column chart. The main character in the story is Jinx. I will write her name in the first column. Another major character is Mr. Deimeister. I'll put his name in the second column. Then there is Jinx's best friend, Vic. There are other, less important characters, but let's just concentrate on these three for now. What do we know about these characters? I think we know something about their personalities and interests. I'll put these down the left side of the chart. Now we can start filling in the information. What is Jinx's personality like? She is funny, can make fun of herself, and she definitely does not seem shy. I'll write this in the chart. What do you know about Mr. Deimeister? Add students' ideas to the chart, continuing to fill it in as they give information.

	Jinx	Mr. Deimeister	Vic
personality	funny, can make fun of herself, outgoing	nervous, caring, good listener	helpful, easy to embarrass, good friend
interests	square dancing	fishing	dancing

Corrective feedback

Circulate around the room as the students use the chart to choose characters to use as the writer and receiver of the letter. Help struggling students think about which character they are most like, as they will be most comfortable writing in that person's voice.

MINI-LESSON

Sentence Variety

- One thing that you can do to make your writing interesting for readers is to use a variety of sentences. Think about how much variety you use when you speak. Usually, the variety in sentence structure is related to variety in your ideas or feelings. I've decided that the writer of my letter is Mr. Deimeister.
- I'm going to create a T-chart to record different types of sentences that Mr. Deimeister might use. On the left I'll describe the sentence, and on the right I'll tell when or why he might use it. I know he asks questions when he is surprised about something. I'll write that information in the chart. He uses long compound sentences when he is explaining his point of view. He uses short simple questions when he is excited about something.

Have students begin their own T-charts using the form on p. 263 of their *Reader's and Writer's Notebook.*

ROUTINE

Quick Write for Fluency

Team Talk

1. **Talk** Have pairs discuss their choices for letter writers.
2. **Write** Each student writes two different types of sentences the letter writer might compose.
3. **Share** Each partner reads the other's sentences. Then each partner asks the other one questions about the sentences.

Routines Flip Chart

Wrap Up Your Day

- ✓ **Build Concepts** What did you learn about Jinx's life?
- ✓ **Generalize** What generalization can you make about Jinx's family?
- ✓ **Predict and Set Purpose** Do you think Jinx will be successful in square dancing? Why or why not? How will you change your reading to check this prediction?

Differentiated Instruction

Advanced

All Types of Sentences Challenge students to come up with as many different types of sentences as possible.

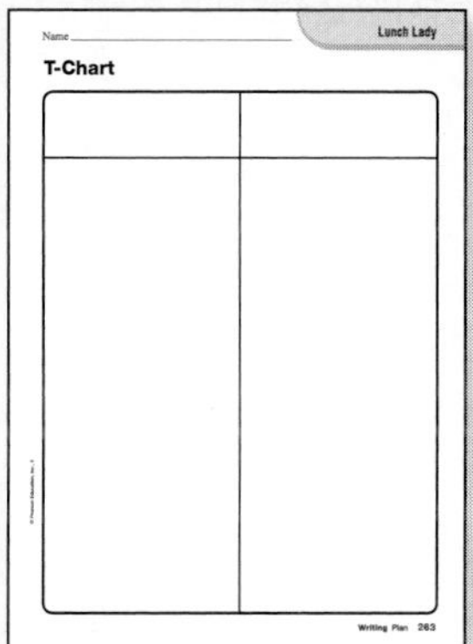

Reader's and Writer's Notebook p. 263

Academic Vocabulary

Compound sentences are two simple sentences joined by a comma and a conjunction.

Tell students that tomorrow they will read about what happens in gym class.

Objectives

- Expand the weekly concept.
- Develop oral vocabulary.

Today at a Glance

Oral Vocabulary
modify, conquer

Comprehension Check/Retelling
Discuss questions

Reading
Tripping Over the Lunch Lady

Think Critically
Retelling

Fluency
Accuracy

Research and Study Skills
Telephone directory

Research and Inquiry
Analyze

Spelling
Prefixes *over-, under-, sub-, super-, out-*

Conventions
Pronouns and antecedents

Writing
Friendly letter

Concept Talk

Question of the Week

How do people overcome obstacles?

Expand the concept

Remind students of the Question of the Week. Discuss how the question relates to Jinx and her desire to square dance. Tell students that today they will read to find out about what happens if and when Jinx gets to square dance in gym class. Encourage students to think about how Jinx's resilient nature helps her triumph over many predicaments.

Anchored Talk

Develop oral vocabulary

Use illustrations to review pp. 52–61 of *Tripping Over the Lunch Lady*. Discuss the Amazing Words *application* and *resilient*. Add these and other concept-related words to the concept map. Use the following questions to develop students' understanding of the concept.

- Jinx's *application* of her desire to have square dancing during gym class shows her determination to overcome obstacles. How have you *applied* yourself to overcome an obstacle in your life?
- Jinx is very *resilient* because she always picks herself up after she falls and starts all over again. How are you *resilient*?

Oral Vocabulary
Amazing Words

Amazing Words

confront	resilient
predicament	modify
ingenious	conquer
triumphant	acclimate
application	persistence

Teach Amazing Words

Amazing Words Oral Vocabulary Routine

1. **Introduce** Write the Amazing Word *conquer* on the board. Have students say it aloud with you. Yesterday we read about how Jinx was not able to *conquer* the trampoline. Have students use the context of the sentence to determine the definition of *conquer*. (When you *conquer* something, you overcome or defeat it.)
2. **Demonstrate** Have students answer questions to demonstrate understanding. How do you know that Jinx could not *conquer* the trampoline? (She kept flying off of it.)
3. **Apply** Have students apply their understanding. What is a synonym for *conquer*?

See p. OV•2 to teach *modify*.

Routines Flip Chart

Apply Amazing Words

As students read pp. 62–67 of *Tripping Over the Lunch Lady*, have them think about the ways Jinx tries to *modify* her gym class. Also think how she tries to *conquer* her reputation for being a jinx.

Connect to reading

Explain that today students will continue to read about Jinx. As they read, they should think about how the Question of the Week and the Amazing Words *modify* and *conquer*, apply to Jinx and her desire to square dance.

ELL **Expand Vocabulary** Use the Day 3 instruction on ELL Poster 17 to help students expand vocabulary.

ELL Poster 17

Objectives

- Generalize to aid comprehension.
- Use the predict and set purpose strategy to aid comprehension.
- Use context clues to determine the meanings of unfamiliar words.

Comprehension Check

Have students discuss each question with a partner. Ask several pairs to share their responses.

✓ **Genre • Analysis**
Why do you think the author chose to use illustrations in *Tripping Over the Lunch Lady*? Possible responses: The illustrations help show you all the crazy things that happen to Jinx. They show that she is like a real person going to a school that seems realistic.

✓ **Generalize • Synthesis**
From what you have read so far, what generalization can you make about Jinx? Use evidence from the text to support your generalization. Possible responses: Jinx always gets into accidents, including getting a concussion from square dancing in gym. The people around Jinx are always getting hurt, including Vic who hurt her foot square dancing with Jinx.

✓ **Predict and set purpose • Analysis**
Make one prediction about what will happen to Jinx at the end of the story. Possible responses: Jinx will get into another accident. Jinx will get someone else hurt. Jinx will learn how to square dance.

✓ **Unfamiliar words • Analysis**
Use what you learned in the story to define the word *jinx*. Restate the word in a sentence. Possible response: Everywhere Jinx goes she brings bad luck with her. So I think *jinx* means "something or someone who brings bad luck." Some people think cracked mirrors are a jinx.

✓ **Connect text to self**
Describe someone you know who is as determined as Jinx. Possible response: My best friend wants to be a professional baseball player. He practices every day so he can be a better player.

Strategy Response Log

INTERACT with TEXT

Have students revisit p. 23 in the Reader's and Writer's Notebook to further explore the genre. Tell them to think about the plot in another story or novel they have read that is also realistic fiction. Ask them to find similarities between the plots of the two stories and then write a summary of those similarities. Remind students to maintain both the meaning and the logical order of the texts in their summaries.

Check Retelling

Have students retell the first part of *Tripping Over the Lunch Lady*, paraphrasing information in the text in a way that maintains its meaning and logical order. Encourage students to use the text features in their retellings.

Corrective feedback

If... students leave out important details,
then... have students look back through the illustrations.

Small Group Time

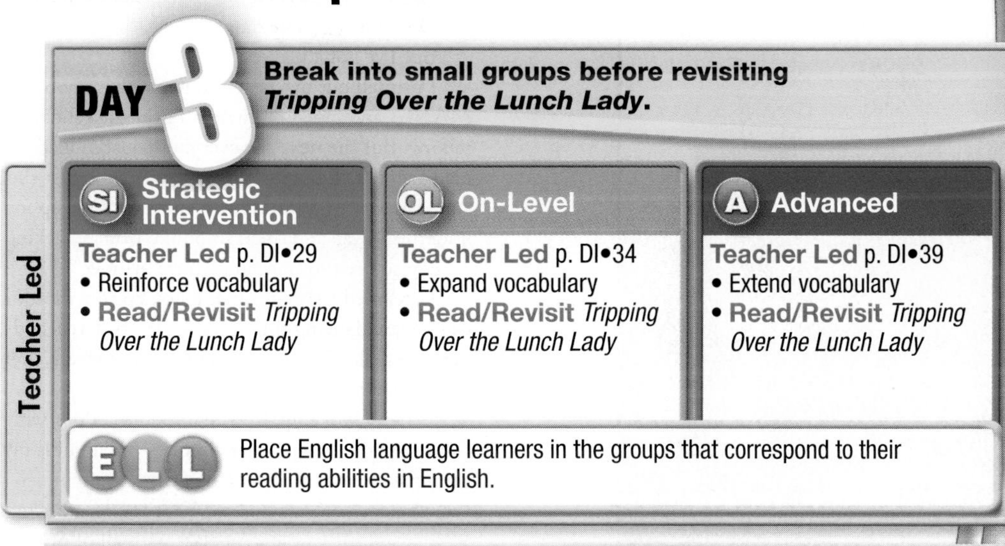

DAY 3
Break into small groups before revisiting *Tripping Over the Lunch Lady.*
Teacher Led
SI Strategic Intervention
Teacher Led p. DI•29
• Reinforce vocabulary
• Read/Revisit *Tripping Over the Lunch Lady*
OL On-Level
Teacher Led p. DI•34
• Expand vocabulary
• Read/Revisit *Tripping Over the Lunch Lady*
A Advanced
Teacher Led p. DI•39
• Extend vocabulary
• Read/Revisit *Tripping Over the Lunch Lady*
ELL
Place English language learners in the groups that correspond to their reading abilities in English.

Practice Stations
- Let's Write
- Get Fluent
- Word Work

Independent Activities
- AudioText: *Tripping Over the Lunch Lady*
- *Reader's and Writer's Notebook*
- Research and Inquiry

English Language Learners

Check retelling To support retelling, review the multilingual summary for *Tripping Over the Lunch Lady* with the appropriate Retelling Cards to scaffold understanding.

Read and Comprehend

45–50 mins.

Objectives

- Draw conclusions to aid comprehension.

OPTION 1 Skills and Strategies, continued

Teach Draw Conclusions

Review **Draw Conclusions** Have students read pp. 62–63. Then ask students why Jinx only ate saltines on gym days. (She didn't want to get sick when she went on the trampoline.)

Corrective Feedback

If... students are having difficulty drawing conclusions from the text, **then...** model how to draw a conclusion.

Model the Skill

What happened to Jinx on the day she ate tuna casserole? (She got sick during gym.) Why do some people eat saltines? (It can make your stomach feel better.)

I'll be carrying Vic's books for a few weeks to class for her.

Her foot cast is pretty cool, though. Bright purple and she let me draw orange daisies all over it already. Everybody is so nosy in this school. Within minutes everyone knew that we were square dancing under the basketball hoop when the broken foot thing happened. You'd pretty much think that would change my mind about square dancing, except technically it was Vic's fault.

We were doing just fine until she thought she heard people coming through the gym doors and turned to run.

Her feet got twisted up with mine. I still feel bad for her, though.

Oh, to be a square dancer.

But I've got a plan.

I printed out five hundred flyers that say SQUARE DANCE MANIA and taped them up all over the school to get people talking. But the next day everybody just looked confused when they read them, including Mr. Deimeister, who just shook his head and stared at me. And it didn't do anything to keep my feet from flying underneath me and the trampoline from smacking me in the face.

I'm so used to trampoline face by now.

I dreamed last night that all of Warren Harding Elementary School was square dancing through the streets. Everybody swung their partners do-si-do. Allemande right to the corners, then we all joined hands and circled to the left.

When I woke up, I was lying on the floor with a sore arm, probably from swinging my partners in my sleep. I guess my dreams of being a gym class hero in square dancing are pretty much squashed since now the whole school knows how Vic's foot got broken.

I spend the whole gym class with all of my friends and enemies skipping around me until Mr. Deimeister says, "The next person to skip around Jinx is running one hundred laps."

Bounce,
bounce,
bounce,
on the evil trampoline.

62

Generalize • Synthesis Based on what you read on page 62, what generalization can you make about Jinx? Possible response: She will never give up on square dancing.

Multidraft Reading

If you chose...

Option 1 Return to Extend Thinking instruction starting on p. 54–55.
Option 2 Read pp. 62–67.
Use the Guide Comprehension and Extend Thinking instruction.

Student Edition pp. 62–63

OPTION 2 Think Critically, continued

Higher-Order Thinking Skills

Review **Draw Conclusions • Synthesis** What conclusion can you draw about what caused Mr. Deimeister's fishing accident? What details from the story allowed you to infer your answer? Possible response: Jinx broke his fishing pole. She dropped a ten-pound weight on his fishing pole when she was in his office dropping off square dancing music.

So, what conclusion can you draw about why Jinx only ate saltines on gym days? (She didn't want to get sick when she went on the trampoline.)

On Their Own

Have students reread the first two paragraphs on p. 62 and draw a conclusion about why Jinx will be carrying Vic's books for a few weeks.

My mom says to give it up.

My dad just laughs.

My little sister sticks her tongue out at me and calls me doofus.

So I've been thinking, just thinking maybe, maybe square dancing isn't the thing. Maybe I can bring peace to the world and less bruises to myself with something else. Maybe jumping rope or jacks in gym might be ok . . .

But then, in gym, Mr. Deimeister says he wants to see me after class.

What's that about? It's been a couple of days since I hurt anybody, and the nurse even stopped me in the hall today to ask if I've been absent.

Anyway in the end I don't get to talk with Mr. Deimeister 'cause he's too busy getting some kid out of the basketball hoop who keeps yelling, "It was just a bet, it was just a bet."

I ate all my lunch today 'cause word got round that we didn't have the trampoline in gym class. I usually don't eat much on gym days. Not since that real bad tuna casserole day that my stomach just couldn't take. (Of course, there was also the unfortunate incident where I tripped over the lunch lady and landed in the sloppy joes . . . but let's not get into that.) Anyway, only saltines on gym day, that's my rule.

But what happened today was better than no trampoline.

It was better than no dodge ball or volleyball. It was better than no field trip to Ice-Skating World or the rock-climbing wall at the Wellness Center. The only thing better than none of these things was no Mr. Deimeister taking us to all those places.

Story is he had a nasty fishing accident over the weekend and he won't be back for a couple of weeks.

It's better than Halloween and summer vacation all rolled up in one. It's better than three desserts and no curfew. It's better than a water main break in school or a snow day that lasts a week.

What's really great is that there isn't a sub either. We all get to go to study groups. No sub gym teacher to carry on the trampoline evil.

63

Predict and Set Purpose • Analysis

What do you predict will happen next in the story? After making your prediction, set a new purpose for reading. Possible response: The students will have gym with a substitute teacher, and Jinx will get hurt. My new purpose for reading is to determine how Jinx will hurt herself.

ELL

English Language Learners

Predict Read aloud the first two sentences from paragraph 7 on p. 62. Then have students look at the illustrations on pp. 62–63. Ask them what they see. (All the flyers are on the floor.) Write this model on the board: *I think* ___ *will happen because* _________. Ask students to make a prediction about what will happen to Jinx's square dancing idea using the model.

DAY 3 Read and Comprehend

Objectives

◎ Use the strategy of predict and set purpose to aid comprehension.

OPTION 1 Skills and Strategies, continued

Teach Predict and Set Purpose

Predict and Set Purpose Have students read p. 64. Then ask what they predict will happen in gym class. (Jinx will square dance and hurt herself.) Based on their prediction, ask students what purpose they can set for reading the next page. (Read to find out *how* Jinx hurts herself.)

Corrective Feedback

If... students are unable to make a prediction and set a purpose,
then... model how to predict and set purposes.

Model the Strategy

Think Aloud: Think about what you already read in the story. What do you think Jinx could have heard that would get her so excited? (She might have heard music.)

Life is good—until I find out it's a lie in fifth period and I'm going to have to dress and head out onto the gym floor like every day before with a substitute teacher who will follow all the lesson plans that Mr. Deimeister left behind.

Vic, whose foot is still healing, limps out beside me.

"Sorry, Jinx, I know you were counting on study group."

"Yeah, I was. But I'll be all right. I've flown off the trampoline before. At least this teacher hasn't seen me do it before."

But then I began to hear something.

It started low as I got closer to the gym door. Then I heard it a little louder. I moved quicker than I ever had getting to gym class.

64

Student Edition pp. 64–65

Review **Draw Conclusions • Analysis** How did Jinx feel at the beginning of page 65? Why did she feel this way? She felt great because the class was finally going to go square dancing, and she thought she would be a star. She was excited, but probably a little nervous because she knows that there is a chance that she could hurt someone in class.

OPTION 2 Think Critically, continued

Higher-Order Thinking Skills

Predict and Set Purpose • Analysis Do you think that Jinx will give up square dancing now that she's been hurt? Possible response: No, because Jinx feels so strongly about it, and she has never quit any other task because she got hurt. Then ask students to set a purpose for reading the rest of the story. My new purpose for reading is to see *how badly* Jinx hurt herself in gym class.

What can you predict might be happening in the gym? (The substitute teacher is playing music for square dancing.) What do you want to find out as you continue to read? (if Jinx gets to go square dancing and if she hurts herself) Setting a purpose to read will help you understand the story better.

There was music coming out of the gym. There was music coming out of *my* gym class.

It was square dance music coming out of that gym class. And beside the boom box playing that music was a bright shiny new gym teacher who had never gotten her nose broken by me!

Everything was going to be different. That little accident with Vic didn't mean anything. I'd be the fifth-grade champ of the world. Just me—all by myself.

All I could do was smile as the substitute explained how we were to line up and which hands we had to grab of each other's to dance. I don't even remember her name, this wonderful teacher who brought square dancing to us.

She started the music again and everybody started moving to the words she called out. All I remember is Josh running at me to swing me around. . . .

In a few minutes I didn't remember anything for a while.

65

Unfamiliar Words • Synthesis If you didn't know the meaning of the word *substitute,* in paragraph 1 on page 64, how could you figure it out? The paragraph says that the teacher will use the plans of Mr. Deimeister. You can also look at the illustrations on p. 65 to see that there is a different teacher in the gym. These clues tell you that *substitute* means "a replacement."

On Their Own

Have students read p. 65 to see if their predictions are correct. Also have them adjust their reading purposes if necessary.

Differentiated Instruction

SI Strategic Intervention

Draw conclusions Have students work in pairs to draw conclusions about how Jinx felt at the beginning of p. 64. Have them find clues in the first four paragraphs that confirm their conclusions. Remind students to think about what they already know about Jinx, look at the clues from the page, and then draw a conclusion. Have pairs share their conclusions with the class.

ELL English Language Learners

Unfamiliar words Have students find the phrase *boom box* on p. 65. Then have them look at the illustrations on pp. 64–65 and use them, along with the text and their prior knowledge, to determine the meaning of this unknown term.

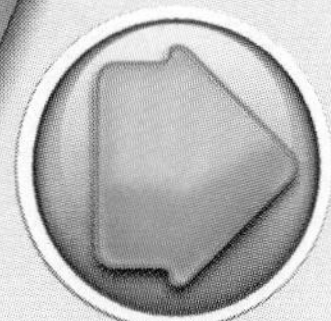

Read and Comprehend

Objectives

- Draw conclusions to improve comprehension.

OPTION 1 Skills and Strategies, continued

Teach Draw Conclusions

Review Draw Conclusions Have students read pp. 66–67. Then ask students what conclusion they can draw about Jinx. (Even though she doesn't succeed, Jinx can still laugh at herself.)

Corrective Feedback

If... students are having difficulty drawing a conclusion,
then... model drawing a conclusion.

Model the Skill

Think Aloud We have learned a lot about Jinx in this story. Summarize some things we know about her. (She gets hurt a lot, and other people get hurt when they are near her. She is always trying to find a way to be good at things.

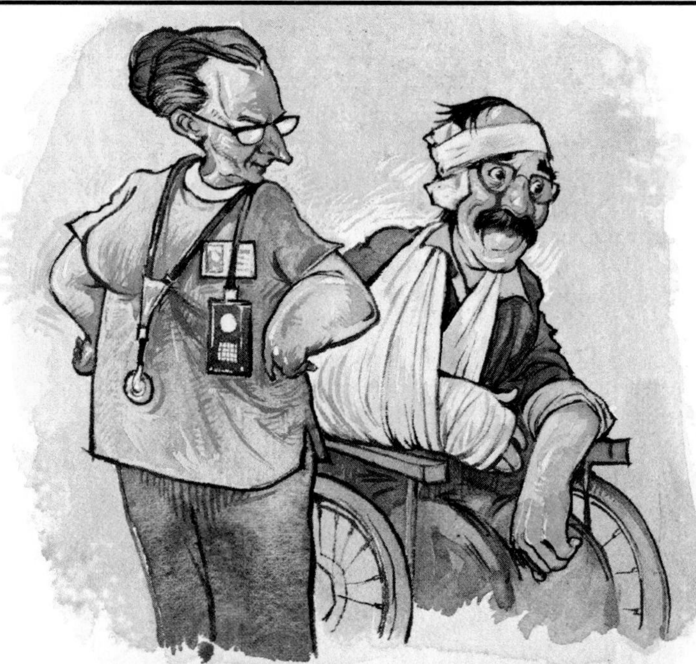

They say I have a concussion and a sprained ankle. Josh only got a big bruise on his forehead.

I had to stay in the hospital for two days. I've had a lot of visitors, though. Most of my gym class came the second day and brought square dance music for me.

The nurses weren't happy.

I even got a visit from Mr. Deimeister, who was on the third floor and wheeled himself down to visit me. He smiled when he rolled himself into my room and heard the music.

"I thought you had a concussion, kid," he said, looking at my bandaged foot.

I shrugged. "How do you get hurt *fishing*?"

He shrugged back. "I didn't know my reel would snap. I must have broken it somehow and not known it. Anyway, I was reeling

66

Student Edition pp. 66–67

OPTION 2 Think Critically, continued

Higher-Order Thinking Skills

Review Draw Conclusions • Synthesis Why does Mr. Deimeister think Jinx missed the square dancing class? He sees that she has gotten hurt and assumes that she fell off the trampoline again. Therefore, she wouldn't have had a chance to go to the square dancing class. He does not believe that anyone would be hurt that badly while square dancing.

Author's Purpose • Analysis Why did the author write this story? How did she achieve her purpose? Mention specific textual evidence in your answer. The author wrote this story to entertain her readers. She achieved her purpose by using very conversational and humorous language in the story. Also, the illustrations add a lot of humor to the story. The word *Naaah* on p. 67 made me laugh, as well as the pictures of Jinx and Mr. Deimeister all bandaged up in the hospital.

She thought that if they had square dancing in gym, she would be good at it. She realizes that she won't be a square dancing star.) From all this information, I can draw a conclusion about Jinx. Even though she doesn't succeed, Jinx can still laugh at herself. I can infer that Jinx will continue to try things even though she hasn't succeeded in square dancing.

a big one in, and out of the boat I went. Just a few ribs and some cuts, a concussion and a collapsed lung. I'm okay."

Oh, no. A broken reel?

Naaah.

"So. How was it?"

"How was what?" I say.

"The square dancing. I called the substitute to suggest it. I take it you were the one who left the music in my office."

"Oh yeah, that was me."

"Well, it looks like you missed the square dancing. Sorry. I thought you'd be safe from the trampoline while I was gone."

"Mr. Deimeister, I didn't get here because of the trampoline."

The look on poor Mr. Deimeister's face made me laugh so hard, I almost fell out of the bed. The nurse came in and said she thought I'd had enough visitors, but I kept laughing because I knew then that I was never going to be a square dance champion.

So what else could I do but laugh?

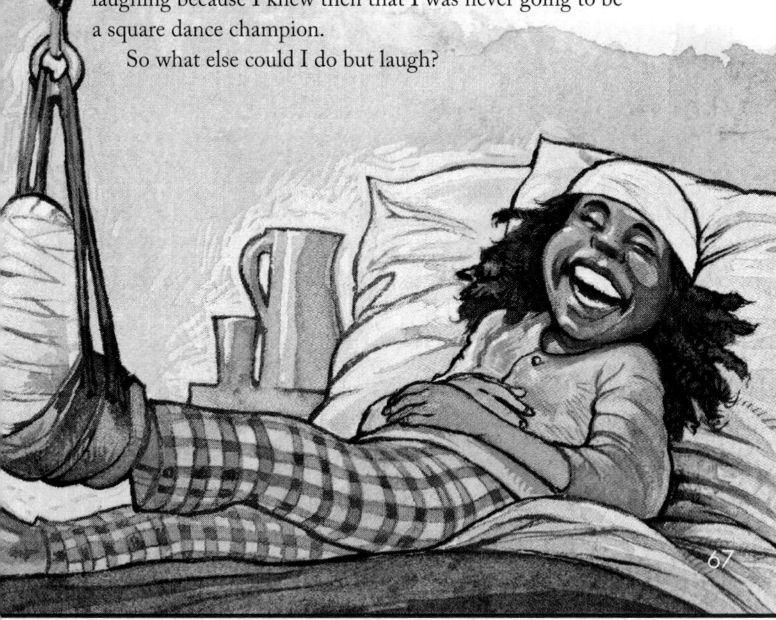

67

On Their Own

Have students look back at p. 59 and reread pp. 66–67 to draw a conclusion about how Mr. Deimeister's reel broke.

Differentiated Instruction

Strategic Intervention

Draw conclusions Tell students that sometimes the illustrations in a story can help them draw conclusions. Ask them to look at the illustration on p. 67 and draw a conclusion about how Jinx feels about herself.

Advanced

Have students brainstorm other ways that Jinx might be able to overcome her problems in gym class.

Comprehension Check

Spiral Review

Literary Elements: Character and Plot • Analysis What character traits does Jinx possess that distinguish her from other characters in the story? Jinx gets into a lot of accidents and sometimes other people get hurt too, but she always maintains a good sense of humor. She tries very hard to overcome her problems by coming up with creative solutions.

Story Structure: Resolution • Analysis Does Jinx resolve her problem? If so, how? Jinx really doesn't resolve her problem. Instead, she realizes that she will never be a square dance champion, but that is okay with her.

Check Predictions Have students return to the predictions they made earlier and confirm whether they were accurate.

English Language Learners

Build vocabulary Read aloud the first sentence on p. 66. Have students use what they know about the word *sprained* as clues to help them figure out the meaning of the word *concussion.*

DAY 3 Read and Comprehend

Objectives

- ◎ Generalize to aid comprehension.
- ◎ Predict and set purpose to aid comprehension.

Check Retelling
SUCCESS PREDICTOR

Objectives
• Describe specific events in the story or novel that result in or hint at future events. • Read independently for a sustained period of time and paraphrase the reading, including the order in which events occur.

Envision It! Retell

READING STREET ONLINE
STORY SORT
www.ReadingStreet.com

Think Critically

1. The main character is nicknamed Jinx by her family. You may have read other stories or seen a movie about someone who, like Jinx, has a nickname. Do you think being known by a nickname is a good thing? Why or why not? **Text to Self**
2. Why do you think the author chose to present the story through the voice of the main character? Do you think it was a good choice? Why or why not? **Think Like an Author**
3. Make a generalization about how the main character feels about herself. Use details from the story to support your ideas. **Generalize**
4. On page 57, Jinx says that she is going to be a square dance star. Based on the incidents in the story, what do you predict the chances of this happening are? **Predict and Set Purpose**
5. **Look Back and Write** Look back at pages 59–60 and pages 66–67. How do events described on pages 59–60 and pages 66–67 connect to each other? Provide evidence from the story to support your answer.

TEST PRACTICE **Extended Response**

68

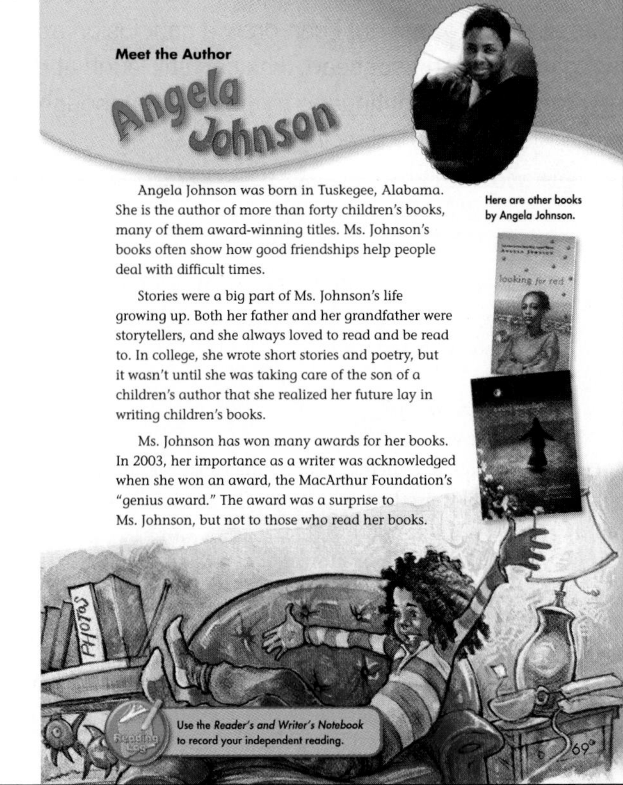
Meet the Author

Angela Johnson

Angela Johnson was born in Tuskegee, Alabama. She is the author of more than forty children's books, many of them award-winning titles. Ms. Johnson's books often show how good friendships help people deal with difficult times.

Stories were a big part of Ms. Johnson's life growing up. Both her father and her grandfather were storytellers, and she always loved to read and be read to. In college, she wrote short stories and poetry, but it wasn't until she was taking care of the son of a children's author that she realized her future lay in writing children's books.

Ms. Johnson has won many awards for her books. In 2003, her importance as a writer was acknowledged when she won an award, the MacArthur Foundation's "genius award." The award was a surprise to Ms. Johnson, but not to those who read her books.

Here are other books by Angela Johnson.

Use the *Reader's and Writer's Notebook* to record your independent reading.

69

Student Edition pp. 68–69

Retelling

Have students work in pairs to retell the selection, using the Envision It! Retelling Cards as prompts. Remind students that they should accurately describe the characters and plot using key vocabulary. Monitor students' retellings.

Scoring rubric

Top-Score Response A top-score response makes connections beyond the text, describes the plot, makes accurate generalizations about the characters, and draws conclusions from the text.

Plan to Assess Retelling

- ☑ **Week 1** Assess Strategic Intervention students.
- ☑ **This week assess Advanced students.**
- ☐ **Week 3** Assess Strategic Intervention students.
- ☐ **Week 4** Assess On-Level students.
- ☐ **Week 5** Assess any students you have not yet checked during this unit.

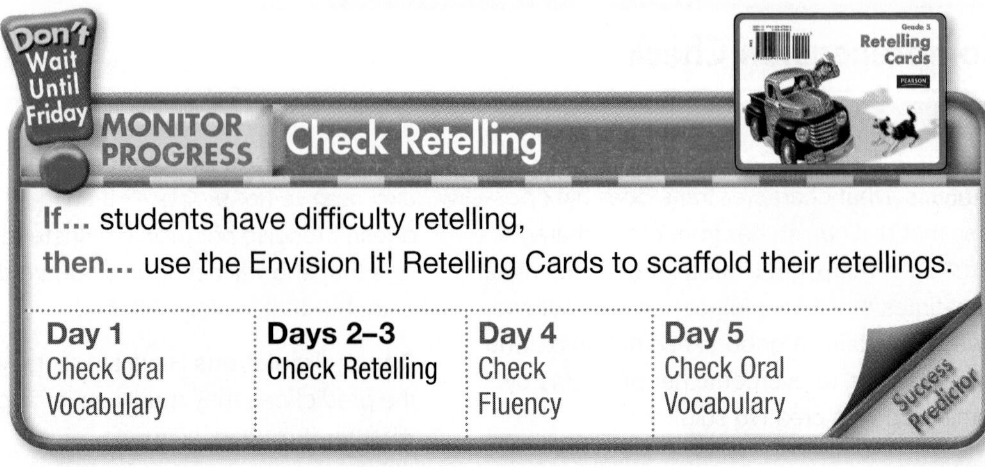

Don't Wait Until Friday
MONITOR PROGRESS
Check Retelling
Retelling Cards
Success Predictor

If... students have difficulty retelling,
then... use the Envision It! Retelling Cards to scaffold their retellings.

Day 1	Days 2–3	Day 4	Day 5
Check Oral Vocabulary	Check Retelling	Check Fluency	Check Oral Vocabulary

Think Critically

Text to self

1. Sometimes it isn't a good thing to be known by a nickname. When the nickname is negative, such as *Jinx,* it can make you feel bad about yourself. Also, it might be harder to overcome your nickname if it is negative.

Think like an author

2. The author wanted to show how the main character, Jinx, was feeling and what she was thinking. It was a good idea because you got to understand how Jinx feels about all the things that happen to her.

Generalize

3. Jinx knows that she gets into a lot of accidents, but she still feels good about herself. You can infer this from the end of the story where she is laughing.

Predict and set purpose

4. Jinx will probably never be a square dance star.

Writing on Demand

5. **Look Back and Write** To build writing fluency, assign a 10–15 minute time limit.

Suggest that students use a prewriting strategy, such as brainstorming or using a graphic organizer, to organize their ideas. Remind them to establish a topic sentence and support it with facts, details, or explanations. As students finish, encourage them to reread their responses, revise for organization and support, and proofread for errors in grammar and conventions.

Scoring rubric

Top-Score Response A top-score response connects Jinx's original idea about square dancing to the outcome of her getting hurt while square dancing.

A top-score response should include:

- Jinx came up with the idea of square dancing and felt that it was meant to be.
- Jinx tried many ways to convince everyone that square dancing would be a great idea.
- Jinx finally gets a chance to square dance, but she ends up getting hurt, just like she always does in gym.

Differentiated Instruction

Strategic Intervention

Writing Have students work in pairs to review the text and illustrations to help them make connections. Have students write down the sequence of events between the two sections of the selection to find the connection.

Meet the Author

Have students read about the author, Angela Johnson, on p. 69. Ask them what she believes helps people overcome obstacles and if this belief can be found in the story.

Independent Reading

After students enter their independent reading information into their Reading Logs or a journal, have them summarize what they have read. Remind students that a summary should be no more than a few sentences about the main idea of a text.

ELL

English Language Learners

Retelling Have students use the retelling strip on p. 68 in the Student Edition to describe the people, places, and objects in the story.

Retelling

Success Predictor

Objectives

- Read grade-level text with accuracy.
- Reread for fluency.
- Understand how to use a telephone directory.

Model Fluency
Accuracy

Model fluent reading Have students turn to p. 56 of *Tripping Over the Lunch Lady.* Have students follow along as you read this page. Explain that you will read the words carefully so that you're reading without making any mistakes, such as word omissions or substitutions. Model accuracy with smooth, fluent reading.

Guide practice Have students follow along as you read the page again. Then have them reread the page as a group without you until they read smoothly and without mistakes. Ask questions to be sure students comprehend the text. Continue in the same way with p. 57.

Reread for Fluency

Corrective feedback **If...** students are having difficulty reading with accuracy,
then... prompt:

- Did you read every word? Where do you see difficult words?
- How can you read with better accuracy?
- Read the sentence again. Make sure you read carefully and do not miss any words.

ROUTINE **Paired Reading**

1. **Select a passage** For *Tripping Over the Lunch Lady,* use p. 59.
2. **Reader 1** Students read the entire page, switching readers at the end of every other paragraph.
3. **Reader 2** Partners reread the passage. This time the other student begins.
4. **Reread** For optimal fluency, have partners continue to read three or four times.
5. **Corrective Feedback** Listen as students read. Provide feedback about their accuracy and encourage them to read the words without making any mistakes.

Routines Flip Chart

Research and Study Skills
Telephone Directory

Teach Discuss with students how they might find the phone number or address for a classmate or a local business to help collect information pertaining to their research plan. Students may use a telephone book. Point out that the same information is also available in online directories. Show students a telephone directory that contains both white and yellow pages. Then describe these terms:

- A **telephone directory** alphabetically lists the names, phone numbers, and addresses for people and businesses in a particular geographical area.
- A telephone directory lists the names of people and businesses in separate sections, often white for people and yellow for businesses.
- A telephone directory contains names in the upper corners of the pages, like guide words in a dictionary or encyclopedia.
- Many directories contain frequently used and important numbers and information in the front of the directory.

Guide practice Provide groups with examples of telephone directories. Discuss these questions:

Why are telephone directories alphabetized? (It makes it easier to find the person or business that you are looking for.)

Why might a telephone directory list people and businesses separately? (to make it easier by looking through only the type of information you need to find, either a person or a business.)

Use the guide words on the tops on the pages to find the listing for your favorite restaurant in your area. What guide words did you use? (Answers will vary.)

On their own Have students complete pp. 265–266 of the *Reader's and Writer's Notebook.*

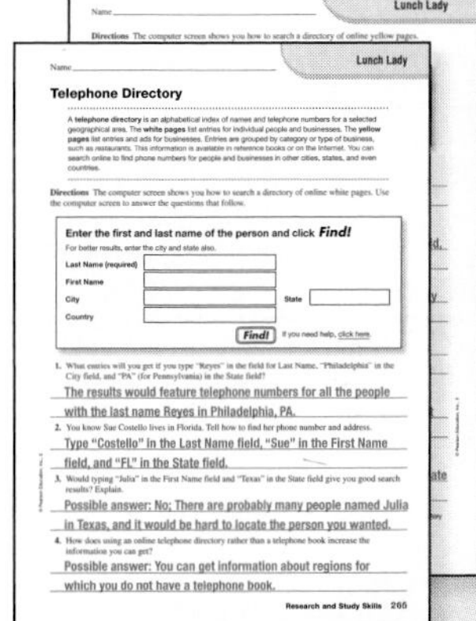
Reader's and Writer's Notebook pp. 265–266

English Language Learners

Professional Development: What ELL experts say about oral reading "Teachers periodically can have students taperecord their oral reading. Ideally, students should be given the option to choose the selection they want to read, to rehearse it, and, when ready, to taperecord their performance....If the child is biliterate, the teacher could suggest that the child make tapes in both languages." —Dr. Georgia Earnest García

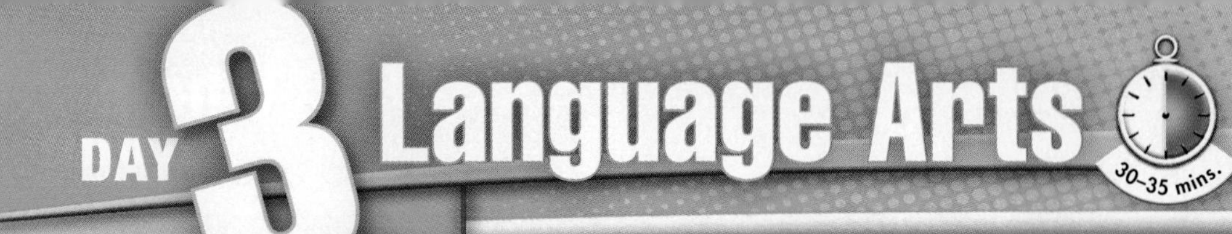

Objectives

- Analyze data for usefulness.
- Identify and correctly use pronouns and antecedents.
- Spell frequently misspelled words.

Research and Inquiry
Analyze

Teach Tell students that today they will analyze their findings. They should ask themselves questions about their research and use the answers to refine their inquiry question.

Model Think Aloud When I researched Nolan Ryan, I found a lot of information and statistics about his baseball career. I ask myself, *What information is most relevant to my topic?* Since I am going to write a description about how Ryan overcame dyslexia, I will need to know more about his dyslexia. I will highlight or put sticky notes on any information about that. I will also make my inquiry question more exact. Now my inquiry question is *How did Nolan Ryan overcome the obstacle of dyslexia to become a major league baseball star?*

Guide practice Have students analyze their findings. Team students who are having trouble narrowing their focus with students who are not having difficulty. Have the pairs ask themselves questions to refine their topics.

On their own Partners can work together to pick the illustration they will use. They may download a photo of the famous person they are studying, find a photo in a magazine or newspaper, or draw a picture of the person. If students want to include a diagram instead, they should make sure they have enough information from their research.

Conventions
Pronouns and Antecedents

Review Remind students that this week they learned about pronouns and antecedents. Review the definitions and examples of pronouns and antecedents:

- A pronoun takes the place of a noun or nouns.
- An antecedent, or referent, is the noun or nouns to which the pronoun refers.
- Each pronoun must agree with its antecedent in number and gender.
- When writing, if a pronoun's antecedent is unclear, the sentence should be rewritten.

Daily Fix-It Use Daily Fix-It numbers 5 and 6 in the right margin.

Connect to oral language Have students fill in the first blank of the sentence with an antecedent and the second blank with the correct pronoun to match it. Ask them to read their complete sentences aloud.

> **Give your trash to ________ , and ________ will sort it for recycling.**

On their own For additional practice, use *Let's Practice It!* p. 198 on the *Teacher Resources DVD-ROM*.

Let's Practice It!
TR DVD•198

Spelling
Prefixes *over-, under-, sub-, super-, out-*

Frequently misspelled words The words *outside* and *because* are words that students often misspell. I'm going to read a sentence. Choose the correct word to complete the sentence and then write it correctly. Have students check their work using a dictionary or other resource.

> **1. I liked the movie ________ it made me laugh. (because)**
>
> **2. We'll have our lunch ________ today. (outside)**

On their own For more practice, use *Reader's and Writer's Notebook* p. 267.

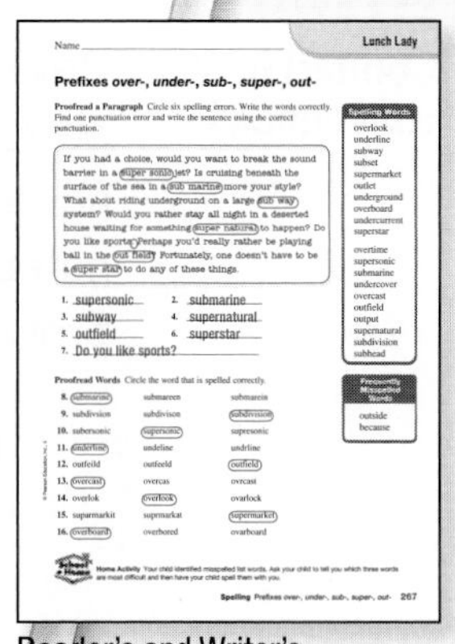

Name ________ Lunch Lady

Prefixes over-, under-, sub-, super-, out-

Reader's and Writer's
Notebook p. 267

Differentiated Instruction

SI Strategic Intervention

Checklist When students are talking with others, writing, and checking their descriptions, have them keep the following short checklist handy, to be sure they are getting and including the essential information:

1. What is the person like?
2. What was the person's obstacle?
3. How did the person overcome it?

Daily Fix-It

5. The students went on field trips, but them didnt like the trips that much. *(they; didn't)*
6. Mr. Deimeister need a good rod for his fishing trip, and he hoped the water would not be ruff. *(needed; rough)*

DAY 3 Language Arts

Objectives

- Understand the criteria for an effective friendly letter.

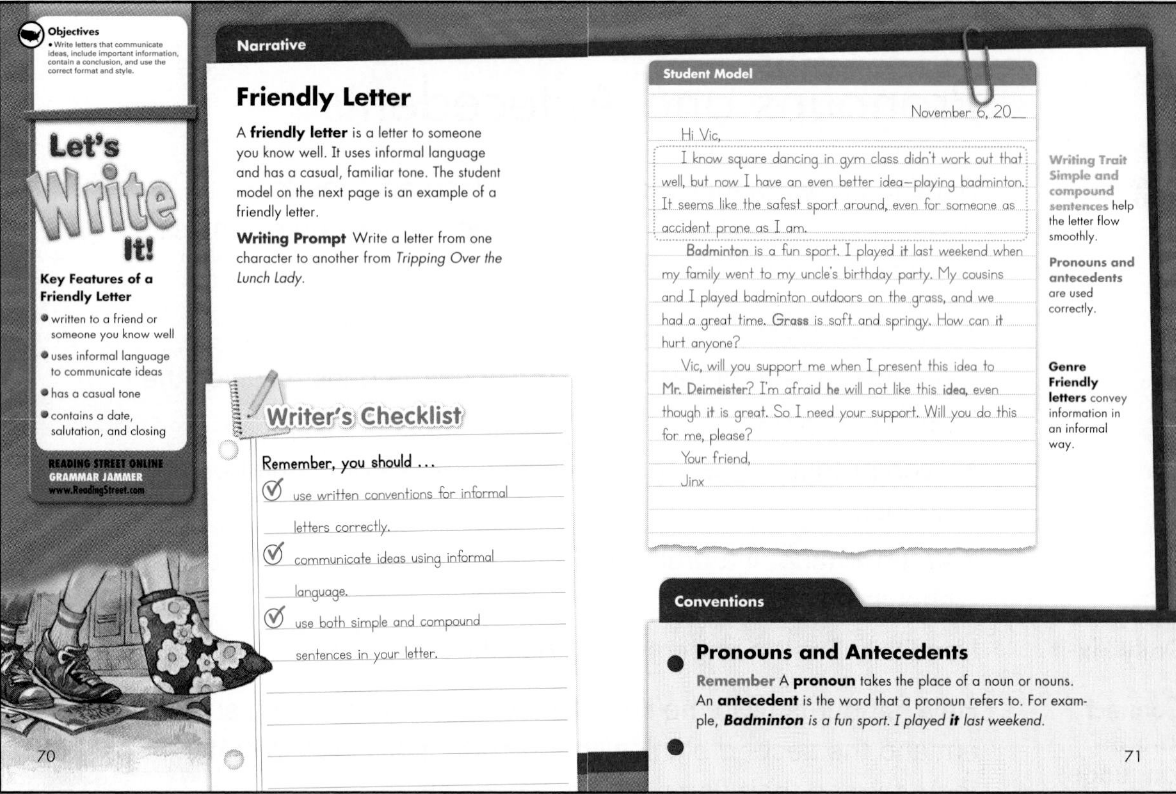

Objectives

- Write letters that communicate ideas, include important information, contain a conclusion, and use the correct format and style.

Let's Write It!

Key Features of a Friendly Letter

- written to a friend or someone you know well
- uses informal language to communicate ideas
- has a casual tone
- contains a date, salutation, and closing

READING STREET ONLINE
GRAMMAR JAMMER
www.ReadingStreet.com

Narrative

Friendly Letter

A **friendly letter** is a letter to someone you know well. It uses informal language and has a casual, familiar tone. The student model on the next page is an example of a friendly letter.

Writing Prompt Write a letter from one character to another from *Tripping Over the Lunch Lady.*

Writer's Checklist

Remember, you should ...

- use written conventions for informal letters correctly.
- communicate ideas using informal language.
- use both simple and compound sentences in your letter.

70

Student Model

November 6, 20__

Hi Vic,

I know square dancing in gym class didn't work out that well, but now I have an even better idea—playing badminton. It seems like the safest sport around, even for someone as accident prone as I am.

Badminton is a fun sport. I played **it** last weekend when my family went to my uncle's birthday party. My cousins and I played badminton outdoors on the grass, and we had a great time. **Grass** is soft and springy. How can **it** hurt anyone?

Vic, will you support me when I present this idea to **Mr. Deimeister**? I'm afraid **he** will not like this **idea**, even though **it** is great. So I need your support. Will you do this for me, please?

Your friend,

Jinx

Writing Trait Simple and compound sentences help the letter flow smoothly.

Pronouns and antecedents are used correctly.

Genre Friendly letters convey information in an informal way.

Conventions

Pronouns and Antecedents

Remember A **pronoun** takes the place of a noun or nouns. An **antecedent** is the word that a pronoun refers to. For example, ***Badminton*** *is a fun sport. I played* ***it*** *last weekend.*

71

Student Edition pp. 70–71

Let's Write It!
Friendly Letter

Teach Use pp. 70–71 in the Student Edition. Direct students to read the key features of a friendly letter that appear on p. 70. Remind them that they can refer to the information in the Writer's Checklist as they write their own friendly letter. The letters should include all important information and include a conclusion that demonstrates a sense of closure. Refer to the student model on p. 71 for examples.

Read the student model on p. 71. Point out the simple and compound sentences in the model.

Connect to conventions Review the definitions of pronouns and antecedents, as found at the bottom of p. 71. Remind students that pronouns and antecedents must agree in number and gender. Help them locate the blue pronouns and antecedents in the student model, discussing why each example shows proper agreement.

Writing—Friendly Letter
Writing Trait: Sentences

Display rubric

Display Scoring Rubric 17 from the *Teacher Resources DVD* and go over the criteria for each trait under each score. Then, using the model in the Student Edition, choose students to explain whether the model should score a 4 for one of the traits and why. If a student offers that the model should score below 4 for a particular trait, the student should support that response. Remind students that this is the rubric that will be used to evaluate the friendly letter they write.

Scoring Rubric: Friendly Letter

	4	3	2	1
Focus/Ideas	Each paragraph presents an important idea that is well developed	Most paragraphs are focused on an important idea, but the ideas could be better developed	The letter rambles because the paragraphs do not clearly focus on single ideas	Paragraph focus and development of ideas are missing from the letter
Organization	All letter parts are there, and written conventions have been used correctly	All letter parts are there, but there are some errors in written conventions	Letter parts are missing or written without proper conventions	Little or no resemblance to how a friendly letter should be written
Voice	Casual style and informal language are just right for a friendly letter	Style and language are mostly good for a friendly letter	Style and language are uneven or not appropriate for a friendly letter	Style and language do not hold together or are not appropriate
Word Choice	Excellent word choice that reveals an attempt to closely match the writer's way of talking	Some good word choice that shows some attention was paid to the writer's way of talking	Lacks clear language or indication of attempts to match the writer's way of talking	Vague, dull, or misused words and no relationship to the writer's way of talking
Sentences	Well-crafted sentences with plenty of variety	Smooth sentences; not as much variety	Many short, choppy sentences; too many similar sentences	Many fragments and run-ons
Conventions	Excellent control and accuracy; all pronouns agree with antecedents	Good control; pronoun-antecedent agreement nearly always correct	Errors that may prevent understanding; some lack of pronoun-antecedent agreement	Frequent errors that interfere with meaning; no pronoun-antecedent agreement

T-chart

Have students get out the T-charts that they worked on yesterday. Encourage them to review the types of sentences they have recorded on the chart, and to continue thinking about which types of sentences might be used by their letter writer and why.

Write

You will be using your T-charts as you write the draft of your friendly letter. When you are drafting, don't worry if your letter does not sound exactly as you want it. You will have a chance to revise it tomorrow.

Differentiated Instruction

Advanced

Colloquialisms Challenge students to come up with one or two colloquialisms that their letter writer might use. Remind students that this type of language is only appropriate in casual writing such as a friendly letter.

English Language Learners

Friendly letters Have pairs of students look for examples of informal language used in the student model on p. 71. As an example, point out the informal greeting, "Hi Vic," explaining that this sounds like Jinx talking to her friend.

Objectives

- Write a first draft of a friendly letter.
- Understand the proper tone for a friendly letter.
- Develop a style that matches the letter writer's way of speaking.

Writing, continued

Casual Tone

Introduce Remind students that a friendly letter is written to someone you know well. The tone of the letter should be casual. One way to approach it is to write the letter as if you were talking to the receiver of it. Use language that sounds natural coming from the letter writer. Display the Drafting Tips for students. Emphasize that while they write they should be thinking about the types of sentences and language they use, trying to match the voice of the letter writer.

December 3, 20__

Dear Jinx,

I am glad that you got to go home from the hospital. I will be here a few more days, but that's okay. I like having people take care of me.

I have been thinking about square dancing and I think it is too soon to give up on it. Did you know that square dancing requires the participation of a person known as the caller? The caller tells the square dancers when to do certain moves, and they are like the leader of the dancing. I think you would make an excellent caller!

I will see you back at school in a few days. We can talk more about turning you into a caller. Until then, I trust you are safe and sound in gym class. I hope you will stay off the trampoline or I fear their could be more injuries.

Yours sincerely
Mr. Deimeister

Unit 4 Tripping Over the Lunch Lady — Writing: Model 17A

Writing Transparency 17A, TR DVD

Drafting Tips

- ✔ To get started, review the sentences on your T-Chart.
- ✔ Make sure you share important information in each paragraph of your letter. The purpose of the letter is to convey ideas, not just to chat. Your letter should leave the reader feeling a sense of closure because he or she has been informed of important ideas or information.
- ✔ Don't worry about grammar and mechanics when drafting. You'll focus on these things during the proofreading stage.

I'm going to write my letter from Mr. Deimeister to Jinx. I want to open by connecting with her. Since the last place they saw each other was the hospital, I'll talk about that. I will share some information about Mr. Deimeister's continued stay in the hospital. I see from my T-chart that he uses longer sentences when he is explaining something, so I'll use a compound sentence when he reports his situation to Jinx.

Direct students to use the drafting tips to guide them in writing their drafts. Remind them to use a variety of sentences.

ROUTINE

Quick Write for Fluency

Team Talk

1. **Talk** Pairs talk about the types of sentences they will use or have used in their friendly letters.
2. **Write** Each person writes one simple sentence and one compound sentence that could be used in the letter, being sure to use an antecedent and a pronoun in one of the sentences.
3. **Share** Partners read each other's sentences and check for correct simple and compound structure and pronoun-antecedent agreement.

Routines Flip Chart

Wrap Up Your Day

- ✔ **Build Concepts** What did you learn about what happened to Mr. Deimeister?
- ✔ **Generalize** What generalization can you make about Jinx's relationship with Mr. Deimeister?
- ✔ **Predict and Set Purpose** What prediction can you make about Jinx's future with square dancing?

Differentiated Instruction

Strategic Intervention

Give students the following frames that will help them remember how to structure compound sentences. Remind them that they can start with two simple sentences and then combine them into a compound sentence.

(simple sentence), and (simple sentence).

(simple sentence), or (simple sentence).

(simple sentence), but (simple sentence).

Preview DAY 4

Tell students that tomorrow they will read about the physical and mental benefits of square dancing.

Objectives

- Expand the weekly concept.
- Develop oral vocabulary.

Today at a Glance

Oral Vocabulary
acclimate, persistence

Genre
Persuasive text: Essay

Reading
"Square Dancing: Good for the Heart and Mind"

Let's Learn It!
Fluency: Accuracy
Vocabulary: Context clues
Listening/Speaking: Persuasive speech

Research and Inquiry
Synthesize

Spelling
Prefixes *over-, under-, sub-, super-, out-*

Conventions
Pronouns and antecedents

Writing
Friendly letter

Concept Talk

Question of the Week

How do people overcome obstacles?

Expand the concept Remind students that this week they have read about how people can overcome the obstacles in their lives. Tell students that today they will read about how square dancing has physical, mental, and emotional benefits.

Anchored Talk

Develop oral vocabulary Use illustrations to review pp. 62–67 of *Tripping Over the Lunch Lady*. Have students discuss the Amazing Words *modify* and *conquer* in groups. Add these and other concept-related words to the concept map. Then have them discuss the following questions and identify points of agreement and disagreement among group members, use context to determine or clarify the meaning of the Amazing Words, and develop their understanding of the concept.

- Sometimes people have to *modify* a task to be able to succeed. Jinx wanted to modify gym so that she could square dance, which is something she thought she would be good at. What are some other ways things can be *modified* to overcome an obstacle? Should some things not be *modified?*
- Jinx wanted to *conquer* her inability to be successful at gym. What are some things in your life that you would like to *conquer*?

Strategy Response Log

Have students review the characteristics of realistic fiction on p. 23 of the *Reader's and Writer's Notebook.* Then have them compare *Tripping Over the Lunch Lady* to another example of realistic fiction that they have read or know about.

Oral Vocabulary
Amazing Words

Amazing Words

confront	resilient
predicament	modify
ingenious	conquer
triumphant	acclimate
application	persistence

Amazing Words Oral Vocabulary Routine

Teach Amazing Words

1. **Introduce** Write the Amazing Word *persistence* on the board. Have students say it aloud with you. Yesterday we read that Jinx had *persistence* when it came to introducing square dancing to her gym class. Have students determine the definition of *persistence.* (When you have *persistence,* you do not give up, especially when faced with difficulties.)
2. **Demonstrate** Have students answer questions to demonstrate understanding. How can you tell that Jinx has *persistence* about the square dancing class? (She printed out five hundred flyers, and she continually talked to Mr. Deimeister about it.)
3. **Apply** Have students apply their understanding. Why is *persistence* a good way to overcome obstacles?

See p. OV•2 to teach *acclimate.*

Routines Flip Chart

Apply Amazing Words

Have students discuss how *persistence* and *acclimate* apply to *Tripping Over the Lunch Lady.* Before students read *Square Dancing: Good for the Heart and Mind* on pp. 72–73, have them establish a purpose for reading. Students can read to find out the benefits of square dancing.

Connect to reading

As students read today's selection about the benefits of square dancing, have them think about how the Question of the Week and the Amazing Words *persistence* and *acclimate,* apply to square dancing.

ELL **Produce Oral Language** Use the Day 4 instruction on ELL Poster 17 to extend and enrich language.

Poster 17

English Language Learners

Cognates Point out that both of today's Amazing Words have Spanish cognates: *acclimate = acclimate; persistence = persistencia*

Objectives

- Introduce persuasive techniques.

Let's Think About Genre

Persuasive Text: Essay

Introduce persuasive essay

Explain that what we read is structured differently depending on the author's reasons for writing and what kind of information he or she wishes to convey. Different types of texts are called genres. Tell them that the persuasive essay is one type of genre.

Discuss the genre

Explain that authors write for many reasons. One is to *persuade*—to convince you to think or act in a certain way. The author of a persuasive text will have a distinct point of view. Ask: What types of things do you read or see that are persuasive and give a point of view? Possible responses: advertisements, movie reviews

On the board, make a list of persuasive techniques as you discuss the following:

- Imagine you read a persuasive essay that says that everyone should learn square dancing, the author learned square dancing, and you should learn square dancing too. What can you identify as the author's viewpoint? Possible response: The author thinks everyone should square dance.
- If you read that square dancing is the best form of dancing ever created, is that realistic? Possible response: No, it sounds like an exaggeration or an opinion instead of a fact.
- Would it be a misleading statement for the author to say that doctors think square dancing is good for your health? Why? Possible response: Yes, it would be misleading. Doctors say that exercise in general is good for your health, not square dancing specifically.
- Would it be a contradictory statement if a person who got hurt while square dancing said that it was good for you? Why? Possible response: Yes, it would be contradictory because receiving an injury is not good for your health.
- Parallelism is a technique authors use to show relationships among ideas. Authors write sentences that have the same grammatical form throughout. Write these sentences on the board: *Dancing is fun. Dancing is exciting.* Ask: How can I write one sentence to show a relationship between these two ideas? Possible response: *Dancing is fun and exciting.*

- Authors use a technique called comparison to link our feelings about one thing to another thing. Have students finish this sentence: *Dancing is like* ________. Tell students to complete this sentence by comparing dancing to something they like or dislike, based on how they feel about dancing. Possible response: *Dancing is like walking on hot coals.*
- Another technique that authors use is showing a causal relationship. Showing causality connects two ideas that may or may not be related. Write this sentence on the board: *He became the most popular kid in school because he learned to square dance.* Ask: What two ideas are being linked? Which one caused the other? Possible response: Popularity and square dancing are being linked. The dancing caused the popularity.

Guide practice Have students work with a partner to write persuasive sentences using each of these techniques. Then have pairs exchange papers, identify each technique, and explain how they know.

Connect to reading Tell students that they will now read a persuasive essay about square dancing. Have the class look for the persuasive techniques the author uses.

Academic Vocabulary

essay a composition written on a certain subject

Small Group Time

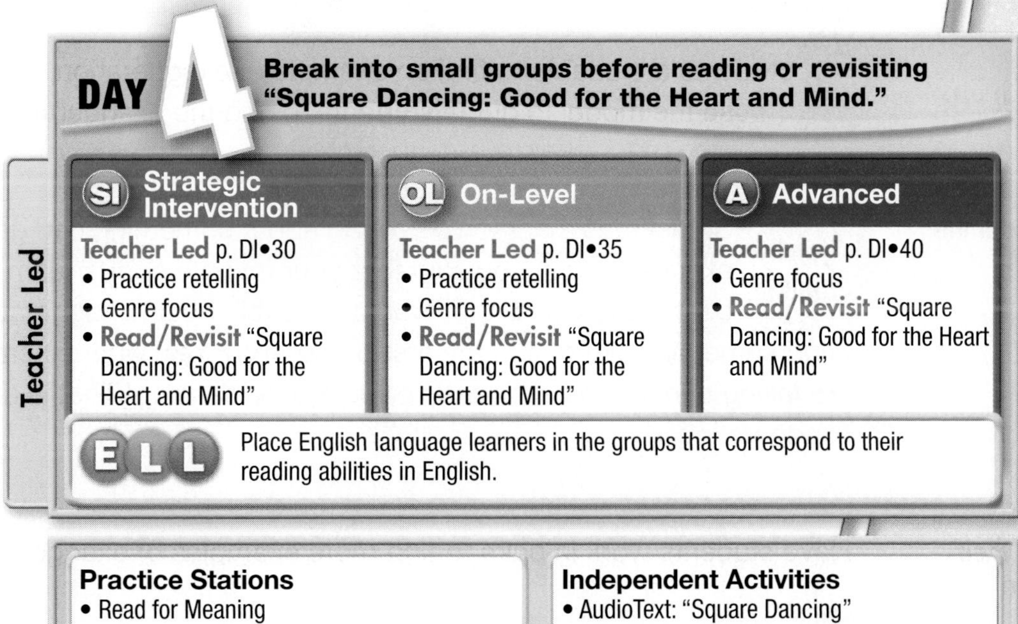

DAY 4
Break into small groups before reading or revisiting "Square Dancing: Good for the Heart and Mind."
Teacher Led
SI Strategic Intervention
Teacher Led p. DI•30
• Practice retelling
• Genre focus
• Read/Revisit "Square Dancing: Good for the Heart and Mind"
OL On-Level
Teacher Led p. DI•35
• Practice retelling
• Genre focus
• Read/Revisit "Square Dancing: Good for the Heart and Mind"
A Advanced
Teacher Led p. DI•40
• Genre focus
• Read/Revisit "Square Dancing: Good for the Heart and Mind"
ELL
Place English language learners in the groups that correspond to their reading abilities in English.
Practice Stations
• Read for Meaning
• Get Fluent
• Words to Know
Independent Activities
• AudioText: "Square Dancing"
• Reader's and Writer's Notebook
• Research and Inquiry

ELL

English Language Learners

Persuasive techniques Talk about exaggeration. Tell students: I went fishing last week. I caught a fish so big it ate the boat. Tell students that this is an *exaggeration*. Have volunteers make up their own exaggeration. Use the fishing sentence as a starting-off point and have students fill in their own exaggerations: *I caught a fish so big it* ____.

Objective

- Recognize persuasive techniques.

Objectives
• Identify the author's viewpoint or position and explain the relationship among ideas in the argument.
• Recognize exaggerated, contradictory, or misleading statements in text. • Make connections between and among texts.

Social Studies in Reading

Genre
Persuasive Text

- A persuasive text tries to convince the reader to do or think something.
- The author of a persuasive text has a distinct point of view and position. Sometimes, an author will repeat words or phrases to help support his argument.
- Persuasive texts may contain exaggerated, contradictory, or misleading statements.
- Read "Square Dancing: Good for the Heart and Mind." Look at elements that make this selection a persuasive text. What is the author's position or viewpoint?

Square Dancing:
Good for the Heart and Mind
by Victoria Barrett

All across the country, people of all ages are taking part in the best dance ever: square dancing! Square dancing is all about good music. Square dancing is all about exercise. Square dancing is all about a great time spent with friends and family.

Where else can you spin around with your partner to the accompaniment of a fiddle? Where else can you learn the do-si-do? These are just some of the reasons that the square dance is the best dance.

Square dancing has a long and very interesting history. Early European settlers brought with them their dances when they came to America. After farming all day, the settlers gathered in barns or fields to party. Over time, the dances changed as more steps were added.

As time passed, square dancing slowly moved westward. In places such as Texas, square dancing became quite popular. Today, people can take classes or join square-dancing clubs. Square dancing is so popular in Texas that in 1991 it became the official state dance. Have you tried square dancing? If not, here are a number of reasons why you should:

Good exercise. Square dancing requires dancers to spin, turn, and move their feet. All that movement keeps the heart and muscles in good shape. All doctors will agree that square dancing has plenty of health benefits. It's true!

It's good for your memory. Circle to the left, bow to the corner, circle to the right, bow to your partner. Can you remember all of that? There are dozens of different square dances, and each dance has its own steps and movements. Remembering all the steps is great exercise for your brain.

It's fun! Square dances are fantastic places to meet new people. You can come to square dances with your friends and family members. You can meet other people who like to dance. If you've never square danced before, you get the chance to try something new.

There are many reasons why people should try square dancing. It's good exercise, it helps your memory, and almost anyone can do it. Square dancing is the most fun you'll have in your entire life! All you need is a dance floor and some music, and you'll be doing the do-si-do before you know it.

Let's Think About...
How does the author use cause and effect in her argument? **Persuasive Text**
1

Let's Think About...
Which sentences in the story are exaggerated, contradictory, or misleading statements? **Persuasive Text**
2

Let's Think About...
Reading Across Texts Are any of the reasons Jinx gives to Mr. Deimeister for holding a square dance similar to the ones in this article?

Writing Across Texts Design a flyer for the square dance held at Jinx's school, including reasons why people should come to the square dance.

72 73

Student Edition pp. 72–73

Guide Comprehension
Skills and Strategies

Teach the genre

Persuasive Text: Essay Have students read "Square Dancing: Good for the Heart and Mind" on pp. 72–73. As they read, have them look for exaggeration in the selection. Then say: Find an example of exaggeration on page 72.

Corrective feedback

If... students are unable to find an example of exaggeration,
then... use the model to guide students to find the exaggeration.

Model the skill

Think Aloud Sometimes a person's opinion about something can get exaggerated. If you said that your favorite sports team was the best in the world, that would probably be an exaggeration. Can I find something like that in the first paragraph? Yes, where it says, *people are taking part in the best dance ever: square dancing!* That is an exaggeration.

On their own

Have students work in pairs to find more examples of exaggeration.

Extend Thinking

Think Critically

Higher-order thinking skills

Generalize • Analysis Identify the author's viewpoint. Make one generalization about square dancing that supports this position. Possible response: Everyone should learn to square dance. Most people will have fun square dancing.

Predict and Set Purpose • Analysis What do you think the writer hopes might happen after a person read this selection? Possible response: They would be persuaded to think that square dancing is great and would try to find a place to go square dancing.

Let's Think About...

1. The effect that Texas made square dancing the official state dance because it's so popular is used as evidence of square dancing's appeal.
2. Exaggeration: *square dancing is the best dance ever* and *square dancing is the most fun you'll ever have in your entire life;* Misleading: *All doctors will agree that square dancing has plenty of health benefits;* Examples of contradictory statements are in paragraph 1 where the author says that square dancing is all about good music, exercise, and a great time spent with friends and family.

Reading Across Texts

Have students create a T-chart to list the reasons Jinx gives Mr. Deimeister for having a square dancing class and the reasons that Victoria gives in the persuasive essay.

Writing Across Texts

Have students use their T-charts to design a flyer for the square dance held at Jinx's school. Remind students to include all the reasons why people should come to the square dance.

Differentiated Instruction

SI Strategic Intervention

Persuasive text In a small group setting, review the first paragraph of "Square Dancing: Good for the Heart and Mind" on p. 72. Write this repeated phrase on the board: *Square dancing is all about* ___. Have volunteers fill in the sentence with information from the selection. Ask students how repeating this phrase makes the reader feel about square dancing. *(It makes people feel that square dancing is great.)*

Advanced

Persuasive text Have students review the text on pp. 72–73 to find contradictory statements.

ELL

English Language Learners

Persuasive text Remind students that this genre is meant to convince you of something. Ask students about their favorite dance. Write the names of the dances on the board. Ask students what makes these dances the best and write that information next to the names. Based on this information, help students come up with a persuasive sentence or sentences about their favorite dances.

Read and Comprehend

Objectives

- Read with fluency and accuracy.
- Use context clues to determine meanings of common idioms.
- Present a persuasive speech.

Check Fluency: WCPM
SUCCESS PREDICTOR

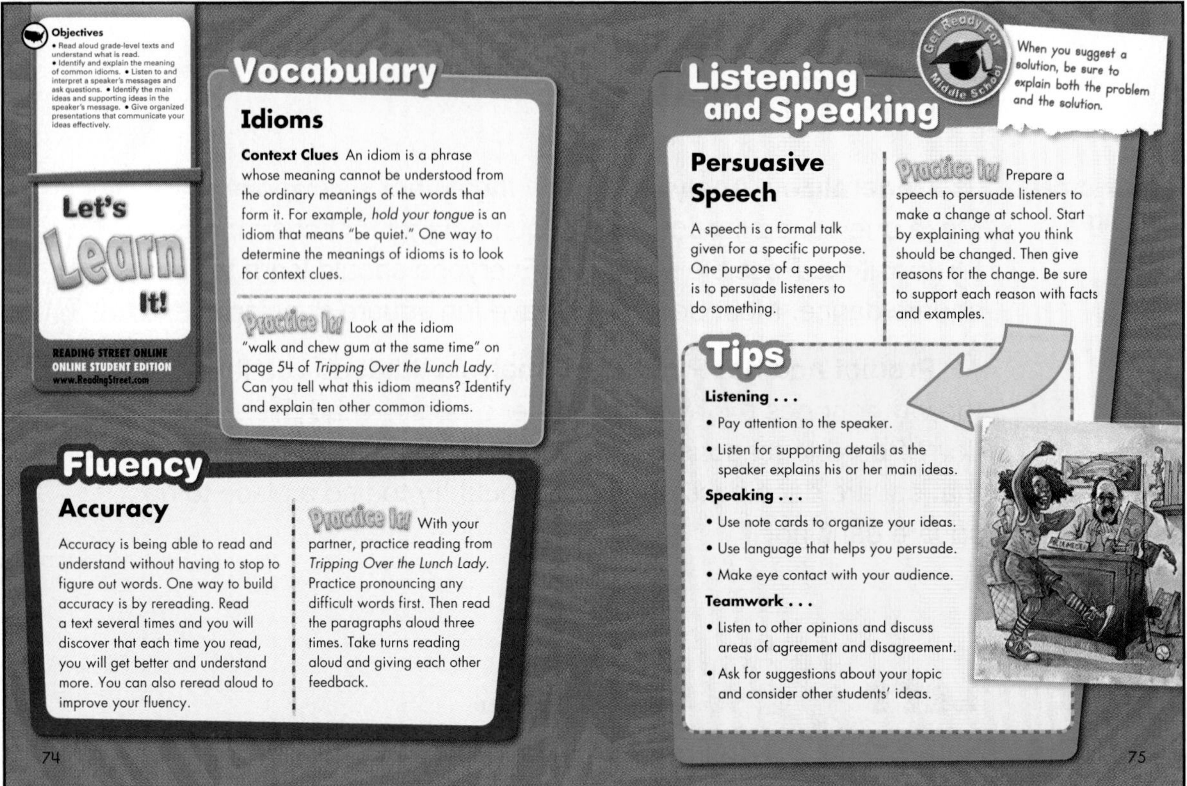

Objectives
• Read aloud grade-level texts and understand what is read. • Identify and explain the meaning of common idioms. • Listen to and interpret a speaker's messages and ask questions. • Identify the main ideas and supporting ideas in the speaker's message. • Give organized presentations that communicate your ideas effectively.

Let's Learn It!

READING STREET ONLINE
ONLINE STUDENT EDITION
www.ReadingStreet.com

Vocabulary

Idioms

Context Clues An idiom is a phrase whose meaning cannot be understood from the ordinary meanings of the words that form it. For example, *hold your tongue* is an idiom that means "be quiet." One way to determine the meanings of idioms is to look for context clues.

Practice It! Look at the idiom "walk and chew gum at the same time" on page 54 of *Tripping Over the Lunch Lady*. Can you tell what this idiom means? Identify and explain ten other common idioms.

Fluency

Accuracy

Accuracy is being able to read and understand without having to stop to figure out words. One way to build accuracy is by rereading. Read a text several times and you will discover that each time you read, you will get better and understand more. You can also reread aloud to improve your fluency.

Practice It! With your partner, practice reading from *Tripping Over the Lunch Lady*. Practice pronouncing any difficult words first. Then read the paragraphs aloud three times. Take turns reading aloud and giving each other feedback.

Listening and Speaking

Get Ready For Middle School

When you suggest a solution, be sure to explain both the problem and the solution.

Persuasive Speech

A speech is a formal talk given for a specific purpose. One purpose of a speech is to persuade listeners to do something.

Practice It! Prepare a speech to persuade listeners to make a change at school. Start by explaining what you think should be changed. Then give reasons for the change. Be sure to support each reason with facts and examples.

Tips

Listening . . .
- Pay attention to the speaker.
- Listen for supporting details as the speaker explains his or her main ideas.

Speaking . . .
- Use note cards to organize your ideas.
- Use language that helps you persuade.
- Make eye contact with your audience.

Teamwork . . .
- Listen to other opinions and discuss areas of agreement and disagreement.
- Ask for suggestions about your topic and consider other students' ideas.

74 75

Student Edition pp. 74–75

Fluency
Accuracy

Guide practice Use the Student Edition activity as an assessment tool. Make sure the reading passage is at least 200 words in length. As students read aloud with partners, walk around to make sure their reading is accurate and that they are able to read and understand without mistakes.

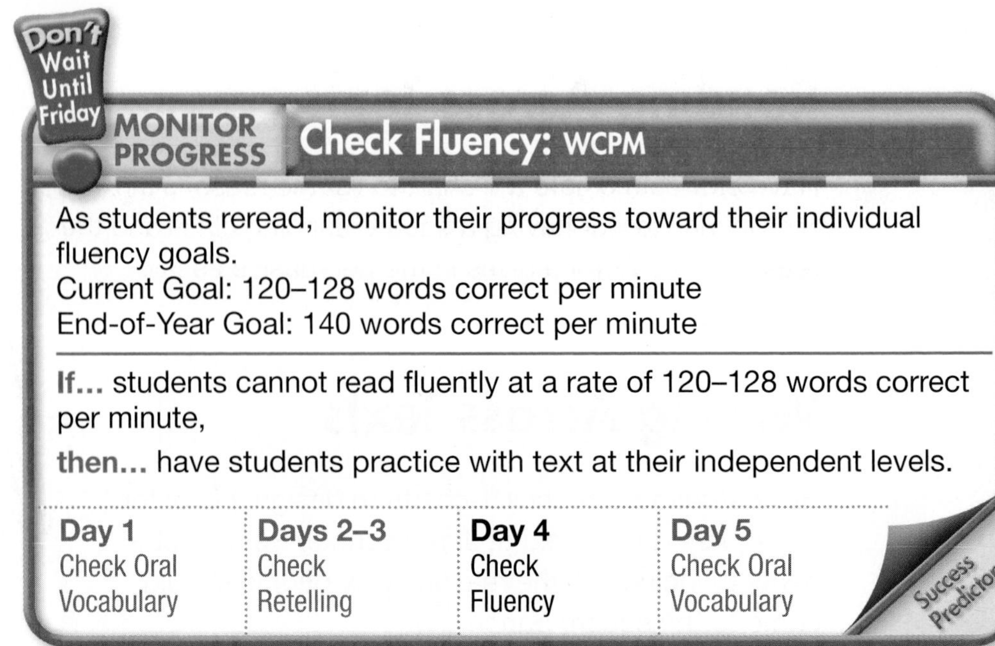

Don't Wait Until Friday

MONITOR PROGRESS **Check Fluency: WCPM**

As students reread, monitor their progress toward their individual fluency goals.
Current Goal: 120–128 words correct per minute
End-of-Year Goal: 140 words correct per minute

If... students cannot read fluently at a rate of 120–128 words correct per minute,
then... have students practice with text at their independent levels.

Day 1	Days 2–3	Day 4	Day 5
Check Oral Vocabulary	Check Retelling	Check Fluency	Check Oral Vocabulary

Success Predictor

Vocabulary
Idioms

Teach context clues

Context Clues Write this sentence on the board: *You know how people say that some folks can't walk and chew gum at the same time*?

Point out that this is an idiom—an expression that can't be understood from the ordinary meaning of the words that form it. Context clues can help you figure out what it means.

Guide practice

Have students identify an idiom in *Tripping Over the Lunch Lady*. Ask volunteers for some context clues to what this idiom means.

On their own

Walk around the room as students explain the meaning of the idioms they have identified. Check to make sure that they are using context clues to help them.

Listening and Speaking
Persuasive Speech

Teach

Tell students that their persuasive speeches will be about something they want to change at school. They will need to persuade their listeners that they have a good reason to make this change. Tell students that one of the most important aspects of making a persuasive speech is to present their arguments in an organized way.

Guide practice

Have students brainstorm ideas and decide what they want to change. Remind them that they need to support their ideas with facts and examples. Before they make their speeches, remind students that good speakers maintain eye contact with listeners, speak at an appropriate rate and volume with clear enunciation, make natural gestures with their hands and body, and use proper conventions of language while speaking. Also remind the students to listen attentively to the speaker to accurately interpret the speaker's verbal and nonverbal message. Have them determine the main idea and supporting ideas in the speaker's speech.

On their own

Students can write their speeches and organize them on note cards. Have students work in groups taking turns presenting their speeches. Encourage students to discuss areas of agreement and disagreement after each speech.

Persuasive Speech

Remind students that they should look directly at their listeners when they present their speech. By making eye contact, they communicate their ideas more effectively.

ELL

English Language Learners

Idioms In a small group, practice understanding another idiom that could describe Jinx: *Jinx is all thumbs.* Explain that it means *clumsy.* Use the illustrations to show the meaning. Then help students locate sentences in the selection that show how clumsy Jinx is.

Objectives

- Prepare a descriptive report.
- Identify and correctly use pronouns and antecedents.
- Spell words with the prefixes *over-*, *under-*, *sub-*, *super-*, and *out-*.

Research and Inquiry

Synthesize

Teach

Have students synthesize their research findings and results into a written description that summarizes what they learned. Their presentations should include a description of the person, the obstacle he or she had to overcome, and how he or she overcame this obstacle. Encourage students to incorporate the picture of the person into their description.

Guide practice

Have students use a word-processing program to prepare for their presentations on Day 5. Have them draw a picture of the person they are describing or print out a photograph to accompany their presentations. Encourage them to arrange the description and photograph on a poster board so they are ready for their presentation.

On their own

Remind students that their descriptions should focus on the obstacle their famous person overcame. Have them decide which extraneous biographical information should be omitted. Other details may enhance the description and should be included.

Conventions
Pronouns and Antecedents

Test practice Remind students that grammar skills, such as making sure pronouns agree with antecedents, are often assessed on important tests. Remind students that pronouns take the place of nouns and that an antecedent is the noun or nouns to which a pronoun refers. Students should remember these rules about pronouns and antecedents:

- Each pronoun must agree with its antecedent in number and gender.
- When writing, if a pronoun's antecedent is unclear, the sentence should be rewritten.

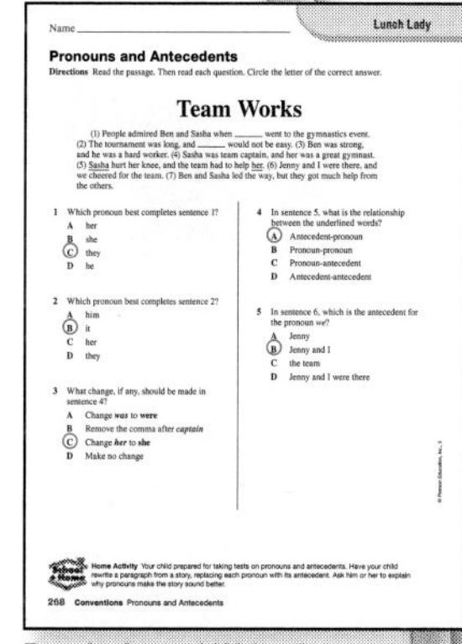
Lunch Lady
Pronouns and Antecedents
Team Works

Reader's and Writer's Notebook p. 268

Daily Fix-It Use Daily Fix-It numbers 7 and 8 in the right margin.

On their own For additional practice, use *Reader's and Writer's Notebook* p. 268.

Spelling
Prefixes *over-, under-, sub-, super-, out-*

Practice spelling strategy Write each list word on a small piece of paper. Fold the papers and mix them up. Then take turns with a partner picking a word and asking each other to spell it. A correct spelling means the speller keeps the paper. For an incorrect spelling, the paper goes to the partner. Keep playing until all the words have been spelled. The partner with more papers is the winner.

On their own For additional practice, use *Let's Practice It!* p. 199 on the *Teacher Resources DVD-ROM.*

Let's Practice It! TR DVD•199

Daily Fix-It

7. Jinx hurt her head and had a ankle that was sprained? *(an; sprained.)*
8. The reel snap and caused mr. Deimeister to fall out of the boat. *(snapped; Mr.)*

Objectives

- Revise draft of a friendly letter.
- Apply revising strategy of adding.
- Include a variety of sentences that reflect the voice of the letter writer.

Writing—Friendly Letter
Revising Strategy

MINI-LESSON

Revising Strategy: Adding

- Yesterday we wrote friendly letters from one character in *Tripping Over the Lunch Lady* to another character. Today we will revise our drafts. The goal is to make your writing clearer, more interesting, and more informative.
- Display Writing Transparency 17B. Remind students that revising does not include corrections of grammar and mechanics, which will be done tomorrow as they proofread their work. Then introduce the revising strategy of adding.
- When we revise, we ask ourselves, *Have I left out anything that could make my writing clearer and more interesting?* The revising strategy of adding is the process by which we include details that help us convey important information. Let's look at the first paragraph of my letter. If I were Jinx, I would want to know why Mr. Deimeister has to stay in the hospital. I could add information here. I could also add that he likes hospital food to explain why he is not upset about staying longer.

Writing Transparency 17B, TR DVD

Tell students that as they revise they should look for places to add information that will clarify the letter or make it more interesting to read. As they add information, they should also think about using a variety of sentences, including both simple and compound sentences.

Revising Tips

- ✔ Add details to make your writing clearer and more interesting.
- ✔ Think about whether you need to add to the end of the letter to create a clear sense of closure.
- ✔ Look for ways to vary your sentences.

Peer conferencing

Peer Revision Have pairs of students exchange papers for peer revision. Students should write three questions about the partner's writing. Their questions should focus on where their partner could revise by adding details to make the writing clearer and more interesting. Refer to *First Stop* for more information about peer conferencing.

Have students revise their compositions using the questions their partner wrote during Peer Revision as well as the key features of a friendly letter to guide them. They should be especially focused on using casual, natural-sounding language. Be sure that students are using the revising strategy of adding.

Corrective feedback Circulate around the room to monitor students and have conferences with students as they revise. If you notice students correcting errors, remind them that they will have time to edit tomorrow. They should be working on content and organization today.

ROUTINE Quick Write for Fluency — Team Talk

1. **Talk** Pairs discuss what they learned about Jinx's personality (not her physical self) from reading *Tripping Over the Lunch Lady*. What kind of person is she?
2. **Write** Each person comes up with three adjectives that describe Jinx and uses the adjectives in three sentences about her. The sentences should be written as if they were in a friendly letter to someone that tells about Jinx.
3. **Share** Partners check each other's sentences for the type of casual tone that should be used in a friendly letter.

Routines Flip Chart

Wrap Up Your Day

- **Build Concepts** What did you learn about the history of square dancing?
- **Oral Vocabulary** Monitor students' use of oral vocabulary as they respond: How did square dancing help early European settles adjust to America?
- **Text Features** Discuss how bullet points help students understand text.

Write Guy *Jeff Anderson*

Life in a Fishbowl

When a teacher can't confer with every student, a "fishbowl conference" with one willing student can allow other students to observe, listen, and explore how to appropriately respond to others' writing. It's important to reflect what the student is doing well and what might be revised and improved.

Differentiated Instruction

Strategic Intervention
If students have trouble creating the right tone for their letters, have them work with a partner to act out a conversation.

English Language Learners
Adding As students think about using the revising strategy of adding, give them some questions to ask. Students should make sure their letter answers the questions *Why? Who? When? How?*

Remind students to think about how people adapt to overcome obstacles.

Objectives

- Review the weekly concept.
- Review oral vocabulary.

Today at a Glance

Oral Vocabulary

Comprehension
◎ Generalize

Lesson Vocabulary
◎ Unfamiliar words

Word Analysis
Suffixes *-ly, -ian*

Literary Terms
Hyperbole

Assessment
Fluency
Comprehension

Research and Inquiry
Communicate

Spelling
Prefixes *over-, under-, sub-, super-, out-*

Conventions
Pronouns and antecedents

Writing
Friendly letter

Check Oral Vocabulary SUCCESS PREDICTOR

Concept Wrap Up

Question of the Week

How do people overcome obstacles?

Review the concept Have students look back at the reading selections to find examples that best demonstrate how people overcome obstacles.

Review Amazing Words Display and review this week's concept map. Remind students that this week they have learned ten Amazing Words related to adapting. Have students use the Amazing Words and the concept map to answer the question *How do people overcome obstacles?*

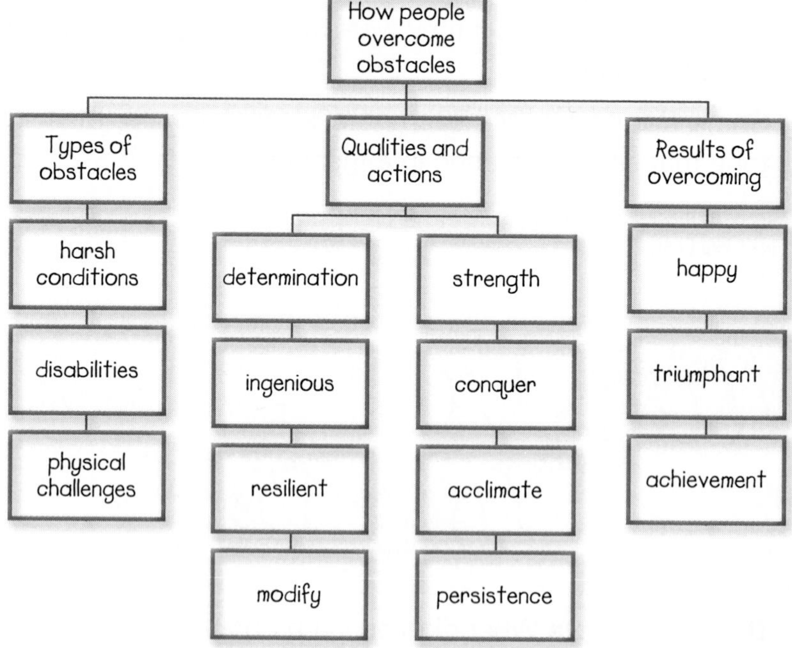

ELL Check Concept and Language Use the Day 5 instruction on ELL Poster 17 to monitor students' understanding of the lesson concept.

ELL Poster 17

Amazing Ideas

Connect to the Big Question

Have pairs of students elicit and consider suggestions from each other in a discussion about how the Question of the Week connects to the Big Question: *How do people and animals adapt to different situations?* Tell students to use the concept map and what they have learned from this week's Anchored Talks and reading selections to form an Amazing Idea—a realization or "big idea" about Adapting. Then ask each pair to share their Amazing Idea with the class.

Amazing Ideas might include these key concepts:

- When people confront challenges, they often come up with ingenious ideas to conquer them.
- It helps to be resilient when you are trying to adapt to a challenge.
- Persistence is a good trait to have when trying to overcome obstacles.

Write about it

Have students write a few sentences about their Amazing Idea, beginning with "This week I learned…"

MONITOR PROGRESS **Check Oral Vocabulary**

Have individuals use this week's Amazing Words to describe overcoming obstacles. Monitor students' ability to use the Amazing Words and note which words you need to reteach.

If… students have difficulty using the Amazing Words,
then… reteach using the Oral Vocabulary Routine, pp. 47a, 50b, 62b, 72b, OV•2.

Day 1	Days 2–3	Day 4	Day 5
Check Oral Vocabulary	Check Retelling	Check Fluency	Check Oral Vocabulary

Success Predictor

Amazing Words

confront	resilient
predicament	modify
ingenious	conquer
triumphant	acclimate
application	persistence

ELL

English Language Learners

Concept map Work with students to add new words to the concept map.

DAY 5 Wrap Up your Week

20–25 mins.

Objectives

- ◎ Review generalizing.
- ◎ Review using context clues to determine the meaning of unfamiliar words.
- Review suffixes *-ly, -ian.*
- Review hyperbole.

Comprehension Review

Generalize

Student Edition p. EI•7

Teach generalize

Envision It!

Review the definition of generalization on p. 48. Remind students that to generalize is to make a broad statement that applies to several examples. For additional support have students review p. EI•7 on generalizing.

Guide practice

Have partners review *Tripping Over the Lunch Lady* to make or infer some generalizations about Jinx. Then have pairs look for information in the text that supports each generalization.

On their own

For additional practice, use *Let's Practice It!* p. 200 on the *Teacher Resources DVD-ROM.*

Let's Practice It!
TR DVD•200

Vocabulary Review

Unfamiliar Words

Teach unfamiliar words

Remind students that unfamiliar words are words whose meaning we can determine to by using context clues.

Guide practice

Review with students how to look at the context of the text to determine the meaning of *substitute* on p. 64 of *Tripping Over the Lunch Lady.*

On their own

Have students work in pairs to write context sentences for *sprained, frilly, promenading,* and *Dalmatian.* Partners can trade sentences and identify the context clues that help them determine each word's meaning.

Word Analysis Review

Suffixes *-ly, -ian*

Teach suffixes Review the definition of suffixes and affixes, with students. Discuss the definition of these words: *safely* and *veterinarian.*

Guide practice Display the following words: *perfectly*, *technically, technician,* and *librarian.* Use the Strategy for Meaningful Word Parts to teach the word *perfectly.*

ROUTINE **Strategy for Meaningful Word Parts**

1. **Introduce word parts** Have students circle the base word and suffix in *perfectly*.
2. **Connect to meaning** Define each word part. *Perfect* means "not having any faults." The suffix *-ly* means "characteristic of."
3. **Read the word** Blend the meaningful word parts together to read *perfectly*. Then use the meanings of the word parts to determine the meaning of the new word. *Perfectly* means "in a perfect way."

Routines Flip Chart

On their own Have students work in pairs to circle the roots or base words and suffixes in each word and define the words.

Literary Terms Review

Hyperbole

Teach hyperbole Have students reread p. 57 of *Tripping Over the Lunch Lady*. Remind students that hyperbole is when something is overstated or exaggerated.

Guide practice Find an example of hyperbole on p. 57. Discuss the fourth paragraph with the students. Discuss why the author used this exaggeration about the goldfish. Have students point out another example of hyperbole on p. 59.

On their own Have students reread p. 65 to find a third example of hyperbole.

Lesson Vocabulary

Dalmatian a dog that has a white coat with black or brown spots

frilly clothing that has ruffles

promenading to be walking for show

sprained to be injured by a sudden twist

substitute a person or thing taking the place of another

ELL

English Language Learners

Generalize Review elements of *Tripping Over the Lunch Lady* with students. What always happened to Jinx on the trampoline? (She fell off.) Write this sentence on the board: *Jinx always fell off the trampoline.* What usually happened to the people around Jinx? (They got hurt.) Write this sentence on the board: *People around Jinx usually got hurt.* Have volunteers read the sentences. Explain that the clue words *always* and *usually* tell that these sentences are generalizations.

Objectives

- Read grade-level text with fluency.

Assessment

Check words correct per minute

Fluency Make two copies of the fluency passage on page 75k. As the student reads the text aloud, mark mistakes on your copy. Also mark where the student is at the end of one minute. To check the student's comprehension of the passage, have him or her retell what was read. To figure words correct per minute (WCPM), subtract the number of mistakes from the total number of words read in one minute.

Corrective feedback

If... students cannot read fluently at a rate of 120–128 WCPM or with comprehension,
then... make sure they practice with text at their independent reading level. Provide additional fluency practice by pairing nonfluent readers with fluent readers.

If... students already read at 140 WCPM,
then... have them read a book of their choice independently.

Plan to Assess Fluency

- [x] **Week 1** Assess Advanced students.
- [x] **This week assess Strategic Intervention students.**
- [ ] **Week 3** Assess On-Level students.
- [ ] **Week 4** Assess Strategic Intervention students.
- [ ] **Week 5** Assess any students you have not yet checked during this unit.

Set individual goals for students to enable them to reach the year-end goal.

- Current Goal: 120–128 WCPM
- Year-End Goal: 140 WCPM

Small Group Time

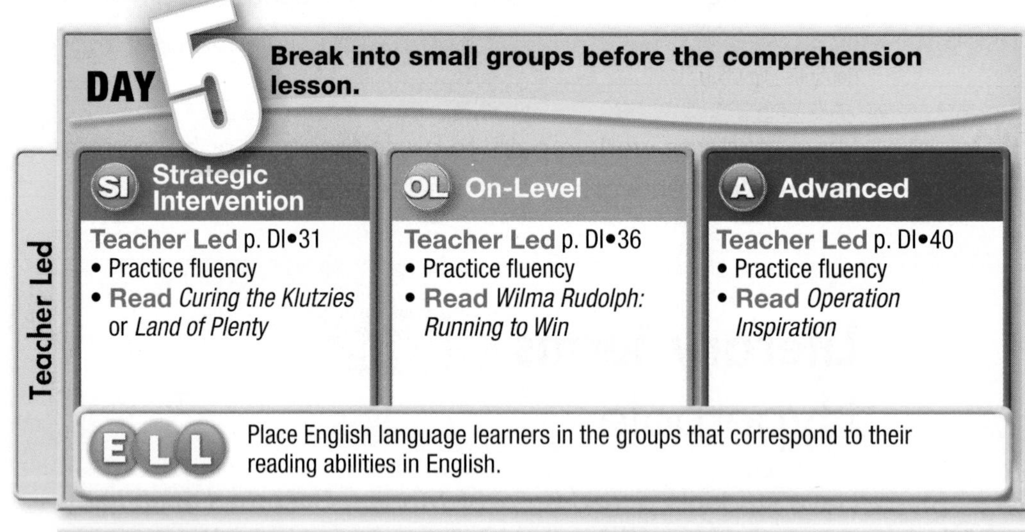

DAY 5 **Break into small groups before the comprehension lesson.**

Teacher Led

SI Strategic Intervention	OL On-Level	A Advanced
Teacher Led p. DI•31 • Practice fluency • **Read** *Curing the Klutzies* or *Land of Plenty*	**Teacher Led** p. DI•36 • Practice fluency • **Read** *Wilma Rudolph: Running to Win*	**Teacher Led** p. DI•40 • Practice fluency • **Read** *Operation Inspiration*

ELL Place English language learners in the groups that correspond to their reading abilities in English.

Practice Stations
- Words to Know
- Get Fluent
- Read for Meaning

Independent Activities
- Grammar Jammer
- Concept Talk Video
- Vocabulary Activities

Name ____________________

The President's Secret

In the 1932 election, when Franklin Roosevelt was chosen president of 11
the United States, he had a secret. He was disabled and couldn't walk on his 26
own. He spent most of his time in a wheelchair. 36

Roosevelt's disability was caused by a horrible disease called polio. He 47
came down with it when he was 39 years old. Polio killed many people, and 62
left many more disabled. 66

Roosevelt was a rich man who fought to find a way to walk unaided 80
again. He worked hard for other people's recovery too. Although he failed, 92
his battle with the disease made him a tougher, more determined person. 104

But why didn't Americans know that Roosevelt needed a wheelchair? 114
Roosevelt didn't want them to know. He and his advisers were afraid that 127
people would think he wasn't strong enough to be president. 137

Roosevelt had what was called a "gentlemen's agreement" with reporters 147
who worked for America's newspapers and radio networks. Reporters agreed 157
not to write or talk about Roosevelt's disability. Newspapers agreed not to 169
publish photographs that showed Roosevelt in a wheelchair. As a result, 180
during Roosevelt's years as president, no such story or photograph was 191
published. Even today, such photos are hard to find. 200

Many historians believe that Roosevelt was one of the greatest presidents. 211
He led the United States through tough times, including World War II. But the 225
big question still remains. In 1932, would Americans have voted for Roosevelt 237
if they had known that he used a wheelchair? 246

MONITOR PROGRESS

- **Check Fluency**

Objectives

- Read grade-level text with comprehension.

Assessment

Check generalize

Generalize Use "Mack's Solution" on p. 75m to check students' understanding of generalizing.

1. What generalization does the author make in the first paragraph? Possible response: Mack and his pals always go sledding on Saturdays in winter.
2. What is one generalization you could make about Mack? Name one detail from the story that supports your generalization. Possible response: Mack is usually clever and smart. In the passage, he tries to trick his mom into not making him put the sleds away.
3. Based on the details in the passage, make a generalization about what Mack's family does for fun. Possible response: I can infer that Mack's family always goes sledding, based on the details that they have three sleds, and know which kind of sled works best.

Corrective feedback

If... students are unable to answer the comprehension questions, **then...** use the Reteach lesson in the *First Stop* book.

Name ______________________________

Mack's Solution

Mack yanked off his weighty winter coat and galoshes. He and two pals had been sledding like they always do on Saturdays in winter, but today they quit because the snow was melting rapidly into slush.

"Did you put the sleds away?" Mom inquired.

Mack frowned because he hadn't. He and his pals had used his family's three classic, old-fashioned sleds made out of wood with metal runners. They were so much better than plastic sleds and perfect for speeding down slick hills. But they were awkward to put away, so Mack left the sleds propped on the front porch.

"But it's my birthday," whined Mack. "That's why I shouldn't have to put sleds away," he said. "Today's special for me!"

"And that's why we're having a party," said Mom. "And that's why everything has to be just right. And . . . "

Before Mom could finish, Mack said, "That's why I should put away the sleds."

Mom smiled as Mack put back on his coat. Mack opened the front door and said, "Oh, no! The snow melted quickly. There's a river of water across our yard. How will people walk into our house for the party?"

Mom looked outside. "It is bad out front," she said.

Then Mack saw the sleds. "We'll use the sleds to make a wooden path over the water. The runners are high enough so people's feet won't get wet."

Mom thought about it and said. "That sounds a bit dangerous. Let's tell our guests to enter through the garage. The driveway isn't so wet."

Then she smiled at Mack and said, "But your suggestion was a clever one."

Mack grinned, and Mom added, "For finding another reason why *not* to put away the sleds."

Mack and Mom laughed. And Mack put the sleds away.

MONITOR PROGRESS

- **Generalize**

Objectives

- Communicate inquiry results.
- Administer spelling test.
- Review pronouns and antecedents.

Research and Inquiry
Communicate

Present ideas Have students share their inquiry results by reading their description and presenting their illustration.

Listening and speaking Remind students how to be good speakers and how to communicate effectively with their audience.

- Speak clearly and loudly.
- Keep eye contact with audience members.
- Enunciate clearly, and use natural hand gestures as appropriate.
- Speak with good grammar, and use language appropriate for your audience.
- Respond to relevant questions with details from your research.

Remind students about these tips for how to be a good listener.

- Pay close attention to understand both the speaker's verbal and nonverbal messages.
- Wait until the speaker has finished before raising your hand to ask a question.

Spelling Test

Prefixes *over-, under-, sub-, super-, out-*

Spelling test To administer the spelling test, refer to the directions, words, and sentences on p. 49c.

Conventions

Extra Practice

Teach Remind students that an antecedent is the noun or nouns to which a pronoun refers. Pronouns must agree with their antecedents in number and gender.

Guide practice Read these sentences aloud. Have sentences name the pronoun that should replace each proper noun the second time it is used.

Bob likes to fish, but Bob lost his fishing gear.

Sue has seven cats living at Sue's house.

The Garcias think the Garcias will vacation in Hawaii this year.

My brother and I asked Mom to take my brothers and I to the movie.

Daily Fix-It Use Daily Fix-It numbers 9 and 10 in the right margin.

On their own Write these sentences about events in *Tripping Over the Lunch Lady*. Have students fill in the blanks with the correct pronoun.

1. **Jinx scared Tony Friedman so badly that ____ choked on some gum.** (he)
2. **Jinx went to Mr. Deimeister's office to talk to ____ about square dancing.** (him)
3. **Everyone had to spot Jinx so that ____ wouldn't get hurt.** (she)
4. **Vic and Jinx had an accident while ____ were trying to square dance together.** (they)
5. **Jinx's Uncle Jeff had problems like hers when ____ was young.** (he)

For additional practice, use *Let's Practice It!* p. 201 on the *Teacher Resources DVD-ROM*.

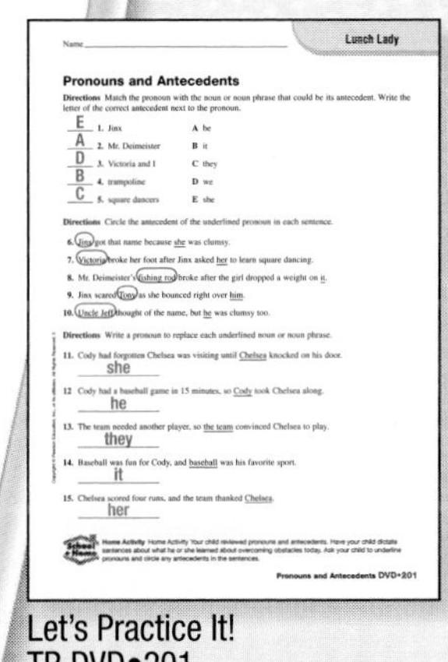
Name ____________ Lunch Lady

Pronouns and Antecedents

Directions Match the pronoun with the noun or noun phrase that could be its antecedent. Write the letter of the correct antecedent next to the pronoun.

E 1. Jinx — A he
A 2. Mr. Deimeister — B it
D 3. Victoria and I — C they
B 4. trampoline — D we
C 5. square dancers — E she

Directions Circle the antecedent of the underlined pronoun in each sentence.

6. Jinx got that name because she was clumsy.
7. Victoria broke her foot after Jinx asked her to learn square dancing.
8. Mr. Deimeister's fishing rod broke after the girl dropped a weight on it.
9. Jinx scared Tony as she bounced right over him.
10. Uncle Jeff thought of the name, but he was clumsy too.

Directions Write a pronoun to replace each underlined noun or noun phrase.

11. Cody had forgotten Chelsea was visiting until Chelsea knocked on his door. she
12. Cody had a baseball game in 15 minutes, so Cody took Chelsea along. he
13. The team needed another player, so the team convinced Chelsea to play. they
14. Baseball was fun for Cody, and baseball was his favorite sport. it
15. Chelsea scored four runs, and the team thanked Chelsea. her

Home Activity Your child reviewed pronouns and antecedents. Have your child dictate sentences about what he or she learned about overcoming obstacles today. Ask your child to underline pronouns and circle any antecedents in the sentences.

Pronouns and Antecedents DVD•201

Let's Practice It!
TR DVD•201

Daily Fix-It

9. Josh got a big bruise on he forehead because of there square dancing accident. *(his; their)*
10. vic tried to make square dancing a sucess. *(Vic; success)*

DAY 5 Wrap Up your Week 20–25 mins.

Objectives

- Proofread revised drafts of friendly letters, including correct use of commas and pronoun and antecedent agreement.
- Create and present final drafts.

Writing—Friendly Letter
Conventions

Review revising Remind students that yesterday they revised their friendly letters, paying particular attention to adding details to make the writing more clear and interesting. Today they will proofread their compositions.

MINI-LESSON

Proofread for Conventions

- **Teach** When we proofread, we look closely at our work, searching for errors in mechanics such as spelling, capitalization, punctuation, and grammar. Today we will focus on making sure that commas, pronouns, and antecedents are used correctly throughout our letters.
- **Model** Let's look at the rest of the letter we started yesterday. Display Writing Transparency 17C. Explain that you will look for errors in the use of commas. I see a problem in my closing. The closing of a friendly letter is always followed by a comma. In addition, I see two sentences that are compound sentences and need a comma before the conjunctions *and* and *or*. Model returning to the beginning to look for pronoun-antecedent agreement errors. Find the error in the first paragraph. Explain to students that they should reread their letter a number of times, each time looking for different types of errors: spelling, punctuation, capitalization, and grammar.

Writing Transparency 17C, TR DVD

Proofread Display the Proofreading Tips. Ask students to proofread their letters, using the Proofreading Tips and paying particular attention to commas. Circulate around the room answering students' questions. When students have finished editing their own work, have pairs proofread one another's letters.

Proofreading Tips

- ✔ Be sure that commas appear in the date, greeting, and closing of the letter.
- ✔ Check for correct use of pronoun and antecedent agreement.
- ✔ Check for correct spelling, capitalization, and grammar.

Present

Have students incorporate revisions and proofreading edits into their letters to create a final draft.

Give students two options for presenting: An oral presentation to the class or a final version of the letter attached to a properly addressed envelope. For oral presentations, students should remember to relax and present the letter in a casual voice. Students producing a final letter with envelope should remember to use correct capitalization, abbreviation, and punctuation in the addresses on the envelope. When students have finished, have each complete a Writing Self-Evaluation Guide.

ROUTINE Quick Write for Fluency — Team Talk

1. **Talk** Pairs discuss what they learned about the story characters they chose to focus on when writing their friendly letters.
2. **Write** Each person writes a sentence about the letter writer and a sentence about the recipient they featured. Each sentence should state something about the character they would not have noticed if they hadn't had to think about the characters while writing the letter.
3. **Share** Partners read their sentences to one another.

Routines Flip Chart

Teacher Note

Writing Self-Evaluation Guide Make copies of the Writing Self-Evaluation Guide on p. 39 of the *Reader's and Writer's Notebook* and hand out to students.

English Language Learners

Support editing Point out the commas in the date, greeting, and closing of the student model on p. 71. Students should remember to include these parts of the letter and to punctuate them as shown.

Poster preview Prepare students for next week by using Week 3, ELL Poster 18. Read the Poster Talk-Through to introduce the concept and vocabulary. Ask students to identify and describe objects and actions in the art.

Selection summary Send home the summary of *Exploding Ants*, in English and the students' home languages, if available. Students can read the summary with family members.

Preview NEXT WEEK

How do animals adapt to survive? You will read about how different animals have adapted in different ways to help them survive.

Assessment Checkpoints for the Week

Weekly Assessment

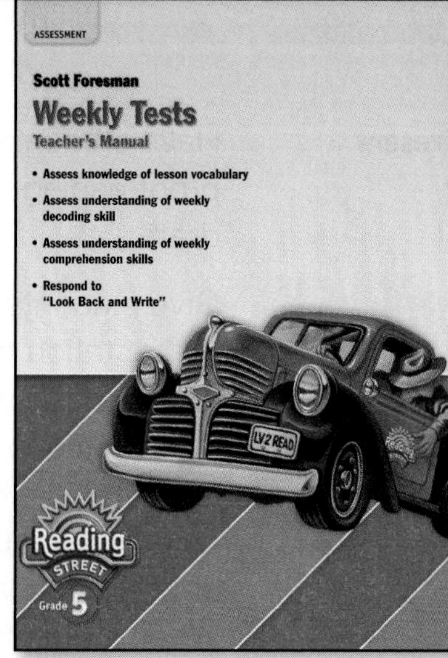

Weekly Tests

Use pp. 119–126 of *Weekly Tests* to check:

- ✔ **Word Analysis** Suffixes *-ly, -ian*
- ✔ **Comprehension Skill** Generalize
- ✔ Review **Comprehension Skill** Draw Conclusions
- ✔ **Lesson Vocabulary**

Dalmation	sprained
frilly	substitute
promenading	

Differentiated Assessment

Advanced

On-Level

SI Strategic Intervention

Fresh Reads for Fluency and Comprehension

Use pp. 97–102 of *Fresh Reads for Fluency and Comprehension* to check:

- ✔ **Comprehension Skill** Generalize
- ✔ Review **Comprehension Skill** Draw Conclusions
- ✔ **Fluency** Words Correct Per Minute

Managing Assessment

Assessment Handbook

Use *Assessment Handbook* for:

- ✔ **Weekly Assessment Blackline Masters for Monitoring Progress**
- ✔ **Observation Checklists**
- ✔ **Record-Keeping Forms**
- ✔ **Portfolio Assessment**

Teacher Notes

Pacing Small Group Instruction

5-Day Plan

DAY 1	• Reinforce the concept • Read Leveled Readers Concept Literacy Below Level
DAY 2	• Generalize • Predict and Set Purpose • Revisit Student Edition pp. 52–61
DAY 3	• Unfamiliar Words • Revisit Student Edition pp. 62–67
DAY 4	• Practice Retelling • Read/Revisit Student Edition pp. 72–73
DAY 5	• Reread for fluency • Reread Leveled Readers

3- or 4-Day Plan

DAY 1	• Reinforce the concept • Read Leveled Readers
DAY 2	• Generalize • Predict and Set Purpose • Revisit Student Edition pp. 52–61
DAY 3	• Unfamiliar Words • Revisit Student Edition pp. 62–67
DAY 4	• Practice Retelling • Read/Revisit Student Edition pp. 72–73 • Reread for fluency • Reread Leveled Readers

3-Day Plan: Eliminate the shaded box.

DAY 1

Build Background

- **Reinforce the Concept** Connect to the weekly question *How do people overcome obstacles?* Ask students to think of someone they know or have heard about who had to overcome a major challenge or obstacle. For example, athletes who have injuries to their spines have formed wheelchair basketball teams. They have found a way to keep playing the game they love no matter what happens to them. Other athletes run marathons and other races with prosthetic legs. This week's concept is *overcoming obstacles.* Some people never give up. For them, limits aren't stopping places. Instead, they are starting places. Discuss the words on the concept map on p. 46–47 in the Teacher Edition.

- **Connect to Reading** Point out to students that the real test for people is not what happens to them but what they do about it after it happens. This week you will read about ways people have overcome their physical problems and challenges. You will learn how their lives are like and unlike your own.

Objectives

- Interpret a speaker's messages (both verbal and nonverbal).

DAY 1

For a complete literacy instructional plan and additional practice with this week's target skills and strategies, see the **Leveled Reader Teaching Guide.**

Concept Literacy Reader

- **Read** *Curing the Klutzies*
- **Before Reading** Preview the selection with students, focusing on key concepts and vocabulary. Have students set a purpose for reading.
- **During Reading** Read the first two pages of the selection aloud while students track the print. Then have students finish reading the selection with a partner.
- **After Reading** After students finish reading the selection, connect it to the weekly question *How do people overcome obstacles?*

Below-Level Reader

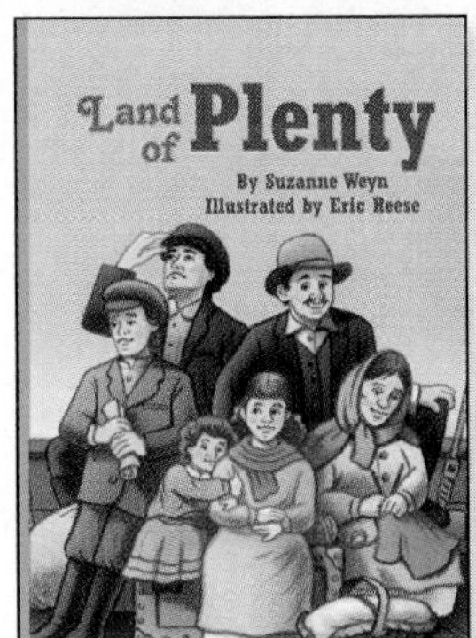

- **Read** *Land of Plenty*
- **Before Reading** Ask students to preview the text by looking at the illustrations. Then have students set a purpose for reading.
- **During Reading** Choral read the first four pages, and ask students to finish on their own if they are able. Have partners discuss the following questions:
  - What problems do Colleen and her family face? *(a long journey to life in a new and unknown land)*
  - Why is passing through Castle Garden so important? *(Immigrants must be officially registered or they will be sent back.)*
- **After Reading** Have students look at and discuss the concept map. Connect the Below-Level Reader to the weekly question *How do people overcome obstacles?* In *Land of Plenty,* how do Colleen and her family overcome obstacles? *(They make up their minds to start over in an unfamiliar land.)*

MONITOR PROGRESS

If... students have difficulty reading the selection with a partner,
then... have them follow along as they listen to the Leveled Readers DVD-ROM.

If... students have trouble understanding the immigrants' situation,
then... reread the first few pages and discuss why immigrants passed through Castle Garden.

Objectives

- Interpret a speaker's messages (both verbal and nonverbal).

DAY 2

Student Edition p. EI•7

More Reading

Use additional Leveled Readers or other texts at students' instructional levels to reinforce this week's skills and strategies. For text suggestions, see the Leveled Reader Database or the Leveled Readers Skills Chart on pp. CL 24–CL 29.

Reinforce Comprehension

Skill Generalize Review with students *Envision It!* p. EI•7 on generalizing. Then use p. 48 to review the definition. Remind students that words like *always* or *never* can be a clue to generalizations characters make in the story.

Strategy Predict and Set Purpose Review the definitions of predict and set purpose. Remind students to use illustrations and text features to help them predict before they read and to use their predictions to set a purpose for reading. For additional support, refer students to *Envision It!* p. EI•20.

Revisit *Tripping Over the Lunch Lady* on pp. 52–61. Have students begin reading aloud with a partner. As they read, have them apply the comprehension skill and strategy to the selection.

- Why does the name "Jinx" fit the narrator? *(Jinx means "bad luck." She keeps doing clumsy things, getting into difficulties, and getting hurt.)*
- What generalizations does Jinx make about using the trampoline and playing basketball? *("I'm never going to be able to keep my feet together and fly perfectly on the trampoline" and "I'm never going to be able to make a basket without breaking somebody's bones.")*
- What clue word helps you recognize her generalizations about these sports? *(never)*
- What generalization does she make about her chance to be a great square dancer? *(Possible answers: It was in my genes; I knew then it was meant to be.)*

Use the During Reading Differentiated Instruction for additional support for struggling readers.

MONITOR PROGRESS

If... students have difficulty reading along with the group,
then... have them follow along as they listen to the AudioText.

Objectives

- Make inferences about text.

SI Strategic Intervention

DAY 3

Reinforce Vocabulary

Unfamiliar Words/Context Clues Tell students that when they come across an unfamiliar word, they can use context clues to help them figure out the meaning. Write the following from *Tripping Over the Lunch Lady* on the board: "Dad pats me on the head like an old skunky stray." If I don't know what *skunky* means, I can look at other words in the sentence for clues. "Pats me on the head" is what you do with a dog or cat. A *stray* is an animal that doesn't have a home. I know that *skunk* is an animal with a strong smell. I can put these clues together to figure out that *skunky stray* probably means "a smelly old animal without a home." This shows how Jinx feels about herself right now.

Revisit *Tripping Over the Lunch Lady* on pp. 62–67. Review *Words!* on p. W•7. As students finish reading the story, encourage them to use context clues to figure out the meaning of any unfamiliar words.

- Point out the word *genes* on p. 57. What context clues do you see that might give you an idea for the meaning of *genes*? *(Jinx had just been looking at a picture of her mother square dancing. She says right after that "It was in my genes.")*
- Based on those clues, what do you think the word *genes* means? *(*Genes *probably means "something that passes on talents from parents to kids.")*

Use the During Reading Differentiated Instruction for additional support for struggling readers.

MONITOR PROGRESS

If... students need more practice with the lesson vocabulary,
then... use *Envision It! Pictured Vocabulary Cards.*

Objectives

- Use context to determine the meaning of unfamiliar words.

Student Edition p. W•7

More Reading

Use additional Leveled Readers or other texts at students' instructional levels to reinforce this week's skills and strategies. For text suggestions, see the Leveled Reader Database or the Leveled Readers Skills Chart on pp. CL 24–CL 29.

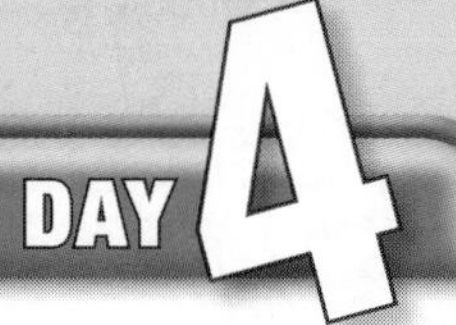

Practice Retelling

- **Retell** Have pairs of students use the Retelling Cards to retell *Tripping Over the Lunch Lady.* Monitor retelling and prompt students as needed. If students struggle, model a fluent retelling.

Genre Focus

- **Before Reading or Revisiting** "Square Dancing: Good for the Heart and Mind" on pp. 72–73, read aloud the genre information about persuasive text on p. 72. Persuasive text appears in ads and articles and may have bullets, subheadings, and illustrations. Persuasive writers sometimes make misleading or exaggerated statements to convince you of something.

Then have students preview "Square Dancing: Good for the Heart and Mind." Ask:

- What does the title tell you about how the writer feels about square dancing? *(excited; very positive)*
- What features do you see? *(checkered background, bulleted text with headings, an illustration)*

Then have students set a purpose for reading based on their preview.

- **During Reading or Revisiting** Lead a choral reading of the persuasive text. Stop to discuss unfamiliar words such as *accompaniment* and *do-si-do.*
- **After Reading or Revisiting** Have students share their reactions to the text. Then guide them through the Reading Across Texts and Writing Across Texts activities. Which words and phrases probably exaggerate the truth in this article? *(all, best dance ever, all doctors will agree, great exercise for your brain, your entire life)*

MONITOR PROGRESS

If... students have difficulty retelling the selection,
then... have them review the story using the illustrations.

Objectives

- Identify the author's viewpoint or position in the argument.

SI Strategic Intervention

DAY 5

For a complete literacy instructional plan and additional practice with this week's target skills and strategies, see the **Leveled Reader Teaching Guide.**

Concept Literacy Reader

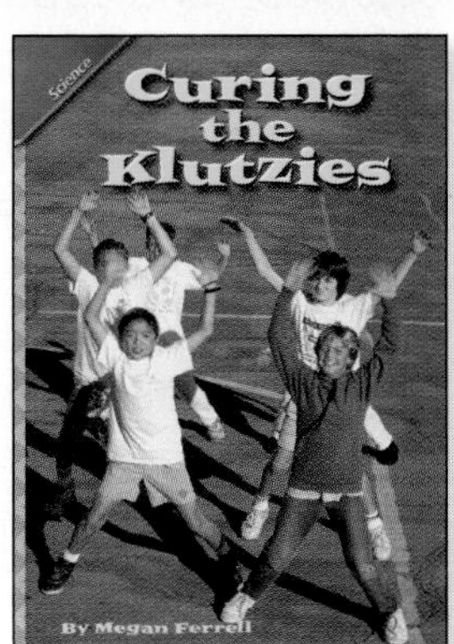

- **Model** Model the fluency skill of accuracy for students. Ask students to follow along in their books and listen carefully as you read—haltingly and with errors or miscues—the first two pages of *Curing the Klutzies.* Then read the passage a second time. Have students notice how the words flow more smoothly and how your reading becomes more accurate.
- **Fluency Routine**

1. Have students reread passages from *Curing the Klutzies* with a partner.
2. For optimal fluency, they should reread three to four times.
3. As students read, monitor fluency and provide corrective feedback. Have students note how their accuracy increases with repeated readings.

See *Routines Flip Chart* for more help with fluency.

- **Retell** Have students retell *Curing the Klutzies.* Prompt as necessary.

Below-Level Reader

- **Model** Ask students to listen carefully as you read aloud pp. 3–5 of *Land of Plenty,* twice: once very quickly and with some errors, the second time slower and with accuracy.
- **Fluency Routine**

1. Have students reread passages from *Land of Plenty* with a partner or individually.
2. For optimal fluency, they should reread three to four times.
3. As students read, monitor fluency and provide corrective feedback. Encourage students to slow down to avoid missing words or misreading them.

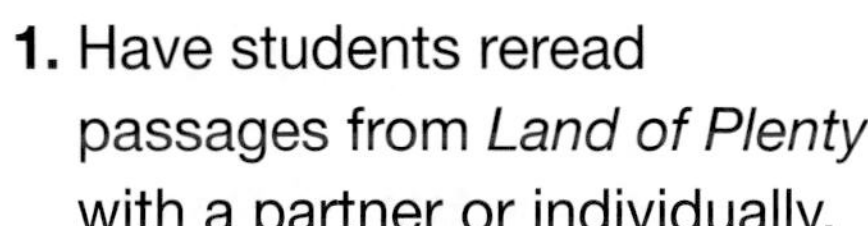

See *Routines Flip Chart* for more help with fluency.

- **Retell** For additional practice, have students retell *Land of Plenty* page-by-page, using the illustrations. Prompt as necessary.

- What are these pages mostly about?
- What do the characters do?

MONITOR PROGRESS

If... students have difficulty reading fluently,
then... provide additional fluency practice by pairing nonfluent readers with fluent ones.

Objectives

- Read aloud grade-level stories with fluency.

Pacing Small Group Instruction

5-Day Plan

DAY 1	• Expand the concept • Read On-Level Reader
DAY 2	• Generalize • Predict and Set Purpose • Revisit Student Edition pp. 52–61
DAY 3	• Unfamiliar Words • Revisit Student Edition pp. 62–67
DAY 4	• Practice Retelling • Read/Revisit Student Edition pp. 72–73
DAY 5	• Reread for fluency • Reread On-Level Reader

3- or 4-Day Plan

DAY 1	• Expand the concept • Read On-Level Reader
DAY 2	• Generalize • Predict and Set Purpose • Revisit Student Edition pp. 52–61
DAY 3	• Unfamiliar Words • Revisit Student Edition pp. 62–67
DAY 4	• Practice Retelling • Read/Revisit Student Edition pp. 72–73 • Reread for fluency • Reread On-Level Reader

3-Day Plan: Eliminate the shaded box.

DAY 1

Build Background

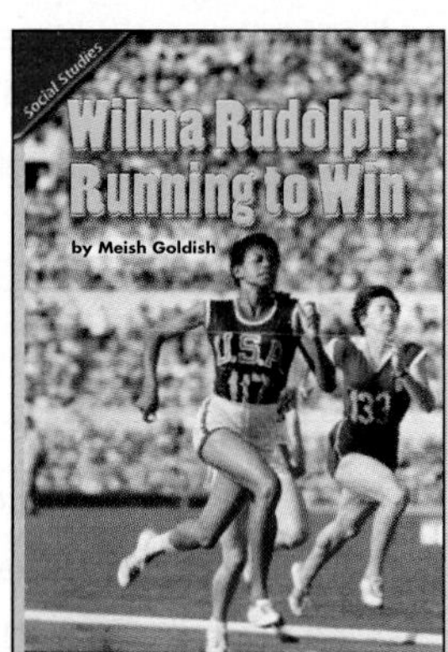

■ **Expand the Concept** Connect the weekly question *How do people overcome obstacles?* and expand the concept. Everyone faces different obstacles and challenges and overcomes them in different ways. Some people triumph over almost impossible obstacles. Discuss the meaning of the words on the concept map on p. 46–47 in the Teacher Edition.

On-Level Reader

For a complete literacy instructional plan and additional practice with this week's target skills and strategies, see the **Leveled Reader Teaching Guide.**

■ **Before Reading** *Wilma Rudolph: Running to Win,* have students preview the reader by looking at the title, cover, and pictures in the book. Ask:

- Who is Wilma Rudolph? *(an athlete, probably track and field)*
- What challenges do you think she overcame? *(probably something about how hard it was for her to be physically active)*

Have students create a sequence chart with the title "Wilma Rudolph's Life." As you read, briefly record in your sequence chart each challenge Wilma faced and how she overcame it. For example, "Stricken with polio, Rudolph learned to walk with braces." Think about how Wilma Rudolph kept overcoming one obstacle after another.

■ **During Reading** Have students follow along as you read the first three pages. Then let them complete the book on their own. Remind students to add events to their sequence charts as they read.

■ **After Reading** Have partners compare the events on their sequence charts.

- According to this book, what are the most important events in Wilma Rudolph's life?
- How does the topic relate to the weekly question *How do people overcome obstacles?*

Objectives

- Interpret a speaker's messages (both verbal and nonverbal).

DAY 2

Expand Comprehension

Skill Generalize Use p. 48 to review the definition of generalize. For additional review, see p. EI•7 in *Envision It!* Remind students to look for clue words such as *always* and *never,* which usually signal a generalization.

Strategy Predict and Set Purpose Review the definitions of predict and set purpose. Encourage students to use illustrations to predict before they read and to use their prediction to set a purpose for reading. During reading, use the Extend Thinking questions and *Envision It!* p. EI•20 for additional support.

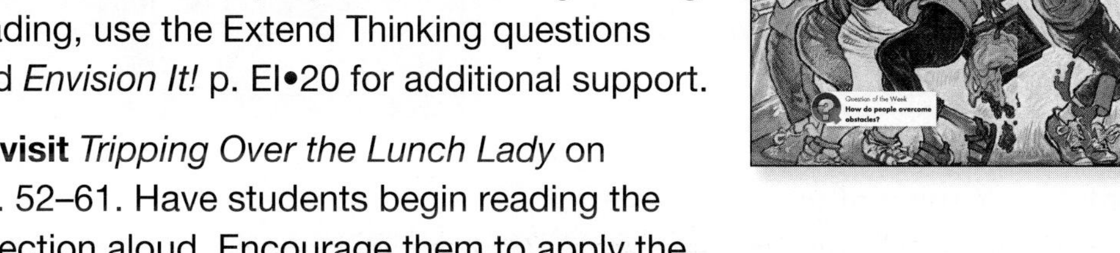

Revisit *Tripping Over the Lunch Lady* on pp. 52–61. Have students begin reading the selection aloud. Encourage them to apply the comprehension skill and strategy as they read.

- The name "Jinx" comes from a generalization that Jinx's uncle made about her. What is that generalization? *(Possible response: Jinx is always falling, hurting herself, doing clumsy things, and having accidents.)*
- Do you think that Jinx's belief that she's meant for square dancing is right or wrong? Why? *(Possible response: Wrong. So far all the details support the generalization that Jinx is uncoordinated or a klutz.)*

Objectives

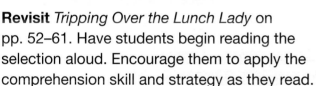

- Make inferences about text.
- Use textual evidence to support understanding

Student Edtion p. EI•7

More Reading

Use additional Leveled Readers or other texts at students' instructional levels to reinforce this week's skills and strategies. For text suggestions, see the Leveled Reader Database or the Leveled Readers Skills Chart on pp. CL 24–CL 29.

Expand Vocabulary

Unfamiliar Words/Context Clues Remind students that context clues can be actions as well as words in a story. Then review *Words!* on p. W•7. Ask students to turn to p. 57 in the story *Tripping Over the Lunch Lady*. Have them read the sentence: "It was in my genes." Ask:

- If you didn't know what *genes* meant, how could you use context clues to help you figure out the meaning? *(Look at the sentences before and after this one to see what words or actions can provide clues to the meaning.)*
- What do you learn about Jinx that helps you figure out the meaning of *genes*? *(Jinx was just looking at a picture that showed her mother square dancing. Jinx must think she inherited her mother's talent for this type of dance.)*
- Based on the context clues in the story, how would you define *genes*? *(something that allows you to inherit talents from your parents)*

Revisit *Tripping Over the Lunch Lady* on pp. 62–67. As students finish reading the selection, encourage them to apply the skill and strategy to help them figure out the meanings of unfamiliar words such as *Heimlich, direct pressure,* and *Dalmatian.*

Critical Thinking Encourage students to think critically. Have students recall what happened in the selection.

- Think about what Jinx's name means. Explain whether you think she is jinxed or creates her own good or bad luck.
- How would you describe Jinx's personality?

Objectives

- Use context to determine the meaning of unfamiliar words.

Student Edition p. W•7

More Reading

Use additional Leveled Readers or other texts at students' instructional levels to reinforce this week's skills and strategies. For text suggestions, see the Leveled Reader Database or the Leveled Readers Skills Chart on pp. CL 24–CL 29.

Practice Retelling

- **Retell** To assess students' comprehension, use the Retelling Cards. Monitor retelling and prompt students as needed.

Genre Focus

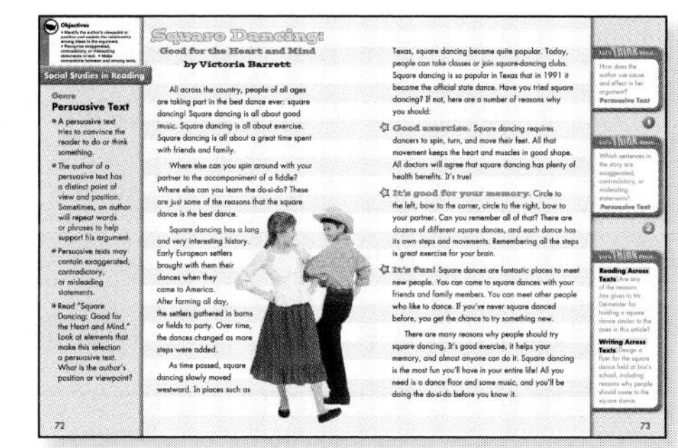

- **Before Reading or Revisiting** "Square Dancing: Good for the Heart and Mind" on pp. 72–73, read aloud the genre information about persuasive text on p. 72. Have students preview "Square Dancing: Good for the Heart and Mind" and set a purpose for reading. Ask: What do you see in the title, illustration, or headings that could be overstated or misleading? *(possible responses: the heading "It's good for your memory"; the happy look of the boy in the illustration)*
- **During Reading or Revisiting** Read aloud and have students follow along, tracking the print.

- What generalizations appear in the first paragraph? *(All the statements could be called generalizations.)*
- What clue word helps you identify the generalizations? *(all)*
- Generalizations can sometimes be overstatements, or exaggerations. What else is probably exaggerated in this article? *(Possible responses: Square dance is the best dance; it helps your memory; it's the most fun you'll have in your entire life.)*

- **After Reading or Revisiting** Have students share their reaction to the persuasive text. Then have them write a persuasive paragraph that exaggerates what is good about something they love to do.

Objectives

- Identify the author's viewpoint or position in the argument.

On-Level Reader

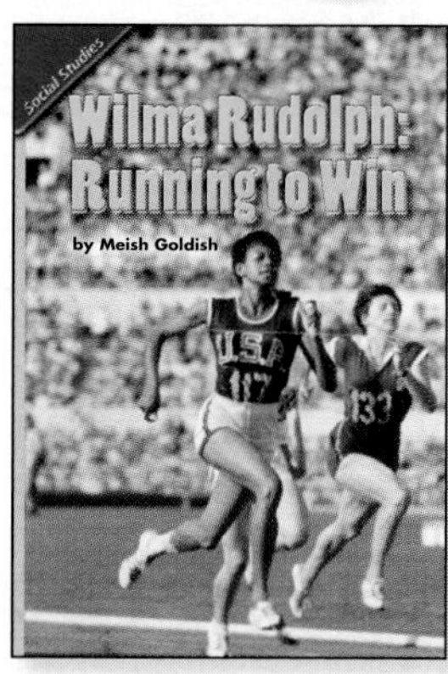

- **Model** Model the fluency skill of accuracy for students. Read aloud the first two pages of the On-Level Reader *Wilma Rudolph: Running to Win.* First read quickly and without focus, skipping words and mispronouncing others. Then reread the text slowly and with focus, demonstrating how your reading becomes more accurate.

- **Fluency Routine**

  1. Have students reread passages from *Wilma Rudolph: Running to Win* with a partner.
  2. For optimal fluency, they should reread passages three to four times.
  3. As students read, monitor fluency and provide corrective feedback. Point out that students can preview a passage to help them identify any words, ideas, or phrasing that might give them difficulty. Have students note how rereading a text two or three times can help them become smoother, faster, and more accurate readers.

See the *Routines Flip Chart* for more help with fluency.

- **Retell** For additional practice, have students use the illustrations to retell *Wilma Rudolph: Running to Win.* Prompt as necessary.

• What is this book mainly about?

• What is the author trying to teach us?

Objectives

• Read aloud grade-level stories with fluency.

DAY 1

Build Background

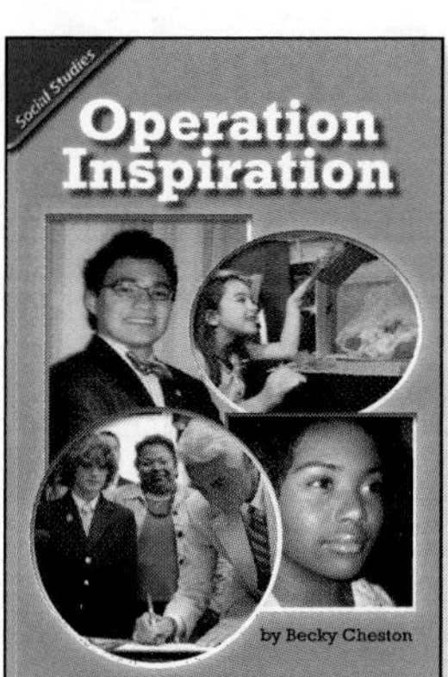

■ **Extend the Concept** Expand on the weekly question *How do people overcome obstacles?* Recall what you have read about the Civil Rights movement in the United States and the actions of people such as Rosa Parks and Dr. Martin Luther King, Jr. How did they manage to accomplish so much? *(possible answers: by letting nothing stop them, overcoming obstacles such as hatred, unfair laws, prejudice, and military force)*

Advanced Reader

For a complete literacy instructional plan and additional practice with this week's target skills and strategies, see the **Leveled Reader Teaching Guide.**

■ **Before Reading** *Operation Inspiration*, tell students to recall the Read Aloud "Sense." What made Beethoven keep going after he started losing his hearing? *(He found ways to keep working and communicating.)* Today, you will read a book about remarkable people who have accomplished nearly impossible goals.

Have students use the illustrations to predict what they will learn. Then have students set a purpose for reading.

■ **During Reading** Have students read the Advanced Reader independently. Encourage them to think critically. For example, ask:

- What qualities do all the people in the book share? *(determination, resourcefulness, caring about others, inspiring other people)*
- What do you think motivates people to sacrifice their time and effort for others? *(possible answers: the desire to make a difference, to help others who are less fortunate, to do what needs to be done)*
- What do you find most remarkable about their accomplishments? Explain.

■ **After Reading** Have students review the concept map and explain how *Operation Inspiration* helps students answer the weekly question *How do people overcome obstacles?* Prompt as necessary. What generalization can you make about the people in this book? *(All were inspired or highly motivated; all did things that no one would expect for their age or experience.)*

■ **Now Try This** Assign "Now Try This" at the end of the Advanced Reader.

Objectives

- Interpret a speaker's messages (both verbal and nonverbal).

Pacing Small Group Instruction

15–20 mins.

5-Day Plan

DAY 1	• Extend the concept • Read Advanced Reader
DAY 2	• Generalize • Predict and Set Purpose • Revisit Student Edition pp. 52–61
DAY 3	• Unfamiliar Words • Revisit Student Edition pp. 62–67
DAY 4	• Persuasive Text • Read/Revisit Student Edition pp. 72–73
DAY 5	• Reread for fluency • Reread Advanced Reader

3- or 4-Day Plan

DAY 1	• Extend the concept • Advanced Reader
DAY 2	• Generalize • Predict and Set Purpose • Revisit Student Edition pp. 52–61
DAY 3	• Unfamiliar Words • Revisit Student Edition pp. 62–67
DAY 4	• Persuasive Text • Read/Revisit Student Edition pp. 72–73 • Reread for fluency • Reread Advanced Reader

3-Day Plan: Eliminate the shaded box.

More Reading

Use additional Leveled Readers or other texts at students' instructional levels to reinforce this week's skills and strategies. For text suggestions, see the Leveled Reader Database or the Leveled Readers Skills Chart on pp. CL 24–CL 29.

Extend Comprehension

Skill Generalize Review the definition of generalize. Remind students that it is possible to over-generalize or exaggerate. Generalizations should always be evaluated for accuracy. Based on the information in *Operation Inspiration,* do you think it is accurate to say that all people could do more to make the world a better place? Why? *(possible answer: yes, because some of the people in the story were ordinary people with no special skill)*

Strategy Predict and Set Purpose Review the definition of the strategy. Remind students to recall their purpose for reading and to revise their predictions as they read the rest of *Tripping Over the Lunch Lady*. During reading, use the Extend Thinking questions and the During Reading Differentiated Instruction for additional support.

Revisit *Tripping Over the Lunch Lady* on pp. 52–61. As students begin reading, encourage them to use the comprehension skill and strategy.

- State and support a generalization about Jinx's personality. *(Possible answers: She wants to be the best at something; she is determined once she makes up her mind; she is willing to look foolish to achieve a goal.)*
- In general, how are Jinx and Mr. Deimeister similar? *(Both are determined once they make up their minds.)* How are they different? *(Mr. Deimeister seems to be good at fishing; Jinx is not really good at anything physical.)*

Critical Thinking Encourage students to think critically as they read "Tripping Over the Lunch Lady."

- What advice would you give Jinx about how to be less clumsy?
- What activities do you think Jinx might be really successful in doing?

Objectives

- Make inferences about text.

DAY 3

Extend Vocabulary

Unfamiliar Words/Context Clues Point out to students that context clues can be specific words, characters' actions, or even students' own knowledge. All these clues can help them figure out the meaning of an unfamiliar word. Then have students turn to p. 54 and read the sentence beginning "Right around the time he was having the Heimlich done on him . . ."

- Jinx talks about something called *the Heimlich.* What context clues can help me figure out the meaning of this term? *(In the paragraph right before this, Tony is choking on his gum. Also, Gus is screaming to apply "direct pressure." Finally, Jinx says that they had just had a first-aid class.)*
- How can you use your own knowledge to help you understand the way this term is used? *(Students may know that Heimlich is the man who developed a technique for saving a choking person. In this technique, you apply direct pressure to the person's diaphragm to force air out of the lungs, expelling objects that block breathing.)*
- Based on all these clues, what do you think *the Heimlich* means? *(It is a first-aid technique developed by Heimlich to save someone who is choking.)*

Revisit *Tripping Over the Lunch Lady* on pp. 62–67. Discuss how using different types of context clues can help students figure out the meaning of unfamiliar words. Remind students to use the strategy as they finish reading *Tripping Over the Lunch Lady*.

Critical Thinking Have students recall what they have read. Encourage them to think critically. For example, ask:

- Even though Jinx is clumsy, what strengths does she have? *(possible answers: determination, cheerfulness, sense of humor, ambition to achieve something great)*
- How might the story have ended differently if Jinx had been really good at square dancing?

Objectives

- Use context to determine the meaning of unfamiliar words.

More Reading

Use additional Leveled Readers or other texts at students' instructional levels to reinforce this week's skills and strategies. For text suggestions, see the Leveled Reader Database or the Leveled Readers Skills Chart on pp. CL 24–CL 29.

DAY 4

Genre Focus

■ **Before Reading or Revisiting** "Square Dancing: Good for the Heart and Mind" on pp. 72–73, read the panel information on persuasive text. Have students preview the text features and set a purpose for reading.

■ **During Reading or Revisiting** Have students read independently.

- How does this article over-generalize, or exaggerate? *(It makes square dancing seem as if it were more fun, better for you, and easier to learn than it is.)*

■ **After Reading or Revisiting** Have students discuss Reading Across Texts. Then have them do Writing Across Texts independently.

Objectives

- Identify the author's viewpoint or position in the argument.

DAY 5

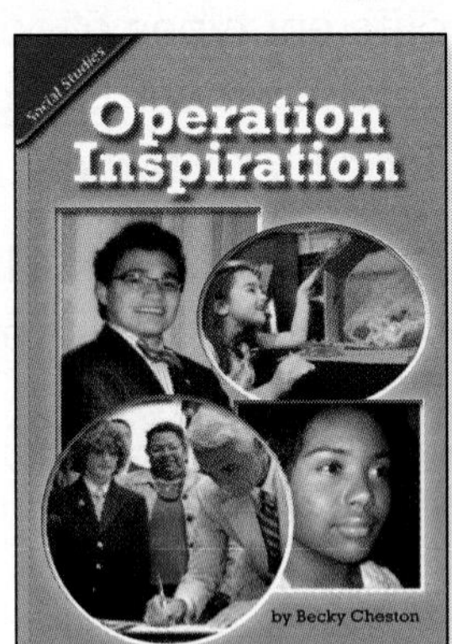

■ **Reread for Fluency** Have students silently reread passages from the Advanced Reader *Operation Inspiration.* Then have them reread aloud with a partner or individually. As students read, monitor fluency and provide corrective feedback. If students read fluently on the first reading, they do not need to reread three to four times. Assess the fluency of students in this group using p.75j.

■ **Retell** Have students retell the main ideas and key details from the Advanced Reader *Operation Inspiration.*

■ **Now Try This** Have students complete their projects. You may wish to review their work to see if they need additional ideas. Have them share their finished work with classmates.

Objectives

- Read aloud grade-level stories with fluency.

The ELL lessons are organized by strands. Use them to scaffold the weekly curriculum of lessons or during small group time instruction.

Academic Language

Students will hear or read the following academic language in this week's core instruction. As students encounter the vocabulary, provide a simple definition or concrete example. Then ask students to suggest an example or synonym of the word and identify available cognates.

Skill Words	Generalize (*generalizar*) essay friendly letter	climax antecedent compound sentence
Concept Words	confront predicament	ingenious triumphant

**Spanish cognates in parentheses*

Concept Development

How do people overcome obstacles?

- **Preteach Concept**
  - **Prior Knowledge** Have students turn to pp. 46–47 in the Student Edition. Do you see the tools the man is holding and wearing? Why do you think he has so many? What might happen if he did not have these tools?
  - **Discuss Concept** Elicit students' knowledge and experience of overcoming obstacles. What have these people done to make it easier to live in the cold? What are some other ways people make life easier for themselves? Supply background information as needed.
  - **Poster Talk-Through** Read aloud the Poster Talk-Through on ELL Poster 17 and work through the Day 1 activities.
- **Daily Concept and Vocabulary Development** Use the daily activities on ELL Poster 17 to build concept and vocabulary knowledge.

Objectives

- Internalize new basic and academic language by using and reusing it in meaningful ways in speaking and writing activities that build concept and language attainment.

Content Objectives

- Use concept vocabulary related to overcoming obstacles.

Language Objectives

- Express ideas in response to art and discussion.

Daily Planner

DAY 1	• **Frontload Concept** • **Preteach** Comprehension Skill, Vocabulary, Phonics/Spelling, Conventions • **Writing**
DAY 2	• **Review** Concept, Vocabulary, Comprehension Skill • **Frontload Main Selection** • **Practice** Phonics/Spelling, Conventions/Writing
DAY 3	• **Review** Concept, Comprehension Skill, Vocabulary, Conventions/Writing • **Reread Main Selection** • **Practice** Phonics/Spelling
DAY 4	• **Review Concept** • **Read ELL/ELD Readers** • **Practice** Phonics/Spelling, Conventions/Writing
DAY 5	• **Review** Concept, Vocabulary, Comprehension Skill, Phonics/Spelling, Conventions • **Reread ELL/ELD Readers** • **Writing**

**See the ELL Handbook for ELL Workshops with targeted instruction.*

Concept Talk Video

Use the Concept Talk Video Routine (*ELL Handbook,* p. 477) to build background knowledge about overcoming obstacles.

Language Objectives

- Understand and use basic vocabulary.
- Learn meanings of grade-level vocabulary.

Basic Vocabulary

■ **High-Frequency Words** Use the vocabulary routines and the high-frequency word list on p. 452 of the *ELL Handbook* to systematically teach newcomers the first 300 sight words in English. Students who began learning ten words per week at the beginning of the year are now learning words 161–170.

Lesson Vocabulary

■ **Preteach** Introduce the Lesson Vocabulary using this routine:

1. Distribute copies of this week's Word Cards (*ELL Handbook,* p. 125).
2. Display ELL Poster 17 and reread the Poster Talk-Through.
3. Using the poster illustrations, model how a word's meaning can be expressed with other similar words: The farmer wanted all of the weeds *uprooted,* or pulled out of the ground.
4. Use these sentences to reveal the meaning of the other words.
   - The information was *accurate*. (correct)
   - It was *extraordinary* how big the crops got. (incredible)
   - The amount of fruit had *dwindled*. (gone down, almost none left)
   - It was *unexplainable* how the hat had disappeared. (not explainable)
   - He wanted to see if the vegetable was *edible*. (safe to eat)

Objectives

- Internalize new basic and academic language by using and reusing it in meaningful ways in speaking and writing activities that build concept and language attainment.
- Learn new language structures, expressions, and basic and academic vocabulary heard during classroom instruction and interactions.
- Monitor understanding of spoken language during classroom instruction and interactions and seek clarification as needed.

- **Reteach** Ask questions to check and reinforce students' understanding of the vocabulary.
  - If something is wrong, is it *accurate?* (no)
  - How strong is something that has *extraordinary* strength? (very strong)
  - What would you need to do if your supply of pencils *dwindled?* (buy more pencils)
  - Is something that is *unexplainable* easy to understand? (no)
  - What is something that is *edible?* (a piece of fruit)
  - What would you do if you wanted a weed *uprooted?* (pull on it)

  Have students speak using the lesson vocabulary. For each word, students can name a synonym. Have them use circumlocution to explain the meaning of *dwindled*. *(I don't have very much of something. I used to have a lot of it, but now I am almost out.)*

- **Writing** Use a 3-column chart to help students organize ideas. Label the chart *Obstacle-Predicament-Triumphant.* Under *Obstacle,* instruct students to note an obstacle. Under *Predicament,* ask students to briefly describe a problem the person facing the obstacle would confront. Under *Triumphant,* students should explain how the predicament is overcome. Then have students write simple and compound sentences about the situation described in the chart.

Beginning/Intermediate Work with this group to write clues to help them understand what an obstacle is. Then, ask them to give an example of an obstacle that they have faced and how they overcame it. You may want to give an example of an obstacle you've overcome first.

Advanced Ask students to think of examples of stories and/or books they've read where a main character has overcome an obstacle.

Advanced High Instruct students to write a short story about a situation from their chart.

Objectives

- Speak using learning strategies such as requesting assistance, employing non-verbal cues, and using synonyms and circumlocution (conveying ideas by defining or describing when exact English words are not known).
- Use visual, contextual, and linguistic support to enhance and confirm understanding of increasingly complex and elaborated spoken language.

Language Objectives

- Produce drawings, phrases, or short sentences to show understanding of Lesson Vocabulary.
- Use strategies to acquire new vocabulary.

ELL Teacher Tip

Emphasize sentence meaning. Encourage students to try to understand and convey ideas rather than focusing only on separate words.

Graphic Organizer

Three-Column Chart

Obstacle	Predicament	Triumphant

Listening Comprehension

Content Objectives

- Monitor and adjust oral comprehension.

Language Objectives

- Discuss oral passages.
- Use a graphic organizer to take notes.

Graphic Organizer

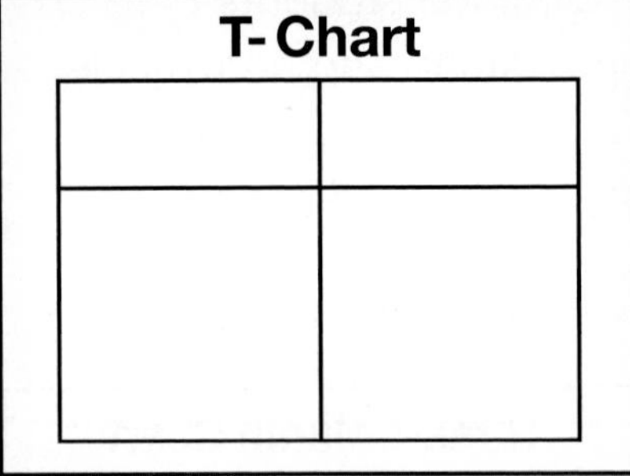

ELL Teacher Tip

Keep students engaged in listening by asking prediction questions throughout the reading of the text: *What do you think will happen next? How do you think the character will react?*

Read Aloud

Beautiful Music

Ludwig van Beethoven loved to play the piano. He loved to write music. He was very good. People loved to listen to his music.

One day, Beethoven noticed he could no longer hear the music. In fact, he could not hear at all. He had to confront the truth. He was deaf.

Beethoven found himself in a predicament. He knew he still had a gift. He knew he could still write and play music. But how could he do it?

He had an ingenious idea. He cut off the legs of his piano. He laid under the piano to feel the vibrations. Each sound the piano made had its own special vibration. He used the vibrations and his memory of how music sounded to write new music. Beethoven wrote beautiful music.

Prepare for the Read Aloud The modified Read Aloud above prepares students for listening to the oral reading "Sense" on p. 47b.

- **First Listening: Listen to Understand** Write the title of the Read Aloud on the board. This is a story about Ludwig van Beethoven. Though he became deaf, Beethoven still wrote beautiful music. What helped him to write the music? How did he tell what the different sounds were after he became deaf? Afterwards, ask the questions again and have students share their answers.
- **Second Listening: Listen to Check Understanding** Using a T-Chart (*ELL Handbook,* p. 493), have students list what Beethoven was able to do before he lost his hearing. Then, have them list what he could do after he lost his hearing. Discuss with students what changed and what stayed the same.

Objectives

- Use visual, contextual, and linguistic support to enhance and confirm understanding of increasingly complex and elaborated spoken language.
- Demonstrate listening comprehension of increasingly complex spoken English by following directions, retelling or summarizing spoken messages, responding to questions and requests, collaborating with peers, and taking notes commensurate with content and grade-level needs.

Phonics and Spelling

- **Prefixes *over-, under-, sub-, super-, out-***
  - **Preteach** Write these word pairs on the board: *cooked, overcook, rank, outrank, marine, submarine, charge, supercharged, state, understate.* Underline the prefixes. A prefix is a word part that is added to the beginning of a word. Adding a prefix makes a new word because prefixes change a words meaning. Point out the spelling rule: adding a prefix does not change the spelling of the base word.
  - **Teach/Model** Write the meaning of each prefix on the board: *over-: beyond, too much; under-: below; sub-: underneath; super-: great, exceptional; out-: more, to a greater degree. Cook* means "to prepare food by applying heat." The prefix *over-* means "beyond." So *overcook* means to "cook too much." Repeat this routine with other words listed above.
  - **Assess** Have students write these prefixes and base words on index cards: *over-, shoot, under-, arm, sub-, zero, super-, human, out-, side.* Tell students to use the index cards to make words with prefixes. Have students follow the spelling rule as they add prefixes.

Word Analysis: Suffixes

- **Teach/Model** When a suffix is added to the end of a word, it changes the meaning or part of speech of that word. The suffix *-ly* forms adjectives or adverbs that mean "in a ____ way," and the suffix *-ian* forms adjectives or nouns that mean "of or from a certain place or group." Write *safely* on the board. Safely. What base word do you see in *safely?* (safe) *Safe* means "free from danger." So *safely* means "in a way that is free from danger."
- **Practice** Write these words on the board: *slowly, politely, politician, magician.* Provide practice for students at their language proficiency levels.

Leveled Support

Beginning/Intermediate Read the words aloud with students. Then have students underline the base words and circle the suffixes.

Advanced/Advanced High Have students work in pairs to identify the base words. Have them define the words and write sentences with them.

Objectives

- Use visual, contextual, and linguistic support to enhance and confirm understanding of increasingly complex and elaborated spoken language.

Content Objectives

- Identify the suffixes *-ly* and *-ian*.
- Identify the prefixes *over-, under-, sub-, super-, out-*.
- Discuss the meanings of the prefixes *over-, under-, sub-, super-, out-*.

Language Objectives

- Use English spelling rules.
- Apply phonics and decoding skills to vocabulary.
- Discuss meaning of words with morphemes.

ELL Teaching Routine

- For more practice with prefixes, use the Multisyllabic Word Strategy Routine (*ELL Handbook,* p. 473).

Content Objectives

- Generalize to aid comprehension.
- Identify details that support generalizations.

Language Objectives

- Write sentences that show generalizations.
- Learn and use routine language for classroom communication.

Language Opportunity: Classroom Language

Generalize is a word that students can use in various classroom circumstances. Have students use the classroom word *generalize* to talk about other subjects. For example, we can generalize about gravity from a science experiment or generalize about even numbers when we do math problems with them.

ELL English Language Learners

Comprehension
Generalize

- **Preteach** When we generalize, we infer or form an opinion or conclusion about something or someone. When we read, often we can make generalizations about characters based on their actions. We can form opinions about them or their situation. Have students turn to Envision It! on p. EI•7 in the Student Edition. Read the text together aloud. Have students identify how the boy on the bicycle makes a generalization.

- **Reteach** Distribute copies of the Picture It! (*ELL Handbook,* p. 126). Have students look at the images. Remind students that generalizations can be made by using facts, past experiences, examples, and reasoning. Have the students reread the passage with a partner. Have the partners tell three facts about Harriet Tubman. Then ask the students to develop a generalization about Harriet Tubman based on the facts. (Harriet Tubman was courageous.)

Leveled LS Support

Beginning/Intermediate Read the passage to the students. Have the students tell three facts about Harriet Tubman and write them on the board. What does this tell us about Harriet Tubman? Guide the students in using the facts to write a generalization about Harriet Tubman (e.g. She was courageous. She was clever.)

Advanced/Advanced High Have students read the passage with a partner. Ask students to work with their partner to write a generalization about Harriet Tubman. Share the generalizations as a class. After you share each generalization, have the students tell facts from the passage that support it.

MINI-LESSON

Expressing Feelings

Tell students that we often generalize to express feelings. For example, if we say that Harriet Tubman was courageous, we are expressing a feeling about her based on the facts in a text. Have students use pp. 72–73 of the Student Edition to generalize about Square Dancing and express their feelings about it. Use a sentence frame: *In general, I feel that square dancing is _______.*

Objectives

- Understand the general meaning, main points, and important details of spoken language ranging from situations in which topics, language, and contexts are familiar to unfamiliar.

ELL English Language Learners

Reading Comprehension *Tripping Over the Lunch Lady*

Student Edition pp. 52–53

- **Frontloading** Read the title aloud and discuss some reasons why people trip. Ask students if they have ever tripped over anything. I've tripped over a few things before, but I've never tripped over a lunch lady. I wonder how someone could trip over a lunch lady. Guide students on a picture walk through *Tripping Over the Lunch Lady.* Ask students to predict what will happen in the story. Have them record their predictions. During reading, pause and invite students to adjust their predictions. Have students use the story predictions chart to record their predictions.
- **Sheltered Reading** Ask questions such as the following to guide students' comprehension:
  - p. 54: What scared Tony Friedman so bad? (the narrator went flying over his head)
  - p. 57: What is in the narrator's genes? (square dancing)
  - p. 59: What did the narrator drop off in Mr. Deimeister's office? (square dance music)
  - p. 66: How did the narrator get a concussion? (Josh must have swung her until she fell down and hit her head.)
- **Fluency: Read with Accuracy** Remind students that reading accurately means saying the words correctly. Read the first paragraph on p. 57. Model accurate reading. Then have students work cooperatively to practice fluent reading while sharing information. They can work in pairs, taking turns reading p. 54 of the Student Edition with accuracy. Have students listen and then retell the main character traits based on the reading.
- **After Reading** Help students summarize the text with the Retelling Cards. Ask questions that prompt students to summarize the important parts of the text.

Objectives

- Ask and give information ranging from using a very limited bank of high-frequency, high-need, concrete vocabulary, including key words and expressions needed for basic communication in academic and social contexts, to using abstract and content-based vocabulary during extended speaking assignments.
- Read linguistically accommodated content area material with a decreasing need for linguistic accommodations as more English is learned.

Content Objectives

- Monitor and adjust comprehension.

Language Objectives

- Read with accuracy.
- Summarize text using visual support.
- Share information cooperatively.

Audio Support

Students can prepare for reading *Tripping Over the Lunch Lady* by using eSelection or the AudioText CD. See the AudioText CD Routine (*ELL Handbook,* p. 477)

ELL Teaching Routine

For more practice summarizing, use the Retelling/Summarizing Narrative Routine (*ELL Handbook,* p. 475).

ELL English Language Learners

For additional leveled instruction, see the **ELL/ELD Reader Teaching Guide.**

Comprehension: *Strength of Spirit*

- **Before Reading** Distribute copies of the ELL and ELD Readers, *Strength of Spirit,* to students at their reading level.
  - **Preview** Read the title aloud with students: This is a nonfiction text about two people who overcame great obstacles in their lives. Invite students to look through pictures and name what they see. Have them predict what might be the obstacles these people faced.
  - **Set a Purpose for Reading** Let's read to see how these people overcame their obstacles.
- **During Reading** Follow the Reading Routine for both reading groups.

1. Read the entire Reader aloud slowly.
2. Reread pp. 2–8, pausing to build background or model comprehension. Have Beginning students finger-point as you read. Use the questions in the chart to check students' comprehension.
3. Have students reread pp. 2–8 in pairs, taking turns reading alternate pages.
4. Repeat the steps for pp. 9–12 of the Reader.

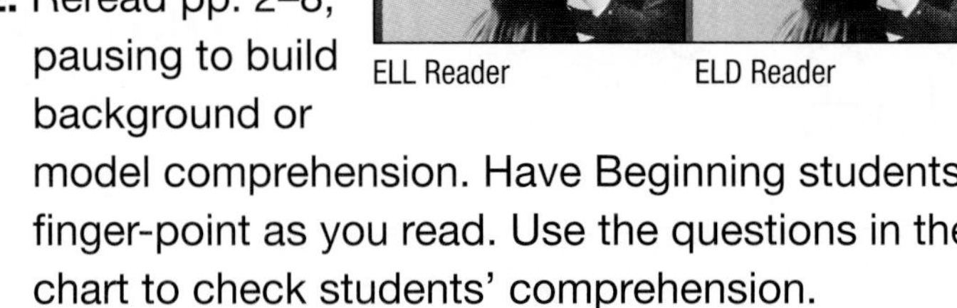

ELL Reader ELD Reader

- **After Reading** Use the exercises on the inside back cover of each Reader and invite students to share their writing. What makes each of these people extraordinary? Record their answers on the board and invite them to point to pictures in the book to support their answers.

ELD Reader Beginning/Intermediate

- **p. 3** What happened to Helen Keller when she was young and got sick? (She became deaf and blind.)
- **p. 7** What college did Helen Keller attend? (Ratcliffe College)

Writing How did Helen Keller overcome her challenges? Find a sentence in the book that tells about something Keller did to overcome her challenges. Copy the sentence. Then read it aloud to your partner.

ELL Reader Advanced/Advanced High

- **p. 3** What obstacle did Helen Keller have to overcome? (an illness left her deaf and blind)
- **p. 7** At age 20, what did Helen Keller become the first blind person to do? (attend Ratcliffe College)

Study Guide Distribute copies of the ELL Reader Study Guide (*ELL Handbook,* p. 130). Reread the text aloud with students. Instruct students to make a mental note of the challenges and achievements of each person. After reading, instruct students to go back and find the mental notes and fill-in the chart with their answers. (See *ELL Handbook,* pp. 209–212.)

Objectives

- Express opinions, ideas, and feelings ranging from communicating single words and short phrases to participating in extended discussions on a variety of social and grade-appropriate academic topics.
- Share information in cooperative learning interactions.

eReaders 

Conventions
Pronouns and Antecedents

- **Preteach** A pronoun is a word that is used to substitute for a noun. The word it replaces is called its antecedent. Each pronoun must agree with its antecedent in number, person, and gender. Point out the sentences patterns which include both subject and object pronouns. Use sticky notes to make a list of pronouns and their antecedents. Show students a match of pronoun and antecedent and ask if the match is correct or incorrect. Example: *he his; she hers; he hers.*
- **Practice** Write these sentence frames on the board. Ask students to provide the antecedent for each.

He gave ______ sandwich to ______ brother. *(his; his)*

She held ______ doll. ______ doll is very special to ______. *(her; her; her)*

We went to the store to spend ______ money on candy. *(our)*

- **Reteach** Have students speak using the grammatical structure of pronouns and antecedents. Antecedents come before pronouns. Be sure when students speaks that they don't say the pronouns without clear antecedents. Then ask students to write sentences with the grammatical structure. Write select sentences on the board and ask if the pronoun and antecedent agree.
- **Practice** Have students create a sentence frame missing either the pronoun or the antecedent. Have students write with a variety of patterns, including both subject and object pronouns. Have students write their frames on the board. Ask other students to complete the frames and read aloud. Have students edit completed sentences for agreement between pronouns and antecedents.

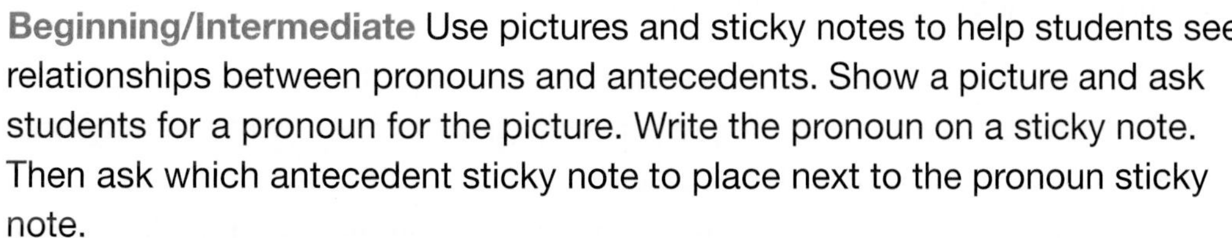

Leveled Support

Beginning/Intermediate Use pictures and sticky notes to help students see relationships between pronouns and antecedents. Show a picture and ask students for a pronoun for the picture. Write the pronoun on a sticky note. Then ask which antecedent sticky note to place next to the pronoun sticky note.

Advanced/Advanced High Have students use a chart to create as many pronouns and antecedents as they can recall.

Objectives

- Edit writing for standard grammar and usage, including subject-verb agreement, pronoun agreement, and appropriate verb tenses commensurate with grade-level expectations as more English is acquired.

Content Objectives

- Decode and use pronouns and antecedents.
- Correctly form pronouns and antecedents.

Language Objectives

- Write using a variety of sentence patterns.
- Speak using a pattern of pronouns and antecedents.
- Write phrases and sentences with pronouns and antecedents.
- Speak using the grammatical structure of pronouns and antecedents.
- Use grammatical structures in writing.

Transfer Skills

Spanish, Chinese, and Vietnamese speakers and other English learners may use subject pronouns as objects until practice in English clarifies the different pronoun forms.

Grammar Jammers

For more practice with pronouns, use the Grammar Jammers for this target skill. See the Grammar Jammers Routine (*ELL Handbook,* p. 478) for suggestions on using this learning tool.

Content Objectives

- Identify simple and compound sentences.

Language Objectives

- Write simple and compound sentences.
- Write using connecting words.
- Edit for subject-verb agreement.
- Know when to use informal language.
- Use peer support to grasp language structures.

Mini-Lesson: Informal Language

Tell students that, in informal speech, we often speak in sentence fragments rather than in simple sentences or compound sentences. Ask students when it is acceptable to use informal language rather than formal language. *(speaking with a friend, speaking with a family member, writing a note or a list, and so on)*

ELL English Language Learners

Simple and Compound Sentences

- **Introduce** Explain that a simple sentence is a sentence that has one subject part and one predicate part. Explain that sometimes the information in two sentences can be closely connected. In such cases, we can write the two sentences as one sentence. This is often referred to as a compound sentence. A compound sentence is a sentence that contains two or more simple sentences joined by a connecting word: *and*, *or*, or *but*. The words *by*, *and*, *or*, and *but*, which join two sentences together, are called conjunctions. We place a comma before a conjunction.

Writing Model

Write these sentences on the board.

We went to the game. We yelled for our team.

We went to the game, and we yelled for our team.

We were careful riding our bikes. We missed our turn.

We were careful riding our bikes, but we missed our turn.

- **Practice** Have students write compound sentences correctly using each of the connecting words *and, or,* and *but.*
- **Write** Have students write the above sentences on the board. In place of the conjunction, students should draw a line to indicate the missing conjunction. Have students write the sentences on their paper and fill in the conjunctions. Have peers support each other as they learn the language structures of compound sentences. Have peers check sentences for connecting words and two complete sentences that have been joined. Tell students that the subjects and verbs in both parts of a compound sentence must agree, Have students edit for subject-verb agreement.

Beginning/Intermediate Have students draw pictures illustrating two ideas. Help students write a sentence for each picture. Then, write a compound sentence to show how the two sentences become one.

Advanced/Advanced High Have students draw pictures for the sentences. Ask students to write a sentence for each picture. Then, write a compound sentence explaining the drawing.

Objectives

- Edit writing for standard grammar and usage, including subject-verb agreement, pronoun agreement, and appropriate verb tenses commensurate with grade-level expectations as more English is acquired.
- Share information in cooperative learning interactions.

This Week's ELL Overview

Grade 5 • Unit 4 • Week 3
Exploding Ants
76a–103s
and DI•66–DI•75

ELL Handbook

- Maximize Literacy and Cognitive Engagement
- Research Into Practice
- Full Weekly Support for Every Selection

Exploding Ants
- Multi-Lingual Summaries in Five Languages
- Selection-Specific Vocabulary Word Cards
- Frontloading/Reteaching for Comprehension Skill Lessons
- ELD and ELL Reader Study Guides

- Transfer Activities
- Professional Development

Daily Leveled ELL Notes

ELL notes appear throughout this week's instruction and ELL Support is on the DI pages of your Teacher's Edition. The following is a sample of an ELL note from this week.

English Language Learners

Beginning Have students draw pictures for the grids. Then have them write the Lesson Vocabulary word.

Intermediate Ask students to draw a picture or write a phrase using the word.

Advanced Assign students to write a sentence that gives a non-example.

Advanced High Have these students supply the word's meaning. Encourage them to look up the words in the glossary of the Student Edition.

ELL by Strand

The ELL lessons on this week's Support for English Language Learners pages are organized by strand. They offer additional scaffolding for the core curriculum. Leveled support notes on these pages address the different proficiency levels in your class. See pages DI•66–DI•75.

	The Three Pillars of ELL Instruction		
ELL Strands	**Activate Prior Knowledge**	**Access Content**	**Extend Language**
Vocabulary pp. DI•67–DI•68	Preteach	Reteach	Leveled Writing Activities
Reading Comprehension p. DI•72	Frontloading	Sheltered Reading	After Reading
Phonics, Spelling, and Word Analysis p. DI•70	Preteach	Teach/Model	Leveled Practice Activities
Listening Comprehension p. DI•69	Prepare for the Read Aloud	First Listening	Second Listening
Conventions and Writing pp. DI•74–DI•75	Preteach	Leveled Practice Activities	Leveled Writing Activities
Concept Development p. DI•66	Activate Prior Knowledge	Discuss Concept	Daily Concept and Vocabulary Development

This Week's Practice Stations Overview

Grade 5 • Unit 4 • Week 3
Exploding Ants
76a–103s

Six Weekly Practice Stations with Leveled Activities can be found at the beginning of each week of instruction. For this week's Practice Stations, see pp. 76h–76i.

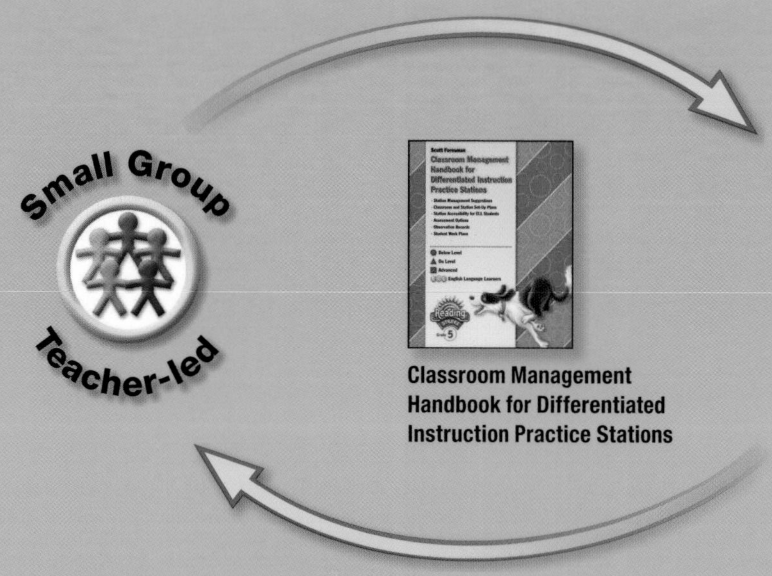

Classroom Management Handbook for Differentiated Instruction Practice Stations

Practice Stations

Daily Leveled Center Activities

 Below
 Advanced
 On-Level

Practice Stations Flip Charts

	 Word Wise	 Word Work	 Words to Know	 Let's Write	 Read for Meaning	 Get Fluent
Objectives	• Spell words with prefixes *over-, under-, sub-, super-,* and *out-.*	• Identify words with prefixes *over-, under-, sub-, super-,* and *out-.*	• Determine the meaning of unfamiliar words.	• Write a friendly letter.	• Make a generalization based on information in the story.	• Read aloud with accuracy.
Materials	• *Word Wise* Flip Chart Activity 18 • Teacher-made word cards • paper • pencil	• *Word Work* Flip Chart Activity 18 • Teacher-made word cards • paper • pencil	• *Words to Know* Flip Chart Activity 18 • newspaper • dictionary • paper • pencil	• *Let's Write* Flip Chart Activity 18 • paper • pencil	• *Read for Meaning* Flip Chart Activity 18 • Leveled Readers • paper • pencil	• *Get Fluent* Flip Chart Activity 18 • Leveled Readers

This Week on Reading Street!

Adapting

Question of the Week

How do animals adapt to survive?

Daily Plan

Don't Wait Until Friday

Whole Group

- Graphic Sources
- Synonyms
- Fluency/Rate
- Research and Inquiry

MONITOR PROGRESS Success Predictor

Day 1	Days 2–3	Day 4	Day 5
Check Oral Vocabulary	Check Retelling	Check Fluency	Check Oral Vocabulary

Small Group

Teacher-Led

- Reading Support
- Skill Support
- Fluency Practice

Practice Stations

Independent Activities

Customize Literacy More support for a balanced literacy approach, see pp. CL•1–CL•47

Customize Writing More support for a customized writing approach, see pp. CW•1–CW•10

Whole Group

- Writing: Formal Letter
- Conventions: Pronouns
- Spelling: Homophones

Assessment

- Weekly Tests
- Day 5 Assessment
- Fresh Reads

You Are Here! Unit 4 Week 3

This Week's Reading Selections

Main Selection
Genre: **Expository Text**

Paired Selection
Genre: **Expository Text**

Leveled Readers

ELL and ELD Readers

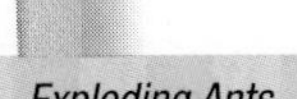

Resources on Reading Street!

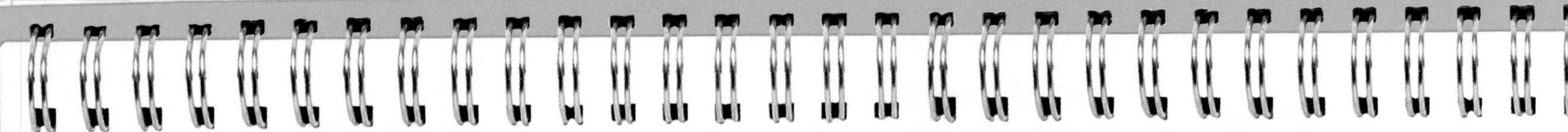

	Build Concepts	Comprehension
Whole Group	 Let's Talk About pp. 76–77	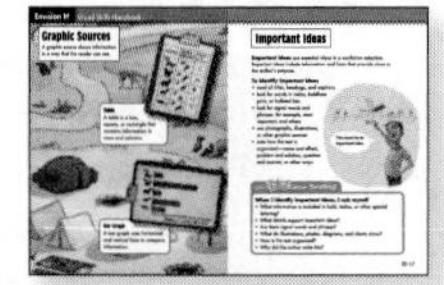 Envision It! Skills/ Strategies 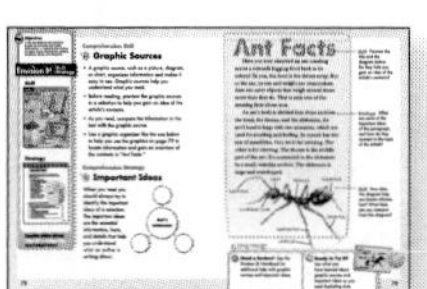 Comprehension Skills Lesson pp. 78–79
 Go Digital	• Concept Talk Video	• Envision It! Animations • eSelections
Small Group and Independent Practice	 Exploding Ants pp. 82–83  ELL and ELD Readers  Leveled Readers	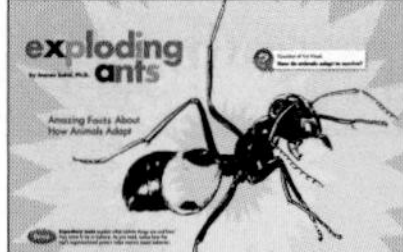 Exploding Ants pp. 82–83  ELL and ELD Readers  Leveled Readers 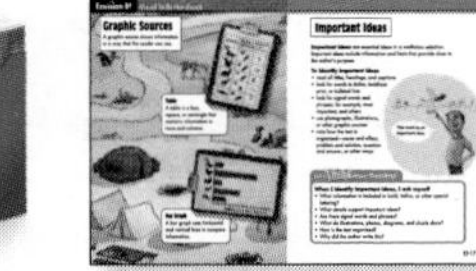 Envision It! Skills/ Strategies  Reader's and Writer's Notebook 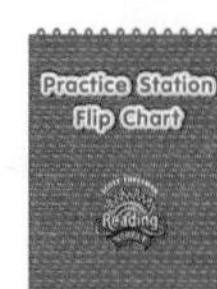 Practice Station Flip Chart
 Go Digital	• eReaders • eSelections	• Envision It! Animations • eSelections • eReaders
Customize Literacy	• Leveled Readers	• Envision It! Skills and Strategies Handbook • Leveled Readers
 Go Digital	• Concept Talk Video • Big Question Video • eReaders	• Envision It! Animations • eReaders

Question of the Week

How do animals adapt to survive?

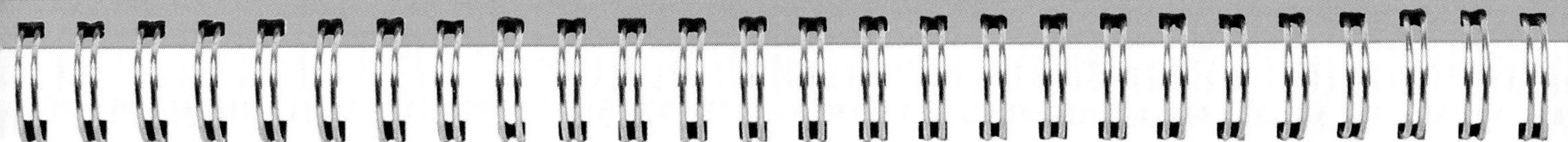

Vocabulary

Envision It! Vocabulary Cards

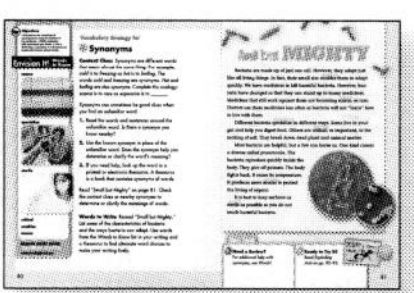
Vocabulary Skill Lesson pp. 80–81

- Envision It! Vocabulary Cards
- Vocabulary Activities

Envision It! Vocabulary Cards

Exploding Ants pp. 82–83

Practice Station Flip Chart

Words!

Reader's and Writer's Notebook

- Envision It! Vocabulary Cards
- Vocabulary Activities
- eSelections

- Envision It! Vocabulary Cards

- Vocabulary Activities

Fluency

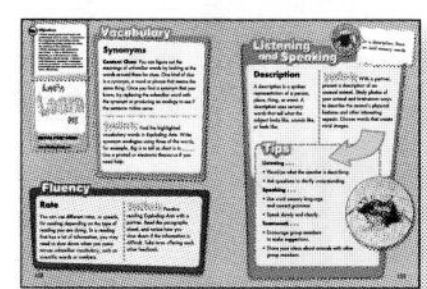
Let's Learn It! pp. 102–103

- eSelections
- eReaders

Exploding Ants pp. 82–83

Practice Station Flip Chart

Leveled Readers

ELL and ELD Readers

- eSelections
- eReaders

- Leveled Readers

- eReaders

Conventions and Writing

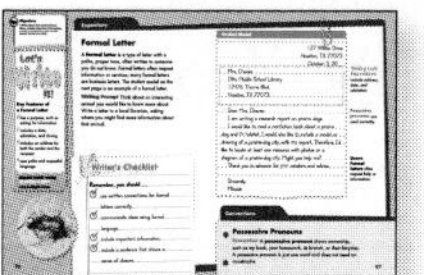
Let's Write It! pp. 96–97

- Grammar Jammer

Reader's and Writer's Notebook

Exploding Ants pp. 82–83

Practice Station Flip Chart

- Grammar Jammer

- Reader's and Writer's Notebook

- Grammar Jammer

My 5-Day Planner for Reading Street!

Don't Wait Until Friday MONITOR PROGRESS

	Check Oral Vocabulary **Day 1** pages 76j–79f	Check Retelling **Day 2** pages 80a–89e
Get Ready to Read	**Concept Talk,** 76j **Oral Vocabulary,** 77a adaptations, predators, defenses, fearsome **Listening Comprehension,** Read Aloud, 77b	**Concept Talk,** 80a **Oral Vocabulary,** 80b mimicry, camouflage **Word Analysis,** 80c Suffix *-ize* **Literary Terms,** 80d Metaphor **Text Features,** 80d Headings
Read and Comprehend	**Comprehension Skill,** ◎ Graphic Sources, 77c **Comprehension Strategy,** ◎ Important Ideas, 77c READ **Comprehension,** 78–79 **Model Fluency,** Rate, 78–79 **Introduce Lesson Vocabulary,** 79a critical, enables, mucus, scarce, specialize, sterile	**Vocabulary Skill,** ◎ Synonyms, 80e **Vocabulary Strategy,** Context Clues, 80e **Lesson Vocabulary,** 80–81 critical, enables, mucus, scarce, specialize, sterile READ **Vocabulary,** 80–81 **Model Fluency,** Rate, 80–81 READ **Main Selection,** *Exploding Ants,* 82–89a
Language Arts	**Research and Inquiry,** Identify Questions, 79b **Spelling,** Homophones, 79c **Conventions,** Possessive Pronouns, 79d **Handwriting,** Cursive Letter *l* and *L*, 79d **Writing,** Formal Letter, 79e–79f	**Research and Inquiry,** Navigate/Search, 89b **Conventions,** Possessive Pronouns, 89c **Spelling,** Homophones, 89c **Writing,** Formal Letter, Choose a Topic, 89d

Question of the Week

How do animals adapt to survive?

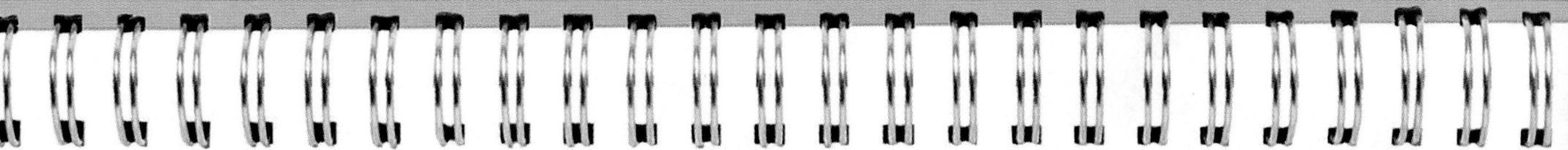

Check Retelling	Check Fluency	Check Oral Vocabulary
Day 3 pages 90a–97c	**Day 4** pages 98a–103e	**Day 5** pages 103f–103q
Concept Talk, 90a **Oral Vocabulary,** 90b spiny, survival **Comprehension Check,** 90c **Check Retelling,** 90d	**Concept Talk,** 98a **Oral Vocabulary,** 98b protrude, formidable **Genre,** Expository Text, 98c	**Concept Wrap Up,** 103f **Check Oral Vocabulary,** 103g adaptations, predators, defenses, fearsome, mimicry, camouflage, spiny, survival, protrude, formidable **Amazing Ideas,** 103g Review ◎ Graphic Sources, 103h Review ◎ Synonyms, 103h Review Word Analysis, 103i Review Literary Terms, 103i
READ **Main Selection,** *Exploding Ants,* 90–95 **Retelling,** 94–95 **Think Critically,** 95a **Model Fluency,** Rate, 95b **Research and Study Skills,** Magazine/Periodical, 95c	READ **Paired Selection,** "The Art of Mimicry," 98–101a **Let's Learn It!** 102–103a Fluency: Rate Vocabulary: Synonyms Listening and Speaking: Description	**Fluency Assessment,** WCPM, 103j–103k **Comprehension Assessment,** ◎ Graphic Sources, 103l–103m
Research and Inquiry, Analyze, 95d **Conventions,** Possessive Pronouns, 95e **Spelling,** Homophones, 95e **Let's Write It!** Formal Letter, 96–97a **Writing,** Formal Letter, Drafting, 97b–97c	**Research and Inquiry,** Synthesize, 103b **Conventions,** Possessive Pronouns, 103c **Spelling,** Homophones, 103c **Writing,** Formal Letter, Revising, 103d–103e	**Research and Inquiry,** Communicate, 103n **Conventions,** Possessive Pronouns, 103o **Spelling Test,** Homophones, 103o **Writing,** Formal Letter, Possessive Pronouns, 103p **Quick Write for Fluency,** 103q

Grouping Options for Differentiated Instruction
Turn the page for the small group time lesson plan.

Planning Small Group Time on Reading Street!

Look for this Small Group Time box each day to help meet the individual needs of all your students. Differentiated Instruction lessons appear on the DI pages at the end of each week.

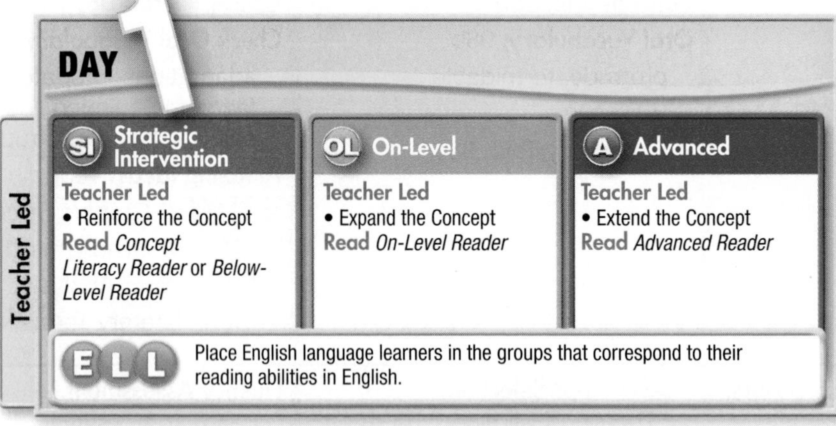

ELL Reader Advanced Advanced High

ELD Reader Beginning Intermediate

ELL Poster

	Day 1
SI Strategic Intervention	**Reinforce the Concept,** DI•51–DI•52 Read **Concept Literacy Reader** or **Below-Level Reader**
OL On-Level	**Expand the Concept,** DI•57 Read **On-Level Reader**
A Advanced	**Extend the Concept,** DI•62 Read **Advanced Reader**
ELL English Language Learners	DI•66–DI•75 **Frontload Concept** **Preteach Skills** **Writing**

You Are Here! Unit 4 Week 3

Reading Street Response to Intervention Kit

Reading Street Practice Stations Kit

Question of the Week

How do animals adapt to survive?

SI Strategic Intervention
Surviving the Elements: Animals in Their Environments
Amazing Ants
By Carol M. Elliott

Below-Level Reader

Concept Literacy Reader

Exploding Ants pp. 82–83

Changing for Survival: Bird Adaptations
by Lillian Duggan

On-Level Reader

Advanced Reader

The Art of Mimicry pp. 98–99

Small Group Weekly Plan

Day 2	Day 3	Day 4	Day 5
Reinforce Comprehension, DI•53 Revisit **Main Selection**	**Reinforce Vocabulary,** DI•54 Read/Revisit **Main Selection**	**Reinforce Comprehension,** Practice Retelling DI•55 Genre Focus Read/Revisit **Paired Selection**	**Practice Fluency,** DI•56 Reread **Concept Literacy Reader** or **Below-Level Reader**
Expand Comprehension, DI•58 Revisit **Main Selection**	**Expand Vocabulary,** DI•59 Read/Revisit **Main Selection**	**Expand Comprehension,** Practice Retelling DI•60 Genre Focus Read/Revisit **Paired Selection**	**Practice Fluency,** DI•61 Reread **On-Level Reader**
Extend Comprehension, DI•63 Revisit **Main Selection**	**Extend Vocabulary,** DI•64 Read/Revisit **Main Selection**	**Extend Comprehension,** Genre Focus DI•65 Read/Revisit **Paired Selection**	**Practice Fluency,** DI•65 Reread **Advanced Reader**
DI•66–DI•75 **Review Concept/Skills** **Frontload Main Selection** **Practice**	DI•66–DI•75 **Review Concept/Skills** Reread **Main Selection** **Practice**	DI•66–DI•75 **Review Concept/Skills** Read **ELL/ELD Readers** **Practice**	DI•66–DI•75 **Review Concept/Skills** Reread **ELL/ELD Reader** **Writing**

Week 3

Practice Stations for Everyone on Reading Street!

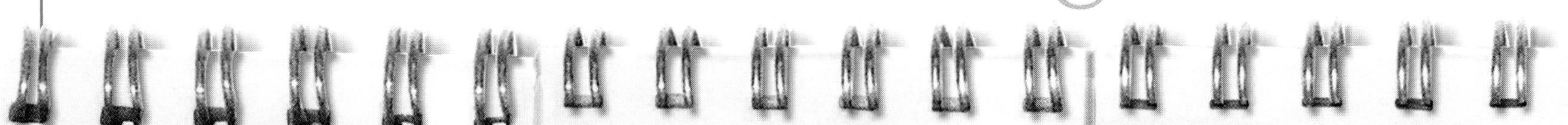

Word Wise
Prefixes *over-*, *under-*, *sub-*, *super-*, and *out-*

Objectives
- Spell words with prefixes *over-*, *under-*, *sub-*, *super-*, and *out-*.

Materials
- *Word Wise* Flip Chart Activity 18
- Teacher-made word cards
- paper
- pencil

Differentiated Activities
● Choose six word cards. Write your words in a list. Circle the prefix in each word. Write sentences using each word. Think other words you know with these prefixes. Add them to your list.

▲ Choose eight word cards, and write your words in a list. Circle the base word in each word. Notice how the prefix changes the word's meaning. Write sentences using each of your words.

■ Choose ten word cards, and write your words in a list. Circle the base word in each word, and notice how the prefix changes word meaning. Write sentences using each of your words.

Technology
- Online Dictionary

Word Work
Prefixes *over-*, *under-*, *sub-*, *super-*, and *out-*

Objectives
- Identify words with prefixes *over-*, *under-*, *sub-*, *super-*, and *out-*.

Materials
- *Word Work* Flip Chart Activity 18
- Teacher-made word cards
- paper
- pencil

Differentiated Activities
● Find two word cards with each prefix. Make a five-column chart with prefixes *over-*, *under-*, *sub-*, *super-*, and *out-* as headings. Write the words in the correct column. Quietly say each word aloud.

▲ Make a five-column chart with the prefixes as headings. Choose twelve word cards. Write your words in the columns. Quietly say each word aloud. Add other words with these prefixes to the chart.

■ Make a five-column chart with the prefixes as headings. Write each word card in the correct column. Quietly say each word aloud, and add other words you know with these prefixes to the chart.

Technology
- Modeled Pronunciation Audio CD

Words to Know
Unfamiliar Words

Objectives
- Determine the meaning of unfamiliar words.

Materials
- *Words to Know* Flip Chart Activity 18
- newspaper
- dictionary
- paper
- pencil

Differentiated Activities
● Use a newspaper to find four unfamiliar words. Write the words in a list. Use context clues to try to determine word meanings. Check definitions in a dictionary. Write a sentence using each word.

▲ Read a newspaper, and make a list of six unfamiliar words. Use context clues to try to determine word meanings, and then check definitions in a dictionary. Write a sentence using each word.

■ Read a newspaper to come up with a list of eight unfamiliar words. Use context to try to determine word meanings, and use a dictionary to check definitions. Write a sentence using each word.

Technology
- Online Dictionary

Use this week's materials from the Reading Street Leveled Practice Stations Kit to organize this week's stations.

Key
- ● Below-Level Activities
- ▲ On-Level Activities
- ■ Advanced Activities

Practice Station Flip Chart

Let's Write!
Friendly Letter

Objectives
- Write a friendly letter.

Materials
- *Let's Write!* Flip Chart Activity 18
- paper
- pencil

Differentiated Activities
● Choose a character from a favorite book or story. Write a friendly letter to the character. Ask the character questions. Tell what you have been busy doing. Include a mix of short and long sentences.

▲ Choose two characters from a book or story. Write a letter from one character to the other. Ask the character questions, and tell what your character has been doing. Use a mix of simple and compound sentences.

■ Choose two characters from a book. Write a letter from one character to the other. Then write the second character's response. Include a mix of simple and compound sentences in the letters.

Technology
- Online Graphic Organizers

Read for Meaning
Generalization

Objectives
- Make a generalization based on information in the story.

Materials
- *Read for Meaning* Flip Chart Activity 18
- Leveled Readers
- paper
- pencil

Differentiated Activities
● Choose and read a book from those your teacher provided. Make a generalization based on what you have read. Write a sentence that states your generalization. Write a sentence with a detail to support your generalization.

▲ Choose and read a book from those your teacher provided. Make a generalization based on information. Write a short paragraph stating your generalization. Include details to support the generalization.

■ Choose and read a book from those your teacher provided. Make two generalizations about characters or events. Write a paragraph stating each generalization, and include text evidence to support both generalizations.

Technology
- Leveled-Reader Database

Get Fluent
Practice fluent reading.

Objectives
- Read aloud with accuracy.

Materials
- *Get Fluent* Flip Chart Activity 18
- Leveled Readers

Differentiated Activities
● Work with a partner. Choose a Concept Literacy Reader or Below-Level Reader. Take turns reading a page from the book. Use the reader to practice accuracy. Provide feedback as needed.

▲ Work with a partner. Choose an On-Level Reader. Take turns reading a page from the book. Use the reader to practice accuracy. Provide feedback as needed.

■ Work with a partner. Choose an Advanced Reader. Take turns reading a page from the book. Use the reader to practice accuracy. Provide feedback as needed.

Technology
- Leveled Reader Database
- Reading Street Readers CD-ROM

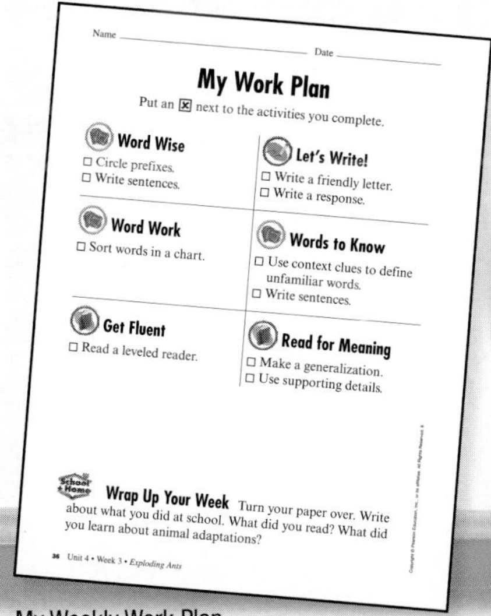
Name ______ Date ______

My Work Plan

Put an ☒ next to the activities you complete.

Word Wise
- ☐ Circle prefixes.
- ☐ Write sentences.

Let's Write!
- ☐ Write a friendly letter.
- ☐ Write a response.

Word Work
- ☐ Sort words in a chart.

Words to Know
- ☐ Use context clues to define unfamiliar words.
- ☐ Write sentences.

Get Fluent
- ☐ Read a leveled reader.

Read for Meaning
- ☐ Make a generalization.
- ☐ Use supporting details.

Wrap Up Your Week Turn your paper over. Write about what you did at school. What did you read? What did you learn about animal adaptations?

Unit 4 • Week 3 • Exploding Ants

My Weekly Work Plan

Week 3

Objectives
- Introduce the weekly concept.
- Develop oral vocabulary.

Today at a Glance

Oral Vocabulary
adaptations, predators, defenses, fearsome

Comprehension
◎ Graphic sources
◎ Important ideas

Reading
"Ant Facts"

Fluency
Rate

Lesson Vocabulary
Tested vocabulary

Research and Inquiry
Identify questions

Spelling
Homophones

Conventions
Possessive pronouns

Handwriting
Cursive letters *l* and *L*

Writing
Formal letter

Concept Talk

Question of the Week
How do animals adapt to survive?

Introduce the concept To further explore the unit concept of Adapting, this week students will read, write, and talk about how animals adapt to survive in the wild. Write the Question of the Week on the board.

ROUTINE Activate Prior Knowledge **Team Talk**

1. **Think** Have students think about why animals might have to adapt, or change, in order to survive or continue to live.
2. **Pair** Have pairs of students discuss the Question of the Week by considering suggestions from each other.
3. **Share** Call on a few students to share their ideas with the group. Guide the discussion and encourage elaboration with prompts such as:
   - What examples of an animal changing to survive did you discuss?
   - What kinds of animals live near where you live? How are those animals suited to live in your area?

Routines Flip Chart

Anchored Talk

Develop oral vocabulary Have students turn to pp. 76–77 in their Student Editions. Look at each of the photos. Then, use the prompts to guide discussion, create the *How animals adapt to survive* concept map, and establish purposes for reading.

- How has the lizard on the branch adapted to its environment? (It has turned green like the branch.) Some animals use mimicry, or imitation, to adapt. Let's add *Mimicry* and *Adaptations* to our concept map.
- Has the fish in the photo changed in order to defend itself? (Yes, it has blown itself up into a spiny, scary form.) Let's add *Defenses* to the concept map.

Amazing Words

You've learned 1 7 0 words so far.

You'll learn 0 1 0 words this week!

adaptations	camouflage
predators	spiny
defenses	survival
fearsome	protrude
mimicry	formidable

Objectives
• Listen to and interpret a speaker's messages and ask questions.
• Identify the main ideas and supporting ideas in the speaker's message.
Oral Vocabulary
Let's Talk About
Adaptations
Share what you know about ways animals adapt.
Listen to and interpret a classmate's knowledge of adaptations.
Determine main and supporting ideas in your classmates' messages about adaptations.
READING STREET ONLINE
CONCEPT TALK VIDEO
www.ReadingStreet.com
You've learned
1 7 0
Amazing Words
so far this year!
76
77

Student Edition pp. 76–77

Writing on Demand 

Writing Fluency

Ask students to respond to the photos on pp. 76–77 by writing as well as they can and as much as they can about how animals adapt in order to survive.

- How has the lion adapted to its environment? (It is tan colored to match the grass and is moving very low to the ground so it can't be seen.)
- After discussing the photos, ask: How do animals adapt?

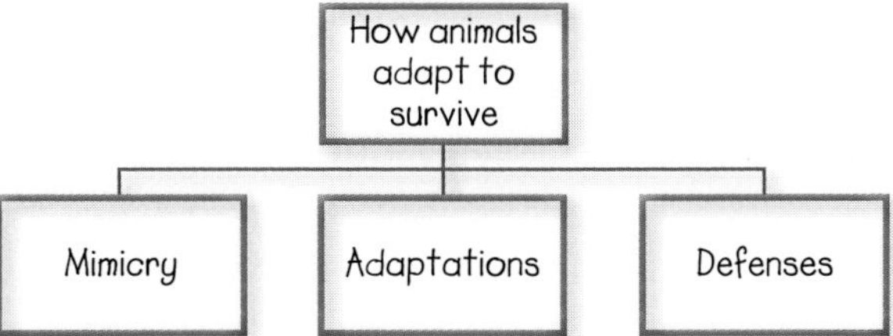

Connect to reading Tell students that this week they will be reading about animals adapting for survival reasons. Encourage students to add concept-related words to this week's concept map.

ELL Preteach Concepts Use the Day 1 instruction on ELL Poster 18 to assess and build background knowledge, develop concepts, and build oral vocabulary.

ELL Poster 18

ELL

English Language Learners

ELL support Additional ELL support and modified instruction is provided in the *ELL Handbook* and in the ELL Support lessons on pp. DI•66–DI•75.

Listening comprehension English learners will benefit from additional visual support to understand the key terms in the concept map. Use the pictures on pp. 76–77 to scaffold understanding.

Frontload for Read Aloud Use the modified Read Aloud on p. DI•69 in the ELL Support lessons to prepare students to listen to "Escape Artists" (p. 77b).

Objectives
- Develop listening comprehension.
- Build oral vocabulary.

Check Oral Vocabulary
SUCCESS PREDICTOR

Oral Vocabulary
Amazing Words

Introduce Amazing Words "Escape Artists" on p. 77b is about animal survival mechanisms. Tell students to listen for this week's Amazing Words—*adaptations, predators, defenses,* and *fearsome*—as you read.

Model fluency As you read "Escape Artists," model appropriate rate by reading at a speed that is appropriate to the text and will improve the listener's comprehension.

Teach Amazing Words

Amazing Words Oral Vocabulary Routine

adaptations
predators
defenses
fearsome

1. **Introduce** Write the word *predators* on the board. Have students say the word aloud with you. In "Escape Artists," we learn that a puffed-up puffer fish scares away its *predators.* Supply a student-friendly definition.
2. **Demonstrate** Have students answer questions to demonstrate understanding. Have them break into groups. Have students consider suggestions from group members. What animals are *predators* to mice? What do *predators* such as hawks feed on?
3. **Apply** Ask students to give an antonym of *predators.*

See p. OV•3 to teach *adaptations, defenses,* and *fearsome.*

Routines Flip Chart

Apply Amazing Words To build oral language, have students discuss the Amazing Words.

Don't Wait Until Friday **MONITOR PROGRESS** **Check Oral Vocabulary**

During discussion, listen for students' use of Amazing Words.

If... students are unable to use the Amazing Words to discuss the concept,
then... use Oral Vocabulary Routine in the Routines Flip Chart to demonstrate words in different contexts.

Day 1	**Days 2–3**	**Day 4**	**Day 5**
Check Oral Vocabulary	Check Retelling	Check Fluency	Check Oral Vocabulary

Escape Artists

by Emily Costello

You don't always have to be strong to survive in the wild. Many animals have adaptations that keep them from being some other animals' dinners.

Some animals have adaptations that are hidden. They appear only when an animal is threatened. Octopuses squirt ink to create a "smoke screen" while they make their escape. Puffer fish "supersize" themselves by gulping water until they resemble a spiny balloon. Silly looking? You bet. But a puffed up puffer fish can scare away its predators, and that's nothing to laugh at.

Other animals have defenses that are always visible and fearsome —even when the animal isn't under attack. Great white sharks have 3,000 teeth. Bulls have long horns. They can ram through anything that bugs them. Monarch butterflies have bold warning signs—colored marks on their wings that tell other animals they taste bad if eaten. Whatever their defense, these animals have one message they want to get across: "Don't mess with me!"

For badgers and coyotes, the striped skunk's black-and-white fur is a clear warning sign. It says: "Stay away!" Animals that don't heed the warning get a whiff of the skunk's in-your-face defenses. First, the skunk gives a warning by raising its tail and stomping with its front paws. If that doesn't work, it pretends to charge its predator. As a last resort, the skunk will let loose a terrible-smelling spray. Getting rid of the stink can take weeks. Most predators, like dogs, usually learn their lesson for a lifetime. But owls can't smell skunk's spray, and successfully hunt them.

Camouflage is an adaptation that helps some animals hide. The flower mantis is a little bug with a huge appetite. One mantis can eat 15 crickets in a single day, sometimes catching one prey while still eating another. The bugs perch on flowers whose colors are like their own. This makes it hard for them to be seen by insects they'd like to eat or bats that would like to eat them.

How would you feel if your pizza suddenly looked like a tuna casserole? You might lose your appetite. Amazing, some "tasty" animals use mimicry. They pretend to be a "yucky" species to avoid being eaten. Take the saltwater comet fish. When a scary grouper or snapper swims by, the 6-inch-long fish sticks its head in its burrow and spreads out its rear fin to reveal a fake "eye." That fools the bigger fish into thinking it's seeing a

(continued on p. 103s)

DAY 1 Read and Comprehend

30–35 mins.

Objectives

- ◎ Understand and use graphic sources in expository text.
- ◎ Use the important ideas strategy to aid comprehension.
- • Read grade-level text at an appropriate rate.

Skills Trace

◎ **Graphic Sources**

Introduce U3W5D1; U4W3D1; U5W2D1

Practice U3W5D2; U3W5D3; U4W3D2; U4W3D3; U5W2D2; U5W2D3

Reteach/Review U1W5D2; U3W5D5; U4W3D5; U5W2D5; U5W3D2; U5W5D2

Assess/Test Weekly Tests U3W5; U4W3; U5W2

Benchmark Tests U5

KEY:

U=Unit W=Week D=Day

Skill ↔ Strategy

Graphic Sources

Important Ideas

Introduce graphic sources

Graphic sources are pictures, diagrams, or charts that organize information visually to help you understand what you read. How might looking at graphic sources before you read help give you an overview of the text or help you to locate information? (Graphic sources often support the information discussed on that page.) How might a graphic source help you understand an idea in a selection? (by providing a visual aid to comprehension) Have students turn to pp. EI•8–EI•9 in the Student Edition to review graphic sources. Then read "Ant Facts" with students.

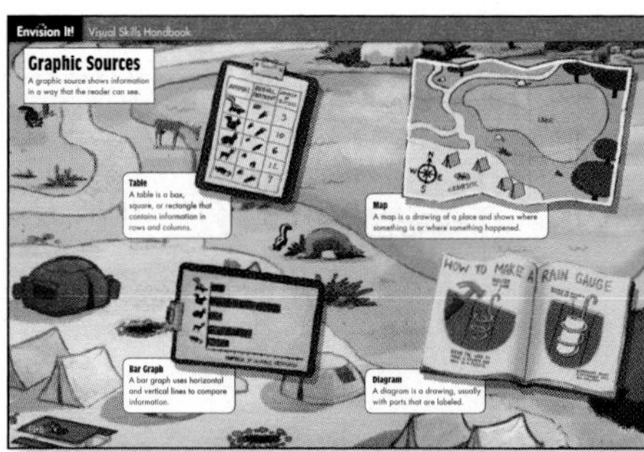

Student Edition pp. EI•8–EI•9

Model the skill

Think Aloud: Today we are going to read about how ants adapt to survive. Look at the illustration on page 79. What is pictured here? (an ant with its body parts labeled) I can see what these tiny ants look like because the image has been enlarged. Now when I read the article, I'll know what these body parts look like.

Guide practice

Ask students to identify the mandible and the foreleg on the ant illustration. Then ask them to tell how many sections an ant's body has. Have students read "Ant Facts" on their own.

Strategy check

Important Ideas Remind students that if they have difficulty understanding "Ant Facts," they can use the strategy of determining important ideas. Model the strategy of rereading to identify important ideas and supporting details.

Model the strategy

Think Aloud: When I first read about how ants can carry things that weigh more than they do, I didn't understand how this could happen. But then I reread the selection. Now I can see that an ant has a uniquely designed body. I think this might allow ants to carry heavy things. This is an important idea. Have students review the strategy of determining important ideas on p. EI•17 of the Student Edition.

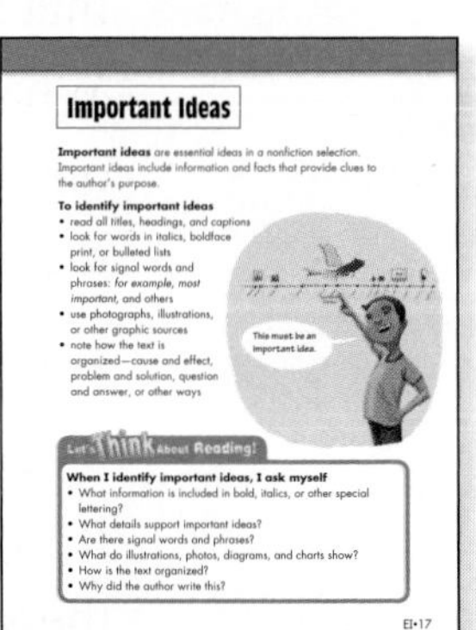

Student Edition p. EI•17

On their own

Have students summarize "Ant Facts" using the important ideas strategy, while maintaining logical order and meaning. Use p. 269 in the *Reader's and Writer's Notebook* for additional practice.

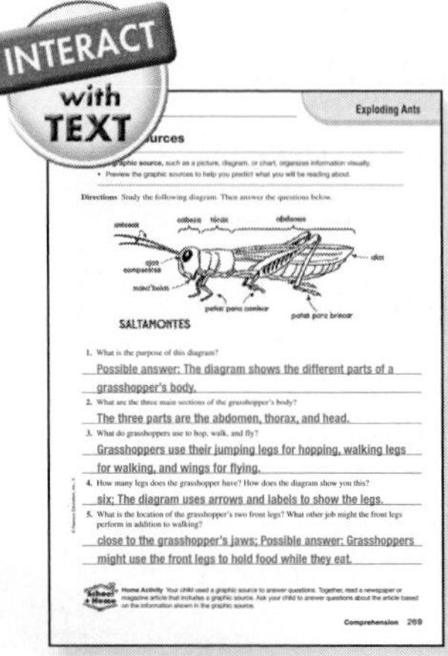

Reader's and Writer's Notebook, p. 269

Envision It! Animations 

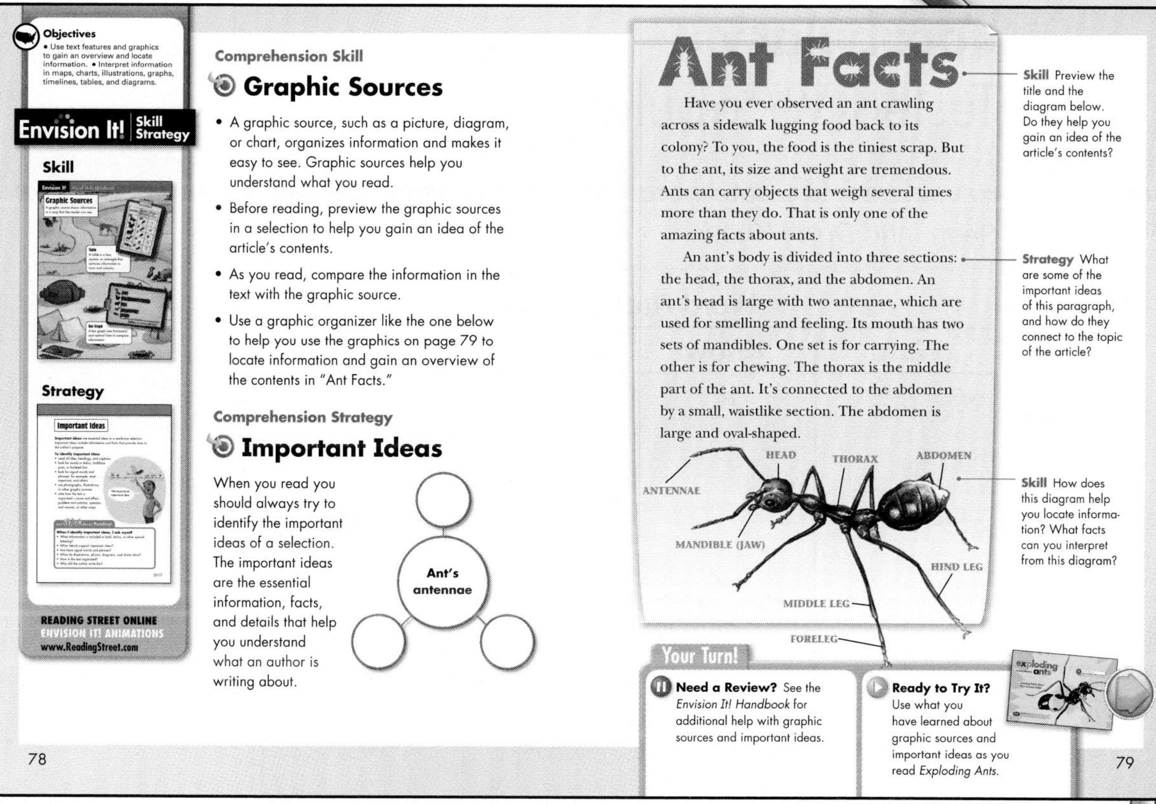

Objectives
• Use text features and graphics to gain an overview and locate information. • Interpret information in maps, charts, illustrations, graphs, timelines, tables, and diagrams.

Envision It! Skill Strategy

Skill

Strategy

READING STREET ONLINE
ENVISION IT! ANIMATIONS
www.ReadingStreet.com

Comprehension Skill

Graphic Sources

- A graphic source, such as a picture, diagram, or chart, organizes information and makes it easy to see. Graphic sources help you understand what you read.
- Before reading, preview the graphic sources in a selection to help you gain an idea of the article's contents.
- As you read, compare the information in the text with the graphic source.
- Use a graphic organizer like the one below to help you use the graphics on page 79 to locate information and gain an overview of the contents in "Ant Facts."

Comprehension Strategy

Important Ideas

When you read you should always try to identify the important ideas of a selection. The important ideas are the essential information, facts, and details that help you understand what an author is writing about.

78

Ant Facts

Have you ever observed an ant crawling across a sidewalk lugging food back to its colony? To you, the food is the tiniest scrap. But to the ant, its size and weight are tremendous. Ants can carry objects that weigh several times more than they do. That is only one of the amazing facts about ants.

An ant's body is divided into three sections: the head, the thorax, and the abdomen. An ant's head is large with two antennae, which are used for smelling and feeling. Its mouth has two sets of mandibles. One set is for carrying. The other is for chewing. The thorax is the middle part of the ant. It's connected to the abdomen by a small, waistlike section. The abdomen is large and oval-shaped.

Skill Preview the title and the diagram below. Do they help you gain an idea of the article's contents?

Strategy What are some of the important ideas of this paragraph, and how do they connect to the topic of the article?

Skill How does this diagram help you locate information? What facts can you interpret from this diagram?

Your Turn!

Need a Review? See the *Envision It! Handbook* for additional help with graphic sources and important ideas.

Ready to Try It? Use what you have learned about graphic sources and important ideas as you read *Exploding Ants*.

79

Student Edition pp. 78–79

Skill Yes; they tell me this article describes amazing things about ants.

Strategy Ants can carry things that weigh more than they do. This important idea relates to the topic of the article because this is a fact about ants.

Skill Possible response: It tells me that this page contains information about an ant's body. I can find names of parts easily; Ants have 6 legs and 3 body sections.

Model Fluency
Rate

Model fluency Have students listen as you read paragraph 1 of "Ant Facts" orally at an appropriate rate. Explain that you will adjust the speed of your reading so that listeners can comprehend the concepts in the text.

ROUTINE Oral Rereading

1. **Read** Have students read paragraph 1 of "Ant Facts" orally.
2. **Reread** To achieve optimal fluency and comprehension, students should reread aloud the text three to four times at any appropriate rate.
3. **Corrective Feedback** Have students read aloud without you. Provide feedback about their rate of reading text and encourage them to read at a speed that will help listeners with comprehension.

Routines Flip Chart

ELL

English Language Learners

Graphic sources Provide oral practice by having students talk about visual tools they use in everyday life. Then list these graphic sources on the board and have students discuss how these sources present information:

- Bus or train schedules
- Road maps
- Packaging on foods that gives nutritional information

Objectives

- Activate prior knowledge of words.
- Identify questions for research.

Vocabulary
Tested Vocabulary

Lesson Vocabulary

Have students create word rating charts using the categories *Know, Have Seen,* and *Don't Know*.

Word Rating Chart

Word	Know	Have Seen	Don't Know
critical	✔		
enables		✔	
mucus			✔
scarce	✔		
specialize		✔	
sterile			✔

Activate prior knowledge

Read each word to students and have the rate their knowledge of the word by placing a checkmark in one of the three columns: *Know* (know and can use); *Have Seen* (have seen or heard the word; don't know meaning); *Don't Know* (don't know the word).

Have students confirm the meanings of the words they checked in the *Know* column by using a print or electronic dictionary, and then have them provide sentences for the words. By the end of the week, have them revise their charts and demonstrate their understanding by using each word in a sentence.

Preteach Academic Vocabulary

ELL **Academic Vocabulary** Write the following words on the board:

synonym	**possessive pronoun**
figurative language	**formal letter**
metaphor	**conventions**

Have students share what they know about this week's Academic Vocabulary. Use the students' responses to assess their prior knowledge. Preteach the Academic Vocabulary by providing a student-friendly description, explanation, or example that clarifies the meaning of each term. Then ask students to define the Academic Vocabulary term in their own words.

Research and Inquiry
Identify Questions

Teach Discuss the Question of the Week: *How do animals adapt to survive?* Tell students they will research how animals adapt. On Day 5 they will present a poster with a picture of the animal they have researched and a description of its special adaptations.

Model Think Aloud: I'll start by brainstorming a list of questions about how animals can adapt to survive. I know that all wild animals have particular adaptations that help them survive. I'm interested in lions. Some possible questions could be: *Do lions have predators? What adaptations help lions survive? Do they always live in groups?*

Guide practice After students have selected an animal and developed inquiry questions, help them generate research plans for gathering information about their chosen animals. Explain that tomorrow they will use magazines and other sources to research their question and prepare to talk to an expert.

On their own Have students work individually to create a research plan.

Small Group Time

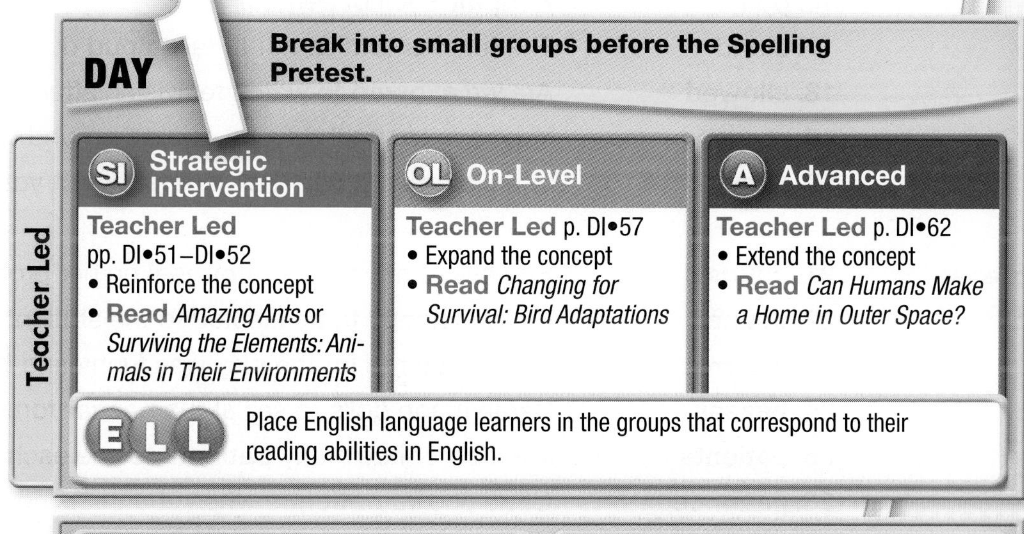

DAY 1 Break into small groups before the Spelling Pretest.

Teacher Led

SI Strategic Intervention	OL On-Level	A Advanced
Teacher Led pp. DI•51–DI•52 • Reinforce the concept • Read *Amazing Ants* or *Surviving the Elements: Animals in Their Environments*	Teacher Led p. DI•57 • Expand the concept • Read *Changing for Survival: Bird Adaptations*	Teacher Led p. DI•62 • Extend the concept • Read *Can Humans Make a Home in Outer Space?*

ELL: Place English language learners in the groups that correspond to their reading abilities in English.

Practice Stations	Independent Activities
• Read for Meaning • Get Fluent • Word Work	• Concept Talk Video • *Reader's and Writer's Notebook* • Vocabulary Activities

INTERNET GUY
Don Leu

21st Century Skills

Weekly Inquiry Project

Day 1 Identify Questions
Day 2 Navigate/Search
Day 3 Analyze
Day 4 Synthesize
Day 5 Communicate

Differentiated Instruction

Advanced
Have students look at the questions they generated and write a prediction for each one.

ELL

English Language Learners
Multilingual vocabulary Students can apply knowledge of their home languages to acquire new English vocabulary by using the Multilingual Vocabulary Lists (*ELL Handbook*, pp. 431–444).

Objectives

- Spell homophones correctly.
- Use and understand possessive pronouns.
- Write cursive capital letter *L* and lowercase *l* in words.

Spelling Pretest
Homophones

Introduce Tell students that homophones are words that sound alike, but they have different meanings and are spelled differently. This week, we will spell homophones.

Pretest Use these sentences to administer the spelling pretest. Say each word, read the sentence, and repeat the word.

1. cent	Ana has two nickels, one dime, and one **cent.**
2. sent	Ricardo **sent** a letter to his grandmother.
3. scent	My favorite **scent** for perfume is vanilla.
4. threw	Kim **threw** the ball as far as she could.
5. through	Is she **through** reading that book?
6. weather	The **weather** is cold, rainy, and cloudy today.
7. whether	He can't say **whether** he wants to see that movie.
8. their	Carla and Rosario are taking **their** dog on vacation.
9. there	Please put the plates **there** on the table.
10. they're	**They're** walking to school together this morning.
11. chili	Richard makes the best **chili** I have ever tasted.
12. chilly	I took my coat because it was **chilly** outside.
13. tide	The ocean is at low **tide** now.
14. tied	Minh **tied** the string to the cat's toy.
15. pale	John's face is **pale** after staying inside all winter.
16. pail	Her **pail** is full of berries.
17. aloud	The teacher told us not to talk **aloud** during a test.
18. allowed	Are we **allowed** to watch television after chores?
19. course	You have to run the entire **course** around the field.
20. coarse	The cloth of the bag feels **coarse** when you touch it.

Challenge words

21. counsel	She asked her aunt for **counsel** on her problem.
22. council	Emily is happy to be elected to the student **council**.
23. bizarre	Tim's costume for the play was funny and **bizarre.**
24. bazaar	Sarah made dolls to sell at the **bazaar** tomorrow.
25. patients	The doctor has many **patients** to see each day.
26. patience	Olivia shows **patience** when she trains her puppy.

Self-correct After the pretest, you can either display the correctly spelled words or spell them orally. Have students self-correct their pretests by writing misspelled words.

On their own For additional practice use *Let's Practice It!* p. 202 on the *Teacher Resources DVD-ROM*.

Let's Practice It!
TR DVD•202

Conventions
Possessive Pronouns

Teach Display Grammar Transparency 18, and read aloud the explanation and examples in the box. Possessive pronouns have two forms: one is used by itself and one is used before a noun.

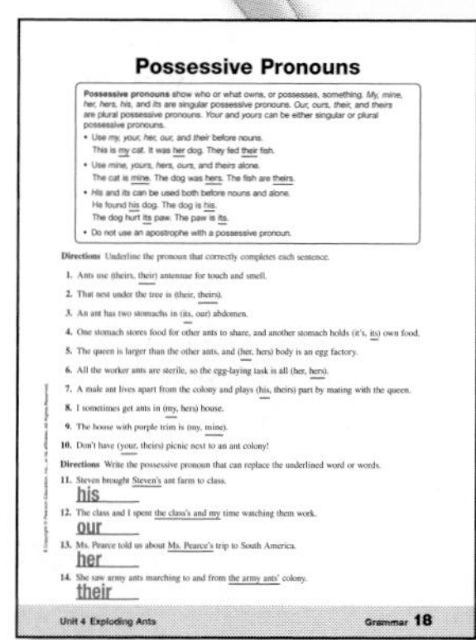

Possessive Pronouns

Possessive pronouns show who or what owns, or possesses, something. *My, mine, her, hers, his,* and *its* are singular possessive pronouns. *Our, ours, their,* and *theirs* are plural possessive pronouns. *Your* and *yours* can be either singular or plural possessive pronouns.

- Use *my, your, her, our,* and *their* before nouns.
  This is my cat. It was her dog. They fed their fish.
- Use *mine, yours, hers, ours,* and *theirs* alone.
  The cat is mine. The dog was hers. The fish are theirs.
- *His* and *its* can be used both before nouns and alone.
  He found his dog. The dog is his.
  The dog hurt its paw. The paw is its.
- Do not use an apostrophe with a possessive pronoun.

Directions Underline the pronoun that correctly completes each sentence.

1. Ants use (theirs, their) antennae for touch and smell.
2. That nest under the tree is (their, theirs).
3. An ant has two stomachs in (its, our) abdomen.
4. One stomach stores food for other ants to share, and another stomach holds (it's, its) own food.
5. The queen is larger than the other ants, and (her, hers) body is an egg factory.
6. All the worker ants are sterile, so the egg-laying task is all (her, hers).
7. A male ant lives apart from the colony and plays (his, theirs) part by mating with the queen.
8. I sometimes get ants in (my, hers) house.
9. The house with purple trim is (my, mine).
10. Don't have (your, theirs) picnic next to an ant colony!

Directions Write the possessive pronoun that can replace the underlined word or words.

11. Steven brought Steven's ant farm to class. his
12. The class and I spent the class's and my time watching them work. our
13. Ms. Pearce told us about Ms. Pearce's trip to South America. her
14. She saw army ants marching to and from the army ants' colony. their

Unit 4 Exploding Ants Grammar **18**

Grammar Transparency 18, TR DVD

Model When I think about what possessive pronoun to use, I remember that the pronoun refers to a noun close by. Then I decide whether the noun is singular or plural. And if I'm referring to a specific person, I use *her* and *hers* with a female and *his* with a male. If I'm referring to an animal, I use *its.* Look at the first item. Will a noun follow the pronoun? Which pronoun should I use?

Guide practice Guide students through the items. In items 1–10, help students decide which of the two pronouns to use.

Daily Fix-It Use Daily Fix-It numbers 1 and 2 in the right margin.

Connect to oral language Have students complete items 11–14 by choosing a pronoun to replace the underlined words.

Handwriting
Cursive Letter *L* and *l*

Model letter formation Display the capital cursive letter *L* and lowercase letter *l*. Follow the stroke instruction pictured to model letter formation.

Model letter size Explain that both the lowercase and capital *L* touch the top line and the bottom line. Write the following sentence: *In Lima, a llama named Liliana licked a lollipop.* Make sure that both the capital and lowercase letters touch the top and bottom lines.

Guide practice Have students write these phrases: *lucky Larry learning* and *likeable Leila laughing*. Circulate around the room, guiding students as they script.

Academic Vocabulary

conventions agreed upon rules describing the use of words in a language

possessive pronoun word that takes the place of a possessive noun and shows who or what owns something

Daily Fix-It

1. A skunk sprays a bad-smelling sent to keep enemys away. *(scent; enemies)*
2. That serves as there protecsion. *(their protection)*

English Language Learners

Language production: Possessive pronouns Ask a student to hold up an object that belongs to him or her. Use the student's name and the name of the object (Lupe's pencil) to form a possessive noun and then change to a possessive pronoun (her). Write the possessive noun and pronoun on the board. Then have pairs use possessive pronouns to describe what a partner is holding. Record their initial answers on the board; then call on students to be the scribes. Model corrective feedback when needed.

Objectives

- Understand and identify the features of a formal letter.

Writing—Formal Letter

Introduce

MINI-LESSON

Read Like a Writer

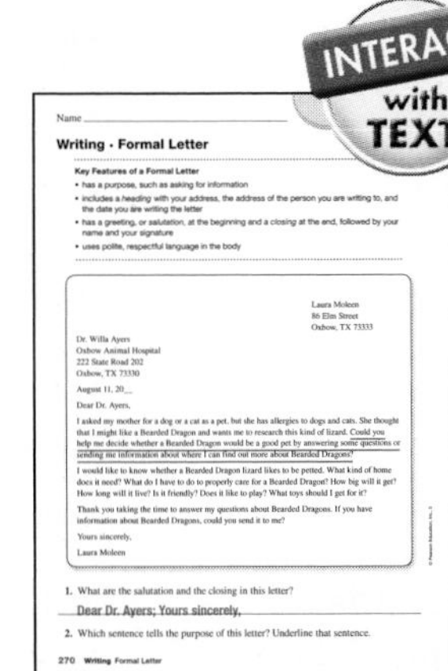

Name ______

Writing • Formal Letter

Key Features of a Formal Letter

- has a purpose, such as asking for information
- includes a *heading* with your address, the address of the person you are writing to, and the date you are writing the letter
- has a greeting, or salutation, at the beginning and a closing at the end, followed by your name and your signature
- uses polite, respectful language in the body

Laura Moleen
86 Elm Street
Oxbow, TX 73333

Dr. Willa Ayers
Oxbow Animal Hospital
222 State Road 202
Oxbow, TX 73330

August 11, 20__

Dear Dr. Ayers,

I asked my mother for a dog or a cat as a pet, but she has allergies to dogs and cats. She thought that I might like a Bearded Dragon and wants me to research this kind of lizard. Could you help me decide whether a Bearded Dragon would be a good pet by answering some questions or sending me information about where I can find out more about Bearded Dragons?

I would like to know whether a Bearded Dragon lizard likes to be petted. What kind of home does it need? What do I have to do to properly care for a Bearded Dragon? How big will it get? How long will it live? Is it friendly? Does it like to play? What toys should I get for it?

Thank you taking the time to answer my questions about Bearded Dragons. If you have information about Bearded Dragons, could you send it to me?

Yours sincerely,
Laura Moleen

1. What are the salutation and the closing in this letter?
Dear Dr. Ayers; Yours sincerely,
2. Which sentence tells the purpose of this letter? Underline that sentence.

270 Writing Formal Letter

Reader's and Writer's Notebook p. 270

- **Introduce** This week you will write a **formal letter.** A formal letter is used at important times, such as when you apply for a job or request information from your bank. It has a specific structure and conventions.

Prompt	Think about an interesting animal you would like to know more about. Write a letter to a local librarian, asking where you might find more information about that animal.
Trait	Conventions
Mode	Expository

- **Examine Model Text** Have students read the formal letter, "Dragon Letter" on p. 270 of the *Reader's and Writer's Notebook.*

- **Key Features** A formal letter begins with a **heading**. It includes your name and address, the title of the person you're writing to with his or her last name, address, and the date.

  A formal letters opens with a greeting, or **salutation**, usually *Dear [title] [last name]* followed by a colon.

  The content or **body** of the letter is to the point and divided into short, clear paragraphs. The first paragraph states the purpose of the letter. Paragraph two gives important details. The last paragraph asks for action you want the person to take, provides closure, and thanks the person you are writing to.

  The language is polite and respectful. You don't need long words to be formal, but you should not use informal language such as contractions, slang, or text abbreviations.

  The letter ends with a **closing**. You normally write *Sincerely yours* or *Yours sincerely* followed by a comma, sign your name, and then print or type your name clearly below your signature.

MINI-LESSON

5-Day Planner
Guide to Mini-Lessons

DAY 1	Read Like a Writer
DAY 2	Conventions of Letters
DAY 3	Drafting a Letter
DAY 4	Revising Strategy: Clarifying
DAY 5	Proofreading for Possessive Nouns

Review key features

Review the key features of formal letters with students. You might want to post the key features in the classroom for students to refer to as they work on their letters.

Key Features of a Formal Letter

- has a purpose, such as asking for information
- includes a *heading* with your address, the address of the person you are writing to, and the date you are writing the letter
- has a greeting, or *salutation,* at the beginning and a *closing* at the end, followed by your name and your signature
- the *body* of the letter uses polite, respectful language

ROUTINE Quick Write for Fluency — Team Talk

1. **Talk** Have pairs take two or three minutes to discuss something they would like to know more about and to whom they might write to get that information.
2. **Write** Each person writes a short paragraph describing what he or she wants to know and how to find out more.
3. **Share** Partners read their paragraphs to one another.

Routines Flip Chart

Wrap Up Your Day

- ✔ **Build Concepts** What did you learn about adapting?
- ✔ **Oral Vocabulary** Have students use the terms that they learned are used in formal letters in context sentences.
- ✔ **Homework** Send home this week's Family Times newsletter in *Let's Practice It!* pp. 203–204 on the *Teacher Resources DVD-ROM*.

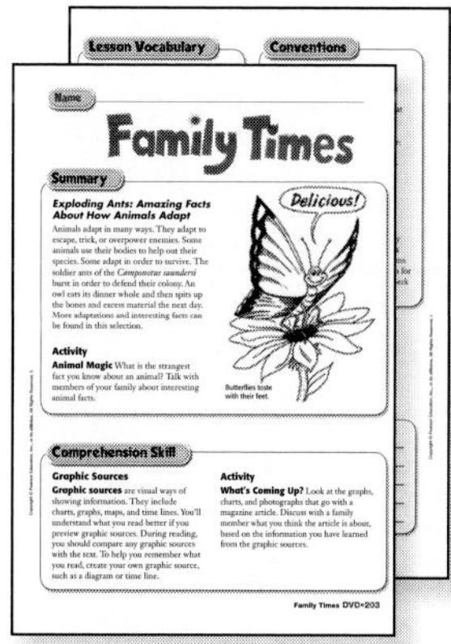

Let's Practice It!
TR DVD•203–204

Write Guy *Jeff Anderson*

Teaching Trait-by-Trait

In a writing conference, choose one aspect of a student's draft, not many things. This will help the student more. Maybe there is one skill that I can help him improve. I'd hate to see that lost in a swarm of my other comments.

ELL

English Language Learners

Preteach writing Make sure that students understand the meaning of a formal letter. Emphasize that these are used in business or important personal occasions. Ask whether they have ever seen a formal letter. Discuss how each type reflects the need for a formal letter.

Academic Vocabulary

Formal letters are formal in tone and are written to a person the writer doesn't know personally.

Preview DAY 2

Tell students that tomorrow they will read about how ants and other animals have adapted to survive.

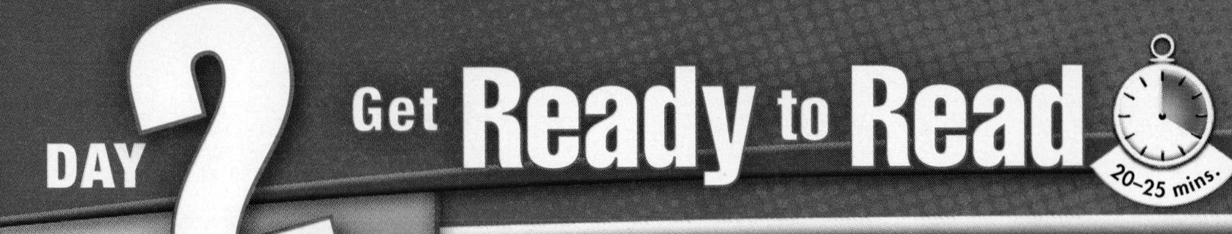

Objectives

- Expand the weekly concept.
- Develop oral vocabulary.

Today at a Glance

Oral Vocabulary
mimicry, camouflage

Word Analysis
Suffix *-ize*

Literary Terms
Figurative language: Metaphor

Text Features
Headings

Lesson Vocabulary
◉ Synonyms

Reading
"Small but Mighty"
Exploding Ants

Fluency
Rate

Research and Inquiry
Navigate/Search

Spelling
Homophones

Conventions
Possessive pronouns

Writing
Formal letter

Concept Talk

Question of the Week

How do animals adapt to survive?

Expand the concept Remind students of the Question of the Week. Tell students that today they will begin reading *Exploding Ants.* As they read, encourage students to think about some of the strange ways animals have adapted in order to survive.

Anchored Talk

Develop oral language Use the photos on pp. 76–77 and the Read Aloud, "Escape Artists," to talk about the Amazing Words: *adaptations, predators, defenses,* and *fearsome.* Add these and other concept-related words to the concept map to develop students' knowledge of the topic. Have students get into groups. Then have them use the following questions to elicit and consider suggestions from each group member and develop their understanding of the concept.

- Why are *adaptations* a necessary part of an animal's *defenses*?
- Discuss how animals can be both *predators* and prey, or food.
- Why do animals sometimes assume *fearsome* shapes or attitudes?

Oral Vocabulary
Amazing Words

Amazing Words

adaptations	camouflage
predators	spiny
defenses	survival
fearsome	protrude
mimicry	formidable

Amazing Words Oral Vocabulary Routine

Teach Amazing Words

1. **Introduce** Write the Amazing Word *camouflage* on the board. Have students say it aloud with you. Invite students to use the context of the word in the questions below to determine its meaning. Relate *camouflage* to the photographs on pp. 76–77 and "Escape Artists." Why might an animal need *camouflage* in the wild? How does *camouflage* protect a small animal from harm? Have students determine the definition of the word. *Camouflage* is a disguise in appearance or behavior designed to protect an animal by helping it blend in with its surroundings.
2. **Demonstrate** Have students answer questions to demonstrate understanding. What kind of *camouflage* could an insect use? How does *camouflage* help a snow rabbit?
3. **Apply** Have students apply their understanding. How might you use *camouflage* in a forest? What would you wear?

See p. OV•3 to teach *mimicry.*

Routines Flip Chart

Help students establish a purpose for reading as they read "Small but Mighty" on p. 81. Have them think about how insects can use *camouflage* and *mimicry* to protect themselves.

Connect to reading

Apply Amazing Words

Explain that today students will read about some adaptive insect behaviors. As they read, they should think about how this week's Question of the Week and the Amazing Words *camouflage* and *mimicry* apply to ants.

ELL **Reinforce Vocabulary** Use the Day 2 instruction on ELL Poster 18 to teach lesson vocabulary and the lesson concept.

ELL Poster 18

Objectives

- Use the meaning of the suffix *-ize* to determine the meaning of unfamiliar words.
- Understand figurative language.
- Understand and use text features to aid comprehension.

Word Analysis
Suffix *-ize*

Teach suffix *-ize*

Tell students that the Greek suffix *-ize* means "to make or become." The suffix can be added to nouns and adjectives to form verbs. Choose the word *special* from the first column below to add the suffix *-ize*.

Model the skill

Think Aloud I can add the suffix *-ize* to the word *special* to form the word *specialize*. *Special* means "better, greater, or otherwise different," and the suffix *-ize* means "to make or become." So I can tell that *specialize* means "to become better at something."

Base word	Verb with *-ize*
critic	
fantasy	
harmony	
special	
minimal	

Guide practice

Have students create verbs with the words from the chart. Explain that some spelling changes will be needed, such as dropping a final *y* or *e*.

On their own

Have students use the suffix to determine the meaning of the new words they created. Then have them use a printed or electronic dictionary to confirm the meaning of each word and determine the word's part of speech. Follow the Strategy for Meaningful Word Parts to teach the word *sterilize.*

ROUTINE Strategy for Meaningful Word Parts

1. **Look for meaningful word parts** Display the word *sterilize*. Circle the suffix *-ize* and underline the base word *sterile,* noting that the final *e* has been dropped.
2. **Connect to meaning** Define *sterile* as "free from bacteria." The suffix *-ize* means "to make or become." Combined, they mean "to make free from bacteria."
3. **Read the word** Blend the meaningful word parts together to read the word *sterilize*.

Continue the Routine with the words *minimize* and *harmonize*.

Routines Flip Chart

Literary Terms
Metaphor

Teach metaphor Tell students that figurative language goes beyond the literal, or everyday, meaning of words. A metaphor is an example of figurative language. A metaphor makes a comparison between two seemingly unlike things that are actually alike in at least one way without using *like* or *as*.

Model metaphor Think Aloud Ask students to turn to p. 100 and read the second paragraph. In "The Art of Mimicry," there is a simile that describes how the lyrebird uses mimicry. The author says, "This bird is like a one-man band!" How could you rephrase this simile to become a metaphor? (This bird is a one-man band.)

Guide practice Read aloud this sentence from p. 87 of Exploding Ants: *Soon their abdomens are as large as small grapes*. Ask students to restate this simile as a metaphor. *(Soon their abdomens are small grapes.)*

On their own Have students look for examples of metaphor and figurative language in other selections of their Student Edition.

Text Features
Headings

Teach headings Expository nonfiction often uses text features such subheads, also called headings, to help readers increase their understanding of a text by making it easier to locate specific information and giving a general overview of the contents of the text.

Model the strategy 

I see that headings are used to introduce some sections of *Exploding Ants*. The headings tell me that I am reading about a different topic and help me to locate information easily.

Guide practice Have students continue to preview the headings in *Exploding Ants*. Ask students to locate the name of the species of ants that can explode, and to tell how the headings helped them find it.

On their own Ask students how the section on p. 84 might be similar to or different than the information found under the heading on p. 86. Ask: How do headings influence the relationships between ideas?

Academic Vocabulary

figurative language any use of language that gives words a meaning beyond their usual, everyday, literal definitions and that thereby adds an extra dimension to meaning

metaphor a type of literary comparison of two unlike things that differs from simile in that it does not use *like* or *as*

Objectives

- ◎ Use a thesaurus or context clues to find synonyms.
- Use a thesaurus to find meanings of unfamiliar words and create anologies.
- Read grade-level text at an appropriate rate.

Vocabulary Strategy for ◎ Synonyms

Teach synonyms

Tell students that when they encounter an unfamiliar word, they can use the strategy of looking for context clues, including synonyms. A synonym is a word that has the same or nearly the same meaning as another word. Explain how a printed or electric thesaurus can help students find synonyms for unfamiliar words. One way to understand the relationships between synonyms is by using analogies. Refer students to *Words!* on p. W•3 in the Student Edition for additional practice.

Student Edition p. W•3

Model the strategy

Write on the board: *In fact, their small size enables them to adapt quickly.*

I know that some synonyms for *enable* are *allow* and *permit*. I can add the letter *s* to each word to make synonyms for *enables*: *allows* and *permits*. I know both of those words, so now I also know the meaning of *enables*. I can also make an analogy with two sets of synonyms: *Enables* is to *permits* as *speaks* is to *talks*.

Guide practice

Write this sentence on the board: *Others are critical, or important, to the making of soil.* Have students determine the meaning of *critical* by using the context clue, the synonym *important*. If they are unable to find synonyms in the text, have them look up the word in a printed or electronic thesaurus.

On their own

Read "Small But Mighty" on p. 81. Have students use a printed or electronic thesaurus to find synonyms for the lesson vocabulary. Then have students produce analogies with the lesson vocabulary and other known synonyms. For additional practice use *Reader's and Writer's Notebook* p. 271.

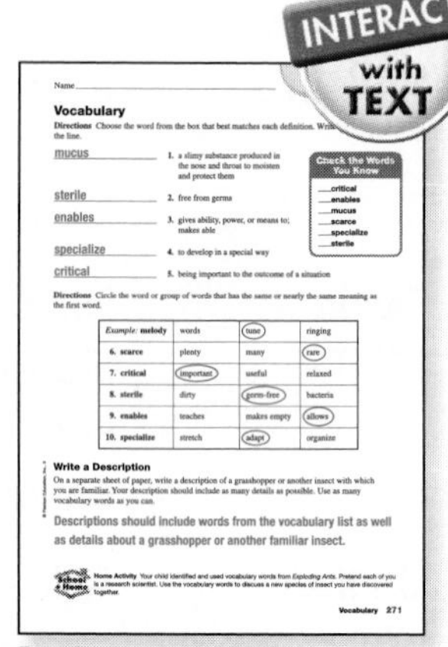

Reader's and Writer's Notebook p. 271

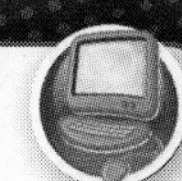

Objectives
• Determine the meanings of synonyms by using the context of the sentence. • Write analogies with synonyms you know. • Use a dictionary, a glossary, or a thesaurus to locate information about words.
Envision It! Words to Know
scarce
specialize
sterile
critical
enables
mucus
READING STREET ONLINE
VOCABULARY ACTIVITIES
www.ReadingStreet.com

Vocabulary Strategy for

Synonyms

Context Clues Synonyms are different words that mean almost the same thing. For example, *cold* is to *freezing* as *hot* is to *boiling*. The words *cold* and *freezing* are synonyms. *Hot* and *boiling* are also synonyms. Complete this analogy: *scarce* is to *rare* as *expensive* is to ______.

Synonyms can sometimes be good clues when you find an unfamiliar word.

1. Read the words and sentences around the unfamiliar word. Is there a synonym you know nearby?
2. Use the known synonym in place of the unfamiliar word. Does the synonym help you determine or clarify the word's meaning?
3. If you need help, look up the word in a printed or electronic thesaurus. A thesaurus is a book that contains synonyms of words.

Read "Small but Mighty" on page 81. Check the context clues or nearby synonyms to determine or clarify the meanings of words.

Words to Write Reread "Small but Mighty." List some of the characteristics of bacteria and the ways bacteria can adapt. Use words from the *Words to Know* list in your writing and a thesaurus to find alternate word choices to make your writing lively.

80

Small but MIGHTY

Bacteria are made up of just one cell. However, they adapt just like all living things. In fact, their small size enables them to adapt quickly. We have medicines to kill harmful bacteria. However, bacteria have changed so that they can stand up to many medicines. Medicines that still work against them are becoming scarce, or rare. Doctors use these medicines less often so bacteria will not "learn" how to live with them.

Different bacteria specialize in different ways. Some live in your gut and help you digest food. Others are critical, or important, to the making of soil. They break down dead plant and animal matter.

Most bacteria are helpful, but a few can harm us. One kind causes a disease called pneumonia. The bacteria reproduce quickly inside the body. They give off poisons. The body fights back. It raises its temperature. It produces more mucus to protect the lining of organs.

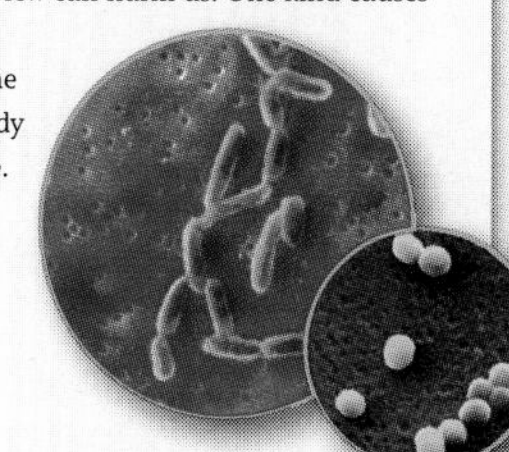

It is best to keep surfaces as sterile as possible so you do not touch harmful bacteria.

Your Turn!

Need a Review? For additional help with synonyms, see *Words!*

Ready to Try It? Read *Exploding Ants* on pp. 82–93.

81

Student Edition pp. 80–81

Reread for Fluency
Rate

Model fluent reading Read paragraph 1 of "Small but Mighty" aloud at a slow, steady rate. Tell students that you are reading a bit more slowly than usual because of the many new, unknown facts in the selection and to increase comprehension.

ROUTINE **Oral Rereading**

1. **Read** Have students read paragraph 1 of "Small but Mighty" orally.
2. **Reread** To achieve optimal fluency and comprehension, students should reread aloud the text three or four times.
3. **Corrective Feedback** Have students read aloud without you. Provide feedback about their rate and encourage them to adjust their rate depending on the content of the passage.

Lesson Vocabulary

critical extremely important
enables makes someone or something able to do an action
mucus slimy substance produced in the nose and throat to moisten and protect
scarce hard to get; rare
specialize to do one thing extremely well
sterile free from bacteria and other living things; totally clean

Academic Vocabulary

synonym a word that means nearly the same thing as another word

Differentiated Instruction

Strategic Intervention

Thesaurus Have students identify synonyms for words in this week's lesson vocabulary. Help students master the skill of using a printed or electronic thesaurus.

ELL

English Language Learners

Synonyms Point out that many words have multiple synonyms. Students can build on their knowledge of basic vocabulary to map increasingly complex vocabulary.

Build Academic Vocabulary Use the lesson vocabulary pictured on p. 80 to teach the meanings of *specialize, scarce,* and *sterile.* Call on pairs to write the words on sticky notes and use them to label the images of the words on the ELL Poster.

Objectives

- Understand the elements of expository text.
- Use text features to preview and predict.
- Set a purpose for reading.

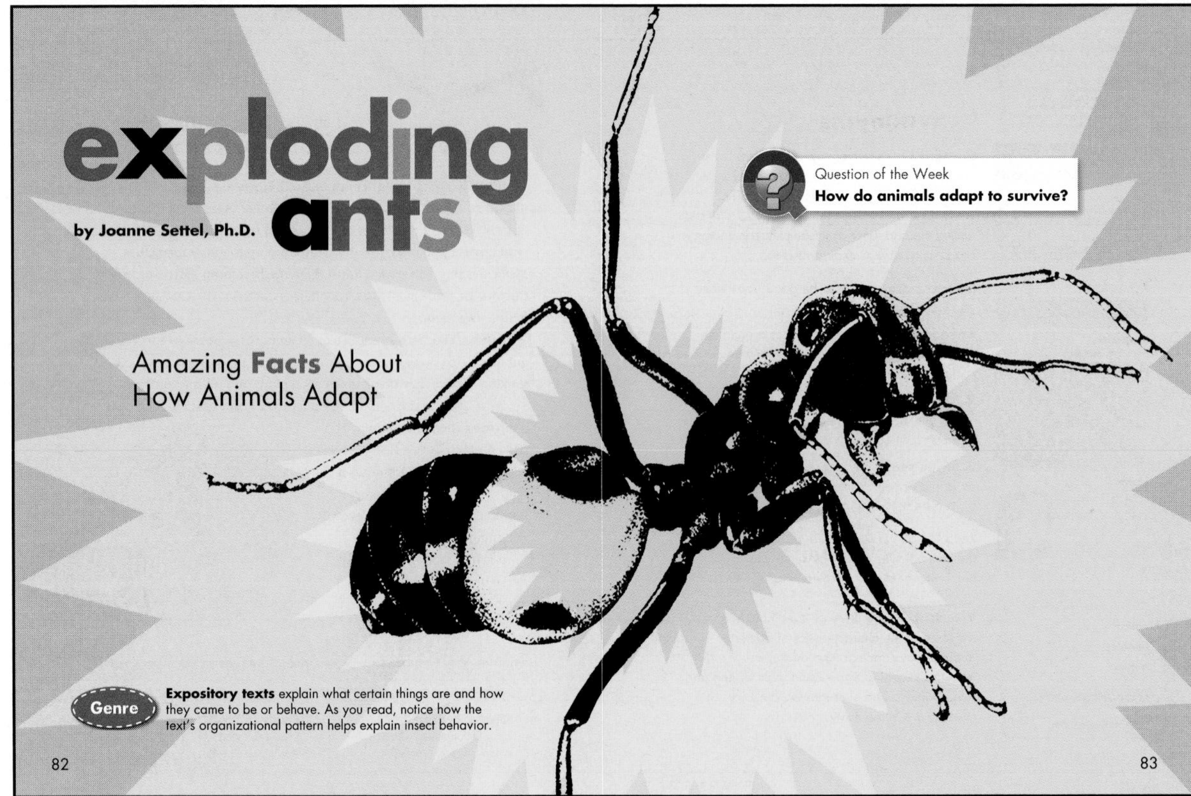

exploding ants
by Joanne Settel, Ph.D.
Amazing Facts About How Animals Adapt
Question of the Week
How do animals adapt to survive?
Genre
Expository texts explain what certain things are and how they came to be or behave. As you read, notice how the text's organizational pattern helps explain insect behavior.
82
83

Student Edition pp. 82–83

Build Background

Discuss animal adaptations

Team Talk Have students turn to a partner and discuss the Question of the Week and these questions about animal adaptations by eliciting and considering suggestions from each other.

- What are the basic needs of all animals?
- How does nature give animals the means of satisfying their needs?
- Can you describe one way that a wild animal adapts to its environment?

Connect to selection

Have students present their answers to the class. Encourage students to listen attentively and ask questions to clarify the speaking students' perspective. Possible responses: All animals need food, shelter, and safety from predators and weather. Nature gives animals the means of satisfying their needs by ensuring that they adapt to the climate and food sources available to them. One way an animal adapts to its environment is by eating available food sources. For additional opportunities to build background, use the Background Building Audio.

Prereading Strategies

Genre Explain that an informational article is one type of **expository text.** Expository texts, which can also be called expository nonfiction, often include explanatory features such as headings, illustrations, and other graphic sources.

Preview and predict Have students preview the title, subheads, illustrations, and photographs. Have them predict what they will find out as they read.

Set purpose Prior to reading, have students set their own purposes for reading this selection. To help students set a purpose, ask them to think about the ways that animals adapt in order to survive.

Strategy Response Log

INTERACT with TEXT

Have students use p. 24 in the *Reader's and Writer's Notebook* to review and use the strategy of important ideas.

Small Group Time

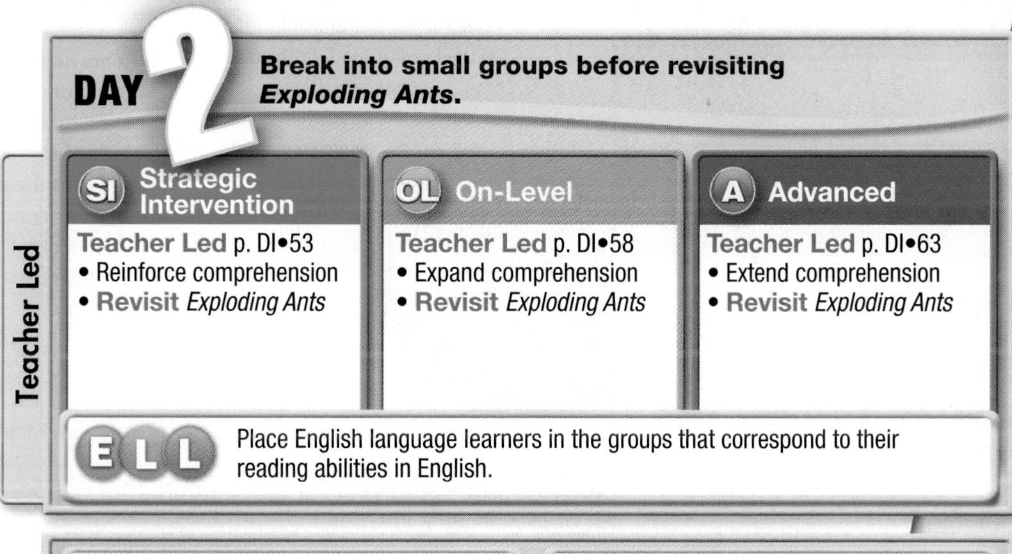

DAY 2 **Break into small groups before revisiting *Exploding Ants.***

Teacher Led

SI Strategic Intervention	OL On-Level	A Advanced
Teacher Led p. DI•53 • Reinforce comprehension • Revisit *Exploding Ants*	Teacher Led p. DI•58 • Expand comprehension • Revisit *Exploding Ants*	Teacher Led p. DI•63 • Extend comprehension • Revisit *Exploding Ants*

ELL Place English language learners in the groups that correspond to their reading abilities in English.

Practice Stations	Independent Activities
• Words to Know • Get Fluent • Word Wise	• Background Building Audio • *Reading and Writer's Notebook* • Research and Inquiry

Differentiated Instruction

Strategic Intervention

Set purpose Work with students to set a purpose for reading, or if time permits, have students work with partners to set purposes.

Advanced

Headings Have students make a T-chart to show how each of an animal's needs are met by nature.

Multidraft Reading

For **Whole Group** instruction, choose one of the reading options below. For each reading, have students set the purpose indicated.

Option 1
Day 2 Read the selection. Use Guide Comprehension to monitor and clarify understanding.
Day 3 Reread the selection. Use Extend Thinking to develop higher-order thinking skills.

Option 2
Day 2 Read the first half of the selection, using both Guide Comprehension and Extend Thinking instruction.
Day 3 Read the second half of the selection, using both Guide Comprehension and Extend Thinking instruction.

English Language Learners

Build background To build background, review the selection summary in English (*ELL Handbook* p. 133) Use the Retelling Cards to provide visual support for the summary.

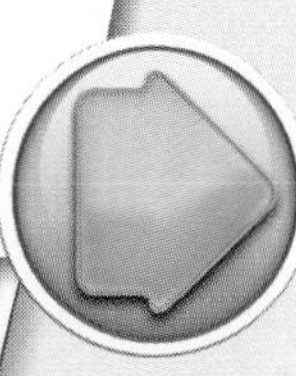

DAY 2 Read and Comprehend

Objectives

- Use graphic sources to gain an overview of a text and locate information.

OPTION 1 Guide Comprehension Skills and Strategies

Teach Graphic Sources

Graphic Sources Direct students' attention to the photo of the lizard and snake on p. 84, and have students identify the information provided by this graphic source. This graphic source shows how a snake (a predator) captures a lizard (its prey).

Corrective Feedback

If... students are unable to extract information from the photograph, **then...** model understanding graphic sources.

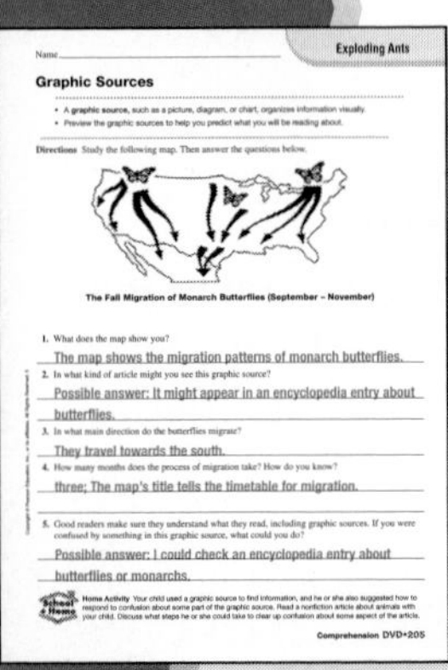

Let's Practice It!
TR DVD•205

Model the Strategy

Think Aloud The text on this page explains that animals often do things we consider gross in order to survive. The photo shows a snake, a predator, wrapping its body around a lizard, its prey.

Why animals do gross things

Animals often do things that seem gross to us. They eat foods that people would find nauseating. They make their homes in disgusting places and feed on mucus and blood. They swell or blow up their body parts.

But while these behaviors are nasty to us, they are critical to life on Earth. They make it possible for many kinds of living things to find food, shelter, and safety. Different species make use of every possible space and gobble down every nutritious crumb of food in the natural world. If every species of animal ate the same kind of food, or lived in the same place, there simply wouldn't be enough to go around. It would become impossible for all of the species to survive. So instead, animals specialize. One predator eats flesh, while another feeds on blood.

As a result, when it comes to eating, nothing is wasted. Almost every part of every living animal, from skin to dung to mucus, can provide food for some other species. All of these things contain good nutrients. An animal that has the right digestive organs and chemicals can easily break them down.

84

Student Edition pp. 84–85

OPTION 2 Extend Thinking Think Critically

Higher-Order Thinking Skills

Graphic Sources • Analysis Look at the photograph of the fish on page 84. How does this graphic source help you gain an overview of the contents of this page? Possible response: The photograph shows a puffer fish that is all puffed up, showing its spines. This photo tells me that this page is likely about how animals do weird or gross things to defend themselves.

Questioning • Analysis Reread paragraph 2 of page 85. What are some literal questions you could ask to help you monitor and adjust your comprehension about how animals use their bodies in the same way that we use tools? Possible response: How do different animals carry objects from place to place? How do different animals defend themselves when they do not have hands? How do different animals catch and kill their prey without using weapons?

How does this picture help you guess what the text will be about? (It shows me a disgusting thing that an animal has to do to survive.) Where do you think you could find out about gross way animals kill prey? (on this page)

Similarly, when it comes to finding shelter, animals make use of any hole or space or building material that they can find. For example, the smelly, slimy holes and organs inside the body of a bigger animal can often provide a warm, protective home for small animals like insects.

Finally, animals often put their body parts to good use. Animals don't have bags to carry things around, tools to open things, knives to cut things, or weapons to defend themselves. Instead, they use their own bodies in ways that seem gross to us. By stretching, swelling, and bursting open, they can trick predators, store food, swallow big gulps, and defend their nests.

85

Genre • Synthesis When rereading expository text, it is important to synthesize all the new ideas that you read and make logical connections between ideas in the text. Synthesize the ideas you learned in paragraph 2 on page 84 by summarizing.

Possible response: Animals specialize to get the most benefit from the available natural resources. What logical connections can you make between the idea of adapting and the idea of survival? Possible response: Animals must adapt to their surroundings or they will not be able to survive.

On Their Own

Have students reread pp. 84–85 and describe how graphic sources help us gain an overview of the contents of the text, as well as help us locate information on the page. For additional practice with graphic sources, use *Let's Practice It!* p. 205 on the *Teacher Resources DVD-ROM.*

Differentiated Instruction

Strategic Intervention

Fact and opinion Explain that authors sometimes begin an article by discussing the opinions some people have about a subject. Have students discuss why the author began with opinions, rather than with facts. (to intrigue readers; to cleverly construct an argument)

Advanced

Critical thinking Have students discuss why an animal might swell up its body. Have them answer the question: How would a predator react to that sight?

Connect to Science

Some animals, like hermit crabs, use parts of other animals for shelter. The hermit crab finds a seashell it likes, and the shell becomes its new home.

English Language Learners

Activate prior knowledge Create a word web to record students' knowledge of animal defenses against predators. What can an animal do to trick or scare off its enemies? Why would this be useful? Record students' answers in the web, and add to them as they read the selection.

DAY 2 # Read and Comprehend

Objectives

- Identify and summarize important ideas.

OPTION 1 Skills and Strategies, continued

Teach Important Ideas

Important Ideas Have students read about repletes on p. 86. Then ask students to identify and summarize one important idea, or main idea from this section of *Exploding Ants.* (The only purpose of the worker ants called repletes is to feed and to be fed in turn.)

Corrective Feedback

If... students are unable to identify and summarize an important idea from this section of the text,
then... model identifying and summarizing an important idea in a way that maintains meaning and logical order.

Model the Strategy

Think Aloud: What is this part of the article about? It has information about worker honey ants that store food and are sometimes fed by other honey ants.

Swelling, expanding and exploding Bodies

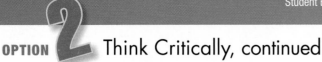

Living honey jars

The swollen sacs of nectar that hang from the roof of a honey ant nest are actually alive. They're the fat bodies of ants that have turned themselves into living honey jars.

The "honey jars" are worker ants that store food and are known as *repletes*. Repletes spend their lives hanging upside-down from the roof of their nest waiting to feed or be fed. Their bodies provide sterile, airtight food containers.

It is when the colony has lots of extra food that the repletes get fed. Each replete receives regurgitated, or spit-up, food from hundreds of ordinary worker ants. The food consists of a golden liquid filled with a predigested mix of termite parts and plant nectar.

As they take in more and more food, the repletes swell. Soon their rear ends or abdomens are as large

86

Student Edition pp. 86–87

Figurative Language • Synthesis What metaphor does the author use in paragraph 2 of page 86? The repletes are called "honey jars." Why is this an appropriate comparison? The repletes store sweet nectar, like honey in jars.

OPTION 2 Think Critically, continued

Higher-Order Thinking Skills

Important Ideas • Analysis Summarize the important idea of paragraphs 2, 3, and 4 on page 87. Possible response: When food runs low, the repletes use their stored food to feed the colony. What are some details from the text that support this main idea? Possible responses: The ants touch the repletes' antennae when they want food. Honey ants live in dry deserts. The "honey" stored in these ants is sweet.

That's an important idea in this part of the article. I can summarize this main idea with the following sentence: Repletes are worker ants that store food they eat and are fed.

as small grapes. The swollen ants then climb to the roof of the nest and continue to eat. They remain on the roof for months, hanging by their claws, barely able to move. If for some reason a replete falls down, other workers must help drag its large, balloonlike body back up to the ceiling.

When food supplies outside the nest run low, the repletes become the feeders. Hungry nest mates now gather round for food. They touch the repletes' antennae with their own. The repletes then regurgitate big drops of golden honey.

The extra food provided by the repletes is important to the colony survival. Honey ants live in large colonies in dry desert regions of North America, Africa, and Australia, where food is often scarce. Storing food in their living honey jars enables the colony to make it through the hottest, driest desert seasons.

The sweet "honey" of the honey ant repletes is not only food for other ants, but also for some people. The aborigines in Australia consider the swollen honey ants to be sweet treats and pop them into their mouths like candy.

87

Cause and Effect • Analysis What caused the honey ant to adapt in this particular way? Possible response: The honey ants live in the desert, where food is scarce, so they needed a way to store nutrients.

On Their Own

Have students relate the graphics on pp. 86–87 to the text. Ask them to explain how text and pictures work together to show an important idea, and then have them summarize that main idea, maintaining meaning and logical order.

Differentiated Instruction

SI Strategic Intervention

Important ideas Explain that important ideas can be stated directly or can become clear to us from details in the passage.

A Advanced

Critical thinking Have students name two other animals that store food in interesting ways.

Connect to Science

A biome is an ecological system with its own kind of climate, plants, animals, and other living things. The desert biome lies in regions that get less than 50 cm of precipitation per year.

ELL English Language Learners

Vocabulary Explain that the adjective *replete* means "filled with or overflowing." In this article, *replete* is used as a noun. Also point out that the words *sac* and *sack* sound the same and have similar meanings. *Sac* means "a baglike part on an animal or plant that holds liquid."

Important ideas Explain that students can look for key words and phrases to help them locate important ideas: *store food, regurgitation, colonies, desert.*

DAY 2 Read and Comprehend

Objectives

- Use a thesaurus to produce analogies with known synonyms.

OPTION 1 Skills and Strategies, continued

Teach Synonyms

Synonyms Have students locate a synonym for the word *contracts* on p. 89. *(tightens)* Then have students use a printed or electronic thesaurus to find a synonym for the word *bursting*. (Possible response: *breaking*) Then ask students to produce an analogy that describes the relationships between the words. *(Contracts is to tightens as bursting is to breaking.)*

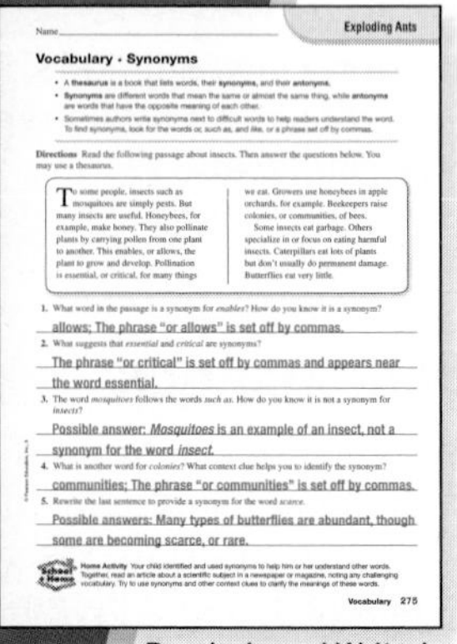

Name__________ Exploding Ants

Vocabulary • Synonyms

- A **thesaurus** is a book that lists words, their **synonyms**, and their **antonyms**.
- **Synonyms** are different words that mean the same or almost the same thing, while **antonyms** are words that have the opposite meaning of each other.
- Sometimes authors write synonyms next to difficult words to help readers understand the word. To find synonyms, look for the words *or, such as,* and *like*, or a phrase set off by commas.

Directions Read the following passage about insects. Then answer the questions below. You may use a thesaurus.

To some people, insects such as mosquitoes are simply pests. But many insects are useful. Honeybees, for example, make honey. They also pollinate plants by carrying pollen from one plant to another. This enables, or allows, the plant to grow and develop. Pollination is essential, or critical, for many things we eat. Growers use honeybees in apple orchards, for example. Beekeepers raise colonies, or communities, of bees.

Some insects eat garbage. Others specialize in or focus on eating harmful insects. Caterpillars eat lots of plants but don't usually do permanent damage. Butterflies eat very little.

1. What word in the passage is a synonym for *enables*? How do you know it is a synonym?
allows; The phrase "or allows" is set off by commas.
2. What suggests that *essential* and *critical* are synonyms?
The phrase "or critical" is set off by commas and appears near the word essential.
3. The word *mosquitoes* follows the words *such as*. How do you know it is not a synonym for *insects*?
Possible answer: *Mosquitoes* is an example of an insect, not a synonym for the word *insect*.
4. What is another word for *colonies*? What context clue helps you to identify the synonym?
communities; The phrase "or communities" is set off by commas.
5. Rewrite the last sentence to provide a synonym for the word *scarce*.
Possible answers: Many types of butterflies are abundant, though some are becoming scarce, or rare.

Home Activity Your child identified and used synonyms to help him or her understand other words. Together, read an article about a scientific subject in a newspaper or magazine, noting any challenging vocabulary. Try to use synonyms and other context clues to clarify the meanings of these words.

Vocabulary 275

Reader's and Writer's Notebook p.275

Corrective Feedback

If... students have difficulty finding synonyms or producing an analogy, **then...** model finding synonyms and producing an analogy.

Model the Skill

Think Aloud I know that *tightens* is a synonym of *contracts*. The other two words, *bursting* and *breaking,* describe what happens when an ant is defending itself. Now let's create an analogy.

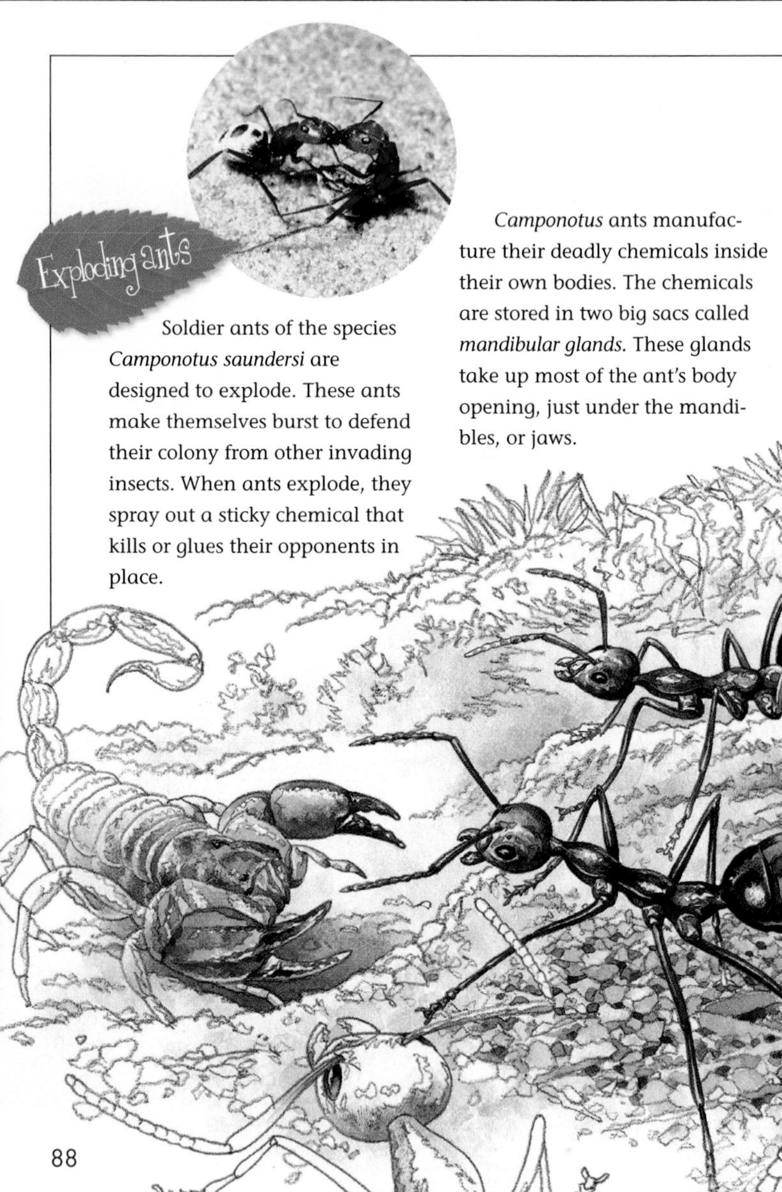

Exploding ants

Soldier ants of the species *Camponotus saundersi* are designed to explode. These ants make themselves burst to defend their colony from other invading insects. When ants explode, they spray out a sticky chemical that kills or glues their opponents in place.

Camponotus ants manufacture their deadly chemicals inside their own bodies. The chemicals are stored in two big sacs called *mandibular glands*. These glands take up most of the ant's body opening, just under the mandibles, or jaws.

88

Student Edition pp. 88–89

Draw Conclusions • Evaluation How successful is the adaptation of the soldier ant? Provide evidence to support your answer. Possible response: The adaptation is very successful in defending the colony and preserving the species, but not successful in preserving the lives of the individual soldiers.

OPTION 2 Think Critically, continued

Higher-Order Thinking Skills

Synonyms • Synthesis Use the text and a printed or electronic thesaurus to complete the following analogy: *Jumping* is to *leaping* as *spewing* is to ______. Possible responses: spraying, gushing.

When an ant is attacked, it *contracts,* or *tightens.* This action causes the ant to *burst,* or *break,* open. So *contracts* is to *tightens* as *bursting* is to *breaking*.

On Their Own

Ask students to use a thesaurus to look for synonyms of unknown words. For additional practice, see *Reader's and Writer's Notebook* p. 275.

When an intruder approaches, the *Camponotus* ant will release small amounts of its special chemical to warn away the invader. If the intruder actually attacks, however, the *Camponotus* ant takes the next step. It violently contracts, or tightens, its muscles, bursting open and spewing out its deadly chemicals.

Camponotus ants aren't the only insect with this unusual behavior. It turns out that soldiers of the termite species *Globitermes sulfureus* are also exploders, bursting open when threatened and spraying a sticky yellow liquid all over their opponents.

89

Differentiated Instruction

Strategic Intervention

Context clues If students have difficulty finding a synonym for the word *mandibles,* have them look for a clue word, such as *or* and *like*.

A Advanced

Critical thinking Write the word *mandibles* on the board. Tell students that the Latin root *mandere* means "to chew." Discuss how knowing the meaning of the root *mandere* can help them figure out the meaning of related words.

Background Knowledge • Evaluation • Text to World On pages 88 and 89, we learn about two kinds of insects that make huge sacrifices to defend their colonies. What are some huge sacrifices that people make for their loved ones? Possible responses: Parents might work long hours to buy food for their children. A person might sacrifice his or her free time to help a sibling with homework.

Check Predictions Have students look back at the predictions they made earlier and discuss whether they were accurate. Then have students preview the rest of the selection and either adjust their predictions accordingly or make new predictions.

ELL

English Language Learners

Important ideas Point out the synonyms *burst* and *explode*. Ask students if they can think of other words with a similar meaning. Encourage them to use a thesaurus if needed.

If you want to teach this selection in two sessions, stop here.

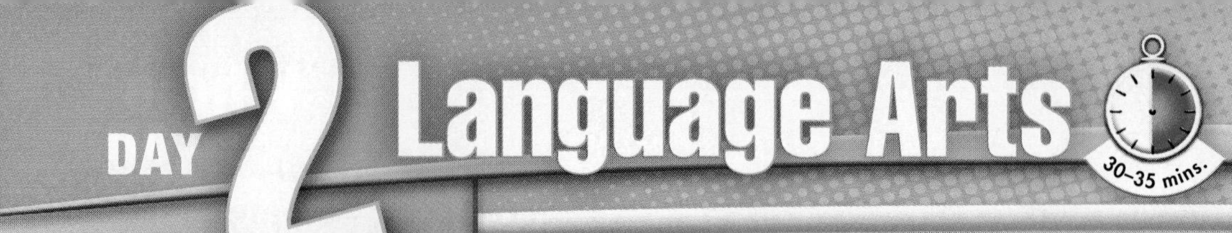

Objectives

- Find pertinent information from online sources.
- Recognize and correctly use possessive pronouns.
- Practice correctly spelling homophones.

Research and Inquiry
Navigate/Search

Teach Before they ask any experts, have students search reference texts and the Internet to gain some background knowledge about their animal. Tell them to look for facts about the ways their animal adapts to its environment. This may include unique behaviors, such as when a skunk sprays intruders. Many mammals travel in groups or packs for protection, which is another kind of adaptation. Students should write down facts only—not opinions.

Model

When looking for information on lions, I've found this statement: *A male lion may be driven out of the pride.* That is a factual statement that helps me answer my inquiry question. I will write it down. On another site about lions, I read the sentence: *Lions are cool animals.* That statement is an opinion that has nothing to do with my inquiry. I won't use that. Gathering facts will help me prepare questions for a local expert at the zoo.

Guide practice Ask students to evaluate the relevance, validity, and reliability of each source. Blogs and other highly personal Web sites may not be reliable sources of information. However, an electronic encyclopedia entry about the animal would be a relevant, reliable source. Some zoos or organizations may also have information about animal adaptations on their Web site.

Remind students to print out or copy any good photographs so they can use them when they put their posters together on Day 4.

On their own Have students call a local zoo to find an expert to interview. They should write a list of questions before they call or visit. It may help to practice on a partner before doing the real interview. If possible, students should try to visit the zoo to see their animal in action. Remind them to bring a camera so they can take photos for their poster.

Conventions
Possessive Pronouns

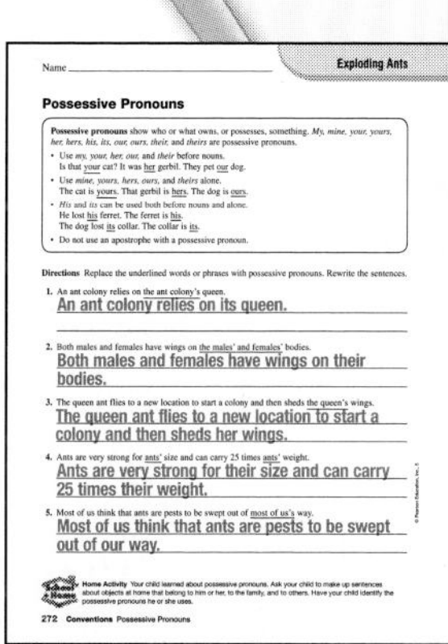
Name ____ Exploding Ants

Possessive Pronouns

Possessive pronouns show who or what owns, or possesses, something. *My, mine, your, yours, her, hers, his, its, our, ours, their,* and *theirs* are possessive pronouns.

- Use *my, your, her, our,* and *their* before nouns.
  Is that your cat? It was her gerbil. They pet our dog.
- Use *mine, yours, hers, ours,* and *theirs* alone.
  The cat is yours. That gerbil is hers. The dog is ours.
- *His* and *its* can be used both before nouns and alone.
  He lost his ferret. The ferret is his.
  The dog lost its collar. The collar is its.
- Do not use an apostrophe with a possessive pronoun.

Directions Replace the underlined words or phrases with possessive pronouns. Rewrite the sentences.

1. An ant colony relies on the ant colony's queen.
   An ant colony relies on its queen.
2. Both males and females have wings on the males' and females' bodies.
   Both males and females have wings on their bodies.
3. The queen ant flies to a new location to start a colony and then sheds the queen's wings.
   The queen ant flies to a new location to start a colony and then sheds her wings.
4. Ants are very strong for ants' size and can carry 25 times ants' weight.
   Ants are very strong for their size and can carry 25 times their weight.
5. Most of us think that ants are pests to be swept out of most of us's way.
   Most of us think that ants are pests to be swept out of our way.

Home Activity Your child learned about possessive pronouns. Ask your child to make up sentences about objects at home that belong to him or her, to the family, and to others. Have your child identify the possessive pronouns he or she uses.

272 **Conventions** Possessive Pronouns

Reader's and Writer's Notebook p. 272

Teach Write on the board: <u>his</u> strength and the <u>ant's</u> body. The first phrase means "the strength of him" and the second means "the body of the ant." Point out the possessive in each phrase.

Guide practice Write the following sentences on the board:

> **It's a shame that the owl broke <u>it's</u> wing.**
>
> **It's a shame that the owl broke <u>its</u> wing.**

The word *i-t-apostrophe-s* is a contraction, a shortened form of two words, *it is*. The contraction *it's* is never used to show possession. Write *No* after the first sentence. Then explain no possessive pronoun has an apostrophe. Write *Yes* after the second sentence.

Daily Fix-It Use Daily Fix-It numbers 3 and 4 in the right margin.

Connect to oral language Have students look for possessive pronouns in *Exploding Ants.* (*their,* pp. 84–85; *its,* pp. 87, 89–91).

On their own For additional practice, use *Reader's and Writer's Notebook* p. 272.

Spelling
Homophones

Teach Remind students that homophones are words that sound the same but have different spellings and meanings.

Guide practice Write *sent, cent,* and *scent.* In each of these words, the sound /s/ is spelled differently. It is spelled *s* in *sent, c* in *cent,* and *sc* in *scent.* Today we are going to look at the homophones on our words list and identify the parts that are spelled differently. Pairs of students should write each spelling word and underline the word parts in each set of homophones that are spelled differently.

On their own For additional practice, use the *Reader's and Writer's Notebook* p. 273.

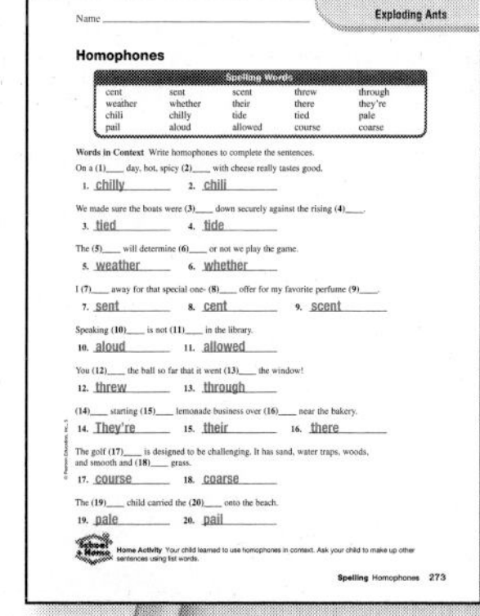
Name ____ Exploding Ants

Homophones

Spelling Words				
cent	sent	scent	threw	through
weather	whether	their	there	they're
chili	chilly	tide	tied	pale
pail	aloud	allowed	course	coarse

Words in Context Write homophones to complete the sentences.

On a (1)____ day, hot, spicy (2)____ with cheese really tastes good.
1. chilly 2. chili

We made sure the boats were (3)____ down securely against the rising (4)____.
3. tied 4. tide

The (5)____ will determine (6)____ or not we play the game.
5. weather 6. whether

I (7)____ away for that special one- (8)____ offer for my favorite perfume (9)____.
7. sent 8. cent 9. scent

Speaking (10)____ is not (11)____ in the library.
10. aloud 11. allowed

You (12)____ the ball so far that it went (13)____ the window!
12. threw 13. through

(14)____ starting (15)____ lemonade business over (16)____ near the bakery.
14. They're 15. their 16. there

The golf (17)____ is designed to be challenging. It has sand, water traps, woods, and smooth and (18)____ grass.
17. course 18. coarse

The (19)____ child carried the (20)____ onto the beach.
19. pale 20. pail

Home Activity Your child learned to use homophones in context. Ask your child to make up other sentences using list words.

Spelling Homophones 273

Reader's and Writer's Notebook p. 273

Daily Fix-It

3. Because clear scales cover the eyes of a snake. It's eyes are always open. (*snake, its*)
4. Snakes raises their body temperature by laying in the sun. (*raise; lying*)

ELL

English Language Learners

Conventions To provide students with practice on subject and object pronouns, use the modified grammar lessons in the *ELL Handbook* and the Grammar Jammer! online at: www.ReadingStreet.com

Remembering possessive pronouns English language learners might have difficulty choosing possessive pronouns that agree in number and gender with the noun. To help them, make a 2-column chart showing each personal subject pronoun (*I, you, he, she, it, we, you, they*) and the matching possessive pronoun (*my, mine, your, yours, his, her, hers, its, our, ours, your, yours, their, theirs*).

Objectives

- Choose a topic.
- Begin a draft of a formal letter.
- Use the proper conventions in constructing and writing a formal letter.

Writing—Formal Letter
Writing Strategy: Choose a Topic

Introduce the prompt

Remind students of what they learned about formal letters. A formal letter is written in the correct letter format. It contains a heading, inside address, salutation, body, closing, and signature. The letter should be short and to the point. It should be written in a respectful tone and contain no unnecessary information. Read aloud the writing prompt.

Select a topic

Writing Prompt

Think about an interesting animal you would like to know more about. Write a letter to a local librarian, asking where you might find more information about that animal.

In the writing process, the first thing to do is choose a topic. I remember that last summer, I visited the zoo and saw many interesting animals. I'll make a quick list of some animals I saw and would like to learn more about.

- zebra
- meerkat
- polar beer
- lion

I'll read over my list. I always thought meerkats were interesting animals. I remember how they stood up on their hindlegs and watched their surroundings. I wonder why they do that? I'll write a letter to my local librarian asking where I can find more information about meerkats.

Narrow the topic

Now you will choose a topic to write about. First, make a list of several animals that you would like to learn more about. When you're finished, pick one animal that interests you the most and that you would like to learn more about.

Corrective feedback

Circulate around the room, helping students list topic ideas. If students are having difficulty coming up with a topic, have them look through books about animals or talk with a partner to come up with ideas. Remind students to choose an animal that they find interesting.

MINI-LESSON

Conventions of Letters

- Tell students that as they begin their drafts, they will focus on the conventions for a formal letter. To help them keep in mind the key features, draw an outline of a formal letter on the board with its parts labeled: writer's address and date, receiver's address, salutation, body, closing, and signature.
- The upper right-hand corner will contain the letter writer's address and the date. Below that, in the left-hand corner, write the name of the person who will receive the letter, the name of the library, and the address of the library.
- Have students begin their own outline of a formal letter using the form on p. 274 of their *Reader's and Writer's Notebook.* Tell students that they may make up names and addresses for the librarian and the library. Have students leave the body until last.

ROUTINE Quick Write for Fluency — Team Talk

1. **Talk** Have pairs discuss an animal they would like to learn more about.
2. **Write** Each person writes a sentence saying why they think the animal is interesting.
3. **Share** Partners read each other's sentences.

Routines Flip Chart

Differentiated Instruction

Advanced

Challenge students to find out the name of a children's librarian at their local library and address the letter to that person. They should also find out the correct address of the library and use it to write their letter.

Name ______ Exploding Ants

Writing • Formal Letter

Sender's Name ______
Address ______
City, ST Zip ______
Date ______

Recipient's Name ______, [Title]
Address ______
City, ST Zip ______

Salutation ______

Opening: Statement of Purpose:

Supporting Details:

Desired Action:

Thank you in advance for:

Closing ______
Signature ______

274 Writing Formal Letter

Reader's and Writer's Notebook p. 274

Teacher Tip

Do a periodic check of students' Quick Writes to make sure they are on task and communicating effectively with their partners.

Wrap Up Your Day

- ✔ **Build Concepts** What did you learn about repletes?
- ✔ **Graphic Sources** How does the picture on p. 87 help you understand how repletes store food?
- ✔ **Important Ideas** What is the most important idea on p. 88?

Tell students that tomorrow they will read about how owls and snakes have adapted.

Objectives
- Expand the weekly concept.
- Develop oral vocabulary.

Today at a Glance

Oral Vocabulary
spiny, survival

Comprehension Check/Retelling
Discuss questions

Reading
Exploding Ants

Think Critically
Retelling

Fluency
Rate

Research and Study Skills
Magazine/Periodical

Research and Inquiry
Analyze

Spelling
Homophones

Conventions
Possessive pronouns

Writing
Formal letter

Concept Talk

Question of the Week

How do animals adapt to survive?

Expand the concept

Remind students of the Question of the Week. Discuss how the question relates to the way ants find food and shelter, as well as how they defend themselves. Tell students that today they will read about snakes and how they have adapted. Encourage students to think about the various causes and effects of these adaptations.

Anchored Talk

Develop oral vocabulary

Use text features—headings and other graphics—to review pp. 84–89 of *Exploding Ants.* Discuss the Amazing Words *mimicry* and *camouflage*. Add these and other concept-related words to the concept map. Have students get into groups. Then have them use the following questions to develop their understanding of the concept.

- Animals can use *mimicry* to avoid becoming the prey of bigger and stronger animals. How can animals use the defense of *mimicry*?
- Think about some animals that use *camouflage* to protect themselves. How can *camouflage* work as a defense?

Oral Vocabulary
Amazing Words

Amazing Words

adaptations	camouflage
predators	spiny
defenses	survival
fearsome	protrude
mimicry	formidable

Amazing Words Oral Vocabulary Routine

Teach Amazing Words

1. **Introduce** Write the word *survival* on the board. Have students say it with you. Invite students to use the context of the word in the questions below to determine its meaning. Yesterday, we learned that the *survival* of an animal sometimes depends on a strange-looking adaptation. Have students determine a definition of *survival*. (*Survival* means the act of staying alive.)
2. **Demonstrate** Break into groups. Have students elicit and consider suggestions from group members to demonstrate understanding. How does the puffer fish fool its enemies to increase its chances of *survival*? (It expands its body so that it seems larger and more powerful than it is.)
3. **Apply** Have students apply their understanding. What must all animals do to ensure their *survival*?

See p. OV•3 to teach *spiny*.

Routines Flip Chart

Apply Amazing Words

Help students establish a purpose for reading as they read pp. 90–93 of *Exploding Ants.* Have them consider how the Amazing Words *spiny* and *survival* apply to animal adaptations in the wild.

Connect to reading

Explain that today students will read about the adaptive behaviors of snakes and owls. As they read, students should think about how this week's Question of the Week and the Amazing Words *spiny* and *survival* apply to these behaviors.

ELL Expand Vocabulary Use the Day 3 instruction on ELL Poster 18 to help students expand vocabulary.

ELL Poster 18

Objectives

- ◎ Obtain information from graphic sources.
- ◎ Use important ideas to clarify understanding.
- ◎ Use background knowledge to identify synonyms.

Comprehension Check

Have students discuss each question with a partner. Ask several pairs to share their responses.

☑ **Genre • Analysis**
Why do you think the author included so much scientific information in this article? Possible response: Using scientific facts makes the author believable and the article a reliable source of information.

☑ **Graphic Sources • Evaluation**
In the article, the author chooses to focus on an unusual species of ant with a unique adaptive behavior. How do the photographs and illustrations help you to understand what this insect does to store food? Do these graphic sources do a good job of helping you locate information? Possible response: The illustrations show me what the repletes look like as "honey jars." For example, I can see the size of their abdomens compared with the rest of their bodies. Yes, the graphics help me know where to find information because they show what the text is talking about.

☑ **Important Ideas • Analysis**
What is an important idea you learned about when reading the section "Why animals do gross things"? Possible response: The behaviors we may think of as gross are actually very clever defense strategies that are important to their survival.

☑ **Synonyms • Synthesis**
Use what you learned about survival needs in *Exploding Ants* to understand the word *nutritious* and identify one or two synonyms for it. Check your synonyms in a dictionary or thesaurus. Possible response: Two synonyms for *nutritious* are *healthful* and *strengthening*. I learned that all animals need nutritious foods in order to survive.

☑ **Connect text to world**
Honey ants and soldier ants include members that have particular functions. Why do many animal species have workers that do certain jobs? Possible responses: Without specialized workers the whole group or colony might not survive.

Strategy Response Log

Have students list 2–3 important ideas presented in *Exploding Ants* on p. 24 in the *Reader's and Writer's Notebook*.

Check Retelling

Have students retell the first two sections of *Exploding Ants*. Encourage students to use the graphic sources to gain an overview as they summarize in their retellings.

Corrective feedback

If... students leave out important details,
then... have students look back through the headings and graphic sources in this part of the selection.

Small Group Time

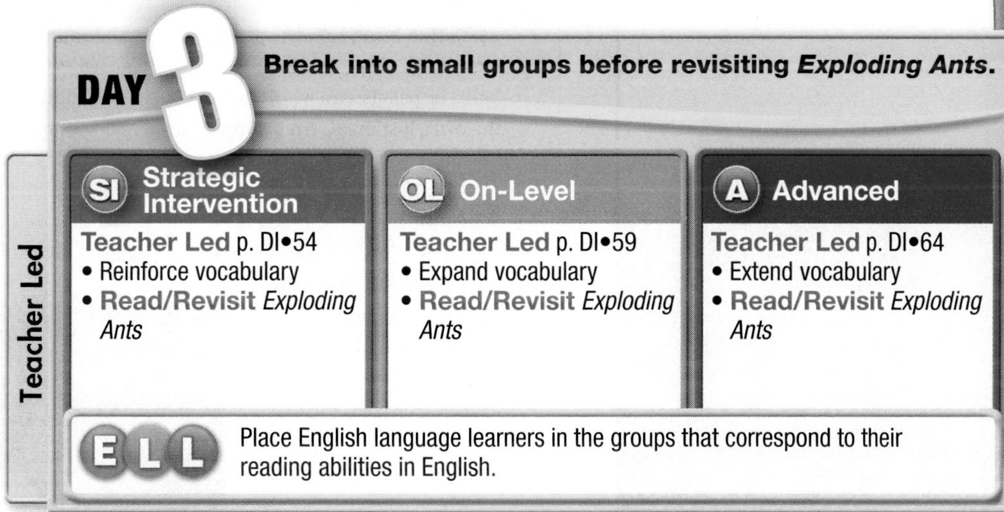

DAY 3
Break into small groups before revisiting Exploding Ants.
Teacher Led
SI Strategic Intervention
Teacher Led p. DI•54
• Reinforce vocabulary
• Read/Revisit Exploding Ants
OL On-Level
Teacher Led p. DI•59
• Expand vocabulary
• Read/Revisit Exploding Ants
A Advanced
Teacher Led p. DI•64
• Extend vocabulary
• Read/Revisit Exploding Ants
ELL
Place English language learners in the groups that correspond to their reading abilities in English.

Practice Stations
- Let's Write
- Get Fluent
- Word Work

Independent Activities
- AudioText: *Exploding Ants*
- *Readers's and Writer's Notebook*
- Research and Inquiry

English Language Learners

Check Retelling To support retelling, review the multilingual summary for *Exploding Ants* with the appropriate Retelling Cards to scaffold understanding.

DAY 3 Read and Comprehend

45–50 mins.

Objectives

- Understand and evaluate the author's purpose.

OPTION 1 Skills and Strategies, continued

Teach the Author's Purpose

Review Author's Purpose In a selection, the author's purpose is either to inform, entertain, persuade, or express a feeling. Knowing the author's purpose helps you monitor and adjust your comprehension of a selection. Ask students to identify the author's purpose on p. 90. (to inform)

Corrective Feedback

If... students have difficulty identifying the author's purpose,
then... model how to determine an author's purpose in a selection.

Model the Skill

The author includes facts and details about what owls eat and how they digest.

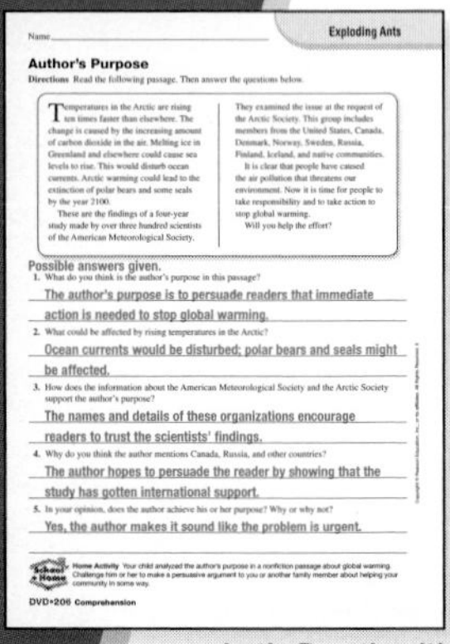

Name__________ Exploding Ants

Author's Purpose

Directions Read the following passage. Then answer the questions below.

Temperatures in the Arctic are rising ten times faster than elsewhere. The change is caused by the increasing amount of carbon dioxide in the air. Melting ice in Greenland and elsewhere could cause sea levels to rise. This would disturb ocean currents. Arctic warming could lead to the extinction of polar bears and some seals by the year 2100.

These are the findings of a four-year study made by over three hundred scientists of the American Meteorological Society. They examined the issue at the request of the Arctic Society. This group includes members from the United States, Canada, Denmark, Norway, Sweden, Russia, Finland, Iceland, and native communities.

It is clear that people have caused the air pollution that threatens our environment. Now it is time for people to take responsibility and to take action to stop global warming.

Will you help the effort?

Possible answers given.

1. What do you think is the author's purpose in this passage?
   The author's purpose is to persuade readers that immediate action is needed to stop global warming.
2. What could be affected by rising temperatures in the Arctic?
   Ocean currents would be disturbed; polar bears and seals might be affected.
3. How does the information about the American Meteorological Society and the Arctic Society support the author's purpose?
   The names and details of these organizations encourage readers to trust the scientists' findings.
4. Why do you think the author mentions Canada, Russia, and other countries?
   The author hopes to persuade the reader by showing that the study has gotten international support.
5. In your opinion, does the author achieve his or her purpose? Why or why not?
   Yes, the author makes it sound like the problem is urgent.

School + Home **Home Activity** Your child analyzed the author's purpose in a nonfiction passage about global warming. Challenge him or her to make a persuasive argument to you or another family member about helping your community in some way.

DVD•206 Comprehension

Let's Practice It!
TR DVD•206

Double Day Read! Multidraft Reading

If you chose...

Option 1 Return to Extend Thinking instruction starting on p. 84–85.
Option 2 Read pp. 90–93. Use the Guide Comprehension and Extend Thinking instruction.

Student Edition pp. 90–91

Getting it down

A ball of bones

Every evening before it goes off to hunt, an owl spits up a few balls of fur and bones. The balls, or pellets, are what's left of the owl's last meal. An owl preys on small animals, such as mice, moles, shrews, birds, and insects. When the feathered predator captures its prey, it doesn't take the time to kill its victim and then pick out the fleshy, nutritious parts. It simply swallows the animal whole. Then the owl digests all the soft stuff, the muscles and organs. The rest, the fur, feathers, teeth, and bones, are wastes. The owl gets rid of these by regurgitating a pellet.

Owls normally spit up two pellets a day. Over time the pellets pile up and form large heaps under the owl's roosting, or resting, site. By examining these

90

OPTION 2 Think Critically, continued

Higher-Order Thinking Skills

Review Author's Purpose • Analysis On page 91, the author is very specific about the quantity of food a barn owl eats each day. What is the author's purpose in providing these facts? How effective are these details in helping to achieve the author's purpose?

The author's purpose is to inform readers about how owls get nutrition from the environment. These details successfully support the author's purpose because they offer clear, factual information that informs the reader.

I learned that owls kill small prey and eat them whole and then spit out pellets of things they can't digest. These are facts about owls, so I think the author's purpose is to inform.

On Their Own

Have students evaluate how well the author achieves her purpose. For additional practice, use *Let's Practice It!* p. 206 on the *Teacher Resources DVD-ROM*.

OWL PELLETS

pellets, scientists can learn all about an owl's diet. A pellet of a barn owl, for example, usually contains entire skeletons of two or three mammals, lots of fur, and insect parts. That means that a barn owl gulps down around six small mammals a day.

Six small mammals at two to six ounces each seems like a lot of meat for a bird that weighs less than one pound. The twelve-ounce owl, however, doesn't get fat on this feast. Most of its food is just the fur and bones that get chucked up as round pellets.

91

Draw Conclusions • Analysis What conclusion can you infer about why the author included the illustration on page 91? Possible response: I can infer that the author included the illustration to show the size and contents of the pellets the owl spits up and to help the reader better comprehend the text.

Context Clues • Synthesis Use the context to determine the meaning of the verb phrase *chucked up* on page 91? What other phrase on page 90 has the same meaning? The phrase *chucked up* means "thrown up." *Spit up* on p. 90 shares a similar meaning.

Differentiated Instruction

 **Strategic Intervention**

Identify author's purpose Tell students that it is often helpful to understand the important ideas of a section of text before trying to determine the author's purpose. Model identifying text that reveals the author's purpose.

A Advanced

Explore a topic Have students use the Internet to find out more about owls and other predatory birds.

Connect to Science

The human body adapts to a wide range of environmental conditions. This enables us to survive in most regions of the world, despite climate and humidity. The human body has also developed behaviors to help us survive in extreme temperatures, such as staying in motion to ward off cold and fanning ourselves to survive in extreme heat.

English Language Learners

Two-part verbs Have students look at the two-part verb *chucked up*. Explain that two-part verbs are phrases in which both words are needed to make meaning. Ask students to work in pairs to make lists of other two-part verbs they have encountered: *give up, stand up,* and *act out*.

Objectives

- Use graphic sources to gain an overview of a text and locate information.

OPTION 1 Skills and Strategies, continued

Teach Graphic Sources

Graphic Sources Direct students' attention to the illustration of the snake on p. 93, and ask them to identify the information provided by this graphic source. (This graphic source shows how large snakes will curl around their prey and squeeze them to death as they are swallowing.)

Corrective Feedback

If... students are unable to extract information from the illustration, **then...** model understanding graphic sources.

Model the Skill

Think Aloud The text explains how snakes can stretch their jaws open to eat very large meals. The illustration shows a snake coiled around a large animal, swallowing it.

Big, big gulps

Gulping down a whole pig or chicken may sound like an impossible task for a snake. But it's no big deal for a twenty-foot python. In fact, many snakes often swallow food much bigger than their own heads. Even very small snakes may feast on mice, rats, birds, frogs, and whole eggs.

The snake's ability to swallow big prey results from the special design of its jaw. The bones of its mouth are loosely joined to its skull. A stretchy strip of tissue called a *ligament* holds together the two halves of the lower jaw. When the snake swallows its dinner, its mouth can stretch wide open. The lower jawbones spread apart and each bone moves separately to pull the prey into the mouth.

Snakes generally try to gulp down their food headfirst. This causes the prey's legs to fold back as the snake swallows. In addition, the snake's sharp teeth are curved

92

Student Edition pp. 92–93

OPTION 2 Think Critically, continued

Higher-Order Thinking Skills

Graphic Sources • Evaluation How does the illustration on the bottom of page 93 help you monitor and adjust your comprehension of a snake's adaptive features? Possible response: The illustration helps me clarify how a snake's jaw stretches to let it swallow a large animal, which confused me before.

Important Ideas • Synthesis Look back at the three sections of *Exploding Ants*. Maintaining meaning, summarize the important, or main, idea that links all three sections. Possible response: However strange they might seem to humans, animal adaptations serve a purpose in helping animals survive.

The text does not mention the snake coiling around its prey to squeeze the life out of it, but the illustration clarifies that piece of information, which helps me gain a better understanding of what I've read.

backward, preventing the squirming prey from wiggling back out. As the snake works its food down its throat, it pushes its windpipe out of its mouth. This means that it doesn't have to stop breathing as it swallows.

Because snakes eat such big meals, they don't need to eat every day. Most snakes only have to grab a meal once a week, and some only eat once every month. Large pythons hold the record, however. After feasting on a pig or chicken, these huge snakes can go for more than a year without any other food!

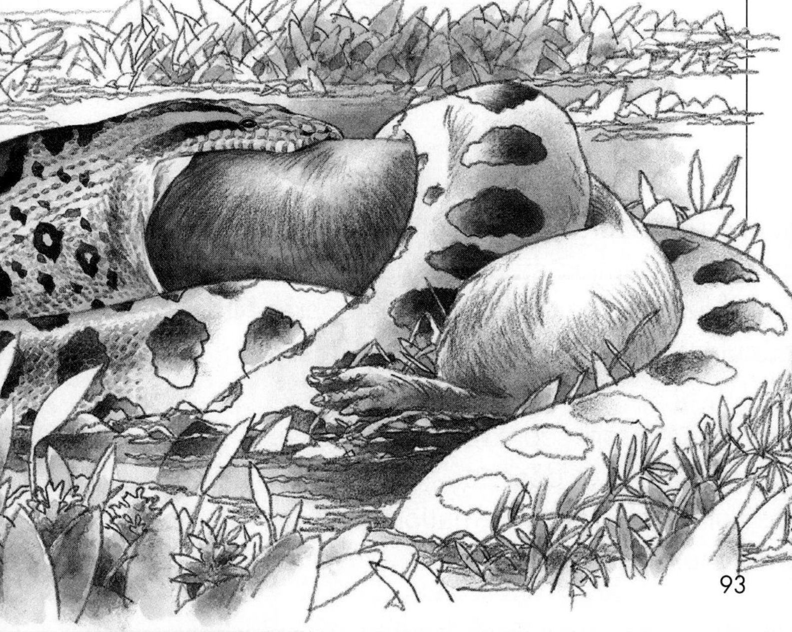

93

On Their Own

Have students look back at the pages they have read. Have them use the graphic sources to locate specific ideas and facts that were confusing to them and to gain a general overview of the information they have read.

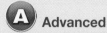

Differentiated Instruction

SI Strategic Intervention

Graphic sources Have students work in pairs to review the graphic sources and to clarify any misunderstandings about the text.

A Advanced

Extend critical thinking Have students identify a part of the human body that contains ligaments, such has those in a snake's jaw. Challenge students to describe the purpose of these ligaments. (ankles, knees)

Connect to Science

The anaconda of South America and the Asiatic Reticulated Python are the world's largest snakes. The python can reach a length of 33 feet—truly an animal extreme!

Comprehension Check

Spiral Review

Draw Conclusions • Evaluation Based on the information presented by the author in the text, what conclusion can you draw about why it would be a useful adaptation for a large snake to only have to eat once a year? Possible response: I can conclude that it would be a useful adaptation for a snake to only have to eat once a year because it limits the amount of time and energy the snake spends hunting.

Monitor and Clarify • Analysis What is something in the text that you do not understand or that confuses you? How might you clarify your understanding of this concept? Possible response: I don't understand how a snake can push its windpipe out of its mouth when it is swallowing. I could use the Internet or other print resources to clarify my understanding of how this adaptation works.

Check Predictions Have students return to the predictions they made earlier and confirm whether they were accurate.

ELL

English Language Learners

Idioms Explain that the phrase *grab a meal* means "to eat." Ask students how often most snakes grab a meal. (once a week)

Objectives

- ◎ Use graphic sources to understand expository text.
- ◎ Identify important ideas to aid comprehension.

Check Retelling
SUCCESS PREDICTOR

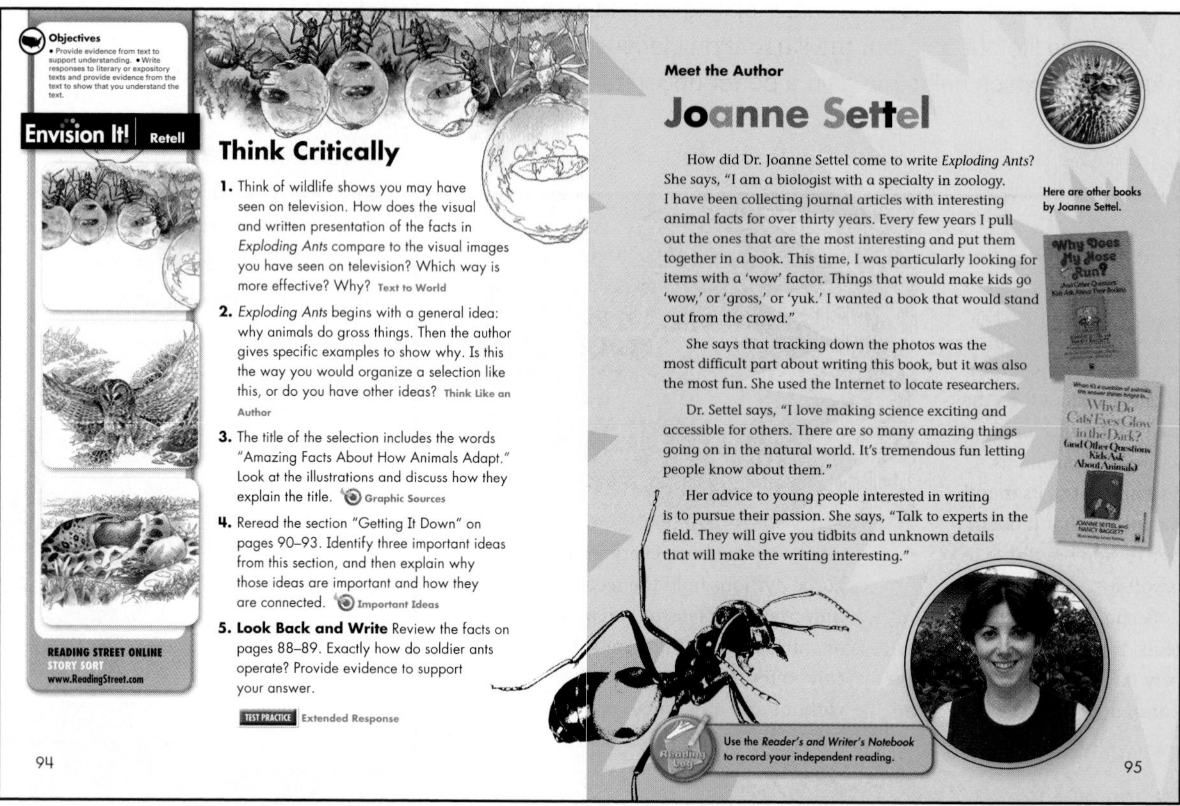

Objectives
• Provide evidence from text to support understanding. • Write responses to literary or expository texts and provide evidence from the text to show that you understand the text.

Envision It! Retell

Think Critically

1. Think of wildlife shows you may have seen on television. How does the visual and written presentation of the facts in *Exploding Ants* compare to the visual images you have seen on television? Which way is more effective? Why? Text to World
2. *Exploding Ants* begins with a general idea: why animals do gross things. Then the author gives specific examples to show why. Is this the way you would organize a selection like this, or do you have other ideas? Think Like an Author
3. The title of the selection includes the words "Amazing Facts About How Animals Adapt." Look at the illustrations and discuss how they explain the title. ◎ Graphic Sources
4. Reread the section "Getting It Down" on pages 90–93. Identify three important ideas from this section, and then explain why those ideas are important and how they are connected. ◎ Important Ideas
5. **Look Back and Write** Review the facts on pages 88–89. Exactly how do soldier ants operate? Provide evidence to support your answer.

TEST PRACTICE Extended Response

READING STREET ONLINE
STORY SORT
www.ReadingStreet.com

94

Meet the Author

Joanne Settel

How did Dr. Joanne Settel come to write *Exploding Ants?* She says, "I am a biologist with a specialty in zoology. I have been collecting journal articles with interesting animal facts for over thirty years. Every few years I pull out the ones that are the most interesting and put them together in a book. This time, I was particularly looking for items with a 'wow' factor. Things that would make kids go 'wow,' or 'gross,' or 'yuk.' I wanted a book that would stand out from the crowd."

She says that tracking down the photos was the most difficult part about writing this book, but it was also the most fun. She used the Internet to locate researchers.

Dr. Settel says, "I love making science exciting and accessible for others. There are so many amazing things going on in the natural world. It's tremendous fun letting people know about them."

Her advice to young people interested in writing is to pursue their passion. She says, "Talk to experts in the field. They will give you tidbits and unknown details that will make the writing interesting."

Here are other books by Joanne Settel.

Reading Log
Use the *Reader's and Writer's Notebook* to record your independent reading.

95

Student Edition pp. 94–95

Retelling

Envision It!

Have students work in pairs to retell the selection, using the Envision It! Retelling Cards as prompts. Remind students that they should use graphics to accurately summarize the main topic and paraphrase important ideas using key vocabulary. Monitor students' retellings.

Scoring rubric

Top-Score Response A top-score response makes connections beyond the text, describes the main topic and important ideas using accurate information, and draws conclusions from the text.

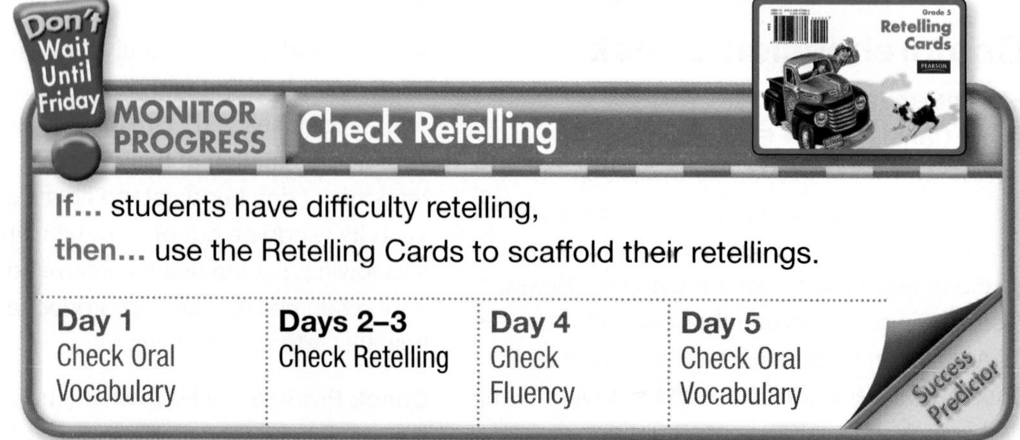

Don't Wait Until Friday
MONITOR PROGRESS
Check Retelling
Retelling Cards

If... students have difficulty retelling,
then... use the Retelling Cards to scaffold their retellings.

Day 1 Check Oral Vocabulary	**Days 2–3** Check Retelling	**Day 4** Check Fluency	**Day 5** Check Oral Vocabulary

Success Predictor

Plan to Assess Retelling

- ☑ **Week 1** Assess Strategic Intervention students.
- ☑ **Week 2** Assess Advanced students.
- ☑ **This week assess Strategic Intervention students.**
- ☐ **Week 4** Assess On-Level students.
- ☐ **Week 5** Assess any students you have not yet checked during this unit.

Think Critically

Text to world 1. Possible response: The visuals in the selection are like snapshots of visual images on TV, except that the visuals in the selection emphasize the facts being presented. I think if I want to remember the scientific facts, then the visuals and writing in the selection are more effective than TV.

Think like an author 2. Possible response: I would organize it by showing a picture of each animal with a caption describing what it is doing and the page number telling where it is covered in the text. This would help readers locate that information.

Graphic sources 3. Possible response: The illustrations show animal adaptations, such as the "living honey jars" and the puffer fish blown up to scare enemies.

Important ideas 4. Possible response: Barn owls eat so much because most of their food is indigestible fur and bones. Snakes have a special kind of jaw that allows them to eat a huge meal all at once. Snakes don't have to eat very often because they eat such big meals. All of these ideas are connected to how the animals get nutrients.

Writing on Demand

5. **Look Back and Write** To build writing fluency, assign a 10–15 minute time limit.

Suggest that students use a prewriting strategy, such as brainstorming or using a graphic organizer, to organize their ideas. Remind them to establish a topic sentence and support it with facts, details, or explanations. As students finish, encourage them to reread their responses, revise for organization and support, and proofread for errors in grammar and conventions.

Scoring rubric

Top-Score Response A top-score response uses factual information about soldier ants.

A top-score response should include:

- They manufacture deadly chemicals in their own bodies.
- The chemicals are stored in two big sacs.
- When threatened, they release a small amount of the chemicals, and when attacked, they spew the chemicals.

Differentiated Instruction

SI Strategic Intervention
Have students work in pairs to brainstorm a list of animal adaptations, both physical and behavioral, that are described in the article.

Meet the Author

Have students read about author Joanne Settel on p. 95. Ask them how and why the author tried to achieve a "wow factor" in *Exploding Ants.*

Independent Reading

After students enter their independent reading information into their Reading Logs, have them paraphrase a portion of the text they have just read. Remind students that when we paraphrase, we express the meaning of a passage using other words and maintaining logical order.

English Language Learners

Support critical response
If students have trouble understanding question 2 about how they would organize the selection, ask which example of animal behavior they found most interesting. Have them tell what part of the selection they think a friend or family member would like to read about first.

Objectives

- Read grade-level text at an appropriate rate.
- Reread for fluency.
- Understand how to locate information in magazines and periodicals.

Model Fluency
Rate

Model fluent reading

Have students turn to p. 84 of *Exploding Ants.* Have students follow along as you read the page. Tell them to listen to you as you read at a natural speaking rate about the adaptive behaviors of animal species. Adjust your rate accordingly as you read the page, slowing as you approach difficult words or concepts.

Guide practice

Have students follow along as you read the page again. Then have them reread the page again until they read at an appropriate rate and with no mistakes. Continue in the same way on p. 85.

Reread for Fluency

Corrective feedback

If... students are having difficulty reading at the correct rate,
then... prompt:

- Do you think you need to slow down or read more quickly?
- Read the sentence more quickly. Now read it more slowly. Which helps you understand what you are reading?
- Tell me the sentence. Read it at the rate that would help me understand it.

ROUTINE **Oral Rereading**

1. **Read** Have students read page 92 of *Exploding Ants* orally.
2. **Reread** To achieve optimal fluency, students should reread the text three or four times.
3. **Corrective Feedback** Have students read aloud without you. Provide feedback about their rate and encourage them to adjust their rate depending on what they are reading to enhance comprehension. Listen for use of appropriate rate.

Routines Flip Chart

Research and Study Skills
Magazine/Periodical

Teach

Ask students what kinds of print reference sources might contain factual information that fits into their research plan. Show a relevant magazine or newspaper to the class and use it to review these terms:

- A **periodical** is a magazine that contains current information in the form of articles, opinion columns, letters, reports, advertisements, and reviews.
- Magazines and newspapers list their contents on the first few pages, much like a book's table of contents.
- The headline or title expresses the topic of the article. Magazines and newspapers present their most important or interesting information first.
- Most magazines follow the 5Ws and How format. The article will tell you *Who?, What?, Where?, When?, Why?,* and *How?*
- Both magazines and newspapers will often include photos, illustrations, and captions to help clarify the information in the article.

Provide groups with examples of different kinds of magazines and newspapers. Have each group select a specific article using the table of contents and show its article to the class, telling how they found their article and why they selected it.

Discuss these questions:

Guide practice

How are the magazines organized? (The most interesting or biggest stories are presented first.)

How can you use text features such as heads and subheads to find what you need? Possible response: I can search for headings or sections that mention what I want to know.

Find the title of an article that grabs your attention. What do you think you might learn from this article? (Answers will vary.)

After students discuss their periodicals, ask specific questions about the articles they have read.

On their own

Have students complete pp. 276–277 of the *Reader's and Writer's Notebook.*

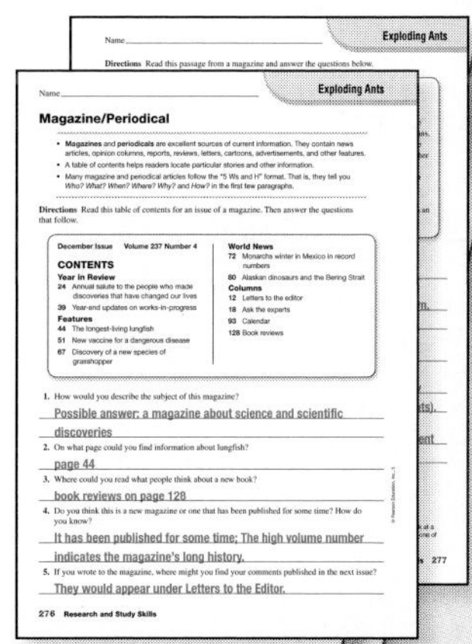
Name

Exploding Ants

Magazine/Periodical

- **Magazines** and **periodicals** are excellent sources of current information. They contain news articles, opinion columns, reports, reviews, letters, cartoons, advertisements, and other features.
- A table of contents helps readers locate particular stories and other information.
- Many magazine and periodical articles follow the "5 Ws and H" format. That is, they tell you *Who? What? When? Where? Why?* and *How?* in the first few paragraphs.

Directions Read this table of contents for an issue of a magazine. Then answer the questions that follow.

December Issue Volume 237 Number 4

CONTENTS

Year in Review
24 Annual salute to the people who made discoveries that have changed our lives
39 Year-end updates on works-in-progress

Features
44 The longest-living lungfish
51 New vaccine for a dangerous disease
67 Discovery of a new species of grasshopper

World News
72 Monarchs winter in Mexico in record numbers
80 Alaskan dinosaurs and the Bering Strait

Columns
12 Letters to the editor
18 Ask the experts
93 Calendar
128 Book reviews

1. How would you describe the subject of this magazine?
Possible answer: a magazine about science and scientific discoveries
2. On what page could you find information about lungfish?
page 44
3. Where could you read what people think about a new book?
book reviews on page 128
4. Do you think this is a new magazine or one that has been published for some time? How do you know?
It has been published for some time; The high volume number indicates the magazine's long history.
5. If you wrote to the magazine, where might you find your comments published in the next issue?
They would appear under Letters to the Editor.

276 Research and Study Skills

Reader's and Writer's Notebook pp. 276–277

English Language Learners

Professional Development
What ELL experts say about sheltered reading: "Often, beginning and intermediate English Language Learners may not understand what their classroom teachers say or read aloud in English. These students benefit when teachers shelter, or make comprehensible, their literacy instruction." —Dr. Georgia Earnest García

Magazines and periodicals
Help students select periodicals from the media center. Point out titles of magazines and articles that seem useful for the student, depending on his or her inquiry topic. Work with students to locate articles with relevant information to their topics. Help students locate words and phrases that are associated with their topic and questions.

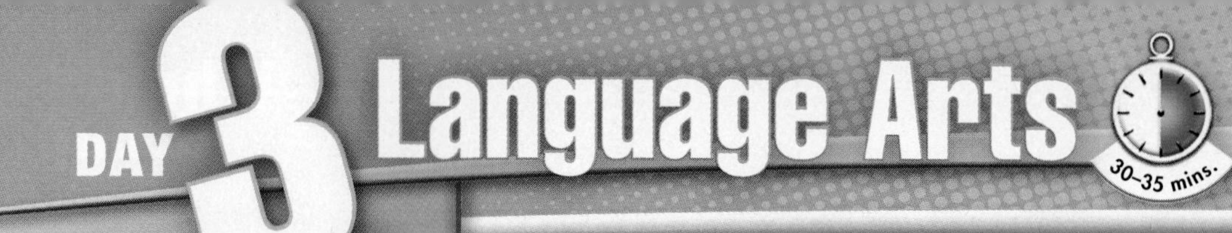

Objectives

- Analyze data for usefulness.
- Identify and correctly use possessive pronouns.
- Spell frequently misspelled words.

Research and Inquiry
Analyze

Teach

Tell students that today they will analyze their findings and focus on photographs and articles that are the most relevant to their posters. To refine their inquiry topics, have them ask themselves secondary questions to narrow the focus of their research.

Model

Think Aloud I had thought that all lions lived in prides, or groups. But when I talked to a zoologist, I learned more about the social habits of lions. He said that although lions do live in prides, there are also outcast lions, usually males, that roam regions such as Central Africa and the Kalahari Desert. I want to focus on this as I create my poster. I ask myself, *How can I make my inquiry question more specific?* I will rewrite my inquiry question so I can focus on these nomadic lions. Now my inquiry question is: *What allows lions of Central Africa and the Kalahari Desert to lead a nomadic life?*

Guide practice

Have students analyze their findings. They should focus on one interesting or unusual adaptation instead of trying to include many different facts about their animal.

On their own

Remind students that they will need to include a photo or an illustration of their chosen animal in their posters. If students are having trouble, suggest that they talk to you or work with other students.

Conventions
Possessive Pronouns

Review

Remind students that this week they learned about possessive pronouns. Review the definition of possessive pronouns.

- Possessive pronouns show who or what possesses, or owns, something.
- Use *my, your, her, our,* and *their* before nouns.
- Use *mine, yours, hers, ours,* and *theirs* alone.
- Use *his* and *its* before nouns and alone.
- No possessive pronouns use an apostrophe.

Daily Fix-It

Use Daily Fix-It numbers 5 and 6 in the right margin.

Connect to oral language

Display the following sentences and have students read from the board, guiding them to select the appropriate pronoun:

They took ________ dog with them when they moved. (their)

"This cake is ________," I said, giving him a piece. (yours)

The cat has mud on ________ paws. (its)

On their own

For additional practice use *Let's Practice It!* p. 207 on the *Teacher Resources DVD-ROM*.

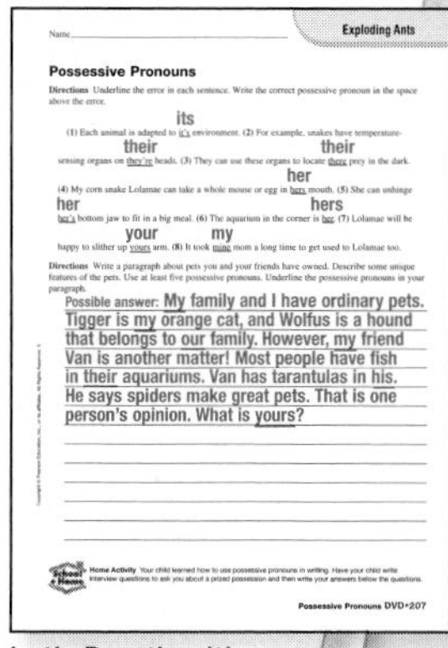

Name________________ Exploding Ants

Possessive Pronouns

Directions Underline the error in each sentence. Write the correct possessive pronoun in the space above the error.

(1) Each animal is adapted to it's [its] environment. (2) For example, snakes have temperature-sensing organs on they're [their] heads. (3) They can use these organs to locate there [their] prey in the dark. (4) My corn snake Lolamae can take a whole mouse or egg in hers [her] mouth. (5) She can unhinge her's [her] bottom jaw to fit in a big meal. (6) The aquarium in the corner is her [hers]. (7) Lolamae will be happy to slither up yours [your] arm. (8) It took mine [my] mom a long time to get used to Lolamae too.

Directions Write a paragraph about pets you and your friends have owned. Describe some unique features of the pets. Use at least five possessive pronouns. Underline the possessive pronouns in your paragraph.

Possible answer: My family and I have ordinary pets. Tigger is my orange cat, and Wolfus is a hound that belongs to our family. However, my friend Van is another matter! Most people have fish in their aquariums. Van has tarantulas in his. He says spiders make great pets. That is one person's opinion. What is yours?

Home Activity Your child learned how to use possessive pronouns in writing. Have your child write interview questions to ask you about a prized possession and then write your answers below the questions.

Possessive Pronouns DVD•207

Let's Practice It!
TR DVD•207

Spelling
Homophones

Frequently misspelled words

The homophones *their, there,* and *they're* are words that students often misspell. I'm going to read a sentence. Choose the right homophone to complete the sentence and then write it correctly. Have students check their own work with an electronic or print dictionary.

1. **Put your book over ________.** (there)
2. **________ late for the game.** (they're)
3. **We went to ________ house for dinner.** (their)

On their own

For more practice, use the *Reader's and Writer's Notebook* p. 278.

Reader's and Writer's Notebook p. 278

Differentiated Instruction

 Strategic Intervention

Possessive pronouns If students have difficulty, make the lesson visual. Write the sentences on the board or on sentence strips. Make word cards for several possessive pronouns, including those that complete the sentences. Then have students suggest a pronoun to complete a sentence, place the card in the sentence, and read the complete sentence. Have other students decide whether it is correct.

Daily Fix-It

5. Their are a snake under that chair! *(There is)*
6. That is mine snake named sue. *(my; Sue)*

Objectives

- Develop draft of a formal letter.

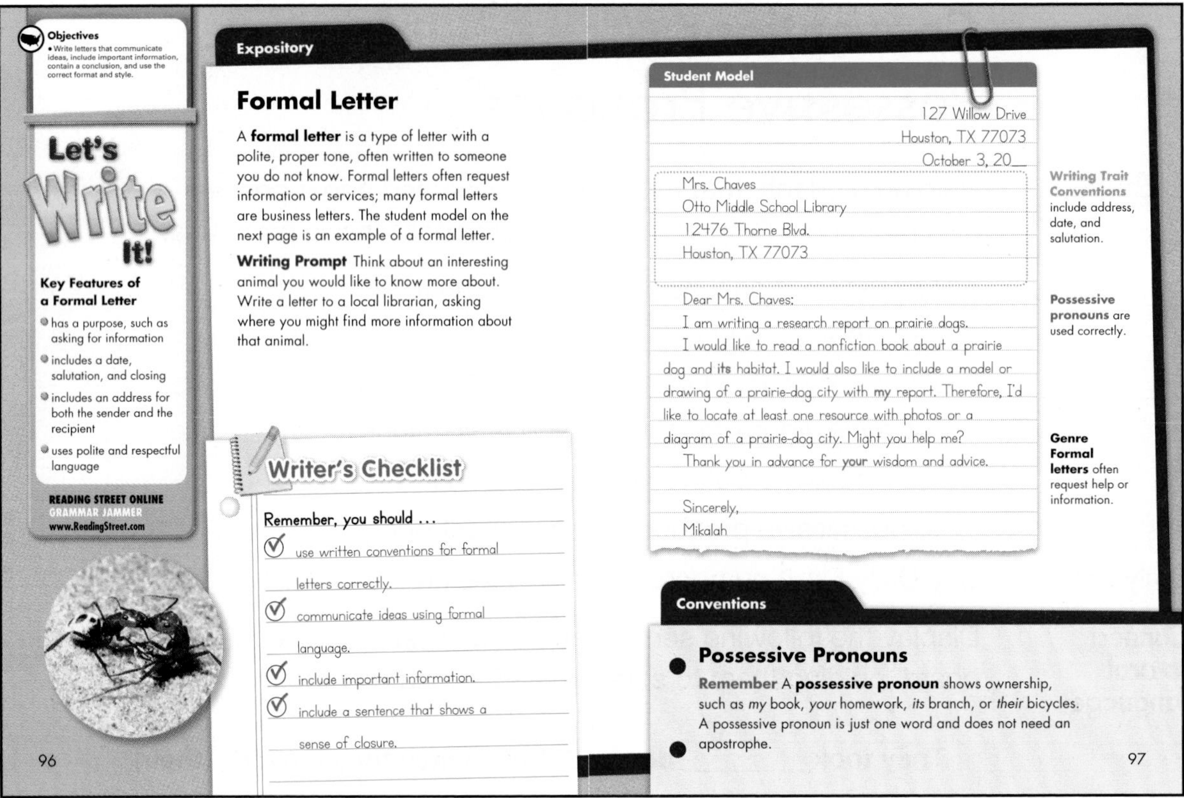

Objectives

- Write letters that communicate ideas, include important information, contain a conclusion, and use the correct format and style.

Let's Write It!

Key Features of a Formal Letter

- has a purpose, such as asking for information
- includes a date, salutation, and closing
- includes an address for both the sender and the recipient
- uses polite and respectful language

READING STREET ONLINE
GRAMMAR JAMMER
www.ReadingStreet.com

Expository

Formal Letter

A **formal letter** is a type of letter with a polite, proper tone, often written to someone you do not know. Formal letters often request information or services; many formal letters are business letters. The student model on the next page is an example of a formal letter.

Writing Prompt Think about an interesting animal you would like to know more about. Write a letter to a local librarian, asking where you might find more information about that animal.

Writer's Checklist

Remember, you should ...

- use written conventions for formal letters correctly.
- communicate ideas using formal language.
- include important information.
- include a sentence that shows a sense of closure.

96

Student Model

127 Willow Drive
Houston, TX 77073
October 3, 20__

Mrs. Chaves
Otto Middle School Library
12476 Thorne Blvd.
Houston, TX 77073

Dear Mrs. Chaves:

I am writing a research report on prairie dogs. I would like to read a nonfiction book about a prairie dog and its habitat. I would also like to include a model or drawing of a prairie-dog city with my report. Therefore, I'd like to locate at least one resource with photos or a diagram of a prairie-dog city. Might you help me?

Thank you in advance for your wisdom and advice.

Sincerely,
Mikalah

Writing Trait Conventions include address, date, and salutation.

Possessive pronouns are used correctly.

Genre Formal letters often request help or information.

Conventions

Possessive Pronouns

Remember A **possessive pronoun** shows ownership, such as *my* book, *your* homework, *its* branch, or *their* bicycles. A possessive pronoun is just one word and does not need an apostrophe.

97

Student Edition pp. 96–97

Let's Write It!
Formal Letter

Teach

Use pp. 96–97 in the Student Edition. Direct students to read the key features of a formal letter which appear on p. 96. Remind students that they can refer to the information in the Writer's Checklist as they write their own formal letter.

Read the student model on p. 97. Point out the use of possessive pronouns in the model.

Connect to conventions

Remind students that possessive pronouns show ownership, or *possession.* Point out the correct use of possessive pronouns in the model. Remind students that possessive pronouns do not need an apostrophe.

Writing—Formal Letter
Evaluation

Display rubric

Display Scoring Rubric 18 from the *Teacher's Resources DVD* and go over the criteria for each trait below each score. Using the model in the Student Edition, choose students to explain why model should score a 4 for one of the traits. If a student offers that model should score below 4 for a particular trait, the student should offer support for that response. Remind students that this rubric will be used to evaluate the formal letter they write.

Scoring Rubric: Formal Letter

	4	3	2	1
Focus/Idea	Clear purpose and ideas; strong focus on request	Adequate description of purpose and ideas; adequate focus on request	Unclear purpose and ideas; little focus on request	No purpose; no focus on request
Organization/ Paragraphs	Appropriate formal letter format; ends with a sense of closure	Reasonable format chosen; some sense of closure	Incorrect format; poor sense of closure	No attempt at formal letter format; no sense of closure
Voice	Strong, polite voice; writer's personality conveyed	Reasonable strong voice; polite voice	Weak or impolite voice	No voice; writer not engaged
Word Choice	Strong use of precise and appropriate words	Use of some precise and appropriate words	Lacks precise or appropriate words	No attempt at using precise or appropriate words
Sentences	Clear, concise sentences; strong variety of sentence beginnings	Reasonably clear, concise sentences; variety of sentence beginnings	Unclear, lengthy sentences; weak variety of sentence beginnings	Many fragments and run-ons; no variety of sentence beginnings
Conventions	Excellent control and accuracy; punctuation and use of possessive pronouns correct	Good control, few errors; most punctuation and/or possessive pronouns correct	Errors that hamper understanding; many punctuation or possessive pronouns errors	Errors that obstruct meaning; punctuation and possessive pronoun errors

Outline

Have students take out the outline of a formal letter that they worked on yesterday. If their outlines are not complete, allow additional time to fill in the address blocks for the sender and the recipient, the date, salutation, the body, closing, and signature.

Write

You will be using your outline as you write a draft of your formal letter. When you are drafting, don't worry if your letter does not sound exactly as you want it. You will have a chance to revise it tomorrow.

English Language Learners

Cognates Point out the Spanish cognates for this week's lesson in formal letter conventions: *letra/letter, saludo/salutation,* and *lenguaje formal/formal language*

Activate prior knowledge Note the similarities between formal letters in English and Spanish in layout: Before the salutation, include both your name and address at the top of the page with the name and address of the person to whom you are writing placed next. Both use formal writing. In the case of Spanish, the use of the formal Usted rather than the informal tu is used to address the recipient as *you*. Both have slight differences in the salutation depending on whether you know the person you are writing to. Both have letter closings followed by your signature.

In Spanish, a person's title appears after the person's name (Maria Florian, Director), a form also acceptable in English.

Date conventions The appearance of the date varies significantly. While many countries give day-month-year, such as 19 August 2009, or 19-10-09, the U.S. uses month-day-year. ELLs might need extra practice with U.S. date conventions.

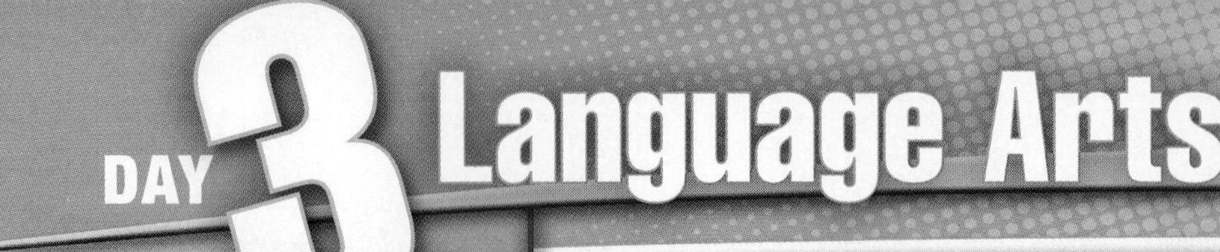

Objectives

- Write a first draft of a formal letter.
- Use the proper conventions in writing a formal letter.

Writing, continued
Writer's Craft: Formal Letter

MINI-LESSON

Drafting a Letter

Introduce Remind students that a formal letter is written to someone you do not know. A formal letter should be written in polite and respectful language. The purpose of the letter should be clearly stated in the first paragraph. What is it that you want the person who will receive your letter to do? Are you asking for help or information? Paragraph two gives important details. Why do you need the person's help or information? The last paragraph asks the person to do something, provides closure, and thanks the person you are writing to. Display the Drafting Tips for students.

Mary Moleen
86 Elm Street
Oxbow, TX 73333

Richard Townsend
Librarian
Oxbow Public Library
12 First Street
Oxbow TX 73334

Dear Richard:

I am a 5th grade student at Oxbow Elementary School. Were currently studiing animals. My teacher recommended that I contact you about the animal I am studying.

I have learned many facts about meerkats so far. Meerkats are small mammals. They live in very hot places. They live in packs. Meerkats seems to do silly things.

I would like to discover more interesting facts about meerkats. Do you know of books or Web sites where I can find more information? Please let me know at your convenance if you can help me with my research. Thanks for your time.

sincerely yours
Mary Moleen

Unit 4 Exploding Ants — Writing: Model 18A

Writing Transparency 18A, TR DVD

Drafting Tips

✔ To get started, use the outline for writing a formal letter.

✔ State the purpose of your letter in paragraph one.

✔ Include important details in paragraph two.

✔ Remember to thank the person you are writing to.

I'm going to begin writing my letter to the librarian asking for information about meerkats. In my first draft, I work toward including the parts of a formal letter, such as the addresses, date, salutation, closing, and signature. I will also tell the librarian what I want and why. I will not slow myself down by revising and proofreading as I write. I will proofread and fix my sentences at the next stage.

Display Writing Transparency 18A for the week and explain the process of drafting using the Writing Transparency. Have students use the drafting tips as a guide as they draft their formal letters. Remind them that their formal letter must include a heading that contains the writer's address followed by the date, the receiver's address, the salutation, the body, the closing, and a signature.

ROUTINE **Quick Write for Fluency** Team Talk

1. **Talk** Pairs talk about the information they are requesting and why.
2. **Write** Each person writes two sentences; the first sentence tells what they are requesting; the second sentence tells why.
3. **Share** Partners read each other's sentences.

Routines Flip Chart

Differentiated Instruction

SI Strategic Intervention
To reinforce differences between formal and informal language, have students make a list of shortened forms they use in text messages and their equivalents in formal English.

Wrap Up Your Day

- ✔ **Build Concepts** What did you learn about how owls digest their food?
- ✔ **Graphic Sources** How do the pictures on p. 92 help you understand the size of pythons?
- ✔ **Important Ideas** How does determining the most important idea on a page help you to understand what you read?

Tell students that tomorrow they will read about mimicry.

DAY 4 Get Ready to Read 15–20 mins.

Objectives

- Expand the weekly concept.
- Develop oral vocabulary.

Today at a Glance

Oral Vocabulary
protrude, formidable

Genre
Expository text

Reading
"The Art of Mimicry"

Let's Learn It!
Fluency: Rate
Vocabulary: Context clues
Listening/Speaking: Description

Research and Inquiry
Synthesize

Spelling
Homophones

Conventions
Possessive pronouns

Writing
Formal letter

Concept Talk

Question of the Week

How do animals adapt to survive?

Expand the concept

Remind students that this week they have read about the ways that animals such as ants, owls, and snakes have adapted in order to survive. Tell students that today they will read an expository text about other kinds of animal adaptations.

Anchored Talk

Develop oral vocabulary

Use the text features—illustrations, photographs, captions, and heads—to review pp. 90–93 of *Exploding Ants.* Discuss the Amazing Words *spiny* and *survival.* Add these and other concept-related words to the concept map. Then have them use the following questions to develop their understanding of the concept.

- How do animals like the *spiny* puffer fish protect themselves from predators?
- *Survival* is the main goal of every kind of animal. How do adaptations help animals in the struggle for *survival*?

Strategy Response Log

INTERACT with TEXT

Have students complete p. 24 in *Reader's and Writer's Notebook*. Then have students summarize the important ideas that they found in the selection.

Oral Vocabulary
Amazing Words

Amazing Words Oral Vocabulary Routine

Teach Amazing Words

1. **Introduce** Write the concept word *formidable* on the board. Have students say it aloud with you. We read about how animals display *formidable* powers of adaptation to the environment. Does the author include any context clues that help me understand this word? (There are photographs that show the threatening or imposing ways animals have of defending themselves against predators.)
2. **Demonstrate** Break into groups. Have students elicit and consider suggestions from group members to demonstrate understanding. What *formidable* defense does the *Camponotus* soldier ant use? (chemicals that explode onto the predator)
3. **Apply** Have students apply their understanding. How does a snake's *formidable* teeth help it to gulp down a meal?

See p. OV•3 to teach *protrude*.

Routines Flip Chart

Apply Amazing Words

Help students establish a purpose for reading as they read "The Art of Mimicry" on pp. 98–101. Have them think about how the Amazing Words apply to the selection.

Connect to reading

As students read today's selection about animals who use mimicry and camouflage, have them set purposes for reading and think about how this week's Question of the Week and the Amazing Words *protrude* and *formidable* apply to animal adaptations.

ELL **Produce Oral Language** Use the Day 4 instruction on ELL Poster 18 to extend and enrich language.

ELL Poster 18

Amazing Words

adaptations	camouflage
predators	spiny
defenses	survival
fearsome	protrude
mimicry	formidable

ELL

English Language Learners

Cognates Point out that *formidable,* one of today's Amazing Words, has a Spanish cognate. The word *formidable* is also used by Spanish speakers.

Objectives

- Introduce expository text.

Let's Think About Genre

Expository Text: Text Structure

Introduce the genre Explain to students that expository text is nonfiction writing that may be organized in a number of ways and for a variety of purposes. Ask students to share what they already know about expository texts.

Discuss the genre Inform students that the purpose of an expository text will determine how the writer chooses to organize it. The organization influences the relationships among ideas. The way in which an expository text is organized is called its *text structure.*

An expository text intended to inform can be organized in several ways. One way is through cause and effect. This means ideas will be set up to highlight the cause and effect relationships. Point out that students have read a number of selections that have this type of text structure. Remind students that a single cause can have multiple effects.

On the board, make a T-chart. Ask the following questions:

- What is a cause-and-effect relationship? Possible response: A relationship in which one event or action is the result of another event or action.
- The weather turns cold, so birds fly south. Which part of this sentence is the cause and which is the effect? Possible responses: The weather is the cause, and the flight of the birds is the effect.
- Which words can signal a cause-and-effect relationship? Possible responses: *because, so, if…then, as a result, since, cause(s), therefore*

Cause	Effect

Guide practice Have students work in pairs to fill in the chart with causes and effects they can identify from their readings, synthesizing ideas they have learned. Ask them to compare the text structure of two or three expository texts and how each organization influences the relationships among ideas. Make sure they summarize or paraphrase texts in ways that maintain meaning and logical order across texts. They should consider suggestions from their partners in the discussions.

Connect to reading Tell students that they will now read an article that is organized by cause-and-effect structure. Have students think about how survival needs determine various effects in animal appearance and behavior.

Small Group Time

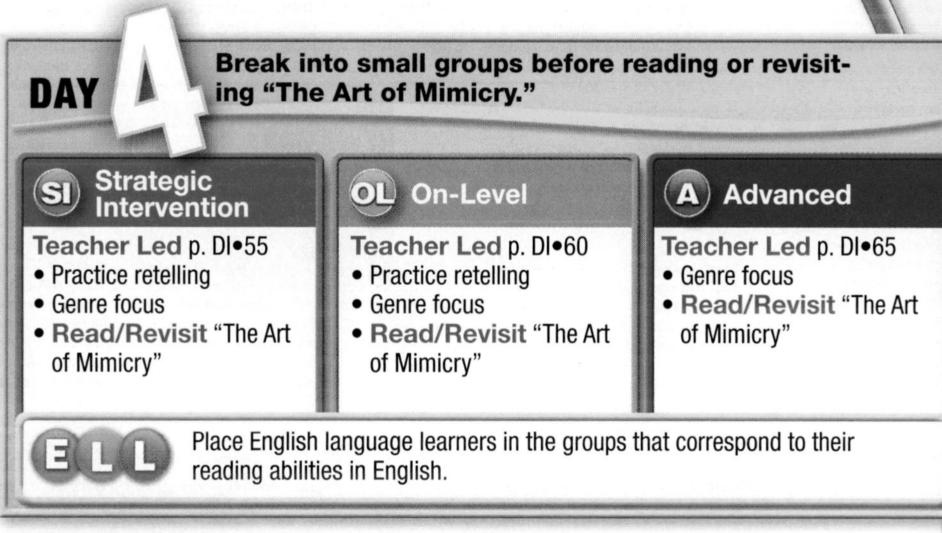

DAY 4 **Break into small groups before reading or revisiting "The Art of Mimicry."**

Teacher Led

SI Strategic Intervention	OL On-Level	A Advanced
Teacher Led p. DI•55 • Practice retelling • Genre focus • **Read/Revisit** "The Art of Mimicry"	**Teacher Led** p. DI•60 • Practice retelling • Genre focus • **Read/Revisit** "The Art of Mimicry"	**Teacher Led** p. DI•65 • Genre focus • **Read/Revisit** "The Art of Mimicry"

ELL Place English language learners in the groups that correspond to their reading abilities in English.

Practice Stations
- Read for Meaning
- Get Fluent
- Words to Know

Independent Activities
- AudioText: "The Art of Mimicry"
- *Reader's and Writer's Notebook*
- Research and Inquiry

DAY 4 Read and Comprehend

45–50 mins.

Objectives

- Understand cause and effect in expository text.
- Synthesize ideas across texts.

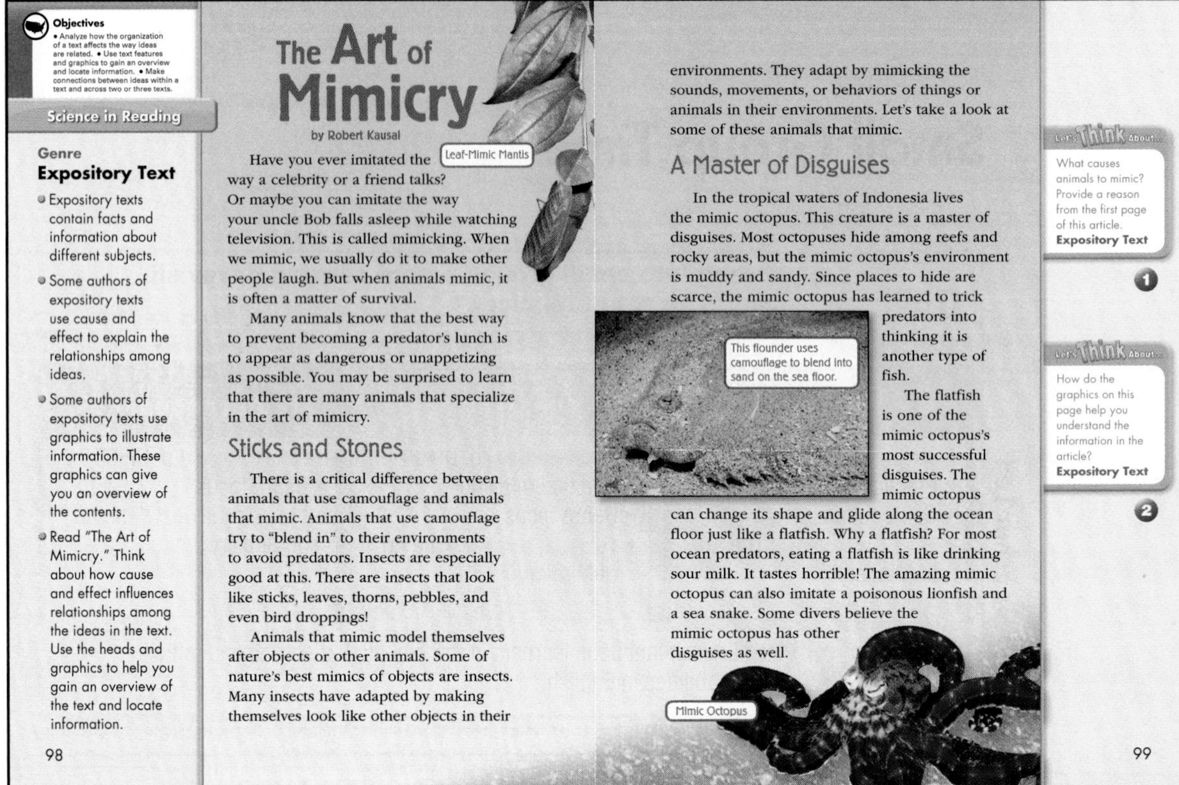

Objectives
• Analyze how the organization of a text affects the way ideas are related. • Use text features and graphics to gain an overview and locate information. • Make connections between ideas within a text and across two or three texts.

Science in Reading

Genre
Expository Text

- Expository texts contain facts and information about different subjects.
- Some authors of expository texts use cause and effect to explain the relationships among ideas.
- Some authors of expository texts use graphics to illustrate information. These graphics can give you an overview of the contents.
- Read "The Art of Mimicry." Think about how cause and effect influences relationships among the ideas in the text. Use the heads and graphics to help you gain an overview of the text and locate information.

The Art of Mimicry

by Robert Kausal

Have you ever imitated the way a celebrity or a friend talks? Or maybe you can imitate the way your uncle Bob falls asleep while watching television. This is called mimicking. When we mimic, we usually do it to make other people laugh. But when animals mimic, it is often a matter of survival.

Many animals know that the best way to prevent becoming a predator's lunch is to appear as dangerous or unappetizing as possible. You may be surprised to learn that there are many animals that specialize in the art of mimicry.

Sticks and Stones

There is a critical difference between animals that use camouflage and animals that mimic. Animals that use camouflage try to "blend in" to their environments to avoid predators. Insects are especially good at this. There are insects that look like sticks, leaves, thorns, pebbles, and even bird droppings!

Animals that mimic model themselves after objects or other animals. Some of nature's best mimics of objects are insects. Many insects have adapted by making themselves look like other objects in their environments. They adapt by mimicking the sounds, movements, or behaviors of things or animals in their environments. Let's take a look at some of these animals that mimic.

A Master of Disguises

In the tropical waters of Indonesia lives the mimic octopus. This creature is a master of disguises. Most octopuses hide among reefs and rocky areas, but the mimic octopus's environment is muddy and sandy. Since places to hide are scarce, the mimic octopus has learned to trick predators into thinking it is another type of fish.

The flatfish is one of the mimic octopus's most successful disguises. The mimic octopus can change its shape and glide along the ocean floor just like a flatfish. Why a flatfish? For most ocean predators, eating a flatfish is like drinking sour milk. It tastes horrible! The amazing mimic octopus can also imitate a poisonous lionfish and a sea snake. Some divers believe the mimic octopus has other disguises as well.

Leaf-Mimic Mantis

This flounder uses camouflage to blend into sand on the sea floor.

Mimic Octopus

Let's Think About...
What causes animals to mimic? Provide a reason from the first page of this article.
Expository Text
1

Let's Think About...
How do the graphics on this page help you understand the information in the article?
Expository Text
2

98 99

Student Edition pp. 98–99

Guide Comprehension

Teach the genre

Expository Text: Text Structure Have students read "The Art of Mimicry" on pp. 98–101. As they read, have them look for examples of cause and effect. Then ask: What is an example of a cause-and-effect relationship that is discussed on page 99?

Corrective feedback

If... students are unable to identify an example of cause and effect, **then...** use the model to guide students in identifying causes and effects.

Model the skill

I see the word *since,* which signals a cause. I'll read the sentence aloud: *Since places to hide are scarce, the mimic octopus has learned to trick predators into thinking it is another type of fish.* The explanation of how the octopus mimics another animal is the effect of having few places to hide. So, this sentence is one example of cause and effect on this page.

On their own

Have students work in pairs to identify other cause-and-effect relationships explained on pp. 98–99.

Extend Thinking
Think Critically

Higher-order thinking skills

Main Idea • Synthesis How does the main idea in "The Art of Mimicry" compare to the main idea in *Exploding Ants?* Possible response: The main ideas are basically the same—that animals adapt to their environments in order to survive. *Exploding Ants* focuses on examples of surprising adaptations, while "The Art of Mimicry" focuses on comparing one type of animal adaptation (modeling) to another (camouflage).

Cause and Effect • Analysis Using the language of cause and effect, explain why insects tend to be good at camouflage. Possible response: Because insects are so small, an insect's best defense is to blend in with an object in its environment.

Graphic Sources • Synthesis Using the text, picture, and caption on page 98, how would you describe the mantis's adaptation to its environment? Possible response: The mantis uses mimicking to appear just like the leaf on which it feeds.

Let's Think About...

1. Animals mimic to appear dangerous or unappetizing to predators.
2. When I look at the flounder, I can see how camouflage helps it almost disappear.

Differentiated Instruction

SI Strategic Intervention

Synthesizing information Have students practice extracting information from text and graphics to make statements about their reading. Explain that additional details can be found in captions. Have students list observations they can make from the graphic sources in the selection, and compare these observations to the language of the main text.

A Advanced

Graphic sources Have students use the Internet to find other photographs that display animal mimicry and camouflage.

Connect to Science

When people build homes and businesses in rural areas, the animals living there must adapt to the changed environment or move to a different place. Make a list of animals in your area that have adapted to survive.

English Language Learners

Cause and effect Have students read aloud the first two paragraphs to find an example of something an animal does to protect itself (the effect) and why the animal acts that way (the cause). Have students share their examples. If no signal words are included in the text, have students provide them.

Objectives

- Summarize important ideas in expository text.
- Make connections across texts.

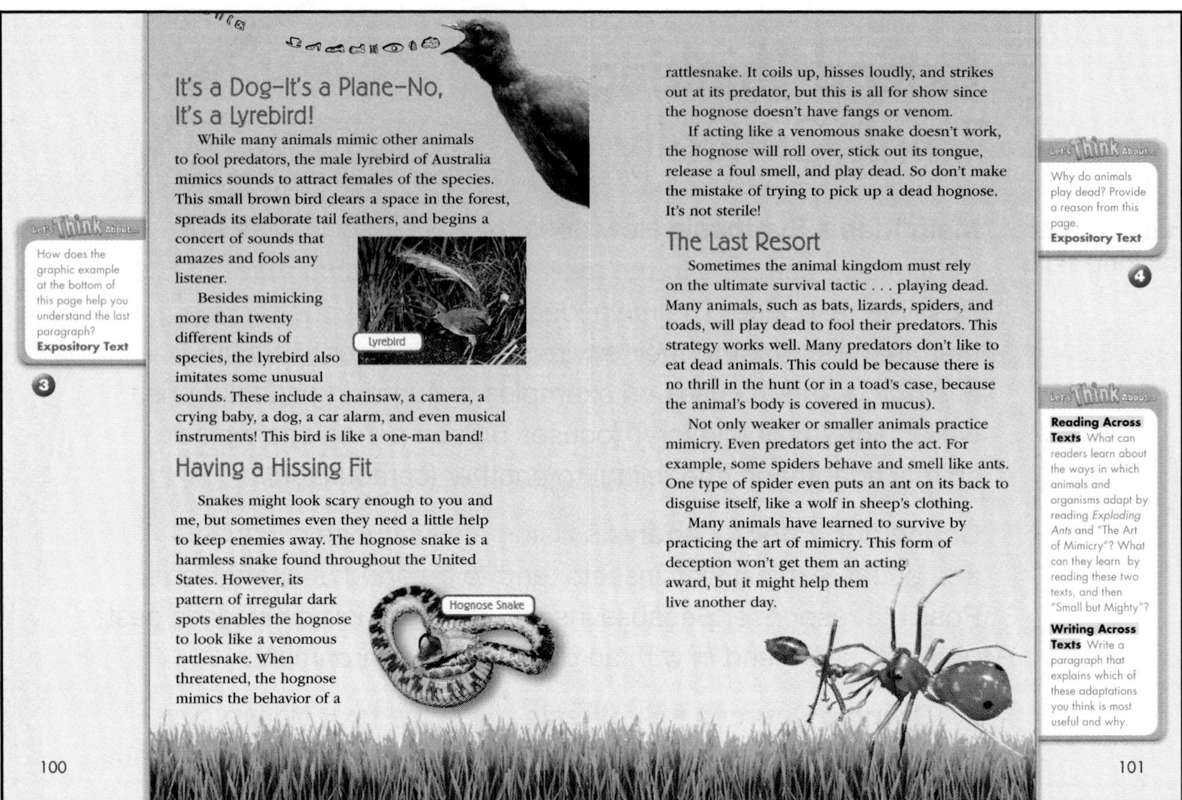

It's a Dog–It's a Plane–No, It's a Lyrebird!

While many animals mimic other animals to fool predators, the male lyrebird of Australia mimics sounds to attract females of the species. This small brown bird clears a space in the forest, spreads its elaborate tail feathers, and begins a concert of sounds that amazes and fools any listener.

Besides mimicking more than twenty different kinds of species, the lyrebird also imitates some unusual sounds. These include a chainsaw, a camera, a crying baby, a dog, a car alarm, and even musical instruments! This bird is like a one-man band!

Having a Hissing Fit

Snakes might look scary enough to you and me, but sometimes even they need a little help to keep enemies away. The hognose snake is a harmless snake found throughout the United States. However, its pattern of irregular dark spots enables the hognose to look like a venomous rattlesnake. When threatened, the hognose mimics the behavior of a rattlesnake. It coils up, hisses loudly, and strikes out at its predator, but this is all for show since the hognose doesn't have fangs or venom.

If acting like a venomous snake doesn't work, the hognose will roll over, stick out its tongue, release a foul smell, and play dead. So don't make the mistake of trying to pick up a dead hognose. It's not sterile!

The Last Resort

Sometimes the animal kingdom must rely on the ultimate survival tactic . . . playing dead. Many animals, such as bats, lizards, spiders, and toads, will play dead to fool their predators. This strategy works well. Many predators don't like to eat dead animals. This could be because there is no thrill in the hunt (or in a toad's case, because the animal's body is covered in mucus).

Not only weaker or smaller animals practice mimicry. Even predators get into the act. For example, some spiders behave and smell like ants. One type of spider even puts an ant on its back to disguise itself, like a wolf in sheep's clothing.

Many animals have learned to survive by practicing the art of mimicry. This form of deception won't get them an acting award, but it might help them live another day.

Let's Think About...

How does the graphic example at the bottom of this page help you understand the last paragraph? **Expository Text** 3

Let's Think About...

Why do animals play dead? Provide a reason from this page. **Expository Text** 4

Let's Think About...

Reading Across Texts What can readers learn about the ways in which animals and organisms adapt by reading *Exploding Ants* and "The Art of Mimicry"? What can they learn by reading these two texts, and then "Small but Mighty"?

Writing Across Texts Write a paragraph that explains which of these adaptations you think is most useful and why.

100 101

Student Edition pp. 100–101

Guide Comprehension

Skills and Strategies

Teach the genre

Expository Text: Text Structure Remind students that as they read, they should use the structure of the text to find the most important ideas. Ask: What important defense has nature given the hognose snake?

Corrective feedback

If... students cannot identify and summarize the important idea,
then... use the model to guide students in identifying the important idea.

Model the skill

The title of the section is "Having a Hissing Fit." The author says that the snake is harmless. I know from my reading that the rattlesnake, though, is poisonous. So, by looking similar to a rattlesnake and imitating it by coiling up, hissing, and striking when under attack, the hognose snake defends itself from predators by convincing predators that it's a rattlesnake. This is the important idea of that section.

On their own

Have students summarize other important ideas in the selection. Then have students synthesize and make logical connections among the important ideas in "The Art of Mimicry," *Exploding Ants,* and "Small But Mighty" on p. 81. (Possible response: The bacteria described in "Small But Mighty," the animals in "The Art of Mimicry," and the animals in *Exploding Ants* all make remarkable adaptations in order to survive.)

Extend Thinking
Think Critically

Higher-order thinking skills

Important Ideas • Analysis What is the main difference between the use of camouflage and the use of mimicry by animals? Make a logical connection. Possible response: Animals use camouflage to blend in with their environment and use mimicry to imitate another animal or object.

Draw Conclusions • Analysis Why might the lyrebird mimic sounds that aren't animal sounds? Possible response: The lyrebird might have adapted to living in areas where humans also live. Lyrebirds would hear sounds made by humans and then imitate those sounds.

Let's Think About...

3 I can see how the snake coils up and looks scary when it hisses.

4 Some animals pretend to be dead because their predators won't eat a dead animal.

Reading Across Texts

Have students create a T-chart of facts they learned about animal adaptations by reading *Exploding Ants* and "The Art of Mimicry." Have them draw lines to connect ideas from each column. Then have students add a third column of facts they learned from "Small but Mighty." Again, have them draw lines to connect ideas across all three columns.

Writing Across Texts

Have students use their charts to plan their paragraphs about animal adaptations. Have students discuss their paragraphs with a classmate as they write them.

Differentiated Instruction

SI Strategic Intervention
Have student pairs add facts to their T-charts. Students can reread the selections together to make sure they have included the important ideas about animal adaptations.

A Advanced
Have students choose a region of the world and find out several facts about one animal's adaptations to the environment within that region. They can write a paragraph about their findings.

Connect to Science

The Hawk Moth caterpillar can mimic a snake in order to scare off its enemies. The caterpillar also uses camouflage to blend in with leaves.

ELL

English Language Learners
Graphic organizer Provide support to students when creating a T-chart. Help them choose two heads for their T-charts. Then have them work together to add details in each column.

Objectives

- Read with fluency and comprehension.
- ◎ Use context clues to determine the meaning of synonyms.
- Create a description.

Check Fluency: WCPM
SUCCESS PREDICTOR

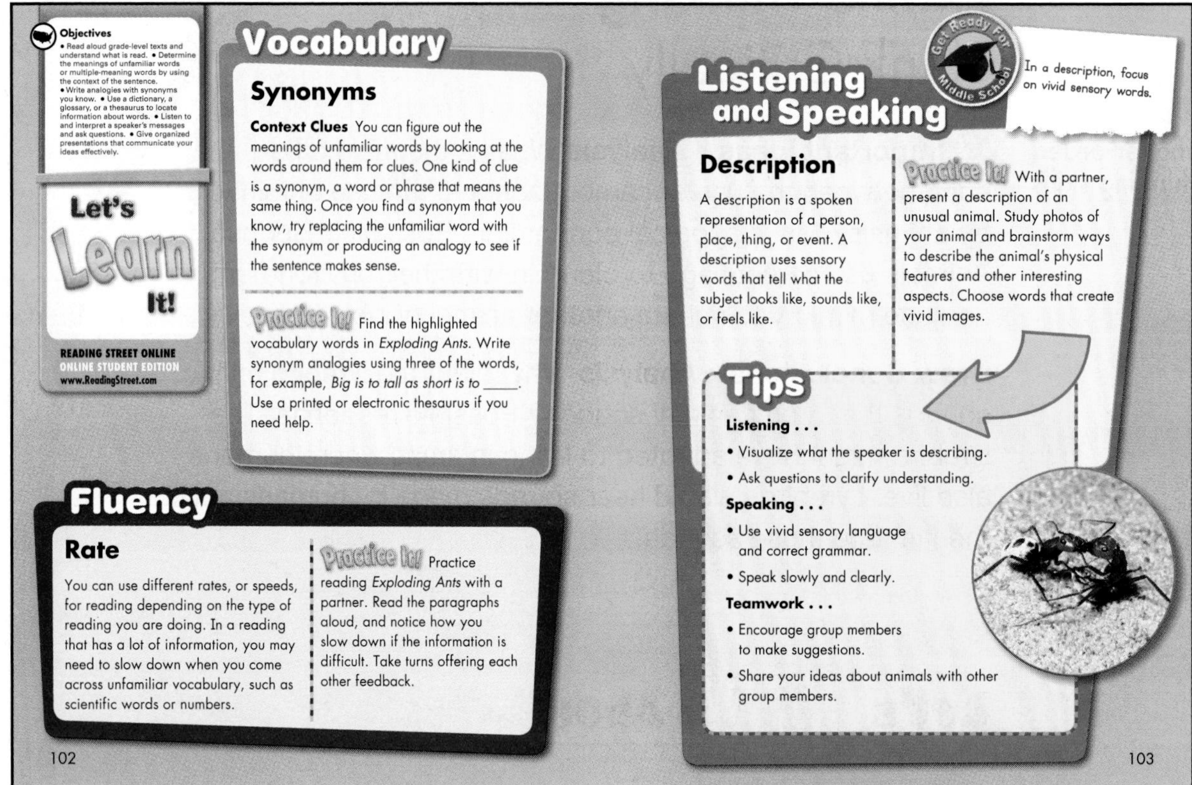

Student Edition pp. 102–103

Fluency
Rate

Guide practice Use the Student Edition activity as an assessment tool. Make sure the reading passage is at least 200 words in length. As students read aloud with partners, walk around to make sure their reading rate changes appropriately according difficulty of the passage and that students comprehend what they read.

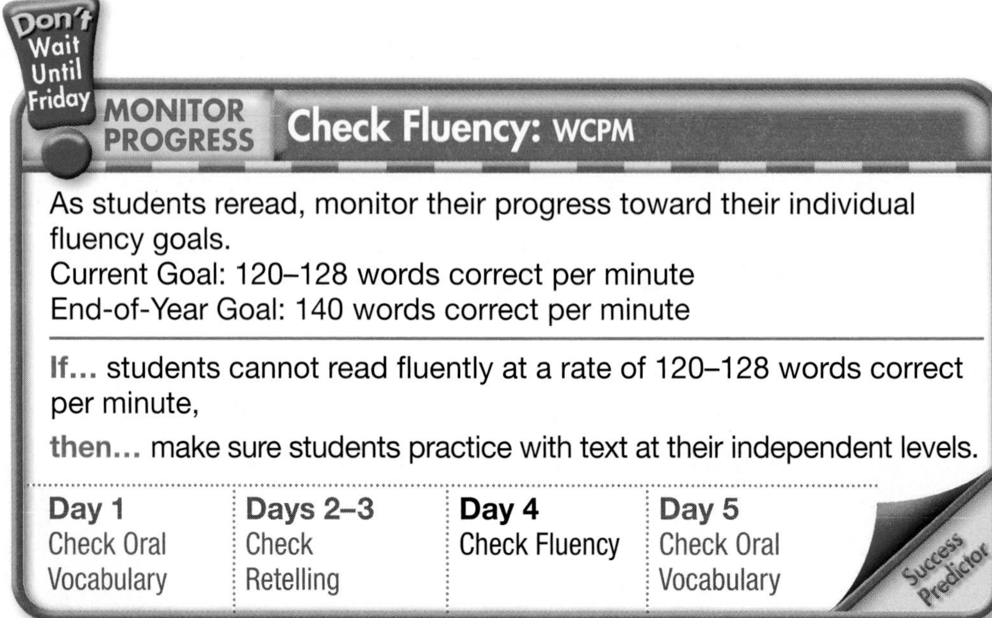

Don't Wait Until Friday — **MONITOR PROGRESS** — **Check Fluency: WCPM**

As students reread, monitor their progress toward their individual fluency goals.
Current Goal: 120–128 words correct per minute
End-of-Year Goal: 140 words correct per minute

If... students cannot read fluently at a rate of 120–128 words correct per minute,
then... make sure students practice with text at their independent levels.

Day 1	**Days 2–3**	**Day 4**	**Day 5**
Check Oral Vocabulary	Check Retelling	Check Fluency	Check Oral Vocabulary

Success Predictor

Vocabulary
 Synonyms

Teach context clues

Context Clues Write on the board: *Adaptations are critical to an animal's survival. Food and shelter are crucial also.* Write the analogy: *critical is to crucial as modeling is to* ______. Explain that you have provided the synonym *crucial* as a context clue to help students understand the word *critical.* Have students complete the analogy with the word *mimicry.*

Guide practice

Have students use a print of electronic thesaurus to find synonyms for the remaining vocabulary words. Have students produce an analogy for each vocabulary word and then write context sentences.

On their own

Have volunteers read their sentences aloud. Have other students identify the synonym and the context clues that helped them determine the meaning of the vocabulary word.

Listening and Speaking
Description

Teach

Tell students that in order for a description to be clear and effective, they must be organized and use vivid sensory words that help the listener visualize the subject. Remind listeners to visualize what the speaker is describing and to be ready to ask questions based on the description.

Guide practice

Remind students that good speakers maintain eye contact with listeners, speak at an appropriate rate and volume with clear enunciation, make natural gestures with their hands and body, and use proper conventions of language while speaking. Also remind the students to listen attentively to the speaker and to take notes to help them accurately interpret the speaker's verbal and nonverbal message. Listeners should determine the main idea and supporting ideas in the speaker's description.

On their own

Have students present their description with their partners.

Description

Remind students they should work cooperatively to share ideas with other group members, whether they are presenting orally or listening to another speaker. Tell students that listening carefully to each other and making suggestions will improve the outcome of the presentations.

ELL

English Language Learners

Practice pronunciation Assist pairs of students by modeling the correct pronunciation of the words from the thesaurus, then having students repeat after you.

Objectives

- Use a poster to present information.
- Review possessive pronouns.
- Spell homophones correctly.

Research and Inquiry
Synthesize

Teach

Have students synthesize their research results by creating a poster that summarizes their findings. They should type up relevant information about the animal's adaptations and include it either as a short description or as a bulleted list. They may want to refer to the picture in their description.

Guide practice

Check to see that students have chosen relevant pictures, and encourage them to write descriptions or lists that support the visual elements of the poster. They should emphasize the key adaptations that help the animal survive in its environment.

On their own

Have students work with a partner to be sure the pictures and text on their posters clearly communicate the animal's adaptations. Encourage them to practice their presentations with each other.

Conventions
Possessive Pronouns

Test practice Remind students that grammar skills, such as recognizing and using possessive pronouns correctly, are often assessed on important tests.

Remind students that a possessive pronoun takes the place of a possessive noun and shows who or what owns, or possesses, something, Possessive pronouns include *my, mine, your, yours, her, hers, his, its, our, ours, their,* and *theirs.*

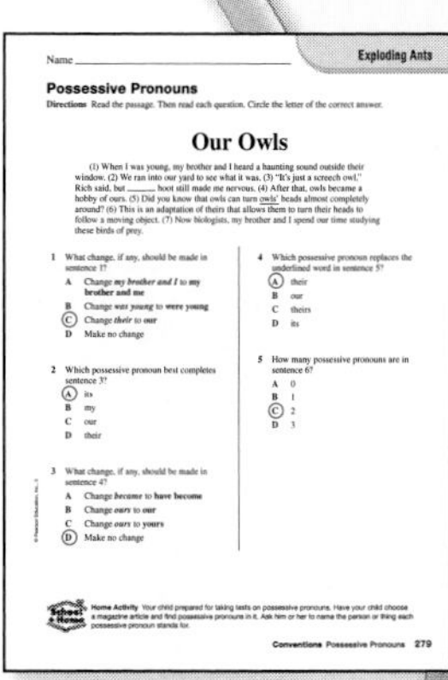
Name ______ Exploding Ants

Possessive Pronouns

Directions Read the passage. Then read each question. Circle the letter of the correct answer.

Our Owls

(1) When I was young, my brother and I heard a haunting sound outside their window. (2) We ran into our yard to see what it was. (3) "It's just a screech owl," Rich said, but ______ hoot still made me nervous. (4) After that, owls became a hobby of ours. (5) Did you know that owls can turn owls' heads almost completely around? (6) This is an adaptation of theirs that allows them to turn their heads to follow a moving object. (7) Now biologists, my brother and I spend our time studying these birds of prey.

1 What change, if any, should be made in sentence 1?
A Change *my brother and I* to **my brother and me**
B Change *was young* to **were young**
(C) Change *their* to **our**
D Make no change

2 Which possessive pronoun best completes sentence 3?
(A) its
B my
C our
D their

3 What change, if any, should be made in sentence 4?
A Change *became* to **have become**
B Change *ours* to **our**
C Change *ours* to **yours**
(D) Make no change

4 Which possessive pronoun replaces the underlined word in sentence 5?
(A) their
B our
C theirs
D its

5 How many possessive pronouns are in sentence 6?
A 0
B 1
(C) 2
D 3

School + Home **Home Activity** Your child prepared for taking tests on possessive pronouns. Have your child choose a magazine article and find possessive pronouns in it. Ask him or her to name the person or thing each possessive pronoun stands for.

Conventions Possessive Pronouns 279

Reader's and Writer's Notebook p. 279

Daily Fix-It Use Daily Fix-It numbers 7 and 8 in the right margin.

On their own For additional practice, use the *Reader's and Writer's Notebook* p. 279.

Spelling
Homophones

Practice spelling strategy Remind students that they must use the context of the sentence carrying the homophone in order to spell it correctly. Have partners write a sentence using each spelling word. Then have one student read aloud his or her sentence while the other student spells each homophone. Students can use an electronic or print dictionary to check their answers.

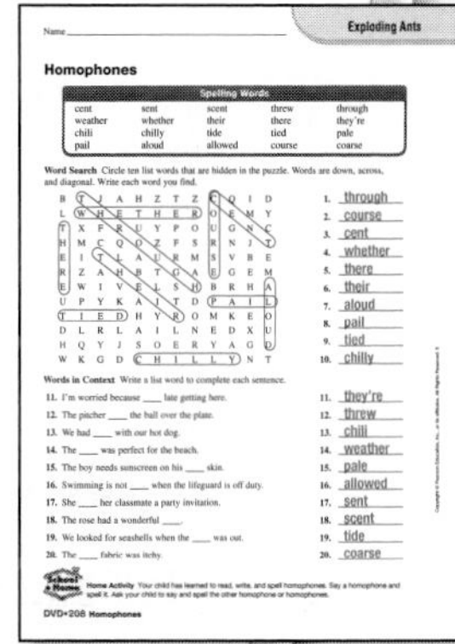
Name ______ Exploding Ants

Homophones

Spelling Words				
cent	sent	scent	threw	through
weather	whether	their	there	they're
chili	chilly	tide	tied	pale
pail	aloud	allowed	course	coarse

Word Search Circle ten list words that are hidden in the puzzle. Words are down, across, and diagonal. Write each word you find.

B T J A H Z T Z C Q I D
L W H E T H E R O E M Y
T X F R U Y P O U G N C
H M C Q O Z F S R N J T
E I T L A U R M S V B E
R Z A H B T G A E G E M
E W I V E L S H B R H A
U P Y K A I T D P A I L
T I E D H Y R O M K E O
D L R L A I L N E D X U
H Q Y J S O E R Y A G D
W K G D C H I L L Y N T

1. through
2. course
3. cent
4. whether
5. there
6. their
7. aloud
8. pail
9. tied
10. chilly

Words in Context Write a list word to complete each sentence.

11. I'm worried because ___ late getting here. — they're
12. The pitcher ___ the ball over the plate. — threw
13. We had ___ with our hot dog. — chili
14. The ___ was perfect for the beach. — weather
15. The boy needs sunscreen on his ___ skin. — pale
16. Swimming is not ___ when the lifeguard is off duty. — allowed
17. She ___ her classmate a party invitation. — sent
18. The rose had a wonderful ___. — scent
19. We looked for seashells when the ___ was out. — tide
20. The ___ fabric was itchy. — coarse

School + Home **Home Activity** Your child has learned to read, write, and spell homophones. Say a homophone and spell it. Ask your child to say and spell the other homophone or homophones.

DVD•208 **Homophones**

Let's Practice It! TR DVD•208

On their own For additional practice, use *Let's Practice It!* p. 208 on the *Teacher Resources DVD-ROM*.

Daily Fix-It

7. That fish is pail so it will blend in with the sandy ocean botem. *(pale; bottom)*
8. Animal bodies and behaviors are adapted to its environments. *(Animals'; their)*

Objectives

- Revise a draft of a formal letter.

Writing—Formal Letter
Revising Strategy

MINI-LESSON

Revising Strategy: Clarifying

- Yesterday you wrote a formal letter to a librarian requesting information about an interesting animal that you would like to know about. Today we will revise our drafts. The goal is to make the purpose of your letter and your ideas clear.

- Display Writing Transparency 18B. Remind students that revising does not include correcting errors in grammar and mechanics. Tell them that this work will be done when they proofread their work. Then introduce the revising strategy of clarifying.

Writing Transparency 18B, TR DVD

- Clarifying is the strategy in which you replace words with ones that make your ideas clearer. The first paragraph should clearly state the purpose of the letter. I will add the teacher's name and the reason that I am contacting Mr. Richard Townsend. In the second paragraph, I will explain what I already know about meerkats, so Mr. Townsend won't give me information I already have. In paragraph three, the word *Thanks* is too informal. I will change it to *Thank you*.

  Then have students revise the drafts of the letters they wrote yesterday to find places where they can make their ideas clearer.

Tell students that as they reread their drafts looking for ways to make their letters clearer and more focused, they should think about the action they want from the person who receives the letter to perform. What it is they would like to achieve with the letter?

Peer conferencing

Peer Revision Have pairs of students exchange letters for peer review. Each student reads the partner's letter and writes a few sentences summarizing what the partner's letter is specifically requesting.

Remind students that a formal letter communicates ideas, using formal language. Have them clarify any slang or casual language by using formal language. The last paragraph should also reflect a sense of closure.

Corrective feedback

Circulate around the room to monitor students and have conferences with them as they revise. Remind students correcting errors that they will have time to edit tomorrow. They should be working on content and organization today.

ROUTINE **Quick Write for Fluency** Team Talk

1. **Talk** Pairs discuss the unusual ways that animals adapt to survive.
2. **Write** Each person writes a few sentences explaining one animal's unusual adaptation.
3. **Share** Partners read each other's sentences.

Routines Flip Chart

Wrap Up Your Day

- ✔ **Build Concepts** Have students discuss how mimicry helps an animal survive.
- ✔ **Oral Vocabulary** Monitor students' use of oral vocabulary as they respond: How do adaptations help animals survive?
- ✔ **Text Features** Discuss how headings help students understand text.

Writers Write!

Student writers succeed in classrooms where they write. Simple, isn't it? Are you trying to meet some mandate or standard with such blinders on that you're forgetting daily writing? Students need to read every day and to write every day. Teachers do not need to read and assess everything that students write.

Differentiated Instruction

SI Strategic Intervention
If students have difficulty revising, have pairs work together to read their letters aloud and listen for places where more information is needed. Have partners suggest words that help clarify ideas.

Remind students to think about how animals adapt to survive.

Objectives
- Review the weekly concept.
- Review oral vocabulary.

Today at a Glance

Oral Vocabulary

Comprehension
◉ Graphic sources

Lesson Vocabulary
◉ Synonyms

Word Analysis
Suffix *–ize*

Literary Terms
Figurative language: Metaphor

Assessment
Fluency
Comprehension

Research and Inquiry
Communicate

Spelling
Homophones

Conventions
Possessive pronouns

Writing
Formal letter

Check Oral Vocabulary
SUCCESS PREDICTOR

Concept Wrap Up

Question of the Week

How do animals adapt to survive?

Review the concept

Have students look back at the reading selections to find examples that best demonstrate how animals adapt to their environment.

Review Amazing Words

Display and review this week's concept map. Remind students that this week they have learned ten Amazing Words related to animal adaptations. Have students use the Amazing Words and the concept map to answer the question *How do animals adapt to survive?*

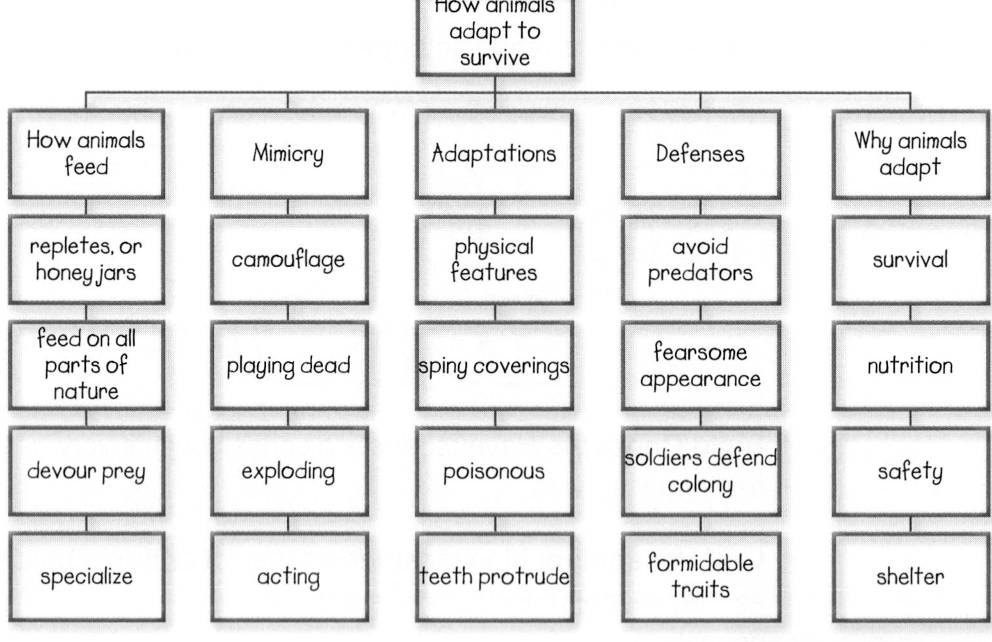

ELL Check Concepts and Language Use the Day 5 instruction on ELL Poster 18 to monitor students' understanding of the lesson concept.

ELL Poster 18

Amazing Ideas

Connect to the Big Question

Have pairs of students elicit suggestions from each other about how the Question of the Week connects to the Big Question: *How do people and animals adapt to different situations?* Tell students to use the concept map and what they have learned from this week's Anchored Talks and reading selections to form an Amazing Idea—a realization or "big idea" about adaptation in animal species. Then ask each pair to share their Amazing Idea with the class. Encourage students to listen to each other attentively and interpret each student's Amazing Idea. Have students ask questions of the speaking student to help clarify his or her perspective.

Amazing Ideas might include these key concepts:

- Both people and animals have to adapt to protect themselves.
- Nature is very inventive in providing living beings with defenses.
- Because animals specialize, there is a place for many species in our world.

Write about it

Have students write a few sentences about their Amazing Idea, beginning with "This week I learned...."

It's Friday

MONITOR PROGRESS Check Oral Vocabulary

Have individuals use this week's Amazing Words to describe animal adaptations. Monitor students' ability to use the Amazing Words and note which words you need to reteach.

If... students have difficulty using the Amazing Words,

then... reteach using the Oral Vocabulary Routine, pp. 77a, 80b, 90b, 98b, OV•3.

Day 1	**Days 2–3**	**Day 4**	**Day 5**
Check Oral Vocabulary	Check Summarizing	Check Fluency	Check Oral Vocabulary

Success Predictor

Amazing Words

adaptations	camouflage
predators	spiny
defenses	survival
fearsome	protrude
mimicry	formidable

ELL

English Language Learners

Concept map Work with students to add new words to the concept map.

Objectives

- Review graphic sources.
- Review synonyms.
- Review suffix -ize.
- Review figurative language and metaphor.

Comprehension Review

Graphic Sources

Teach graphic sources

Envision It!

Review the types of graphic sources discussed on p. 78. Remind students that graphic sources are tools that show information visually. Some graphic sources found in expository text include illustrations, captions, diagrams, labels, graphs, maps, and schedules. For additional support, have students review pp. EI•8–EI•9 on graphic sources.

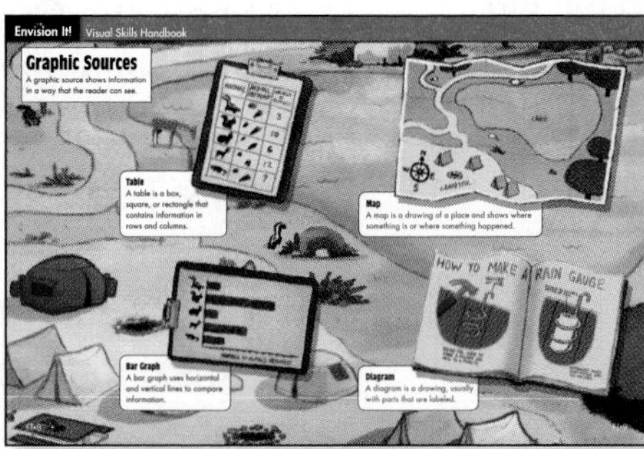

Student Edition pp. EI•8–EI•9

Guide practice

Have partners identify the graphic sources in *Exploding Ants.* Have student pairs look at the diagram and labels on p. 89 and discuss how this graphic source helps them gain an overview of the text and locate information. Then have pairs review the other graphic sources in *Exploding Ants* and explain how each adds information to the text.

On their own

For additional practice with graphic sources, use *Let's Practice It!* p. 209 on the *Teacher Resources DVD-ROM.*

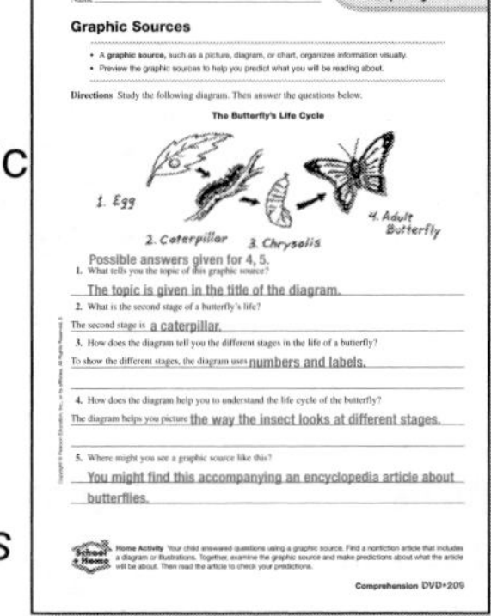
Name ______ Exploding Ants

Graphic Sources

- A **graphic source,** such as a picture, diagram, or chart, organizes information visually.
- Preview the graphic sources to help you predict what you will be reading about.

Directions Study the following diagram. Then answer the questions below.

The Butterfly's Life Cycle

1. Egg 2. Caterpillar 3. Chrysalis 4. Adult Butterfly

Possible answers given for 4, 5.

1. What tells you the topic of this graphic source?
   The topic is given in the title of the diagram.
2. What is the second stage of a butterfly's life?
   The second stage is a caterpillar.
3. How does the diagram tell you the different stages in the life of a butterfly?
   To show the different stages, the diagram uses numbers and labels.
4. How does the diagram help you to understand the life cycle of the butterfly?
   The diagram helps you picture the way the insect looks at different stages.
5. Where might you see a graphic source like this?
   You might find this accompanying an encyclopedia article about butterflies.

School + Home **Home Activity** Your child answered questions using a graphic source. Find a nonfiction article that includes a diagram or illustrations. Together, examine the graphic source and make predictions about what the article will be about. Then read the article to check your predictions.

Comprehension DVD•209

Let's Practice It!
TR DVD•209

Vocabulary Review

Synonyms

Teach synonyms

Remind students to look for synonyms in a text that can serve as context clues when they come across unfamiliar words and to consult a print or electronic thesaurus for more synonyms.

Guide practice

Review with students how to find the correct meaning of *enables* using a thesaurus. Explain that there may be more than one synonym for a word.

On their own

Have students work with partners to write analogies using the words *critical, mucus, scarce, specialize,* and *sterile* and their synonyms. Partners can trade their lists of analogies and confirm that the words are synonyms by consulting a print or electronic thesaurus.

Word Analysis Review
Suffix *-ize*

Teach suffix *-ize* Review suffixes and how Greek affixes can be added to nouns and adjectives to form verbs: *critic, criticize.*

Guide practice Display the following words: *specialize, terrorize,* and *socialize.* Use the Strategy for Meaningful Word Parts to determine the meaning of the word *specialize.*

ROUTINE Strategy for Meaningful Word Parts

1. **Introduce the word parts** Display the word *specialize.* Underline *special* and circle *-ize.*
2. **Connect to meaning** Define *special as* "particular." The suffix *-ize* means "to make or become."
3. **Read the word** Blend the word parts together to read *specialize*. Combined, they mean "to concentrate on a particular thing."

Continue the Routine with the words *terrorize* and *socialize*.

Routines Flip Chart

On their own Have students work in pairs to identify the base word in *terrorize* and *socialize* and determine the meaning of each word.

Literary Terms Review
Metaphor

Teach metaphor Have students review p. 86 of *Exploding Ants*. Remind them that a metaphor is a comparison of two seemingly unlike things that are actually alike in at least one way. For example, an animal that eats constantly could be called "an eating machine."

Guide practice Find an example of metaphor from *Exploding Ants. (honey jars)* Discuss why the author uses this metaphor in place of literal language.

On their own Have students make a T-chart with the headings *Figurative Language* and *Literal Language*. Ask them to record common metaphors and then translate them into literal phrases.

Lesson Vocabulary

critical extremely important
enables makes someone or something able to do an action
mucus slimy substance produced in the nose and throat to moisten and protect
scarce hard to get; rare
specialize to do one thing extremely well
sterile free from bacteria and other living things; totally clean

ELL

English Language Learners

Figurative language If students have trouble unpacking metaphors and other types of figurative language, ask, What is the writer comparing? Why are these two things alike in one or more ways? Which words help me to see this likeness?

Suffix *-ize* Supply students with a list of verbs with the suffix *-ize*. Have students circle the ending of each word. How does the ending change the base word? Then ask them to use the verb in a sentence.

DAY 5 Wrap Up your Week

15–20 mins.

Objectives

- Read grade-level text with fluency.

Assessment

Check words correct per minute

Fluency Make two copies of the fluency passage on page 103k. As the student reads the text aloud, mark mistakes on your copy. Also mark where the student is at the end of one minute. To figure words correct per minute (WCPM), subtract the number of mistakes from the total number of words read in one minute. To check the student's comprehension of the passage, have him or her retell what was read.

Corrective Feedback

If... students cannot read fluently at a rate of 120–128 WCPM or with comprehension,
then... make sure they practice with text at their independent reading level. Provide additional fluency practice by pairing nonfluent readers with fluent readers.

If... students already read at 140 WCPM,
then... then have them read a book of their choice independently.

Plan to Assess Fluency

- ☑ **Week 1** Assess Advanced students.
- ☑ **Week 2** Assess Strategic Intervention students.
- ☑ **This week assess On-Level students.**
- ☐ **Week 4** Assess Strategic Intervention students.
- ☐ **Week 5** Assess any students you have not yet checked during this unit.

Set individual goals for students to enable them to reach the year-end goal.

- Current Goal: 120–128 WCPM
- Year-End Goal: 140 WCPM

Small Group Time

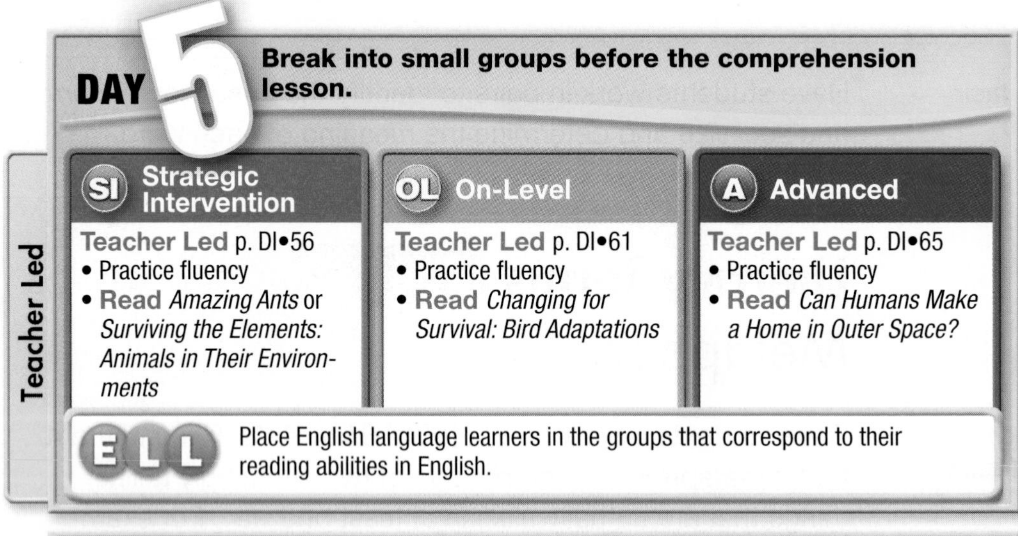

DAY 5
Break into small groups before the comprehension lesson.
Teacher Led
SI Strategic Intervention
Teacher Led p. DI•56
• Practice fluency
• Read Amazing Ants or Surviving the Elements: Animals in Their Environments
OL On-Level
Teacher Led p. DI•61
• Practice fluency
• Read Changing for Survival: Bird Adaptations
A Advanced
Teacher Led p. DI•65
• Practice fluency
• Read Can Humans Make a Home in Outer Space?
ELL
Place English language learners in the groups that correspond to their reading abilities in English.

Practice Stations

- Words to Know
- Get Fluent
- Read for Meaning

Independent Activities

- Grammar Jammer
- Concept Talk Video
- Vocabulary Activities

Name ______________________________

See How They Survive!

Survival for some animals means acting or looking like something else. 11
Brown-headed cowbirds, for instance, are the only birds in North America 22
that always lay their eggs in other birds' nests. More than 200 other species 36
are known to raise cowbirds' eggs. 42

The cowbird leaves a single egg in each nest. This egg usually hatches 55
before the other bird's eggs, giving the cowbird chick a good chance of 68
getting the most food. Some birds throw out the cowbird egg, but more raise 82
the chick along with their own. 88

In many insects, bright colors serve to scare away birds and other 100
animals. Large, black and orange Monarch butterflies, which migrate every 110
year between Mexico and breeding grounds in the north of North America, 122
feed on milkweed. These plants contain a poison. Any bird that fails to 135
heed the Monarch's bright orange warning color may learn too late that the 148
Monarch is not a treat but instead a dangerous meal. 158

The Viceroy butterfly looks so much like the Monarch that many people 170
can't tell them apart. Even though the Viceroy is not poisonous, its orange- 183
and-black warning colors protect it from most birds and other animals that 194
avoid the Monarch. This kind of defense, called *mimicry,* is common in the 207
insect world. 209

Survival in nature, then, is often more than meets the eye. 220

MONITOR PROGRESS

- **Check Fluency**

DAY 5 Wrap Up your Week 15–20 mins.

Objectives

- Read grade-level text with comprehension.

Assessment

Check graphic sources

Graphic sources Use “The Arctic Hare” on p. 103m to check students’ understanding of using graphic sources to find information.

1. Why is the arctic hare’s fur white in the winter? (It blends with the snow to camouflage it from predators.)
2. What is the main idea of this passage? (The arctic hare’s fur helps it survive.)
3. How does the graphic source “Climate in Eureka, Nunavut, Canada from 1971–2000” help the reader? (It helps the reader see the temperature and the amount of snow where the arctic hare lives.)
4. Using the chart “Climate in Eureka, Nunavut, Canada from 1971–2000,” what is the temperature in January where the arctic hare lives? (–37.1°C)

Corrective feedback

If... students are unable to answer the comprehension questions,
then... use the Reteach lesson in the *First Stop* book.

Name ______________________________

The Arctic Hare

The arctic hare lives in the frozen areas of North America, Newfoundland, and Greenland. The arctic hare's fur helps it survive both the cold winters.

The arctic hare's fur is its best defense against the freezing weather. In winter, the arctic hare grows two layers of fur. The short, thick bottom layer is called the underfur. On top of the underfur is another layer of long, silky fur. These two layers insulate the arctic hare.

The ever-changing color of the arctic hare's fur also protects the animal from predators. In the winter, it is bright white. The white fur blends perfectly with the snow and camouflages the arctic hare from its predators. In the cool summer, the arctic hare's color depends on where it lives. An arctic hare that lives where the summers are short has a sandy-brown or gray tone. An arctic hare that lives where the summers are longer has a brown and blue-gray tone. These colors help the arctic hare hide from its predators against the snow-free ground.

Although the arctic hare lives in a frigid and dangerous environment, its fur enables it to survive.

Climate in Eureka, Nunavut, Canada from 1971–2000

	January	April	June	September
Daily Average Temperature (°C)	–37.1	–27.4	2.3	–7.7
Snowfall (cm)	3.2	4.3	3.5	11
Average Depth of Snow (cm)	15	18	5	3

MONITOR PROGRESS

• Graphic Sources

DAY 5 Wrap Up your Week 10–15 mins.

Objectives
- Communicate inquiry results.
- Administer spelling test.
- Review possessive pronouns.

Research and Inquiry
Communicate

Present ideas Have students share their inquiry results by presenting their posters and giving brief talks about their research. Have students explain how the pictures illustrate the animals' survival adaptations.

Listening and speaking Remind students how to be good speakers and how to communicate effectively with their audience.

- Speak clearly and loudly, carefully enunciating words and using language appropriate for your audience to be sure everyone understands the presentation.
- Gesture at your poster as you talk about it.
- Keep eye contact with audience members.
- Respond to relevant questions with appropriate details.

Remind students of these tips for being a good listener.

- Listen to and interpret all of a speaker's messages, both verbal and nonverbal, in order to fully understand the presentation.
- Wait until the speaker has finished before raising your hand to ask a relevant question.

Spelling Test
Homophones

Spelling test To administer the spelling test, refer to the directions, words, and sentences on p. 79c.

Conventions
Extra Practice

Teach Remind students that possessive pronouns show who or what possesses, or owns, something.

- Use *my, your, her, our,* and *their* before nouns.
- Use *mine, yours, hers, ours,* and *theirs* alone.
- Use *his* and *its* before nouns and alone.

Guide practice Have students work with a partner to use possessive pronouns in the following sentences. Guide students in selecting the correct possessive pronouns.

- This rabbit is my/mine pet. (my)
- This rabbit is your/yours. (yours)
- This rabbit is us/our pet. (our)
- This rabbit is her/hers pet. (her)
- This rabbit is happy in it's/its cage. (its)
- This rabbit is theirs/there's. (theirs)

Daily Fix-It Use Daily Fix-It numbers 9 and 10 in the right margin.

On their own Write these sentences. Have students look back in *Exploding Ants* to find correct possessive pronouns to fill in the blanks. Students should complete *Let's Practice It!* p. 210 on the *Teacher Resources DVD-ROM.*

1. **They make ____ homes in disgusting places and feed on mucus and blood.** (their)
2. **They swell or blow up ____ body parts.** (their)
3. **Most of ____ food is just the fur and bones that get chucked up as round pellets.** (its)

Daily Fix-It

9. On saturday morning you can bring you dog for training. *(Saturday; your)*
10. Dogs are allways aloud in the pet store. *(always allowed)*

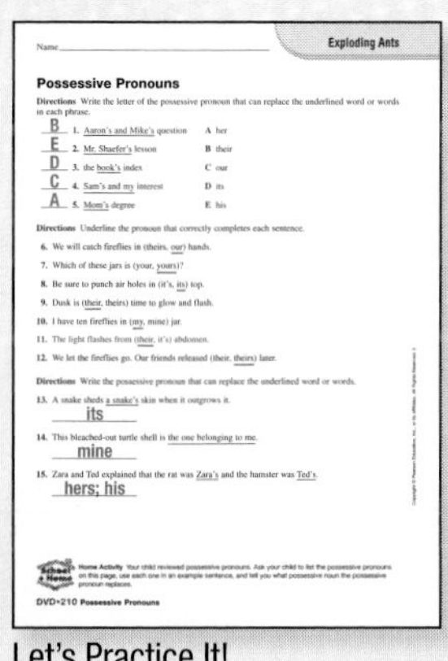
Name____________ Exploding Ants

Possessive Pronouns

Directions Write the letter of the possessive pronoun that can replace the underlined word or words in each phrase.

B 1. Aaron's and Mike's question — A her
E 2. Mr. Shaefer's lesson — B their
D 3. the book's index — C our
C 4. Sam's and my interest — D its
A 5. Mom's degree — E his

Directions Underline the pronoun that correctly completes each sentence.

6. We will catch fireflies in (theirs, our) hands.
7. Which of these jars is (your, yours)?
8. Be sure to punch air holes in (it's, its) top.
9. Dusk is (their, theirs) time to glow and flash.
10. I have ten fireflies in (my, mine) jar.
11. The light flashes from (their, it's) abdomen.
12. We let the fireflies go. Our friends released (their, theirs) later.

Directions Write the possessive pronoun that can replace the underlined word or words.

13. A snake sheds a snake's skin when it outgrows it. its
14. This bleached-out turtle shell is the one belonging to me. mine
15. Zara and Ted explained that the rat was Zara's and the hamster was Ted's. hers; his

Home Activity Your child reviewed possessive pronouns. Ask your child to list the possessive pronouns on this page, use each one in an example sentence, and tell you what possessive noun the possessive pronoun replaces.

DVD•210 Possessive Pronouns

Let's Practice It!
TR DVD•210

DAY 5 Wrap Up your Week 20–25 mins.

Objectives

- Proofread formal letters.
- Create a final draft.

Writing—Formal Letter
Possessive Pronouns

Review Revising Remind students that yesterday they revised their formal letters to a librarian, paying particular attention to clarifying their ideas. Today they will proofread their formal letters. Display Writing Transparency 18C.

MINI-LESSON

Proofreading for Possessive Nouns

- **Teach** When we proofread, we look closely at our work, searching for errors in spelling, capitalization, punctuation, and grammar. Today we will focus on proofreading for conventions and correct use of possessive pronouns.

- **Model** When we revise a formal letter, we make sure the letter begins with a heading that includes the date. A formal letter must also include the name of the person you're writing to. Look at the writer's address at the top. The date is missing. Next, I notice that the salutation in Mrs. Moleen's letter begins with *Dear Richard* and uses a comma instead of a colon. The salutation should include a last name along with a title, such as *Mr., Mrs., Ms.,* or *Miss*. I notice that the first and third paragraphs contain the possessive pronouns *my* and *your*.

  I see spelling errors in paragraphs one and three. There is a missing comma after *snakes* in paragraph two. The word *sincerely* should be capitalized and I'll add a comma after *yours.*

- **Proofread** Have students proofread their formal letters.

Writing Transparency 18C, TR DVD

Proofread Display the Proofreading Tips. Ask students to proofread their formal letters, paying particular attention to conventions and possessive pronouns. Circulate around the room answering students' questions. When students have finished editing their own work, have pairs proofread one another's formal letters.

Proofreading Tips

- ✔ Be sure you use possessive pronouns correctly.
- ✔ Check for the correct use of conventions in a formal letter.
- ✔ Check capitalization.
- ✔ Reread for spelling errors.

Present

Have students incorporate revisions and proofreading edits into their formal letters to create a final draft.

Give students two options for presenting: An oral presentation to the class or, if you have provided the student with the name of a real librarian, consider mailing the letters, providing you have cleared it with the librarian first.

ROUTINE **Quick Write for Fluency** Team Talk

1. **Talk** Pairs discuss what they learned about writing formal letters and how they could use this knowledge in the future.
2. **Write** Each person writes a paragraph summarizing what they learned.
3. **Share** Partners read their summaries to one another.

Routines Flip Chart

Teacher Note

Writing Self-Evaluation Guide Make copies of the Writing Self-Evaluation Guide on p. 39 of the *Reader's and Writer's Notebook* and hand out to students.

ELL

English Language Learners

Poster preview Prepare students for next week by using Week 4 ELL Poster 19. Read the Poster Talk-Through to introduce the concept and vocabulary. Ask students to identify and describe objects and actions in the art.

Selection summary Send home the summary of *The Stormi Giovanni Club,* in English and the students' home languages, if available. Students can read the summary with family members.

Preview NEXT WEEK

How do people adapt to new places? You will read a play about a girl who attends a new school.

Assessment Checkpoints for the Week

Weekly Assessment

Use pp. 127–134 of *Weekly Tests* to check:

✔ **Word Analysis** Suffix *-ize*

✔ **Comprehension Skill** Graphic Sources

✔ Review **Comprehension Skill** Author's Purpose

✔ **Lesson Vocabulary**

critical	scarce
enables	specialize
mucus	sterile

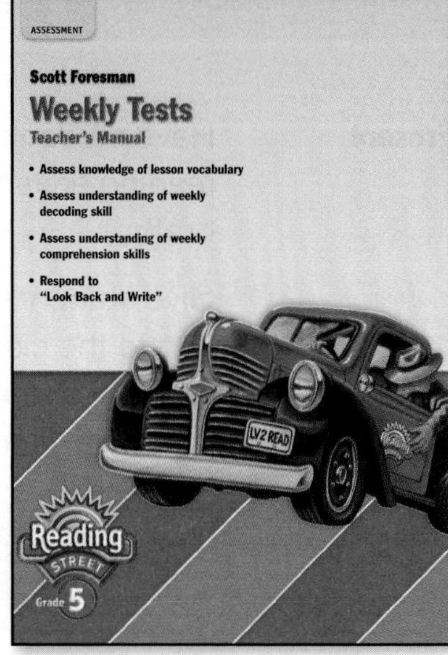

Weekly Tests

Differentiated Assessment

Advanced

On-Level

SI
Strategic Intervention

Use pp. 103–108 of *Fresh Reads for Fluency and Comprehension* to check:

✔ **Comprehension Skill** Graphic Sources

✔ Review **Comprehension Skill** Author's Purpose

✔ **Fluency** Words Correct Per Minute

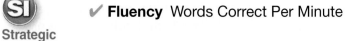

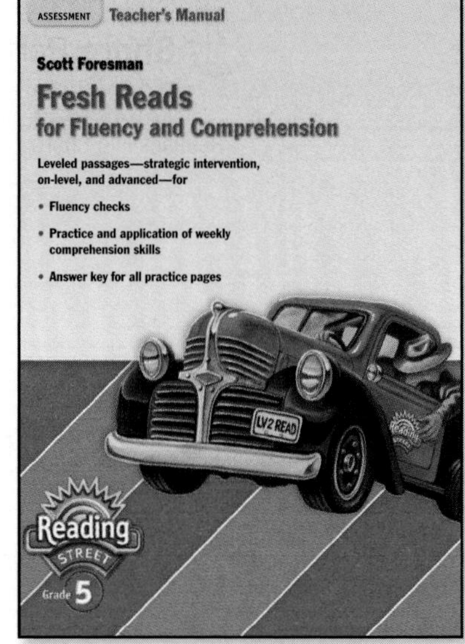

Fresh Reads for Fluency and Comprehension

Managing Assessment

Use *Assessment Handbook* for:

✔ **Weekly Assessment Blackline Masters for Monitoring Progress**

✔ **Observation Checklists**

✔ **Record-Keeping Forms**

✔ **Portfolio Assessment**

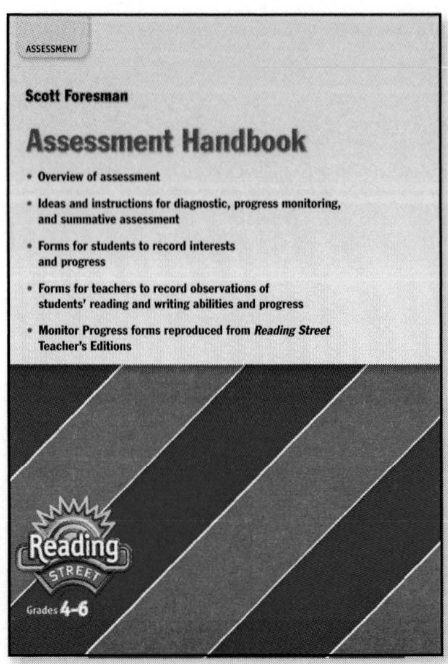

Assessment Handbook

Read Aloud (continued)

Escape Artists

Continued from p. 77b

sharp-toothed moray eel. The bigger fish then usually swims off to look for a meal that isn't as scary.

Pacing Small Group Instruction

5-Day Plan

DAY 1	• Reinforce the concept • Read Leveled Readers Concept Literacy Below Level
DAY 2	• Graphic Sources • Important Ideas • Revisit Student Edition pp. 82–89
DAY 3	• Synonyms • Revisit Student Edition pp. 90–93
DAY 4	• Practice Retelling • Read/Revisit Student Edition pp. 98–101
DAY 5	• Reread for fluency • Reread Leveled Readers

3- or 4-Day Plan

DAY 1	• Reinforce the concept • Read Leveled Readers
DAY 2	• Graphic Sources • Important Ideas • Revisit Student Edition pp. 82–89
DAY 3	• Synonyms • Revisit Student Edition pp. 90–93
DAY 4	• Practice Retelling • Read/Revisit Student Edition pp. 98–101 • Reread for fluency • Reread Leveled Readers

3-Day Plan: Eliminate the shaded box.

DAY 1

Build Background

- **Reinforce the Concept** Connect to the weekly question *How do animals adapt to survive?* Discuss with students what they know about how animals adapt to winter. For example, some animals migrate to warmer climates, others grow thicker fur, and still others sleep through the coldest part of winter. Then discuss how animals might have to change if their environment becomes drier or wetter. This week's concept is *animal adaptation.* Animals have to adapt, or change, to survive in their environments. Discuss the words on the concept map on p. 76–77 in the Teacher Edition.

- **Connect to Reading** Ask students to think of an animal that lives in an extreme environment, such as a desert or swamp. Discuss with them what physical traits the animals might need to live in such places. This week you will read about many different kinds of animals that have adapted to their environments in order to survive. What ways might animals have adapted to survive? *(possible answers: camouflage; ability to go without drinking for long periods of time; poison to defend themselves and kill prey; different types of claws and teeth)*

Objectives

- Interpret a speaker's messages (both verbal and nonverbal).

DAY 1

For a complete literacy instructional plan and additional practice with this week's target skills and strategies, see the **Leveled Reader Teaching Guide.**

Concept Literacy Reader

- **Read** *Amazing Ants*
- **Before Reading** Preview the book with students, focusing on key concepts and vocabulary. Then have them set a purpose for reading.
- **During Reading** Read the first two pages of the book aloud while students track the print. Then have students finish reading the book with a partner.
- **After Reading** After students finish reading the book, connect it to the weekly question *How do animals adapt to survive?*

Below-Level Reader

- **Read** *Surviving the Elements: Animals in Their Environments*
- **Before Reading** Have students preview the book, using the pictures. Then have students set a purpose for reading.
- **During Reading** Do a choral reading of the pages.
  - Name two differences between animals in the Arctic and animals in the desert. *(possible responses: Arctic = thick winter coats, hibernate; Desert = stay cool; need little water)*
  - How have animals adapted to survive in savannas? *(Possible response: Elephants get water from the baobab tree, and lions live in prides.)*
  - How have animals adapted to survive in rain forests? *(Possible response: Some animals live in trees to avoid predators.)*
- **After Reading** Have students look at and discuss the concept map. Connect the Below-Level Reader to the weekly question *How do animals adapt to survive?* What are some general ways that animals adapt to their environments?

MONITOR PROGRESS

If... students have difficulty reading the selection with a partner,
then... have them follow along as they listen to the Leveled Readers DVD-ROM.

If... students have trouble understanding how animals specialize,
then... reread p. 16 and discuss how elephants are specialists in getting water from baobab trees.

Objectives

- Interpret a speaker's messages (both verbal and nonverbal).

Reinforce Comprehension

Skill Graphic Sources Review with students *Envision It!* pp. EI•8–EI•9 on Graphic Sources. Then use p. 78 to review the definition of graphic sources.

Graphic sources can help you understand information in a text. Photographs and illustrations can help you visualize something the writer describes, while diagrams can show you the parts of something or how something works. Charts provide a quick, visual way to present a lot of information in a small space.

Strategy Important Ideas Review the definition of important ideas. For additional support, refer students to *Envision It!* p. EI•17.

Revisit *Exploding Ants* on pp. 82–89. Have students begin reading aloud with a partner. As they read, encourage them to apply the comprehension skill and strategy to the selection.

- What kinds of graphic sources are used in this selection? *(photographs and drawings)*
- How do these sources help you understand the text? *(They give examples of how animals get food and protect themselves.)*
- What details does the diagram on p. 89 show? *(It shows the different parts of the exploding ant.)*
- How do diagrams help you understand the text better? *(They show more details about the parts of animals that are talked about in the text.)*

Use the During Reading Differentiated Instruction for additional support for struggling readers.

MONITOR PROGRESS

If... students have difficulty reading along with the group,
then... have them follow along as they listen to the AudioText.

Objectives

- Use graphics to gain an overview of the contents of text.
- Summarize main ideas in a text in ways that maintain meaning.

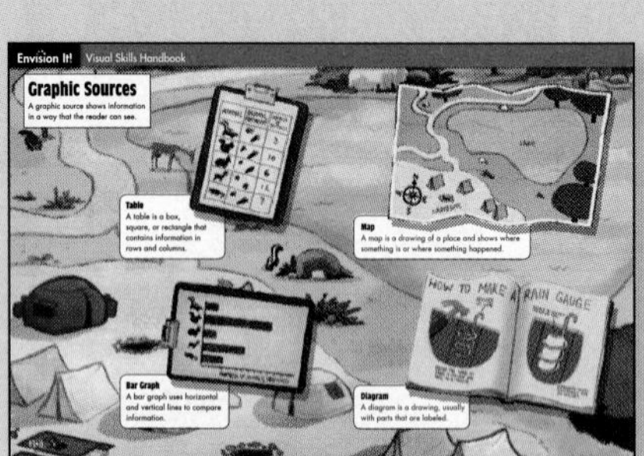

Student Edition pp. EI•8–EI•9

More Reading

Use additional Leveled Readers or other texts at students' instructional levels to reinforce this week's skills and strategies. For text suggestions, see the Leveled Reader Database or the Leveled Readers Skills Chart on pp. CL 24–CL 29.

DAY 3

Reinforce Vocabulary

Synonyms/Context Clues Say the following sentence aloud as you write it on the board: "Many animals adapt by camouflaging themselves in their environment, or blending in to hide." Underline the word *camouflaging* and circle the word *or* and the phrase *blending in to hide.*

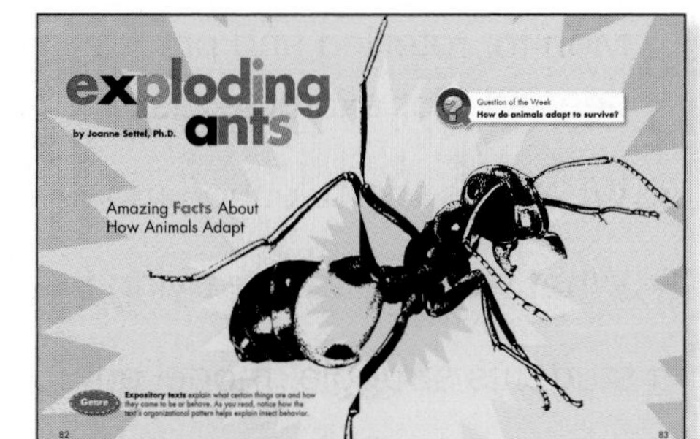

When I see the word *camouflaging,* I look for context clues to help me find the word's meaning. Sometimes writers provide synonyms, or words and phrases that mean the same thing as the unfamiliar word. Clue words such as *or* can help me find synonyms. In this sentence, I see that the phrase *blending in to hide* is a synonym for *camouflaging.*

Revisit *Exploding Ants* on pp. 90–93. Review *Words!* on pp. W•3 and W•7. As students finish reading the selection, encourage them to look for context clues with synonyms to help them figure out unfamiliar words.

- Point out the word *mandibles* on p. 88.
- What clue word in the same sentence can help you find a synonym for *mandibles?* *(or)*
- What is the synonym? *(jaws)*
- What does *mandibles* mean? *(the jaws of the ant)*

Use the During Reading Differentiated Instruction for additional support for struggling readers.

MONITOR PROGRESS

If... students need more practice with the lesson vocabulary,
then... use *Envision It! Pictured Vocabulary Cards.*

Student Edition, p. W•3

More Reading

Use additional Leveled Readers or other texts at students' instructional levels to reinforce this week's skills and strategies. For text suggestions, see the Leveled Reader Database or the Leveled Readers Skills Chart on pp. CL 24–CL 29.

Objectives

- Use context and synonyms to determine the meaning of an unknown word.
- Use context to determine the meaning of unfamiliar words.

Practice Retelling

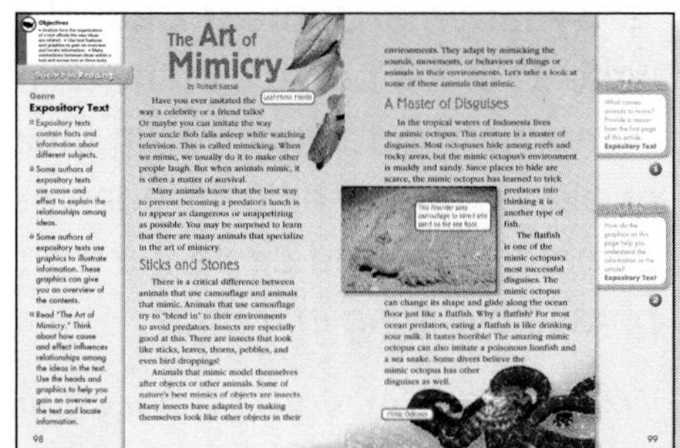

Genre
Expository Text
- Expository texts contain facts and information about different subjects.
- Some authors of expository texts use cause and effect to explain the relationships among ideas.
- Some authors of expository texts use graphics to illustrate information. These graphics can give you an overview of the contents.
- Read "The Art of Mimicry." Think about how cause and effect influences relationships among the ideas in the text. Use the heads and graphics to help you gain an overview of the text and locate information.

98

The Art of Mimicry

Have you ever imitated the way a celebrity or a friend talks? Or maybe you can imitate the way your uncle Bob falls asleep while watching television. This is called mimicking. When we mimic, we usually do it to make other people laugh. But when animals mimic, it is often a matter of survival.

Many animals know that the best way to prevent becoming a predator's lunch is to appear as dangerous or unappetizing as possible. You may be surprised to learn that there are many animals that specialize in the art of mimicry.

Sticks and Stones

There is a critical difference between animals that use camouflage and animals that mimic. Animals that use camouflage try to "blend in" to their environments to avoid predators. Insects are especially good at this. There are insects that look like sticks, leaves, thorns, pebbles, and even bird droppings!

Animals that mimic model themselves after objects or other animals. Some of nature's best mimics of objects are insects. Many insects have adapted by making themselves look like other objects in their environments. They adapt by mimicking the sounds, movements, or behaviors of things or animals in their environments. Let's take a look at some of these animals that mimic.

A Master of Disguises

In the tropical waters of Indonesia lives the mimic octopus. This creature is a master of disguises. Most octopuses hide among reefs and rocky areas, but the mimic octopus's environment is muddy and sandy. Since places to hide are scarce, the mimic octopus has learned to trick predators into thinking it is another type of fish.

The flatfish is one of the mimic octopus's most successful disguises. The mimic octopus can change its shape and glide along the ocean floor just like a flatfish. Why a flatfish? For most ocean predators, eating a flatfish is like drinking sour milk. It tastes horrible! The amazing mimic octopus can also imitate a poisonous lionfish and a sea snake. Some divers believe the mimic octopus has other disguises as well.

Expository Text 1

Expository Text 2

99

- **Retell** Have students work in pairs and use the Retelling Cards to retell *Exploding Ants.* Monitor retelling and prompt students as needed. For example, ask:

- What was the selection mostly about?
- What was the author trying to teach us?

If students struggle, model a fluent retelling.

Genre Focus

- **Before Reading or Revisiting** "The Art of Mimicry" on pp. 98–101, read aloud the genre information about expository text on p. 98. Some texts tell you how to do something, others explain how something works, and still others provide information on an interesting topic. Some expository text includes graphics to help the reader understand the material. Then have students preview "The Art of Mimicry." Look at the captions. What information do they give you? *(the names of the animals; in one case, an explanation of what the animal is doing)* Then have students set a purpose for reading based on their preview.
- **During Reading or Revisiting** Have students read along with you while tracking the print or do a choral reading of the article. Stop to discuss any unfamiliar words, such as *venomous* and *sterile.*
- **After Reading or Revisiting** Have students share their reactions to the article. Then guide them through the Reading Across Texts and Writing Across Texts activities.

MONITOR PROGRESS

If... students have difficulty retelling the selection,
then... have them review the selection using the photos and text features.

Objectives

- Synthesize ideas across two or three texts representing similar or different genres.

For a complete literacy instructional plan and additional practice with this week's target skills and strategies, see the **Leveled Reader Teaching Guide.**

Concept Literacy Reader

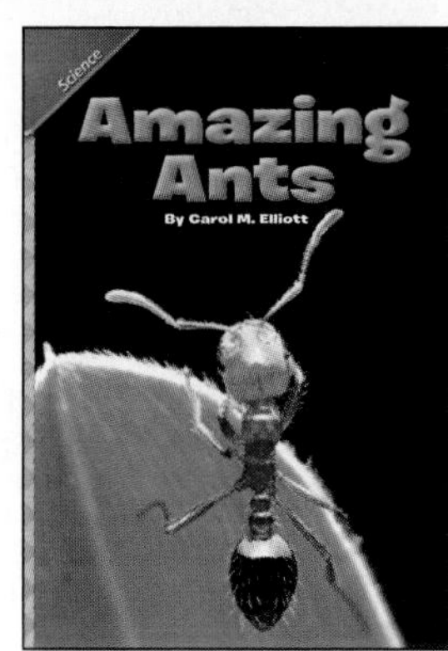

- **Model** Model the fluency skill of rate for students. Ask students to listen carefully as you read aloud the first several pages of *Amazing Ants.* Have students note how you slow down your rate to make sure listeners can hear important information.
- **Fluency Routine**
  1. Have students reread passages from *Amazing Ants* with a partner.
  2. For optimal fluency, students should reread three to four times.
  3. As students read, monitor fluency and provide corrective feedback. Encourage students to practice pronouncing difficult words before they read aloud so that they can read at a steady rate.

See *Routines Flip Chart* for more help with fluency.

- **Retell** Have students retell *Amazing Ants.* Prompt as necessary.

Below-Level Reader

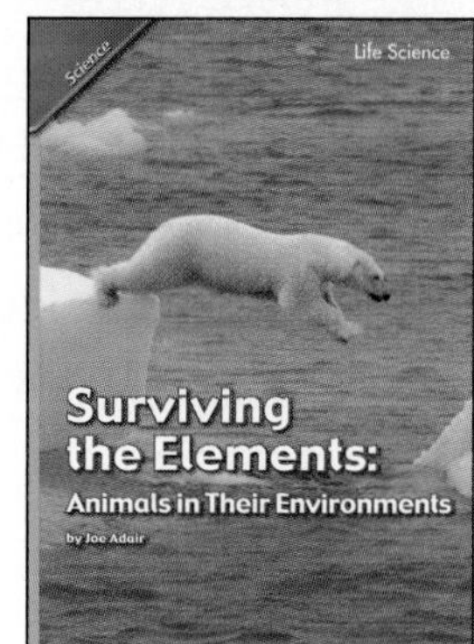

- **Model** Ask students to listen carefully as you read aloud the first two pages of *Surviving the Elements: Animals in Their Environments,* emphasizing rate.
- **Fluency Routine**
  1. Have students reread passages from *Surviving the Elements: Animals in Their Environments* with a partner or individually.
  2. For optimal fluency, students should reread three to four times.
  3. As students read, monitor fluency and provide corrective feedback. Point out that when you read scientific information that may be new to both readers and audience, it's important to slow down so that everyone grasps the concepts and understands the text.

See *Routines Flip Chart* for more help with fluency.

- **Retell** For additional practice, have students retell *Surviving the Elements: Animals in Their Environments* page-by-page, using the pictures. Prompt as necessary.

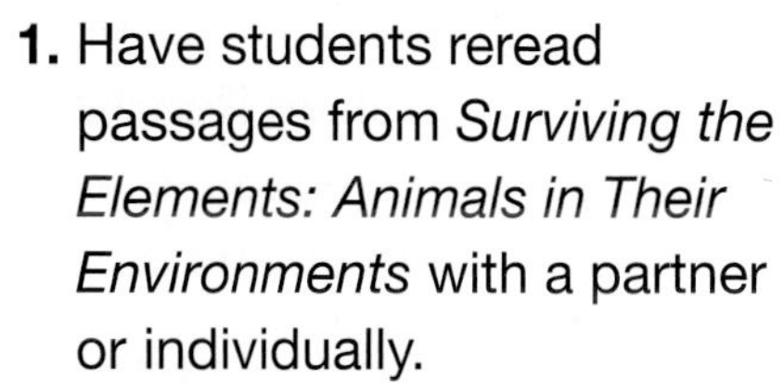

MONITOR PROGRESS

If... students have difficulty reading fluently,
then... provide additional fluency practice by pairing nonfluent readers with fluent ones.

Objectives

- Read aloud grade-level stories with fluency.

Pacing Small Group Instruction

5-Day Plan

DAY 1	• Expand the concept • Read On-Level Reader
DAY 2	• Graphic Sources • Important Ideas • Revisit Student Edition pp. 82–89
DAY 3	• Synonyms • Revisit Student Edition pp. 90–93
DAY 4	• Practice Retelling • Read/Revisit Student Edition pp. 98–101
DAY 5	• Reread for fluency • Reread On-Level Reader

3- or 4-Day Plan

DAY 1	• Expand the concept • On-Level Reader
DAY 2	• Graphic Sources • Important Ideas • Revisit Student Edition pp. 82–89
DAY 3	• Synonyms • Revisit Student Edition pp. 90–93
DAY 4	• Practice Retelling • Read/Revisit Student Edition pp. 98–101 • Reread for fluency • Reread On-Level Reader

3-Day Plan: Eliminate the shaded box.

OL On-Level DAY 1

Build Background

■ **Expand the Concept** Connect the weekly question *How do animals adapt to survive?* and expand the concept. Animals need to adapt to their environments for many reasons: to find shelter, to get food and water, and to protect themselves from predators. Discuss the meaning of the words on the concept map on p. 77.

On-Level Reader

For a complete literacy instructional plan and additional practice with this week's target skills and strategies, see the **Leveled Reader Teaching Guide.**

■ **Before Reading** *Changing for Survival: Bird Adaptations* have students preview the reader by looking at the title, cover, and pictures in the book. Ask:

- What is the topic of this book? *(how birds adapt to survive in their environments)*
- Why do you think the pictures show different types of environments? *(because the book will be about birds that live in different places)*

Have students create a KWL chart with the topic head *Birds.* Have them fill out the columns for What I Know (K) and What I Want to Know (W).

This book tells a lot about different types of birds. As you read, look for facts you learned to add to the third column of your chart (L). Jot down facts you think are most important.

■ **During Reading** Have students follow along as you read aloud pp. 3–9. Then let them finish reading the book on their own. Remind students to add facts to the What I Learned column on their KWL charts as they read.

■ **After Reading** Have partners compare information from their KWL charts.

- What was the most interesting bird adaptation you learned about in this book?
- How does the book relate to the weekly question *How do animals adapt to survive? (It tells how different birds adapt to survive in different habitats.)*

Objectives

- Interpret a speaker's messages (both verbal and nonverbal).

On-Level

DAY 2

Expand Comprehension

Skill Graphic Sources Use p. 78 to review the definition of graphic sources. For additional review, see pp. EI•8–EI•9 in *Envision It!* Remind students that graphic sources can help them understand a text by displaying information in a chart or diagram or by showing examples in photographs and drawings.

Strategy Important Ideas Review the definition of important ideas. Encourage students to look for important ideas in the headings and topic sentences that will help them understand the topic as they read. For additional support, use the Extend Thinking questions and refer students to *Envision It!* p. EI•17.

exploding ants
by Joanne Settel, Ph.D.
Amazing Facts About How Animals Adapt

Revisit *Exploding Ants* on pp. 82–89. As students begin reading aloud, encourage them to apply the comprehension skill and strategy to the selection.

- What information does the photograph on p. 89 give you that you cannot get from the text? *(what a honey ant nest looks like from the outside)*
- What information does the diagram on p. 89 give you? *(It shows what the inside of an exploding ant looks like; it shows the location of two important body parts.)*

Objectives

- Use graphics to gain an overview of the contents of text.
- Summarize main ideas in a text in ways that maintain meaning.

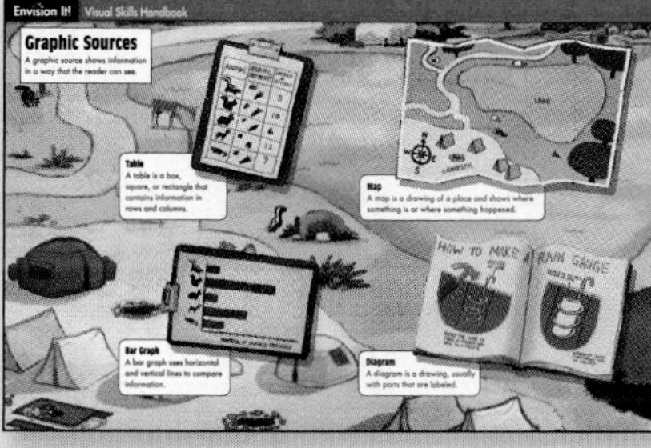

Student Edition pp. EI•8–EI•9

More Reading

Use additional Leveled Readers or other texts at students' instructional levels to reinforce this week's skills and strategies. For text suggestions, see the Leveled Reader Database or the Leveled Readers Skills Chart on pp. CL 24–CL 29.

Student Edition, p. W•3

More Reading

Use additional Leveled Readers or other texts at students' instructional levels to reinforce this week's skills and strategies. For text suggestions, see the Leveled Reader Database or the Leveled Readers Skills Chart on pp. CL 24–CL 29.

Expand Vocabulary

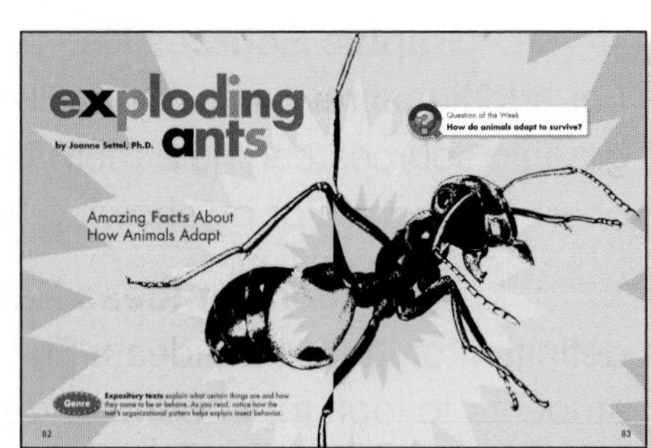

Synonyms/Context Clues Remind students that synonyms for unfamiliar words can often be found by looking for clue words, such as *like* and *or.* Write this sentence on the board: "Each replete receives regurgitated, or spit-up, food from hundred of ordinary worker ants." Then ask:

- What clue word do you see in this sentence? *(or)*
- What word or phrase can you find that is a synonym for the word *regurgitated? (spit-up)*
- What does this tell you about the meaning of *regurgitated food* in this sentence? *(It means food that has been eaten and spit up by worker ants.)*

Then read the following sentence on p. 88: "The chemicals are stored in two big sacs called *mandibular glands.*"

- Read the rest of the paragraph on page 88. What synonym can you find to help you figure out what *mandibular* means? *(The next sentence says the glands are just under the "mandibles, or jaws."* Jaws *is a synonym for* mandibles.*)*
- Now what do you think *mandibular glands* means? *("glands that are near the ant's jaws")*

Revisit *Exploding Ants* on pp. 90–93. As students finish reading the selection, encourage them to apply the strategy to help them figure out unfamiliar words.

Have students recall the information they read in the selection. Encourage them to think critically.

- How would the text be different without the diagrams? *(The information would be harder to visualize and understand.)*
- If you were writing this article, what graphics or information would you add?

Objectives

- Use context and synonyms to determine the meaning of an unknown word.
- Use context to determine the meaning of unfamiliar words.

DAY 4

Practice Retelling

- **Retell** To assess students' comprehension, use the Retelling Cards. Monitor retelling and prompt students as needed.

Genre Focus

- **Before Reading or Revisiting** "The Art of Mimicry" on pp. 98–101, read aloud the genre information about expository text on p. 98. Have students preview the selection and set a purpose for reading. Ask:

- What features do you see? *(headings, pictures, captions)*
- What purpose do you think the headings serve? *(Each heading begins a section about a different animal and its adaptation.)*

- **During Reading or Revisiting** Have students read along with you while tracking the print.

- What information does the photo at the top of p. 98 give you? *(It shows an example of a mimicking insect.)*
- What advantage does the octopus gain by imitating a flatfish? *(It looks like something that tastes bad, so predators leave it alone.)*
- What do animal mimics depend on when a predator comes along? *(that the predator will be fooled by the disguise or that the predator has had a bad experience with the real animal)*

- **After Reading or Revisiting** Have students share their reaction to the article. Then have them write the first page of a short expository piece about an animal they know well.

Objectives

- Synthesize ideas across two or three texts representing similar or different genres.

On-Level Reader

- **Model** Model the fluency skill of rate for students. Read aloud the first page of the On-Level Reader *Changing for Survival: Bird Adaptations,* emphasizing rate. Have students note that when you read expository text, you cannot read too quickly or you may miss important facts and details.
- **Fluency Routine**
  1. Have students reread passages from *Changing for Survival: Bird Adaptations* with a partner.
  2. For optimal fluency, students should reread passages three to four times.
  3. As students read, monitor fluency and provide corrective feedback. Have students note that the text contains many facts and details about body structures. Point out that reading at a slower rate helps the listener more easily understand the information and also makes it less likely that the reader will make mistakes.

See *Routines Flip Chart* for more help with fluency.

- **Retell** For additional practice, have students use pictures as a guide to retell *Changing for Survival: Bird Adaptations.* Prompt as necessary.

- What is this selection mostly about?
- What did you learn from this selection?

Objectives
- Read aloud grade-level stories with fluency.

DAY 1

Build Background

■ **Extend the Concept** Expand on the weekly question *How do animals adapt to survive?*

Humans have the ability to adapt to a wide variety of conditions. We now live in nearly every environment on Earth.

Advanced Reader

For a complete literacy instructional plan and additional practice with this week's target skills and strategies, see the **Leveled Reader Teaching Guide.**

■ **Before Reading** *Can Humans Make a Home in Outer Space?* have students look at the pictures to predict what they will learn from the text. Then have students set a purpose for reading.

■ **During Reading** Have students read the Advanced Reader independently. Encourage them to think analytically. For example, ask:

- What are some other ways scientists could try to prevent an asteroid from crashing into Earth? *(Possible answer: Find a way to destroy the asteroid first.)*
- Do you think space colonization will be possible in your lifetime? Why or why not? *(Possible answers: Yes, if countries decide to put their resources into space colonies; no, the problems are too big to overcome in such a short time.)*

■ **After Reading** Have students review the concept map and explain how information in the Advanced Reader helps them answer the weekly question *How do animals adapt to survive?* Prompt as necessary.

- What other adaptations can you think of that humans will have to make to live in space colonies?
- Think of science fiction movies and TV shows where people live in outer space. What are some of the problems people would have to solve to make these stories realistic?

■ **Now Try This** Assign "Now Try This" at the end of the Advanced Reader.

Objectives

- Interpret a speaker's messages (both verbal and nonverbal).

Pacing Small Group Instruction

15–20 mins.

5-Day Plan

DAY 1	• Extend the concept • Read Advanced Reader
DAY 2	• Graphic Sources • Important Ideas • Revisit Student Edition pp. 82–89
DAY 3	• Synonyms • Revisit Student Edition pp. 90–93
DAY 4	• Expository Text • Read/Revisit Student Edition pp. 98–101
DAY 5	• Reread for fluency • Reread Advanced Reader

3- or 4-Day Plan

DAY 1	• Extend the concept • Advanced Reader
DAY 2	• Graphic Sources • Important Ideas • Revisit Student Edition pp. 82–89
DAY 3	• Synonyms • Revisit Student Edition pp. 90–93
DAY 4	• Expository Text • Read/Revisit Student Edition pp. 98–101 • Reread for fluency • Reread Advanced Reader

3-Day Plan: Eliminate the shaded box.

More Reading

Use additional Leveled Readers or other texts at students' instructional levels to reinforce this week's skills and strategies. For text suggestions, see the Leveled Reader Database or the Leveled Readers Skills Chart on pp. CL 24–CL 29.

Extend Comprehension

Skill Graphic Sources To broaden students' understanding of graphic sources, encourage them to think about which graphics are best suited to display different types of information.

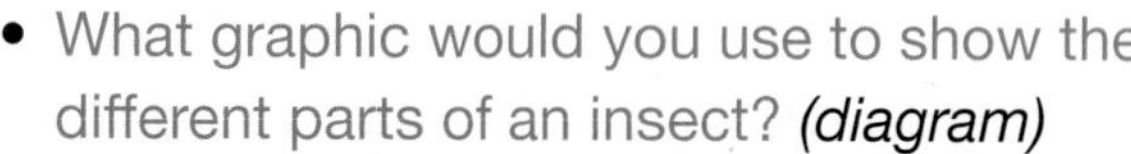

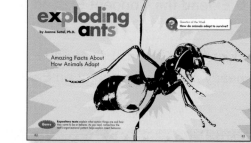

- What graphic would you use to show the different parts of an insect? *(diagram)*

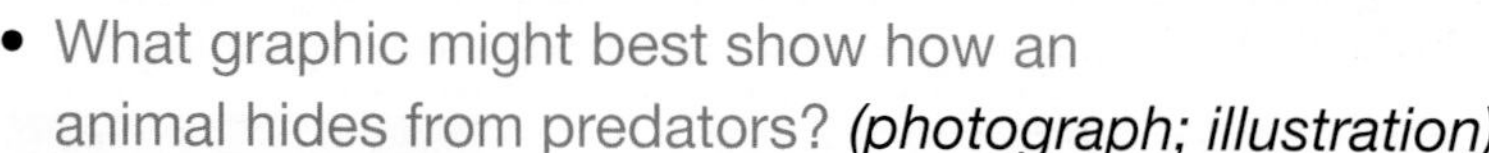

- What graphic might best show how an animal hides from predators? *(photograph; illustration)*

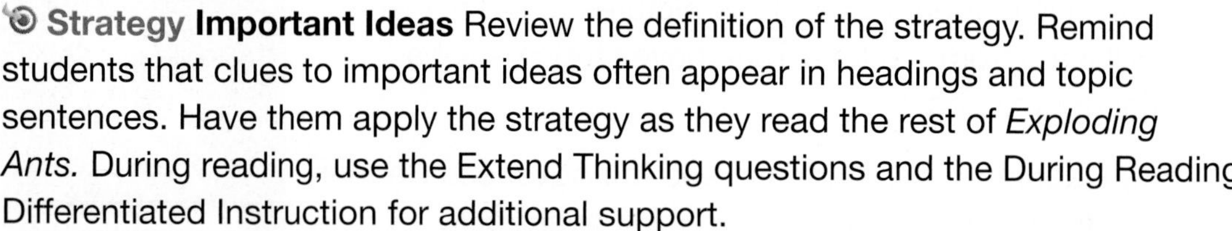

Strategy Important Ideas Review the definition of the strategy. Remind students that clues to important ideas often appear in headings and topic sentences. Have them apply the strategy as they read the rest of *Exploding Ants.* During reading, use the Extend Thinking questions and the During Reading Differentiated Instruction for additional support.

Revisit *Exploding Ants* on pp. 82–89. Have students apply the comprehension skill and strategy as they read the selection.

- Do you think that photographs or drawings do a better job of showing the unusual traits of animals on pp. 84 and 85? Explain. *(Most students will probably say photographs do a better job because they show the actual animal rather than someone's depiction of the animal.)*
- Why do you think both photographs and drawings are used in the section about "honey jar" ants? *(The photographs show what the ants look like in real life, but the drawing more clearly illustrates what is described in the text.)*

Critical Thinking Encourage students to think critically as they read *Exploding Ants.*

- What other graphics do you think would be helpful in illustrating this text?
- If you were a scientist studying the animals on these pages, what more would you like to know?

Objectives

- Use graphics to gain an overview of the contents of text.
- Summarize main ideas in a text in ways that maintain meaning.

Advanced

DAY 3

Extend Vocabulary

Synonyms/Context Clues Have students read the following sentences on p. 5 from *Can Humans Make a Home in Outer Space?:* "What would happen if an asteroid collided with our planet? For one thing, you wouldn't want to be close by to find out. Some scientists believe that an asteroid crashed into Earth 65 million years ago, wiping out the dinosaurs."

- Point out the word *collided.* What is one way that I can figure out the meaning of this word? *(by looking for synonyms in the passage)*
- What synonym can I find for *collided? (the final sentence says the "asteroid crashed into Earth." "Crashed into" is probably a synonym for* collided.*)*
- What can I conclude that *collided* means? *("crashed into")*

Revisit *Exploding Ants* on pp. 90–93. Discuss how synonyms can help students figure out the meaning of difficult words and phrases such as *mandibular glands, violently contracts,* and *regurgitating.* Remind students to use the strategy as they read the selection.

Critical Thinking Have students recall what they learned from *Exploding Ants.* Encourage them to think critically.

- Why might swallowing prey whole be an advantage for some animals?
- Suppose there were only photographs in the book. How would this affect your understanding of the text?

Objectives

- Use context and synonyms to determine the meaning of an unknown word.
- Use context to determine the meaning of unfamiliar words.

More Reading

Use additional Leveled Readers or other texts at students' instructional levels to reinforce this week's skills and strategies. For text suggestions, see the Leveled Reader Database or the Leveled Readers Skills Chart on pp. CL 24–CL 29.

DAY 4

Genre Focus

- **Before Reading or Revisiting** "The Art of Mimicry" on pp. 98–101, read the sidebar information on expository text. Ask students preview to the selection and set a purpose for reading.
- **During Reading or Revisiting** Ask students to share examples of how the graphics illustrate the expository text. Then ask: Why is the lyrebird shown with tiny illustrations of seemingly disconnected items? How does this relate to the text? *(The items are shown in a line coming out of the bird's mouth. The text tells me that the lyrebird can imitate many unusual sounds, so the illustration is meant to represent the lyrebird's amazing ability.)*
- **After Reading or Revisiting** Have students discuss Reading Across Texts. Then have them do Writing Across Texts independently.

Objectives

- Synthesize ideas across two or three texts representing similar or different genres.

DAY 5

- **Reread For Fluency** Have students silently reread passages from the Advanced Reader *Can Humans Make a Home in Outer Space?* Then have them reread aloud with a partner or individually. As students read, monitor fluency and provide corrective feedback. If students read fluently on the first reading, they do not need to reread three to four times. Assess the fluency of students in this group using p. 103j.
- **Retell** Have students summarize the main idea and key details from the Advanced Reader *Can Humans Make a Home in Outer Space?*
- **Now Try This** Have students complete their space mission plans. You may wish to review their work before they share their finished plans with classmates.

Objectives

- Read aloud grade-level stories with fluency.

The ELL lessons are organized by strands. Use them to scaffold the weekly curriculum of lessons or during small group time instruction.

Academic Language

Students will hear or read the following academic language in this week's core instruction. As students encounter the vocabulary, provide a simple definition or concrete example. Then ask students to suggest an example or synonym of the word and identify available cognates.

Skill Words	closure (*clausura*)	reading rate
	possessive pronoun	homophones
	suffix (*sufijo*)	graphic sources
Concept Words	adapt (*adaptar*)	escape (*escape*)
	exploding	survive

**Spanish cognates in parentheses*

Concept Development

How do animals adapt to survive?

- **Preteach Concept**
  - **Prior Knowledge** Have students turn to pp. 76–77 in the Student Edition. Do you know what this animal is? Yes, it's a chameleon. Why do you think chameleons change color? How can that help protect them? Use the discussion to have students use basic classroom vocabulary *animal*, *adapt,* and *survive*.
  - **Discuss Concept** Elicit students' knowledge and experience of how animals adapt to survive. What are some other ways that animals protect themselves? How can adaptations help animals survive? Supply background information as needed.
  - **Poster Talk-Through** Read aloud the Poster Talk-Through on ELL Poster 18 and work through the Day 1 activities.
- **Daily Concept and Vocabulary Development** Use the daily activities on ELL Poster 18 to build concept and vocabulary knowledge.

Objectives

- Internalize new basic and academic language by using and reusing it in meaningful ways in speaking and writing activities that build concept and language attainment.
- Learn new language structures, expressions, and basic and academic vocabulary heard during classroom instruction and interactions.

Content Objectives

- Use concept vocabulary related to adaption.

Language Objectives

- Express ideas in response to art and discussion.
- Use basic vocabulary in classroom interactions.

Daily Planner

DAY 1	• **Frontload Concept** • **Preteach** Comprehension Skill, Vocabulary, Phonics/Spelling, Conventions • **Writing**
DAY 2	• **Review** Concept, Vocabulary, Comprehension Skill • **Frontload Main Selection** • **Practice** Phonics/Spelling, Conventions/Writing
DAY 3	• **Review** Concept, Comprehension Skill, Vocabulary, Conventions/Writing • **Reread Main Selection** • **Practice** Phonics/Spelling
DAY 4	• **Review Concept** • **Read ELL/ELD Readers** • **Practice** Phonics/Spelling, Conventions/Writing
DAY 5	• **Review** Concept, Vocabulary, Comprehension Skill, Phonics/Spelling, Conventions • **Reread ELL/ELD Readers** • **Writing**

**See the ELL Handbook for ELL Workshops with targeted instruction.*

Concept Talk Video

Use the Concept Talk Video Routine (*ELL Handbook,* p. 477) to build background knowledge about adapting to survive. For more listening practice, see *Use Classroom Resources* (*ELL Handbook,* pp. 406–407).

Language Objectives

- Understand and use basic vocabulary.
- Learn meanings of grade-level vocabulary.

Basic Vocabulary

- **High-Frequency Words** Use the vocabulary routines and the High-Frequency Word list on p. 452 of the *ELL Handbook* to systematically teach newcomers the first 300 sight words in English. Students who began learning ten words per week at the beginning of the year are now learning words 171–180.

Lesson Vocabulary

- **Preteach** Introduce the Lesson Vocabulary using this routine:

1. Distribute copies of this week's Word Cards (*ELL Handbook,* p. 131).
2. Display ELL Poster 18 and reread the Poster Talk-Through.
3. Using the poster illustrations, model how a word's meaning can be expressed with other similar words: The snail is covered with *mucus,* or slime.
4. Use these sentences to reveal the meaning of the other words.
   - It is *critical* that no food is wasted. (very important)
   - Food is sometimes *scarce*. (hard to find)
   - The mucus *enables* the snail to glide. (makes it able)
   - Ants *specialize* in gathering food. (do something really well)
   - Ants' saliva makes their food *sterile*. (without germs, safe to eat)

Objectives

- Use accessible language and learn new and essential language in the process.
- Expand and internalize initial English vocabulary by learning and using high-frequency English words necessary for identifying and describing people, places, and objects by retelling simple stories and basic information represented or supported by pictures, and by learning and using routine language needed for classroom communication.

ELL English Language Learners

- **Reteach** Ask questions to check and reinforce students' understanding of the vocabulary.
  - What parts of an ant *enable* it to walk? (legs)
  - What can a bird do if food is *scarce* in a place? (fly to another place)
  - Is food *critical* to animals? (Yes, they need food to live.)
  - Is *mucus* more like glue or like sand? (glue)
  - what does a doctor *specialize* in? (medicine, treating people)
  - If I got hurt and needed a bandage, why should it be *sterile*? (to protect from germs)
- **Writing** Place students in mixed proficiency groups. Put the Word Cards facedown and have each group draw one or two cards. In a jigsaw activity, assign students to create a Word Grid (*ELL Handbook,* p. 493) of the words they picked. Circulate to provide assistance as needed. Afterwards, have groups share their grids. Before students begin, model using the graphic organizer: Word: critical; Meaning: very important; Picture: healthy food, such as fruits and vegetables; Example: Fruit is critical for a good diet; Non-example: Cookies are not critical for a good diet.

  Then have students speak using the content vocabulary on p. 80 of the Student Edition. They can use *critical*, *scarce*, *enables*, and *specialize* to talk about an animal and how it survives in its environment.

Beginning Have students draw pictures for the grids. Then have them write the Lesson Vocabulary word.

Intermediate Ask students to draw a picture or write a phrase using the word.

Advanced Assign students to write a sentence that gives a non-example.

Advanced High Have these students supply the word's meaning. Encourage them to look up the words in the glossary of the Student Edition.

Objectives

- Internalize new basic and academic language by using and reusing it in meaningful ways in speaking and writing activities that build concept and language attainment.
- Write using newly acquired basic vocabulary and content-based grade-level vocabulary.

Language Objectives

- Produce drawings, phrases, or short sentences to show understanding of Lesson Vocabulary.
- Speak using content vocabulary.

Graphic Organizer

Word	Meaning (or picture)
Example	Non-example

ELL Teacher Tip

Shared reading is rich with interactions between the teacher and students. Because students actively participate in the reading process, this is an excellent opportunity to encourage English learners to use oral language in a relaxed and informal setting. The basic components of shared reading include think-alouds, guided discussions, active reading (choral reading), and multiple readings.

Content Objectives

- Monitor and adjust oral comprehension.

Language Objectives

- Discuss oral passages.
- Use a graphic organizer to take notes.

ELL English Language Learners

Listening Comprehension

Read Aloud

Animal Disguises

Many animals have adaptations to keep them from being some other animal's dinner.

Some adaptations appear only when the animal is threatened. Octopuses squirt ink to create a "smoke screen." Puffer fish "supersize" themselves by gulping water. They get big enough to look like a spiny balloon.

Other animals have defenses that are always visible and fearsome. Great white sharks have 3,000 teeth. Bulls have long horns. These animals have one message: "Don't mess with me!"

The striped skunk's black-and-white fur sends a warning: "Stay away!" Animals that don't respect the warning get a whiff of the skunk's in-your-face defense. Getting rid of the stink can take weeks.

Some "tasty" animals pretend to look "yucky" or dangerous to avoid being eaten. The saltwater comet fish sticks its head in its burrow. It spreads out its rear fin to reveal a fake "eye." The bigger fish thinks it's seeing a sharp-toothed moray eel.

Prepare for the Read Aloud The modified Read Aloud above prepares students for listening to the oral reading "Escape Artists" on p. 77b.

- **First Listening: Listen to Understand** Write the title of the Read Aloud on the board. This is about the different ways animals disguise their appearance in order to protect themselves. Listen to find out the different ways. Which disguise is most surprising to you? Why? Afterwards, ask the questions again and have students share their answers.
- **Second Listening: Listen to Check Understanding** Using an Outline Form graphic organizer (*ELL Handbook*, p. 495), work with students to take notes regarding the different ways animals disguise themselves. Invite students to share their notes with the class.

Objectives

- Use strategic learning techniques such as concept mapping, drawing, memorizing, comparing, contrasting, and reviewing to acquire basic and grade-level vocabulary.

Modeled Pronunciation Audio CD

ELL

ELL English Language Learners

Phonics and Spelling

■ **Homophones** Copy and distribute p. 282 of the *ELL Handbook*.

- **Preteach** Tell students this joke: What is black and white and read all over? A newspaper! Explain that this joke is based on a pair of homophones (*red* and *read*), two words that sound the same but are spelled differently and mean completely different things.
- **Teach/Model** Write the following homophone pairs on the board: *pair, pear; flour, flower; ceiling, sealing; week, weak*. Explain the meaning of each word and point out the two different spellings. Emphasize that the two words in each pair are pronounced in exactly the same way.
- **Practice** Dictate pairs of sentences using homophones from p. 282 of the *ELL Handbook*. For example, *Mo* threw *the ball. The ball went through the window*. Monitor students' work for accurate English spellings of the words.

Word Analysis: Suffix *-ize*

■ **Suffix *-ize*** Use this routine to teach how to form words that end in the suffix *-ize.*

- **Preteach and Model** On the board write *sterile*. Remind students that the word *sterile* means "free of germs." Point out that students can make a new word, *sterilize*, by adding the suffix *-ize*. Discuss the meaning of *sterilize*: to kill all of the germs on something. Have students write the new word, dropping the letter *e* at the end of *sterile* and adding *-ize*. Make sure students can write *sterilize* correctly. We can add the suffix *-ize* to nouns and adjectives to make them into verbs.
- **Practice** Write these words on the board: *special*, *final*, *modern*. Have students use the suffix *-ize* to form new words and make a sentence using one of the new words.

Leveled Support

Beginning/Intermediate Have Beginning students form new words and call on Intermediate students to tell what the new word means.

Advanced/Advanced High Have students work in pairs to form new words and make sentences using the new words.

Objectives

- Distinguish sounds and intonation patterns of English with increasing ease.

Content Objectives

- Identify and define words with suffix *-ize.*
- Identify homophones.
- Review synonyms.

Language Objectives

- Apply phonics and decoding skills to vocabulary.
- Discuss the meaning of words with suffix *-ize.*
- Use linguistic and contextual support to understand spoken language.
- Spell English Words.

Language Opportunity: Listening

Give students word cards with homophones: one on the front and one on the back. Say a sentence and ask students to listen for the correct homophone and hold up the card with the correct side. Students should listen to the context and language in determining the correct homophone for the sentence.

Content Objectives

- Identify graphic sources to aid comprehension.

Language Objectives

- Demonstrate and expand reading skills.
- Learn and use academic vocabulary.
- Read environmental print.
- Use graphic sources to discuss information from a reading.
- Use information from a reading to label a diagram.

Language Opportunity: Academic Vocabulary

Graphic sources, picture, diagram, and *chart* are academic vocabulary that students use in various classes. Turn to pp. 78–79 in the Student Edition to review information about graphic sources. Then have students use the academic language *graphic source* and *diagram* as they discuss the picture of the ant on p. 79.

ELL English Language Learners

Comprehension
Graphic Sources

- **Preteach** Graphic sources show information in a way that the reader can see. Have students turn to Envision It! on p. EI•8 in the Student Edition. Read aloud the text together. Have students demonstrate reading skills as they point to and read aloud the different graphic sources used in the spread and explain what kind of information is given by each.

- **Reteach** Distribute copies of the Picture It! (*ELL Handbook*, p. 132) to have students expand their ability to interpret graphic sources. Ask students to describe the diagram. Then read the text aloud twice. During the second reading, have students listen for labels to use on the diagram. Have them demonstrate their use of the reading skill by labeling the parts on the diagram. (1. eggs 2. caterpillar 3. pupa or cocoon 4. butterfly)

Leveled Support

Beginning/Intermediate Reread the paragraph as students read along. Guide them as they underline words for the four images in the diagram. Then have students write the labels.

Advanced/Advanced High Have students reread the paragraph, looking at the diagram as they read. Remind them to look for words that they can use to label the diagram's four parts. Have them write the labels.

MINI-LESSON

Environmental Print

Turn to p. EI•9 in the Student Edition to point out the environmental print. The map and diagram both have environmental print, such as labels and captions. Provide other graphic sources for students to examine and have them explain what they learn from the environmental print. Ask them to list other places in which they have used maps and diagrams and seen labels and captions.

Objectives

- Express opinions, ideas, and feelings ranging from communicating single words and short phrases to participating in extended discussions on a variety of social and grade-appropriate academic topics.

ELL English Language Learners

Reading Comprehension
Exploding Ants

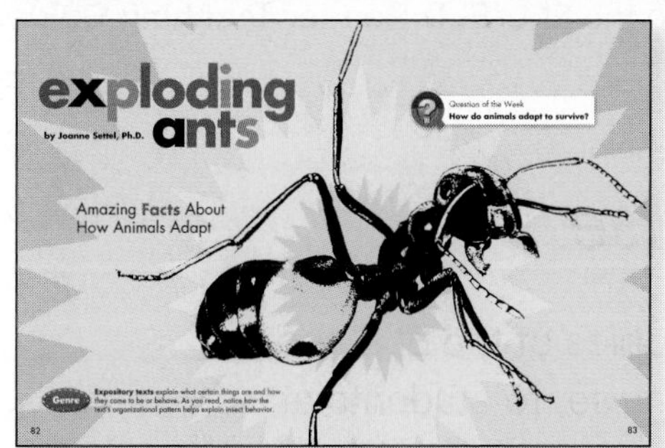

Student Edition pp. 82–83

- **Frontloading** Have students look through *Exploding Ants,* pp. 82–87 in the Student Edition. Distribute copies of the English summary of *Exploding Ants* (*ELL Handbook*, p. 133). Have students read the summary aloud with you. Encourage them to ask questions about any ideas or unfamiliar words. Preview the selection by having students look at the pictures. Distribute the Story Prediction Chart (*ELL Handbook*, p. 482). for students to fill out as they read the selection.

  Sheltered Reading Ask questions to guide comprehension:
  - p. 78: Why do animals sometimes do things that we find gross? (to find food and shelter, and to be safe) In your opinion, why do you think many people consider these things gross? (because the animals are eating food already chewed up by another animal)
  - p. 80: How do *repletes* help a honey ant colony survive? (Repletes store honey nectar, which the other ants eat when food is scarce.)
  - p. 82: Why do some soldier ants explode? (They use their body as a weapon. When it explodes, it sprays deadly chemicals on intruders.)
  - p. 84: In your opinion, why do you think owls swallow small animals whole instead of picking out the nutritious parts? (because it's safer for owls to eat quickly)

- **Fluency: Reading Rate** Remind students that they should read with an even rate that is neither too slow nor too fast. Read the last paragraph on page 78 quickly, and then reread it at a slower rate. Which reading was easier to understand? Why? Have pairs choose a paragraph on p. 79. Have students listen and offer feedback on their partner's reading rate. For more practice, use the Fluency: Timed Reading (*ELL Handbook*, p. 475).

  After Reading Have students retell the text using the picture support of the Retelling Cards.

Objectives
- Understand the general meaning, main points, and important details of spoken language ranging from situations in which topics, language, and contexts are familiar to unfamiliar.

Content Objectives
- Monitor and adjust comprehension.
- Make and adjust predictions.

Language Objectives
- Retell stories supported by pictures.
- Read grade-level text at an appropriate rate.
- Use visual and contextual support to read text.

Audio Support
Students can prepare for reading *Exploding Ants* by using the eSelection or the AudioText CD. See the AudioText CD Routine (*ELL Handbook,* p. 477).

Mini-Lesson: Visual and Contextual Support
Have students use support both from visuals and the text itself to better understanding information in the reading. Turn to pp. 86 and 87 in the Student Edition, for example, and ask questions that can be answered using support from the drawings and photographs as well as from the text.

For additional leveled instruction, see the **ELL/ELD Reader Teaching Guide.**

Comprehension: *Masters of Disguise*

- **Before Reading** Distribute copies of the ELL and ELD Readers, *Masters of Disguise*, to students at their reading level.
  - **Preview** Read the title aloud with students: This is a nonfiction book about insects who disguise their appearance. Invite students to look through the pictures and name what they see. Have them predict different ways insects can disguise themselves based on the picture clues and their prior knowledge.
  - **Set a Purpose for Reading** Let's read to learn different ways insects can disguise their appearance.
- **During Reading** Follow the Reading Routine for both reading groups.

ELL Reader ELD Reader

1. Read the entire Reader aloud slowly.
2. Reread pp. 1–5, pausing to build background or model comprehension. Have Beginning students finger-point as you read. Use the questions in the chart to check students' comprehension.
3. Have students reread pp. 1–5 in pairs, taking turns reading alternate pages.
4. Repeat steps 2–3 for pp. 6–8 of the Reader.

- **After Reading** Use the exercises on the inside back cover of each Reader and invite students to share their writing. In a whole-group discussion, ask students What are some different ways animals can disguise themselves? Record their answers on the board and invite them to point to pictures in the book to support their answers.

ELD Reader Beginning/Intermediate

- **pp. 4–5** What do syrphid flies look like? (They look like wasps and bees.) Read aloud the sentence that gives you the answer. (sentence on p. 4)
- **p. 7** What does a Viceroy butterfly look like? (a Monarch) Read aloud the sentence that gives you the answer. (sentence on p. 7)

Writing What insect disguise is most interesting to you? Find the sentence in the book that tells about this insect disguise. Copy the sentence. Then read it aloud to your partner.

ELL Reader Advanced/Advanced High

- **pp. 4–5** Why do some predators not attack syrphid flies? (They look like wasps and bees.)
- **p. 7** How are Viceroy butterflies like Monarchs? (they look alike)

Study Guide Distribute copies of the ELL Reader Study Guide (*ELL Handbook*, p. 136). Scaffold comprehension of graphic sources by having students look back through the Reader for information about what the insects look like. Review the responses together. (See *ELL Handbook*, pp. 209–212.)

Objectives

- Understand the general meaning, main points, and important details of spoken language ranging from situations in which topics, language, and contexts are familiar to unfamiliar.

Conventions
Possessive Pronouns

- **Preteach** This is my book. This book is mine. The words *my* and *mine* are possessive pronouns. They show that I have this book. Possessive pronouns show who or what has or owns something.
- **Teach/Model** Present the concept and provide examples. Use *my, your, her, our,* and *their* before nouns. Use *mine, yours, hers, ours,* and *theirs* alone. *His* and *its* can be used before nouns and alone.
- **Practice** Have students place school supplies on their desks.

Leveled Support

Beginning Have students point to and name items using phrases. For example, *my book, your paper,* and *his pencil.*

Intermediate Have students name items using these sentence frames: This is _____. These are _____.

Advanced/Advanced High Have students name items using complete sentences.

- **Reteach** Continue to use school supplies and have students create three sentences modeling the three types of examples displayed on the chart.

Before nouns	Alone	Both
This is <u>your</u> pen. It is <u>her</u> doll.	The shoes are <u>mine</u>. The doll is <u>hers</u>.	The pen is <u>his</u>. This is <u>his</u> home.

Beginning Have students develop examples using these sentence frames: This is _____. The _____ is _____. The _____ are _____. These are _____.

Intermediate Have students develop examples using complete sentences.

Advanced/Advanced High Have students write a paragraph using as many possessive pronouns as they can.

Objectives

- Learn new language structures, expressions, and basic and academic vocabulary heard during classroom instruction and interactions.
- Use visual, contextual, and linguistic support to enhance and confirm understanding of increasingly complex and elaborated spoken language.
- Speak using a variety of grammatical structures, sentence lengths, sentence types, and connecting words with increasing accuracy and ease as more English is acquired.

Content Objectives

- Decode and use possessive pronouns.
- Correctly form possessive pronouns.

Language Objectives

- Speak using the pattern of possessive pronouns.
- Write phrases and sentences with possessive pronouns.

Transfer Skills

Students who speak Asian languages may try various forms for possessive pronouns—*the hat of her, you hat*—or may not always state the pronoun (*Mo Yun took off hat*). Provide practice with possessive pronouns.

Support for English Language Learners

Content Objectives

- Identify strong conclusions that provide a sense of closure.

Language Objectives

- Know when to use formal English.
- Write concluding paragraphs providing a sense of closure.
- Share feedback for editing and revising.

Mini-Lesson: Use Formal English

Read the writing model with students, pointing out that single word and a fragment are used for emphasis. Is this formal English? Fragments and single words are usually part of the conversational style of informal English. Have students change the fragments in the writing model to complete sentences and then name other instances in which formal English is preferred, such as research reports.

ELL English Language Learners

Writing with a Sense of Closure

- **Introduce** Display the paragraph model and read it aloud. Review that a conclusion is at the end of a paragraph. What is this paragraph about? (exploding ants) Underline the final sentence. This is the conclusion. A strong conclusion provides a sense of closure. It makes clear why the topic discussed in the paragraph is important or significant.

Writing Model

Some insects, such as the *Camponotus* soldier ants, are designed to explode. Yes, that's right. Explode. They do so in order to drive intruders away. If not for the soldier ants, the colony would not be able to defend itself from intruders.

- **Practice** Write this incomplete paragraph on the board. Work together to create a concluding sentence that provides a sense of closure. (Because snakes eat such big meals, they don't need to eat every day.)

Snakes swallow their food whole. Their ability to do this results from the special design of their jaw. The jaw bones are loosely joined to the skull, so they can stretch far apart.

- **Write** Have students write a paragraph about one of the animal adaptations studied this week. For ideas, they can use *Exploding Ants or Escape Artists.*

Beginning Have students write the name of an animal from *Exploding Ants* or *Escape Artists* at the top of their paper. Then have them draw details about the animal's adaptation and dictate to you one sentence for each drawing. Write out their sentences and have students copy them.

Intermediate Supply students with this sentence frame for a conclusion: [Adaption] is useful for [name of animal] because _____. Have partners work together to write supporting details in the form of a paragraph. For prewriting, students can use a Main Ideas graphic organizer for planning their details.

Advanced/Advanced High Have students develop their paragraph with a conclusion independently. Then have pairs exchange papers and provide feedback for revising and editing. Encourage partners to star the detail they find most interesting and point out any areas that are difficult to understand.

Objectives

- Understand the general meaning, main points, and important details of spoken language ranging from situations in which topics, language, and contexts are familiar to unfamiliar.
- Share information in cooperative learning interactions.
- Write using newly acquired basic vocabulary and content-based grade-level vocabulary.

UNIT 4 21st Century Writing

E-Pen Pals

Writing Project Correspond by e-mail with an e-pen pal to share advice about adjusting to school.

Purpose Enhance skills in writing formal e-mail and using word processing applications

Audience Teacher and a younger student in your school

Introduce genre and key features

In this workshop, we will write an e-mail to an e-pen pal giving advice about how to adjust to the new experiences they will have in school. We will match our class with a class of younger students in our school and send them e-mails. We will draft, revise, and edit our e-mails using tools at the e-mail account site.

Key Features of an E-mail

- is sent over the Internet from one computer to another
- contains a greeting, body, closing, and signature just like a friendly letter
- requires use of an exact e-mail address
- calls for use of correct English both as a courtesy and to be understood

Academic Vocabulary

E-pen pal An e-pen pal is a person with whom one communicates by e-mail on a regular basis.

Differentiated Instruction

SI Strategic Intervention

Compare E-mail to Letter Ask students to explain similarities between a letter and an e-mail. Display an example of each form and have students circle parallel parts in the forms (date, greeting, body, etc.).

ELL

English Language Learners

English Conventions of Punctuation Using 21st Century Writing TC8, point out the conventions for using a comma after the greeting and closing of an e-mail and for using quotation marks. Ask students to tell how these conventions differ in their first language.

UNIT 4 21st Century Writing

Objectives

- Understand and identify the features of an e-mail.
- Organize ideas to prepare for writing.

1 Plan and Prewrite

MINI-LESSON

Read Like a Writer

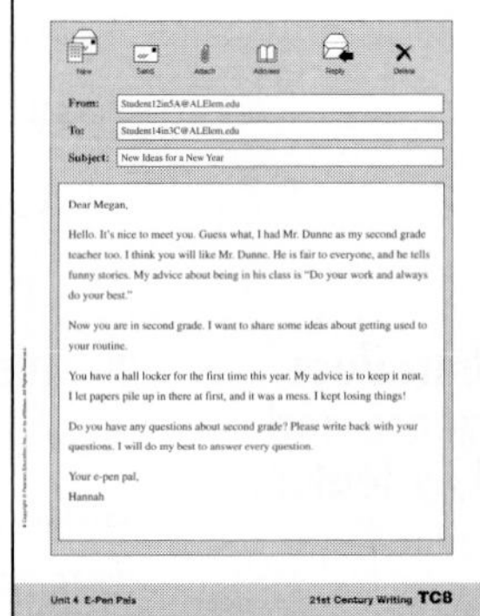

New Send Attach Address Reply Delete

From: Student12in5A@ALElem.edu

To: Student14in3C@ALElem.edu

Subject: New Ideas for a New Year

Dear Megan,

Hello. It's nice to meet you. Guess what, I had Mr. Dunne as my second grade teacher too. I think you will like Mr. Dunne. He is fair to everyone, and he tells funny stories. My advice about being in his class is "Do your work and always do your best."

Now you are in second grade. I want to share some ideas about getting used to your routine.

You have a hall locker for the first time this year. My advice is to keep it neat. I let papers pile up in there at first, and it was a mess. I kept losing things!

Do you have any questions about second grade? Please write back with your questions. I will do my best to answer every question.

Your e-pen pal,
Hannah

Unit 4 E-Pen Pals — 21st Century Writing TC8

21st Century Transparency TC8, TR DVD

- **Examine Model Text** Use a projector to display 21st Century Transparency TC8. Point out and discuss the parts of an e-mail and appropriate conventions for entering text in each part. Online e-mail service programs can vary slightly. In this program, the e-mail address of the sender appears in the first box on the e-mail form. The sender types the e-mail address of the person who is to receive the e-mail in the second box. In the "Subject" box, the sender types a phrase that sums up what the e-mail is about. The message or letter is typed in the large box below these boxes. To get from one box to another, press the "tab" key or use the mouse to position the cursor.

- Read aloud the e-mail, asking students to identify the e-mail addresses, subject, date, greeting, closing, and signature. Remind students that an e-mail to an e-pen pal is like a friendly letter and should use standard English grammar, spelling, and mechanics.

Make a list You will write e-mails to a younger pen pal who attends our school. These e-mails will give friendly advice about ways to adapt to new experiences in a new school year. Your e-mail will tell about some ways you have found to adapt as you started each new grade in school. First, we need to list some ways that each new school year differs from the last one. Have students brainstorm the different expectations, routines, and activities they have encountered as they advanced to fifth grade.

Ask students to describe techniques and attitudes that have helped them adapt to changes in their school routine. Summarize their responses in categories such as "Meet New People," "Learn New Routines," and "Solve Problems."

Differentiated Instruction

SI Strategic Intervention

Identifying Problems and Solutions Help students organize their ideas for their e-mails by having them describe how they adjusted to a new school year when they were younger. Write an example on the board in a word web and, as students respond, write their comments in outer circles of the web. Have students make their own webs for problems on their lists.

Teacher Tip

Student Safety Online Before students compose their e-mails, familiarize yourself with your school's policy about e-mail communications among students. Discuss with students the need to avoid sending personal information such as telephone numbers and street addresses over the Internet.

UNIT 4 21st Century Writing

Objectives

- Brainstorm and organize into categories details about adapting to a new school.
- Fill out required information in an e-mail form.
- Type a correct greeting.

1 Plan and Prewrite

MINI-LESSON

Brainstorming Details of an E-mail

Think Aloud To write advice about how to adapt to a new experience, I need to remember details of how I adapted to the conditions when I started something new. I can write them quickly as I think of them. Then I can organize them in categories similar to the ones listed on the board.

- Using a projector, model brainstorming details about adapting to a new experience and then list the details under appropriate column headings, or display 21st Century Transparency TC9.
- Have students brainstorm independently, listing details or explanations about their experiences. Then have them refer to their notes as they use a word processing application to create a chart with headings and organize details into categories.

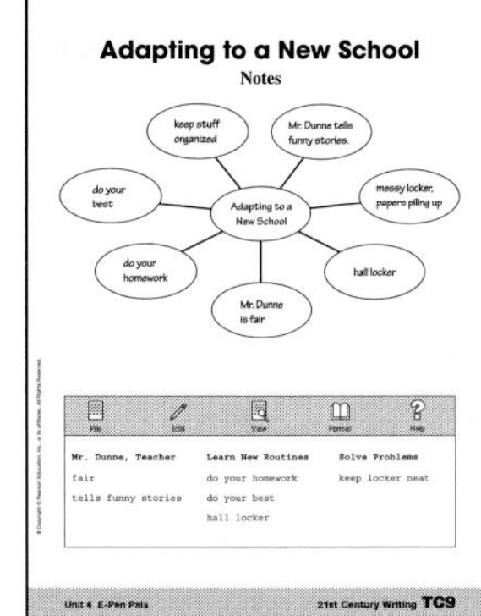

21st Century Transparency TC9, TR DVD

Plan and Prewrite

Assigning e-pen pals

Analyze the list of students from the partner class for this workshop to match each student in your classroom with an e-pen pal. Assign each student his or her individual e-mail address and the e-mail address and name of his or her e-pen pal. Explain that everyone will begin by filling out the fields in the e-mail form.

Using an e-mail format

Display the "compose message" screen of the e-mail application students will use on a projector. Be sure you fill out the boxes on the e-mail form correctly, or your e-mail cannot be sent. Here is how I fill out the forms to send an e-mail. I enter my e-mail address carefully in the first box and then move the cursor to the box labeled "To." I type the e-mail address of my e-pen pal in this box. Then I move the cursor to the box labeled "Subject" and type a phrase describing what the e-mail is about. Fill in each field with appropriate examples. Next, I move the cursor to the message box and type in the greeting. In the greeting, I use the name of my e-pen pal. Enter a standard greeting and point out proper punctuation.

Have students open an e-mail form and type their e-mail address, their e-pen pal's e-mail address, the topic of their e-mail, and a greeting.

Academic Vocabulary

Greeting In a friendly letter or e-mail, the greeting identifies the recipient and opens the letter.

Technology Tip

E-Pen Pal Sites If you and the teacher of the cooperating class have registered at an educational e-pen pal site, connect your classes online and establish e-mail addresses for students.

English Language Learners

Building Vocabulary Encourage students to tell about their experiences in adapting to a new grade in school. To assist them, provide sentence frames such as: *I had to learn to ___.*

As students respond, write their completed sentences on the board, adding vocabulary as necessary. Read each sentence aloud, and have students echo read it.

Objectives

- Write a first draft of an e-mail giving advice.
- Combine sentences to improve logic and flow of text.
- Revise drafts for clarity and adequate detail.

Draft

Write a First Draft

Getting started Give students the name of their e-pen pal and have them access their e-mail site to write a greeting and an introductory paragraph for their e-mail. Remind them that they are offering help to someone going through an experience they have already had. Suggest that they try to remember their concerns when they were in that grade. Remind them that a friendly letter should open with a few sentences that introduce them to the e-pen pal.

Have students look at their chart and list and think of a beginning for their e-mail. Then they can relate their advice to the younger student about school. Encourage them to refer back to details in their prewriting notes as they write.

Examine model text Display 21st Century Transparency TC8 and review the body of the e-mail.

This student begins by introducing herself and sharing something in common with her e-pen pal. Then she gives advice about how to adapt to this teacher's second-grade classroom. Last, the student asks her e-pen pal to write back. She ends with a closing and signature.

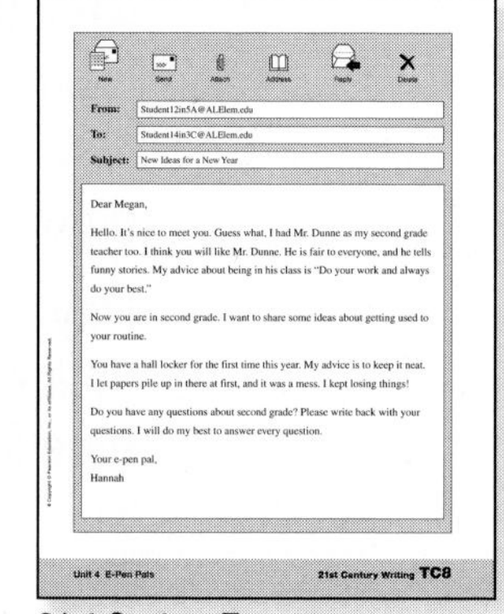

From: Student12in5A@ALElem.edu
To: Student14in3C@ALElem.edu
Subject: New Ideas for a New Year

Dear Megan,

Hello. It's nice to meet you. Guess what, I had Mr. Dunne as my second grade teacher too. I think you will like Mr. Dunne. He is fair to everyone, and he tells funny stories. My advice about being in his class is "Do your work and always do your best."

Now you are in second grade. I want to share some ideas about getting used to your routine.

You have a hall locker for the first time this year. My advice is to keep it neat. I let papers pile up in there at first, and it was a mess. I kept losing things!

Do you have any questions about second grade? Please write back with your questions. I will do my best to answer every question.

Your e-pen pal,
Hannah

Unit 4 E-Pen Pals 21st Century Writing TC8

21st Century Transparency TC8, TR DVD

Develop draft Remind students that in a draft they get ideas down in rough form. There will be time to change it by rearranging, adding, or subtracting when they revise.

Revise

MINI-LESSON

Combine Sentences

- One way to revise writing is to combine sentences that are related. In a written explanation, many ideas are related to each other. By combining short sentences using conjunctions, you can make your writing smoother and show how ideas are related. Conjunctions are joining words such as *and, but, or,* and *so.*

Short, choppy sentences: He is fair to everyone. He tells funny stories.
You're probably wondering. "Can I do it?"

Combined sentences: He is fair to everyone, and he tells funny stories.
You're probably asking yourself, "Can I do it?"

Discuss with students how combining the sentences shows the relationship between ideas and makes the writing sound smoother. Summarize the function of the conjunctions *and* (to add), *but* (to contrast), *or* (to show a choice), and *so* (to give a reason).

Peer conferencing Have students share their drafts with their partners for peer revision. Ask each partner to note sentences that are incomplete, choppy, or unrelated and ideas that need more detailed explanation. Encourage students to write at least two suggestions for revision.

Revise drafts Now we will revise our e-mail drafts. When we revise, we try to make our writing clearer and more interesting. As you revise, think about your partner's comments and look for ways to combine sentences to make a relationship clear.

Corrective feedback

If... students have difficulty identifying relationships between ideas,
then... write the sentences in question on the board and discuss whether they show a similarity, a difference, a choice, or a cause and effect. Help students diagram the relationship between them. For example, draw an arrow from a cause to an effect or place a + between similarities. Give students appropriate conjunctions to use with each relationship.

Differentiated Instruction

Strategic Intervention

Practice Sentence Combining Review compound sentences and the conjunctions *and, but, or, for, nor*, and *yet*. Have partners combine simple sentences you write on the board using a comma and conjunction, then explain the relationship they have shown by their choice of conjunction.

Teacher Tip

Copying and Pasting Revisions call for moving text. Show students the operations for highlighting text and copying it. Explain that the computer "remembers" the last text copied and pastes it when the paste command is given.

ELL

English Language Learners

Learn Conjunctions Have students create a word card for each common conjunction *(and, but, or, so, for, yet)* and write a brief definition and a symbol that suggests it on the back of the card (for example, "add ideas" and "+" for *and*, "unlike ideas" and "–" for *but)*. Write simple related sentences on the board and read them aloud. Have students continue the sentences by holding up the correct conjunction to join them.

Objectives

- Correct spelling errors and errors with commonly confused words.
- Identify word groups that do not express complete ideas.
- Fill out required information in an e-mail form.
- Edit drafts.
- Type a correct closing.

Edit

MINI-LESSON

Using the Computer to Edit

- The spelling checker will highlight words in your draft that it determines are misspelled. Reread these words to check whether you have made an error. Some e-mail programs have dictionaries that can make suggestions. Have students use the spelling checker in the e-mail program to check their draft. Then type the following passage and display it on a projector:

  I let papers pil up in their at first. And it was a mess.

  First, I will use the spelling checker to check for errors. Use the spelling checker and identify the results. The spelling checker caught the word *pil,* which is spelled incorrectly. I will insert an *e* at the end. Make the change. If you use the wrong word, the spelling checker will not catch the error. You will have to proofread your e-mail for this kind of error. The word *their* is spelled correctly, but it is the wrong word. *Their* should be *there*. These words are homophones; they sound the same, but they are spelled differently and have different meanings. Make the change.

- Most e-mail programs have a spelling checker, but not a grammar checker. I will have to check the passage for grammar on my own. Read the passage aloud. The second group of words does not sound correct by itself. The word *and* can join two sentences that add their ideas together. A comma goes before the word *and*. This means I should delete the period after *first,* add a comma, and change the uppercase letter *A* to a lowercase *a*. Make the correction. Read the corrected sentence aloud.

- Ask students to edit their own draft using the spelling checker in the e-mail program. Then have them read their drafts to check for errors in grammar, punctuation, and capitalization.

Corrective feedback

If... students have difficulty correcting common homophone errors such as *your/you're, there/their/they're, and its/it's,*
then... review the meaning of each homophone and have students complete sentences on the board using the correct homophone. They can then review their drafts.

Edit

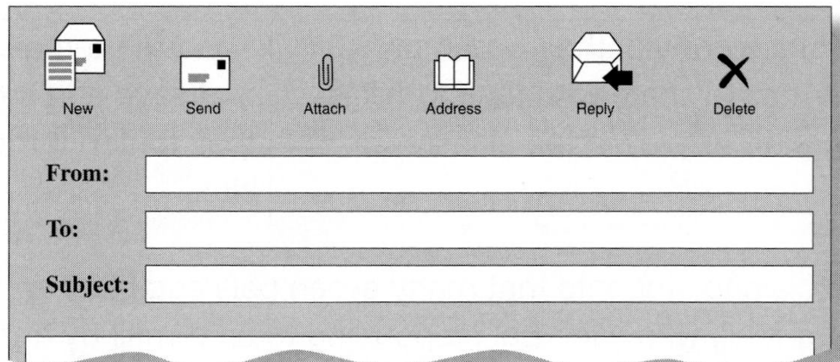

Add a closing Your e-mail will end with a closing and your name. The closing is a word or phrase such as "Sincerely" or "Your e-pen pal" followed by a comma. On the line below the closing, you type your name. Model adding an appropriate closing and signature line. Then instruct students to write their closing and add their names to their e-mails.

Check format Have students use a checklist like the following to check their e-mail:

- ☑ The To and Subject lines are completed correctly.
- ☑ The e-mail address is correct.
- ☑ The e-pen pal's name is correctly spelled in the greeting.
- ☑ The greeting ends with a comma.
- ☑ Each paragraph of the e-mail has a space before and after it.
- ☑ The closing line ends with a comma.
- ☑ I typed my name below the closing.

Send e-mails Have students send their e-mails. Explain that you will check the e-mails to be sure they are correct and appropriate and then send them on to each e-pen pal.

Academic Vocabulary

Closing The closing of an e-mail is a phrase placed below the last line of the e-mail and followed by a comma. Example: *Your friend,*

Homophones Homophones are words that sound alike but have different spellings and meanings. Example: *there/their/they're*

Differentiated Instruction

Strategic Intervention

Practice with Homophones Have partners use a dictionary to define these homophones: *their/there/they're, your/you're, to/too/two, for/fore/four, its/it's.*

Dictate sentences with missing homophones and have students supply and spell the correct word.

Teacher Tip

Using a Spelling Checker Many e-mail programs have a spelling checker that highlights errors with a colored wavy line. Show students how to get an explanation of the highlighted error.

English Language Learners

Identifying Incomplete Thoughts Point out key relationship words that make a word group incomplete by itself: *if, although, because, until.* Point out the need for more information to complete ideas in examples: *If you get lost (What should you do?) When you join a club (What will happen then?)*

Have students complete each sentence by answering the question. Model correct punctuation of the new sentence.

Objectives

- Plan and journal for future e-mails.
- Analyze and evaluate the process of writing an e-mail.

Publish and Present

Options for presenting

Students may choose from the following options for presenting their e-mail.

Print a copy of their e-pen pal e-mail to share with their families and to display in the classroom.	Send the e-mail to their e-pen pal and save and store the e-mail in their folder at the school e-mail site.

Continuing correspondence

Explain to students that many e-pen pals establish an ongoing exchange of e-mail, with each pal responding to an e-mail by answering questions and commenting on information that has been sent. When students' e-pen pals respond, it will be your student's turn to write a second e-mail.

E-pen pals can remain in touch and share ideas by e-mail. An older student can serve as a mentor, or adviser, to a younger student. Discuss with students additional subjects on which they might like to give advice to their e-pen pals.

Encourage students to record in journals what they have learned as they adjusted to new situations and possible subjects that might be discussed with a younger student. They can refer to their journals when replying to their e-pen pals.

Have your students discuss what they found most rewarding and most challenging about setting up and writing an e-mail that gives advice to a younger e-pen pal.